THE QUEST FOR THE MESSIAH

7.

Nik Kiehom   TAU   1996

THE
QUEST

FOR THE

MESSIAH

The History, Literature and Theology
of the Johannine Community

John Painter

Second Edition

T&T CLARK
EDINBURGH

T&T CLARK LTD
59 GEORGE STREET
EDINBURGH EH 2 2LQ
SCOTLAND

First edition 1991
Second edition 1993

ISBN 0 567 29246 0

British Library Cataloguing-in-Publication Data
A Catalogue record for this book is available
from the British Library

Printed and bound in Great Britain by Redwood Books, Trowbridge, Wiltshire

AMICO DOCTORIQUE

Charles Kingsley Barrett

Contents

Preface to the Second Edition

My interest in the Johannine Literature is long standing, going back to my days as a student. This interest received decisive direction in Durham between 1965 and 1967 under the supervision of C. K. Barrett. Published in this form *The Quest for the Messiah* (henceforth *Quest*) is a token of thanks for stimulation, support and friendship through the years.

Since Durham days my teaching responsibilities have ranged widely covering Hellenistic Judaism, Early Christianity to 451, and some aspects of Contemporary Christian Thought but my research interests have persistently returned (after brief interludes) to the mysterious, enchanting and perplexing area of Johannine studies. *Quest* is a manifestation of my own journey in this area. It has been a journey in quest of a more adequate grasp of John's distinctive understanding of belief in Jesus the Messiah in the context of early Christianity. John (henceforth Jn) has also made an impact on my understanding of Christians living in the West at the end of the twentieth century. Naturally this perspective cannot find expression in the present book but without this impact on my own understanding I doubt that my interest would have been sustained and even now be undiminished.

Obviously the present book is a manifestation of that ongoing interest. It began with a view to the writing of a commentary that would combine historical, literary, social and theological perspectives. Much work has been done in preparation for this project but the commentary must be deferred to allow for other commitments to be fulfilled. Because of this it seemed to be a good idea to bring together the material for this monograph, especially as a surprising convergence of themes had emerged in studies that I had been preparing for some years. Consequently *Quest* can be used like a commentary by consulting particular chapters for a discussion of various passages. But, unlike most commentaries, a sustained argument is developed in *Quest*.

This second edition of *Quest* affords the opportunity to correct typographical errors that have come to my attention; to clarify the argument in places by presenting the material in a more persuasive order and fashion; to expand in a more systematic way some aspects of the theme, especially concerning the Son of Man and the apocalyptic ideology of Jn; and to take account of the literature that has appeared since the first edition was completed. The long second chapter ("Johannine Christianity"), which provides the overall context into which the detailed chapters fit, is now even longer. Chapter 4 ("Quest Stories in John 1–4") is presented in a clearer and more logical way, laying the foundation more solidly for the exposition of the theme of the quest for the Messiah. While some chapters have been more thoroughly revised than others and there is a more coherent treatment of the Johannine Son of Man, every chapter has been significantly revised.

John Ashton's fine book, *Understanding the Fourth Gospel* came into my hands after the first edition of *Quest* had already been published. I now take the opportunity to refer to it, especially in additional notes. The discerning reader will recognize that we agree on many points, though not concerning a Bultmann/Fortna type of Signs source. We agree on the importance of Qumran for the thought world of Jn and the writing of the Gospel in stages, in at least two editions followed by redaction, but not on the evangelist's membership of the Qumran sect. The theme of the quest for the Messiah is of course distinctive to *Quest*.

Some of the material has been published before appearing in *Quest*. All of this has been reshaped and some of it has been very substantially expanded to fit the theme of this book. More than half of the book is completely new having been written especially for *Quest*. Essays that have been published previously were originally prepared as independent papers to be delivered at various international meetings of New Testament scholars. At the time I was not completely aware of the way they would fit together though I was attempting to work through the Gospel and to discern its place and importance in early Christianity. The original order of preparation did not fit the chronology of the Gospel but often arose in terms of set themes at conferences. In these papers I sought to discern the key to the perspective of the Gospel. Appropriately it was a paper on the Farewell Discourses prepared for *SNTS*[1] Toronto in 1980 that set the process in motion. This was followed by a paper on the Prologue at *SNTS* Canterbury 1983; another on "The Opponents in 1 John" at *SNTS* Basel in 1984; on John 10 at *SNTS* Atlanta in 1986; and John 6 at *SNTS* Cambridge in 1988. This paper, together with one on "Quest and Rejection Stories in John" prepared for the *SBL*[2] meeting at Sheffield in 1988 began to provide a further element in the perceived structure that would bind these studies together. Glimmerings of this were already present in the paper on John 10 and a essay on John 5 in honour of my friend Eric Osborn published in *ABR*[3] in 1987.

---

[1]*Studiorum Novi Testamenti Societas.*
[2]*Society of Biblical Literature.*
[3]*The Australian Biblical Review* (Melbourne).

PREFACE

The papers prepared for *SNTS* meetings have all appeared in *NTS*[4] except the paper on John 10 which appeared in the *SNTS* monograph *The Shepherd Discourse of John 10 and its Context*. The *SBL* paper appeared in *JSNT*[5]. The chapter on John 9 was based on an earlier article that had appeared in *JTSA*[6] in 1979 and in significantly revised form in *JSNT* in 1986. Chapter 12 was originally a contribution in honour of Leon Morris in 1974. Three other publications also contribute to this volume: A paper on "Quest Stories in John 1–4" in *JSNT*; another on "Quest Stories in John and the Synoptics" presented at the 1990 *Colloquium Biblicum Lovaniense* and now in the volume *John and the Synoptics*; and "The Enigmatic Johannine Son of Man" which appeared in *The Four Gospels 1992*. I am grateful for permission to make use of material from these papers in *Quest*.

The concentration of papers that were first delivered at meetings of *SNTS* in various parts of the world will alert the reader to the debt that I owe to this illustrious Society and its members. Certainly without it one rich part of my life would have been impossible as would the writing of this book. In particular I acknowledge the contribution of the "John Seminar". It has been the context in which a number of the papers were first delivered and in which I have learned much from my colleagues. In particular I acknowledge the debt I owe to a group of my seminar colleagues: Johannes Beutler, SJ; R. Alan Culpepper; R. T. (Bob) Fortna; D. Moody Smith. I am also grateful to La Trobe University for periods of leave and funding assistance without which the writing of this book would not have been possible.

In *Quest* abbreviations follow the practice of *New Testament Studies*. Commentaries on the Gospel of John are cited by author's name and *John*. Full details of all works referred to in text and notes are given in the Bibliography of works cited. I am grateful to Dr. Geoffrey Green for accepting this manuscript for publication by T&T Clark and for the cooperation of his staff as the camera ready copy for the revised edition was prepared. The courtesy, efficiency and speed of operation were impressive.

John Painter
La Trobe University
Melbourne

---

[4] *New Testament Studies* (Cambridge).
[5] *Journal for the Study of the New Testament* (Sheffield).
[6] *Journal of Theology for Southern Africa* (Cape Town).

1

The Quest for the Messiah

Jn is a puzzle, a puzzle of historical, literary, social and theological dimensions. The historical and theological aspects have frequently been the focus of study as have certain literary aspects related to the book as an historical work. Contemporary studies have thrown new light on the literary and social perspectives. In this study some attempt is made to bring together the historical, literary, social and theological dimensions. In doing this the aim is not to provide a history of past research[1] or even a conspectus of some present consensus. Rather what is in view is the setting out of a synthesis in which certain new insights provide the basis for understanding the fundamental unity of the Johannine tradition. In some scholarly circles it has become customary to view Jn as an amalgam of competing ideologies. This is sometimes seen as a consequence of an aggressive editing of an alien source or sources, leaving traces of literary, historical and theological contradictions. Alternatively it can be suggested that Jn underwent a single or a series of unsympathetic redactions.[2] While recognizing the importance of the data which provide a basis for these hypotheses this book follows a different line of approach.

The approach was significantly developed in research in Durham (UK) in the mid-1960s under the supervision of C. K. Barrett. There I became convinced that the Gospel was shaped in conflict between Jewish believers in Jesus as the Messiah and the synagogue. Subsequently this position was given detailed expression by J. Louis Martyn in his creative and original treatment which proved to be convincing to many Johannine scholars.[3] The essential evidence upon which Martyn based his thesis had been treated in the commentaries,[4] but without using it to develop an

---

[1] For this see Robert Kysar, *The Fourth Evangelist and his Gospel* and "The Fourth Gospel. A Report on Recent Research".

[2] That Jn underwent redaction is evident from 21.24-25. What is in question is the suggestion that this was unsympathetic in the sense that the redactor(s) sought to modify the views of the evangelist. Rather it is argued that redaction and publication were carried out by the Johannine school in sympathy with the intentions of the evangelist.

[3] Martyn's *History and Theology in the Fourth Gospel* was first published in 1968.

[4] See the first edition of the commentary by C. K. Barrett (1955) where the use of $\dot{\alpha}\pi o\sigma\upsilon\nu\dot{\alpha}\gamma\omega\gamma o\varsigma$ in 9.22; 12.42; 16.2 is given attention in relation to *birkat hamminim*. In the second edition (1978) the discussion is related to Martyn's work.

hypothesis about the factors shaping the Gospel as a whole. This Martyn did, not only in his original book but in successive articles.[5]

At the same time R. E. Brown was working on his important commentary in which he gave expression to the hypothesis of the development of the Gospel in a number of stages over a lengthy period of time. The basic hypothesis has become increasingly persuasive to me because some process rather than an instant writing seems to be inherently probable and the hypothesis has the power to solve many problems raised by the text of the Gospel as it has come down to us. An hypothesis of the development of the Gospel in stages is almost a natural development of my own original research where I had argued for a process of development from the Gospel to 1 John. Dialogue with the work of Brown and others and further study of the Gospel itself led me to recognize that the Gospel itself overlapped this process. Brown has given full expression to his views in a series of articles, then in the daringly fertile monograph *The Community of the Beloved Disciple* and finally in his commentary on *The Johannine Epistles*.

While readers will recognize that much of the discussion in *Quest* has been carried on in dialogue with the work of R. E. Brown, the seminal contributions are to be found in the first edition of the commentary by C. K. Barrett first published in 1955. A decisive step in recognizing that the text of the Gospel implied a process of composition was taken in the preparation of a paper for the 1980 *SNTS* meeting in Toronto. The paper took as its starting point Barrett's suggestion that two versions of the Farewell discourse had been included in the Gospel.[6] Barrett's seminal suggestion about the role of a Johannine school also implies a process of composition in relation to the history of the school.[7] In Barrett's work these seminal suggestions foreshadow the detailed work by others that would follow a decade or more later. They remain undeveloped in his own work, perhaps because his focus has been turned first to Paul and now to Acts, but failure to develop them further in the second edition of the commentary (1978) suggests that he finds too little evidence so that work done in this area is all too hypothetical.

The hypothetical nature of the historical reconstruction attempted in *Quest* is self-evident. Three responses may be made to those who are critical of such attempts. 1). The evidence which suggests this reconstruction is to be found largely within the Gospel itself, though this

---

[5]See especially "Glimpses into the History of the Johannine Community".
[6]*John*, (1955), 379 and (1978[2]), 454-5.
[7]See chapter 2 "Johannine Christianity", 96–8 below.

is integrated with external evidence wherever possible. 2). The reconstruction makes sense of what otherwise would remain perplexing problems. 3). There are no hypothesis free readings of the Gospel. A "straightforward" reading of the Gospel as a self-contained whole may seem to be more or less hypothesis free. But the reader cannot help being aware that the story has a real person as the major character. How does the story relate to the life of that person? Neither the answer that the story is straight history nor that the relation of the story to history does not matter is self-evident. Few today would wish to argue that any one of the Gospels provides a straightforward account of Jesus' life. It is no more likely that the story has no relation to the life of Jesus. How then are we to understand the balance between historical narrative and imaginative story? Hypotheses are inevitably involved here. The assumption that to read the Gospel simply as a self-contained story is to be preferred because it involves a minimal hypothesis is not self-justifying. That the story should have no relation to the history of Jesus and no relevance to the evangelist and his time is most unlikely. Further, what justifies a more complex hypothesis is the way it enables the reader to cope with perplexing problems within the Gospel such as the *aporia* in Jn 13.31 which presupposes that 18.1 should follow immediately.

Other work important for *Quest* is associated with the names of Rudolf Bultmann[8] and C. H. Dodd.[9] Both saw the Gospel as the work of a brilliant thinker who rethought the gospel tradition in response to a new challenge. Though the challenge was described differently by each and important consequences flow from these differences, their positions have more in common than is often thought. Both sought to discern the *Weltanschauung* that underpins the language of the Gospel. Bultmann found this in the evangelist's historicizing of Gnostic myth while Dodd argued that the evangelist had radically reinterpreted a (Middle) Platonic metaphysic. I remain convinced that discerning the *Weltanschauung* or

---

[8]With most Johannine scholars today this study does not follow Bultmann's source hypothesis. Nevertheless Bultmann's interpretation of the thought of the evangelist remains a profound and sustained contribution. It is so because he was determined to find the conceptual key to the Johannine categories and to discern how and where Jn fitted in early Christianity. See especially "Die Bedeutung neuerschlossenen mandäischen Quellen für das Verständnis des Johannesevangeliums", *ZNW* 24 (1925), 100-46; "Johannesevangelium" in *RGG*[3] III (Tübingen 1955), 840-50; and my *Theology as Hermeneutics: Rudolf Bultmann's Interpretation of the History of Jesus*.

[9]A host of other more recent works have been drawn on in specific ways as noted in *Quest*.

metaphysic presupposed by the evangelist is a key to a profound interpretation of his thought. Bultmann, Dodd, Barrett and others rightly stress the evangelist was a profound and creative interpreter of the Christian tradition. Bultmann, Dodd, Martyn and others correctly stress the concrete nature of that interpretation. So specific was the expression of the evangelist's thought that it needed to be reworked in changing situations. If this is true the tasks of reconstructing those situations and laying bare the presupposed *Weltanschauung* are not optional but essential to any precise understanding of the evangelist's thought.

Study of Jn as a book, a work of literature, is the fruit of our time. A number of clues suggest that Jn is a self-consciously literary work.[10] The author has referred to the principle of selection for material used in "this book" (20.30), an idiom taken up in the appended chapter, 21.25. Further, while the Synoptic Gospels have been studied in relation to the literary forms of the material used by the evangelists,[11] comparable studies have not been made of Jn.[12] There is, perhaps, good reason for this. Jn cannot readily be dissected in a way that reveals what probably are the underlying units of tradition, oral or written. For this reason it has been fashionable to refer to this Gospel as the seamless robe, a description (used by D. F. Strauss) intended to draw attention to the uniform wholeness of the Gospel. Yet there are notable exceptions to this impression. There is evidence that the evangelist has built up episodes in his overall story on the basis of small self-contained traditional story units, such as 5.2-9a; 6.2-15; 6.16-21; 9.1-11(13). Here *Quest* is in the tradition of the work of C. H. Dodd and Barnabas Lindars in recognizing in Jn Synoptic-like tradition which is probably independent of the Synoptics although this tradition cannot be isolated in detail and reconstructed to its full extent. There are also narrative breaks (*aporiai* such as 14.31, which presupposes that 18.1 should follow immediately), and thematic discontinuities. These can be understood as evidence of a process of composition in a series of editions.

Recent literary studies have however emphasized literary devices and themes which hold the book together. There is what Bultmann called the misunderstanding device used by the evangelist[13] and the characteristic use

---

[10]On this question as a whole see R. Alan Culpepper, *Anatomy of the Fourth Gospel.*

[11]See especially Rudolf Bultmann, *History of the Synoptic Tradition.*

[12]Though see the work of Johannes Beutler "Literarische Gattungen im Johannesevangelium. Ein Forschungsbericht 1919-1980" in *ANRW* II.25.3, 2506-2568.

[13]See Bultmann, *The Gospel of John*, 127 n1, 135 n1, 181f.

of irony, which has been featured in a recent study.[14] Much work still needs to be done on the literary techniques of the evangelist both in the telling of the stories and in his exposé of the teaching of Jesus. Louis Martyn has demonstrated the dramatic development of scenes in the telling of the story of the healing of the lame man (Jn 5) and of the blind man (Jn 9).[15] More work needs to be done in this area.

Some recent literary studies celebrate the passing of historical critical methods and the rise of two new paradigms, "literary criticism and social world criticism". But the assertion that cracks emerging in the foundations of the old methods opened so widely that they have now given way[16] is unjustifiably triumphalistic and, even in the USA where this movement is strongest, owes more to wishful thinking than to reality. This comment is made, not from a perspective that rejects insights from a literary perspective, but with the insistence that the new should be joined with the old in a critical way. Jn is a literary work *from the first century*. It is unrealistic to treat it as if it were a twentieth century composition and as if everything depended on the reader, as is argued by some "reader response" critics. If that were the case then any text read by a twentieth century reader would be read as a twentieth century text though the way this happens would depend on the particular reader so that we would have a variety of readings according to the number of readers. But with a text like Jn any reading presupposes at least a knowledge of Hellenistic Greek. If a reader begins with a translation prepared by others it is then a different work in which the possible meanings have already been modified by the translation. Consequently literary critics make use of historical critical methods, at least in a limited way, even when this is not acknowledged.

I. QUEST AND REJECTION STORIES IN A DUALISTIC CONTEXT

If we recognize the concrete nature of human cultures, as a literary work from the first century Jn should be read in terms of the literary conventions of that time and in terms of its specific cultural context. *Quest* is written

---

[14]See Paul D. Duke, *Irony in the Fourth Gospel*.

[15]See his *History and Theology in the Fourth Gospel*. See also chapter 5, "The Paradigm of Rejection" and chapter 8, "The Son of Man: The Light of the World" below. The development of the story along the lines of scenes in a drama suggests a self-consciously literary author. This work is to be attributed to the evangelist, not the author of a continuous narrative source as argued by Haenchen.

[16]Thus F. Segovia, *The Fourth Gospel from a Literary Perspective, Semeia* 53 (1991), 1.

on the assumption that while human reality provides a common basis making cross-cultural communication possible, positive communication (understanding) presupposes that the other culture is taken seriously *in its own terms*. Some reader response critics are concerned about the question of the literary *genre* of the text[17] and units within the text. This is a positive step in the direction of the recognition of the continuing role of historical methods. In *Quest* we are concerned to understand Jn as a whole and to perceive within the whole the place of types of stories, recognizable within ancient literature.

The evangelist's use of quest and rejection stories[18] throws light on both his situation and intention.[19] According to Robert Tannehill, pronouncement stories, of which quest and objection stories are sub-types, are concentrated in the Synoptic Gospels and in the Graeco-Roman political and philosophical biographies. There are, according to the studies he has edited, virtually no examples in the Jewish sources of the period or in other early Christian sources. This suggests some influence of Graeco-Roman biography, direct or indirect, on the evangelists.[20] The most common of the pronouncement stories, correction and objection stories, deal with situations of conflict, revealing the struggle between competing value systems in the ancient world. In the political and philosophical biographies a self-conscious struggle is revealed. The same is obviously true of the use of these stories in the Gospels. They are rightly considered in the general category as conflict stories.

Given that quest stories are (according to Tannehill) virtually restricted to the Synoptics (we add the examples in Jn), we have before us another aspect of the Johannine puzzle. It could be that quest stories came to the Synoptic evangelists more or less in their present form, though the absence of these stories from other contemporary sources than the Gospels and the concentration of these stories in Lk and Jn does not support this view. It is clear that the fourth evangelist shaped the quest stories of Jn. We will seek to discern what quest stories reveal about the situation and

---

[17]For example, F. Segovia thinks "the Gospel to be an example of ancient biography of the holy man as son of God type." *Semeia* 53,.3.

[18]See chapter 4, "Quest Stories in John 1–4" and chapter 5, "The Paradigm of Rejection" below for an exposition of quest and rejection stories and their place in Jn.

[19]See R. C. Tannehill (ed.), *Pronouncement Stories*. My own work, making use of Tannehill's analysis, is a feature of *Quest* though I prefer "rejection" to Tannehill's category "objection".

[20]This is one more piece of evidence that suggests that the last word has not yet been said on the relation of the Gospels to Graeco-Roman biographies. See now Richard Burridge, *What are the Gospels?*

orientation of the evangelist and his implied or intended readers.[21] Further, in the case of at least one quest story, the quest of the crowd (6.1-35(36)), the quest story has become the basis of a rejection story (6.1-66) which has been laid over the quest story like a second layer. Here quest has given way to rejection.

The expulsion from the synagogue marks a turning-point. Quest stories belong to the pre-expulsion situation while rejection stories are post-expulsion stories. The rejection stories were developed by making use of the tradition which portrayed Jesus' conflict with Jewish authorities which led to his arrest, trial, and execution. In Jn, however, the tradition portraying Jesus' conflict with Jewish authorities is used in a way that takes account of the conflict experienced by the Johannine community, culminating in their expulsion from the synagogue. Nowhere is this clearer than in John 9. Louis Martyn was right in using this chapter as a window into the history of the Johannine community. The evidence suggests that the quest and rejection stories were introduced in different editions of the Gospel. But in the final analysis these are not competing interests because the evangelist came to the view that the rejection of the Messiah was essential to the fulfilment of the age-old quest for the Messiah.

One of the purposes of *Quest* is to feature the quest and rejection stories to see what light they throw on the composition of the Gospel, the situation of the evangelist, the audiences in view and the understanding of the message the evangelist wished to communicate. The quest and rejection stories reveal something of the situation in which they were told and the orientation intended by the storyteller. That the situation of the evangelist can be illuminated by the way the stories are told might seem to be a precarious hypothesis. Might not the way the stories are told indicate an ideal situation, that is, where the author would like his readers to be? This comment certainly contains a caution. Language always reveals something of the speaker/author, whatever the speaker/author is speaking/writing about and it is easy to confuse the situation that shaped

---

[21]The distinction between "implied reader" and "intended reader" (and actual readers) is important. The completed text of the Gospel implies a particular readership which will understand what is written and needs the explanations that are provided in the text. It *need not* follow that such readers were the intended recipients or the original actual readers of the Gospel. The clues within the Gospel which imply a reader may have been laid unintentionally by the author or even in spite of his intentions. Nevertheless it is helpful to explore these clues to see if we can progress from implied to intended or even actual readers.

the language with the situation which the speaker/author wishes to shape with the language. Does the language in Jn reveal the situation of the speaker/author, or the orientation? A case in point is the story in John 9. Does the language of synagogue expulsion reveal the situation of the Johannine community or does it reflect the author's intention to call on members of the synagogue to face expulsion? It is the argument of *Quest* that it does both. In the first instance the language conveys the fact. In the next it calls on those who remain as secret believers within the synagogue to confess their faith openly and to face expulsion. It is also intended to reassure those who have braved excommunication that though they have been rejected by men they have been chosen by God.[22]

What of the dualistic language?[23] Does the language reveal a situation or an orientation? Again the answer is probably, "both!" In the case of the Qumran community the dualistic language, which (especially 1 QS III.13–IV.26) offers parallels as close to Jn as can be found, the language reflects the rejection of the rest of Judaism by the community and its exclusive identification of itself with the covenant people of God. In their case the orientation might have led to the social reality of separation. On the other hand it is possible that it was only after the community was alienated from the rest of Judaism that it developed the dualistic language which now dominates some of the writings of the community. In the case of Jn it seems that the community did not choose separation but was expelled from the synagogue. A good case can be made for thinking that the characteristic use of dualistic language is a consequence of that expulsion though it seems likely that the influence of a dualistic tradition contributed to the breach with the synagogue. This language gives expression to a social reality and, once it has been formed, it becomes the language of orientation, calling on all who will hear to join the user's side of the great divide. The language can only function this way because it is understood in terms of a dualistic worldview which provides the context for the Johannine quest for the Messiah.

Quest stories in Jn are of two major types.[24] First there are the manifold quest stories portraying individuals of every kind, a variety of

---

[22]See chapter 8, "The Son of Man: The Light of the World" below.

[23]Bultmann rightly saw the Johannine dualism as *a* key to the understanding of the Gospel. Wayne Meeks ("The Man from Heaven in Johannine Sectarianism") has shown it to be a key to understanding the social reality of the Johannine community. Further work needs to be done to show that the dualistic language reflects a dualistic world view related to apocalyptic understanding.

[24]For the second type see p. 22 below.

questers and a variety of quests, for the Messiah, for wine, for the Kingdom, for water, healing and life, for bread, and ultimately for Jesus. Indeed it is in the last quest story of chapters 1-12 that the object of the quest is clearly named, "Sir, we would see Jesus", 12.21. Naturally the evangelist insists that Jesus is actually the real object of all of these quests, whether the questers are conscious of this or not. This is part of the point in his use of the symbolic "I am..." sayings. In these Jesus identifies himself with whatever it is that is sought. Further, the narrative in Jn begins with the portrayal of the widespread quest for the Messiah, 1.19ff. That quest appears not only to be widespread, it is diffuse, ill-defined, and even expressed in contradictory ways. The purpose of the Gospel is to convince the readers that Jesus is the Christ. In doing this the evangelist seeks to clarify the nature of the quest. It is the quest for the Messiah. But for this to be a clarification the evangelist must reinterpret messiahship in terms of his understanding of Jesus. From this point of view the evangelist and his Gospel give expression to this quest and in the Gospel the reader comes finally to recognize the Messiah in Jesus. Consequently the Gospel is a self-conscious reinterpretation of the meaning of messiahship. It is also a reinterpretation of the quest for the Messiah as the quest for life, for eternal life. According to John the Messiah is none other than the revealer of God, the one in whom God is known and in whom eternal life is present, Jn 20.30-31.

II. THE QUEST FOR THE MESSIAH

The title, *The Quest for the Messiah,* has the virtue of highlighting the elusiveness of the Messiah. The Messiah must be sought. This is as true for the contemporary student who must seek to discern the concept or concepts of messiahship that are presupposed as it is for the questers in the story. It is not only the question of "who is the Messiah?", but also, "what is he like?" This state of confusion is well captured in the title of the recent book, *Judaisms and Their Messiahs at the Turn of the Christian Era.*[25] There it is argued that there were competing conceptions of messiahship in the first century. It is also recognized that the earliest Christian conceptions are rightly considered as Jewish. In this study we will survey the concepts which emerge on the pages of Jn, and seek to discern what understanding of messiahship is actually promoted through this telling of the story of Jesus. Naturally it is of interest to discern whether existing concepts are actually transformed by the evangelist in the process. In this regard we can ask whether the quest in view is Jewish and

---

[25]Edited by Jacob Neusner, William Scott Green and Ernest S. Frerichs.

Christian or an exclusively Christian quest. That is, does the understanding of messiahship that is promoted have precedent in other Jewish sources or is it found only in early Christian sources?

The focus on the quest for the Messiah appears at the beginning of Jn (1.19-51).[26] From the beginning it is clear that it is the quest for the Messiah, 1.19-20. Here we encounter for the first time the Jewish term Messiah transliterated (Μεσσίας) and translated into Greek (Χριστός), Jn 1.41. The series of incidents introduced by 1.19 alerts the reader to the widespread quest for the Messiah amongst widely divergent groups of people. That the Baptist's activity should provoke an official delegation to ask if he is the Messiah suggests something about perceived criteria for recognizing the appearance of the Messiah. From this point of view Jn presents a number of notable miracles which are designated signs and these are the basis for a widespread belief in Jesus, see 2.23-25. This material has given rise to the hypothesis of a signs source with a distinctive view of Jesus.[27]

III. THE SIGNS OF THE MESSIAH

Jn 20.30-31 indicates that the Gospel was written to promote the belief that Jesus is the Christ through the presentation of the signs of Jesus recorded in the Gospel. Thus we might naturally expect to find a tradition concerning the signs of the Messiah. It is therefore surprising to discover that there is no *evidence* independent of the Gospels of such an expectation within the Judaism contemporary with Jesus. It is this problem that is central to the recent impressive study by Hans-Jürgen Kuhn.[28] Kuhn recognizes Jn 1.35-42,44-50[29] as the introduction to the Signs Source. Because there is no evidence of a Jewish tradition of the signs of the Messiah he rejects the view that the community in which the source was formed considered Jesus to be the Davidic Messiah. In his critique of the work of Georg Richter he notes that the title "prophet" is not ascribed to

---

[26]See chapter 4, "Quest Stories in John 1–4" below.

[27]For a discussion of the signs source hypothesis see "Johannine Christianity" V.2 below.

[28]*Christologie und Wunder: Untersuchungen zu Joh 1.35-51.* This detailed study provides an overview of the exegesis of Jn 1.35-51 from 1700; a detailed literary analysis of the passage and its *genre*; a critique of the prophet Christology of Georg Richter and the *theios aner* Christology of Jürgen Becker followed by Kuhn's critical evaluation.

[29]He considers Jn 1.43,51 to be redactional.

Jesus in 1.35-51 and rejects Richter's view that the source portrayed him as the eschatological Mosaic prophet (of Deut 18.15-20).[30]

Kuhn's critique is also applicable to the work of Louis Martyn[31] and Robert Fortna.[32] While Martyn does not presuppose Fortna's source theory he perceives its compatibility with his own reconstruction of Johannine history[33] which Fortna evidently accepts.[34] Fortna asserts that the notion of messiahship presupposed by the Signs Gospel is not the political, Davidic liberator, the military victor but a healer, a worker of miracles, Elijah, the prophet like Moses, arguing that both Elijah and Moses worked miracles.[35] The weakness in this position is the failure to provide any evidence that the returning Elijah or the prophet like Moses were expected to work signs. This is simply assumed. In response to the alternative of a *theios aner* christology in either the Fourth Gospel or its predecessor Fortna adds a lengthy note. Here he concludes:

> In the end, however, the comparison is self-contradictory, for in both the pre-Johannine and Johannine christologies there is some correspondence with the divine-man figure but also divergence from it.[36]

The divergence is evidently significant enough for Fortna to reject the view that the divine-man provides the key to the christology of the signs source. Fortna, however, does not appear to be sensitive to the problem of the absence of evidence of a signs tradition in relation to messianic expectation.

Kuhn follows Bultmann, Becker and others in postulating a *theios aner* (divine man) christology for the source. He relates this to the Son of God designation of the Signs Source, which was more appropriate to the Jewish and early Christian context. Consequently he argues for the merging of

---

[30]*Christologie und Wunder*, 270-351.

[31]*History and Theology in the Fourth Gospel* and *The Gospel of John in Christian History* (especially chapters 1 and 3).

[32]*The Gospel of Signs*, 223-25, 228-34 and *The Fourth Gospel and its Predecessor*, 38, 225-34.

[33]Martyn, *History*, 92-3 n141.

[34]Fortna, *Predecessor*, 224.

[35]*Predecessor*, 38. In 287 n114 Fortna notes: "Clearly, the messianic expectations held by both author and audience of SQ were neither Davidic nor apocalyptic. The role that Jesus fills was to be seen not in the political conquests of a king or supernatural display of a cosmic saviour but in the miracles of Elijah, in the signs of the prophet like Moses." Fortna's views are similar to those of Wolfgang J. Bittner (*Jesu Zeichen im Johannesevangelium*) except that Bittner dismisses the signs source hypothesis.

[36]*Predecessor*, 229 n9.

Jewish and non-Jewish Hellenistic concepts in the christology of the source. All of this is argued in some detail and with great erudition. We need not be concerned that an Hellenistic perspective (a *theios aner* christology) dominates the signs source which, according to Bultmann, originated in a Palestinian Jewish baptist sect.[37] The possibility of Hellenistic influence on Palestinian Judaism no longer needs to be argued. But at this point the *theios aner* tradition is ambiguous.[38] It first needs to be recognized that the *theios aner* overlapped Hellenistic Jewish portrayals of Moses. Tiede argues that this arises as much from the influence of the Old Testament as from the concept of the *theios aner*. Further, there is in fact no clear typology of the *theios aner* and little evidence of the use of this category in Hellenistic Jewish sources. The piecing together of the evidence for the *theios aner* is drawn from sources widely divergent in time and place and without attention to whether they are pre-Johannine. Nor does the evidence suggest an inseparable or even characteristic connection between the *theios aner* and aretologies. More serious again is the association of the signs in Jn with Jesus perceived in messianic and prophetic terms. We cannot rule out the possibility that *theios aner* influences may have shaped messianic and prophetic categories in Jn, a process that might have taken place when the Johannine tradition moved into the *diaspora*. It is however more likely that, as in the case of Moses traditions, we are looking at parallel developments. Even in the Old Testament itself Moses and some of the prophets exhibit powers comparable to those of the *theios aner*. Thus prophetic categories overlap what we know of the *theios aner*, even though they should be understood in different contexts because the prophet does not act in his own power.[39]

---

[37]R. Bultmann, *John*, 106 says "The (signs) *source* showed Jesus as the θεῖος ἄνθρωπος, whose miraculous knowledge overwhelms those who meet him."

[38]On this matter see Carl H. Holladay, *Theios Aner in Hellenistic Judaism: A Critique of the use of this Category in New Testament Christology*, especially 233-42 where he sums up his conclusions. See also the work of D. L. Tiede, *The Charismatic Figure as Miracle Worker* (Missoula, 1972) and D. Moody Smith"The Milieu of the Johannine Miracle Source" now in his *Johannine Christianity*, esp 67-74.

[39]While Bultmann, Kuhn and others attributed the view of Jesus as a *theios aner* to the signs source, Ernst Käsemann, *The Testament of Jesus*, worked out the implications of this type of christology and attributed it to the completed Gospel. Marianne Meye Thompson, *The Humanity of Jesus in the Fourth Gospel* correctly criticizes Käsemann's view mainly by showing the unsuitable nature of his definition of human and offering a more persuasive characterization. She rightly argues that Jn assumes that Jesus is

It is, as Fortna has observed, the differences that preclude the adoption of a *theios aner* christology in relation to the Johannine presentation of the signs.

The tradition of signs as validation of the mission of the prophet is well established by Wolfgang Bittner.[40] These data constitute one of the fundamental strengths of Georg Richter's position in attributing a prophet christology to the source. But Kuhn noted that the prophet title is not ascribed to Jesus in the catalogue of titles used in 1.35-51. Bittner's criticism that the stated purpose of the Gospel is expressed in terms of Christ (20.30-31) not the prophet is also relevant in that this is thought to be the original conclusion of the signs source. Consequently he dismisses not only the *theios aner* but also the prophet christology arguing that neither Jn nor his source has a prophet christology. Jesus is not portrayed as a liberating sign-prophet. Jesus is the Christ but not a political liberator. Rather he is a "helper" Messiah, a view similar to that of Fortna. Bittner attempts to provide a bank of evidence for this view by appealing to traditions in Isaiah, especially Isaiah 11. While his work has the virtue of taking the Johannine categories seriously (John wrote of the Christ, not a *theios aner* or "the prophet"), his approach seems to have over-compartmentalized the categories. It is also difficult to justify the weight given to Isaiah 11 and other texts which are meant to support the specific connection between signs and the helper Messiah when these texts are not in focus in Jn.

The assumption that the Messiah will perform signs is stated in Jn 7.31. Cf. Matt 11.2. In Jn 1.35-51, though not referred to as a sign, Jesus manifests divine knowledge (1.47-50). Such knowledge is, according to the Samaritan woman, a characteristic of the coming Messiah (4.25) though she did not recognize Jesus' earlier manifestation of such powers as evidence of his messiahship but only an indication that he was a prophet (4.16-19). This, and other evidence, draws attention to a mass of ill-defined expectations prevalent in the first century, much of which could be, and probably was designated messianic. Here we should probably distinguish what is narrowly (or precisely) messianic from what is broadly messianic, or messianic in the popular perception of the day in which there was a merging of different views. The evidence of Jn 6.14-15 is important

---

human but argues that God is encountered in him. This is the position maintained by my own work. See my *John*, 20. The stress on Jesus' relation to and dependence on the Father fits the prophetic model better than the *theios aner* even if the stress is made in order to assert Jesus' authority. The paradigm of his authority is one of dependence.

[40] *Jesu Zeichen im Johannesevangelium*, 24-27, 34ff., 151-7.

here. Because the views expressed there do not represent either the evangelist or the early Christian communities it seems likely that the tradition reports a popular Jewish response to Jesus. There we are told that those who saw the feeding sign confessed Jesus to be *the* coming prophet and, although the report of Jesus' insight into their intention to make him king is a Johannine motif, the identification of the prophet with the messianic king is not. This is confirmed by the account of Jesus' withdrawal, rejecting the attempt to make him king. At this point John must reject popular messianic views in order to clarify the christology of the Gospel.

There is also the evidence of the "sign-prophets" referred to by Josephus,[41] and the warnings of Jesus' Apocalyptic discourse concerning the signs worked by the false Christs and false prophets (Mk 13.22 and parallels).[42] Matt's redaction of Q (Matt 11.2-19=Lk 7.18-35) adds the description "the works of the Messiah" ($\tau\grave{\alpha}$ $\check{\epsilon}\rho\gamma\alpha$ $\tauο\hat{υ}$ $X\rho\iota\sigma\tauο\hat{υ}$). According to Matt 11.2, what John the Baptist hears of in prison is "the works of the Messiah". In response he sends messengers to ask Jesus if he is indeed the coming one. Jesus' answer describes his works in words that echo Isaiah 35.5-6; 61.1. For Matthew and the early Christians these texts described the works of the Messiah. Hence we might suspect that, though the evidence now escapes us, there was the expectation that the Messiah would demonstrate his credentials with signs.[43] Naturally this situation changed after the disastrous Jewish war which saw the destruction of the holy place (the Temple) and the holy city. It may be that the absence of a messianic signs tradition from the Jewish sources is a consequence of this event and of the early Christian proclamation of Jesus as a wonder-working Messiah, see Acts 2.22,36.

That Jesus is portrayed in prophetic terms in Jn is difficult to deny in the light of the emphasis on his authority vested in his mission from the Father. The signs are taken as evidence that he is (sent) from God, 3.2; 9.33. Jesus himself appeals to his works ($\check{\epsilon}\rho\gamma\alpha$) as evidence of his

---

[41] See Josephus *AJ* xix.162; xx.167-172, 188; *BJ* ii.258-263; vi.285-286. In *BJ* vi.286 Josephus mentions a multitude of such prophets. That they were perceived to be prophets by the masses is clear from his reluctant naming them as such though he himself uses the term $\gamma\acuteο\eta\varsigma$ of them. See chapter 6, "The Messiah and the Bread of Life" below and the discussion in Wolfgang J. Bittner, *Jesu Zeichen im Johannesevangelium*, 57-74.

[42] In keeping with these traditions but in a new context the author of 1 Jn attributes the false confessions of faith to the anti*christ* and the Spirit of Error, 1 Jn 4.1-6.

[43] See Schürer, *History* II, 598-606, especially 603-6.

relation to the Father, 5.36. Clearly these terms (signs and works) overlap to some extent. It is almost true to say that "works" is the word Jesus uses and that "signs" belongs to the language of others.[44] Certainly Jesus' works include the signs he worked. But no action of Jesus is called a sign except a miracle of healing or providing food and drink. Thus, contrary to Bittner[45] and many others, it is argued in this study that "signs" refers only to Jesus' miraculous works. The signs are taken to be evidence of his messiahship. Hence, in spite of 2.23-25; 4.48; 6.26, it is not true to say that the evangelist has a negative view while the source had a positive view of the signs. After all the evangelist chose to narrate a number of them and to provide impressive summaries concerning many others all in the service of leading his readers to true belief in Jesus as the Messiah, 20.30-31. Indeed it is also true to say that because of the signs the failure to believe was the more reprehensible, 12.37-43. Certainly belief involved accepting Jesus' testimony to himself but belief in his works is seen to be a significant positive step in this direction, 10.38.

The work of Wayne Meeks[46] suggests that the concept of the coming eschatological Mosaic prophet was merged with that of the coming messianic king. But even this is only a starting point for Jn. Indeed we must say that other concepts have also been used in a way that interacts with messiahship, especially the Father/Son relation and the Son of Man. Consequently in Jn's christology the notion of prophetic mission has been radically transformed by the notion of the pre-existence (before Abraham, before the beginning of creation) of the Son who is sent into the world by the Father and is glorified and exalted to return to the Father by way of the cross. One can only say that at this point Johannine christology and Jewish messianic expectations widely diverge though the former has its

---

[44]Surprisingly Jesus' brothers use the term "works" (7.3) when refering to his "supposed" miracles. The use of "good work" by the Jews in 10.33 is not a real exception because they repeat Jesus' words. The question of the crowd (6.28) is a more interesting though they too pick up Jesus' language from 6.27 ("Do not work for the food that perishes"). They ask, "What must we do in order that we may work the works of God?" On the other hand Jesus uses the term "signs" in 4.48; 6.26. Both statements appear to be critical and, if anything, the latter is more critical than the former. At least signs and wonders are there (4.48) a basis of belief. In 6.26 it is not signs and belief that the crowd seeks but food.

[45]See *Jesu Zeichen*. Bittner argues that an event, miraculous or otherwise, that is announced in advance, is a sign. Though Jesus did not announce his signs in advance it is Bittner's argument that God announced them in Scripture.

[46]*The Prophet-King*, 67, 99.

roots in the latter, especially in the merging of the diversity of expectations that could broadly be called messianic.

IV. MESSIAHSHIP AND CHRISTOLOGY

The task of correlating the evidence of Jn with what we know of the first century is complex. The fragmentary evidence inside and outside the Gospel supports the view that there were widespread messianic expectations in the time of Jesus, though this view is contested by R. A. Horsley.[47] Horsley takes the sparse and fragmentary evidence to mean that messianic expectations were not widespread.

> It is becoming increasingly evident that there was little interest in a Messiah, Davidic or otherwise, let alone a standard messianic expectation, in the diverse Palestinian Jewish literature of late Second Temple times.

> Hence the unavoidable conclusion remains that ideas or expectations of a "Messiah" of any sort were not only rare but unimportant among the literate groups in late Second Temple Jewish Palestine.

This is an extreme position. The evidence should be read in a more nuanced way.

1. The evidence is fragmentary and such evidence as we have suggests that there were competing and overlapping messianic expectations.[48]

2. Christian christology takes its point of *departure* from messianic expectations and should not be read back into those expectations.[49] Nor can it be read out of those expectations. In addition to messianic expectations, other elements from the emerging Christian movement were essential for the emergence of christology.

3. Fragmentary though the evidence is concerning the Messiah this must be assessed in relation to the fragmentary evidence concerning Judaism in Palestine in the first century.

---

[47]"'Messianic' figures and movements in first-century Palestine" in *The Messiah: Developments in Earliest Judaism and Christianity*, ed. J.H. Charlesworth, 276-295, especially 278-80, 295.

[48]This is a major thesis of *Judaisms and their Messiahs at the turn of the Christian Era*, ed J. Neusner *et al.* and especially the essay by Wm Scott Green, 1-13. See also E. P. Sanders, *Judaism: Practice and Belief 63 BCE–66 CE*, 295–98.

[49]See J. H. Charlesworth, "From Messianology to Christology: Problems and Prospects", in *The Messiah*, 6. This section of *Quest*, "Messiahship and Christology" now finds support in his views.

4. Specific reference to the *mashiah* (anointed one) occurs only 38 times in the Hebrew Scriptures[50] and it seems that none of these is a reference to "the Messiah", though there are broadly messianic passages (Ps 2; 2 Sam 7; Isa 7; 9; 11; Zech 9; Dan 9.26). These passages were interpreted messianically by Jews in the two centuries prior to 70 CE and:

> "the Messiah" appears with unusual frequency and urgency only during this period, especially from the first century B.C.E. to 135 C.E.[51]

5. The tendency to insist that when "the Messiah" occurs it always refers to the Davidic kingly Messiah obscures the situation.[52] Certainly Pss of Sol 17 provide evidence of the future idealised Davidic king. Reference to the two Messiahs of the Qumran Texts,[53] and the interpretation of the Danielic Son of Man in 1 Enoch; 4 Ezra; 2 Baruch[54] as an individual heavenly messianic figure sufficiently fills out the complex messianic expectations of the time.

6. It is important to note that, in this complexity of messianic expectations, references to the messianic figures in the various texts appear to presuppose that the readers are familiar with them and their roles. To some extent this observation counters the force of the fragmentary nature of the evidence.

7. The relative absence of reference to the Messiah in the Mishnah is explained by Jacob Neusner in terms of a reaction to two disastrous wars and a concentration on sanctification rather than eschatological salvation.[55] He does not mention a third factor: the Jewish need to define itself over against the messianism/christology of the burgeoning Christian movement.

8. Horsley's rejection of eschatological expectations in relation to the Messiah are a consequence of an over narrow understanding of eschatology in terms of the end of the world.[56] Not surprisingly this is seen to be incompatible with movements to bring about social change. Both J. J.

---

[50]Wm Scott Green, "Messiah in Judaism" in *Judaisms and their Messiahs*, ed J. Neusner *et al.*, 2.

[51]J. H. Charlesworth, *op. cit.*, 12.

[52]Thus, correctly, J. J. Collins, "Messianism in the Maccabean Period" in *Judaisms and their Messiahs*, ed. J. Neusner *et al.*, 97, 106 n4. Wm Scott Green notes that although G. Vermes argues for a singular Davidic interpretation of "the Messiah", four other interpretations are possible. *Ibid.*, 13 n26.

[53]See 1 QS IX.11; 1 QSa II.12; 4 QPBless; CD XIV.19; XIX.10 and J. J. Collins, "Messianism in the Maccabean Period", *op cit.* 109 n43.

[54]See J. J. Collins, "The 'Son of Man' in First Century Judaism", *NTS* 38/3 (1992), 448-66, especially 464-6.

[55]*Messiah in Context: Israel's History and Destiny in Formative Judaism* (see my review in *Abr-Nahrain* 28 (1990), 139-42) and his essay, "Mishnah and Messiah" in *Judaisms and their Messiahs*, 265-282.

[56]*Op. cit.* 280-2.

Collins[57] and P. D. Hanson[58] affirm the complexity and importance of the eschatological understanding of Messiah.

9. Horsley gives too much weight to the evidence of Josephus. His observation that Josephus is our most important source for the period fails to take account of his post-Jewish war perspective. From this perspective the Mishnah also tends to ignore the Messiah. It is thus not surprising that the Messiah is absent from his account of Judaism in *Antiquities* and *Apion*.[59] Consequently Horsley's reading of Josephus is at this point somewhat uncritical. His failure to acknowledge eschatological implications in the proffered Exodus type signs of which Josephus writes is a consequence of equating eschatology with the end of the world. But this is a very strange view of eschatology within Judaism. Rather the proffered deliverance is to be understood in eschatological terms because it is identified with the paradigmatic divine deliverance of the past which has become the ideal deliverance of the future. What is offered (though not delivered) is not just deliverance, but divine deliverance which allows no room for looking beyond the act itself to any further progress.

10. Pervasive and complex messianic views are presupposed by the re-entry of the figure of the Messiah into Talmudic Judaism. Had the Messiah been as insignificant for Judaism as Horsley argues it is unthinkable that Judaism would have incorporated messianic expectation into the Talmuds, given the polemical and apologetic use of messianic motifs by Christians.

11. The use of Messiah in the Gospels (especially Jn, which alone uses the transliteration *Μεσσίας*, 1.41; 4.25) is also unintelligible if there were no widespread messianic expectation within Judaism . Here christology is built on and develops out of messianic expectation. If such messianic expectation were rare and unimportant this operation would make little sense.

This evidence throws light on the way Jesus was perceived by others rather than on the way he viewed himself. Amongst others Jesus was perceived in messianic terms. Like the sign prophets mentioned by Josephus the perception of the messianic role of Jesus was based on the signs that he performed. The irony is that, whereas the deaths of the other perceived messianic figures shattered the hopes associated with them, exposing them as an illusion, the death of Jesus led to a reaffirmation of his messiahship and its transformation into christology. The messianic perception of Jesus survived his death and was transformed into christology because of the belief in his resurrection. This pattern of transformation took place generally within the early Christian movement and in a somewhat distinctive form in Jn.

---

[57]*Op. cit.*, 97.
[58]"Messiahs and Messianic Figures in Proto-Apocalypticism" in *The Messiah*, ed. J. H. Charlesworth, 67, 75.
[59]Wm Scott Green, *op. cit.* 3.

The Gospel purports to tell the story of Jesus in the context of Palestine around the year 30 CE. The shaping of the Johannine tradition probably went on in Palestine until some time in the 60s. There is reason to believe that the evangelist, perhaps with a group of disciples, migrated to some place in the *diaspora*, perhaps Ephesus. There, until the publication of the Gospel in the last decade of the first century, the tradition continued to be shaped by the evangelist, and finally by a member or members of his school. Throughout this time the quest for the Messiah continued and it is likely that there were varying perceptions of messiahship. It would probably be a mistake to see this in terms of clear cut transitions from one concept to another. Rather it seems more appropriate to think of one perception being laid over another. It is likely that Davidic messiahship was at first primary and that this involved the notion of political deliverance. According to Jn Jesus struggled against that perception of Messiahship.[60] Against this background we can discern the criteria of Davidic messiahship being applied to Jesus.[61] While there are aspects of Jesus' mission that point in the direction of political liberation,[62] it is inconceivable that any signs source should have presented him in these terms because it would have involved the admission of dismal failure. Laid over this is the portrayal of Jesus as the prophet, or perhaps it is better to say, the perception of Jesus as the prophet like Moses. But this too is related to kingship and deliverance (Jn 6.14-15).

Arising out of the perception of the Davidic Messiah as the king of Israel is the title "Son of God" (Jn 1.49). In the underlying miracle tradition, if Son of God was used it was a messianic designation. It is only in the Gospel that it is given ontological status through the extensive treatment of the Father/Son relation where it takes on the sense of ontological sonship. Then, in the diaspora, this sense of sonship might have been interpreted in terms of the divine man (*theios aner*). Consequently, in the later strata of the Gospel[63] and in the Johannine letters, Christ no longer signifies Messiah, but is an alternative for Son of

---

[60]See Jn 1.49; 6.14-15; 11.45-53; 12.12-19; 18.33-38; 19.13-15,19-22.

[61]See Jn 1.49; and my "Christ and the Church in John 1.45-51" in *L'Evangile de Jean* ed. M. de Jonge, 359-62 and "The Church and Israel in the Gospel of John" *NTS* 25, 103-12.

[62]Jn 2.13-22; 12.12-19.

[63]Those references in the Gospel which speak of "Jesus Christ" (Jn 1.17; 17.3) no longer use messianic language but use the term Christ to refer to a divine being, though in the Gospel the paradox of the Word made flesh is maintained in the double name, "Jesus Christ". The double name signifies that "Jesus Christ has come in the flesh", or that "the Word became flesh".

God. But it should be stated unequivocally that neither in the Gospel nor in the Epistles is the category *theios aner* used.[64] Rather the category is applied (by modern scholars) to Jesus as a man who is declared to be Son of God in an ontological rather than an honorary sense. Consequently the finished Gospel allows for a number of levels of perception so that Jesus is understood as the fulfillment of various messianic conceptions. Ultimately the evangelist is intent to show that, whatever the conceptual starting-point of the quest for the Messiah, it finds its fulfillment in Jesus. That means that the conception is finally clarified by the reality of Jesus revealed in this Gospel. But to do this the evangelist must set Jesus against the various criteria developed to legitimate the various concepts of the Messiah. In some cases this is done with subtle irony, where the reader knows what the opponents of Jesus in the story do not know, that in fact Jesus does come from Bethlehem, the city of David (7.42).

V. THE LEGITIMATION OF CHRISTOLOGY

The major legitimation of Jesus is to be found in the signs that he worked. In this regard Jn does not differ greatly from Mk or Q where the miracles (especially the exorcisms) though not called signs, are taken as the evidence of the inbreaking of the Kingdom of God in the ministry of Jesus. In Jn the miracles are portrayed as legitimating signs but in a way that is incongruous with the lack of evidence to suggest that the Davidic Messiah or the prophet like Moses were expected to perform notable signs. Yet it is only to be expected that they would be able to demonstrate their legitimate authority. Thus, even if the tradition did not teach that the Messiah would perform signs, some demonstration of authority would be expected and descent from David would not be sufficient evidence by itself. It is here that the role of the signs emerges. But what can the signs demonstrate, from a Jewish point of view, from a Jewish Christian point of view, and from a Gentile Christian point of view? It is interesting to notice that nothing in Jn goes beyond a Jewish and Jewish Christian debate about the signs. Naturally that leaves open how Gentiles and Gentile Christians might understand that tradition.

---

[64]It is misleading to use this term of the christology of the Gospel which bears little resemblance to the Hellenistic figure. Rather by it we refer to the Word become flesh, Jesus Christ having come in the flesh. Perhaps it would be less misleading to use the later dogmatic formula, the God-Man, though this would be anachronistic. Here the hyphen takes seriously both the divine and the human. In the figure of the *theios aner* we have something of a composite figure.

Jn leaves no doubt that Jesus performed notable signs. This fact is reluctantly acknowledged by his Jewish opponents (9.18-23). It is the basis for the unexpected acknowledgement of Jesus as a teacher come from God (3.2), a recognition which led to the exclusion from the synagogue of the once blind man (9.24-34), and even causes division amongst the Pharisees (9.16) and the Jews (10.19-21). All of this suggests that, even if there was no tradition concerning signs to be worked by the Messiah, a collection of notable signs would have been useful in the dialogue with the synagogue. Contrary to Bultmann, Fortna, and Kuhn, amongst a host of others, the argument put forward in *Quest* is that the evangelist made use of a loose collection of Synoptic-like miracle stories,[65] not an extensive signs source. These traditions were worked up, together with fragments of traditional sayings, into the present Gospel. But this was not done all at once. Rather the evidence suggests a lengthy process and a number of stages, beginning in Palestine and being completed somewhere in the *diaspora*, perhaps Ephesus. In the process the quest is reinterpreted. From the quest for the Messiah it becomes the quest for life. The form in which life is sought remains appropriate to the Jewish quest. The dominant symbols for the life that is sought are the symbols which Judaism had come to use of the Law.[66] For Judaism life was to be found in the Law. For Jn life was to be found only in Jesus. Naturally this perspective opened the Gospel up to all those who found themselves to be lost or yearning for a dimension of life which transcended bare material existence. For such questers Jn has an alluring appeal and it is at this point that Dodd's reading of Jn is relevant.

VI. CHRISTOLOGY AND THEOLOGY

The christological focus of the Gospel is commonly recognized today. Yet what the evangelist had to say to his readers was profoundly theological in the most precise sense. He set out to talk of God in the only way he considered possible, that is, in terms of christology. For him christology

---

[65]The catenae referred to by Paul J. Achtemeier ("Towards the isolation of the Pre-Markan Miracle Catenae", *JBL* 89 (1970), 265-91) are more in keeping with what I envisage than Bultmann's extensive signs source. But Achtemeier's theory of the *Sitz-im-Leben* of the catenae ("The Origin and Formation of the Pre-Markan Miracle Catenae", *JBL* 91 (1972), 198-221) is unconvincing. In general my proposal fits well with the unrelated traditions and short collections proposed by Barnabas Lindars, *Behind the Fourth Gospel*, 38.

[66]See chapter 6, "The Messiah and the Bread of Life" and chapter 8, "The Son of Man: The Light of the World" below.

is the symbol for God in relation to his world and it is significant that the Gospel opens with the Prologue which speaks of God in relation to creation in terms of the *Logos*, creative, revealing and incarnate. The Prologue deserves full treatment in any book dealing with the message and theology of the Gospel. Indeed it seems clear that the Prologue offers an incisive insight into the message of the Gospel.

In the second type[67] of quest story Jesus is himself portrayed as the quester. These stories mesh into the distinctive Johannine presentation of Jesus and his mission, as the one sent from above, sent by the Father.[68] Consequently his quest is not one of self-expression or self-fulfilment. It is rather a quest laid upon him by another, a mission in that sense. The mission of the Son is the mission from the Father. The Father seeks and the Son seeks, yet there are not two quests but one. But that is only one side of the paradox. As we have seen, Jn presents a picture of the widespread and diffuse quest for the Messiah. Those who seek and find discover that underlying their quest is the quest of the Messiah for them and that his quest is an expression of the quest of the seeking Father (Jn 1.43; 3.15-16; 4.23; 6.36-40). The paradox is completed by the recognition that the Messiah's mission is successful and the quest of those who seek him is successful only when the Messiah has been rejected. The nature of his messiahship was revealed when he was lifted up (8.28) and his mission was fulfilled by drawing all men to himself (12.20-32). Those who are seeking him discover, in finding him, that they have been drawn by him.

The presentation of Jesus' quest might well belong to the second edition where the focus has moved from the quest for the Messiah to the rejection of the Messiah. The quest for the Messiah remains the central focus of Jn 1–4, though even here some modifications are evident, in the addition of the Prologue; Jn 1.51; the theme of the lifting up of the Son of Man in 3.13ff. and the theme of the judgement expressed in the light/darkness language that follows in 3.19-21; and the eschatological note that sounds in 4.21-24. But these modifications are minor in relation to the change that is signalled by Jn 5. Here, in the first miraculous sign followed by a discourse, we encounter for the first time in narrative form the theme of conflict and rejection. The reader is informed as if by an afterthought (Jn 5.9c) that the healing took place on the Sabbath. This then becomes the basis of controversy, accusation, persecution, and ultimately, the first attempt to kill Jesus. It is presented as the first of successive attempts by

---

[67]For the first type see p. 8 above.

[68]This theme will be treated extensively in the following chapters.

the Jewish authorities to kill Jesus.[69] As such it provides an account of the basis of the opposition to Jesus. It is, first, the accusation that Jesus' work broke the Sabbath. But, second, this led Jesus to identify his work with the work of the (my) Father (5.17) and to affirm, "I and my Father are one" (10.30). It was in the conflict with the synagogue that Jn developed the identification of his christology with theology.

Jn 5–12 is focussed on the rejection of the Messiah. The series of rejection stories shows how baseless is this rejection and how misguided is the thought and action leading to that rejection. Yet the theme of quest does not altogether disappear. Sometimes we are led to follow a quest that turns to rejection (as in Jn 6). With irony the evangelist is able to present the rejection of Jesus in terms of the quest to kill him (as in Jn 7–8). The quest of Mary and Martha to bring Jesus to save Lazarus leads paradoxically to the intensified rejection of him (Jn 11–12). The quest of the crowd to make Jesus king also contributes to this (12.12-19) and is followed by the quest of the Greeks to see Jesus (12.20-26), a quest that remains unfulfilled in the narrative but is promised eschatological fulfilment (12.31-32). Chapter 12 ends on the note of the failure of the signs to evoke faith (12.37), and this is justified by an appeal to Isaiah 6. Yet it is said that many of the rulers believed in him (12.42).[70] Perhaps the validity of this faith is put in question by the reference to the "many" (see 2.23-25). It is certainly made questionable by reference to their silence for fear of the Jews and the note that "they loved the glory of men rather than the glory of God" (12.42-43 and see 3.19-21). This is followed by Jesus' justification of his mission from the Father (12.43-50).

In addition to the theological perspective *Quest* also attempts to take account of the new literary studies, because the evangelist has given expression to his theology by telling a story. The message is expressed in dramatic and self-consciously literary ways. Social and sociological insights are also significant because, not only has the evangelist firmly embedded his theology in the story of Jesus but has also intermingled that

---

[69]See chapter 7, "The Hidden Messiah in John 7–8" below.

[70]This is certainly a formal contradiction of 12.37. Such formal contradictions can be taken as evidence of the evangelist's point of view coming into conflict with the source. Such a view does not seem to be necessary here. Rather the evangelist questions the effectiveness of the signs, by themselves, to produce adequate faith. What is needed in addition to this is Jesus' own understanding of his mission as set out in 12.43-50. Thus, throughout the Gospel, faith that begins with the signs is challenged to press on to take account of Jesus' words (5.36; 10.37-39) which elucidate his relation to the Father.

story with the story of his own community. Naturally, distinguishing the two stories remains a task both precarious and controversial. The rewards for attempting the task are compensation enough reminding us, amongst other things, that the Logos became flesh and is encountered in the midst of human society.

VII. CRISES IN THE QUEST FOR THE MESSIAH

The theme of rejection prepares the way for the passion. But before this can be narrated Jesus must farewell his disciples and prepare them for the coming crises. The farewell scene is to be understood in terms of a recognizable literary *genre*.[71] The evangelist has made use of this in an impressive fashion. In the farewell scene the evangelist displays a literary finesse in portraying Jesus' washing of the disciples feet in a way that recalls the washing and anointing of his own by Mary (Jn 12.1-8; 13.1-20). This suggests that the description of the resurrection of Jesus is also consciously set over against the description of the raising of Lazarus. The farewell discourses themselves have been built up in an impressive fashion. Here, as elsewhere, there is evidence that the Gospel was written in stages. The evangelist has produced the discourses in stages so that Jesus is able to prepare the Johannine community for the successive crises that it is to face.

The first of these crises was the crucifixion of the Messiah. Jn takes up the early Christian theme that Jesus gave his life for his friends and that this is a manifestation of his love, indeed of the divine love for the world. The death of Jesus is also portrayed as his necessary departure to the Father, thus enabling the coming of the Spirit Paraclete. The farewell discourses indicate that the crisis caused by the departure of Jesus left the sorrowing disciples. Their sense of abandonment was exacerbated by the failure of Jesus' imminent return to materialize. The Spirit Paraclete appears as the comforter who brings the presence of the absent Jesus to the sorrowing disciples. It is also the Spirit Paraclete who prepares the disciples for their mission in the world. This mission is presented in a number of stages. It is mission in the face of intense Jewish persecution. In this context the Spirit produces the knowledge of Jesus and the authentic witness to him within the believing community[72] and in the face of the hostile world. The hostility of the Jewish world to the disciples of Jesus is portrayed as the most important context for the formation of this Gospel. It is true that the completed Gospel looks back bitterly on the

---

[71]See F.F. Segovia, *Farewell*, 1-58.
[72]See R. Bultmann, *Th.N.T.* II, 92.

expulsion from the synagogue as a traumatic past event. Consequently there is a stratum of discourse that looks forward hopefully to this new situation while at the same time recognizing the perils that lurk in the future.

VIII. PERSPECTIVE AND OVERVIEW

The chapters that follow take account of the evidence that the Gospel is the product of a long and specific history. It reflects the history of Jewish believers in Jesus who were eventually ostracized from the synagogue for their faith. In this process the evangelist has developed a distinctive understanding of Jesus' miracles as signs. In the first instance the signs appear to have been used as a basis for missionary proclamation in the synagogue context. What christology this proclamation implied is difficult to say given the absence of any evidence of a tradition that the Messiah or the Mosaic prophet would work signs. Yet the appropriateness of legitimating signs seems obvious enough. This is supported by what Paul says in 1 Cor 1.22ff.:

> For since the Jews ask ($a\hat{\iota}\tau o\hat{\upsilon}\sigma\iota\nu$) for signs and the Greeks seek ($\zeta\eta\tauo\hat{\upsilon}\sigma\iota\nu$) wisdom, but we preach Christ crucified, to the Jews a stumbling block ($\sigma\kappa\acute{a}\nu\delta a\lambda o\nu$), and to the Gentiles foolishness ($\mu\omega\rho\acute{\iota}a\nu$), but to those who are called, whether Jews or Greeks, Christ the power ($\delta\acute{\upsilon}\nu a\mu\iota\nu$) of God and the wisdom ($\sigma o\phi\acute{\iota}a\nu$) of God.

From this perspective it seems likely that the signs would have been a relevant and persuasive form of proclamation to the Jewish synagogue, whether in the diaspora or in Palestine. Jn adopts this approach but ultimately it is Jesus' self-witness, as proclaimed by the Gospel, that has the last word. It is here that the mystery of Jesus' Messiahship is ultimately revealed and the quest for the Messiah reaches fulfilment. Yet it is only through the rejection and departure of the Messiah that the quest is fulfilled. Only when he has been rejected, when he has departed, do the disciples remember what Jesus has taught and believe in a way that brings the quest for the Messiah to fulfilment (Jn 2.22; 12.16).

Paradoxically, in Jn the quest for the Messiah necessitates his rejection if the quest is finally to reach fulfilment. Nowhere is this clearer than in the response of Caiaphas to the spectacular success of Jesus through the raising of Lazarus (Jn 11.45-53). We are told that many of the Jews believed in him when they saw what he did. Others reported to the Pharisees what Jesus did. The chief-priests and the Pharisees came together in council and said:

"What shall we do because this man does many signs? If we permit him (to behave) in this way, all will believe in him, and the Romans will come and destroy our holy place[73] and nation."

Caiaphas, the high priest replied:

"You do not know anything, nor do you reckon that it is expedient for us that one man should die for the people and that the whole nation should not perish."

We are then reminded that as high priest Caiaphas spoke prophetically:

He prophesied that Jesus was about to die for the nation, and not for the nation only but to gather into one the children of God who were scattered abroad.

Naturally this last comment is meant to be understood as the omniscient interpretation of the narrator[74] who brings to light the hidden meaning of the words of Caiaphas, meaning of which he had no idea and it is only in this sense that his words can be understood as prophecy. That gathering together of the scattered children of God is prefigured in the coming of the Greeks with their request: "Sir, we wish to see Jesus" (Jn 12.20). This formally unfulfilled quest story looks forward to fulfilment in the eschatological moment of judgement of which Jesus speaks:

"And I if I am lifted up from the earth will draw all men to myself". (Jn 12.31-32)

Only when he was rejected would Jesus be lifted up. Only then would the quest to seek and find him be fulfilled. Hence the title of this book, *The Quest for the Messiah* already presupposes the rejection of the Messiah. All quests prior to his rejection are only fulfilled in a preliminary fashion. This is the paradox, that the faith of the many in Jesus that is frequently noted (2.23-25; 11.45,48) does not yet perceive who Jesus is, that the quest for the Messiah is still in progress. Only when he is lifted up is the Messiah truly revealed and the quest for the Messiah reaches its true fulfilment. Of course this fulfilment is also a product of the work of the Spirit Paraclete, whose coming the withdrawal (exaltation) of Jesus makes possible.

---

[73]Here the Greek is simply "our place" ($\dot{\eta}\mu\tilde{\omega}\nu...\dot{o}\nu$ $\tau\dot{o}\pi o\nu$), but "the place" is clearly a reference to the Temple. See Jn 4.20 where the Samaritan woman refers to the place ($\dot{o}$ $\tau\dot{o}\pi o s$) where Jews say people must worship. This too is a reference to the Temple. Compare Jer 7.14; Neh 4.7; 2 Macc 5.19; Acts 6.14; 21.28 and *Bikkurim* 2.2 where the place, though focused on the Temple, may include Jerusalem.

[74]Omniscience here is not only the benefit of hindsight but also the narrator's insight into what the Gospel proclaims as the saving work of God.

A summary of the way the following chapters fit together can now be given. The development of the theme of the quest for the Messiah is intimately related to the history and character of Johannine Christianity. Because of this a chapter is devoted to "Johannine Christianity", the evidence, the scope, and something of its character. This chapter is a summary which signals the context for the more specific studies which follow and is, to some extent, justified by them.[75] Though the Prologue is probably a late addition to the Gospel it is the intended Prologue. The Prologue *genre* is well known in Hellenistic literature. In it the narrator provides the reader with a glimpse of his omniscient view. It is a God's eye view which places the reader in a position of advantage over the characters in the story (apart from Jesus). The reader knows from the beginning what the disciples will come to know only by the end of the story when Jesus has been lifted up and the Spirit has been given. Attention is also turned to the light the Prologue throws on the history of Johannine Christianity.

Jn 1–4 forms a structural unit dealing with the quest for the Messiah while Jn 5–12 develops the theme of the rejection of the Messiah. The basis for this rejection is laid down in Jn 5 and is the subject of the chapter, "The Paradigm of Rejection". In Jn 6 the themes of quest and rejection are intertwined in a way that suggests a reworking of the theme of quest. Ironically some of the motifs that have been used in setting out the quest for the Messiah reappear in Jn 7–8 as the opponents of Jesus *seek* to arrest and kill him. This chapter is entitled "The Hidden Messiah". Jn 9 is rightly a focal point in that, as in Jn 5, we have an instance of a miracle story that becomes the basis of a rejection story. Whereas Jn 5 deals with the rejection of Jesus, Jn 9 portrays the rejection of the blind man who had been healed by Jesus. The overt conflict depicted in Jn 9 is captured in the title "The Son of Man: The Light of the World" so that attention is drawn to the centrality of the symbolic dualism of light and darkness. Jn 10 continues the theme of conflict with Jesus taking up the critique of the Jewish leaders through a parable (aptly entitled "The Good Shepherd") and multiple interpretations of it. In these studies we are concerned to discern the history of the tradition thus throwing light on the history of the Johannine community and to draw out the contribution these chapters make to Johannine theology and particularly the theme of the quest for the Messiah.

---

[75] A detailed treatment of the various themes of this chapter is not practicable because each of them calls for a lengthy monograph.

Jn 5 and 10 form a literary *inclusio* suggesting that at some stage the public ministry of Jesus concluded with Jn 10.42. Jn 11–12 appear to be a secondary conclusion to the public ministry providing a further basis for the rejection, trial and execution of Jesus. Literary, historical and theological problems find focus in the study of the Farewell discourses which provide both a rationale for the stages of theological development in the Gospel and something of a trajectory in the direction of the Johannine Epistles. A study of the opponents in 1 John traces the trajectory as far as we can follow it to the schism in the Johannine community providing a detailed discussion of the basis of the schism. Finally, the implications of these studies for the theme of the quest for the Messiah are drawn together with a view to assessing their importance for an understanding of Johannine history, literature and theology.

While the theme of the quest for the Messiah runs through this book, attention has also been paid to the way the various parts of the Gospel fit together and contribute to this theme. The form of *Quest* is not that of a synthesis or simply a logically developed argument. Rather it respects the integrity of the Gospel itself and, in this respect, inclines somewhat in the direction of a commentary. Not all issues and problems are treated however, nor is a section by section commentary given, though each chapter of the Gospel (apart from the passion and resurrection narratives) is the subject of study in a chapter of *Quest*. A fuller treatment of the passion and resurrection narratives, though relevant to the theme of *Quest*, must await further research.

In *Quest* three major and related tasks are undertaken. There is *first* the recognition of the evidence that suggests a process of composition which leads on to the attempt to detect the underlying tradition. Arising from this there is an attempt to see if something of the process of composition can be reconstructed. While it is possible to recognize the way the underlying tradition surfaces from time to time, there is no attempt to isolate and reconstruct the source(s) in detail. The compositional methods of the evangelist have made this too uncertain to be practicable. The attempt to outline the development of the composition of the Gospel should be seen in terms of the recognition of watersheds rather than a precise detailed account of the development.

Second, there is the task of recognizing the evidence that suggests that the Gospel was shaped in the history of the Johannine believers. The impact of that history has left its mark in the Gospel and the developing Gospel can be seen as a response to a series of crises. The crises are identified by evidence in the Gospel itself especially where differences from the Synoptics can be understood in terms of what we know from other sources of the history of the early Christian movement. The resulting reconstruction, hypothetical as it is, is nothing like a complete history. Rather it identifies the critical situations in which the Gospel was written.

Third, Quest is concerned with the interpretation of the Gospel in its completed form. Hence the chapters of *Quest* follow the sequence of the Gospel and can be consulted as a commentary, though this is not exhaustive but from the perspective of the quest for the Messiah. The first and second tasks are intimately related and have implications for the third task. Though the findings of the third task can stand alone, the discernment of them is aided by the conclusions concerning the development of the tradition and the history of the Johannine believers. Theories about sources and the development of tradition and the history of the Johannine believers are used only in as much as they illuminate the meaning of the text as it now stands.[76] In this task an awareness of Hellenistic rhetoric and Jewish and Greek literary conventions is also invaluable.

IX. THE JEWS AND THE QUEST FOR THE MESSIAH

The quest for the Messiah in Jn is portrayed from the point of view of those who had found Jesus to be the Messiah and through their confession of faith in him had come into conflict with the synagogue and eventually into an enforced schism from it. Their reaction was to vilify the Jews calling them children of the devil. Indeed this charge is placed on the lips of Jesus who calls the Jews children of the devil while they assert that he is a Samaritan and demon possessed, 8.39-59. These terms reveal the bitterness involved in the parting of the ways between the Johannine Christians and the synagogue. Apparently the bitterness was mutual. From this point of view it can be said with some justification that Jn is the most anti-Jewish book in the New Testament.[77] But such an accusation demands clarification.

Jn is certainly not an anti-Semitic work. It is clearly stated in the Gospel that Jesus was himself a Jew and it is accepted in this study that the Johannine Christians were Jewish. Naturally what we mean by Jewish

---

[76]See pp.61–87 and 98–119.

[77]In many ways Matt reveals an equally bitter attitude. The woes pronounced on the scribes and Pharisees in Matt 23 are in fact aimed at their successors in rabbinic or synagogue Judaism after 70 CE. While Matt cannot have known the influence that the words "His blood be upon us and upon our children" (Matt 27.25) would have in subsequent history, they certainly broaden the base of the blame for Jesus' death beyond those who were directly involved.

demands closer attention. In the first place it signifies those who trace their history through Moses and back to Abraham. Such ethnicity involves more than genetic descent. From Abraham to Moses to David and Jews of the first century there was a history of tradition and culture. To be Jewish is to be an essential part of that history. Those Jews who believed Jesus to be the Messiah understood such belief to arise from the mainstream of that history but those who rejected the claim saw it as a break with the tradition. Thus the confession of faith in Jesus as the Messiah set believers apart from other Jews. Being rejected by the synagogue they were not treated as Jews and came to regard those who had rejected them as the Jews.

The bitterness reflected in Jn reveals an urgent struggle between two groups each of which understood its very existence to be threatened. With the destruction of Jerusalem and the Temple, focal points of Jewish identity had been destroyed. Thus Judaism was in search of new marks of identity. These marks were not intended for the use of others to enable them to recognize Jews. The marks were intended for Jews to enable them to recognize themselves as Jewish and to provide a formula for survival without holy city (Jerusalem) and holy place (Temple). What emerged was a form of orthodoxy which could find no place for those who confessed Jesus as Messiah. They were rejected unequivocally, even brutally. The bitterness of the reaction to such rejection is at least intelligible even if it is not excusable. In our age of ecumenism such hostility has rightly been condemned and, given the history of anti-Semitism since Constantine, it is not surprising or unreasonable that focus should fall on this side of the bitterness. Historically, however, it is important to recognize that the bitterness was originally mutual and that in the early period the believers in Jesus were the powerless minority.

In condemning the bitterness and hostility the differences that separated the two groups can be minimized to a point that fails to do justice to history. The conflict was more than a clash of personalities and it is the task of modern scholars to examine whether the opposed positions depicted in Jn actually represent the situation that led to the parting of the ways between the Johannine community and the synagogue. It is also important to see how far these positions were (and are) essential to Judaism and Christianity as distinct from differences arising from a violent clash between two groups. Here Jn's quest for the Messiah is crucial. Jn interpreted messiahship in terms of the unique divine sonship of Jesus as the emissary from the Father. This view, together with Jn's teaching about the Spirit/Paraclete, moved the church firmly in a trinitarian direction which the synagogue refused to follow. Consequently we should

30

recognize that a real and significant difference was the basis of the breach between the Johannine community and the synagogue. In rejecting the bitterness with which the debate was enacted it would be a mistake to ignore or minimize the real differences that provoked it. We should, however, guard against anachronistically reading full-blown trinitarian debates back into the Gospel. In Jn christological development has its source in Jewish messianic expectations and Wisdom speculation and lacks the precision of later definitions. It would be surprising if it violated belief in one God[78] though it may have strained the credulity of the opponents.

The Johannine community was born in a bitter schism. Before long that community was itself rent by a schism. In this case neither the continuing Johannine community nor its opponents were excommunicated by the other side.[79] Rather the opponents appear to have withdrawn from fellowship with the Johannine community. One of the major causes of this schism was the confession of faith in Jesus. The author of 1 Jn and his supporters maintained that the confession of faith in Jesus involved the acceptance that "Jesus Christ has come in the flesh". This apparently took account of the giving of his life for the life of the world. The opponents either denied this or at least saw nothing significant in Jesus' actual life and death. Consequently this schism also took place over the meaning of Jesus as the Christ. The conflict led to bitter invective against the opponents and we might suspect that they returned the abuse. The author of 1 Jn terms his opponents "false prophets". They are of "the anti-Christ" and their confession is a manifestation of the Spirit of Error. Consequently we see that the invective against those who dissented from within the Christian community was equally as bitter as the conflict with the Jews. Again it is important to be able to distinguish the bitterness with which the debate was carried on from the importance of the issues that were debated.

---

[78]See the Foreword to the second edition of J. D. G. Dunn, *Christology in the Making*.

[79]Jn 9.22,34 indicates an active exclusion. See also 12.42 and 16.2. But 1 Jn 2.19 describes what was apparently a voluntary withdrawal.

2

Johannine Christianity

Discussion of Johannine Christianity is dependent on the recognition of a discrete collection of distinctive Johannine writings, the Gospel, three Epistles, and the Apocalypse. While the Apocalypse stands apart from the rest of the Johannine literature[1] there is good reason for recognizing that it belongs there. It shares more Johannine characteristics than any New Testament book outside the Johannine corpus[2] and early tradition recognized it as an essential part of that corpus. It has, however, become increasingly clear that these books are not straightforwardly the compositions of a single author. The Johannine literature appears to be the work of the Johannine school.[3] The writings of the school give expression to Johannine Christianity and the original readers to whom these works were addressed can be described as the Johannine community or communities. In discussing Johannine Christianity we can ask about differences within the school. We can also ask how far the school was characteristic of the Johannine community and whether that community was at all different from other Christian communities of the time. In doing this our primary focus will be on the Gospel and to a lesser extent on 1 Jn.

In the twenty years following the Second World War there emerged what J. A. T. Robinson called "the new look of the Fourth Gospel".[4] Much of the motivation for this development arose from the intense interest in the then recently discovered Qumran Texts and their obvious relevance for Johannine studies. Because of this there was a renewed emphasis on the Jewishness of the Gospel. While this emphasis was not in itself new, it

---

[1] See especially E. S. Fiorenza, "The Quest for the Johannine School: The Apocalypse and the Fourth Gospel", *NTS* 23 (1976-7), 402-27. Fiorenza argues that the Apocalypse is closer to Pauline than Johannine Christianity.
[2] The Apocalypse stands generally with the Johannine literature in the portrayal of Jesus as the Word of God, the emphasis on witness (μαρτυρία), and the focus on the role of the Spirit. For other points of contact see Barrett, *John*, 62, 133-4 and R. E. Brown, *Epistles*, 56 n131.
[3] See R. A. Culpepper, *The Johannine School* for a discussion of the character of the school. It is argued in *Quest* that the Johannine school comprised the evangelist and a small group strongly influenced by his views. The school is to be distinguished from the Johannine community, the intended audience of the Johannine writings, the audience these writings were intended to influence.
[4] The paper, delivered in 1957, is now printed in his *Twelve New Testament Studies*, 94-106.

took on a new significance. Formerly it had been a minority view; it now became the popular position. The context of the formation of the Johannine tradition now came to be seen in the events which led to the expulsion of Jewish believers in Jesus from the synagogue.[5] This tendency was given a systematic treatment in J.L. Martyn's *History and Theology in the Fourth Gospel*, a work that has been influential in the further development of the "new look". Thus, whereas the stress on Jewishness had previously been associated with the suggestion that Jn should not be regarded as a later hellenization of an earlier Jewish Gospel, recognition of the importance of the synagogue struggle was now used to confirm a publication date in the last decade of the first century. There has also been a blurring of the distinction between Jewish and Hellenistic. No consensus has emerged in detailed interpretation and the "new look" has tended to fragment into a variety of positions on specific issues though the term aptly describes the general direction in which the straws of modern scholarship were blowing.

Because of the distinctive character of Johannine Christianity the role of the Jesus tradition can be overlooked. Whatever the difficulties in establishing the precise relation of Jn to the Synoptics, the evidence leaves no doubt that the evangelist is an interpreter of the Jesus tradition. Important as this observation is, it hardly begins to solve the problem of the distinctive nature of Johannine Christianity. Nor do the few points of contact with Paul shed much light on this puzzle, for a solution to which we must turn to other considerations.

The distinctive character of Jn can be accounted for in a number of ways: by reference to a distinctive source; or the thought world which shaped the concepts and language of the evangelist; or the peculiar history of the Johannine community. Most likely we should reckon with some balance combining all of these factors and not neglecting the distinctive contribution made by the evangelist which should not be thought to be simply as an amalgam of these influences. At this point we are concerned with the character and importance of the thought-world of the evangelist. While in the past the view that the most significant thought-world influencing the evangelist was that of Gnosticism[6] or one or more of the

---

[5]This was one conclusion of my own Ph.D. thesis written in Durham 1965-67, *The Idea of Knowledge in the Johannine Gospel and Epistles*, 50, 113 and had been the focus of an earlier but largely ignored article by K. L Carroll, "The Fourth Gospel and the Exclusion of Christians from the Synagogue", *BJRL* 40 (1957-8), 19-32. See also M. von Arble, "Über den Zweck des Johannesevangelium".

[6]The interpretation of the Gospel in the light of Gnostic categories has long been associated with the name of Rudolf Bultmann who developed his

schools of Greek philosophy[7] found many supporters, there has been a shift to emphasize the Jewish context of thought since the discovery of the Qumran Texts. Those texts, however, revealed the extent of hellenization of Palestinian Judaism and the thought world to which we refer is that of the syncretistic (mixed) Judaism of first century Palestine in which gnosticizing tendencies were evident and elements of popular Greek philosophy were present.

I. JOHN AND QUMRAN

In *Quest* it is argued that the syncretistic Judaism of the Hellenistic age, in which Gnostic tendencies had developed,[8] was the context in which the Johannine language and tradition were shaped. That form of Judaism is best known to us in the Qumran Texts.[9] These texts throw light on the character of syncretistic Palestinian[10] Judaism in the first half of the first century and, in the absence of other significant literary evidence from that period, the importance of the Qumran texts is difficult to exaggerate. The Jewish war of 66-74 CE marks a time of change in Judaism so that sources from a later period ought not to be taken as an accurate guide for the earlier period, especially in Palestine. It is not necessary to argue that the evangelist was influenced directly by the Qumran sect, though some relation to it cannot be ruled out.[11] The texts are used to demonstrate the character of Palestinian Judaism in the period and the sectarian character of the Johannine consciousness. Not all of the emphases found in these texts can be peculiar to Qumran. Many of them must have been shared with other groups. Thus, while recognizing differences from Qumran, points of contact are taken to indicate only some relation to sectarian Palestinian

---

thesis in a number of brilliant articles in the 1930s and set out his position in his great commentary on the Gospel.

[7]C. H. Dodd (in *The Bible and the Greeks* and *Interpretation*, 276f., 296) developed a Platonic interpretation of the Gospel based on the writings of Philo and the *Corpus Hermeticum* as an indication of thought world of the readers of the Gospel.

[8]See my "Gnosticism and the Qumran Texts".

[9]See R. E. Brown, "The Qumran Scrolls and the Johannine Gospel and Epistles"; *John* I, lxiii; R. Schnackenburg, *John* I, 134ff.; J. H. Charlesworth (ed), *John and Qumran*; H. Braun, *Qumran und das Neue Testament*, 2 vols; E. Lohse (ed.), *Die Texte aus Qumran*; G. Vermes, *The Dead Sea Scrolls in English*, T. Gaster, *The Scriptures of the Dead Sea Sect*.

[10]Although anachronistic, "Palestine" is a convenient term with which to refer to what were separate territories in the first century.

[11]John Ashton, *Understanding*, (205, 235ff.) sees no advantage in a theory of indirect connection between Jn and Qumran and postulates that Jn had been an Essene. The evidence, however, while not ruling out this possibility, fails to make it a probability.

Judaism. From this perspective the Qumran Texts provide us with our most important evidence concerning the evangelist's thought world.

With John Ashton I agree that Jn's language reflects his world of thought and is not to be understood as in some sense "borrowed".[12] Whether this makes the theory that Jn was once an Essene probable or that the forms of dualism evident at Qumran and in Jn were more widespread is more likely strikes me as being an open question. To have the courage to choose at this point could be unwise.

The texts reveal the influence of hellenization on Judaism. Hellenization was a complex process. Through Alexander's political and cultural conquest Greek language and thought reached every part of the empire. As a consequence and by design this led to the active interaction between Greek culture and the cultures of all conquered peoples. Through this interaction the overarching Greek culture became the channel through which elements of the cultures of conquered nations also flowed to every part of the empire. The Judaism of the Qumran Texts is the syncretistic Judaism of the Hellenistic age. But it is the Judaism of Palestine which expressed itself characteristically in Hebrew and Aramaic. The use of these languages indicates the nationalistic bent of those who produced the texts. Consciously they rejected Greek language and the culture which that language bore. But Judaism had by that time imbibed Hellenistic influence, including the non-Greek elements which it transmitted.

In the texts we become aware of the complexity of the quest for the Messiah in first century Judaism (1 QS IX.9-11 and the *Messianic Anthology)* and the uncertainty with which the quest was pursued at times (CD I.9). Yet in a Jewish context the role of the Law was prominent even if this was understood in an eschatological and dualistic framework.

1. Dualism

Two important elements appear in the Qumran Texts which should probably be attributed to Hellenistic influence. The first is the modified dualism which provides us with the closest literary parallel to Jn. That dualism is commonly attributed to Persian (Zoroastrian) influence.[13] While there were ample opportunities for this to have occurred in the Babylonian exile the evidence suggests that the time for significant influence of Persian dualism on Judaism was subsequent to the conquest by Alexander the Great, thus in the Hellenistic age.

---

[12]Contrary to C. H. Dodd, *Epistles* xvii-xviii, who argues that the evangelist mastered "alien categories".

[13]See the discussion of the complex issue of the attribution of influence in James Barr's, "The Question of Religious Influence: The Case of Zoroastrianism, Judaism, and Christianity".

It is sometimes objected that modified dualism is to be found in the Old Testament,[14] and that the dualism of Qumran and Jn arises from this influence without any need to postulate Persian or other Hellenistic influence. There is some merit in the positive part of that position. Modified dualism is to be found in the Old Testament and a few expressions of this are quite notable. But we find no developed or systematic expression of a dualistic position in the Old Testament such as we find at Qumran and in Jn. In both the Qumran Texts and Jn the dualism is modified by the doctrine of creation; 1 QS XI.11[15] and Jn 1.3 decisively exclude the possibility that there is anything at all not created by God:[16]

All things come to pass by his knowledge;	All things came to be through him,
He establishes all things by his design and without him nothing is done. 1 QS XI.11 cf. III.15 (Vermes 93, 75).	and without him nothing came to be... Jn 1.3.

It can even be suggested that "knowledge" *(da'ath)* in 1 QS XI.11 is the equivalent of the λόγος in Jn 1.1-3. To be fair it must be admitted that "knowledge" is not developed as an ontological principal in the way the λόγος is in the Prologue of Jn but the potential for such development is apparent.

Alongside one such statement in the texts (1 QS III.15), which is remarkably similar to the passage quoted, we find the most thoroughgoing expression of dualism in the texts:

> He (God) has created man to govern the world, and has appointed for him two spirits in which to walk until the time of his visitation: the spirits of truth and falsehood. Those born of truth spring from a fountain of light, but those born of falsehood spring from a source of darkness. All the children of righteousness are ruled by the Prince of Light and walk in the ways of light; but all the children of falsehood are ruled by the Angel of Darkness and walk in the ways of darkness. cf. III.17ff., (Vermes 75f.)

---

[14] See C. K. Barrett, *The Gospel According to St. John* (1978[2]), 34.

[15] 1 QS refers to the text known variously as the Community Rule (Vermes) or the Manual of Discipline (Millar Burrows et al.). English quotations are from G. Vermes, *The Dead Sea Scrolls In English*. The 1 in 1 QS indicates that the manuscript was found in cave 1, the initial discovery of texts from the Qumran sect.

[16] Millar Burrows, *More Light on the Dead Sea Scrolls*, 126f., argues that this verbal parallel is one of the closest between the texts and the New Testament.

It is not surprising that, in a collection of texts such as those from Qumran, we find variant, or even conflicting, understandings. Here in 1 QS III.13–IV.26 (Vermes 75-8) we find them side by side in the same document. 1 QS is obviously a collection of authoritative traditions rather than the logical exposition of a theme by a single author. The evidence suggests that a Jewish monotheistic sect had been strongly influenced by dualism and that the dualism reinforced their sectarian consciousness justifying their separation not only from the world at large but also from Judaism in general. At the same time the experience of separation gave experiential support to the dualistic doctrine. Consequently monotheistic and dualistic interpretations exist side by side, sometimes quite independently, at others modifying each other.

In dealing with the comparison of Jewish ideas with Jn Schnackenburg notes:

> Judaism tends to stress human free will because of the obligation to observe the Law. ... The idea of God's fore-ordinance is not, indeed, unknown to the rabbis, but it does not abolish human freedom. ... The two ideas are left side by side unconnected and hardly interpreted, ... The idea of predestination was thus familiar to rabbinic Judaism, but hardly influential.[17]

His discussion of the Qumran Texts reflects this complexity. On the one hand he acknowledges that

> the idea of God's foreknowledge, his plan and his predestination is strongly expressed.[18]

There are, in the Texts, many predestinarian expressions of God's initiative. Schnackenburg's understanding of predestination as expressed in the Texts is also severely qualified:

> Care is necessary in presuming a belief in absolute predestination *('ante praevisa merita')*, since in other passages the free decision to join the community (of salvation) is stressed (cf. 1 QS 1.11; 5.1,6,8,10,21-22; 6.1e-14; 9.17), members are responsible for their actions, and even their apostasy does not seem impossible (1QS 7.18-24). Of the non-elect it is said . . . that God knew (beforehand) their works (Damasc. 2.7-8). Did God make his decrees in foreknowledge of the works of men *('scientia media')?* It must be wrong to expect such theological precision or even to look for any clear doctrine of predestination.[19]

He is right in insisting that we should not expect to find a philosophically

---

[17]*John* II, 265ff.

[18]*John* II, 267.

[19]*John* II, 268. Schnackenburg comes to a similar conclusion concerning the understanding of predestination in John. C.K. Barrett is in agreement with Schnackenburg.

argued and consistent doctrine of predestination either in the Qumran Texts or in Jn.[20] His main concern at this point is to qualify the understanding of predestination in the Texts to take account of human freedom and moral responsibility.

Given this approach it is surprising that he assimilates the dualism to a predestinarian perspective and thus tends to underplay the force of the dualism at Qumran. This is implied in his suggestion that in the dualistic section (1 QS III.13–IV.26) the emphasis on predestination is even stronger than elsewhere. He argues that

> Even outside the dualistic section (1 QS III.13–IV.26) . . . the idea of God's foreknowledge, his plan and his predestination is strongly expressed.[21]

and

> ...in the section dealing with the two spirits ... the deterministic attitude appears in a much stronger form.[22]

Here we find a confusing identification of dualistic determinism with divine predestination. But the very point of the dualism is to distance God from the cause of evil. Consequently Schnackenburg's approach tends to underplay the force of the dualism at Qumran by subordinating it to the teaching on predestination. While it is true that in Jn and the Qumran Texts all things have their origin in God, nevertheless a significant dualism is sustained. One theme should not be subordinated to the other.

Thus although in 1 QS III.18-20 it is expressly affirmed that God *appointed* the two spirits and in III.25 that he created them, in this same passage it is said that God loves the one and delights in its works and loathes the other and hates its ways (III.26–IV.1) and in the mystery of his understanding has ordained an end to it, IV.18. In Jn there is no specific reference to the origin of the darkness or the devil, the prince of this world, and the origin of the power of darkness remains a mystery. In 1 QS the role of the Spirit of Falsehood/Angel of Darkness is expressly said to be a mystery in the plan of God (רָזֵי אֵל).[23] In neither Jn nor 1 QS is God explicitly made responsible for the darkness/falsehood and the statements concerning control are directed towards the assurance that an end of the darkness/the falsehood has been determined by God.[24]

J. H. Charlesworth, like Schnackenburg, interprets the dualism of

---

[20]R. E. Brown thinks that the determinism of Qumran is neither logically nor speculatively developed. "The Qumran Scrolls and the Johannine Gospel and Epistles" in *The Scrolls and the New Testament* ed. *K. Stendahl.*
[21]*John* II, 267.
[22]*John* II, 269.
[23]1 QS III.23; IV.6,18.
[24]John 12.31; 1 QS IV.18.

Qumran in predestinarian terms because the two spirits are subject to God. Unlike Schnackenburg, however, Charlesworth does not qualify his understanding of predestination at Qumran to include human freedom and responsibility but explicitly asserts that

> to join the community was not a free act of choice but an appointed task carried through by one predestined by nature to be a son of light (3.18).[25]

While this conclusion might be possible on the basis of a consideration of 1 QS II.13–IV.26 in isolation,[26] it ignores explicit indications that to join the community was an act of free choice:

> He shall admit into the Covenant of Grace all those who have freely devoted themselves to the observance of God's precepts, ... (1 QS I.7-8)

> All those who freely devote themselves to His truth shall bring all their knowledge, powers, and possessions into the Community of God,...(1 QS I.11-12)

Thus Schnackenburg is right in asserting that neither in 1 QS nor in Jn does the teaching concerning dualism or predestination exclude human freedom and responsibility. But what of the tendency to assimilate the dualism to the teaching on predestination?

The discussion of the "fountain of light" and the "source of darkness" in 1 QS III.18-20 does *not* explicitly assert that the source of darkness is purposed by God. Dualism is not expressly incorporated into a view of divine predestination. Such a move would destroy the purpose of the dualism which is to distance God from the source of darkness and the Angel of Darkness who leads all the children of falsehood astray.[27] Thus there is an unresolved tension in the Texts between dualism and belief in the one sovereign God. In terms of the present, though the two Spirits were created by God, it is said that God

> loves the one everlastingly and delights in its works for ever; but

---

[25]*John and Qumran*, 79-80. Thus he also understands dualistic determinism in terms of divine predestination.

[26]This section does not deal with conditions of entry into the community. Thus such a conclusion must be drawn from related themes. But if in 1 QS conflicting themes appear side by side an extrapolation along these lines is precarious, especially when it is opposed to explicit statements elsewhere.

[27]In 1 QS III.18-20 the Spirit of Truth is identified with the Prince of Light and the Spirit of Falsehood with the Angel of Darkness as is shown by the way it is said that "those born of the *truth* spring from a fountain of light" and are called "the children of righteousness" who "are ruled by the Prince of Light and walk in the ways of light" while "those born of *falsehood* spring from a source of darkness" and "are ruled by the Angel of Darkness and walk in the ways of darkness". Further, in 1 QS III.25 the two Spirits are referred to as the Spirits of Light and Darkness.

the counsel of the other he loathes and for ever hates its ways.

The tension, which is recognized as a mystery, is unresolved in relation to the origin of the source of darkness and the activity of the Spirit of Falsehood though there is a promised eschatological resolution:

> But in the mysteries of His understanding, and in His glorious wisdom, God has ordained an end of falsehood, and at the time of the visitation He will destroy it for ever. (1 QS IV.18)

Although Schnackenburg assimilates the dualistic determinism of Qumran to his understanding of divine predestination, which is qualified to take account of human freedom and responsibility, he finds it necessary to distance Jn from the teaching at Qumran:

> We need not spend any more time on this doctrine of the two spirits, however, since in its statements it goes far beyond what can be found in John, ...

This judgement needs to be questioned, not only because in 1 Jn 4.2, which should be understood in relation to the Johannine tradition, if not by the same author as the Gospel, the Spirit of Error[28] is mentioned, but also because of the role of the darkness and the devil, the prince of this world in Jn. That the Qumran Texts contain more fully developed passages on the role of the two spirits than Jn does not mean that Jn's dualistic statements should not be taken seriously.

Charlesworth argues that the dualism has been used symbolically by Jn and that the devil has been demythologized.[29] Such an interpretation is an option for the modern interpreter, but not the meaning of the evangelist who accounted for the struggle he experienced in terms of dualism. Charlesworth thinks that the dualism of Qumran has been assimilated into a monotheistic determinism (predestination). He argues for a rigorous determinism in the Qumran Texts but in regard to Jn:

> We conclude, therefore, that no doctrine of predestination is put forward in this Gospel, nor is there any strong emphasis on determinism. Man's destiny is balanced between God's sovereign initiative and man's response.[30]

As we have seen, Schnackenburg also assimilates the dualism into a predestinarian view but balances this with an emphasis on human freedom and responsibility even at Qumran. If in contemporary Jewish sources the ideas of divine sovereignty and human freedom appear side by side in an unresolved tension, as Schnackenburg argues, is it not likely that this is

---

[28]This title should be understood as a more or less Greek equivalent of the Semitic Spirit of Falsehood. Compare the use of Error in the Gospel of Truth.

[29]*John and Qumran*, 92-3.

[30]*John and Qumran*, 95.

true also of the dualistic and monotheistic statements in Jn and the Qumran Texts? If this is the case the dualistic statements should be taken seriously and not simply absorbed into a predestinarian view which is then qualified by statements about human freedom and moral responsibility.

In the Qumran Texts the Spirit of Falsehood not only has led astray all the children of darkness but is active amongst the children of light also. So also in Jn it is not only the Jews as the opponents of Jesus who are led astray by the devil, even Judas, one of the twelve, is turned into the one who would betray Jesus by the devil who enters his heart (Jn 13.2). Consequently there is a strongly dualistic reading of some parts of the Qumran Texts as well as well as the Gospel of Jn.

The Qumran Texts contain the writings of the sect and it would be a mistake to think of them as a homogeneous whole without tensions and even conflicting views. They were the product of the understanding of the sect over the course of a couple of hundred years and not the writing of a single person. Even 1 QS should not be seen as an homogeneous document. It brings together the beliefs of the sect. Consequently we should not be surprised to find blatant and unresolved tensions there. The two Spirits can be characterized in terms of the division between the sect as the sons of light and the world as the place of darkness. This aspect is dominant in 1 QS III.13–IV.26. But because the members of the sect also experienced the struggle with the darkness there is also the recognition that even the members of the sect had to struggle with the deceptions of the Spirit of Falsehood. In all of this the two Spirits are understood in apocalyptic terms as supernatural powers. Alongside these uses we find a more psychological use of the term spirit which impinges on the area in which the apocalyptic use occurs. Here every person is characterized by the spirit given by God so that people are determined by the spirit "of their lot". While this understanding is characteristic of the *Hodayoth* (Hymn Scroll) approximations to it are found in 1 QS IV.20-23.

For the purpose of our discussion it is the apocalyptic understanding of the two Spirits that is important. It corresponds quite closely to the understanding of the Spirit of Truth in Jn and the role of the devil that is found there.

The dualism of the Qumran Texts and Jn probably provides evidence of the influence of an Iranian *Weltanschauung*.[31] It may be that the Iranian dualism was already subject to a monotheistic principle[32] although this

---

[31] This view has the support of such scholars as K. G. Kuhn, W. F. Albright, F. M. Cross, H. Ringgren.

[32] This is the view of R. C. Zaehner, *The Dawn and Twilight of Zoroastrianism*, 41–61.

might have been a consequence of the dualism being mediated through Judaism. Which of these views is adopted makes little difference to the interpretation of Jn. We conclude that, for the evangelist, the belief in one supreme and good God is held in tension with the acknowledgement of a dualistic conflict in which the forces of good and evil are locked. In this deadly conflict mankind is called to play a part. In this context the evangelist identifies the power of darkness as the force that blinded people and prevented them from believing (12.40), as is argued in chapter 12 below.

Although there is nothing approaching the exposition of the ontological dualism of parts of 1 QS III.13–IV.26 in Jn, there is close contact with the antithetical language so that what we have is a conceptual and linguistic point of contact indicating the evangelist's thought world. The point of contact is close in Jn's treatment of the Devil, the prince of this world, Jn 8.44; 12.31,40; 14.30; 16.11. The obvious comparison is with the Spirit of Falsehood, the Angel of Darkness (1 QS III.19; IV.23), cf. 1 Jn 4.6. But while Jn poses, in a most pointed fashion, the problem of the world of darkness in its opposition to God who created all things (Jn 1.10), it (like historical apocalypses) offers no speculation about the source of the darkness. Thus we are talking about the language and concepts inherited by the evangelist which bear the mark of the impact of a dualistic tradition mediated through the syncretistic context of Palestinian Judaism.

In Jn the dualism has influenced the evangelist's use of antithetical language concerning light and darkness, 1.5; 8.12; truth and falsehood, 8.44ff.; flesh and Spirit, 1.12f.; 3.5f.; 6.63; freedom and bondage, 8.31f. The antitheses give expression to a conflict which rages between good and evil, 3.19-21; Jesus and the prince of this world, 12.31 and in which all are called to the crisis of decision for the light or the darkness, Jesus or the devil, 3.19-21; 8.12,31ff. A similar presentation is to be found in parts of 1 QS III.13–IV.26 and 1 QM XIII.9-12.[33] In the order created by God there is a conflict. God supports one side and is opposed to the other, 1 QS III.26–IV.1. Men are divided into two groups and the conflict between the light and darkness is worked out in their lives so that just as the light is opposed to the darkness so are the ways of the sons of light opposed to the sons of darkness. Alongside this ethical dualism we have noted that there is (at Qumran) a kind of ontological dualism, a dualism of being, 1 QS III.17ff. There it seems to be affirmed that men are determined by their origin or source. In the Hymn Scroll (1 QH) mankind is divided into two groups "in accordance with the spirits of their lot", 1 QH XIV.1-12

---

[33] 1 QM indicates the War Scroll (Vermes 124ff.). Like 1 QS the War Scroll was amongst the scrolls found in the first cave.

(Vermes 192).[34] This teaching sits uneasily alongside the view that even the sons of light must struggle with the Spirit of Falsehood and that all men are subject to both the good and the evil inclinations. Likewise Jn, while presenting the view that Jesus calls all to believe (3.16), also says that only those given or drawn by God may come to him, 6.37,44,65; 10.26ff. But the most serious dualism of origins is to be found in Jesus' affirmation that

"You are from below, I am from above;
You are of this world, I am not of this world." Jn 8.23, cf. 3.31.

These references appear to suggest an ontological dualism which determines all that follows. However, Jn 17.6-19 expresses a different point of view because Jesus' disciples were given to him (by the Father) from the world (17.6). Here Jesus, who is about to leave the world and his disciples in it (17.11), prays that they will be kept from the corrupting influence of the evil world. What is more, it is said,

"they are not of the world even as I am not of the world." Jn 17.16.

In Jn 8.39-47 the discussion between Jesus and the Jews picks up the contrast Jesus made (8.38) between his father and theirs. This develops, in a new way, the contrast between "from above" and "from below". The contrast is now between children of God (and Abraham) and children of the devil. The Jews, by their behaviour, manifest their origin as children of the devil. While this might appear to indicate that actions are determined by origin, the argument can be understood as actions reveal origins and hence origins can be chosen. Consequently even these statements appear to focus on the historical conflict in which all are called to decide for or against Jesus as the revealer of God, though the language might reflect the influence of an ontological dualism.

Reference to the historical conflict reminds us that the dualistic influence was dominant because it made sense of the situation of those who used it. In both the Qumran Texts and Jn it gives expression to the sectarian consciousness of those who have rejected the dominant forms of Judaism of the day (the Temple and political and social life) or who have been rejected by synagogue Judaism. This reminds us that for influences to occur they must function usefully for those who are influenced.

Light and darkness are the dominant symbols which give expression to the dualism of both Jn and Qumran.[35] The parallelism with Qumran demands that these symbols be dealt with as a pair in their opposition to each other. In Jn their use is concentrated in chapters 1–12

---

[34] See also 1 QH XIV.25-26; XV.10-22; VII.3,13,16 (Vermes 194-5; 172-4).
[35] See J. H. Charlesworth (ed.), *John and Qumran,* especially 76-106.

(1.4,9; 3.19-21; 8.12; 9.5,39-41; 12.46). The theme of these chapters is *The light shines in the darkness.* This challenge to the darkness causes divisions (7.43; 9.16; 10.19), as people leave the darkness for the light (9.5,25,39,41). But those who belong in the darkness deny Jesus' claims (10.1-41), deny the meaning of his miracles (11.1-54), deny the witness of those who believe (11.55–12.9), retreating irrevocably into the darkness of falsehood and death, 9.39-41. In what follows in chapters 13-17 the division has already taken place, though Judas has yet to divide himself from the community of believers. When this is described the evangelist notes significantly, "and it was night", 13.30. Judas withdrew into the darkness and his doom was sealed.

Having set out some evidence to show how fundamental the light-darkness symbolism is for Jn, attention can now be drawn to more detailed links in the language of the Texts and the Gospel, remembering that the similarities occur in a dualistic framework in both. This framework makes the parallels more significant than they would otherwise be. Especially significant are the expressions:

1.

and walk in the ways of darkness 1 QS III.21 (Vermes, 75) those who walk in darkness 1 QS XI.10 (Vermes, 93)	shall not walk in darkness, Jn 8.12, he who walks in darkness, Jn 12.35, cf. 1 Jn 1.6; 2.11.

2.

Members of the sect thought of themselves as "the sons of light". 1 QS I.9 etc.(Vermes, 72).	For Jn people become "sons of light" by believing, Jn 12.35.

3.

Members of the sect were able to contemplate "the light of life". 1 QS III.7 (Vermes, 75).	For Jn those who follow Jesus "have the light of life", Jn 8.12; cf. 1.4.

4.

God revealed himself "as perfect light", 1 QH IV.23 (Vermes, 162).	God is light and in him is no darkness, 1 Jn 1.5.

Truth and falsehood are also opposed in the Texts and the Gospel. In the texts the most important reference is to the Spirits of Truth and Falsehood, 1 QS III.13-IV.26 (Vermes, 75-8) and see also *Testament of Judah* XX.1-5. In Jn, the Spirit of Truth is used Jn 14.17 etc., but not "the Spirit of Falsehood" though see the Greek equivalent ("the Spirit of error") in 1 Jn 4.6. To some extent (in Jn) the role of the Spirit of Falsehood is performed by the devil, the prince of this world (Jn 12.31; 14.30; 16.11), who is the originator of lies (Jn 8.44) and is opposed by the Spirit of Truth (Jn 16.11ff.). In 1 QM XIII.11 (Vermes, 141) we learn that the Spirit of Falsehood, the Angel of Malevolence is *Belial* which Vermes correctly identifies with Satan.[36] But the teaching about Satan is minute in Jn as compared with the texts.

In both the Texts and the Gospel "the Spirit of Truth" is identified with "the Holy Spirit", 1 QS VIII.18; IX.3; CD II.12.[37] (Vermes, 86, 87, 98); Jn 14.16,17,26. However, the other "title" used of the Spirit in Jn (παράκλητος) is not found in the texts though functions ascribed to the *Paraclete* in the Gospel are ascribed to the Spirit in the texts.[38]

The Texts also contain the view that man will be purified by the truth, 1 QS I.12; IV.20-21 (Vermes, 72, 77) and compare Jn 15.3; 17.17. Of course for one the Law was the truth while for the other the truth was a person, Jesus, Jn 14.6. Thus the formal agreement "Thy word is truth" in 1 QH XI.7 (Vermes, 185) and Jn 17.17 does not indicate a common meaning. Closer is the statement to God "For Thou Thyself art truth" 1 QH IV.40 (see T. Gaster, 149 and E. Lohse, 128f.). Both the Texts and the Gospel refer to "witness to the truth" 1 QS VIII.6 (Vermes, 85) and Jn 5.33; 18.37. The theme is much more prominent in the Gospel where witness to Jesus 1.5ff.,15,29ff.; 15.26-27 etc., is witness to the truth. The Texts also provide parallels to the Hebraic idea of "doing" the truth, Jn 3.21; 1 QS V.3; VIII.2,4; X.17; 1 QM XIII.2-3 (Vermes, 78, 85, 90, 140).

Statements about "knowledge of" or "knowing the truth" 1 QH VI.12; IX.35; X.20.29 (Vermes, 169, 182, 183, 184) can be compared with Jn 8.32 "and you will know the truth". Universal knowledge, such as envisaged in 1 QH VI.12 can be compared with Jn 17.20-23. "The sons of truth" 1 QH VI.29; VII.29-30 (IX.35); X.27 (Vermes, 171, 175, 182, 184) is similar to "everyone who is of the truth", Jn 18.37 cf. 1 Jn 2.21; 3.19.

Flesh and Spirit form another contrasting pair. As in the Old Testament, "flesh" indicates man in his weakness as distinct from God in his power who is Spirit, Isaiah 31.3; 40.6-8; etc. "Flesh" indicates man in his weakness as mortal and sinful, 1 QH IV.29 (Vermes, 163). As such

---

[36]See J. H. Charlesworth, *John and Qumran*, 80.
[37]CD indicates the Damascus Rule, also discovered in Cave 1 but is not designated 1 CD because the document was known previously from the discovery of the Cairo geniza in 1896.
[38]See O. Betz, *Der Paraklet. Fürsprecher im Spätjudentum, im Johannes-Evangelium und in neu gefundenen gnostischen Schriften.*

the flesh requires cleansing through God's truth (Law) and his Holy Spirit, 1 QS IV.20-22 (Vermes, 77f.). Compare with this Jn 1.12f.; 3.5-7. However, the affirmation that "the Word ($\lambda \acute{o} \gamma o s$) became flesh" (Jn 1.14) finds no precedent in this tradition.

Life is also opposed to **death** and the Texts and the Gospel speak of eternal life, 1 QS IV.7 (Vermes, 76) Jn 3.15ff., etc. This theme is much more prominent in Jn. Both speak of life-giving knowledge 1 QS 11.3 (Vermes, 73); Jn 17.3 and contrast the end of the righteous and the wicked in terms of life and death, 1 QS IV.6-8,11-14 (Vermes, 76f.), Jn 3.36; 5.29.

Love and **hate** form a formal antithesis but because of the Hebraic sense of choosing and rejecting it does not follow that there are those who love and others who hate. It is a matter of loving and hating appropriately. Thus "Truth abhors the works of falsehood, and falsehood hates all the ways of truth, and their struggle is fierce for they do not walk together." 1 QS IV.17-18; IX.14ff. (Vermes, 77, 87f.), and Jn 3.19-21. At times love and hate can express the Johannine dualism because what the believers are and love is hated by the world (Jn 15.18-25; 17.14; 1 Jn 3.13). Likewise what the world loves is rejected by the believers, Jn 3.19-21.

The Qumran Texts speak of "the Precept of the Age", 1 QS IX.14,23 (Vermes, 87, 88). The precept concerns correct loving and hating, 1 QS I.3-4 (Vermes, 72). In Jn the "new commandment" was "love one another", Jn 13.34f.; 15.12,17. The theme of hating is not developed though some scholars think that it is implied in the use of "one another" rather than "the neighbour", noting that the Synoptic command to love the enemy is absent from this Gospel.[39] However, this overlooks the theme of God's love for the world and the aim that the world might come to believe and know, 3.16; 17.20ff. At the heart of Jn is a theology of mission[40] expressed in the mission of the Son from the Father and of the believers from Jesus to and for the world, 17.18-26; 20.21.

2. Knowledge

Jn shows a concentration on the use of the language of knowing. In common with both Testaments emphasis is on *verbs* rather than the noun ($\gamma \nu \widehat{\omega} \sigma \iota s$) knowledge. Jn uses the two verbs meaning "to know" 141 times ($\gamma \iota \nu \acute{\omega} \sigma \kappa \epsilon \iota \nu$ 56 times and $\epsilon \iota \delta \acute{\epsilon} \nu a \iota$ 85 times). In the New Testament the noun is used 29 times and the verbs over 540 times. Thus

---

[39]See Ernst Käsemann, *The Testament of Jesus*, 59ff.
[40]See my review of Teresa Okure, *The Johannine Approach to Mission*, *Pacifica* 3/3 (1990) 347-9.

preference for the verb is not peculiar to Jn but the concentration on knowing is unusual. Jn's use exceeds the collective use of the three Synoptics and is only narrowly surpassed by the total use of Paul in all of his letters. The use of the two verbs as equivalents is consistent with the translation practice of the Septuagint.[41] But this concentration of emphasis on the language of knowing is not matched by any book in the Old Testament. Here again the Qumran Texts reveal a contemporary tradition within Judaism which matches the evangelist's concentration on knowledge. In addition to the increased use of the Hebrew verb (*yada'*) the texts give evidence to a greatly increased use of the noun (*da'ath*).

In the Texts there is reference to "the God of knowledge" 1 QS III.15-17; XI.11; 1 QH I.26; XII.9-11 (Vermes, 75, 93, 152, 189) and compare 1 Sam 2.3. Here we find reference to God's design and control of creation and history. But it would be a mistake to identify knowledge here with the λόγος in Jn. Rather the link with λόγος is to be found in the tradition where Wisdom is identified with Law and is personified in her creative role, Proverbs 8; Wisdom 7; Sirach 24.[42] The Qumran community also provides evidence of the creative role of Wisdom 1 QH I.6-20; X.2f.; XIII.1-13 (Vermes, 150-1, 182, 191-2).

God's knowledge as his power in action controlling what is known is widely attested in the Texts. More important for us is the stress on "the God of knowledge" as the source of all knowledge, 1 QS X.11-12; XI.3; 1 QH XII.29 (Vermes, 89-90, 92, 190). He gives knowledge, 1 QS XI.15-20 (Vermes, 94 cf. Daniel 2.20-23). In the Hymns an individual gives thanks for the gift of knowledge 1 QH I.21, X.14-17; XI.15-18,27-35; XIV.8-11,23-27 (Vermes, 151, 183, 186, 187-8, 192-4). Because of the gift he can say "I know", 1 QH XII.11; XIII.18-19; XIV.12,17; XV.12-14,22-24; XVI.1,2,11,15-16 (Vermes, 189, 192-7). Such knowledge is based on the claim to have received the revelation, 1 QH IV.5-6,27-29; V.8,9,11; VII.26-27; IX.26-27; XI.3-4,9,10,15-17,27-28; XII.11-13; XIV.8-12,17,25, etc., (Vermes, 160-3, 165, 175, 181, 185-7, 189, 192-4). Whether the individual speaking is "the Teacher of Righteousness" to whom God revealed his mysteries (1 QpHab VII.4-5; cf.1 QH IV.27-29; Vermes, 236, 163); the "Ruler/Guardian" of the community (1 QS IX.12ff.; CD XIII.7ff. and 1 QH XII.11-13; Vermes, 87-88, 115-6, 189), or can be the affirmation of every member of the community who has

---

[41]The Greek translation of the Old Testament, known as the LXX.

[42]C. H. Dodd, *Interpretation*, 274f., has set out an impressive list of parallels of Jn 1.1-14 from the Wisdom literature. This part of the Prologue looks like a patchwork of quotations. Hence what was said of Wisdom/Law in this tradition of Judaism Jn transfers to Jesus Christ, 1.14-18.

received true knowledge passed down from "the Teacher", cannot be decided with any certainty. For our purpose what is important is the focus on revealed knowledge which is enjoyed by the sect through the revealing work of the Teacher and the Guardians who transmitted his teaching as the tradition of the sect. That knowledge finds its focus in the discourse on the two Spirits (1 QS III.13–IV.26) to which we have frequently referred. Hence saving knowledge is focussed on the dualistic nature of the present order of things and the assurance of the "end of falsehood". That end is bound up with a complex messianic expectation[43] and an eschatological conflict.[44]

Before leaving the theme of knowledge there is a significant phrase that should be noted. In 1 QM XIII.3 the author speaks of those who know God by faith (Vermes, 140). Given the close relation between believing and knowing in Jn and the absence of similar language from other contemporary sources this statement is linguistically significant.

3. Miscellaneous Parallels

The Texts affirm that "God will deliver" members of the sect "because of their faith in the Teacher of Righteousness", 1 QpHab VIII.2-3 (Vermes, 237) and compare Jn 3.15ff.; etc. They also speak of those "who know God by faith", 1 QM XIII.3 (Vermes, 140). Given the centrality of the theme of knowing and believing in Jn this is important. But, like the reference to faith in the Teacher of Righteousness it is a single reference whereas these themes are recurrent in Jn. The Teacher of Righteousness is referred to as "a faithful shepherd" (Vermes, 206) and Jesus as "the good shepherd" in Jn 10.11. Naturally the Old Testament background to the texts and Jn 10 is obvious. See Pss 23(22).1; 80(79).1; Ez 34, etc.

The sectarians had chosen "the way", 1 QS IX.17; X.21 (Vermes, 88, 91) which for them was the study of the Law, 1 QS VIII.13-15 (Vermes, 86). For Jn Jesus is "the way", Jn 14.6. Thus the real comparison is between the role of the Law for the sect with the place of Jesus in Jn.

In the Texts there is reference to "raise an *ensign* for the destruction of wickedness", 1 QH VI.34 (Vermes, 172). The word translated "ensign" (*nes*) is used in Isa 11.12, etc., and is translated σημεῖον in the Septuagint as is the same term in Num 21.8 which is important for Jn 3.15, "as

---

[43] The sect looked for the coming of the Prophet and the Messiahs of Aaron and Israel, 1 QS IX.9-11 (Vermes 87). Apparently the precepts of the Teacher applied until this time.

[44] How the messianic figures relate to this is not clear. It could be that they were to lead the community in the conflict (see especially 1 QM XI, Vermes, 137f.) though other texts look for supernatural leadership in that conflict, see 1 QM XII–XVII (Vermes, 139-46).

Moses lifted up the serpent in the wilderness, even so must the Son of Man be lifted up". In Jn 12.31-33 σημαίνων is used to *signify* the lifting up of the Son of Man through which wickedness is destroyed.

The Damascus Rule refers to "...the fountain of living waters" (*Vermes* 106) and for them "the well is the Law" CD VI.4 (Vermes, 102) while Jesus is the giver of "rivers of living water", identified with the Spirit, Jn 4.14; 7.38. Here, as elsewhere, the influence of the Old Testament is obvious, Num 21.18; Jer 2.13; Ez 47; Ps 36.9; Prov 13.14.

Both the Qumran Texts and the Gospel stress the unity of their respective communities in similar terms, 1 QS V.2,7 (Vermes, 78-79) and Jn 11.52; 17.11,21,23. The complex messianic hope at Qumran throws some light on Jn, especially reference to the coming Prophet and the Messiahs of Aaron and Israel, 1 QS XI.11 (Vermes, 87 and see Deut 18.15,18) and note Jn 1.19-28 for an example of the variety of messianic designations. Jesus is portrayed as the coming Prophet in Jn 1.21; 4.19-30,44,45; 5.45-47; 7.50-52. While these complex messianic expectations were suspected by some scholars, the first hand evidence in the Texts now puts that suspicion beyond doubt, making clear also the lack of conformity in pre-70 CE Judaism.

4. Conclusion on the Gospel and Qumran

Jn shares some striking features with the Qumran Texts but nothing that need indicate direct dependence. Rather the Texts provide evidence of first century Palestinian Judaism and its syncretistic and "sectarian"[45] character. The similarities show how first century Judaism had developed themes and ideas which are to be found in the Old Testament. Jn is influenced by these in the form in which they are to be found in first century Judaism. The evangelist did not make use of the Old Testament in a vacuum but in the context of the way it was understood in the Judaism of the time. The Qumran Texts are an invaluable source of information concerning this understanding.[46] In particular they show a wider context for the

---

[45]"Sectarian" indicates the divisions within first century Palestinian Judaism. To some extent the divisions can be seen in terms of attitudes to hellenization which varied from enthusiastic acceptance to conscious rejection though all groups were hellenized to some extent. See G. W. E. Nickelsburg and M. E. Stone, *Faith and Piety in Early Judaism*, 11ff.

[46]While Jn has few actual quotations from the Old Testament, all from the Palestinian Canon, the Gospel is permeated by contemporary Jewish understanding of and use of Old Testament themes and forms. The influence of the Wisdom literature on the Prologue and discourses is evident. See C. H. Dodd, *Interpretation*, 274f.; on the Prologue and on the discourses see my *John: Witness and Theologian (=JWT)*, 48f. In addition, John's symbolism arises out of debate with the Jewish understanding of the Old

evangelist's use of antithetical language and lend weight to the view that this language manifests an underlying dualistic *Weltanshauung* commonly associated with apocalyptic literature.[47] This comparison is important because it highlights the sectarian character of both the Qumran community and the Johannine Christians.

The relationship to the *Weltanshauung* of apocalyptic is manifest in three aspects of the Johannine dualism:
1. The spatial antithesis between above and below;
2. The temporal tension between this age and the age to come and;
3. The ethical conflict between good and evil, God and the devil, the children of God (the light) and the children of the devil (the darkness).
Jn stands with those (apocalyptic) works that see a conflict between above and below, this age and the age to come, that see this world/age dominated by the forces of evil which would be overcome only in the coming age.

There is first the separation of heaven and earth, above and below, God and the world of men so that no one has ever seen God, Jn 1.18. To overcome this dualism Jesus is presented as the revealer who has come from above. There is second, the separation of the present age from the age to come and this is marked by the references to the coming hour (7.30; 8.20) which arrives with the triumphant "now" of 12.31ff. It is here too that the ethical dualism is apparent, though this has been clear from the Prologue (1.5) and is dominant in 3.19-21. What is more, it is *revelation* that overcomes the dualism as the revealer comes from above and this revelation is the judgement of the world. Here the evangelist has given his own distinctive stamp to apocalyptic themes.

Hence it is not correct to say that the world below is a reflection of the world above.[48] Such a view does not take with sufficient seriousness the conflict between the two realms. Thus when the world below is depicted as a reflection of the world above this is so only in a very limited sense. When, in apocalyptic works, the world above is seen as already revealing what is about to happen on earth, this is related to God's saving intervention on behalf of his people. What is happening in heaven is relevant to earth because it foreshadows what will happen on earth. Such a vision enables a continuing belief in God in the face of the wickedness prevailing in this world which, at least for the moment, is in the grip of the prince of this world, Jn 12.31; 14.30; 16.11. The apocalyptic vision affirms faith in God and his good purpose in the face of (apparently)

Testament. On the Jewish midrashic influence on the development of Jn's discourses see Peder Borgen, *Bread from Heaven*.
[47] See O. Böcher, *Der johanneische Dualismus*, 164.
[48] *Pace* John Ashton, *Understanding*, 370-1, 404-5.

prevailing evil. The vision affirms that in the end God will prevail. The role of the vision was not to suggest that the evil of this world was intended and enacted by God from heaven. Such a conclusion is the consequence of a misconstrual of the function of the two realms in apocalyptic, a misconstrual which does not take seriously the radical distinction between the two ages in terms of the evil of this age and the blessedness of the age to come. Jn has modified the apocalyptic vision in that Jesus, as the emissary from above has entered this world/age as the revelation of the age to come in this age. But he is more than this; he is already, in his coming and going, the decisive intervention of God in this world. This does not, however, exhaust or completely fulfil the purpose of God for this world. Because of this Jn's eschatological views are complex and the perspective of future fulfillment remains important.[49]

Thus Jn seriously differs from the sect which produced the Texts. In spite of conceptual similarities his theology is radically different. What the Law was for the sect Jesus Christ is for the Gospel. Jn can, in part, be interpreted against the background of the question of the nature and authority of the Law. The evangelist was no legalist. For him Jesus had done away with any independent authority that the Law might have been thought to possess. The only function remaining for the Law was to bear witness to Jesus. The very full treatment that the evangelist gives to the question of Jesus' relation to the Law suggests that Jn was formatively shaped with Jewish Christians in mind. What is more the evangelist drew on the language and concepts from his own characteristic world of thought. That thought world, it has been argued, is usefully illuminated for us by the Qumran Texts. These Texts illustrate for us the thought world which was at the evangelist's disposal when he wrote his Gospel.[50] We see however, that the treasury of concepts and language on which he drew does not adequately account for his interpretation of Jesus. Other factors must also be examined.

II. PHILO AND THE HERMETIC TRACTATES

The voluminous writings of Philo provide another significant body of Jewish evidence from the period. His writings exhibit a blend of Judaism with Hellenistic philosophy, particularly Platonism and Stoicism. The most obvious parallel is found in the Prologue in the Johannine use of λόγος. As in Jn, Philo's λόγος functions in relation to symbolism. This

---

[49]See my "Theology and Eschatology in the Prologue of John" and chapter 3 below.

[50]Martin Hengel, *The Johannine Question,* 109-13 is in broad agreement with this position.

relation needs to be qualified. Philo's writings are much more overtly philosophical than Jn. The use of the hypostatized λόγος, the most significant point of contact, is restricted to the Prologue of Jn and might have come to the evangelist in the hymn source which underlies the Prologue.[51] The λόγος is not overtly connected with symbols in Jn, as it is in Philo, though it is presupposed. Whether in the source, or introduced into the Prologue by the evangelist, this use of λόγος is a notable point of resemblance. Philo uses the term over 1300 times with a confusing array of meanings, some deriving from Judaism, others from Stoicism and Platonism, while others appear to be linked with oriental Egyptian theology. Thus, for Philo, λόγος can mean both the Word of God and the notional world (κόσμος νοητός) which gives rise to the visible world (κόσμος αἰσθητός), to be compared with the idea of the immanent λόγος and extrapolated λόγος, the reason and word of Stoicism. The λόγος as the Word of God has clear links with Judaism and it is this that is important for Jn. Though the λόγος is not specifically called the Word *of God* in the Prologue, this is implied in Jn 1.1-2. Thus it seems that Philo, like the evangelist, has been influenced by that form of Hellenistic Judaism known to us in the Wisdom literature and, to some extent, in the Qumran Texts. It is more likely that both the evangelist and Philo were influenced by some form of Hellenistic Judaism than that Jn was directly influenced by Philo.

1. The Higher Religion of Hellenism

Philo was a Jew of the Alexandrian *diaspora* and his writings reflect his situation. Both Philo and the author of Jn have written in Greek. What is more, C. H. Dodd has used Philo and the *Corpus Hermeticum* to illustrate how Jn would have been read and understood by educated *pagans*. Indeed, Philo and the *Hermetica* provide Dodd with the data to reconstruct "the higher religion of Hellenism" for whose adherents, he argues, Jn was written. Dodd attributed the hellenization evident in the Gospel to the evangelist and his purpose in writing. The Gospel is understood as an acknowledgement of the quest for eternal life (my characterization) that was alive in "the higher religions of Hellenism". Only because there was a widespread quest for eternal life could the evangelist hope to find eager readers of his Gospel of eternal life.

Two lines of thought emerge in Dodd's early writings and a third appears alongside the other two in *Interpretation*, and it is the third that is dominant there.

---

[51]In fact I believe that λόγος is part of the evangelist's modification of his source. See chapter 3, "Christology and History in the Prologue" below.

i The polemical purpose. In his commentary on *The Johannine Epistles* Dodd argued that a situation of confusion was developing because "higher pagans" were adopting Christianity, in the same way as they had adopted Judaism, as one cult among others, and ill-informed converts to Christianity were adopting the language of higher paganism to express the faith "in terms of modern thought". The result was confusion. The evangelist set about to overcome the problem by adopting the language himself and

> by a genuine and thoroughgoing reinterpretation, in which alien categories are completely mastered and transformed by the Gospel, and constrained to express the central truth of Christianity in universal terms. It was along the lines laid down in the Fourth Gospel that the problem was in the end successfully solved.[52]

The polemical intention in this statement of purpose is clear. "The Fourth Gospel can best be understood as a brilliant attempt to undercut the whole process..." laying down the lines which were ultimately successful in overcoming the confusion and misunderstanding. The polemical purpose of 1 Jn is clear. Out of the confusion which Dodd has described came teachers, whom the author of 1 Jn considered to be false prophets, who were on the road to the later Gnostic heresies. Their language was akin to that of higher paganism though, according to the author of 1 Jn, it was used in an unworthy and untrue way. He condemned this use though he was prepared to use the same language himself in a redefined sense.[53] In spite of this Dodd considered 1 Jn to be less guarded and more open to Gnosticism than the Gospel. Given the clearly polemical nature of 1 Jn it seems that Dodd has allowed the purpose of that letter to influence his interpretation of the Gospel. Thus the reverse of what he wrote in the Preface to his commentary on the Epistles appears to be true:

> The interpretation, however, which I offer here has in large measure emerged from studies primarily directed towards the understanding of the Fourth Gospel in its contemporary setting.[54]

Apparently it was assumed that Gospel and Epistles were written in the same context and with the same purpose. In *Interpretation* there are traces of the thesis of a polemical purpose in the assertion that the claim to have vision of God, made by Hellenistic mystics, was false, and that certain other statements in the Gospel might be directed against the forerunners of

---

[52]*The Johannine Epistles*, xvii-xviii.
[53]*Ibid.*, xviii-xx.
[54]*Ibid.*, vii, in later editions, viii.

second-century "Gnostic heresies".[55] The emphasis in *Interpretation*, however, falls on the third purpose.

ii The theological purpose. From a very early time Dodd emphasized the necessity of bringing together Hebraic and Hellenistic concepts if the gospel was to be expressed adequately. The event of the incarnation called for an interpretation that neither tradition, by itself, could supply. Nor was an amalgamation of the two adequate. Rather, out of the two a new understanding emerged under the impact of the incarnation. In this development Dodd emphasized the contribution of the distinctive Hellenistic elements:

> The religious quest of the Hellenistic world was not in vain. It attained some genuine religious insight; and it provided early Christian thinkers with an intellectual apparatus for interpreting Christianity to the wider world, and, in doing so, penetrating more deeply into the meaning of the Gospel.[56]

A little earlier Dodd had said that the evangelist's mastery of the language of "higher paganism" had enabled him "to express the central truth of Christianity in universal terms".[57] In *Interpretation* Dodd argues that the categories used by the evangelist enable him to express the relation of both Christ and the believer to God and to develop an understanding of the incarnation.[58]

iii The apologetic purpose. In *Interpretation* focus falls on the apologetic purpose, especially where Dodd discusses the readers the evangelist had in view.[59] He describes them as "a wide public" of "thoughtful persons" in such a varied Hellenistic city as Ephesus. They were already searching for "life", "eternal life", and their religious attitudes are best represented by the *Corpus Hermeticum* and the writings of Philo. By identifying the readers Dodd attempts not only to show how they would have understood the Gospel, but to indicate what the evangelist intended to say to them, the readers he had in view.

The evangelist's intention to communicate the Gospel to such an audience is his reason for placing the Prologue at the beginning of the Gospel:

> The Logos-doctrine is placed first, because, addressing a public nurtured in the higher religion of Hellenism, the writer wishes to

---

[55]*Interpretation*, 166, 314.

[56]*The Johannine Epistles*, pp. xx-xxi .

[57]*Ibid.*, p xviii.

[58]*Interpretation*, 199f., 248f., 262, 284f.

[59]*Ibid.*, 8, 9, 53 n1, 265, 277, 283f., 296, 332, 241 n2, 343, 366, 401, 420 421 n2. Such "questers" (in my view) fit the later stages of Jn.

offer the Logos-idea as the appropriate approach, for them, to the central purpose of the Gospel, through which he may lead them to the historical actuality of its story, rooted as it is in Jewish tradition.[60]

In this way the evangelist led his readers into the historical actuality of the story, rooted in ancient Jewish tradition, which presented Jesus as the Messiah in conflict with the Jewish Law. Though the term *Messias* is used only in Jn in the New Testament, and the evangelist deals systematically with the Jewish objections to Jesus' messiahship, Dodd argues that the Jewish elements have little to do with Jn's christology but are merely the starting point for his reinterpretation of messiahship for a non-Jewish audience.[61]

He argues that the clash between Jesus and the Law moves in the same direction, from the encounter with particular legal questions, such as Sabbath law, to the evangelist's christological developments claiming that Jesus, not the Law, is the divine Wisdom, the light of the world, the light of Man.[62] This theme, though dependent on Jewish tradition, has undergone Hellenistic influence. A further step is taken in this direction when the evangelist uses, not Wisdom, but *logos*.[63] Here the link with Philo's use of *logos* is vital.

In dealing with the theme of "knowledge of God" Dodd refers to the interweaving of Hebraic and non-Hebraic ideas and says:

That the evangelist was not conscious of the duality of his thought we may probably assume.[64]

On this basis we might question whether it was Dodd's view that the evangelist intentionally translated a Jewish gospel into Hellenistic terms.[65] In *The Bible and the Greeks* Dodd had argued that the translation of the OT into Greek had led to the transformation of the meaning of Greek words. Meaning was determined by the use of the Greek word and the context in which it was now used. This was true in the evangelist's use of the language concerning knowledge of God ($\gamma\nu\tilde{\omega}\sigma\iota\varsigma\ \theta\epsilon o\tilde{\upsilon}$). Of this the evangelist might not have been aware, but this does not preclude the conclusion that he set out intentionally to express the gospel message for an audience of adherents of the higher religion of Hellenism. Dodd argues that the evangelist went beyond the use of language in which Greek and

---

[60]*Ibid.*, 296.
[61]*Ibid.*, 87, 92, 346, 361f.
[62] *Ibid.*, 78f., 86.
[63]*Ibid.*, 276f.
[64]*Ibid.*, 158f.
[65]Thus J. S. King, "There and Back Again", *Evangelical Quarterly* 55/3 (July, 1983), 153.

Hebraic nuances had already been united in order to communicate with a particular kind of Hellenistic audience.

Such readers were not Christians and the evangelist presupposes no information that would not be readily available to educated people in the empire. The Gospel was intended as a first serious introduction to Christianity for such readers and as such should be viewed as an *apologia*. While the Gospel antedates the works of those who are known to us as the Christian apologists it is not without precedent. Arguably Philo did for Judaism what Dodd claims the evangelist did for Christianity.

iv Critique. Attractive and persuasive as much of Dodd's argument is, his position must be modified in the light of the following observations.

1. Recognition that the evangelist himself carried on a running debate with Judaism throughout the Gospel must modify Dodd's apologetic theory. Acceptance that the Gospel stands in a closer relation to Jewish Christianity than Dodd allowed seems to be demanded.

2. Failure to discuss sectarian Judaism and, in particular, the significance of the Qumran Texts, is a real weakness. In those texts the symbols of light and darkness (the dominant Johannine symbols) appear in the same polarity as they do in the Fourth Gospel. Contrary to Dodd,[66] there is good reason for discerning Hellenistic influence in these Palestinian Jewish texts.

3. Recognition of these factors suggests that the Gospel was written for Jewish believers in the process of their struggle with the synagogue.[67] This need not exclude the influence of Hellenism on the evangelist, though such influence might have been transmitted to him through Judaism.

4. While Dodd correctly recognized that the evangelist reinterprets Jewish messianic categories and identified "Son of God", "Son of Man", and *logos* as the important Johannine categories, he failed to note that these categories also remain in the Jewish area. Hence it seems that the evangelist was attempting to redefine the understanding of Jews or Christian Jews, or, perhaps, both. This might be considered polemical or apologetic, or theological, but not along the lines suggested by Dodd.

5. Dodd correctly notes that, although the *logos* christology is explicit only in the Prologue, it is implicit throughout the Gospel.[68] It is a key to

---

[66]*Tradition*, 15 n3.

[67]This leaves open the question of how the Gospel might have been understood by "higher pagans". Indeed it is possible that later redactional elements in the Gospel might have been designed to adjust it to a new audience.

[68]*Interpretation*, 267f.

the evangelist's christology. In spite of the links with Philo, this need not indicate that the evangelist was dependent on the Greek understanding of *logos* as mind/thought/word. Rather we should allow that there was a Greek influence on Jewish Wisdom speculation and it was from this latter context that the evangelist drew his resources.

6. Dodd argues that the evangelist intended to universalize an originally Jewish gospel through the use of categories resulting from the encounter of Hebraic and Hellenistic thought. That there is an intent to universalize is perhaps true. This is not, however, achieved through the use of universal categories. The universalization contains within itself the scandal of particularity; that the God who created the world has made himself known and acted to redeem the world in a particular man, a Jew, Jesus of Nazareth. The terms in which the evangelist expressed this thought came to him through Hellenistic Judaism. There is no evidence that he had to master "alien categories" either for the purpose of undercutting the use of them,[69] or for the purpose of translating a Jewish gospel in terms of them. Rather he made use of Hellenistic Jewish thought about Wisdom/Law in order to cope with the synagogue conflict in which he needed to go beyond the traditional proclamation of Jesus' messiahship, interpreting this in terms of his own key categories.

That there were such readers of Jn as Dodd proposes there is no reason to doubt. But it is not clear that the Gospel was written with such readers in mind. Did the author consciously compose what he had to say so that it would be intelligible and clear to such readers in the sense that he intended? It is argued in *Quest* that such readers did respond to the Gospel in the later stages of its development and they found in it the fulfillment of their quest for life, but they misunderstood it and this led to the schism within the Johannine Community.[70] What is more, it seems that this development contributed to the growth of Christian Gnosticism.[71]

2. The Gnostic Problem
The shift of emphasis in Dodd's thinking of the purpose of the Gospel, from polemics to apologetics, is matched by a shift in his understanding of the background of the Gospel. In his commentary on the Epistles he wrote:
> In common with the Fourth Gospel, the First Epistle of John
> shows the influence of Gnostic ways of thought.[72]

This is not the view presented in *Interpretation*, which is the consequence of

---

[69]*The Johannine Epistles*, xvii-xviii.
[70]See chapter 14, "The 'Opponents' in 1 John" below.
[71]The *Nag Hammadi* library now illustrates the character of this movement from the perspective of its later development.
[72]*Epistles, xx.*

not only a shift in terminology, but a real change of position.

In his commentary on the Epistles Dodd outlines his understanding of the development of Gnosticism in relation to "higher paganism", a new movement within paganism which rationalized, universalized, and spiritualized traditional cults and mysteries. In its lowest form superstition was made respectable but, in higher forms, it became a religion of mystical communion with the divine. Just as it had adopted cults and mysteries from the Hellenistic world, it also adopted Judaism and Christianity as additional cults and mysteries. Converts to Christianity also used the language of "higher paganism" to express the faith in terms of modern thought. The consequence of this was confusion, and when the church emerges from the "tunnel" period in the mid-second century it was "surrounded by a medley of sects" varying from eccentric, to half-Christian, to near-Christian, to mere caricatures. Dodd recognizes that this development took place in what he calls the "tunnel" period and his reconstruction makes good sense. Nevertheless a few questions remain.

i Gnosticism and the Johannine literature. The Gospel was written when syncretism between "higher paganism" and Christianity was beginning. The evangelist aimed to think through the new categories to clarify the confusion of the situation and in so doing advanced the understanding of the Christian faith. The confusion continued, however, not only generally, but also in the Johannine situation. It was necessary for another author to write 1 Jn because the language continued to be used in an "unworthy" and "untrue" sense. This author made use of the Gospel, which he did not altogether understand. He was less able than the evangelist and less guarded against Gnostic ideas, especially in the affirmation "God is light". Neither the Gospel nor 1 Jn was able to prevent the continued growth of Gnosticism[73] and, by the mid-second century the church was besieged by Gnostic sects. In spite of the fact that the Gospel, according to Dodd, was designed to undercut this development, the Gnostic sects were attracted to it. This throws some doubt on Dodd's hypothesis. Would not a Gospel specifically designed to encounter and control the development of Gnosticism have been more resistant to Gnostic interpretation? Hence Dodd's later emphasis on apologetics rather than polemics is more credible though even this is questionable as the intended purpose of the Gospel. Rather it should be seen as an actual but unintended (by the evangelist) use of the Gospel.

ii The "higher paganism" and Gnosticism. In his commentary

---

[73]*Ibid.*, xviii-xix.

on the Epistles Dodd discusses the merits of a "narrow" or broader definition of Gnosticism. In the narrow sense Gnosticism is perceived as a term to cover heretical Christian sects from the second century.[74] In the broader sense the term describes a movement, pagan and Christian, which taught salvation through a special kind of knowledge. He concluded that the broader definition had advantages, bringing out the common elements in the diverse phenomena. Thus Dodd says that both Gospel and Epistle show "the influence of Gnostics ways of thought".[75] He also illustrates the position of the opponents of 1 Jn by reference to the second century Gnostic texts, indicating a sense of continuity.[76]

Dodd uses the term "Gnostic" in a narrow and a broader sense. Given that the narrow is included in the broader, his description of the assumptions of *"higher paganism"* should be relevant to his understanding of Gnosticism.

> The material world is evil. The rational part of man is a prisoner in it, and an exile from the world of light; in fact, in some way a separated part of the supernal world, an effluence, or radiation, of that eternal Light which is Reason, or pure Being, or God. By knowledge of the world of light, communicated in esoteric revelations or initiations of one kind or another, the rational spirit of man can liberate itself from its prison of matter and rise to the supernal world. It is then united or identified with, or absorbed in, the Divine.
>
> Many variations were played upon this theme, all of them controlled by the central dogmas: the distinction between the realm of light and the realm of darkness which is the material world, and deification through supernatural knowledge *(gnosis)*.[77]

This summary is similar to the one concerning Gnosticism given by Rudolf Bultmann in his *Primitive Christianity*.[78] Both stress the variety of forms and there are many points of contact in the actual description. Three important differences stand out however:

1. Bultmann qualifies the use of "soul" by indicating that the language of Gnosticism refers to "man's true inner self", while Dodd speaks of "the rational part of man". Bultmann highlights the mythical elements while Dodd's description is more philosophical.

2. Dodd's understanding of the broader movement includes superstition and myth which he distinguishes sharply from the piety of the "higher paganism" described above. Bultmann recognized the mythical character of

---

[74]*Ibid.*, xviii.
[75]*Ibid.*, xx.
[76]*Ibid.*, xix, 61, 76f., 98.
[77]*Ibid.*, xvii.
[78]Fontana edition, 194f.; Thames & Hudson edition, 163f.

Gnosticism, but argued that it gave expression to an understanding of existence new to its time. Hence he was concerned to ask about the meaning and significance of Gnostic myth. It now appears that Bultmann's understanding of the mythical texts corresponds quite closely to Dodd's interpretation of the more philosophical texts.

3. Bultmann's summary involves the role of the descending and ascending redeemer, which is not mentioned by Dodd. Given the "manifold variations", and recognizing that this element appears only in texts influenced by Christianity, it seems unwise to include this element in the broader description of Gnosticism.

In *Interpretation*, without explanation, Dodd adopts the narrow definition of Gnosticism and contrasts it sharply with his understanding of the "higher paganism", now termed "the higher religion of Hellenism". Compared with this the Gnostic systems are less Hellenic, more oriental, and addicted to myth.[79] For Gnosticism *gnosis is* not profoundly religious, as it is for the higher religion of Hellenism. It is rather, knowledge about the structure of the higher world and how to get there, knowledge conveyed in myths. Whatever Jn meant by knowledge, it was not this.[80] Rather, Dodd links knowledge of God in the Gospel with the "higher religion of Hellenism". Hence he has driven a wedge between the later Gnostic sects and the "higher religion of Hellenism" which he had previously seen as two phases in a common movement. More sympathetic study of Gnostic myths suggests that this sharp distinction is not justified.

It is argued in *Quest* that Gnostic tendencies, present within some streams of sectarian Judaism, contributed to the development of the distinctive Johannine language and symbolism. The Johannine tradition, however, developed a christology that would be used in the development of the second century forms of Gnosticism.

III. TRADITION AND HISTORY

Unlike the Qumran Texts Jn was written in Greek. Even so, the most significant single factor in shaping the Johannine tradition was the relation to the synagogue, a relationship which began with dialogue, became a conflict and ended in mutual execration. This process is reflected in the tradition and the observation of clues can lead to the detection of much that at first seems hidden. Yet, in the end Jn remains a mysterious book. Clues that seem to indicate the use of sources and a process of redaction have led to no certain conclusions. Certainly the majority of scholars recognize evidence of a hand (or hands) other than the evangelist's in

---

[79]*Interpretation*, 97, 98, 101.
[80]*Interpretation*, 101, 151, 212.

chapter 21, though even here it is possible to argue that 21.23-24 makes use of a literary technique and does not indicate any process of redaction.[81] Even if we accept the majority view there is no agreement concerning the character or the scope of the redaction(s). Most agree that the evangelist made use of sources. There is, however, no agreement on the identification of the sources, their scope and character, the criteria to be used in their detection and separation, or concerning whether Jn knew and used the Synoptics. This has seriously limited the success of attempts to assess the contribution made by the evangelist.

Any observant reader will detect tensions in Jn. The more important of these concern eschatology (present or realized alongside future apocalyptic); signs (faith based on signs alongside a critical attitude to signs); sacraments (a sacramental attitude alongside non-sacramental or even an anti-sacramental perspective); and chronological or sequential dislocations. It is a moot point whether these tensions exist because the evangelist has failed to assimilate his sources successfully or because the text became disordered and was finally redacted by another hand (or hands), or because Jn has come to us unpolished and to a degree unfinished. Probably sources and redaction have left their mark on Jn. But the tensions could be a consequence of the evangelist's response to situations within and outside his community and, to some extent and in some instances his thought might involve tensions.[82] As for the process of redaction, it is probable that this should be attributed to the Johannine school and is hardly likely to have been antithetical to the intentions of the evangelist (pace Bultmann and others), though new perspectives might well have been introduced. We need to allow for the possibility that the evangelist's contribution to

---

[81] See Paul Minear, "The Original Function of John 21", *JBL* 102(1), March 1983, 85-98.

[82] Today we are inclined to call such tensions a kind of "dialectic". I have in mind the stress in Jn on divine sovereignty and individual responsibility which we find side by side in Jn 6. C. K. Barrett has long been a defender of the dialectical nature of Jn's thought. See especially his essays "The Dialectical Theology of St. John" (*New Testament Essays*, 49–69), "Christocentric or Theocentric? Observations on the Theological Method of the Fourth Gospel" (*Essays on John*, 1--18), "'The Father is greater than I' John 14.28: Subordinationist Christology in the New Testament" (*Essays on John*, 19–36), "Paradox and Dualism" (*Essays on John*, 98–115). It is necessary, however, that the acceptance of tensions in the evangelist's thought should not be allowed to justify all contradictions so that unsympathetic redaction is ruled out in principle without regard to the evidence. For a tension to be regarded as dialectical, not a contradiction, there needs to be at least an indication that the author intends dialectic or evidence of a dialectical tradition on the issue which we could expect the author to know.

the writing of Jn was made over a lengthy period and that he revised and added to earlier "drafts" of his work before his contribution was completed.[83] That is not to suggest that Jn was to his satisfaction, only that at some point his contribution came to an end.

1. A Developing Tradition

The task of plotting the development of the Gospel has been undertaken by a number of scholars, e.g., G. Richter,[84] B. Lindars,[85] R. Schnackenburg, J. Becker,[86] M. E. Boismard[87] and R. E. Brown. Brown posits a minimum of five stages in the development of the tradition.

Stage one is the tradition of words and works of Jesus originating with the BD (beloved disciple) whom Brown originally identified with John the son of Zebedee in an attempt to combine the tradition of authorship with the evidence of the Gospel.[88] Subsequently Brown moved from this position concluding that the internal and external evidence should not be harmonized and that the BD was an outsider from the group of best known disciples. Brown suggests that the BD might have been one of the unnamed disciples of Jn 21.2, originally mentioned as the unnamed disciple of John the Baptist who follows Jesus, Jn 1.35ff.[89]

Stage two saw the development of the oral tradition into its distinctive Johannine form through its use in the teaching and preaching of the Johannine school under the influence of a leading figure whom we may call the evangelist.

Stage three involved the production of a written Gospel by the evangelist. This process involved a limited selection from available oral tradition (which seems to have contained multiple versions of various

---

[83]This position is accepted by Martin Hengel, *The Johannine Question*, 94–5, 102, 205–6 n86.

[84]*Studien zum Johannesevangelium*.

[85]*John* and *Behind the Fourth Gospel*.

[86]*Das Evangelium nach Johannes*.

[87]M.-E. Boismard and A. Lamouille, *L'évangile de Jean*.

[88] It is a problem, for those who reject the traditional view, to explain how the Gospel became associated with John by a witness as reliable as Irenaeus who had access to much earlier evidence, *viz.* the elders of Asia Minor. Perhaps the identification was simply the result of certain deductions drawn from evidence in Jn. The sons of Zebedee are not mentioned in Jn 1–20. The Baptist is referred to simply as John. No confusion would arise if the readers knew that the author was the other John. The sons of Zebedee are mentioned in Jn 21.2 in a group which appears to include the BD though he is not specifically mentioned at this point. As James was martyred early only John is left (apart from two unnamed disciples) as a possible candidate as BD and author of Jn because the others mentioned can be excluded. However this ignores the possibility that one of the two unnamed disciples of Jn 21.2 is the BD.

[89]See *The Community of the Beloved Disciple*, 33f.

traditions as well as traditions not included by the evangelist).

Stage four was a second edition, also by the evangelist. Indeed there might have been successive editions to meet specific needs such as difficulties posed by the continuance of the disciples of the Baptist and the secret believers within the synagogue .

Stage five was the redaction of the Gospel by another hand as is indicated by Jn 21.24. The intention was, consistent with the Johannine school, not to lose tradition developed in stage two and to meet new problems that had emerged. Such problems relate e.g., to the death of the BD and the relation of the Johannine Christians to the Petrine group (Catholic Christians).

Thus Brown identifies three major figures involved in the composition of Jn from the Johannine school: the BD as the source of the tradition; the evangelist as largely responsible for stages two, three and four; and the redactor.[90] In between stages four and five the Epistles were written by another Johannine author. This involves a fourth Johannine figure and a sixth stage in the history of the tradition.

In linking the BD with the founding of the Johannine school but distinguishing him from the evangelist Brown stands with scholars such as Alan Culpepper[91] and Rudolf Schnackenburg.[92] Like Schnackenburg he gave up the identification of the BD as John the son of Zebedee.

Brown's theory of the development of the tradition is treated as representative. It is used because, with the completion of commentaries on the Gospel and Epistles, together with other studies, he has provided a detailed exemplification and justification of his approach. It is precisely the detail and complexity of the theory that has brought criticism from some scholars. This criticism is not always well directed. Brown recognizes that an hypothesis of this sort must allow for some variables and suggests a fairly straightforward course of developments. His stages of development allow for the beginning of the tradition, its oral shaping in transmission, the formation of an ordered written edition, its revision or revisions and finally a redaction. He notes that is is not possible to specify precisely the number of editions. However, unless the author sat down and wrote the Gospel out of his head without reference to any tradition, some such process is inevitable. Given the evidence of Jn 21.24 a redactional stage is indicated. There is also evidence that the Gospel was not written at a "sitting", that it is the result of a literary-historical process.[93] The Prologue appears to have been added to a work previously

---

[90] R. E. Brown, *The Johannine Epistles*, 30 n71.

[91] *The Johannine School*, 265.

[92] *The Gospel According to St. John* III, 375-88.

[93] This is recognized also by M. Hengel, *The Johannine Question*, 95 and 205-6 n86.

beginning at Jn 1.19. Brown argues that there are two versions of the bread of life discourse (Jn 6.35-50 and 6.51-58). While the overall picture is plausible, many of the details are questionable.[94]

Clearly if the origin of the tradition was an eyewitness (BD) the evangelist has access to a unique tradition.[95] Some parts of the Johannine narrative can scarcely be derived from the Synoptics[96] so that the only origin for these can be a distinctive source or sources or the fertile imagination of the evangelist. Other parts are intelligible in terms of the evangelist's imaginative interpretation of Synoptic-like tradition.[97] In all of this we can readily recognize Synoptic-like narrative tradition and occasional Synoptic-like sayings. These may have Synoptic parallels or be comparable to the *genre* of Synoptic sayings or narratives. But it is only as the narratives are developed through dialogues and monologues that they take on their distinctive Johannine character. Likewise it is only as the isolated Synoptic-like sayings are embedded in the discourses that they take on their Johannine character. Some of these brief sayings become Johannine by becoming a major focus and theme. This is true of the so-called "Johannine thunderbolt" and the focus on Jesus as the one sent and the theme of eternal life.[98]

On the basis of such evidence as the Qumran-like dualistic language it is argued that the Gospel was first shaped in Judaea in the shadow of sectarian Judaism. As a consequence of the disastrous Jewish war, culminating in the destruction of Jerusalem in 70 CE, the Gospel was written in Greek, probably from some great urban centre of the *diaspora* such as Ephesus. The Gospel reflects the Jewish search for identity. But the Johannine Christians were subsequently excluded from the synagogue

---

[94]In the Preface to *Community* (p.7) Brown stresses the hypothetical nature of his reconstruction indicating that he will be happy if 60% of it is found convincing. Some readers will be convinced of much more than this and others of less.

[95]Moody Smith concluded that "The distinctive character of the Johannine narrative material within the Gospel strongly suggests a principal source (or sources) and one independent of the Synoptics." In support of this view he appeals to a variety of scholars such as Robert Fortna, E. Bammel, J. Becker. "Johannine Christianity", *NTS* 21/2 (1976) 229.

[96]Jn 2.1-11; 4.4-42; 5.1-9b; 9.1-11; 11.

[97]Jn 1.19-51; 2.13-22; 3.1-11; 4.46-52; 6.1-21; 12.1-8,12-19.

[98]See Matt 11.25-30=Lk 10.21-22 and the use of $\dot{\alpha}\pi o\sigma\tau\dot{\epsilon}\lambda\lambda\epsilon\iota\nu$ and $\pi\dot{\epsilon}\mu\pi\epsilon\iota\nu$ in Mk 9.37; 12.6 and parallels and Matt 15.24; Lk 4.18,43; 10.16 and $\mathring{\eta}\lambda\theta o\nu$ in Mk 2.17; Matt 5.17; 10.34-35; 11.3ff. Only Mk 10.17,30 and parallels, Matt 25.46 and Lk 10.25 treat the major Johannine theme of eternal life. Also significantly, only Jn 3.3,5 explicitly treats the major complementary Synoptic theme of the kingdom of God.

and the rejection stories, which reflect that crisis, provided the Johannine community with the assurance that though rejected by men they were chosen by God.

In what follows a model for understanding the process of the composition of the Gospel features the recognition of evidence of:

    i. the tradition used by the evangelist;

    ii. the shaping of this in three consecutive editions and;

    iii. a final redaction prior to publication.

The model is adopted in the awareness that it is a simplification of the process. Very likely the editions represent a process of ongoing revision, but one in which certain watersheds can be perceived in the way the tradition has been shaped. The "editions" represent these perceived watersheds. The first edition contains the traditions shaped in the period of open dialogue with the synagogue concerning the messiahship of Jesus. This openness probably closed down rapidly after the Jewish war but no precise date can be given. The second edition is bounded by the experience of expulsion from the synagogue and also contains the tradition of dispute and conflict leading up to that expulsion. The *experience* of expulsion takes in reflection on the expulsion and its consequences. The third edition manifests issues bound up with a growing schism within the Johannine community (a schism which had recently occurred when 1 Jn was written). The controversy of the true confession of faith emerged here in a new way.

Brown also thinks of complex stages in interpreting this tradition. They involve crises in the history of the Johannine community and a variety of interpreters. His distinction between the BD and the evangelist calls for justification and the identification of crises calling for the reinterpretation of the tradition requires discussion. Here care is needed to distinguish crises within the life of Jesus from the reflected crises of the Johannine community which are reflected in John's story of Jesus.

2. The Community and Its History

Brown's hypothesis about the development of the tradition can be related to his suggested phases of the history of the Johannine community.

The first phase began when a group of disciples of the Baptist became believers and concluded when the believers were excluded from the synagogue. It includes stages one and two in the development of the tradition.

The second phase saw the writing of the Gospel by the evangelist about 90 CE and stages three and four in the development of the tradition.

The third phase includes the redaction of the Gospel and the writing of the Epistles in about 100 CE. It involved a schism within the community. This corresponds to stage five in the development of the tradition.

The final phase concluded some time in the second century when the

Johannine community and the schismatics both disappeared, absorbed either into the emerging great church or Docetism, Gnosticism and Montanism.

Brown's reconstruction seems to me to be generally convincing. Only a few points need be raised. *Firstly*, there seems to be no good reason for delaying the development of the "higher"[99] christology. This might well have been a contribution of the evangelist in the context of the dialogue with the synagogue.[100] *Secondly*, there is reason to think that the farewell discourses do *not* all belong to the same late stage in the pre-Gospel history. *Thirdly*, the break from the synagogue almost certainly opened the Johannine community to Gentiles. It is not improbable that the Gentile believers understood the tradition in a different light and that this contributed to the division of the community reflected in the Johannine Epistles. *Fourthly*, the redactor, whose hand is clearly responsible for 21.24, probably added the whole of chapter 21 including the references to the BD in 21.7,23-24 and in the rest of the Gospel, 13.23-26; 18.15; 19.25-27; 20.2-10; the *ex eventu* "prophecy" of Peter's martyrdom, 13.38; cf. 21.18-19; and the parenthetical explanations of Jewish terms and customs, 1.38,41; 2.6,13; 6.4; 7.2; 11.55; 19.31,40. Recognition that this material is redactional is significant for the historical reconstruction. It is not suggested that the redactional stratum is contrary to the purpose of the Gospel as it probably was the work of the *Johannine school*. But it is the latest stratum.

Clues to the changing circumstances of the life of the Johannine community are embedded in Jn. The clues exist because of the influence of those circumstances on the shaping of the Johannine tradition.[101]

---

[99]Brown, *ibid.*, 25 n32, on the use of "high" and "low" in relation to christology.

[100]If the evangelist had been a follower of the Baptist he might well have been critical from the very beginning of the Temple, "establishment Judaism" and the view of the people of God by physical descent. The tradition of the Baptist's critique is recorded in Matt 3.7-12 = Lk 3.7-9.

[101] The most detailed attempt to outline the history of the Johannine community is to be found in R. E. Brown's, *The Community of the Beloved Disciple* and is taken further in his *Epistles*. His reconstruction of the pre-Gospel period of the history of the Johannine Christians follows the chronology of Jn. Whatever he intended this gives the impression that the history of the community can simply be read out of the Gospel, suggesting that the evangelist set out to write a history of his community in the guise of a Gospel. This complaint is voiced by Judith Lieu, *The Second and Third Epistles of John*, 167, 214. According to Brown, the movement began when some disciples of the Baptist with Davidic Messianic expectation became disciples of Jesus Jn 1.35-51. They were joined by Christian Jews of anti-Temple persuasion, Jn 2-3; and a group of their Samaritan converts, Jn 4. A 'high christology developed and conflict with the Jews increased,

Hence it is clear that the history of the Johannine community is a second factor (in addition to the thought world of the evangelist) influencing the formation of Jn. Indeed that history helps us to understand why the specific concepts and language, which were available to the evangelist from his thought world, were drawn on by him. Consequently the task of reconstructing the history of the Johannine community is not only of interest for its own sake, it promises to throw light on our interpretation of Jn.[102]

It is now generally accepted that although the Gospels were written to tell the story of Jesus they also reflect the story of the author and his community.[103] From these reflections it is possible to reconstruct something of the history of the communities which shaped the traditions. Even in Jn, however, where the reflections are clearest, there are no straightforward data upon which the history of the Johannine community can be based.[104] Such data as we find appear to come from various stages in the life of the community and different phases of the development of the Gospel.

The identification of clues within Jn is made possible by our knowledge of other evidence of the history of Jesus. Where Jn differs from the Synoptics we are alerted to the possibility of finding traces of the history

---

Jn 6-12; with the consequence that the Johannine Christians were excluded from the synagogue. This chronological development raises questions about the detailed credibility of the reconstruction. See my review of Brown in *ABR* 28 (1980), 70-2. On the history of the Johannine community see also J. L. Martyn, *History and Theology In the Fourth Gospel*, and "Glimpses into the History of the Johannine Community", in *L'Evangile de Jean* ed. M. de Jonge.

[102]Judith Lieu (*Epistles*, 168) questions the validity of seeing the theology as a response to an historical situation. Consequently she tends to play down the role of the historical context in the formation of the theology.

[103]This is acknowledged by Judith Lieu (*Epistles*, 214), though she appears to doubt the possibility of identifying those reflections. "This is not to deny that John does reflect the community's own circumstances; it is to question whether those circumstances can be 'read off' directly from distinctively Johannine passages." Of course they cannot be read off directly. The question is, can they be discerned at all and are they relevant to an understanding of the Gospel?

[104]It is thus essential to recognize the hypothetical nature of all reconstructions. But this is not an excuse for avoiding reconstruction. All interpretations presuppose some reconstruction, even those based on the naive assumption that the Gospel simply tells the story as it happened or the assertion that the story floats free from history and is simply to be read as a story. The former concludes the straightforward identity of story and event and the latter assumes that no history throws light on the story. Neither position is simply a "given".

of Johannine Christianity. Perhaps clues relating to the earliest history of the Johannine Christians are to be found in the treatment of John the Baptist. We are alerted to the clues by the way Jn's treatment differs from the Synoptics. In Jn, the Baptist's role is "reduced" to that of a witness to Jesus.[105] There is no mention of the baptism of Jesus by him nor any indication that he was the prophet of impending doom such as we find in the Synoptics.[106] Rather he disclaims any eschatological significance for himself except as the witness to Jesus, Jn 1.6-8,15,19ff.,29ff.,35ff.; 3.26; 5.33. In giving this witness the Baptist is portrayed as the first true believer through whom belief for all others becomes possible. His words provide the reader with genuine witness to the profound Johannine christology so that his words are indistinguishable from those of the narrator and even Jesus himself, 3.31-36. Thus what was reduction, from one point of view, leads to an expanded role from another. Both the contraction and the expansion point to the history of the Johannine community rather than the history of Jesus though the portrayal of rival missions probably is an insight into the situation of Jesus' mission.

According to Jn the first disciples to join Jesus were former disciples of the Baptist. This does not fit the Synoptic account of the calling of the first disciples, Mk 1.16ff. The events described in Jn 1.35ff. are taken to refer to the history of the Johannine Christians. The first members of their "community" were converts from the Baptist "sect" or group. Jn 3.22f. attests the continuance of the group into the period of Jesus' ministry and Acts 19.1-7 refers to a group of disciples of the Baptist who were led to faith in Jesus and were baptized by Paul. The fourth century Pseudo-Clementine Homilies (2.22-25) suggest that the followers of the Baptist persisted as an independent movement. Of the two disciples of the Baptist who follow Jesus (1.35ff.) one is unnamed and it could be that this disciple is to be identified with the BD who is said to be involved in the writing of the Gospel, Jn 21.24-25.[107] If the Johannine Christians were originally disciples of the Baptist this could throw light on the distinctive

---

[105]Jn 3.22ff. indicates that the two missions (of the Baptist and of Jesus) continued side by side whereas the Synoptics portray successive missions, first the Baptist then Jesus, Mk 1.14. Both Jn and Mk seek to obscure the opposition between the two missions though Jn did not follow Mk's lead by making them successive missions. Even in the context of the reference to their rival missions the Baptist is portrayed as a witness to Jesus, Jn 3.26ff.

[106]See Mk 1.4 but especially Q, Matt 3.7-12=Lk 3.7-9,16-17.

[107]Naturally at this point it would have been inappropriate to refer to him as the BD, though it remains a puzzle as to why this designation should be used for the first time only at the farewell supper, 13.23.

understanding of Jesus that we find in Jn,[108] as well as the distinctive interpretation of of the role of the Baptist. The profoundly true witness of the Baptist to Jesus, providing as it does the foundation for the belief of the first Johannine Christians, significantly supports the claims of the community to know the truth.

There is a case for arguing that Jesus was himself a disciple of the Baptist. After all, he was baptized by him, a fact obscured by Jn even though he made use of the sign that revealed Jesus as the coming one. Some other disciples of the Baptist may have followed Jesus when he began his independent mission. Apologetic tradition in relation to the Baptist might have begun to develop at this stage and tradition that portrays the Baptist as the witness to Jesus fits well here. It is likely that a challenge from a continuing Baptist "sect" was encountered at a later period, perhaps in Ephesus, giving point and emphasis to this tradition.

Plotting the history of the Johannine community with any precision is difficult. It seems that the Johannine response to the crisis of the departure of Jesus was quite distinctive. The crisis was exacerbated by the unfulfilled expectation of Jesus' imminent return. Evidence of this problem is to be discerned in what we have termed the first version of the farewell discourse where there is a nuanced treatment of the theme of Jesus' coming. This constitutes the first crisis in the history of the community. Response to it also constitutes the beginning of a theological trajectory identifiable in terms of the the the Paraclete/Spirit of Truth. The destruction of the Temple may constitute a second crisis, again leading to a theological development and one which might well have provoked further conflict with the synagogue.[109] It is probable that the missionary use of the signs within the synagogue came to an end in the period immediately following the Jewish war (66-74 CE). Around this time, perhaps immediately before the war, the Johannine believers were forced to evacuate from Palestine, perhaps with other Jews.[110] Such evidence as exists suggests that the relationship between *Christian Jews*[111] and Jews

---

[108] See Bultmann, *Gospel of John*, 108. Perhaps it would be better to say that a nucleus of the Johannine Christians, including the evangelist, were once disciples of the Baptist.

[109] See Jn 2.13-22 and 4.16-26.

[110] The strong connection between the thought forms and language of Jn and the Qumran Texts suggests that the Johannine tradition was shaped in Palestine, at least this best explains the evangelist's thought forms and language.

[111] In agreement with J. L. Martyn, *Christian Jews* refers to Jewish believers in Jesus the Messiah who have not separated from the synagogue while *Jewish Christians* refers to Christians of Jewish extraction whose beliefs brought about their separation from Judaism.

deteriorated quite rapidly after the Jewish war. The synagogue conflict reflected in the Gospel is to be taken as evidence of the situation somewhere in the *diaspora*. That the Gospel was written in Greek is a reflection of this context.

In the first place there were *Christian Jews* of various persuasions within the synagogue. Amongst these was the evangelist who was probably associated closely with a group which might loosely be described as the *Johannine school*. After the break from the synagogue the evangelist and his "school" played a formative role in shaping a group of *Jewish Christians* into the *Johannine community*. Both before and after the break from the synagogue the evangelist sought to reinterpret the "traditional Davidic christology" of those who appear in the Gospel as "secret believers" (or crypto-Christians). Thus while the *Johannine school* was unified by the christology of the evangelist the *Johannine community* probably was not. True belief, according to the evangelist, involved more than the traditional confession. One of the primary achievements of the Gospel is its reinterpretation of what the evangelist considered an inadequate christological confession.

Many scholars accept that the evangelist made use of a signs source and that it surfaces in 2.11; 4.54 and 20.30f. where it is recognized by the numbering of the first two signs and 20.30f. is thought to have come from its conclusion. From it the evangelist could have derived his use of the term sign ($\sigma\eta\mu\epsilon\hat{\iota}o\nu$).[112] This observation is supported by the assertion that there is some ambivalence over the evaluation of signs in Jn. In some places signs are evaluated positively as the basis for faith while elsewhere the value of signs is severely questioned as in Jn 2.24-25 following 2.23 and in 4.48. It is argued that the evangelist was more critical of the signs than was the source. But if the evangelist made use of such a source, what was its origin? Bultmann argued that the source was used by the converts from the Baptist sect in an effort to win over those who remained loyal to the Baptist. The contrast in Jn 10.40ff., "John did no sign but all that he said of this man was true",[113] lends support to his view as does the overall treatment of the Baptist in Jn. There is, however, also evidence that suggests that the signs were used in the debate with the synagogue.

---

[112]See the discussion of the signs source below. In fact it is difficult to know whether this use of the term "sign" is derived from a distinctive collection of miracle stories or is an aspect of the evangelist's distinctive contribution. Certainly the use of it has been thoroughly integrated into the Gospel.

[113]See E. Bammel, "John did no miracle", *NTS* 18 (1971), now in C. F. D. Moule (ed.), *Miracles*, 179-202.

The miracle story of Jn 9 may have been derived from a signs source.[114] In its present form in Jn 9 the miracle story has been elaborated to the point that it has become the basis of a symbolic discourse.[115] The miracle story is easily recognized: introduction 9.1-3; miracle 9.6-7; evidence 9.8-11. This follows the general form with which we are familiar from the Synoptics. Such stories were used in the missionary proclamation. The evangelist's elaboration of the story has placed it in the context of dialogue/conflict with the synagogue. Apparently the early missionary preaching using signs was quite successful in attracting members of the synagogue. That would account for the hostility of the response from the synagogue as evidenced in the debate, Jn 9.13-38. From debate the conflict moved to the mutual execration of synagogue and Johannine Christians, 9.22,34,39-41.

At the parting of the ways, when the Johannine community came into being as a separate community of *Jewish Christians*, there were those who were wavering, undecided which way to turn. The decision to exclude any who, "confessed him (Jesus) to be Christ" (αὐτὸν ὁμολογήσῃ Χριστόν) was intended to intimidate the cautious and to discourage converts to the "new movement". Exclusion from the synagogue for confessing (ὁμολογεῖν) that Jesus is the Messiah (Jn 9.22; 12.42) is a clue that assists us in locating the situation of the Johannine Christians as reflected in this part of Jn. Jesus encountered conflict with the Jewish authorities but "excommunication" from the synagogue is an event from the history of the Johannine Christians. Recognition of this is more important than a precise dating of when the event took place. It should be noted that the basis of excommunication here was simply the confession, "Jesus is the Christ", that being the implication of the phrase "to confess him to be Christ" (αὐτὸν ὁμολογήσῃ Χριστόν), with the consequence ἵνα ἀποσυνάγωγος γένηται. Wayne Meeks[116] has argued that the grounds

---

[114]It is noteworthy that Jn includes a number of miracle stories for which there is no Synoptic parallel. The signs source hypothesis provides a solution to the problem of the origin of these stories. All that is necessary for this purpose is a collection of miracle stories, not the elaborate narrative source proposed by Bultmann and developed further by Fortna. See the discussion of the signs source below.

[115]See chapter 8, "The Son of Man: The Light of the World" below.

[116]"Breaking Away", 103. Meeks thinks that the situation of Yavneh and Formative Judaism is more relevant to *Matt* than Jn. But *Matt* and Jn face much the same situation though their responses are different, *Matt* affirming the integrity and continuing significance of the Law which is undercut by the authority of Jesus in Jn. On *Matt*'s affirmation of the Law (including the Sabbath) see J. A. Overman, *Matthew's Gospel and Formative Judaism*, 80-81. For the development of Formative Judaism see Jacob Neusner, "The Formation of Rabbinic Judaism: Yavneh from AD 70-100", *ANRW* II.19.2, 3-42.

for exclusion in Jn do not reflect the introduction of *birkat hamminim* but the decision of the local synagogue rulers to get rid of the troublesome followers of a false Messiah. His reason for this judgement strikes me as artificial:

> John does not speak of people who do not go to synagogue because they cannot conscientiously say the prayers. It speaks of being put out of the synagogue.

Even if Meeks has described the situation accurately, would not those who felt themselves unable to go to synagogue because of recently introduced prayers think of themselves as "excluded"? It may be that Meeks was influenced by his judgement that Jn is to be understood in relation to sectarian Judaism. But this need not exclude a traumatic encounter with Formative Judaism at a later stage. What is more, by focusing on the confession of faith alone he has overlooked the controversy concerning the Law which is regularly the initial cause of conflict in Jn. Only in the context of existing conflict does the focus move to the christological confession. This is especially clear in Jn 5 and 9. It would, however, be a mistake to become preoccupied with identifying the Johannine situation with the introduction of *birkat hamminim*. It is simply the best known relevant factor external to Jn that might throw light on this aspect of the Gospel. What is important is the situation of conflict with Formative Judaism whenever or wherever it happened.

The evidence of the trauma caused by the introduction of measures to exclude those who confessed faith in Jesus suggests that it achieved its purpose reasonably well. On the other hand, the evangelist and his group were intent on persuading the "secret believers" to join them. The theme is prominent in the Gospel. Nicodemus is treated as typical of those who kept their faith secret to maintain their position within Judaism (Jn 3.1ff.; 7.50ff.). He is typical of the rulers who would not confess faith openly for fear of excommunication, 12.42. Secrecy because of fear of the Jews was typical even of the disciples, 20.19. In the end Nicodemus did perform the open act of the burial of the body of Jesus, Jn 19.38ff. His story within the Gospel is the portrayal of one who moves progressively from the darkness (3.2) into the light. The threat of excommunication was a form of intimidation intended to prevent, or at least retard the spread of the new movement. In Jn 9 the parents of the once blind man were so intimidated that they refused to acknowledge how their son had received his sight. The man himself overcame the intimidation because the significance of Jesus' action was inescapable for him.[117] As a result he was excommunicated and became the model of the true believer in this Jewish situation, Jn 9.34-38. Nowhere else in Jn is Jesus absent from so much significant dialogue and action as in Jn 9.8-34. Here the once blind man is the central character and he, not Jesus, takes the brunt of the Jewish reaction. This signals that his story mirrors that of the Johannine Christians.

The evidence suggests that Jn, as we now know it, came into being progressively through the re-interpretation of the tradition in various situations. The dialogue and conflict with the synagogue constituted a highly significant series of events which have left their mark on much of the material in Jn. But this dialogue and conflict did not take place in a moment. Rather it is to be seen as a process over a number of decades. Jesus encountered conflict during his ministry and so did his followers from the very beginning. From the perspective of the later stages of the conflict however, the early stages appear more like a dialogue. What has happened is that the situation of the community has been used in the narration of Jesus' conflict. To put this in another way, the conflict of Jesus has been interpreted in such a way to make it relevant to the Johannine community.[118] That liberty has been taken with the actual historical situation of Jesus is evident from the way we are told of the Jews attempting to kill Jesus in one moment (5.18), but Jesus continues with a lengthy discourse (5.19-47). Later (7.1) we are told that the Jews sought to kill him, yet he moves freely and teaches in the Temple (7.14). In Jn 9 action is taken against the man Jesus healed (9.34) but Jesus moves freely, even rebuking the Pharisees. At this point one can only suspect that the story of the blind man is meant to be understood as the story of the Johannine Christians.

According to Acts the first believers encountered conflict because of the proclamation of the resurrection of Jesus. The conflict was greater for those of anti-Temple persuasion such as Stephen. This conflict was probably one element contributing to the Johannine christological

---

[117]The positive role of the sign in Jn 9 excludes the conclusion that the evangelist had a negative view of signs. But the sign is not viewed as a sheer act of supernatural power. Rather the quality of the act of the sign as a life-giving (restoring) act of goodness is in view. Compare the stress on making the man whole ($\dot{v}\gamma\iota\dot{\eta}\varsigma$) in Jn 5.6,9,11,14,15.

[118]R. Schnackenburg, *John* I, 19-25 draws a distinction between an author who simply puts words on the lips of Jesus and one who seeks to let Jesus be heard by his own generation by interpreting the words of Jesus to them. The distinction is clear in principle but in practice all that may distinguish two authors is their intentions!

development. But there was no break from the synagogue at this stage, which we can call the *first* wave of conflict. The *second* wave of conflict is illustrated in the writings of Paul and in Acts. The issue provoking this phase concerned the conditions for the entry of Gentile believers. Paul advocated entry into the Christian community on the basis of faith in Jesus without the fulfillment of the requirements of circumcision and other aspects of the Mosaic Law commonly demanded by Christian Judaism. This led to conflict within early Christianity because it was clear that acceptance of the Pauline position would lead to the separation of Christianity from Judaism. It was a conflict involving those groups which were engaged in an active mission to the Gentiles and adopting something like the Pauline "Law-free" approach. Wayne Meeks[119] correctly notes that Pauline Christianity did not face the trauma of exclusion from the synagogue because Paul and his associates

> had created an organized movement that was entirely independent of
> the Jewish communities...

There is evidence, however, of early conflict, even in relation to the Pauline mission.

According to Acts 13–14, Jewish reaction against Paul in Pisidian Antioch, Iconium and Lystra was a consequence of the offer of salvation to Jews and Gentiles on equal terms. Unbelieving Jews attacked Paul as a consequence of the popular response and his turning to the Gentiles was a response that provoked more violent reaction. Thus Acts chronicles a conflict between Paul and unbelieving Jews in relation to his policy of openness to Gentile mission without concern for the provisions of the Jewish Law. Both Paul (in Galatians) and Acts 15 indicate that this was an issue between Paul and a sector of the Jerusalem Church. It is hardly likely that this sector was out of step with the opinion of much of the unbelieving Jewish community concerning relationships with Gentiles. Philo was strongly opposed to laxity concerning the ritual requirements of the Law. Thus the total removal of barriers between Jews and Gentiles on the basis of belief in the gospel alone makes the opposition of the Jews to Paul according to Acts altogether intelligible.

The Johannine conflict with the synagogue belongs to the *third* wave. There is no sign that the controversy concerned the conditions of entry for Gentile believers. There is no controversy about the validity of circumcision. The controversy set Jesus against Moses and the Law, but in a way that suggests an internal Jewish conflict rather than one arising out of problems involved in the mission to the Gentiles. The evangelist accepts the validity of the Law as a witness to Jesus but argues that what

---

[119]"Breaking Away", 107-8.

is witnessed to in the Law was fulfilled in Jesus Christ, Jn 1.17; 5.39,45-47. There is a real sense in which the evangelist portrays Jesus as the fulfillment and therefore the end of alternative forms of Judaism just as Formative Judaism sought to exclude alternatives. There is also a point of conflict in detail. This concerns the keeping of the Sabbath, Jn 5.9ff.; 9.14ff.[120] Jesus came into conflict with Jewish authorities over the keeping of the Sabbath. The way this controversy is introduced in Jn indicates that the Johannine community also found this a point of conflict. The issue is used to highlight the fundamental problem of the Johannine christology, Jn 1.17; 5.17. The Jewish authorities saw the breaking of the Sabbath as the breaking of the Law of Moses. To break the Sabbath using the precedent of Jesus was thus to pit Jesus against Moses. In this context the confession that Jesus is the Christ (Messiah) became the crux in the controversy.

Jn refers to the excommunication from the synagogue ($\dot{\alpha}\pi o\sigma\upsilon\nu\acute{\alpha}\gamma\omega\gamma o\varsigma$ $\gamma\acute{\epsilon}\nu\eta\tau\alpha\iota$) of those who "confessed Christ", Jn 9.22. The language concerning excommunication (9.22; 12.42; 16.2) is peculiar to Jn in the New Testament. Nor is there any early parallel to the situation portrayed in Jn, that is, excommunication for the confession that Jesus is the Messiah. Conclusions on the basis of this observation are supported by what we know of the history of the time. Here the confrontation (in the form depicted in Jn) between believing Jews who confessed Christ and the synagogue is thought to belong to the period after the Jewish war (66-74 CE) and probably around 85 CE at the time of the publication of *birkat hamminim*.[121]

---

[120] The Sabbath issue is also in view in Mk 2.23-28; 3.1-6.

[121] This is the name given to the synagogue ban on heretics, including Jews who believed Jesus to be the Messiah. Though there is contention concerning the precise wording and date of the ban (see Wayne Meeks, "Breaking Away", 102-3) it is generally dated about 85 CE. For a more detailed discussion see J. L. Martyn, *History and Theology In the Fourth Gospel*, 148ff., and 156ff. in the second edition. See also the critique of this view by R. Kimelman, "*Birkat Ha-Minim* and the Lack of Evidence for an Anti-Christian Jewish Prayer in Late Antiquity", in *Jewish and Christian Self-Definition*, Vol. 2, 226-44., ed. E.P. Sanders *et al.* and the response and defence by W. Horbury, "The Benediction of the *minim and Early Jewish Christian Controversy*", *JThS* 33/1 (1982). The discussion by Martin Hengel (*The Johannine Question*, 114-15) is helpful though it fails to note that none of the early confrontations to which he refers deals with excommunication for no other reason than the confession that "Jesus is the Christ". Because of local conditions application of the ban probably varied and some flexibility must be allowed. The situation of the Johannine Christians might have been in advance or later than the general ban. The situation is presupposed by Justin in his discussion of the Jewish practice

What is important, however, is not the identification of the crisis in the Johannine community with *birkat hamminim*. The recognition that the Johannine believers were excluded from the synagogue for the confession that Jesus is the Messiah, whenever or wherever that happened, is what is crucial, whether this was part of a general policy or restricted to a particular locality.[122] It makes no sense to defend the *birkat hamminim* hypothesis as if the understanding of Jn depends upon it. Rather the case depends on the recognition that the Johannine believers were excluded for their confession of faith, whatever the circumstances in which it occurred.

The period following the Jewish war was one of crisis for Judaism marked by the traumatic attempt to arrive at a new self-definition. Without the identity-giving focus on Jerusalem and the Temple, with its attendant festivals, the question raised was, "How would Judaism perceive and recognize itself?" With such an identity crisis, previously permitted diversity could no longer be tolerated. Consequently there was a move (Formative Judaism) towards the development of a Jewish orthodoxy which excluded (amongst others) those Jewish believers who confessed Jesus to be the Christ. Exclusion from the synagogue also brought self-definition to the Johannine community. Prior to exclusion from the synagogue there were Christian Jews (Jews who confessed Jesus to be the Christ) of various views in the synagogue. Exclusion from the synagogue produced a community with its own identity.[123] The evidence suggests that the evangelist, and those associated with him (the Johannine School) attempted to mould this group into the Johannine community. That moulding took the form of a reinterpretation of the variety of christological confessions, which had previously been found within the

---

of cursing Christ and Jewish Christians (*Dial.* 16.4; 47.4; 93.4; 95; 96; 108.3; 117; 123; 133.6; 137). This included the liturgical practice (*birkat hamminim*). The situation has been confused because from the fourth century Christians were in a position of power in relation to powerless Judaism and the evidence of earlier Jewish action against Jewish believers in Jesus has largely been obscured.

[122]This point is often missed as it was in a review of the first edition of *Quest* by K. Grayston in *Epworth Review* (May 1993), 112. Grayston's comment assumes that the case stands and falls on the reconstruction of the circumstances and content of *birkat hamminim*. What is crucial, however, is the evidence in Jn.

[123]Jacob Neusner (*Jews and Christians: The Myth of a Common Tradition*) correctly notes that in the second half of the first century Judaism and Christianity were struggling to establish self-identity and each did this over against the other. Hence Formative Judaism and Jewish Christianity are to be seen as siblings of common parents (sectarian Judaism) but having nothing significant in common with each other. Thus Neusner.

synagogue.[124] Consequently Jn provides a distinctive understanding of traditional christological formulae as well as introducing some distinctive forms of its own.

While there was probably pressure to identify and exclude "secret believers", the main purpose of the ban was to threaten, intimidate and discourage those who were attracted to belief in Jesus as Messiah. On the other hand the evangelist was intent on pressing "secret believers" to come out into the open and to join the Johannine community. The focus on the "secret believers" would not have lasted for long. Soon after the schism the group of believers, which had been rejected, retaliated repudiating those who had rejected them, Jn 9.39-41; 15.1-10. The Johannine community repudiated the synagogue claim to the title "people of God" and claimed it for themselves. Only Jews who believed in (abided in) Jesus belonged to the True vine, the Israel of God. This is an internal Jewish controversy between Jewish Christians (now separated from the synagogue) and synagogue Judaism. There is no sign of Gentile presence in this conflict. In all probability this stage of the conflict took place somewhere outside of Palestine in the *diaspora*. Ephesus would fit the situation as well as any suggested location.

Looking beyond the first edition, in the end it is rejection stories that dominate the Gospel. Not only is Jesus rejected, those who confess that Jesus is the Christ are expelled from the synagogue. Thus an ecclesiology is implied. The believers are "the community under the Word" (Käsemann) where the true confession of faith in Jesus is made. Christology determines the way in which the community is portrayed. This is emphasized by the words of Jesus in Jn 15.1, "I am the true vine". Participation in the people of God, is possible only through abiding in him. The branches cut off represent unbelieving Israel. Unlike Romans 9.16-21, which deals with the relation of the Gentile mission to the people of God, there is no suggestion of the grafting of wild branches to represent the incoming of Gentile believers. The evangelist's implied ecclesiology does not lay the foundation for Gentile mission. But in the changed situation, brought about by the break from the synagogue, it seems that the universal implications of the evangelist's christology became apparent and Gentiles were admitted to the community.

Beyond this point the traces of history are more ambiguous. The break from Judaism was likely to bring the Johannine community in contact

---

[124]The focus on the christological confession may have led to further reflection and even more profound claims such as 1.1-18; 5.17. The evangelist seeks to clarify christology, to make clear that Jesus is the Messiah and what messiahship means in the light of Jesus, Jn 20.30.

with Gentiles. Clues within the Gospel, such as the reference to the Greeks seeking Jesus in Jn 12.20,[125] suggest that this was in fact the case. The announcement of their coming to Jesus brought his response, "The hour has come for *the Son of Man* to be *glorified*" (Jn 12.23), a saying which the evangelist interpreted in terms of Jesus' death. Thus, the Gospel, as it stands, assumes the presence of Gentiles in the Johannine community. But there is no debate over the conditions required for their entry and the issues specifically handled in the Gospel reflect internal Jewish conflicts.

The presence of Gentiles is catered for by the writing of the Gospel in Greek. What is more, Jewish names and traditions are explained in notes which appear to have been added to Jn at a late stage for their sake (Jn 1.38,41; 2.6,13; 5.1; 6.4; 7.2; 11.55; 19.31,40). The entry of Gentiles would explain the emergence of a secondary theme. In the controversy with the synagogue the Johannine emphasis was on the dignity and authority of Jesus. This emphasis led to divergences amongst believing Jews and the evangelist supported his interpretation of Jesus (his christology) by appeal to the teaching and interpreting role of the Spirit of Truth. Apparently Gentile believers, who had joined the Johannine community, took this "higher christology"[126] to refer only to the heavenly exalted Christ and emphasized their own experience of the Spirit as those who were enlightened and knew all the truth. In so doing they ignored the historical Jesus and his teaching. In some parts of the Gospel (later strata) the evangelist has responded to this new situation, especially in the Prologue (Jn 1.1-18) and in the Farewell Prayer (Jn 17). But it is in 1 Jn that we find the most detailed evidence of this conflict. The later strata of Jn are a bridge between the fundamentally Jewish context of Jn as a whole and the new Gentile context of the community, now separated from the synagogue, as reflected in 1 Jn.[127] What emerges now is the new quest for the meaning of christology (messiahship) with Jn and 1 Jn affirming (against the secessionists of 1 Jn 2.19) that "Jesus Christ is come in the flesh", Jn 1.14; 1 Jn 4.2.

---

[125]It has been argued that this is to be understood as a group of *diaspora* Jews, see J. A. T. Robinson *NTS* 6 (1960), 120. But this is hardly convincing.

[126] R. E. Brown, *Community of the Beloved Disciple*, 25 n32 defines the christology of pre-existence in Jn as "higher christology".

[127]See chapter 14, "The 'Opponents' in 1 John" below for a more detailed treatment of the relation of the Gospel to 1 Jn. The position set out there was first expressed in my Durham Ph.D. (1965-67) and outlined in *JWT* (1975). "The 'Opponents' in 1 John" was delivered as a paper to the John Seminar at the Basel SNTS Meeting in 1984.

3. Community History – Fact or Fantasy?

The attempt to reconstruct the history of the Johannine community has not gone unchallenged. Those who reject the validity of the historical critical method regard the attempt as pure fantasy. But alternative methods, such as reader response criticism, cannot be complete and exclusive methods for the study of a text from the distant past such as Jn because to read the text involves the application of historical critical methods.[128] More significant is the questioning of the approach adopted in this study in three recent books.[129] When I first wrote on the significance of the relation of Jn to 1 Jn for the reconstruction of the history of Johannine Christianity I made the following statement:

> It appears to be axiomatic to assume that the background presupposed by the Gospel and 1 John is identical. This is true of those who believe that both books come from the same hand, such as Sir Edwyn Hoskyns, "In the First Epistle of John, which must be assumed to have come from the same hand as the Gospel, a somewhat stronger light is thrown upon the readers of the epistle, and therefore, presumably, upon the readers of the Gospel also", and J. A. T. Robinson, "the milieu they (Gospel and Epistles of John) presuppose is so similar that any theory about the nature of the community for which the Gospel was written which will not fit the evidence of the Epistles is bound to be precarious". It is also true of those who believe that the books were written by different authors, Rudolf Bultmann and C. H. Dodd.[130]

---

[128]Jn was not written in English and the meaning of the form of ancient Greek used is discovered only by means of historical methods. The story is also set in the context of the history of that time.

[129]Since the publication of the first edition of *Quest* M. W. G. Stibbe (*John as Story Teller*, 56-61) has questioned the reconstructions of Martyn and Brown, summarizing the arguments of Martin Hengel and J. A. T. Robinson. He fails to take account of the specific situation depicted in Jn 9 which distinguishes the Johannine situation from any of those described by Paul or portrayed in Acts, as has already been argued above.

[130]*JWT*, 114 which reflects the views of my Durham Ph.D. thesis. Bultmann postulated a common Gnostic background for Gospel and Epistles seeing the same Gnostic revelation discourses underlying them. In his commentary on the *Epistles* (p. 1) Bultmann accepted the view of Haenchen that the Gospel was directed against the Jews (the world) while the Epistles were directed to believers. But the common Gnostic context remains constant. Dodd wrote his commentary on the Epistles on the basis of research done on the Gospel (see his Preface to *Epistles*) and indicated that both were to be understood in the same historical context though the author of 1 Jn was less guarded than the evangelist in his use of what was then the "new" language drawn from the higher religion of Hellenism.

Against what then seemed to be a consensus concerning a common historical situation I argued for two successive contexts, the first Jewish and the second dominantly Gentile:

> Differences between the Gospel and 1 John are due to the situations for which they were written; if not by the same author, the authors certainly belonged to the same school and expressed a similar theology.[131]

According to Judith Lieu this has now (1986) become a common position:[132]

> This observation is often used to account for the differences between them (Gospels and Epistles). Thus, for example, in the Epistles the situation is one of internal division and conflict while in the Gospel we are more aware of the external conflict with unbelief epitomized by the Jews; the conclusion can then be drawn that the Gospel was written in the context of dialogue with the Synagogue, a dialogue which is over by the time of the Epistles where the community is on the defensive, erecting barriers against internal dissent – a change of context which may explain the changes in the theology...

This position, which Lieu rejects, fits my own fairly well.[133] Recognizing the validity of speaking about the Johannine literature and the Johannine community which produced it,[134] she argues for a common context and different authors.[135] Consequently, to explain the similarities and differences she sees different theological minds at work in the Gospel and Epistles so that there is no straight chronological line from one to the other though there is a common use of tradition.[136] The tensions in the Gospel are not to be thought of as indications of layers of tradition or redaction but are an expression of the dialectical theology of the evangelist.[137] In her view, reading the Gospel as a unity, which she

---

[131]*John: Witness and Theologian*, 108.

[132]*Epistles*, 168.

[133]Though my treatment was perhaps the first outline of this position, and Lieu's critique presupposes a position something like it, she makes no reference to it. Naturally her running debate is with Raymond Brown's more detailed *The Community of the Beloved Disciple*.

[134]*Epistles*, 166.

[135]I left the question of common authorship open, indicating that, when the different contexts were taken into account, and the differences presupposed by a Gospel and an Epistle, the case against common authorship was unconvincing. This hardly established common authorship though I argued that, "if not by the same author, the authors certainly belonged to the same school and expressed a similar theology". *JWT*, 108.

[136]*Epistles* , 168, 205, 207-8, 209, 211.

[137]*Epistles*, 214-16. Here Lieu is in agreement with C. K. Barrett (see n82

advocates, rules out discerning layers "reflecting the historical development of the community".[138]

Lieu accepts, however, that it is historically probable that the Johannine "community is no longer in dialogue with the synagogue by the time of the writing of the Gospel"[139] and asks how we may distinguish

> "those theological claims which may have led to such exclusion and those which have been used to justify the consequent isolation; did the Johannine community's christology lead to the break with the Synagogue or does it serve to reaffirm the community in the light of the break."[140]

Here she gives more ground than she seems to acknowledge. The Gospel does reveal the history of the exclusion of the Johannine community from the synagogue. Her question of whether the Johannine christology was cause or consequence of the breach is, in my view, almost certainly to be answered, "both!" That the detailed questions cannot be answered with certainty need not be denied nor cause for great anxiety.

Lieu's hypothesis of simultaneous composition of the Gospel and Epistles, denying transition from Jewish to Gentile contexts, itself needs to be examined. Given that she accepts the breach with the synagogue had taken place by the time the Gospel was written it is not implausible that this might have led to greater contact with Gentiles and an increasingly Gentile community. Lieu does not examine whether the language and issues of the Epistles might not betray a Gentile context. She responds only to the observation that there is no use of the Old Testament in 1 Jn.

> "1 John is marked by the absence of any use of the Old Testament...The only possible exception, the reference to Cain and Abel as an ethical example (1 Jn 3.12), is a common one and probably comes from a tradition of Christian catechesis rather than from independent use of the Old Testament. In as much as in the New Testament only 2 and 3 John and Philemon share this failure to use the Old Testament it can hardly be attributed to the possibility that the community to which the Epistle was written was gentile, and in view of the Jewish background often posited for the letter it is particularly striking."[141]

The logic of this argument is puzzling. Apparently Lieu implies that these four books cannot be the only four written to predominantly Gentile

---

above) and Martin Hengel, *Question*, 99.

[138] *Epistles*, 214-15.
[139] *Epistles*, 168.
[140] *Epistles*, 187.
[141] *Epistles*, 181.

readers, hence Gentile readership cannot explain the absence of Old Testament quotation. This implied logic is not valid. More relevant is the question of whether the Old Testament would have been ignored if the readers were predominantly Jewish. What is more Lieu totally ignores the central place that allusion to and quotation of the Old Testament plays in the Gospel. That focus in the Gospel reveals a predominantly Jewish situation, at least in the process of the shaping of the tradition. The absence of the Old Testament from the Epistles reveals a different situation as does the concluding warning of 1 Jn 5.21, "Little children, guard yourself from idols."[142]

Teresa Okure also argues that the Gospel should be read as a unity and that it addresses the same situation as the Epistles. Not only written at the same time to deal with the same crisis, it was written by the same author.[143] Adopting the chronology of J. A. T. Robinson she argues that Gospel and Epistles were written before the destruction of the Temple to a community of predominantly Jewish Christians in Palestine,[144] though she seems to allow for a second edition in Ephesus some thirty years later.[145] Here she needs to address the question "Was the Gospel unaltered and was the purpose of the second edition identical to the first?" She accepts that the author was an eyewitness, apparently the BD, though not necessarily John the Son of Zebedee.[146] The crisis arose because some within the community were not persuaded that the claims of Jesus' messiahship satisfied the criteria of the Jewish Scriptures and traditions and were even more troubled by the Johannine claims concerning Jesus' ontological divine sonship:[147]

> we may infer that certain Jews of the Evangelist's day first became disciples when they heard it preached that Jesus was the Messiah. But after they had had time to 'look into the matter' (cf. 7.52), they decided that Jesus did not meet the Scriptural and traditional criteria set for the Messiah (7.25-27,40-44,52; 12.34). Most importantly, these people appear to have found the teaching on Jesus' ontological divine sonship, the mystery of the incarnation, the most difficult to accept (cf. 6.41-42; 5.18; 8.56-59; 10.33-39; 1 Jn 4.2,15; 5.1,5; 2 Jn 7).

Thus she recognizes that the debates and controversies between Jesus and

---

[142]See my *JWT*, 117.

[143]*The Johannine Approach to Mission: A Contextual Study of John 4.1-32* (1988), 235-81, especially 262, 268, 273-281 and see my review in *Pacifica* 3/3 (1990), 347-9.

[144]*Mission*, 273ff.

[145]*Mission*, 279-81.

[146]*Mission*, 279.

[147]*Mission*, 260 and see 247, 257ff.

the Jews in the Gospel do indeed represent debates from the evangelist's own time:

> But the protagonists in the Evangelist's day need not necessarily be seen as hard-line synagogue Jews set against convinced Christians. The contenders are more likely convinced believers (among whom is the author) and wavering Christians. Nor must we forget that even at Jesus' own level the debates were wholly an in-house affair, since Jesus was debating with his fellow Jews.[148]

While it may be that, in Jn, controversies between Jesus and the Jews do sometimes have some relevance to debates within the Johannine community,[149] their primary reference is to the controversy between Jesus and the Jews which has been "brought up to date" in the light of the controversy between the Johannine community and the synagogue. The evangelist was able to deal with internal conflicts by referring to deficiencies amongst the disciples and their subsequent falling away (Jn 6.60-66).[150] It is not helpful to see Jesus' debates with the Jews as "in-house" simply because Jesus was a Jew. This hardly gives due weight to the diversity of the Judaism of Jesus' day. "In-house" might have been valid in terms of an internal Pharisaic debate, but even here internal divisions might have made this reference more appropriate to an internal debate in the school (house) of Hillel or an internal debate in the school of Shammai.

Martin Hengel agrees with both Lieu and Okure in asserting that Gospel and Epistles address the same situation and that the problem was an internal Johannine community debate.[151] He agrees with Okure against

---

[148]*Mission*, 261.

[149]See R. Schnackenburg, *John* vol. II, 61. Commenting on Jn 6.53 he wrote, "The audience has now changed from unbelieving Judaism in the metaphorical discourse to a heretical group within the church."

[150]There the evangelist makes clear that not only the Jews found difficulties with Jesus' teaching (Jn 6.41-59), so did his disciples (6.60-66).

[151]Teresa Okure appears to think that the question of whether the Gospel and Epistles were "directed against the same or different fronts" means only "insiders" or "outsiders", *Mission*, 235. Certainly most scholars today see both Gospel and Epistles directed to the Johannine community, though both C. H. Dodd and J. A. T. Robinson saw the Gospel as a missionary tract. Dodd saw the Gospel directed to adherents of the higher religion of Hellenism while Robinson thought *diaspora* Jews were the target. But the matter can be viewed differently, as is recognized by Lieu (*Epistles*, 168 quoted on p. 81 above). What is envisaged in this study is a change in the character of the Johannine community from a Jewish to predominantly Gentile community. Because the Gospel was shaped over a lengthy period of time only the late strata reflect the issues of the predominantly Gentile

Lieu concerning the common authorship of the Gospel and Epistles. The evangelist (the Elder) was a Judaean Jew who migrated to Ephesus before the Jewish war. There, at the end of the first century, the Epistles were written. The Gospel had long been in the process of composition. It was published soon after the death of the Elder, suitably edited by his pupils. When it was published the Epistles were circulated with it.[152] By this time the breach with the synagogue was long past.[153] The crises which provoked the writing of the Epistles and the publication of the Gospel were precipitated by the entry into the community of Cerinthus, whom Hengel thinks was a Judaeo-Christian, and the influence of his docetic christology.[154] The Gospel and Epistles were addressed to the predominantly Gentile Johannine community where the false teaching had produced a crisis.[155] Hengel argues:

> the Prologue and the prayer of consecration seem to be among the last keystones in the building of the Gospel, and in my opinion they were added after the acute crises which led to the letters.[156]

Thus Hengel, more than Lieu and Okure, allows for the growth of the Gospel and is prepared to delineate layers, even before the final redaction by the pupils of the Elder after his death. He also notes, in agreement with Okure, that the Gospel tradition was shaped in the teaching of the Elder (for Okure, the BD) which began in Judaea before the Jewish war of 66-74 CE. The breach with the synagogue, also acknowledged by Lieu, long past by the time the Gospel was written, nevertheless left its mark on the Gospel. Against Okure, Hengel argues that the crisis that called forth

community, which are the focus of the Epistles. In fact this appears to be Hengel's position, but he ignores the context(s) underlying the shaping of the earlier phases of the Gospel.

[152]*The Johannine Question* (1989), 73, 105-6, 176-7 n7. See my review in *ABR* 38 (1990), 80-3.

[153]"The 'expulsion' lies quite far in the past and was not dependent on one historical act of excommunication...", *Question*, 119.

[154]*Question*, 60-3.

[155]"Now all this means that the Gospel and letters, which primarily address the school, are not predominantly aimed at Jewish Christians but at Gentile Christians. The immediate controversy with the Jews has long ceased to be the main theme of the school", *Question*, 121. What Hengel has overlooked here is his own recognition of the long process of the composition of the Gospel. The controversy with the Jews, though long past when the Gospel was *published*, has left its mark on the Gospel.

[156]*Question*, 61. See also 95, 105. Here Hengel lists the Prologue, chapters 6 and 10, passages in the farewell discourses and passion narrative as later additions in response to the crisis which provoked the letters.

the Gospel and Epistles was the docetic teaching of Cerinthus.[157] Though Cerinthus is said to be a Judaeo-Christian his position is some distance from the Ebionite trouble-makers proposed by Okure.[158] Indeed, Hengel goes on to describe the problem in terms of

> a group of its members who, influenced by the view taken for granted among educated Greeks that a god was incapable of suffering, separated the man Jesus from the divine Logos, Son of God and Christ and radically devalued his significance for salvation. The three letters of John are fruits of the way in which the old school-head combated the threat. They, together with the Gospel, were probably edited soon after his death by his pupils (or one of them) not long after 100 CE, and this editing appears to be the last visible action of the "school".[159]

This description hardly fits the description of Cerinthus as a Judaeo-Christian. Hengel's attempt to harmonize the two views is found in the suggestion that

> Cerinthus was a Judaeo-Christian teacher coming from outside with some popular philosophical learning of the kind widespread in the Greek-speaking synagogue.[160]

But the success of the intruder (Cerinthus) appears to be dependent on the predominantly Gentile Christian character of the Johannine school.[161] We might ask whether it is necessary to postulate an intruder in a context of predominantly Gentile Christians if the views could already emerge in a Greek speaking synagogue. Surely awareness of this kind of Hellenistic religious philosophy would be a sufficient basis and a predominantly Gentile Christian group could bring this awareness with them when they became members of "the school" (in my terms, "the community").

Hengel's reconstruction recognizes the evangelist as a Judaean Jewish Christian who came to Ephesus in the 60s. The Gospel was shaped over a long period of time. The Epistles were written in a predominantly Gentile Christian context and soon after the evangelist's death the Gospel was edited and published with the Epistles. There is here the potential to trace development from Jewish to predominantly Gentile contexts. In spite of this, and a good deal more hypothetical reconstruction,[162] Hengel concludes:

> Nowadays we already have too many attempts to reconstruct a "history of the Johannine community". They are all doomed to

---

[157]*Question*, 59-63.
[158]*Mission*, 260.
[159]*Question*, 81.
[160]*Question*, 60.
[161]*Question*, 119-24.
[162]*Question*, 94-135 and notes.

failure, because we know nothing of a real history which even
goes back to Palestine, and conjectures about it are idle.[163]

Indeed, what is necessary is for Hengel to take seriously his own analysis of the Judaean origin of the Elder, the breach from the synagogue, and the later layers of the Gospel. Already in these observations there is room to say a good deal about the history of the Elder and those associated with him. For example, if the Prologue and Jn 17 were added to cope with the crises caused by the entry of Cerinthus into the community, that suggests that the bulk of the Gospel had already been shaped in response to other issues. Even if the breach from the synagogue lay in the distant past, the Gospel suggests that the issue had been sufficiently traumatic to leave permanent marks on the Gospel. Thus, although Hengel appears to postulate a common context for Gospel and Epistles his view of the long period of composition for the Gospel makes allowance for the influence of other contexts in its shaping. Whereas Lieu saw different theologies in the Gospel and Epistles Hengel hears in all the voice of one towering theologian, the Elder.[164] With a little unpacking it seem to me that Hengel's views are not so different from my own. Certainly I agree that the Prologue and Jn 17 represent late strata of the Gospel written in response to the same crisis that called forth the Epistles.[165]

IV. THE EVANGELIST

When the Gospel was published chapter 21, identifying the BD as author,[166] had already been added. On the basis of the evidence of $\mathfrak{P}^{52}$ and Papyrus Egerton 2 we may conclude that the Gospel must have been published by 125 CE and probably somewhat earlier. Indeed, the early evidence of the papyri strongly favours Jn in the sense that, of the twenty pre-Constantinian Gospel papyri eleven are Johannine and some of these are the earliest papyri. Of course this has something to do with the provenance of the Gospels because the papyri are from Egypt. But *Matt* is also well represented so that the evidence should not be construed in terms of Gnostic use, though the Gnostics also made wide use of *Matt*. But this only shows the Gnostic propensity to interpret virtually any text. The evidence of early papyri indicates that the title, *ΕΥΑΓΓΕΛΙΟΝ ΚΑΤΑ*

---

[163]*Question*, 205 n85. But Hengel's attempts to demonstrate the evidence for the Palestinian Jewish origin of the Elder are surely not idle

[164]*Question*, ix, 108, and see 96, 99, 104.

[165]See chapter 3, "Christology and History in the Prologue" and chapter 13, "The Farewell of the Messiah" below. But I doubt that Jn 6 as a whole is late. See chapter 6, "The Messiah and the Bread of Life" below.

[166]Though Jn 21 is generally thought to be an addition there is no textual evidence that the Gospel ever circulated without it.

IΩANNHN had been added by the early second century.[167] Thus, when the title was added, John the son of Zebedee or some other John was thought to be the author.

The unanimous tradition of Asia Minor from the time of Irenaeus was that the BD was John the son of Zebedee, author of Gospel, Epistles and Apocalypse.[168] Irenaeus attributed his knowledge of this tradition to the elders of Asia Minor, naming in particular Papias and Polycarp.[169] This attribution of the authorship of the Gospel to Jn is consistent with Gnostic tradition known to Irenaeus,[170] but is not dependent on it. It is probable that Roman tradition also acknowledged John as author at this time. Thus converging traditions, consistent with the title of the Gospel, clarify the identity of the BD which had been left anonymous by the editors of the Gospel.[171]

In spite of this evidence few scholars today think that the Gospel was written by John the son of Zebedee. There are numerous reasons for this.[172] First, there was a tendency in the early Church to attribute works of authority to apostolic authorship.[173] But this does not rule out the

---

[167]See P. W. Comfort, "The Greek Text of the Gospel of John according to the Early Papyri" and Hengel, *Question*, 74-76 and n1 193 including n1 and also 6,9-10. Both Comfort and Hengel draw attention to the early evidence of $\mathfrak{P}^{66}$ and $\mathfrak{P}^{75}$.

[168]See the evidence of Irenaeus (A.h.) which is often repeated by Eusebius (HE). A.h. 3.1.1 =HE 5.8.4; A.h. 2.22.5 = HE 3.23.3; A.h. 3.3.4 = 4.14.3-8 and 3.23.4; Ep. ad Flor. =HE 5.20.4-8. See also A.h.1.8.5; 1.9.1-3; 2.2.5; 2.22.3; 3.31.3 (cf. HE 5.25.1-7); 3.8.3; 3.11.1-4;,7,9; 3.15.2,5,8; 3.16.5,8; 3.22.2; 4.2.3; 4.6.1; 4.10.1; 5.18.2; 5.33.3; *Epideixis* 43.94. From these references it is clear that Irenaeus identified John the disciple of the Lord with the BD as author of the Gospel and Epistles published in Ephesus in the reign of Trajan. For references to John and the Apocalypse see 1.26.3; 4.17.6; 4.20.11; 4.21.3; 4.30.4 and 5.26.1; 5.28.2; 5.34.2; 5.35.2.

[169]Ep. ad Flor. =HE 5.20.4-8; Ep. ad Victor of Rome; A.h. 2.22.5; 3.1.1,4; 5.33.3-4.

[170]See A.h. 1.8.5.

[171]The suggestion that the editors expected the readers to know the identity of the BD is not borne out by 21.24. Had his identity been known there would have been no necessity for the editors to attest the veracity of his testimony. The relevance of this evidence will be discussed a little later.

[172]Hengel says (*Question*, 130) "There are too many historical reasons against supposing that the Gospel was composed by John the son of Zebedee, which was the predominant view from the middle of the second century on. He notes (220 n110) "the twenty-one reasons against John the son of Zebedee being author of the Gospel in P. Parker, 'John the Son of Zebedee and the Fourth Gospel', *JBL* 81, 1962, 35-43."

[173]Note the vast array of pseudepigrapha from the second century on.

possibility of genuine apostolic works. It is also argued, on the basis of reading Eusebius, that Irenaeus was mistaken in identifying the John known by Papias with John the Apostle when in fact it was John the Elder. The text quoted from Papias[174] is in fact ambiguous and the works of Papias are lost so that there is no possibility of checking what he says elsewhere. Because Eusebius intended to discredit Papias it may well be that he wished to show that Papias did not know the Apostle but only some other John. The argument that Eusebius had the benefit of the rest of the works of Papias is not persuasive because Irenaeus had read them also as had others who continued to accept the apostolic authorship of the Gospel. Irenaeus knew Papias while Eusebius lived almost two centuries later. That, with his prejudice against Papias, does not encourage confidence in his opinion on this matter. What is more, Eusebius maintained the apostolic authorship of the Gospel. It was Revelation (of which he had a low opinion) that he attributed to the Elder. In differentiating the authors of these two books Eusebius struck a contemporary note although, in so far as modern scholarship has followed Eusebius it has revised his views, attributing the Gospel to the Elder. But the hypothesis that John the Elder was confused with the Apostle as author of the Gospel is based on little evidence. Schnackenburg considers that this theory should be abandoned.[175]

Many scholars today see different authors responsible for the Gospel and Epistles. Very few think the same author wrote the Gospel and Revelation.[176] But this is precisely what Irenaeus claims, casting doubt on his credibility, even if the two books are closer than at first seems obvious. Then there is the view that both John and James died early. This view probably arose on the basis of the seeming prophecy of Mk 10.38-39. The evidence in support of it is too late to be trusted.[177]

Despite the failure to establish the early death of John the majority of scholars conclude that he did not write the Gospel. C. K. Barrett considers it to be

> a moral certainty that the Gospel was not written by John the son of Zebedee. (*John*, 132)

---

[174]Eusebius, HE 3.39.3ff.

[175]*Gospel* I, 91.

[176]See nn1 and 2 above.

[177]The earliest is Philip of Side (c.430) who appeals to the second book of Papias for evidence that both John and his brother James were killed by the Jews. But how could this have been missed by earlier readers of Papias such as Irenaeus (indeed all the early Fathers) and even Eusebius? Barrett's assessment of this evidence is astute, *John*, 104. Thus against Hengel (*Question*, 21-2 and 158-59 n121) who finds this evidence convincing.

The reason for this is that "the implied author"[178] of the Gospel does not fit the picture of what we know of John the son of Zebedee. Relevant to this discussion is the Judaean/Jerusalem focus of Jn which is thought to be inconsistent with the perspective of a Galilean fisherman. But this is to forget that this fisherman became a disciple of Jesus and a leader in the Jerusalem Church so that the Jerusalem orientation after the crucifixion of Jesus is likely to have been more influential in the writing of this Gospel than his earlier Galilean life.

Nevertheless Rudolf Bultmann concludes his *RGG* article on the Gospel:

> yet so much is certain, that the author of the Gospel of John is
> not John the son of Zebedee and certainly not an eyewitness".
> (*RGG*³ III, 849)

Certainly if the author was not an eyewitness the author was not John, though the reverse of this proposition need not follow. But the evidence reviewed so far does not preclude the identification of the author with John. On what grounds then is this judgement made? What is it that makes the majority of modern scholars certain that the author was not John the son of Zebedee? Raymond Brown asserts that differences from the Synoptics are the product of editorial and theological development which

> make it implausible (nay impossible) that the Fourth Gospel was
> written by an eyewitness of the ministry of Jesus; the role of the
> Beloved Disciple was therefore not that of the evangelist.[179]

Discussion of the role of the BD must be left aside for the moment. What is significant at this stage is the explicit basis upon which Brown rejects authorship by an eyewitness. It is the theologically interpretative character of Jn (by comparison with the Synoptics) that rules this out. This judgement is certainly not peculiar to Brown. But the Synoptics hardly provide an accurate guide to what books written by eyewitnesses would look like. The crucial question here is whether eyewitnesses may be

---

[178]In the new literary criticism this has become a technical term to describe the reader's perception of the author, built up from from the clues in the text which imply a picture of the author, and may be quite different from the actual author. The clues are laid in the text, whether by intent or not, whether to reveal the real author or to lay a false trail. Consequently using such evidence to establish the identity of the actual author is fraught with perils even if we thought that in this class of literature it was unlikely that the author would mislead us because, without intending to do so, the author may have created a fictional *persona*. The implied author is not a character in the narrative, he is implied by it and not necessarily with the intent of the actual author. Indeed actual authors may be surprised by the author implied by what they have written.

[179]*Community*, 178.

significant interpreters rather than straightforward reporters. Elsewhere Brown writes:

> As I understand Johannine tradition, even as the Beloved Disciple reinterpreted the tradition about Jesus rather than simply repeating it, so also the evangelist gave new insights in reinterpreting the tradition that he received from the Beloved Disciple. Undergirding all this freedom is the notion of the Paraclete...(16.12-13) – a statement that implies insights going beyond those available in the ministry of Jesus (see also John 2.22).[180]

Apparently the amount of interpretation allowed to the BD as an eyewitness is one of degree and the Gospel exceeds this. Surely this is a precarious judgement. On the basis of it would we conclude that Plato knew and was the pupil of Socrates? Hengel is right when he notes that those who use the evidence of the freely interpretative work of the evangelist as evidence that it cannot be that of an eyewitness are

> transferring their own, modern, understanding of history and historicity to a first century Palestinian author.[181]

Perhaps the most damaging evidence against the traditional view of authorship is to be found in Jn 21.24. Had Jn the Apostle been the author it is unlikely that this would not have been known or that he would need anyone to defend the veracity of his witness. But the editors do this for the author:

> This is the disciple who bears witness concerning these things and has written these things, and we know that his witness is true.

It is as if it were necessary for less authoritative but better known witnesses to attest the veracity of the testimony of a more authoritative but less well known (unknown?) witness. Certainly it seems unlikely that John the son of Zebedee would have been little known, unless we are to suppose that the Gospel was published some little time after his death. At this point a discussion of the role of the BD is appropriate.

Unlike other early Christian writings such as the letters of Paul, Jn, like each of the Gospels, is strictly anonymous[182] and 21.24 does nothing to lift the veil of anonymity because the identity of the BD remains a mystery.[183] While he could be one of the sons of Zebedee, he could just as easily be one of the two unnamed disciples of 21.2, who can be

---

[180]*Epistles*, 97 n222.

[181]*Question*, 130.

[182]Though the titles are early we can have no confidence that the Gospels were originally published with titles.

[183]It is sometimes argued imprecisely that Jn is pseudonymous, that 21.24 wrongly identifies the evangelist with the BD. But the BD is not identified.

identified variously as John Mark[184] or Lazarus[185] or almost any one. Because of this a start can be made only by seeing what is said about the BD and by forming a picture of the author implied by the Gospel as a whole and in chapter 21 in particular. Of course it is possible that we are only following false trails laid by the actual author and that the BD is unknown precisely because he is a fictional character introduced by the evangelist to characterize the ideal disciple.[186] It seems more likely, however, that the figure of the BD is both ideal and historical.

The editors who identify themselves in 21.24 are probably responsible

---

[184]John Mark and the Gospel share the common name John. The tradition concerning the Last Supper being held in the the family home of Mark is dubious. If historical and the identification proved to be correct it would help to account for the Jerusalem orientation of the Gospel. But there is no support for this view in tradition and it would be ironical indeed if the tradition, having (incorrectly?) ascribed one Gospel to Mark missed the opportunity of identifying the Gospel he had written.

[185]The grounds for this identification are that it is said that Jesus loved Lazarus (11.3,5,11,36). The sisters describe Lazarus as "him whom you (Jesus) love ($\phi\iota\lambda\epsilon\hat{\iota}s$)"; the narrator tells us "Now Jesus loved ($\mathring{\eta}\gamma\acute{a}\pi a$) Martha and her sister and Lazarus"; Jesus speaks to the disciples of "Lazarus our friend ($\phi\acute{\iota}\lambda os$)"; and the Jews at the tomb say of Jesus "See how he loved ($\acute{\epsilon}\phi\acute{\iota}\lambda\epsilon\iota$) him". The use of two different verbs is no problem for the identification because they are used synonymously in the Gospel and while the usual description of the BD uses $\mathring{o}v \mathring{\eta}\gamma\acute{a}\pi a$ (13.23; 19.26; 21.7,20) $\mathring{o}v$ $\acute{\epsilon}\phi\acute{\iota}\lambda\epsilon\iota$ is used in 20.2. It is also rightly noted that the resurrection of Lazarus could be thought of as the basis of the belief that the BD would not die, a belief that proved to be wrong and had to be dealt with by the editors in 21.20-23. But in 11.5 the narrator tells us that "Jesus loved Martha and her sister and Lazarus". This statement by the narrator, who is the reliable guide to the reader, warns against singling out Lazarus and identifying him with the BD though it could be argued that only Lazarus qualifies as "him" ($\mathring{o}v \mathring{\eta}\gamma\acute{a}\pi a$ or $\acute{\epsilon}\phi\acute{\iota}\lambda\epsilon\iota$). But given that the presupposed $\mu a\theta\eta\tau\mathring{\eta}s$ is masculine this argument holds little weight. The identification of the BD with Lazarus is sometimes used to accentuate the ideal rather than the historical role of the BD and this can be combined with the theory that John Mark was the actual evangelist. That the BD was Lazarus has been argued most recently by M. W. G. Stibbe (*John as Story Teller*) who has combined this view with the argument that the actual evangelist was John the Elder. The basis of the present Gospel is then what Stibbe calls "the Bethany Gospel" (pp.77-82).

[186]There are those (e.g. Jülicher, Käsemann, Bultmann, Kragerud) who consider that this disciple is an ideal figure rather than historical. Bultmann thinks that in Jn 1–20 the BD represents Gentile Christianity while in Jn 21 the redactor thinks of an actual person, *John*, 483ff., 701. However, this would make his appearance alongside Peter quite strange. Both are representative figures in this Gospel and both are historical figures. It would be strange to ascribe the Gospel to an ideal figure who had not actually existed or at least who was not thought to have existed.

for the whole of chapter 21.[187] Consequently they are responsible for the use of the title BD in 21.2,20. J. Roloff has helpfully compared the use of this designation to the "Teacher of Righteousness" as found in the Qumran Texts as the designation of the anonymous leading personality of the sect.[188] Neither is likely to be a self-designation yet "BD" also occurs in Jn 13–20 which is apparently the work of the evangelist. Here two conclusions seem possible. Either the evangelist had described his own role in certain events without using "BD" which was later supplied by those who posthumously published his Gospel, or he used "BD" to refer to another person but this was mistakenly understood as a self reference by those who added chapter 21. The latter is the view of Hengel who thinks that the evangelist identified John the Apostle, his teacher and source of tradition in Jn 1–20 but that the redactors wrongly identified the evangelist with the BD in 21.24. The view that those who added Jn 21 have confused the role of the BD is now quite common though not all associate the BD with John the son of Zebedee.[189]

Leading Johannine scholars, such as F. M. Braun, R. E. Brown and Rudolf Schnackenburg, at one stage have all held the view that John the son of Zebedee was the BD but have now abandoned it. Clearly the evidence of the Gospel does not necessitate identifying the BD with John. Brown, like Schnackenburg, now identifies the BD with one of the two unnamed disciples of Jn 21.2.[190] Brown thus makes the BD the source of the tradition used by the evangelist.[191] The difference between the position of Hengel (who identifies the BD with John the son of Zebedee) and Brown (who identifies him with an unknown disciple) is that Hengel gives weight to the second century tradition[192] while Brown now thinks that:

---

[187]This makes sense of 20.30-31 as the original conclusion. It can be argued that Jn 1–21 is a literary unity and that the appearance of redaction in 21.24 is a literary technique to give authority to the Gospel. See Paul Minear, "The Original Functions of John 21", *JBL* 102/1 (1983), 85-98. But literary unity only shows that the redactors did their job well even though they clearly signalled the redaction by leaving the original conclusion and identifying themselves in 21.24.

[188]"Der Johanneische 'Lieblingsjünger' und der Lehrer der Gerichtigkeit", *NTS* 15 (1968-69) 129-51, especially 143-50.

[189]As we have seen, Mark Stibbe identifies the BD with Lazarus and the actual evangelist with John the Elder.

[190]*Community*, 33-4.

[191]Yet Brown acknowledges that both the BD and the evangelist were interpreters of the tradition.

[192]*Question*, ix, etc.

the external and internal evidence are probably not to be harmonized.[193]

But an approach that gives priority to the internal evidence must at least provide a persuasive account of how the incorrect tradition (external evidence) arose. Here Hengel's hypothesis is more persuasive because it provides a basis for the incorrect identification of John the son of Zebedee with the BD.[194]

Amongst those who treat the BD as an historical figure there is a growing consensus distinguishing the BD from the evangelist. Yet the identification of the evangelist with the BD is the most natural way to read Jn 21.24[195] even if it is allowed that an amanuensis did the actual writing.[196] Theories which make the BD only the source or beginning of

---

[193]*Community*, 33-4.

[194]I remain convinced that the evidence of Irenaeus constitutes a serious obstacle for those who wish to set aside John the son of Zebedee from any relation to the Gospel. Attempts to discredit Irenaeus frequently appear to be motivated by doubts about what he says rather than serious grounds for doubting the basis of his evidence.

[195]Alan Culpepper (*Anatomy,* 45f.) outlines four different ways in which Jn 21.24f. may be taken:

1. The BD identified himself as author indicating the community should not expect him to live until the parousia. This one person theory is generally rejected because Jn 21 is recognized as an addition; 21.23 implies the death of the BD; the 'we' of 21.24 is distinguished from the author; the author would hardly refer to himself as the BD. The view of Paul Minear ("The Original Functions of John 21", *JBL* 102/1, 1983, 85-98 and *The Martyrs Gospel*) is a variation on 1. above. Minear stresses the unity of Jn 1–21 arguing that the reinstatement of Peter in Jn 21.1-17 presupposes the account of his threefold denial. But this only shows that the redaction was skilfully done, indeed from within the Johannine school.

2. The evangelist, as a member of the Johannine school, attributed the Gospel to the BD his mentor and source. This two person theory implies that Jn is pseudonymous, falsely attributed to someone other than the true author.

3. An editor added 21.24-25 to Jn correctly identifying the BD as author. This two person theory is the most straightforward way of reading 21.24-25 and would be rejected only if it raises serious objections.

4. An editor adding 21.24-25 identified the BD as the evangelist when in fact he was the source of the evangelist's material. This view involves the detection of an error in the ascription of authorship but is the view held by many scholars today such as R. E. Brown. However, if 19.35 is attributed to the evangelist rather than the editor, the evangelist thus indicates his dependence on the BD.

[196]Taking "who has written these things" (Jn 21.24) in the weaker sense of "has caused to have written". It is pressing the point too far to suggest this phrase is used to indicate the remote, even if important, source of the tradition along the line suggested by Brown. Here Hengel's hypothesis is

the tradition and ascribe the greater interpretative role to the evangelist[197] would seem to put such a strain on Jn 21.24 that it must be questioned as a reliable guide to the solution of questions concerning the composition of the Gospel. If we allow that the BD was the evangelist we may allow a pervasive role to the editors who added Jn 21. This is implied by the reference to the death of the BD and the need to identify him as author and verify his authority suggesting that he is already a distant figure for the readers by the time the Gospel was published.

At this point a summary of the role of the BD in Jn may throw light on the question of whether the internal and external evidence can be harmonized or at least if one can provide an intelligible basis for the other. The BD appears (by name) for the first time at the farewell supper. He is the confidant of Jesus, leaned on his breast[198] and spoke to him, 13.23ff. Here already the contrast with Peter begins. The BD is close to Jesus and knows what he is saying while Peter is distant and ignorant. After the report of the empty tomb he ran with Peter to the tomb and was the first to believe that Jesus was risen, 20.1-10.[199] At this point it is not said that Peter believed, thus reinforcing the contrast between the two. In this narrative he is also called "the other disciple" (δ $\dot{\alpha}\lambda\lambda o\varsigma$ $\mu\alpha\theta\eta\tau\dot{\eta}\varsigma$), a description used of the disciple who was known to the High Priest and who gained Peter's admittance to the hearing before Annas, 18.15ff. If this identification is correct he might be the unnamed disciple of the two disciples of the Baptist who subsequently followed Jesus, 1.35ff.[200] In all of these incidents the BD appears alongside Peter in a more favourable position. Of the disciples, only the BD is present at the crucifixion and Jesus commits his mother to his care, 19.26-27. Most likely it is he who is spoken of as the witness to the issue of water and blood at the death of Jesus, 19.35. He is present, again with Peter, at the final fishing expedition and it is he who identifies Jesus on the sea shore. There is then an account of the reinstatement of Peter and a contrast between the different fates of Peter and the BD. The account is careful to indicate that Jesus did

superior to Brown's in that the "has written" does apply to the evangelist though the identification of the evangelist with the BD involves a double image, the imposition of the image of the evangelist over the image of John the son of Zebedee.

[197]Thus R. E. Brown, *John* 1, xcviii–cii and F. M. Braun, *Jean le Theologian*, 396f.

[198]Here the relation of the BD to Jesus is portrayed in similar terms to Jesus' relation to the Father in Jn 1.18.

[199] In 20.2 the verb is $\dot{\epsilon}\phi\dot{\iota}\lambda\epsilon\iota$ while $\dot{\eta}\gamma\dot{\alpha}\pi\alpha$ is used elsewhere, 13.23; 19.26; 21.7,20.

[200]See F. Neirynck, "The Anonymous Disciple in John 1", *Ephemerides Theologicae Lovanienses* LXVI/1 (April 1990) 5-37.

not say that the BD would live till he returned, but only "what if...?" The clarification could have been made necessary by the death of the BD in the face of the expectation that he would not die.

The author was "a towering theologian"[201] who does not suffer from a comparison with Paul. It has already been argued that his thought world is best illuminated by the Qumran Texts. The Judaean, Jerusalem focus of Jn and implied connections with the family of the High Priest perhaps do not fit the profile of a Galilean fisherman. But we would need to take into account over thirty years in Judaea after the crucifixion of Jesus. It could be that this period was of greater influence than is generally thought. But just as the Gospel does not identify the BD with John, neither does the implied profile of the evangelist which gives us the picture of a leader in the community engaged in dialogue and struggle with the synagogue who gave voice to the inspired teaching of the risen Jesus thereby shaping and giving distinctive identity to the community. Thus if comparison with the Qumran Texts implies the Judaean origin of the evangelist (and his community?) the history of the community reflected in the Gospel implies a situation in the *diaspora* sometime after the Jewish war. But then it is probable that the evangelist and his community migrated shortly before the Jewish war. We should also allow some responsibility for the image of the implied author to the redactor, recognizing that the final editorial role was somewhat larger than is often thought. But this need not have been contrary to the work of the evangelist given that it was carried on by members of the Johannine school.

From this perspective the brief exposition of an hypothesis by C.K. Barrett has much to commend it.[202] Barrett succinctly notes that, in addition to the traditions outlined, the most important evidence is the existence of the Johannine literature which exhibits such differences as to preclude common authorship and similarities which demand relationship. To account for these he proposes that John came from Palestine to Ephesus where he composed apocalyptic works. These, with his long life, gave rise to the belief that he would live to see the *parousia*. By the time he died he had gathered a school of disciples. His death fanned apocalyptic hopes and provoked reflection on the meaning of eschatology. Around 96 CE one of his disciples incorporated his work into the Apocalypse. One or more other disciples were responsible for the Epistles. Another disciple, a bolder thinker more widely read in Judaism and Hellenism,

---

[201]Hengel, *Question*, ix, 108 and see 96, 99, 104. Barrett (*John*, 127, 134) also speaks of the theological achievement of the evangelist, "perhaps, after Paul, the greatest theologian in all the history of the church".
[202]*John*, 133-4.

composed Jn 1–20 but died before the Gospel was finished. It was used by "gnostics" but was used hesitantly by the Great Church. In time it was seen to be the best weapon against the "gnostics", using their language to vindicate the true gospel. The Gospel was now edited with traditional material being added in chapter 21. The Gospel reveals the hand of the greatest theologian (after Paul) in the history of the church. When it was published the references to the Beloved Disciple were correctly understood to refer to John the son of Zebedee who was incorrectly thought to be the evangelist, Jn 21.24.

This hypothesis, which was first put forward in 1955, has much in common with the more recent and detailed views of Brown, Hengel and others. It has the advantage of providing a basis for the tradition of John the son of Zebedee in Ephesus, but it needs to be developed in several areas. When did John migrate to Ephesus? Did this take place about the time of the Jewish war? If the evangelist knew Mk thoroughly and perhaps Lk as well, as is argued,[203] is it not likely that he also knew tradition handed down in the school from the founder teacher? Need the Gospel and Epistles be written by different authors? Might not different literary *genre* and different situations account for such differences as are recognized? If we allow that John handed on distinctive traditions, might it not have been the case that he contributed rather more to the shaping of the Gospel than has been suggested? If this is accepted it may follow that what remained to be done was to gather these traditions together and edit them for publication after the death of John. In this case the redaction was rather more extensive than Barrett suggests but the role of the additional evangelist is made redundant. John is the evangelist but another disciple(s) had to do extensive work to prepare the Gospel for publication after the death of John. Against this view Barrett could argue that it does not do justice to the apocalyptic views of John. But if John developed apocalyptic works in Palestine around the time of the Jewish war, that leaves time for his own reflection on the Gospel tradition after his migration to Ephesus.[204] Barrett is probably right in thinking that a disciple edited and published the apocalyptic works towards the end of the

---

[203]*John*, 15, 127.

[204]This is Hengel's approach to the problem, though the figure in question is John the Elder not the Apostle. It is also possible to interpret the Apocalypse in a more Johannine way by stressing that some works belonging to the literary *genre* of apocalyptic can be understood in terms of the message for the present time rather than providing a timetable for the future. It is also important to recognize that the evangelist has not abandoned apocalyptic dualism or future eschatology though his primary focus is elsewhere.

century[205] and that another representative of the Johannine school edited and published the Gospel. Indeed it seems a good deal remained to be done when the evangelist died, perhaps mainly by incorporating additional Johannine tradition and adapting the Gospel to a wider and more diverse audience amongst whom the evangelist was not well known. This hypothesis has the merit of taking Jn 21.24 seriously and making sense of the early tradition.

V. SOURCES

The role of the evangelist is assessed differently by scholars. For some he is the editor of extensive sources and the character of his Gospel is a consequence of the sources used.[206] Those who see Jn as independent of the Synoptics commonly attribute his differences from them to his sources. For others it is the evangelist who has given Jn its special character. Those who argue that the Synoptics provided the evangelist with his major sources must attribute the character of his Gospel to the touch of his hand.[207] It is possible, however, to think that the evangelist has created the Gospel while arguing his sources were independent of the Synoptics. C.H. Dodd argued that Jn was independent of the Synoptics but that the tradition which surfaces in Jn is Synoptic-like.[208] Hence John is responsible for the remarkable differences from the Synoptics.

The question of the sources of Jn is one which has been frequently addressed in recent years. As yet there has been little agreement concerning how to go about the task of identifying and separating the sources. Even the old question of whether Jn is in some sense dependent on the Synoptics cannot be answered decisively.[209] Lack of certainty at this level

---

[205] That an apocalyptic genre should emanate from the Johannine school constitutes no great problem once the basic apocalyptic *Weltanschauung* of the Gospel is recognized. Naturally the decision to write a Gospel precludes the possibility of expressing all of the marks of the apocalyptic genre.

[206] R. Bultmann, *John*; R. Fortna, *The Gospel of Signs*; E. Käsemann, *The Testament of Jesus*; E. Haenchen, *John* and see D. M. Smith, "Johannine Christianity", *NTS* 21/2 (1976), 229.

[207] F. Neirynck (*Jean et les Synoptiques*, 390) rightly insists that the complexity of the Gospel arises from the evangelist's redaction not from the sources.

[208] C. H. Dodd (*Historical Tradition and the Fourth Gospel*) argued, case by case, that the traditions that he had isolated were not derived from the Synoptic Gospels but were Synoptic-like. In terms of the role of the evangelist this view is not greatly different from the theory of Synoptic dependence. In either case the evangelist is responsible for the distinctive character of Jn.

[209] This is recognized by Barrett (*John*, 45) though he argues that Jn knew *Mk* well and probably *Lk* also (*John*, 15, 127).

has limited the success of the attempts to elaborate on the evangelist's contribution to the Gospel. Implicit in the argument in *Quest* so far has been the view that the evangelist is largely responsible for Jn and that sources, such as have been used, have been thoroughly assimilated to his point of view.

1. The Synoptic Tradition

At least from the time of Irenaeus Jn has been thought of as the fourth Gospel to have been written.

> Matthew for his part published also a written Gospel among the Hebrews in their own language, whilst Peter and Paul were in Rome, preaching, and laying the foundation of the Church. And after their departure, Mark, Peter's disciple and interpreter, did himself also publish unto us in writing the things which were preached by Peter. And Luke too, the attendant of Paul, set down in a book the Gospel preached by him. Afterwards John the disciple of the Lord, who also leaned on his breast, – he again put forth his Gospel, while he abode in Ephesus in Asia.[210]

What is more it was thought that he wrote with knowledge of the other three. Having mentioned the publication of *Matt* Eusebius goes on:

> And when Mark and Luke had already published their Gospels, it is said that John, who all the time had used unwritten preaching, at last came also to write, for the following reason. Those three which we have mentioned above having come into the hands of all, including his own, it is said that he accepted them and attested their truth;...[211]

Naturally there is here no suggestion that John used the other Gospels as sources and it is implied that he was already using some form of his Gospel orally. This evidence shows only that John *was thought* to have published his Gospel fourth and with a knowledge of the other three. When critical scholarship destroyed confidence in the tradition of apostolic authorship, denying at the same time that the evangelist had independent access to tradition, it was natural that knowledge of the Synoptics should then be thought of as dependence on them. This remained the common critical scholarly view until the publication of *Saint John and the Synoptic Gospels* by P. Gardner-Smith in 1938[212] and is still supported by notable scholars who have strong evidence in their favour.

Jn is obviously a Gospel as distinct from other forms of early Christian

---

[210]A.h. 3.1.1. also found in Eusebius, H.E. 5.8.2-4.

[211]Eusebius, H.E. 3.24.5-7.

[212]Rudolf Bultmann's great commentary was published in 1950 arguing that Jn was independent of the Synoptics though allowing for assimilation to the Synoptics in the redaction of Jn.

literature.[213] The Gospel form was a Christian innovation and, as far as we know, it was created by Mk. Matt and Lk belong to this *genre* to the extent that they have taken over and made use of Mk. Is this true also of Jn? While Mk appears to entitle his book a Gospel[214] this vocabulary is totally missing from Jn.[215] Neither Matt nor Lk calls his book a Gospel and Lk does not use the noun at all.[216] Perhaps, though they have followed Mk to a great extent, they were less aware than we are in retrospect that Mk had created a new literary *genre* which is appropriately called Gospel.

Jn, like the Synoptics, tells its story beginning with the appearance of John the Baptist[217] and moves towards the arrest, trial, passion, discovery of the empty tomb and resurrection appearances of Jesus. On the way we encounter the gathering of the disciples,[218] and miracles of healing, leading on to the confession of Jesus' Messiahship. This is done against the background of growing opposition which finally results in Jesus' arrest and execution. In addition to the similarities of structure, Jn contains a number of sections with strong similarities to the Synoptic tradition, including the traditions about John the Baptist, the cleansing of the

---

[213]On Jn and the Gospel *genre* see R. Schnackenburg, *John* I, 11-19.

[214] In the ancient world books were often known by the opening words, in Mk's case, "The beginning of the gospel of Jesus Christ.." G. N. Stanton, *The Gospels and Jesus*, 30-3, 143-4 apparently accepted this point of view but has subsequently revised it in his *A Gospel for a New People: Studies in Matthew*, 13–17. He now argues that Mk did not quite make the leap to call his book a Gospel ($\epsilon\dot{v}\alpha\gamma\gamma\dot{\epsilon}\lambda\iota o\nu$ continues to refer to the oral proclamation) but Matt did.

[215] See my *JWT*, 7-8. It should be noted, however, that when Jn was published it apparently went out under the title *EYAΓΓΕΛΙΟΝ ΚΑΤΑ ΙΩΑΝΝΗΝ*. It may even be that the title was added by the editors of Jn 21. See Hengel, *Question*, 74-6.

[216] *Lk*, following the use of the LXX, uses only the verb.

[217]Leaving aside reference in the Prologue to the eternal $\lambda\dot{o}\gamma o\varsigma$ and his role in creation.

[218]Though here, where Jn closely resembles the Synoptic tradition, call stories have been transformed into quest stories. Of Jn's quest stories two have parallels in Synoptic quest stories: the quest of Nicodemus (Jn 2.23–3.11 and Mk 10.17-22=Matt 19.16-22=Lk 18.18-23 and see also the conflict story of Mk 12.28-34=Matt 22.34-40=Lk 10.25-38) and the miracle quest story of the nobleman (Jn 4.46-54 and Matt 8.5-13=Lk 7.1-10 [Q?]); others make use of tradition common to the Synoptics but not as quest stories: Jn 1.19-51; 2.13-22; 6.1-36; 18.1-9; 20.1-18; while others are peculiar to Jn in form and content: 2.1-11; 4.4-42; 11.1–12.19; 12.20-24. Whether or not Jn makes use of Synoptic tradition it is clear that he is largely responsible for the complex development of the quest theme in the Gospel.

Temple, the healing of the nobleman's son, the feeding of the multitude, the storm with Jesus walking on the sea, the healing of a paralytic, the giving of sight to a blind man, the anointing of Jesus' feet, the entry into Jerusalem, the last supper and a final discourse. Some of the agreements in detail are remarkable[219] suggesting some literary relation between Jn and the Synoptics.

Evidence that Jn was dependent on the Synoptics is often found in the overall agreement of order between Jn and Mk,[220] within which close verbal parallels occur:

Mark		**John**	
(a) The work and witness of the Baptist	1.4-8	1.19-36	
(b) Departure to Galilee	1.14f.	4.3	
(c) Feeding of the Multitude	6.34-44	6.1-13	
(d) Walking on the Lake	6.45-52	6.16-21	
(e) Peter's Confession	8.29	6.68f.	
(f) Departure to Jerusalem	9.30f.	7.10-14	
10.1,32,46			
(g) The Entry (transposed in John)	11.1-10	12.12-15	
The Anointing	14.3-9	12.1-8	
(h) The Last Supper, with predictions of			
betrayal and denial	4.17-26	13.1–17.26	
(i) The Arrest	14.43-52	18.1-11	
(j) The Passion and Resurrection	14.53–16.8	18.12–20.29	

It is to be noted further that the cleansing of the Temple (Mk 11.15-17) also occurs in Jn, but at a different point (2.14-16).[221] Barrett notes that the sequence of the feeding and the walking on the lake "is not readily

---

[219] See the description of "perfume" in the anointing of Jn 12.3 and Mk 14.3. But in Mk the woman anoints Jesus' head, not his feet, as in Jn. Such differences in detail, even where there are close resemblances, make the task of identifying Synoptic dependence difficult and the case for dependence less than probable. In this instance it could be argued that Jn has modified his source so that Mary's action in relation to Jesus will strike an harmonic chord with the narrative of the washing of the disciples' feet by Jesus (Jn 13). Thus Mary is shown to do for Jesus what the disciples should do (13.12-17) and is portrayed as an (the?) ideal disciple.

[220] In general Jn 1–12 follows the order of Mk: Prologue and call of the disciples, Mk 1.1-20; Jn 1.1-51; the revelation of Jesus through word and action, Mk 1.21-45; Jn 2.1–4.54; Conflict stories and disputations, Mk 2.1–3.30; Jn 5.1–10.39. In both Mk 3 and Jn 10 Jesus is accused of demon possession. Jn 11.1–12.36 also includes conflict material.

[221] See C. K. Barrett, *The Gospel According to St. John,* (1978²) 43 for this "list, which is certainly not complete,...".

explicable except on the hypothesis of literary relationships". One may ask, however, whether the dependence is direct or indirect, because Mark could have taken over the sequence from his tradition. In some of the studies that follow the relation of particular Johannine passages to the Synoptics will be in view. On the basis of agreements in structure and detail Barrett concludes that the evangelist knew and had thoroughly mastered the contents of Mk and expected his readers to be familiar with them and he probably knew and used Lk also to a lesser degree.[222]

The Louvain school, led by F. Neirynck,[223] has ably defended the position that Jn knew and is dependent on all three Synoptic Gospels. Given the relative dates of Jn and the latest of the Synoptic Gospels this can only mean that Neirynck views the composition of Jn as a single act. Indeed this becomes clear in his discussion of the work of Boismard. Neirynck insists on dealing with the actual documents rather than with hypothetical sources.[224] Thus, while Boismard allows that all three Synoptics were known by the time Jn was completed he insists that it was significantly shaped on the basis of pre-Synoptic sources. But Neirynck argues that Jn is to be understood on the basis of the known Synoptic Gospels and his critique of Boismard's argument is impressive.

Given that the evangelist has thoroughly assimilated whatever sources he has used it is not surprising that criteria for separating sources or levels of redaction will fail to be convincing to all scholars. But this need not mean that the view that Jn is the result of a lengthy process of composition is only an inspired guess. Clues within the text point to this: the addition of the Prologue when the Gospel began at some stage only with 1.19; the break at 14.31 that is taken up again only at 18.1; the addition of Jn 21. Identifying clues leads to the recognition of the process of composition but this does not mean that sources and layers of composition can be identified with precision. Indeed it is the temptation to do this in fine detail that often exposes the hypothesis to harsh criticism. We may have to be content with a general hypothesis that cannot be worked out in fine detail. While this may be seen as taking an easy way out of the problem, the nature of the evidence upon which an hypothesis must be based will not bear the weight of a fully detailed solution.

---

[222]*John*, 127 and see 15-17, 42-54.

[223]See Neirynck, F. *et al.*, *Jean et les synoptiques: Examen critique de l'exégèse de M.-E. Boismard.*

[224]When it comes to Synoptic relations Neirynck supports the two document hypothesis involving the hypothetical Q. See "The Two-Source Hypothesis", in *The Interrelations of the Gospels*, ed. David L. Dungan, 3-22.

Hengel's suggestion that, because of antipathy to the Petrine tradition, the evangelist did not make use of the Synoptics as sources[225] is not altogether clear. He says that the Elder was involved in "critical discussion" with Mk and to a lesser extent Lk also. But he ignored Matt, which he probably knew, because "it was probably at the opposite pole."[226] But how can we say that Jn probably knew Matt if he ignored it? On what evidence is such an assertion based? It is true that if Jn makes use of the Synoptics[227] his treatment indicates some degree of dissatisfaction, even disagreement with them. Hengel's view that there is some evidence of antipathy between Jn and the Petrine tradition has some substance but need not mean that Jn knew the Synoptics. After all, Jn does not simply repeat, he modifies and interprets in a thoroughgoing fashion so that even where there are Synoptic parallels it is impossible to say more than that the source is Synoptic-like. Given a theory that links Jn to the BD, it would be a mistake to limit the tradition available to the evangelist to the Synoptics and to attempt to derive everything from them, no matter how contrived such an explanation may be.[228] Consequently in this study Synoptic-like traditions are recognized in such narratives as 2.1-10; 5.1-9 and 9.1-11, but they are not thought to be derived from the Synoptics. Thus something needs to be said of the distinctive tradition used by the evangelist.[229]

---

[225]*Question*, 75-6, 91-2, 102, 125, 127-30. If Jn did not make use of the Synoptics "as sources", how do we *know* he used them at all?

[226]*Question*, 75. What is meant by saying that Matt is "at the opposite pole" is unclear. In my view Matt and Jn reflect very similar histories. Both reflect bitter conflicts with synagogue Judaism after the Jewish war. Consequent to the exclusion from the synagogue Matt appears to have adopted a Law based mission to the Gentiles. Matt 28.19-20 is to be understood in terms of the intensified demands of the sermon on the mount, the greater righteousness, and against those who set aside the demands of the Law (Matt 5.17-20) while Jn allows a Law free mission.

[227]The discussion by Hans Windisch (*Johannes und die Synoptiker*) remains worthy of consideration on this question.

[228]See the seminar paper by Michael Goulder given at the 1990 Leuven Colloquium and now in *John and the Synoptics*, 201-38. Even Barrett (*John* 17–18) who acknowledges several narratives without Synoptic parallels is inclined to view them as Jn's creation making use of Mk and Lk.

[229]Thus Hengel, *Question*, 91-2, 102 makes reference to a distinctive signs tradition in the Johannine school. Moody Smith suggests that "The distinctive character of the Johannine narrative material strongly suggests a principal source (or sources) and one independent of the Synoptics." "Johannine Christianity", NTS 21/2 (1976), 229. Here, while accepting that there is an independent narrative source I do not think that the clue to it is the distinctive character of the Johannine narrative. Rather the evangelist is responsible for this and the source is Synoptic-like.

The approach to Jn which seeks to explain the Gospel solely on the basis of the Synoptics does not do justice to the differences from the Synoptics. It is hardly convincing to ascribe all of these (narratives without Synoptic parallels, sayings and narrative with points of contact alongside remarkable differences, not to mention perplexing omissions of suitable Synoptic material) to the interpretative imagination of the evangelist. The question of Jn's relation to the Synoptics is complex. There are remarkable similarities alongside striking differences in structure and content. The focus of Jesus' ministry in the Synoptics is in Galilee. In Jn it is on Jerusalem and Jesus moves continually between Galilee and Jerusalem. In the Synoptics Jesus' ministry moves inexorably from Galilee to Jerusalem where the events of the last week of Jesus' life, including the cleansing of the Temple, are played out. Jn places this event at the beginning of Jesus' ministry and in the place of the characteristic exorcisms of Mk and Q Jn announces a climatic cosmic exorcism of 12.31. In the place of the parables, "pithy sayings", talk of the kingdom of God[230] and some forms of the frequent pronouncement stories of the Synoptics the Jesus of Jn encounters and has lengthy dialogues with number of individuals not mentioned in the Synoptics: Nathanael, Nicodemus, the Samaritan woman, Lazarus.

What distinguishes Jn most from the Synoptics is the way incidents lead to dialogues which conclude with monologues where it is often unclear whether it is Jesus or the narrator/evangelist who is speaking. In these discourses the language of Jesus differs radically from that of Jesus in the Synoptics. Rather the style is more akin to that of 1 Jn. While the language is simple and the vocabulary restricted, the style and the form of the assertions are pretentious. The contrast with the Synoptics and the links with 1 Jn suggest that the evangelist is responsible for these peculiarities. The strength of this approach is that it acknowledges the role of the evangelist and the Johannine school in the creation of Jn rather than attributing its peculiar character to some putative source or sources. Clearly if Jn has used the Synoptics he has not used them in the way Matt and Lk appear to have used Mk.[231] The evangelist's freedom in handling his sources is much greater than in the use of Mk by Matt and Lk. Indeed, the differences are so great that it is not possible to demonstrate that the evangelist knew the Synoptics and it may be that he has made use of Synoptic-like tradition in a form independent of Matt, Mk and Lk. The radical differences from the Synoptics, including inexplicable omissions

---

[230] The exception is Jn 3.3,5 but the meaning differs from the characteristic Synoptic theme.
[231] Barrett, *John* 45 makes this point succinctly.

and variations, suggest that this was the case. Redaction critical work can only begin, however, with Jn's differences from the Synoptics.[232]

If Jn was published between 90 and 100 CE it seems unlikely that it reached its present form uninfluenced by one or more of the Synoptics. Naturally that means the tradition might have influenced Jn at some stage of its development in a form prior to its incorporation into any one of the Synoptics or through the direct influence of that tradition on a later form of the Gospel via the evangelist, the redactor, or both. Here the work of Peder Borgen is interesting. Borgen notes Paul's use of tradition (presumably oral) parallel to what is now found in the Synoptics to illustrate the nature of the tradition drawn on by Jn.[233] Tradition in this form was available to the evangelist in the earliest stages of the development of the Gospel. In later stages the evangelist probably did know Mk, Q, and perhaps even Matt and Lk though more likely if the latter two were known it was only in the redactional stage of Jn. By the time Synoptic Gospels were known Jn had already been significantly shaped.[234] An alternative to recognizing some Synoptic influence would seem possible only if Jn were earlier than is generally supposed or was composed in an area remote from them.

2. The Signs Source

Of the special sources identified by Bultmann,[235] Brown[236] and many other scholars allow only for the possibility of a signs source. Though the analysis of the source shows that it was distinctive, it is generally held that it did not completely determine the character of the Gospel because the evangelist was critical of the view of signs and christology in the source.

---

[232]See "Postscript: Purposes related to the Synoptic Gospels", p.131 below.

[233]"John and the Synoptics" in *The Interrelations of the Gospels*, ed. David L. Dungan, 408-37. If Borgen's arguments were not convincing to Neirynck neither did Neirynck's criticisms undermine Borgen's case. See 438-58.

[234]The argument for the relative independence of Jn in relation to the Synoptics may well seem inconclusive but then it should be recognized that proof of independence is an impossibility because absence of evidence does not necessarily mean absence of knowledge. All that can be shown is that the case for Jn's dependence on one or more of the Synoptics in shaping his Gospel is inconclusive and, given the differences and the probable process of composition, must be deemed unlikely.

[235]Bultmann analyzed the evidence and separated the source with some precision. For a systematic reconstruction of Bultmann's signs source see D. M. Smith, *The Composition and Order of the Fourth Gospel*, 34-44.

[236]*The Gospel According to John*, vol. 2, viii which also refers the reader to vol. 1, xxi, 195. See also the works of R. Fortna; W. Nicol; J. Becker; R. Schnackenburg; H-J. Kühn, U. C. von Wahlde. Many other scholars have indicated their acceptance of the signs source hypothesis.

The scope and character of the source, however remain problematical. Some scholars restrict the scope of the source to the numbered signs and what seems to have been the conclusion of the source (2.1-11; 4.46-54; 20.30-31). Bultmann's view of the source was that it was much more extensive and that it originated among the converts from the Baptist sect who used it in an attempt to win those who remained loyal to the Baptist.[237] Given that the Baptist did no signs (Jn 10.41), a signs source would have been an effective missionary tract.

The case for recognizing the use of a signs tradition in the mission to the synagogue in an attempt to win members to faith in Jesus as Messiah has been argued persuasively by Robert Fortna, first in his *The Gospel of Signs* and now, building on his earlier thesis, in *The Fourth Gospel and its Predecessor*. He has postulated a Signs Gospel which incorporates what for Bultmann were two independent sources, the signs source and the passion source. Fortna, like Bultmann, argued that the evangelist was critical of the christology and view of signs in the source. Certainly Fortna has rightly seen that a document (signs source) used in dialogue with the synagogue would not be able to avoid the scandal of the crucifixion of Jesus. Some response to this would have to be made if the signs were to be effective in winning Jews to belief in Jesus. Thus he thinks that although the signs source and passion source were of independent origin they had been combined into a rudimentary Signs Gospel prior to being used by the fourth evangelist. From the Signs Gospel the evangelist produced the Fourth Gospel. The Fourth Gospel is distinguished from the Signs Gospel primarily by the addition of the discourse material. Subsequently the Gospel was redacted and published.

The two Cana miracles specifically designated signs (Jn 2.11; 4.54) stand out within Jn. They are numbered first and second signs. Neither of them is followed by a discourse or dialogue. Rather the narration of the two signs is quite self-contained. Fortna argues that the miraculous draught of fishes, narrated in 21.1-14, might contain the third of the signs from the source.[238] The suggestion is made tentatively in the recognition of the the appended nature of chapter 21. He notes the reference to the third appearance (21.14) which he thinks originally was a reference to the third sign. The term sign is not now used in the narrative at all. Fortna notes that the signs of 2.1-11; 6.1-14; 21.1-14 all deal with the bounty of the messianic age.[239]

---

[237]Bultmann, *The Gospel of John*, 108 n6.
[238]See *Predecessor*, 66-79. In this Fortna follows in the earlier steps of Boismard who suggests that it was originally the third Galilean sign.
[239]*Ibid.*, 253.

It may well be that 21.1-14 does come from Johannine tradition, but the evidence suggests that it fell outside the evangelist's plan of the book and was later appended. Whether it was the third sign in a signs source is a question that cannot be answered with any degree of certainty on the basis of evidence. Stories like it in the Synoptics are often described as misplaced post-resurrection epiphanies. Fortna's suggestion moves in the opposite direction. His hypothesis presupposes a rather inept evangelist who allowed the numbering of the first two signs to remain while excluding the third and removing the numbering on the remaining signs. He also referred to other signs which upset the numbering of the first two (Jn 2.23-25; 3.2). It seems easier to refer to the two numbered signs simply as the two Cana signs. They are numbered because of the focus on Cana which the evangelist wished to highlight.[240]

Fortna is now broadly followed by U. C. von Wahlde[241] who looks at the production of the Gospel in three stages. The first stage involves the narrative signs material and includes (in agreement with Fortna) the passion and resurrection stories. He shows awareness of the similarity of his approach to that of Robert Fortna, especially his *The Fourth Gospel and its Predecessor* and throughout this study he carries on a running dialogue with Fortna. Naturally, in spite of strong similarities in approach,[242] they differ on points of detail. Von Wahlde aims to set his source critical work on what he claims is an "objective" basis.[243] It is

---

[240]The two signs form an *inclusio* marking the unity of the section concluding with 4.54. Thus 5.1 begins a new section where the focus is no longer on quest but on the rejection of Jesus.

[241]*The Earliest Version of John's Gospel.* See also his, "The Terms for Religious Authorities in the Fourth Gospel: A Key to Literary Strata?" *JBL* 98 (1979), 231-53; "The Witnesses to Jesus in John 5.31-40 and Belief in the Fourth Gospel", *CBQ* 43 (1981), 385-404.

[242]Though von Wahlde does not call his earliest version a signs Gospel, it involves both the signs and the passion and subsequent "versions" are by different authors. Both Fortna and von Wahlde envisage three stages. Thus von Wahlde is closer to Fortna than his explicit statements suggest.

[243]Von Wahlde asserts (p. 30), "These linguistic characteristics are the most objective criteria available and therefore the most reliable." Again (p. 35) he writes, "because the terms are so numerous in the gospel, they provide a means which is both objective and at the same time widespread within the gospel for determining a core of the first two editions of the gospel". The claims to objectivity go on throughout the book. The argument would have been more plausible had he distinguished formal and material evidence. Even formal evidence does not provide "objective criteria" as such. Whether it can provide a basis for distinguishing sources must be debated and is put in question by the studies of E. Ruchstuhl and E. Schweizer. Von Wahlde's use of this evidence is also questionable.

unfortunate that he uses this term because all of the criteria he has chosen to use are open to objection. How could it be otherwise? The two primary linguistic criteria used by von Wahlde are (what he claims to be) two separate sets of terms for the Jewish authorities and for Jesus' miracles.

He asserts that in the earliest material the authorities are called the Pharisees, chief priests and rulers while in the second stratum they are the Jews. In support of his view that the terms manifest two separate strata he remarks (p. 34) "the terms from the two groups are never intermixed." How could they be? The terms of the first group are sectional while the "Jews" is comprehensive, including all. It would not make sense to say, "the Pharisees and the Jews". Further, according to von Wahlde the "Jews" of the second stratum are said to be the opponents of Jesus.[244] "Never is there division among the Jews." (pp. 56-7) But what are we to make of the references to "the Jews" in Jn 10.19-21? This reference (10.19-21) is given to support the assertion:

> There is also division among the people even though the vast majority of them believe in Jesus (7.31, 40-44; 10. 19-21;[245] 11.45-50). There is none of this in the material of the second edition. (p. 57)

To maintain his position von Wahlde interprets "Jews" in different senses. When the term is used of the Judaeans generally, as he argues it is in 10.19-21, it belongs to the first version. When it is used of the Jewish authorities, unified in their opposition to Jesus, he argues that it belongs to the second version. This is certainly not a formal distinction and it is open to objection. If the "Pharisees" (Jewish leaders) can be divided (Jn 9.16), why not the Jewish leaders ("Jews", Jn 10.19-21)? It is arbitrary to assign these references to different strata of the Gospel. Rather it should be recognized that the evangelist uses "the Jews" in a variety of ways which the reader can discern from the context.

The treatment of the two sets of terms to describe the miracles fares no better. According to von Wahlde, "signs" belongs to the earliest version and "works" to the later versions. But this can only be maintained by

---

[244]The Jews who determined to cast out of the synagogue any one who confessed (Jesus is the) Christ (9.22) fit this view but, contrary to von Wahlde's argument, the Pharisees appear in exactly the same role in 12.42. See "The root of unbelief, 12.36b-43" chapter 11,VI below.

[245]Here the note is added "Note the neutral use of 'Jews' in the sense of 'Judeans'." How objective is this evidence? It is not a matter of recognizing the use of one set of terms in one version and another set of terms in the next. Rather von Wahlde must argue that the same term is used in different ways in the two versions. This is hardly an objective distinction and his argument is open to objection.

distinguishing certain uses of "signs" and "works" which do not fit this pattern. The demands for a sign in 2.18 and 6.30 are said to belong to the second version. In support of this view it is argued that both of these uses of "sign" appear in conjunction with the "Jews" used in a context of hostility, an indication of the second version. The demand for a sign is used in conjunction with reference to the Jews in 2.18, though the level of hostility has been reduced by the evangelist.[246] But there is neither reference to the Jews nor a context of hostility in 6.30. The assumption here is that Jesus is speaking to the crowd ($\check{o}\chi\lambda o\varsigma$) which followed him (6.2), which he fed and left, and which subsequently followed and found him again (6.22,24-25). It is this crowd which requests of him, $K\acute{u}\rho\iota\epsilon$, $\pi\acute{a}\nu\tau o\tau\epsilon$ $\delta\grave{o}\varsigma$ $\dot{\eta}\mu\hat{\iota}\nu$ $\tau\grave{o}\nu$ $\check{a}\rho\tau o\nu$ $\tau o\hat{u}\tau o\nu$. This is hardly the response of the Jewish authorities. Indeed the Jews do not appear until 6.41. If the "Jews" here are simply taken as a synonym for the "crowd" the meaning is surely not the Jewish authorities (the meaning of von Wahlde's second version) but must indicate a Jewish crowd. I find this suggestion implausible. Even if we allowed that this is correct, it does not fit von Wahlde's view that the Jews of the second version are the hostile Jewish authorities.

It is important to note that following Jesus' identification of himself with the bread of life, for which the crowd has made request, there is a sequence of semi-connected sayings (6.36-40) leading up to the rejection of Jesus by the Jews. The note of rejection is introduced through the use of the term $\dot{\epsilon}\gamma\acute{o}\gamma\gamma\upsilon\zeta o\nu$. In my view this is a new beginning, introducing a new response.[247] That the demand for a sign should be relegated to the second edition is also unconvincing in the light of the evidence of this demand in the Synoptic tradition.[248] The inherent probability is that this goes back to the earliest tradition.

That apart from Jn 7.3 the term "works" always appears on the lips of Jesus while "signs" is the term used by others is challenged by von Wahlde[249] with a view to showing this does not explain the Johannine use of signs and works. His aim rather is to show that "works" is part of the

---

[246]This assessment is based on a comparison with the Synoptic accounts of the "cleansing". By placing this event at the beginning of Jesus' ministry Jn has changed the role of this event in his story from the cause of Jesus' arrest (Synoptics) to become a revelatory event in the experience of the disciples, Jn 2.17,22. The demand for a sign by the Jews lacks hostility because it is the cue for Jesus to proclaim the coming sign of his resurrection which would lead to the belief of the disciples.

[247]See chapter 6, "The Messiah and the Bread of Life" below.

[248]See von Wahlde, 37 n26.

[249]*Ibid.*, 36 n23.

vocabulary peculiar to the second version. He instances 10.33 as an exception where characters other than Jesus use "works". Formally he is correct. In 10.33 it is the Jews who use the term "good work". But they are responding to Jesus' question (10.32) using his language. It is no real exception.[250] In attributing the term "works" to the second version it is also necessary to discern different meanings so that a minority of uses can be recognized in the first version without prejudicing the hypothesis.

Serious objections can be raised concerning each of von Wahlde's two "primary linguistic criteria". The reason for this failure is that he is mistaken (in my view) in thinking that the versions of Jn were produced by different "authors".[251] Because the versions were produced by the same author linguistic criteria are of little use in separating them,[252] and this is apparent from the difficulties he has in his attempt to make use of linguistic evidence. The evangelist has made use of traditional material which has been thoroughly assimilated. When the tradition does surface it is Synoptic-like and suggests that the evangelist concentrated on a limited number of key terms in the tradition (such as "signs" and "works") and has developed them thematically.

The first sign (2.1-11) alone of the Johannine miracles has no general parallel in the Synoptics,[253] though only the miracles of Jn 6 (the feeding miracle and the walking on the sea) have specific parallels. The other miracles are generally similar to those described in the Synoptics. All (including 2.1-11) manifest the miracle story or miracle quest story form, the latter being the case with the two Cana miracles. The two Cana signs also betray evidence of the evangelist's hand. He has modified them by introducing Jesus' negative response to the request/demand for a sign.[254]

---

[250]It is equally true to say that in Jn Son of Man is a self-designation of Jesus. Jn 12.34 is no real exception. Jn assumes that the crowd (and the reader) know that Jesus' "I" saying of 12.32 presupposes similar "Son of Man" sayings.

[251]Similarly Robert Fortna argues that the Signs Gospel was used as the major source by the evangelist. A brief summary criticism of the signs source hypothesis is provided by Wolfgang J. Bittner, *Jesu Zeichen im Johannesevangelium*, 1-16.

[252]I prefer to speak of "editions" rather than "versions" because I perceive the same author at work. The work of E. Schweizer and E. Ruckstuhl has shown how hazardous it is to use linguistic criteria to distinguish different authors in Jn.

[253]The suggestion that Jn constructed this story on the basis of sayings about a bridegroom and attendants (Mk 2.19-20) and new wine (Mk 2.22) (thus M. Goulder in *John and the Synoptics*, 201-38) is less than convincing.

[254]The negative response to the request is part of the anatomy of a quest story. See chapter 4, "Quest Stories in John 1-4" below.

In the miracle stories generally Jn has also allowed the language of the signs to interact with his portrayal of Jesus' works.[255] His motivation for doing this might have been the concern to wean followers of Jesus from reliance on the spectacular nature of Jesus' miracles, stressing rather the nature of his works as the works of God and ultimately the need to receive Jesus' word. Thus the evangelist portrays Jesus speaking characteristically of his works ($\check{\epsilon}\rho\gamma\alpha$) rather than his signs. But the term "sign" does not belong exclusively to the language of the crowd because Jesus also speaks of signs in 4.48; 6.26, though in each case his use of the term is somewhat critical. His criticism is aimed at attitudes to signs however, not at the signs themselves. Indeed, in 6.26 the criticism is of the failure to respond to the signs. Further, in adopting the Cana "signs" the evangelist has placed the language of "signs" on the lips of the narrator who has also made use of several summary statements about signs (Jn 2.23; 3.2; 12.37; 20.30). This is enough to show that his attitude to signs is not negative. It is true, however, that the narrator speaks of the signs from the perspective of those who may see them rather than of Jesus who performs them. His account of the language of Jesus changes the focus to his works, a term with a wider reference than miracles (Jn 6.28-29). Indeed the whole of Jesus' ministry is conceived as his work (Jn 4.34).[256] But the overlapping use of terms makes clear that the signs are included in the works and can be referred to by this term also.

The term "sign" is not used of Jesus' miracles in the Synoptics. There it appears only in the demand for a sign, Mk 8.11-12; Matt 12.38-42; 16.1-4; Lk 11.29-32; 12.54-56; and in the warning concerning the signs and wonders[257] of the false prophets and false Messiahs, Mk 13.22. This could explain why the Synoptics do not use the term of the miracles of Jesus. Jn also records the request/demand for a sign (2.18; 6.30; 7.3). That request/demand underlies the otherwise harsh responses of Jesus in Jn 2.4; 4.48. Hence the evangelist's negative attitude to the demand for a sign emerges but should not be understood as an indication of a negative

---

[255]The evangelist's distinctive touch is to be seen in this interaction.

[256]For the theme of works see Jn 3.19,20,21; 4.34; 5.17,20,36; 6.27,28,29,30; 7.3,7,21; 8.39,41; 9.3,4; 10.25,32,33,37,38; 14.10,11,12; 15.24; 17.4. Most uses are on the lips of Jesus. The term "sign" is used in Jn 2.11,18,23; 3.2; 4.48,54; 6.2,14,26,30; 7.31; 9.16; 10.41; 11.47; 12.18,37; 20.30. Of these only 4.48; 6.26 are on the lips of Jesus and both sayings are somewhat negative.

[257]The phrase "signs and wonders" ($\sigma\eta\mu\epsilon\hat{\iota}\alpha\ \kappa\alpha\hat{\iota}\ \tau\acute{\epsilon}\rho\alpha\tau\alpha$) is also used in Jn 4.48. There Jesus' words are disparaging and it is no accident that the phrase is used rather than "signs". It is likely that the evangelist was aware of the tradition of the signs and wonders of the false prophets and Messiahs.

view of the signs as such. Jn has made use of two narratives which specifically designate the miracles described as signs (Jn 2.11; 4.54). It is also implied that Jesus' miracles are signs (Jn 2.23; 3.2). The feeding miracle is retrospectively so described (6.14) as is the raising of Lazarus (12.18) and a plural use of σημεῖα (9.16) encompasses the healing of the blind man. Predominantly this talk of signs is in the words of the narrator though both Nicodemus (3.2) and some of the Pharisees (9.16) draw attention to the signs of Jesus, Nicodemus to affirm that Jesus is a teacher come from God, and the group of Pharisees to deny that Jesus is a sinner. Thus here it is the signs of Jesus that cause a division (σχίσμα) amongst the Pharisees[258] while elsewhere it is his word (7.40-44).

Bultmann's (and Fortna's) theory concerning the signs source breaks down because it sets the evangelist against the view of signs in the source, producing a negative view of the signs that cannot be sustained in the Gospel as a whole. It also presupposes that the narrative source was free from discourse. While this was probably true of independent narrative stories it seems highly likely that narrative and discourse were woven together from the beginning of the Johannine development. Rather than a Signs Gospel the evangelist appears to have begun with a loose collection of traditional stories, perhaps mainly miracle stories. These he has worked up into the first edition of the Gospel in which narrative and discourse were already integrated. In doing this the evangelist made significant use of the quest story *genre*. The quest story was eminently suitable in appealing to those the evangelist perceived as searchers after truth. In this situation the evangelist reinterpreted the signs tradition, now shaped into quest stories, in order to portray his understanding of Jesus and the nature of faith. He wrote to strengthen believers in various stages of their struggle with the synagogue. The reaction depicted in Jn 9 indicates the success of this enterprise. Thus the view that the evangelist was working with Synoptic-like tradition (including miracle stories) and, in a number of stages, weaving it into its present form is an alternative to the distinctive signs source hypothesis.

3. The Discourse Source

More controversial is Bultmann's postulated revelation discourses source, *Offenbarungsreden*.[259] The distinctive character of the Johannine discourses is the basis of this theory. The discourses are quite distinct

---

[258]In addition to Jn 9.16 see 7.31,32,45-52; 10.19-22.

[259] For a reconstruction of the *Offenbarungsreden* see D. M. Smith, *The Composition and Order of the Fourth Gospel*, 15-34. For Bultmann's arguments concerning the character of the *Offenbarungsreden* see the commentary on the Prologue in his *John*.

from the Synoptics and even from the narrative material of Jn in terms of theme, vocabulary and style. According to Bultmann each discourse began with a self-revelation (ἐγώ εἰμι) "I am..." saying and developed through a dualistic structure. The source originated in the Baptist sect where the Baptist was thought to be the revealer and the Prologue hymn (part of the source) used by the evangelist had originally celebrated the incarnation of the λόγος in the Baptist.

Bultmann argued that the evangelist had once been a member of the gnosticizing Baptist sect. The form of Gnosticism of which he spoke was "early oriental Gnosticism" where the more mythological developments had been held in check through the encounter with the Jewish doctrine of creation. The evangelist's concepts and language were shaped in that tradition and he made use of a sayings tradition from the sect as his most important source, "the revelation discourses" *(Offenbarungsreden)*. They provided the evangelist with the source of the Prologue and material for the discourses of Jesus. In the Prologue the evangelist identified Jesus with the incarnate λόγος. In the discourses, in the "I am..." formulations, Jesus asserts that he is the revealer of God and the giver of the life for which all people are searching.

Although Bultmann recognized the large contribution made by the evangelist (about 47% of the Gospel), he considered that the peculiarity of the Gospel revealed that the evangelist was strongly influenced by this source, which contributed only about 16% of the Gospel, but was the most formative influence on the evangelist's contribution, revealing his world of thought. The evangelist's language and style were strongly influenced by the source. Because of this Bultmann indicated that, although there was no difficulty in separating the *Offenbarungsreden* from the signs source, this could only be done with great difficulty in relation to the evangelist's interpretation/redaction.

The discourse source hypothesis has not won wide support. Perhaps the primary reason is the admitted difficulty of separating the source from the evangelist's contribution. The discourses are, however, closely related to the signs. Robert Fortna recognized the secondary nature of the discourse material,[260] an observation that makes it unlikely that we have a combination of two sources. Rather, it is argued in this study, we have in the discourses the evangelist's interpretative elaboration of the tradition. The distinctive form of the Johannine discourses is however worthy of note and some attempt must be made to account for it.

The discovery of the Qumran Texts brought a wave of reaction against Bultmann's theory. The very motifs to which Bultmann had appealed as

---

[260]See my review of his *Predecessor* in *Pacifica* 3/3 (1990), 344-6.

evidence of Gnostic influence, especially the dualistic framework of Johannine symbolism, were found in the Jewish texts of Qumran. This convinced many scholars that no appeal to Gnostic influence was necessary. The evidence of these texts has also counted against the once popular view that the evangelist had translated the gospel message into the thought forms of Hellenistic paganism. This position had received classical exposition in C. H. Dodd's *Interpretation of the Fourth Gospel*. His position has not so much been proved wrong as vanished for want of exponents and defenders although C. K. Barrett continues to maintain that the Gospel is a meeting of Jewish and Greek traditions but that, paradoxically, the theology of the Gospel is somehow independent of both.[261] The reaction to the theory of Gnostic influence was not complete at any time. More recently, as a consequence of the study of the Gnostic documents from *Nag Hammadi*,[262] there has been a cautious return to the recognition of Gnostic influences on the Gospel by some scholars. It is recognized that Gnostic tendencies are already evident in the Qumran Texts. Consequently an appeal to these texts does not resolve the Gnostic question.[263]

The form of the Johannine discourses has been analyzed[264] leaving little doubt that it belongs to a particular tradition. However, for many reasons, including those outlined above, the source theory has not been widely accepted. Rather appeal has been made to a discourse *genre* which the evangelist used in constructing his discourses. The *genre* is to be seen in the *egoistic*-discourses of Wisdom.[265] Further important evidence of the *genre* has come to light in the fourth century Gnostic Nag Hammadi library.[266] The evidence suggests that the evangelist constructed the discourses after the pattern of these discourses. It might be that, along with the evidence of the Wisdom literature, we have an indication of the influence of a Gnostic discourse *genre*, an influence mediated to the evangelist via syncretistic Judaism. While this might be true, and it

---

[261]See especially *The Gospel of John and Judaism*, 75-6, and my review in *JTSA* 13 (1975), 76-8.

[262]See *The Nag Hammadi Library*, edited by J.M. Robinson.

[263]Bultmann had already noted this, *Th.NT*. II, 13. He had argued that the Gnostic influence had been mediated to the evangelist through Judaism.

[264]In addition to Bultmann's own work his student H. Becker, *Die Reden des Johannesevangeliums und der Stil der gnostischen Offenbarungsrede* has attempted to show the Gnostic character of the source.

[265] See R.E. Brown, *John*, Vol 1, cxxii-cxxv, 537f., and especially 'The Kerygma of the Gospel According to John', *Interpretation* 21 (1967), 387-400.

[266]See George MacRae, "The Ego–Proclamation in Gnostic sources", in E. Bammel (ed.), *The Trial of Jesus* (London 1970), 122-34.

would account for the distinctive Johannine discourses, much of the evidence used to construct the theory is post-Johannine and cannot escape the criticisms that have been used in relation to other Gnostic evidence. This theory does acknowledge the contribution of the evangelist in terms of the content of the discourses though some of this would have been suggested by the discourse *genre*.

The question of Jewish or Gnostic is simplistic. It is possible that the milieu of the Gospel was both Jewish and Gnostic. Indeed this now seems probable. However, was the milieu Jewish and Gnostic simultaneously or successively? Recognition that the Gospel is the product of a literary process allows for the emergence of successive problems and influences in the tradition.[267] Bultmann had recognized the process up to a point. He recognized 1. the production of sources; 2. the contribution of the evangelist; 3. the disruption of his work; 4. the repairing and editorial work of the ecclesiastical redactor. More recent interpreters[268] have tended to understand the contribution of the evangelist as a process rather than the writing of the Gospel in a short space of time and this allows room for the discussion of some relation to Gnosticism at various points on the Johannine trajectory.

4. The Passion Source

Jn has a distinctive passion story which Bultmann attributes to a distinctive passion source.[269] Robert Fortna considers that the Signs Gospel already included the passion narrative which gives the Johannine passion story its distinctive character. While Bultmann allowed for the considerable influence of the evangelist the passion source provided much of the distinctive material. Bultmann did not, however, attempt to provide a description of the Sitz-im-Leben of this source as he did for the Signs source and the discourse source. The Johannine passion story appears to be both straightforward, without much elaboration, and yet distinctively Johannine. How this can be accounted for remains a matter of

---

[267]Gnostic influences are evident in the form of Judaism that shaped Jn's language and world of thought but, it is argued in *Quest*, that the challenge of a Gnostic christology and anthropology emerged only in the latter stages of the Johannine trajectory.

[268]J. L. Martyn, R. E. Brown, G. Richter, B. Lindars, W. Wilkens. For a good survey of recent scholarship see R. Kysar, "The Fourth Gospel: A Report on Recent Research" in *Aufstieg und Niedergang der Romischen Welt*, Band 25.3, 2389-2480, and his earlier, *The Fourth Evangelist and His Gospel*.

[269]See D. M. Smith, *The Composition and Order of the Fourth Gospel*, 44-51 for a reconstruction of the Passion source.

conjecture.[270]

5. Concluding Remarks

An alternative to an approach based on the delineation of various sources is to recognize the source of the Synoptic-like tradition in the BD and to allow for its distinctive character being formed in the history of the Johannine community through the interpretative influence of the evangelist. Whether or not the evangelist was the BD, the distinctive character of the discourses is to be attributed to him. There is evidence of an attitude to signs and a christology which no longer represented the evangelist's point of view but was representative of views held by others in the Johannine community. The evangelist may once have been comfortable with this tradition and he made use of it in order to work with those who continued to hold such views. His aim was to move them in the direction of his own current position.

The relationship between the signs narrative and the discourse material in Jn is complex, much more complex than is sometimes supposed. C. H. Dodd's analysis of "The Book of Signs" suggests that the discourses grew out of the signs.[271] R. E. Brown refers to "the Johannine custom of having a miraculous work followed by an interpretative discourse"[272] and that in the Book of Signs it is the "discourses which interpret the signs".[273] The Gospel gives this impression and there is enough truth in it to cast doubt on the view that two disparate sources have been combined to form "The Book of Signs". Robert Fortna has worked exclusively on the narrative material of the Gospel because he perceives an "all-but-intolerable tension between narrative and discourse" in Jn.[274] He asserts the priority of the narrative in the sense that it can stand by itself in a way that the discourse material cannot. He also recognizes that the discourse material has much in common with the style in which the evangelist has redacted the narrative source. From these observations the conclusion (which Fortna fails to recognize) can be drawn that the evangelist is responsible for the discourses.[275] That need not mean that there are no

---

[270]See now the discussion by M. W. G. Stibbe, *John as Story Teller*, 156. Stibbe argues that the passion story in Jn is based on the witness (perhaps written) of the BD (Lazarus) and fashioned into a profound christological interpretation by the evangelist (John the Elder).
[271] *Interpretation*, 289-389.
[272] *John* I, 527.
[273] Ibid., I, cxxxix. See also K. H. Rengstorf, σημεῖον, *TDNT* 7 (1971), 252 "If the λόγος interprets the σημεῖον, the σημεῖον authenticates the λόγος."
[274]*Predecessor*, 1.
[275]See my review of *Predecessor* in *Pacifica* 3/3 (1990), 344-6.

clusters of traditional sayings. Dodd has done much to establish that this is indeed the case. But the construction of lengthy dialogues and discourses is the work of the evangelist.

It is not true however that all narratives have become inextricably bound up with discourse. The two miracles specifically designated signs have no connected discourses (Jn 2.1-11; 4.43-54). Some of the most distinctive discourses are developed without any sign as a basis (Jn 3; 4.1-42; 7; 8; 10; 13.31–17.2). Some of the discourses are more appropriately designated dialogues (Jn 4.1-42; 9.1-41). Indeed the dialogues of Jn 9 contain words of Jesus only in 9.3-5,35,37,39,41, that is, seven of the forty-one verses. The discourse of Jn 5 grows out of the "sign" as do the dialogues of 9.1-41. Generally the relation between narrative and discourse is more intricate than is supposed. This evidence weighs against the two source (signs and discourse) hypothesis.[276] Rather the evidence suggests that the evangelist was working freely with source material developing themes in various ways, via sign and sign elaborated by dialogue or discourse, or by discourse alone.

Some account can be given of the development of the Johannine tradition in the context of the history of the Johannine believers. With Bultmann, Brown and others it seems right to conclude that the history began with defection of a group of the Baptist's disciples (amongst whom was the BD) to become followers of Jesus, who himself seems once to have been a disciple of the Baptist. But, while Bultmann thought of this defection occurring some time subsequent to Jesus' death,[277] Brown conceives of this occurring during Jesus' ministry as he does not rule out the possibility that the BD was present at the last supper.[278]

Given that during Jesus' ministry a group of disciples of the Baptist became disciples of Jesus, that same group of disciples might have developed a collection of signs to win over their former fellow disciples to faith in Jesus. Subsequent to the death of Jesus, however, the signs were used in the synagogue to win members of the synagogue to faith in Jesus. It was in this dialogue that the quest stories were shaped with a view to appealing to those who were seeking the Messiah or in search of a new understanding of their lives in changing circumstances. But the dialogue with the synagogue turned bitterly sour and the evangelist became aware of the inadequacy of a theology based on signs alone.

---

[276]J. A. T. Robinson, *The Priority of John,* 303 makes some perceptive comments on the relation of signs and discourse in Jn.

[277] Bultmann, *John*, 108.

[278]*Community*, 32 n42. Indeed he says that the BD, "the hero of the community, may have been an eyewitness of the ministry of Jesus". *Ibid.*, 22 n31.

Throughout the dialogue and conflict the tradition was reinterpreted in response to a variety of crises: the crucifixion and departure of Jesus and the failure of his imminent return; exclusion from the synagogue; the re-emergence of the Baptist sect as a threat to the Johannine community; an influx of Gentile believers who interpreted the divinity of Jesus in such a way as to disregard his humanity. Each of these crises produced revisions of the tradition which were incorporated into the finished Gospel.

Through his interpretation of the tradition the evangelist sought to shape the Johannine community and we must conclude that he was a creative thinker with a sophisticated literary ability.[279] This is confirmed by the interrelatedness of the various parts of Jn and its radical christocentricity.[280] At many points the unique vision of Jn, in the context of first century Christianity, has been recognized and is generally attributed to the Johannine community. The evangelist was not, however, simply a cipher of his community. Through his reinterpretation of the tradition he was shaping the Johannine community. He was influenced by the events through which he and his community passed. But without his Gospel no such community might have emerged. His Gospel must have struck a chord in the minds and experiences of those who received it as their Gospel. To the extent that the Gospel was received as their Gospel the community was shaped by it and the survival of the Gospel signals the success of the evangelist's enterprise. But the history of the Johannine community as reflected in the Johannine Epistles and the transmission of the Gospel indicates that the shaping was not all that the evangelist would have hoped. Not only was he not able to persuade all potential members to join his community, the community once formed was rent by schism. That schism was so serious that no distinctive Johannine community survived beyond the early second century. The heirs of the Johannine tradition either seceded into developing Gnosticism or "made their peace" with the emerging "Great Church".[281] Certainly the "Great Church" came to use Jn as a powerful weapon against Gnosticism and from this time the influence of Jn on Christian theology has been without rival. ⏐

---

[279]There is no need to deny that the Gospel is written in a simple, though correct fashion, using a limited and repetitive vocabulary. Though this is the case the consequent literary work is an impressive, persuasive and dramatic work.

[280]See R. Kysar, *The Fourth Evangelist and his Gospel*, 179f., 260, 273-5.

[281] On this theme see R. E. Brown, *The Community of the Beloved Disciple*.

VI. PURPOSES OF THE GOSPEL

The purpose of Jn appears to be stated succinctly in Jn 20.30f. But is it? Jn was written to promote believing. That much is clear. But is it to promote believing for the first time, or, going on in faith? Both views have their advocates and can be supported. What is clear is that the question cannot be settled by deciding what tense the evangelist used for the verb to believe (πιστεύσητε or πιστεύητε).[282] It is true that the aorist would indicate the inception (beginning) of belief while the present would refer to ongoing belief. It could be argued that acceptance of the aorist tense implied that Jn was a missionary tract while acceptance of the present tense suggested that it was written for believers to strengthen them in their faith. However, the textual evidence does not provide grounds for any certainty in such a decision. Further, closer examination of Jn 20.30f. shows that the tense of the verb is not the issue at stake. The content of belief is crucial. The evangelist intends to lead his readers to believe that Jesus is the Christ the Son of God so that believing in his name[283] they may have eternal life.

Jn is concerned to lead its readers to believe. But more than this, it is concerned to lead them to right belief. The "confession" that Jesus is the Christ became critical in the conflict with the synagogue Jn 9.22; cf. 12.42. The focus on that confession in the statement of purpose is significant. This could mean that Jn was written to lead Jews to believe that Jesus was the Messiah. Of all the writers of the New Testament only Jn uses the transliteration of the Semitic *Messiah* (Jn 1.42; 4.25), which is translated into Greek as *Christ* (Χριστός).[284]

Dodd rightly notes that messiahship is but the starting point for the evangelist's christology.[285] This is indicated by the interpretative gloss that follows "Jesus is the Christ" in Jn 20.31. For Jn' "Christ" is interpreted in terms of Jesus' divine sonship, suggesting that he was writing to those who already accepted Jesus as Messiah in order to lead them on to his own perception of Jesus. While this is the most comprehensive statement of the purpose of Jn at the stage at which 20.30f. was made the conclusion, account needs to be taken of the process of composition prior to that point which reflects a variety of purposes in the completed work. A further stage of development beyond 20.30f. is

---

[282] Aorist or present subjunctive.

[283] See Jn 1.12; 2.23; 3.18 for the precedent of taking "his name" as the object of belief.

[284] C. H. Dodd, *Interpretation*, 87.

[285]*Ibid.*, 346, 361f. However, Dodd's point that the evangelist was making a Jewish Gospel intelligible to a non-Jewish public is dubious.

signalled by Jn 21.24-25. Thus we should talk of purposes. It is likely however, that there was an overriding purpose for the edition of Jn for which 20.30f. was the conclusion.

1. Purposes Related to the Baptist Sect

The treatment of traditions concerning John the Baptist has led to various theories concerning the relation of the Gospel to the Baptist sect. Bultmann argued that the evangelist was a convert from the Baptist sect and that the signs source, used by him, had been developed to win those who remained loyal to the Baptist. While Bultmann interpreted Jn 1.35 as reflecting the conversion of the evangelist he regarded this as an event subsequent to Jesus' life.[286] The development of the signs source took place in this later period along with the polemical motifs in the Prologue (Jn 1.6-8) and elsewhere for which the evangelist was responsible. Thus Bultmann makes the polemic against the Baptist sect a prominent purpose for Jn. Not only was the signs source designed to win Baptist loyalists, the sayings source was (according to Bultmann) originally the collection of revelation discourses from the Baptist sect. The evangelist daringly placed these discourses on the lips of Jesus thus supplanting the Baptist. But in doing this he did more than change the name of the revealer from John (the Baptist) to Jesus.

Bultmann understood the Baptist sect to be a manifestation of early oriental Gnosticism.[287] In this context the Baptist was understood to be one of a succession of revealers. Indeed the Gnostic myth set out the understanding of the true nature and heavenly origin of the essential "self" of all members of the sect. The evangelist radically historicized the myth by identifying Jesus as the unique revealer in whom alone the λόγος was incarnate, thus excluding the notion that there were those who were saved by virtue of their heavenly nature. Thus Bultmann proposed that the Gospel was both an *apologia* to win Baptist loyalists and a polemic against the Gnostic views of the Baptist sect. The polemical purpose should perhaps be seen as subservient to the apologetic aim to make clear that to join the following of Jesus involved more than a substitution of the name Jesus for that of John. The Gnostic views of the sect also needed to be reinterpreted in an acceptable fashion. According to Bultmann this is precisely what the evangelist achieved by taking the sacred discourses of the sect and using them as discourses of Jesus but in a way that supported his own understanding against the views of the sect.

---

[286]R. Bultmann, *John*, 108 nn4, 5.
[287]For Bultmann's account of this see his *John*, especially the detailed commentary on the Prologue.

There is nothing implausible in principle with this hypothesis. It does justice to both the gnosticizing character of the Johannine language and the non- or even anti-Gnostic views of the evangelist. But it is not convincing because it fails to recognize the source of the evangelist's language and *Weltanschauung* in sectarian Judaism best exemplified in the Qumran Texts. When evidence from these texts became available Bultmann appealed to them to demonstrate the penetration of Judaism by Gnosticism.[288] While this is a valid observation it failed to take account of the more important context of apocalyptic views in which messianic expectations were at home. Obviously elements of apocalyptic ideology are conducive to the growth of Gnosticism but it is a mistake to equate the one with the other. For Jn an apocalyptic *Weltanschauung* is the matrix of his language and leading ideas. Naturally the language and ideas have been radically shaped in the Jesus movement and in the events through which the Johannine community passed, especially the dialogue and conflict with the synagogue. Only at a later stage did the evangelist confront something like the Gnostic ideology. This confrontation is reflected only in the later strata of the Gospel such as the Prologue and Jn 17. By making the incarnation the touchstone of the Johannine theology Bultmann has adopted a later emphasis as the key to the development of the Gospel as a whole. But this perspective cannot make sense of the stress on the divine status of Jesus in Jn, especially from 5.17 onwards. It is this stress that provoked the implacable opposition of the Jews to Jesus in the narrative and which led to the breach with the synagogue which is reflected in the Gospel. Only after the breach with the synagogue did the Gnostic problem emerge. Thus it is a mistake to view the Gospel as an occasional piece of writing like the Johannine letters. Rather the Gospel is the product of a lengthy process and reflects a series of situations which give a depth to the interpretation of Jesus and the faith response to him that is given there.

Raymond Brown recognizes that Jn does put the Baptist in his place, dealing with exaggerated claims concerning him but at the same time according him a position of honour amongst the witnesses to Jesus, Jn 1.6-8,31; 3.29.[289] The evidence of Jn 1.35ff. may indicate that the Johannine Christians looked back to the defection of two of the disciples of the Baptist, one of whom might have been the BD, as the foundation of their group. Brown acknowledges that this disciple might have been one of Jesus' disciples and representative of a group of converts. Such a group would have attempted to win those who remained loyal to the Baptist, so

---

[288]*Th.N.T.* II, 13 n*.
[289]Brown, *John* 1, lxix-lxx.

that Bultmann's suggestion about the origin of the signs might well be right.[290] An approach based on signs could well have suggested itself to those who sought to win Baptist loyalists, whose master himself did no signs, Jn 10.41.[291] This seems to have been an early development because the treatment of the Baptist in the body of the Gospel is generally positive though even there the Baptist denies that he is the Christ (1.19-23) and asserts Jesus' superiority. But Jn 10.41 is a transitional summary which might have been part of the conclusion of an early version of the Gospel and thus give us a clue to its purpose at that stage. Yet Brown regards the apologetic against the followers of the Baptist as "one of the latest strata of the Gospel composition".[292]

Recognition of the Prologue as one of the later strata of Jn suggests that the problem of the Baptist sect re-emerged, possibly in Asia Minor, see Acts 18.25; 19.2-6. Polemical statements concerning the Baptist appear in Jn 1.6-8,20,30; 3.27ff. Consequently it appears that there are purposes in relation to the Baptist sect, the first early, positive and the second later and negative, denying that the Baptist was the light or the Christ. These purposes should not be seen as dominating Jn. Rather, the first was possibly the purpose of a collection of miracle stories used by the evangelist while the latter was a subsidiary purpose to Jn as a whole.

2. Purposes Related to the Samaritans

Raymond Brown[293] has used the evidence of Jn 4 in conjunction with Acts 6–8 to argue that a group of Hellenist Christian Jews with their Samaritan converts joined the Johannine community. He argues that Jn 4 departs from what we know of Jesus' ministry in the Synoptics and, according to Acts 8.1-25, it was only through the Hellenist mission that Samaritans were converted and the story reflects "the post-resurrectional history of the Christian movement". The Hellenists, with anti-Temple tendencies and "higher" christology were even more obnoxious to the Jews because of their Samaritan converts. Their coming introduced the Johannine Christians, previously dominated by the converts from the Baptist sect with their Davidic Messiahship, to the anti-Temple attitude and christology of pre-existence which were to become characteristic of Johannine tradition and to lead the Johannine Christians into the bitter struggle with the synagogue.

---

[290]What is in view in this suggestion (*pace* Bultmann) is a loose collection of miracle stories.

[291]There is no reason to doubt this assertion because neither the Synoptics nor Josephus suggest that the Baptist performed signs.

[292] Brown, *John* I, lxix-lxx.

[293] R. E. Brown, *Community*, 22 n31 and 35-40.

What Brown suggests concerning the Samaritans is that their entry into the Johannine community is *reflected* (my word) in the tradition of Jn 4. He does not suggest that Jn 4 was constructed in order to win Samaritans to the faith. On the contrary he points out that in Jn 4.22 "Salvation is of the Jews" assumes an anti-Samaritan pro-Jewish identity while at the same time adopting a negative attitude to the Temple and its cult, Jn 4.21. This attitude is consistent with the Hellenists depicted in Acts.[294] Thus Brown argues that Jn reflects the entry into the Johannine community of Samaritan converts with a group of Hellenists who were responsible for the development of a "higher" christology which was to lead to the conflict with the synagogue depicted in Jn 5–12. The Johannine community as such was not in Samaria and was not concerned with mission to the Samaritans, nor was Jn written to win them as converts.

There are, however, those who argue that Jn was written to win Samaritans, at least as one of its purposes.[295] In addition to drawing attention to the way the conversion of a Samaritan village is treated in Jn 4 it is argued that Jesus is presented in a way that would appeal to Samaritans. He is not presented as the Davidic Messiah but as the Prophet like Moses,[296] the king of Israel,[297] that is, as the Prophet-King.[298] Much more can be said to show elements in common between Jn and the Samaritans. The negative attitude to "the Jews", the presentation of Jesus' signs in parallel with those of the Northern prophets Elijah and Elisha[299] could be illuminated from this perspective as could the charge, not only that Jesus is demon-possessed (also found in the Synoptics, e.g., *Mk* 3.22 and parallels), but also that he is a Samaritan, Jn 8.48-49, a charge that is

---

[294] Brown, *Community*, 38 notes the work of Oscar Cullmann, *The Johannine Circle*. Cullmann identifies the Johannine Christians with the Hellenists of Acts 6–8 which Brown rightly sees as an oversimplification.

[295] See J. Bowman, "Samaritan Studies", BJRL (1958), 298-327 and E. D. Freed, "Did John write his Gospel partly to win Samaritan Converts?" *Novum Testamentum*, 12 (1970), 241-56.

[296] See Jn 6.14; 7.40 and see 1.45 which might refer to Deut 18.15,18.

[297] Jn 1.49; 12.13 and contrast the accusation of 19.19 and the mockery of 19.3.

[298] See Wayne Meeks, *The Prophet-King: Moses Traditions and the Johannine Christology*. On the relation of Jn to the Samaritans see also G. W. Buchanan, "The Samaritan origin of the Gospel of John", in *Religions in Antiquity*, ed Jacob Neusner, 149-75; J. D. Purvis, "The Fourth Gospel and the Samaritans", *Novum Testamentum* 17 (1975), 161-98; C. H. H. Scobie, "The Origins and Development of Samaritan Christianity", *New Testament Studies* 19 (1972-73), 390-414, especially 401-8.

[299] See the article by Buchanan in the note above, 166f. Buchanan points out that, unlike the Northern prophets Amos and Hosea, Elijah and Elisha are pro-Israelite.

not denied.

As impressive as the case appears at first sight it crumbles under closer scrutiny.[300] The charge that Jesus is a Samaritan is equated with the charge of demon possession. Both charges are assumed to be wrong and in Jn the woman acknowledged Jesus to be a Jew and she a Samaritan. More importantly, as we have noted, Jesus affirms the pro-Jewish position, "Salvation is of the Jews". Further, the prophet like Moses of Deut 18.15,18, in conjunction with Exodus 20.17, was used by the Samaritans to identify the *Taheb* ("the one who returns" or "restores"). Not only does Jn not use some equivalent to this, the Samaritan woman speaks of Jesus as "a prophet" (as does the blind man of Jn 9.17) and the question concerning the prophet is put on the lips of Jews in Jn 1.21; 6.14; 7.40. Further, the Samaritan woman refers to Messiah (4.25), the Christ (4.29), rather than the Samaritan *Taheb*.

What links can be found between Jn and the Samaritans are also common to various streams of syncretistic Judaism in the Hellenistic age. Here the Qumran Texts provide important evidence. In these texts we also find the expectation of the messianic Mosaic prophet to whom reference is apparently made in Jn. Margaret Pamment[301] argues that the link between the Samaritans and Jn was the Scriptures which Jn used in the Septuagint along with the rest of the Greek-speaking church. There the evangelist found his christological terms, "Logos, prophet, Christ, king of Israel, son of man, son of God, Lord" and the association of to lift up ($\dot{v}\psi o\hat{v}\nu$) and glorify ($\delta o\xi\dot{a}\zeta\epsilon\iota\nu$) in Isaiah 52.13; sign ($\sigma\eta\mu\epsilon\hat{\iota}o\nu$) used of the miracles of Moses, Exodus 7.3,9; the contrast of above ($\dot{a}\nu\omega$) and below ($\kappa\dot{a}\tau\omega$) meaning heavenly and earthly, Exodus 20.4; Deut 5.8; Joel 3.3.

On the basis of this critique it does not seem probable that one of the purposes of Jn was to win Samaritans. But does Jn reflect the entry of Samaritans, with Hellenists, to the Johannine community? The link with the Hellenists arises out of the account in Acts 6–8 rather than Jn itself and from an attempt to explain the development of the distinctive Johannine christology. On the first point, it is a mistake to allow the account in Acts to dictate the interpretation of Jn where there is no indication that the Samaritans were converted by the Hellenists. Rather Jesus himself, together with his first converts are the evangelists. Further, there is no indication that the Samaritans join the community. In keeping with traditions in the Synoptics some of those who come to believe in Jesus remain in their own locality.

---

[300]See the critique by Margaret Pamment, "Is there evidence of Samaritan influence on the Fourth Gospel", *ZNW* 73 (1982), 221-30.
[301]*Ibid.*, 229f.

The development of the distinctive Johannine christology is certainly a puzzle. But that puzzle is not solved simply by attributing it to a group of anti-Temple Hellenists. It is just as likely that the disciples of the Baptist, who came to be followers of Jesus, were anti-Temple, see Matt 3.7-12; Lk 3.7-9. Thus no further group is necessary to explain the emergence of the anti-Temple attitude in Jn. Brown assumes that this group would have espoused a Davidic christology. That being the case something quite new must be introduced to explain the development of the distinctive Johannine christology. But would the disciples of the Baptist have held this position? It is apparently the view of Nathanael, Jn 1.49. But Nathanael may not have been one of the disciples of the Baptist. It is less clear that *Messiah* in 1.41 must be the Davidic Messiah. It could be that links with syncretistic Judaism (Qumran?) go back through those who had been disciples of the Baptist and that much more complex messianic expectations have their basis there and find expression in Jn.

Our conclusion is that there is no strong reason to think that Jn was written to win Samaritans and Jn does not indicate that there was a significant Samaritan group in the Johannine community. The danger in reconstructing community history from Jn is that not everything there relates directly to the history of the community. It is unlikely that the history of the Johannine community follows the same order as the Johannine story of Jesus. The Synoptics show that Jesus did make contact with Samaritans. It may be that Jn has done no more than to feature one such incident in order to develop an aspect of his understanding of Jesus.

3. Purposes Related to the Jews

Jn was written for Jews. So much seems clear concerning the work for which 20.30-31 was the intended conclusion. This view allows for the possibility that subsequent editions of Jn might have broadened its purpose. In this section we are concerned with the clarification of the Jewish purposes of Jn. The possibilities can be discussed under the following headings:

i. To win Palestinian Jews to faith;

ii. To appeal to Jews of the *diaspora*;

iii. To appeal to secret believers within the synagogue;

iv. Opposition to and condemnation of the Jews.

v. To encourage the Johannine believers.

While we could be faced with choosing between these possibilities, it is argued that the Johannine tradition was used for all of these purposes. Again it is a matter of recognizing the process of composition where the various stages were used for different purposes. These different purposes may help to explain the complex way the evangelist uses the term "the Jews".[302]

i Palestinian Judaism. The Gospel reflects a Palestinian Jewish context. The Qumran texts illuminate the language and themes of Jn which reflects a knowledge of Palestine and of Jewish customs there.[303] This material does not in itself show that Jn, at any stage, was intended to win Jews to faith. It might rather reflect the fact that Jn embodies historical tradition rooted in Palestine and conveying accurate information about Judaism in Palestine. After all, Jesus was a Palestinian Jew and it would be extraordinary if nothing in the Johannine tradition went back to him. Thus Jesus is himself presented as a Jew in contrast to the Samaritans (Jn 4.9) and Pilate acknowledges that he himself is not a Jew, Jn 18.35. From this perspective we note also Jn 18.20; 19.20 and it is said "Salvation is of the Jews", Jn 4.22. In common with the Markan passion story Jesus is crucified as "the king of the Jews", Jn 18.33,39; 19.3,14,19,21.[304] The language use concerning "the Jews" represents a non-Palestinian Jewish or non-Jewish point of view. Consequently we note that the narrator speaks from a non-Palestinian perspective. The Palestinian perspective refers rather to Israel and Israelites and the evangelist has used such language when appropriate on lips of Israelites, Jn 1.47,49; 12.13.

The language concerning the Jews has also almost obliterated the various groups, Pharisees, Sadducees, Zealots, Herodians, which appear in the Synoptics. Only the Pharisees,[305] the rulers[306] and chief priests, priests and levites[307] appear as distinct groups in Jn. Even these groups

---

[302]The "Jews" is a term used 70 times in Jn, 5 times each in Matt and Lk and 6 times in Mk. Most of the Synoptic references come from the trial scene and refer to Jesus as "King of the Jews". In Jn there are five references to Jesus as "King of the Jews" in the trial scene which, in this regard reflects the Synoptic tradition as found in Mk. The majority of references are specifically Johannine.

[303]see R. E. Brown, *John* 1, xlii-xliii, 74f.; W. F. Albright, "Recent discoveries in Palestine and the Gospel of St. John", in *The Background to the NT and its Eschatology*, ed. W.D. Davies and D. Daube, 153-72.

[304]In Jn 1.49; 12.13 we find 'King of Israel' representing the nationalistic viewpoint of Palestinian Jews. See my "The Church and Israel in the Gospel of John", *NTS* 25 1978), 103-12.

[305]Jn 1.24; 3.1; 4.1; 7.32,45,47,48; 8.13; 9.13,15,16,40; 11.46,47,57; 12.19,42; 18.3.

[306]Jn 3.1; 7.26,48; 12.42; the only other ruler ($\check{\alpha}\rho\chi\omega\nu$) in Jn is the ruler of this world, Jn 12.31; 14.30; 16.11.

[307]Jn 7.32,45; 11.47,57; 12.10; 18.3,35; 19.6,15,21. In many of these references the Pharisees appear as a power block with the chief priests. The

tend to be merged in their opposition to Jesus. Thus the Pharisees and chief priests appear as a power block. The same is true of the rulers and the Pharisees. Nicodemus, a Pharisee, is one of the rulers. The rulers and the Pharisees are linked in their opposition to Jesus, Jn 7.48. Thus Pharisees, chief priests and rulers plot to kill Jesus. In the same way the "Jews" represent those groups in their opposition to Jesus.[308] The Jews of Jn 9.18,22 are the Pharisees of Jn 9.13,40; 12.42. By attributing the opposition to Jesus to the rulers, the chief priests and the Pharisees, the evangelist was isolating the opposition and allowing for a more positive response to Jesus from other sectors.[309] Where opposition is simply portrayed as of the Jews we probably should note the later perspective of Jn where there is no point in distinguishing those in authority because Jewish opposition has become total.[310]

There are important indications that some Jews believed in Jesus, Jn 8.31; 11.45; 12.9,11. They are important not only because it said that Jews believe but the basis for that belief (in 11.45; 12.9,11) is indicated as being the sign of the raising of Lazarus. Belief on the basis of Jesus' signs is an important theme in the tradition embodied in Jn, though this is qualified in the completed Gospel. This suggests that there was a stage of openness when Jews were able to respond positively to Jesus as one who performed signs which were recognized as indications that he was from God. There are strands in Jn that indicate that even the Pharisees and rulers were not monolithic in their opposition to Jesus. Nicodemus, a Pharisee and ruler recognized Jesus as "from God" on the basis of his signs, Jn 2.23-25; 3.1. There were rulers who believed but feared the Pharisees, Jn 12.42. Consequently there is evidence in Jn which portrays Jews responding to Jesus with an openness hard to reconcile with the united front of opposition in which the Jews are portrayed elsewhere. That openness is to be seen in Jn 7.15; 11.19,31,33,36.

In other places the Jews or the Pharisees are portrayed as puzzled and questioning, certainly not implacable in opposition Jn 9.16; 7.35; 8.22; 10.19,24; 11.33. It is probable that this situation of openness with

---

levites appear as a separate group in Jn 1.19, cf. *Lk* 10.32 and Acts 4.36. Hence Jn retains a view of some of the groups while others have disappeared.

[308] Jn 9.22; 18.12,14,31,36,38; 19.7,12,14,21,31.

[309] This means that the Johannine picture of the Jews is not as monolithic as is sometimes supposed though the later levels do reflect the Judaism of post-70 CE led by the rabbis and linked in Jn with the Pharisees and rulers.

[310] But the different uses of "Jews" does not provide a secure basis for distinguishing the versions of the Gospel. See the discussion of the views of U. von Wahlde on the Signs source above.

instances of belief represents the tradition in its pre-70 CE Palestinian form. In this situation the signs of Jesus were used in an attempt to win other Jews to belief in Jesus. The early stages of Jn 9 provide evidence to support this case. Consequently it is argued here that the Johannine tradition embodies signs which were used in Palestine before 70 CE in the attempt to win other Jews to faith in Jesus.

ii Diaspora Jews. Most scholars today date Jn, in its present form, after the Jewish war of 66-74 CE. Given that it is written in Greek it is almost certainly a document of the *diaspora*. Was Jn written as a missionary document to convert Greek speaking Jews of the *diaspora*? This is the view expressed by W. C. Van Unnik[311] and J. A. T. Robinson.[312] Both take their cue from their understanding of the stated purpose in Jn 20.30f., and the focus on the Jews in Jn which has no explicit evidence of mission to the Gentiles such as is found in the letters of Paul.[313] Robinson now dates Jn before 70 CE but this need not influence his view of its purpose.

A number of objections can be raised to the theory that Jn was a missionary document to *diaspora* Jews. Such a purpose is not required by Jn 20.30f., as we have noted. Nor does that theory take account of the polemical level where the Jews stand for the opponents of Jesus and the believers.[314] Consequently it is the Jews that the "believers" fear, Jn 7.13; 9.22;12.42; 19.38; 20.19. Those who interpret Jn as a missionary document have mistaken the purpose of the Johannine tradition at an earlier stage for the purpose of the finished Gospel. The missionary purpose might well have been restricted to the Palestinian life of the Johannine Christians.

iii Secret believers in the synagogue. In the *diaspora* the Johannine Christians were excommunicated from the synagogue. The threat of excommunication was a fearful weapon as is evidenced by Jn 9.22; 12.42. At some stage it was the purpose of the Johannine tradition to encourage secret believers to confess their faith and to face excommunication. In order to do this the evangelist sought to lead those believers to the Johannine perception of Christ as Son of God. Thus, though the threat of excommunication was aimed at those who confessed

---

[311] "The Purpose of St. John's Gospel", *Studia Evang* 1, 382-411.
[312] "The Destination and Purpose of St. John's Gospel", in his *Twelve New Testament Studies*, 107-25.
[313] See A. Wind, 'Destination and Purpose of the Gospel of John', in *NT* 14 (1972), 26-69 for a critique of theories of purpose especially those of Robinson and Van Unnik.
[314] See Jn 9.18,22; 18.12,14,31,36,38; 19.7,12,14,31.

that Jesus was the Christ (Jn 9.22), the evangelist's stress on Jesus' unique relation to God was to provoke a stronger reaction. The focus on this 'higher' christology of divine status and pre-existence was to produce a violent reaction.[315] This is expressed in Jn in terms of plots and decisions to kill Jesus and in the prediction that those who believe in him will not only be excommunicated but martyred.

iv Condemnation of the Jews. J. L. Martyn has seen in Jn 16.2 the response of the synagogue to the Johannine Christians in their city somewhere in the *diaspora* subsequent to the synagogue ban.[316] Another level of Jn was a polemical response to the synagogue. Just as the synagogue rejected the believers so they rejected the synagogue and justified their rejection of it by deeming it to be under the judgement of God, Jn 9.39-41; 15.1-6 and by accusing the Jews of being children of the devil, Jn 8.44,[317] while the Jews accused Jesus of being a Samaritan and demon-possessed, 8.48.

While there is a level of the Johannine tradition in debate with the synagogue concerning the relative authority of Jesus and Moses (Jn 1.17; 5.39,45-47; 9.16,24-25,28-34) and another level where Johannine Christians and synagogue pronounce judgement mutually on each other, it is hardly credible to suggest that Jn was written for this polemical purpose. The evidence suggests that the Johannine tradition was used to encourage secret believers to confess their faith openly and to face persecution. But this was not the task for which the completed Gospel was planned and ultimately the condemnation of the Jews serves a purpose for the Johannine community to assure them that though rejected by the synagogue they are chosen by God.

v Johannine Christians in the *diaspora*. Taking Jn as the work for which 20.30-31 was the conclusion[318] it seems probable that the purpose of the Gospel was one which had the Johannine community in view. It was a *Jewish* Christian community which had recently experienced a violent rejection by the synagogue. Cut off from its roots it was seeking to discover its identity in the world. Through this Gospel the evangelist intended, and in fact succeeded in shaping a community. That community was shaped by the christology of the Gospel. The

---

[315]Jn 5.10,16,18; 7.1,11; 8.48,52,57; 10.31,33; 11.8,54; 16.2.

[316] *History and Theology In the Fourth Gospel.*

[317]See chapter 7,"The Hidden Messiah" and chapter 8,"The Son of Man: The Light of the World" below.

[318]That stage probably lacked not only Jn 21 but also the Prologue and some other minor additions.

Gospel presented Jesus as "the stranger from heaven"[319] and this is the image in which the Johannine community was formed and for this reason it bears some of the marks of a sect.[320] In due course it was necessary for the Johannine Christians to come to terms with other Christian groups and with the Gentile world around them.

Thus we see new purposes being added to Jn in later editions. In such later editions the Prologue, later versions of the Farewell Discourses and Jn 17 were added. They not only reinforce the theme of the pre-existence and divinity of Jesus, which runs through the later strata, but also affirm the real humanity of Jesus through the incarnation, Jn 1.14. In the body of Jn the Jews do not question Jesus' humanity. This is assumed. It is his divinity which is questioned by the Jews. This stress on divinity seems to have led to an ignoring or denial of Jesus' humanity at a later stage, especially as evidenced in 1 Jn 4.1-6. It seems probable that this denial of humanity came from Gentile converts following the break from the synagogue.[321] But the publication of the Gospel was probably prior to the schism reflected in 1 Jn 2.19.

Even here what is suggested is not that Jn was redesigned to convert Gentiles. Rather it was modified to take account of the fact that there were now Gentile believers as well as Jewish believers within the Johannine community. Consequently the view of C. H. Dodd, brilliantly argued in his *Interpretation of the Fourth Gospel*, that Jn was written as an apologetic work to adherents of the higher paganism is to be rejected. His view fails to take account of how much knowledge Jn presupposes. It is right, however, to see the later strata of Jn (and the whole of 1 Jn) in a struggle with nascent Gnosticism. But Jn is a church book, written for those who believe, to enable faith to grow so that the Johannine community might, not only survive, but fulfill God's purpose for it in the world. Thus Jn is a missionary document in the sense that it gives expression to a theology of mission for the believing community.[322] The Johannine community is commissioned to perpetuate the mission of Jesus to the world. In order to do this it was necessary to bind the believers to the revelation of God in Jesus and it was to fulfill this purpose that Jn was written. Naturally this theology of mission is tightly bound to the christology of the Gospel which is portrayed as the ideal image of the

---

[319]See M. de Jonge, *The Stranger from Heaven*.

[320]The term is used here in the sociological sense of a group withdrawn from the institutions of society at large and seeking to make itself into an alternative community.

[321] See chapter 14, "The 'Opponents' in 1 John" below.

[322]See Jn 17.18,20f.; 20.21 and Teresa Okure, *Mission* and my review in *Pacifica* 3/3 (1990), 347-9.

community, "As the Father has sent me, in the same way I am sending you".

In the Epilogue (Jn 21) the redactor has used traditional material to encourage the mutual acceptance of the Johannine and Petrine Christians. This is the point of the recommissioning of Peter as the undershepherd of Jesus while at the same time witnessing to the authority and role of the BD. It is probably at this stage that explanations concerning certain Jewish names, customs, rites and festivals were added for the sake of Gentile readers[323] along with the references to the BD in Jn 13–20

4. Postscript: Purposes Related to the Synoptic Gospels.

It is clear that the evangelist assumed that his readers knew gospel tradition not included in Jn but found in the Synoptics.[324] Such knowledge does not necessarily presuppose the Synoptic Gospels but only wider tradition than is to be found in Jn. Thus it cannot be shown that the Johannine Christians possessed another Gospel besides Jn.[325] But given the theology of Jn the evangelist would not have been satisfied with the Synoptics had he known them. Perhaps Jn was the only Gospel for Johannine community, but even if one or more of the Synoptics had been available, the evangelist would have written his Gospel. It was fashioned in the fires which forged that community and it was a Gospel designed to meet their specific needs while at the same time giving evidence of the dangers which would have to be faced by such a distinctive, adventurous and creative response to Jesus.

VII. THE GOSPEL AND THE GOSPELS

Jn, like each of the Synoptics, belongs to the Gospel *genre*, and without chapter 21 is, like them, an anonymous Gospel. But while we might suspect that the Gospel *genre* was derived from Mk, it is possible that the Johannine variation was developed independently of Mk.[326] Jn is clearly a Gospel though neither the noun ($\epsilon\dot{v}\alpha\gamma\gamma\acute{\epsilon}\lambda\iota o\nu$) nor the verb ($\epsilon\dot{v}\alpha\gamma\gamma\epsilon\lambda\acute{\iota}\zeta o\mu\alpha\iota$) is used. The absence of characteristic Markan and Pauline language warns against identifying the evangelist with the Pauline

---

[323] Jn 1.38,41; 2.6,13; 5.1; 6.4; 7.2; 11.55; 19.31,40,42. Of course to call these Jewish is also to remind the reader that, though they are of Jewish extraction, these things are not Christian.

[324] Jn does not mention the baptism of Jesus but 1.31-34 appears to presuppose the readers know that tradition. Jn also appears to take for granted that the readers know Jesus was born in Bethlehem. An instance of implicit irony depends on this knowledge.

[325] See J. A. T. Robinson, *The Priority of John*.

[326] See for example the argument of H. Koester, "From Kerygma-Gospel to Written Gospels", *NTS* 35 (1989) 361-81.

stream of early Christianity (*pace* Goulder) or the communities for which Mk was their Gospel. Jn and the Jesus of Jn express themselves in language from another world of thought.

Yet if Jn is not self-consciously derived from Mk or one of the Synoptics there is a need for some other explanation of it as an expression of the Gospel *genre*. Indeed, it would be strange if Jn were thought to be dependent on Matt or Lk rather than Mk because, as an expression of the Gospel *genre* Jn is closer to Mk than either of the other two. In Jn, as in Mk, the story is told to lead the reader to belief in Jesus, uncomplicated by detailed ethical teaching. Though Jn gives an account of much more of the teaching of Jesus than does Mk the impression is misleading because, as Bultmann has noted, in Jn, what Jesus teaches is the necessity of belief in him as the way to God and eternal life. Thus Jn 20.30-31 forms an equally fitting conclusion to Mk as it does for Jn. Yet when it comes to a detailed comparison Jn lacks so many of the characteristic Markan features and in their place has distinctive features of his own.

The question of the relationship of the Gospels to Graeco-Roman biographies,[327] though rejected by some scholars in favour of a distinctive Gospel *genre*, refuses to be settled. Recently the question has been dealt with by Richard Burridge[328] who has argued that the criteria for recognizing *genre* should be seen to operate in a flexible fashion, different from the approach implied in the attempts to establish Gospels as a unique *genre* or as a sub-*genre* of biography with equally precise criteria. The latter approach is then forced to distinguish a different *genre* for each of the Gospels. While this approach may be useful in recognizing differences between the Gospels, it does not establish the recognized existence of such sub-*genres*. Rather than do this Burridge argues that the Gospels share sufficiently the criteria of family resemblances[329] to justify being recognized as Graeco-Roman biographies. He argues that the generic features used to identify such biographies should "be as wide-ranging and comprehensive as possible."[330] He lists four major features each with a comprehensive list which we can summarize as follows:

---

[327] Perhaps better referred to as βίοι to distinguish them from the expectations associated with modern biographies.

[328] *What are the Gospels?* From here on the discussion assumes that by biographies what is in view is the Graeco-Roman phenomenon and no account will be taken of distinctions from modern biographies.

[329] Here Burridge appeals to the work of Alastair Fowler (*Kinds of Literature: An Introduction to the Theory of Genres and Modes*, 42) who makes use of Wittgenstein's concept of "family resemblance" in defining *genre*.

[330] *What are the Gospels?*, 109.

(i) **Opening features:** title, opening words, prologue/preface.

(ii) **Subject:** appropriate to the *genre*.

(iii) **External features:** mode, metre, size, structure, scale, appearance, units, sources, methods.

(iv) **Internal features:** setting and topics, style, tone, mood, attitude, values, function of the text, social setting, occasion of writing, purpose.[331]

By using these features, or at least a sufficient group of them, the author produces expectations in the minds of the readers which constitute the recognition of a *genre*. Burridge's detailed work shows variations within the widely recognized biographies and then goes on to show in detail that the Gospels fall within the parameters of permissible variations in recognizable biographies.

While Burridge's work will not convince everyone, there are certain points that can now be accepted as well established. The Gospels are not free of a biographical concern. The very decision to write Gospels demonstrates that the early Christians believed that a knowledge of the life and work of Jesus was of some importance. There is probably some point in recognizing the Gospels as "folk literature" rather than "high literature", and thus as "popular biographies" though it would be false to think of popular literature as completely separate from the more self-consciously literary works. We should rather think of interaction and mutual influence. But this does not invalidate the distinction between the more scholarly and sophisticated literature and the popular literature to which the Gospels belong. Such literature is best seen in the category of the literature of popular persuasion.[332] It is clear, however, that the Gospels as biographies[333] have their own distinctive features having been formed under the impact of the oral preaching of the early believers.[334] This draws our attention to the rhetorical purpose of the Gospels. They belong to the literature of persuasion.

Essential to the recognition of the place of the Gospels within the literature of persuasion is the way they tell the story of Jesus from the

---

[331]*Ibid.*, 111.

[332]I prefer this description to "propaganda" because of the negative connotations attached to this term. Propaganda literature is normally thought to be a one-sided manipulative distortion used to ensnare the unwary.

[333]We might question whether there are any "straightforward biographies". Certainly Burridge has shown considerable variations within works of this kind.

[334]It is not necessary to renounce the insights of the earlier generation of scholars such as Dibelius, Bultmann, and Dodd, who saw the formation of the Gospels taking place under the impact of the oral *kerygma*. Where their work was inadequate was in the denial that this development had anything in common with the Graeco-Roman biographies.

perspective of faith in the risen Jesus. This perspective is implicit in the Synoptics. It is explicit in Jn. In two places the narrator turns the reader's attention to the belief of the disciples following the resurrection or glorification of Jesus (2.22; 12.16) making quite clear that this belief/understanding was not possible during Jesus' ministry at the precise point these interjections are made in the narrative. Indeed the purpose of these interjections is to make explicit the post resurrection/glorification perspective of the Gospel. Once this is recognized other *specific* post-resurrection/glorification references can be seen, 1.14,15,18; 3.13. Of course the understanding available to the reader in the Gospel as a whole is post-resurrection/glorification but the narrative generally assumes the situation of Jesus' ministry. It is only in these few instances that the narrator leaps ahead and speaks explicitly from the point of view of the resurrection/glorification.

That Jn has signalled this in the comments of the narrator shows that he was aware of what he was doing. That the Gospels do this is clear though only Jn signals that he was reflecting self-consciously on this process. Indeed, he goes further than this in affirming that the believing understanding emerges only with the coming of the Spirit/Paraclete (Jn 7.37ff.; 14.11; 16.7), whose coming was linked to the departure or glorification of Jesus. Consequently Jn's understanding of his Gospel reveals the essential post-resurrection/glorification perspective and the point of view of faith as the faith produced by the coming of the Spirit/Paraclete at that.

Thus if the Graeco-Roman biographies have contributed to the development of the Gospels, as seems probable, it is likely that the *genre* has been significantly modified under the impact of the early Christian belief in the risen Jesus and the proclamation of him as such. In addition we need to take account of the Jewish literary traditions, especially the *Testaments* and apocalyptic works. It is a feature of *Quest* that it argues that Jn owes more to apocalyptic motifs, indeed to an apocalyptic *Weltanschauung*, than is normally recognized.[335] But this recognition should not be opposed to Hellenistic influences such as the biographies and such specific aspects of them as the quest and conflict stories. In these particulars Jn and the Synoptics manifest the influence of the Graeco-Roman biographies. In other ways as well they manifest features of the Hellenistic literature of persuasion. Much of this, perhaps all of it, might have been mediated to the evangelists through Judaism. Whatever the particular mixture of influences and resources we detect it is clear that the

---

[335]I am glad to see here the general agreement of John Ashton, *Understanding* (404-5, 434ff).

early Christian belief in Jesus as the risen one has significantly shaped the Gospels and in the end each author has given his Gospel its own distinctive mark. The degree of distinctiveness that we see in Jn, compared with the Synoptics, suggests that Jn was shaped independently of them.

3

Christology and History in the Prologue

The Prologue is one of the more remarkable passages in the New Testament. Because of the distinctive form and content of the Prologue it is often suggested that the evangelist made use of a hymn in writing the Prologue. If this is true, what was the origin of the hymn? How did it come to the evangelist and why did he use it? What was in the hymn and what was added by the evangelist? Answers to these questions are fundamental to a precise understanding of the Prologue and could throw light on the history of the Johannine community.

I. THE HYPOTHESIS

The hypothesis set out in this chapter is that, in the conflict with the synagogue, the evangelist made use of a "sectarian" Jewish hymn in praise of Wisdom/Torah as the basis of his Prologue. Prior to being used by the evangelist the hymn had been edited and used by a "Hellenist" Christian community which was familiar with the Pauline identification of Christ with Wisdom and the antithesis of Law and grace. This is reflected in their editing of the hymn which then proclaims that new Law/Christ, not the old Law of Moses, is the Wisdom of God. To these emphases, which are not Johannine, the evangelist made his own modifications so that the edited hymn became a suitable introduction to his Gospel. Because the Prologue was one of the later strata added to the Gospel, the evangelist has not introduced new motifs which appeared in his source into the body of the Gospel. Some of these, though suited to the theme of creation, were not readily applicable to the gospel story. But this is not true of the Law/grace antithesis. It fitted the evangelist's perspective admirably so that the absence from the rest of the Gospel of the antithesis expressed in precisely these terms is a clue pointing to the history of the source prior to its use by the evangelist. Significant themes for the Gospel were to be found already in the source. That is why the evangelist used it. Others were introduced by his interpretative editing. The importance of this discussion of the Prologue is that it shows the evangelist in his quest for an adequate christology in the context of debate with sectarian Judaism, the synagogue and another early Christian view.

II. SOURCE THEORIES: A RESPONSE TO OBJECTIONS

Three arguments are frequently used against the source theory:[1]

1. The Prologue is a unified piece of writing.
2. It exhibits a unity of theme and subject matter with the Gospel as a whole and makes an excellent introduction to it.
3. There is no scholarly consensus about the form and content of the source amongst those who maintain that the evangelist used a source. These arguments have considerable weight. They indicate that the Prologue, however it came to be, is now an excellent introduction to the Gospel. But the implications of this observation can be overstated as can the emphasis on scholarly disagreement.

The lack of consensus concerning the *precise* separation of the source is a problem. But this need not mean that no source was used. Recognition of the possibility that the evangelist made use of a hymn is partly dependent on the recognition of the existence of hymns in this period and of the use of them in other New Testament writings.[2] Should this be seen as a fairly common practice then the possibility that John also made use of a hymn is unlikely to be excluded.[3]

No consensus exists concerning the detailed separation of the source. This does not mean that there is no consensus at all. A high degree of agreement can be seen on a number of points by the cross-section of scholarly opinion provided by R. E. Brown[4] to which can be added Brown's own analysis and that of J. T. Sanders.[5] My own views on this are complicated because I argue that a Jewish hymn was redacted by a Hellenistic Christian community before being used by Jn but broadly agree with this cross-section of opinion. In the following table only those verses (or parts of verses) belonging to the original hymn are shown though in relation to my analysis those verses added by the pre-Johannine Hellenistic redaction are also shown but in parentheses.

---

[1] C. K. Barrett, *John* (1955), 126; (1978[2]), 150.

[2] Similar hymns are detected in Romans 1.1-4; Philippians 2.6-11; Colossians 1.15-20. See J. T. Sanders, *The New Testament Christological Hymns*; R. P. Martin, *Carmen Christi*.

[3] R. Schnackenburg, *John* I, 224f. says that there is now a scholarly consensus that the evangelist made use of a hymn.

[4] R. E. Brown, *John* I, 22.

[5] *The New Testament Christological Hymn*, 20-5.

Bernard	1-5	10-11	14			18
Bultmann[6]	1-5	9-12b	14	16		
De Ausejo	1-5	9-11	14	16		18
Gaechter	1-5	10-12	14	16	17	
Green	1,3-5	10-11	14a-d			18
Haenchen	1-5	9-11	14	16	17	
Käsemann	1,(2?)3-5	10-12				
Schnackenburg	1,3-4	9-11	14abe	16		
Brown	1-5	10-12b	14	16		
Sanders	1-5	9-11				
Painter	1-3ac, 4-5	10-12b	14abc[7](e)	(16)	(17)	

There is a consensus that 6-8, 15 were added by the evangelist. Many would also identify 9, 12c-13,[8] 17-18 as additions by the evangelist.[9] The problem with 17-18 is that they lack the poetic form of the source yet they include a high proportion of non-Johannine words. The same is true of the latter part of 14 and 16. The consensus concerning 6-8, 15 is crucial and has far-reaching implications for an understanding of the Prologue.

Thus the Prologue is not as unified as it appears at first sight. Verses 6-8, 15 stand out from the rest drawing attention to the contrast between the poetry of much of the Prologue and the prose of these verses; between affirmation/confession and argument/polemics of these verses. The poetic form of 1-5 is marked and there is evidence of only minor editing by the evangelist,[10] who probably added only 3b to reinforce the statement that nothing exists which was not created by the λόγος. That 3b is an addition is shown by the repetition and by its polemical character. The evangelist added this to exclude any possibility of cosmological dualism to which the Gospel was susceptible because of the use of dualistic statements which challenge the reader to choose between good and evil. When 3b is removed the form of interlocking themes in 1-5 is then clear.

---

[6]Brown fails to note that Bultmann strongly suggested that verse 2 was added by the evangelist, Bultmann, *John*, 35 n3.

[7]The source was modified in 1 and 14 by the evangelist's use of λόγος rather than σοφία and some other modifications appear to have been made to 14abc also.

[8]Jn 1.12c-13 are clearly Johannine. For the expression "believe in his name" of 12c see 2.23; 3.18; 20.31 and the emphasis on the role of "the name" in Jn. For the theme "born of God", see 3.3,5; 1 Jn 2.20, 29; 3.1ff.,9ff.; 4.47; 5.1ff., 18f.

[9]R. E. Brown, *John* I, 21f.

[10]See R. Bultmann, *John*, 13ff.

ἐν ἀρχῇ ἦν ὁ λόγος,	In the beginning was the Logos,
καὶ ὁ λόγος ἦν πρὸς τὸν θεόν,	and the Logos was with God,
καὶ θεὸς ἦν ὁ λόγος.	and divine[11] was the Logos.
οὗτος ἦν ἐν ἀρχῇ πρὸς τὸν θεόν.	He was in the beginning with God.
πάντα δι' αὐτοῦ ἐγένετο,	All things through him became.
ὃ γέγονεν ἐν αὐτῷ ζωὴ ἦν,	What became in him was life,
καὶ ἡ ζωὴ ἦν τὸ φῶς τῶν ἀνθρώπων·	and the life was the light of men;
καὶ τὸ φῶς ἐν τῇ σκοτίᾳ φαίνει,	and the light in the darkness shines,
καὶ ἡ σκοτία αὐτὸ οὐ κατέλαβεν.	And the darkness did not receive/ overcome it.

The poetic form of the source might have been more marked than any reconstruction can recover because of the difficulty of identifying all of the additions and because there might also have been deletions.

Attention has been drawn to the evidence of the marked poetic form of much of the Prologue. We should also note the constellation of terms which occur only in the Prologue in the Gospel, and especially those terms which occur nowhere else in the Johannine literature. Peculiar to the Prologue is the use of λόγος as a christological designation (though see Rev. 19.13 and 1 Jn 1.1); φωτίζει, ἐσκήνωσεν, πλήρης, χάρις, χάριτος καὶ ἀληθείας, πληρώματος, ἐξηγήσατο.[12] The use of the name "Jesus Christ" (elsewhere only in 17.3) is also uncharacteristic of John. The concentration of some of these terms outside the poetic sections suggests a pre-Johannine redaction of the hymn.

Theologically the Prologue also presents a perspective different from the Gospel as a whole. In the Gospel the coming and going of the revealer form a unity but in the Prologue his coming alone appears to be the basis of his revealing work. Although the Gospel teaches the pre-existence of the revealer and speaks of his "descent", the focus is on his "ascent"[13] or "glorification".[14] The Prologue gives an account of the activity of the pre-existent revealer and speaks of his "descent", "coming", or "incarnation".

---

[11]This is the force of the use of θεός without the definite article *in this context*. The point is not to assert some inferior status for the λόγος but to take account of the asserted relationship πρὸς τὸν θεόν.

[12]Both σκηνόω and φωτίζω are used in Revelation, but not christologically. On the use of φαίνει in 1.5 see 5.35, but there its use is qualified to show the subordinate role of the Baptist.

[13]See Jn 1.51; 3.13; 6.62 in the context of 6.33,38,41,42,50,51,58, and also 3.14; 8.28; 12.32,34; 13.31; 20.17. For the significance of this motif see Wayne A. Meeks, *The Prophet King* and "The Man from Heaven in Johannine Sectarianism", *JBL* 91/1 (1972), 44-72; G. C. Nicholson, *Death as Departure: The Johannine Descent-Ascent Schema* .

[14]While it has been argued that the death of Jesus has no essential place in the Fourth Gospel it is at least the necessary means of the revealer's ascent.

But apparently it says nothing of the "ascent". While this was true of the source used by the evangelist, his addition of 18c adopts a post-exaltation perspective by speaking of the Son as being in the bosom of the Father. This modification is so subtle that without the rest of the Gospel the impression given here is that the revealer's descent alone accomplishes his mission.

In the Gospel as a whole ·ᵉ "Scriptures" are seen in a positive light (5.45ff.; 8.56; 12.41), but according to the Prologue there was no effective revelation prior to the incarnation. This is the force of οὐ κατέλαβεν in 1.5 and the recognition that 6-8 imply that all that follows applies to the historical revealer. Given that 6-8 were added by the evangelist this very negative attitude must be attributed to him as a consequence of the bitter struggle with the synagogue. Indeed there is a tension within the Gospel as a whole where we find indications of widespread belief even amongst the leaders and at the same time an emphasis on the unbelief of the Jews, especially the leaders, even the impossibility of their belief, 12.37-43.

The triple introduction of the Baptist is strange, 6-8, 15, 19ff., and only partly explicable in terms of the evangelist's use of a source in 1-18. Had the Baptist been introduced only in 15 and 19ff. this repetition could have been explained in terms of an original beginning, 19ff. to which the Prologue was later added. The introduction of the Baptist at 6-8 seems inappropriate because the incarnation is not specifically mentioned until 14. The witness of the Baptist is appropriately introduced at 15 after the confession of the incarnation but it has the appearance of being pulled from 1.30[15] at the time the Prologue was added. Verse 15 interrupts the first person plural confession ("we beheld...") which is continued in 16, indicating that 15 has been introduced into an existing composition because of the proclamation of the incarnation in 14.

The first introduction of the Baptist and his witness in 6-8 implies that the description of all that follows is the work of the historical, incarnate revealer. Indeed, verse 9 was added by the evangelist to make this

---

[15] Some of the variations between 1.15 and 30 are explicable as characteristic of the evangelist's method of slightly varying earlier sayings when they are later quoted. But the "This was..." (imperfect tense) of 1.15 instead of the "This is..." (present tense) is unusual. Can it be that John (the Baptist) in 1.15 speaks retrospectively from the perspective of the exaltation of Jesus? If we are to think that his words continue from 15-18 this must be the case. But it may be that his words imperceptibly fade into those of the narrator in 16-18 and this could be indicated by the return to the plural which was interrupted by the insertion of 15. Compare the way the words of Jesus fade into those of the narrator in 3.10-21 and the words of John again fade into the words of the narrator in 3.27-36. John, Jesus and the narrator are the authentic witnesses in this Gospel.

specifically clear. From this point of view, the proclamation of the incarnation in 14 comes as an anticlimax.

These observations suggests that the evangelist was working with a source and modifying it to his own purpose. In spite of the resulting "broken logic" at points in the final composition, the Prologue is an admirable introduction to the Gospel as a whole. Either the evangelist found almost all of the major themes of the Gospel in his source or he introduced them to his own edition of it. We would expect no less from such a skilful author. He would not have used the source unless it suited him and he was free to adapt it for his own purpose as an introduction to the Gospel. Recognition of the evangelist's skill as an author need not mean that there is nothing in the Prologue to distinguish a source from his own "free composition".

III. DETECTING THE HYMN SOURCE

So far we have sought to show there is evidence that the evangelist used a source. That the source was a hymn is a conclusion drawn on the basis of the recognition that the poetic structure, confessional character and christological focus are consistent with other passages in the New Testament which are also thought to be based on early Christian hymns. While this approach involves a degree of circularity in that none of this evidence presently exists as a hymn, that there were hymns in this period is unquestionable. The *Hodayoth* of Qumran provides evidence of contemporary Jewish hymns which is especially relevant because of the affinity between the Gospel and the Qumran Texts. Pliny referred to Christians who sing a hymn to Christ as to (a) god. The Odes of Solomon could well be an example of a Gnostic hymn book. Was the hymn source Jewish,[16] Christian,[17] Gnostic,[18] or some combination of the three?[19] The hymn source is to be recognized by its poetic form, peculiar

---

[16]J. R. Harris, *The Origin of the Prologue to St. John* , 6.

[17]For example, R E Brown, *John* I, 18ff.; R. Schnackenburg, *John* I,224ff.

[18]R. Bultmann, "Der religionsgeschichtliche Hintergrund des Prologs zum Johannes-Evangelium", in *ΕΥΧΑΡΙΣΤΗΡΙΟΝ Festschrift fur H. Gunkel*, 2 Teil, 1923 (Vandenhoeck & Ruprecht, Göttingen), 3-26.

[19]R. Bultmann, *John*, 17f., 107f.; and in his *Th.N.T.* II, 13 and n. According to Bultmann both the evangelist and the hymn came from a gnosticizing Jewish Baptist sect. He argued (*John,* 28ff.) that the hymn had its origin in "early Oriental Gnosticism", a description which he took over from Hans Jonas, and to which he added the qualification "early". In such Gnosticism mythological features had been pushed into the background under the influence of the Old Testament, an indication of the Jewish milieu of the source. Because of this the evangelist was not directly opposed to the source in its understanding of God and creation,which was the main point of

vocabulary and distinctive theology/christology. It is confessional in style rather than argumentative and it lacks particular names.[20] Application of these criteria confirms that 3b,6-8,9,12c-13,14d,e,15,16-17,18 do not belong to the source.

1. A Gnostic Hymn[21]

Bultmann argued that the Prologue was a special part of the *Offenbarungsreden* which provided the evangelist with the source for his discourses. But there is nothing in the discourses as tightly structured as the Prologue. Bultmann accounted for this by recognizing the source of the Prologue as a cultic hymn. However, his discourse source theory has won few supporters. It is more likely that the character of the discourses is to be accounted for by the evangelist's use of typically Gnostic literary *genres* which were familiar to him from his milieu.[22] Might not the tradition which provided him with the treasury of language also have supplied him with the idiom, style and *genre* of the Prologue? While this could, theoretically, have happened, the evidence suggests that the evangelist actually edited an existing source. Though the witness of the Baptist fits the context well enough at 15, it actually breaks into the confession of 14, 16. As the evangelist is responsible for 15 this evidence suggests he was editing an existing source, adapting it to a new purpose. Also important is the concentration of vocabulary which is peculiar to the Prologue. This concentration is far too high and full of significant words to be treated as a coincidence. It is puzzling however that, while the poetic form is clearest in 1-14c, the peculiar vocabulary is concentrated in 14d-18. The peculiar vocabulary and theology/christology suggest that the evangelist made use of a source and the poetic form suggests that the source was a hymn. But what are we to make of the differences between 1-

---

later controversy; see also his *Th.N.T.* I, 170; II, 13; and *John*, 28ff. Two important points should be noted. Gnosticism is said to have influenced the evangelist *through* Judaism. Hence it was modified Gnosticism which could take account of creation. Secondly, "early" meant for Bultmann Gnosticism which had been so modified. He does not suggest that fully developed Gnosticism did not yet exist.

[20]See J. H. Bernard, *John,* cxiv who notes that the source can be recognized by: i) In accordance with Semitic poetry we expect short clauses in some form of parallelism; ii) Affirmations rather than argument or polemic; iii) Absence of specific names.

[21]For a critique of Bultmann's Gnostic theory of the influence of Gnosticism on Jn's christology see J-A. Bühner, *Der Gesandte und sein Weg im 4. Evangelium,* 24-47.

[22]See G. W. MacRae, "Nag Hammadi and the New Testament" in *Gnosis: Festschrift fur Hans Jonas,* 156.

14c and 14d-18?[23] It does not seem to be justifiable to attribute 14d-18 to the evangelist because of the high concentration of important non-Johannine vocabulary in these verses.

2. Two Hymns from the Evangelist's Community

Mathias Rissi[24] has made a case for recognizing that the Prologue is based on two hymns; one underlying 1-13 and the other as the basis of 14-18. Both were hymns from the evangelist's community. Rissi observed that:

1. The form/style of the two sections differ;
2. The Baptist is introduced twice, once in each section, in 6ff. and 15;
3. The "incarnation" is mentioned twice, once in each section, in 11 and 14. The theory that the evangelist used and edited two hymns, treating them consecutively, to form the basis of his Prologue could explain these data. Together the two hymns provided a history of the revelation of the Word; the first concentrating on the creative Word and reaching a climax with the "incarnation" while the second was focused on the salvation event in the incarnation.

Rissi's theory would be more convincing if there were more agreement concerning the poetic form of 14-18. Because the poetic form breaks down here most scholars find evidence of the evangelist's editing. Rissi's theory rightly takes account of the concentration of non-Johannine vocabulary in this section. However it does not solve the problems of repetition, to which he drew attention. If the Baptist's witness was introduced into the hymns by the evangelist the two hymn theory does not explain why he introduced this *twice* in the Prologue and again in 19ff. In adapting the hymns for use in his Prologue there was no need for a double reference. This criticism is less applicable to the double reference to the incarnation because this is a consequence of the evangelist's retention of a reference to

---

[23]In verses 1-14c only ($\phi\omega\tau\acute{\iota}\zeta\epsilon\iota$) "enlightens" (9) is non-Johannine, found only in Revelation in the Johannine corpus, though "shines" ($\phi\alpha\acute{\iota}\nu\epsilon\iota$) (5) is also unusual used only in 5.35 of the Baptist but qualified to show the subordinate role of the Baptist; "dwelt" ($\acute{\epsilon}\sigma\kappa\acute{\eta}\nu\omega\sigma\epsilon\nu$) (14b). In 14d,e,16-18 there is a high concentration of non-Johannine terms: "full" ($\pi\lambda\acute{\eta}\rho\eta\varsigma$ 14e); "grace" ($\chi\acute{\alpha}\rho\iota\varsigma$ 14e,16,17); "grace and truth" ($\chi\acute{\alpha}\rho\iota\varsigma\kappa\alpha\acute{\iota}\ \acute{\alpha}\lambda\acute{\eta}\theta\epsilon\iota\alpha$ 14e,17); "fullness" ($\pi\lambda\eta\rho\acute{\omega}\mu\alpha\tau\sigma\varsigma$ 16); "declared" ($\acute{\epsilon}\xi\eta\gamma\acute{\eta}\sigma\alpha\tau\sigma$ 18). In addition there is the unusual (for Jn) "Jesus Christ" (16) found elsewhere only in 17.3 though common in 1 John; and "bosom" ($\kappa\acute{\sigma}\lambda\pi\sigma\nu$ 18) found elsewhere only in 13.23 which refers to the BD and is probably a redactional addition modelling the relation of the BD to Jesus on the relation of Jesus to the Father in the Prologue.

[24]M. Rissi, "Die Logoslieder im Prolog des 4 Evangeliums", *Th.Z.* (1975), 321-36, and "John 1.1-18 (The Eternal Word)", *Interpretation* 31 (1977), 394-401.

the incarnation in each hymn. However, the two hymn theory is faced with the problem of why the evangelist accentuated the dislocations which were a consequence of treating two hymns consecutively by introducing the witness of the Baptist into each of them. I also find it difficult to think that the proclamation of the incarnation in 14 was not the climactic conclusion to the hymn rather than the opening of a second hymn. The proclamation is in the form of a confession of faith. What follows (15-18) is not from the context of worship but from the context of polemics and is not poetic like 1-5. In the light of the criteria already discussed 15-18 should not be assigned to any hymn source.[25]

In the light of these difficulties an alternative theory is called for to account for the differences between 1-14c and 14d-18. That theory will need to give due weight to the recognition that 6-8,15 were added by the evangelist and of the polemical and non-poetic nature of 16-18, which contain a significant concentration of non-Johannine vocabulary.

3. A "Sectarian" Jewish Hymn in Praise of Sophia/Torah

Recognition of the poetic form suggests that the original hymn underlies 1-14c. From this the evangelist's additions must be excluded. On formal and theological grounds 3b appears as an addition. This suggests that the evangelist found it necessary to oppose some form of cosmological dualism. By consensus 6-8,15 were added by the evangelist and it seems to follow that 9 was also added by the evangelist to make the transition from the theme of the eternal $\lambda \acute{o} \gamma o s$ and to speak of the incarnate historical revealer, which was made necessary by the introduction of the Baptist in 6-8. Also to be removed are 12c-13, which are Johannine, see 3.3,5; 1 Jn 2.20,29; 3.1ff.,9ff.; 4.4,7; 5.1ff,18f. This separation is also supported on formal grounds. The christological use of $\lambda \acute{o} \gamma o s$ is Johannine (1 Jn 1.1 and see Rev. 19.13) as is the confession of the incarnation, 1 Jn 4.2; 2 Jn 7. Nevertheless the christological uses of $\lambda \acute{o} \gamma o s$ in 1.1 and 14 form an *inclusio* revealing the limits of the hymn.[26]

J. R. Harris and C. H. Dodd have shown the extensive parallels to the Prologue (especially 1-14) which can be found in the Wisdom literature.[27]

---

[25] See note 20 above.

[26] It is argued that the evangelist has substituted $\lambda \acute{o} \gamma o s$ for $\sigma o \phi \acute{\iota} a$ in the hymn. Thus the hymn was bounded by references to $\sigma o \phi \acute{\iota} a$.

[27] See Harris, *Origin*, 4ff., 10-19, and especially 43; and Dodd, *Interpretation*, 274f. Dodd lists parallels only to verses 1-14. The significance of the Wisdom literature is also discussed by Rudolf Bultmann in his 1923 article on the Prologue. Here, however, he already appeals to the older mythology isolated by Bousset and Reitzenstein which, he claims, underlies the fragmentary expressions of the myth in the Wisdom literature, the myth which, he argues, underlies the Prologue. Thus, while much of his

The first fourteen verses appear to be a patchwork of phrases in praise of Wisdom. On the basis of this observation Harris argued that the hymn upon which the Prologue was based was a Jewish hymn in praise of Wisdom and not the composition of the evangelist.[28] When the evangelist's editorial additions have been removed, including the restoration of Wisdom for the substituted λόγος, what remains is a Jewish hymn in praise of Wisdom. This observation, which was made by Harris in a cautious and qualified way, and without having removed the evangelist's additions, now appears convincing to me. A more comprehensive picture of the indebtedness of the Prologue to the Wisdom ideology can be grasped by looking at the broader contexts of the passages noted below where the reconstructed hymn with its parallels in the Wisdom literature is set out as follows:

The Prologue Hymn Source[29]	Wisdom Parallels
1 In the beginning was *Wisdom*	Prov 8.22-23; Wisd 6.22; Sir 24.9
And *Wisdom* was with *God*	Prov 8.23,30; Wisd 9.4,9
And *God* (divine) was *Wisdom*	
2 The same (She) was in the beginning with *God*	
3a All things through her *became* (ἐγένετο)	Prov 3.19; 8.30; Wisd 7.21-27; 8.1; 9.1-2; 1 QS X.11.
4 What *became* in her was *life*	Prov 3.18; 8.35
And the *life* was the *light* of men	Wisd 7.26; Prov 6.23; Test Levi 14.4; (Sir 17.11)
5 And the *light* in the *darkness* shines,	
And the darkness did not extinguish it (οὐ κατέλαβεν)	Wisd 7.29-30
10 In the *world* she was	Wisd 8.1; Sir 24.6
And the *world* through her became (ἐγένετο)	
And the *world* did not know her	Prov 1.29; Bar 3.23,28,31
11 Unto her *own* (τὰ ἴδια) she came,	
And her *own* (οἱ ἴδιοι) did not *receive* (οὐ παρέλαβον) her.	Sir 24.8-12; 1 Enoch 42.1-2

---

comparative analysis in relation to Wisdom is in agreement with the work of Rendel Harris, the argument of his essay is opposed to the position of Harris.

[28]"Our hypothesis that the Logos of the Fourth Gospel is a substitute for a previously existing Sophia involves (or almost involves) the consequence that the Prologue is a hymn in honour of Sophia, and that it need not be in that sense due to the same authorship as the Gospel itself." Harris, 6.

[29]The translation given here is over-literal in an attempt to bring out the parallelism of the original with the connecting word chains.

12a But as many as *received*(ἔλαβον) her,
12b She gave to them authority children of God
(τέκνα θεοῦ) to become (γενέσθαι),   Wisd 7.14,27; Sir 6.20-22;
15.7
14a/b And Wisdom tabernacled among us   Sir 24.8,10; (nb σκηνή); Wisd
(nb. ἐσκήνωσεν)   9.10; Bar 3.37; (cf. Prov 8.31)
14c and we beheld her glory.   (cf. Sir 24.23) Baruch 4.1

The original hymn praised Wisdom/Torah as God's agent in creation, in whom was light and life, but who was rejected by the world, and even by Israel as a whole. However, Wisdom/Torah was received by the few, the "wise" and the "holy", amongst whom Wisdom came to dwell (ἐσκήνωσεν), revealing her glory. The indomitable light of Wisdom is asserted by the οὐ κατέλαβεν of verse 5, while the rejection is asserted by οὐ παρέλαβον (verse 11), yet leaving room for limited acceptance ὅσοι δὲ ἔλαβον in verse 12. The play on words is characteristic of the source, κατέλαβεν, παρέλαβον, ἔλαβον. This theme was developed on the basis of the tradition of the *Shekinah* in relation to the Tabernacle and Temple and in the hymn it might well have indicated the rejection of the Jerusalem temple and constituted a rival claim. Thus the hymn manifests sectarian Jewish piety. The sectarian character of the community is indicated by the affirmation that Wisdom was rejected not only by the world (which was to be expected), but also by Israel. The community considered itself to be the "wise" and "holy", the children of Wisdom, and "the children of light", as Wisdom is the source of light, because Wisdom dwelt amongst them. Hence the world, and even Israel, was in darkness.

IV. A "HELLENIST" INTERPRETATION IN PRAISE OF SOPHIA/CHRIST

Recognition that 14d-18 is comment on the original hymn is based on its formal difference from the hymn and the Christian and anti-Jewish polemical character. Such polemical editing would be consistent with the evangelist but for three facts:

1. There is a concentration of non-Johannine vocabulary in 14e,16-18.
2. The evangelist's addition of 15 severs 14 from 16 where the "we" confession is continued, indicating that the evangelist was editing an existing text.
3. The Law/grace antithesis is not Johannine but Pauline, indicating that this editorial material was added in a "Hellenist" community where the Pauline antithesis was known and affirmed. That the community was strongly influenced by Paul suggests that it would have been dominantly Gentile in character.

The absence of the terminology of "grace" from the Johannine literature is notable.[30] Apart from verse 17 the Law/grace antithesis is known to us only in the Pauline literature in the New Testament. James shows awareness of the faith/works antithesis, but was opposed to it, which probably indicates an opposition to his understanding of Paul. Hence we must attribute the editing of the hymn to a "Hellenist" Christian community where the Pauline Law/grace antithesis was known and accepted. However, they did not make the cross central, as it was for Paul in his edition of the hymn of Phil. 2.6-11. Perhaps this suggests a Christian Wisdom tradition such as Paul encountered at Corinth.[31]

The "Hellenist" edition of the hymn added 14e,16-17 and identified Jesus Christ with Wisdom. Having picked up the confession of the glory of Wisdom this interpretation confessed it to be:

full of grace and truth. (14e)

Because of her fulness have we all received
and grace upon grace;
because the Law was given through Moses,
grace and truth came through Jesus Christ. (16-17)

As W. D. Davies argued, "Jesus in the totality of His teaching and of His person ... had not merely replaced the 'old Torah' but had assumed for Paul the significance of a 'New Torah'."[32] Given this identification, a hymn in praise of Wisdom/Torah was taken over and used in praise of Wisdom/Christ. This context throws light on and gives force to the contrast between the Law of Moses and the grace and truth of Jesus Christ in 1.17. Davies (177) went on to argue that this development in Pauline circles "illuminates for us both the origin and meaning of the cosmological significance that the Apostle ascribed to his Lord". This comment is applicable to the hypothesis that a "sectarian" Jewish hymn in praise of Wisdom in her role in creation and revelation was taken over and used as a hymn in praise of Jesus Christ. Whether this occurred in a community which was strictly Pauline or one that was "Hellenist" in a more general way it is difficult to say because Paul's relation to the "Hellenists" needs to be clarified.[33] The "Hellenists" appear in Acts 6.1ff. and the peculiar

---

[30]The use of χάρις in the form of a Hellenistic greeting as in 2 Jn 3 is no parallel. Compare Rev 1.4; 22.21.

[31]See my "Paul and the πνευματικοί at Corinth", in *Paul and Paulinism: Essays in honour of C. K. Barrett* , 237-50.

[32]*Paul and Rabbinic Judaism*, 147-76 and especially 177. According to 1 Cor 1.24 Christ is the Wisdom of God.

[33]Should Paul be understood against the background of Palestinian or diaspora Judaism? Does the background make any difference? Paul's relation to the "Hellenist" movement is suggested by his relation to the Church at

character of the movement could be manifest in Stephen's speech (Acts 7, with its criticism of the Temple) and the Epistle to the Hebrews.[34]

In its "Hellenist" form the hymn praised Christ as the Wisdom of God for his role in creation (1-5) and redemption (10-12b,14a-c,e,16) and went on polemically to contrast the grace of Christ with the Law of Moses (17). It recognized the revealing work of Wisdom, prior to the coming of the historical revealer as partly successful, 10-12b. The "dwelling" of Wisdom amongst them, with the subsequent revelation of glory,[35] is now understood in terms of the *appearance* of the historical revealer. There is no mention of his death. Through his appearance the Law of Moses has become obsolete. In this way the universal effectiveness of the revelation brought by Jesus Christ is stressed. If the revelation had previously enjoyed partial success, his coming now engendered an enthusiastic hope of complete success.[36] Whether that coming was thought to involve "becoming man" or merely the "taking of a body" as a disguise in the Gnostic sense (see *Gospel of Truth* 31.1ff.) it is not possible to say with certainty, though the latter is probable in the light of the evangelist's addition of σὰρξ ἐγένετο. If this tradition was not strictly docetic there was, at least, a tendency to ignore the significance of Jesus' earthly life and *death*. Already, when adding the Prologue, the evangelist recognized the necessity to stress the reality of Jesus' earthly life, though the seriousness of his conflict with the docetic tradition was not to become apparent until a later stage, provoking the Johannine Epistles. This reconstruction of the Hellenist interpretation of the hymn fits the interpretation of the crisis faced in 1 and 2 Jn as precipitated by the influence of Gentile believers in the Johannine community after their expulsion from the synagogue.[37]

Antioch which (according to Acts) arose from the dispersal of that movement.

[34] On the Hellenists in relation to John see Oscar Cullmann, *The Johannine Circle*; and on the relation of Hebrews to the Hellenists see Wm. Manson, *The Epistle to the Hebrews*.

[35] See Ernst Käsemann, *The Testament of Jesus*, 6, 10 13, 20, 22, 26f. I suggest that the "naive docetism" which Käsemann attributed to the evangelist might well have been true of the "Hellenist" editing of the Prologue. But the evangelist interpreted the revelation of glory in terms of self-giving love, involving the death of the revealer. See Margaret Pamment, "The Meaning of δόξα in the Fourth Gospel", *ZNW* 74 1/2 (1982), 12-16 and my *John*, 58.

[36] This attitude was probably encouraged also by the third version of the Farewell Discourse. See chapter 13,"The Farewell of the Messiah" below.

[37] See chapter 14, "The 'Opponents' in 1 John" below.

V. THE EVANGELIST'S INTERPRETATION

The evangelist has added 3b,6-8,12c-13,14d, 15, and 18. But more than this, he has replaced σοφία with λόγος and introduced the theme of the incarnation in 14a. Delbert Burkett[38] has objected to the treatment of Wisdom and Logos as interchangeable in the Prologue of John. In support of his case he notes that "Wisdom" is not used in the Gospel or Epistles and appeals to C. H. Dodd's view that the Wisdom literature provides no precedent for the Johannine assertion that "the Word was God". Burkett concludes that this "should warn against making an automatic jump from John's 'Word' to 'Wisdom'". This objection is facile:

1. No attempt is made by Burkett to provide a precedent in Jewish literature for the affirmation that "the Word was God".

2. The appeal to the views of C. H. Dodd concerning the lack of precedent for "the Word was God" in the Wisdom literature (see *Interpretation*, 275) is made ignoring the context of this assertion, coming as it does after the demonstration of the widespread Wisdom parallels to the Prologue, leading to the conclusion that "in composing the Prologue the author's mind was moving along lines similar to those followed by Jewish writers of the 'Wisdom' school".[39]

3. In some of the Wisdom parallels "Wisdom" and "Word" are interchanged; Wisdom 9.1-2,10; 18.15; Sir 24.1-3.

> Who madest all things by thy word; and by thy wisdom thou formedst man. (Wisdom 9.1-2)

In three passages first Wisdom, then Word and finally Wisdom again, are spoken of in royal terms in a way that suggests the overlapping use of the two terms:

> Send her (Wisdom) forth out of the holy heavens, and from the throne of thy glory bid her come,... (Wisdom 9.10)

> "Thine all powerful Word leaped from heaven out of the royal throne,... (Wisdom 18.15)

> I (Wisdom) came forth from the *mouth* of the Most High, and covered the earth as a mist. I dwelt in high places, and my throne is in the pillar of cloud. (Sir 24.3-4)

4). Both "Wisdom" and "Word" were used as synonyms for the Law in Jewish writings of the period.[40]

---

[38]*Son of Man*, 33.

[39]*Interpretation*, 274f.

[40]According to W. F. Albright (*From the Stone Age to Christianity*, .146, 285, 371ff.; *JBL* 60 (1941), 206-8), who drew on the work of L. Dürr, the view of the Word in Judaism "goes back to a dynamystic conception of third millenium BC. which makes the voice of God act as a distinct entity with

The evidence suggests that Jn changed "Wisdom" in the source hymn into "Word" (λόγος) in the Prologue[41] and where the hymn proclaimed the creation of all things the evangelist added:

and apart from him was made not one thing that was made. (3b)

Following the affirmation of the light of the eternal λόγος the evangelist prepares for the manifestation of the historical revealer by introducing the work of a witness:

A man appeared, sent from God, his name was John;
He came as a witness to bear witness concerning the light,
that all may believe through him.
He was not the light,
but (he came) to bear witness concerning the light. (6-8)

The evangelist then proclaimed the historic entry of the true light into the world:

The true light, which shines on every man,
was coming into the world. (9)

Where the hymn proclaimed that those who received Wisdom were given the authority to become children of God the evangelist added:

to those who believed in his name,
who were (born) not of bloods, nor the will of the flesh, nor the will of man but were born of God. (12c-13)

And the λόγος became flesh"(14a)

The hymn confessed the glory of Wisdom which the evangelist interpreted in terms of the incarnate λόγος:

glory as of the only begotten from the Father (14d).

With the announcement of the dwelling of Wisdom in the hymn the evangelist made explicit the announcement of the incarnation of the λόγος and this led to the reintroduction of the witness of the Baptist, this time reporting his words:

John bears witness concerning him and cried saying,
"This was he of whom I said,
The one coming after me has become before me,
because he was before me." (15)

Then at the end of the Hellenist contrast of Law and grace, Moses and Jesus Christ, the evangelist concludes his interpretation:

No one has ever seen God,
the only begotten God,

---

power of its own. In second Temple Judaism Wisdom came to overshadow Word." For reasons of his own Jn reasserts the tradition of Word.

[41]Consequently the hypothesis outlined here is not the object of Burkett's criticism because what is argued here is the overlap of meaning and use of σοφία and λόγος not their exact equivalence. Had the latter been the case there would have been no point in exchanging one term for the other.

who is in the bosom of the Father,
he has revealed (him). (18)

The evangelist's emphases in the Prologue can now be analysed.

1. Λόγος Christology

That it was the evangelist who modified a Wisdom christology is indicated
by the following observations. The first fourteen verses of the Prologue
are a patchwork of statements in praise of Wisdom. While the λόγος
christology is not found outside the Prologue in the Fourth Gospel,
making a *prima facie* case that it came to the evangelist in the source, this
is unlikely as we know of no such christology outside the Johannine
literature. We are familiar with Wisdom christology, especially in the
writings of Paul. Though 1 Jn 1.1ff. and Rev 19.13 do not provide exact
parallels for the λόγος christology of the Prologue, they do indicate that
we are dealing with a Johannine development. Perhaps of more importance
is the evangelist's treatment of Jesus' relation to his words in the body of
the Gospel. Jesus speaks the Word/words of God, to receive his words is
to receive him and to receive him is to receive the Father who sent him.
The Fourth Gospel as a whole has an implicit λόγος christology.[42]
Because of his relation to God, God is communicated in him and for this
reason he is the λόγος. It was crucial for Jn to use λόγος rather than
σοφία in the Prologue because he set the christology of the Gospel in
opposition to the Wisdom/*Torah* ideology of Judaism (Jn 1.17) and a
defective Wisdom christology. The use of λόγος expressed the theme of
revelation dynamically, drawing together a number of themes, thus uniting
the creative Word (Gen 1.1; Ps 33.6), the prophetic Word and the incarnate
Word who himself is the Word of God, speaks the Word of God and is
proclaimed in the preaching of the Church.[43]

2. Exclusion of Cosmic Dualism

The evangelist's addition of 3b suggests the need to exclude cosmic
dualism, a problem that might have been encouraged by the dualistic
language of the Gospel. Jn's assertion of the incarnation of the λόγος
against the background of 3b might indicate that a devaluation of the
material creation was one reason for the disregard of the human Jesus. The
addition of 3b reveals something of the Hellenists who transmitted the
hymn, being a response to their views.

3. The Witness of the Baptist

The threefold witness of the Baptist (6-8,15,19ff.) suggests that the

---

[42]See C. H. Dodd, *Interpretation*, 265-8 and my *JWT*, 26.
[43]See my *JWT*, 26-7.

Prologue was a late addition and that the Gospel originally began at 1.19ff. Some modifications to 1.19ff. were probably made to take account of the new beginning.[44] The natural place to introduce the witness of the Baptist is at verse 15. The reference at verses 6-8 raises questions, yet its position there is the work of the evangelist. Some answers can be discovered by paying attention to the way the Baptist is presented. In this presentation the characteristic Johannine terminology of witness is dominant. Through this theme the role of the Baptist, as it appears in the Synoptics, is transformed. In each of the three passages (1.6-8,15,19ff.) it is denied that the Baptist is the revealer and he admits his own subordinate role as a witness, giving Bultmann strong evidence for recognizing a polemic against those who confessed the Baptist as revealer.[45] Thus 6-8 was placed immediately following the first mention of the light (4-5) to deny that the Baptist is the light, 6-8. Such a denial, "he was not that light", makes sense only if there were those who claimed that he was.[46] In 6-8 the evangelist has intentionally contrasted what he says about the Baptist with what is said of the λόγος in 1-5 suggesting that the evangelist wrote 6-8 when he edited the hymn for the Prologue.

ἐν ἀρχῇ ἦν ὁ λόγος,	ἐγένετο ἄνθρωπος,
καὶ ὁ λόγος ἦν πρὸς τὸν θεόν,	ἀπεσταλμένος παρὰ θεοῦ,
καὶ ὁ θεὸς ἦν ὁ λόγος.	ὄνομα αὐτῷ Ἰωάννης·
οὗτος ἦν ἐν ἀρχῇ πρὸς τὸν θεόν.	οὗτος ἦλθεν εἰς μαρτυρίαν...,
πάντα δι᾽ αὐτοῦ ἐγένετο...	ἵνα πάντες πιστεύσωσιν δι᾽ αὐτοῦ.
ἐν αὐτῷ ζωὴ ἦν,	οὐκ ἦν ἐκεῖνος τὸ φῶς,
καὶ ἡ ζωὴ ἦν τὸ φῶς τῶν ἀνθρώπων·	ἀλλ᾽ ἵνα μαρτυρήσῃ περὶ τοῦ φωτός.
	Ἦν τὸ φῶς τὸ ἀληθινόν,
καὶ τὸ φῶς ἐν τῇ σκοτίᾳ φαίνει,	ὃ φωτίζει πάντα ἄνθρωπον,
καὶ ἡ σκοτία αὐτὸ οὐ κατέλαβεν.	ἐρχόμενον εἰς τὸν κόσμον.

Set out in this way the contrast between the two is clear:

i. The λόγος was in the beginning whereas John appeared (ἐγένετο). The verb ἐγένετο is also used of the creation (ἐγένετο) of all things by the λόγος. The λόγος is creator, John is creature.

ii. The λόγος was with God, John was a messenger from God.

---

[44]See J. A. T. Robinson, "The relation of the Prologue to the Gospel of St. John", *NTS* 9 (1962-63), 120-9; and B. Lindars, *The Gospel of John*, 82. The Prologue might well have been added about the same time as John 17.

[45]*The Gospel of John*, 17f. Bultmann refers to the earlier work (1898) of W. Baldensperger, *Der Prolog des vierten Evangeliums*.

[46]While the witness of the Baptist fits into the theme of witness in the Gospel, no other witness is defined negatively in the way the Baptist is; first by the narrator, he is not the light (1.8); then by himself, "I am not the Christ" (1.20).

iii. The λόγος is called God, the man is called John.

iv. The λόγος is creator, John is witness.

v. *All* things were made by the λόγος, *all* are to believe in the incarnate λόγος through the witness of John.

vi. The λόγος is the light, John is not the light but the witness to the light.

vii. Both passages characterize the light, it shines in the darkness; it shines on every person coming into the world.

viii. The consequences of the work of both the λόγος (light) and John are described as "not received/extinguished" and "that all may believe through him"

The contrast is too marked to be accidental/coincidental. Nevertheless the Baptist emerges as the foundational and ideal witness through whom all will believe.[47]

4. A Copernican Shift

It could be argued that the placing of the witness of the Baptist at 6ff. was solely for the purpose of denying that he was the light (1.8) mentioned in 4b-5. But the evangelist also added 9, which speaks of the coming of the historical revealer, and 12c-13 which deal with the faith which is a consequence of the revealer's coming. The consequence of these additions is that 1-5 speak of the work of the eternal λόγος prior to the coming of the historical revealer while 9ff. deals with the coming and work of the historical revealer. Certainly the use of the present tense φαίνει (1.4) indicates that the light of the eternal λόγος always shines in the darkness. However, the situation prior to the coming of the historical revealer is indicated by the aorist tense in the phrase καὶ ἡ σκοτία αὐτὸ οὐ κατέλαβεν (1.5). The statement probably has multiple meanings, indicating that the darkness did not extinguish the light, but neither did it receive or understand it. The appearance of the Baptist as the witness to the shining of the light in the historical revealer makes possible the coming of faith (1.6-8). The effect of placing the coming of the historical revealer immediately after this statement is to indicate that the revelation prior to his coming was totally unsuccessful. This is surprising in view of a more positive relation to the Old Testament in the Gospel, 5.45ff.; 8.56; 12.41, which seems to indicate some success for the revelation in that period. On the other hand the revealer says, "All who came before me were thieves and robbers", 10.8.

---

[47]The role of the ideal witness, outlined in principle in the Prologue, is set in the narrative context of the story of Jesus (see the discussion of Jn 1.19-34 in chapter 4 below) and assessed by Jesus (see the discussion of Jn 5.33-35 in chapter 5 below). There he also appears as an ideal believer.

Before the evangelist added 6-9 everything prior to 1.14 referred to the eternal shining of the light of Wisdom. Thus the Hellenist interpretation of the hymn recognized the limited success of the revelation prior to the coming of the historical revealer, 10-12b. The evangelist's rejection of that position is the more surprising in the light of his substitution of λόγος for σοφία. While the relation of λόγος/σοφία/Torah is not without precedent (see Wisdom 9.1-2; and the relation of Wisdom 9.10; 18.15; and Sirach 24.3-4) his use of λόγος is distinctively Johannine, introducing the theme of revelation[48] in antithesis to the Law. It is the theme of the self-revelation of God in his creative activity and in created reality.[49] Given this theme it is all the more paradoxical that the light should shine ineffectually in the darkness. Even the revelation in the historical revealer meets with only limited success, 9ff. though his *coming is* the divine response to the world of darkness which cannot comprehend the light of the eternal λόγος. The incarnate revealer brings effective revelation as the light *enters* the world in the form of the judgement of the world, calling forth faith and giving the believers the power to leave the darkness and come to the light, 3.19ff.; 9.39ff.

5. The Incarnation

Outside the Johannine literature there is no exact parallel to the incarnational language of verse 14. Paul comes close to it in Gal. 4.4.[50] In common with Jn and Hebrews he wrote of the sending of the pre-existent Son. But in place of "the Word became flesh" he wrote "born of a woman", γενόμενον for ἐγένετο and ἐκ γυναικός for σάρξ. There may be little difference in meaning between the two statements. But the evangelist's incarnational language was to become technical and the touchstone for the true faith amongst Johannine Christians, 1 Jn 4.1ff.; 2 Jn 7, and in due course, for the whole of Christendom. In the first century, however, both the christological use of λόγος[51] and the incarnational

---

[48] R. Bultmann, *John,* 32 n1 says that "the 'Logos doctrine' of the Prologue gives expression to the idea of revelation which dominates the whole Gospel". See also 35.

[49] For the evangelist the revelation is an expression of the self-giving love of God (3.16) for which the "Word" is a more adequate expression because of the identification of the speaker with his words, his self-revelation in his words.

[50] ἐξαπέστειλεν ὁ θεὸς τὸν υἱὸν αὐτοῦ, γενόμενον ἐκ γυναικός, γενόμενον ὑπὸ νόμον. In later confessions "born of a woman" becomes "born of the virgin Mary".

[51] No doubt the evangelist was aided by Jewish traditions about the Word (Genesis 1.1ff.; Psalm 33.6; Sirach 39.17; Wisdom 9.1; 4 Ezra 6.38ff.; Psalm 107.20; Wisdom 16.12). Thus it can be argued that the Prologue is

formula are distinctively Johannine. They were fashioned by the evangelist in his conflict with the synagogue and his docetic opponents and are not part of the tradition which he took over from his background in "sectarian" Judaism or from the "Hellenist" interpretation. By the time the Johannine Epistles were written the confession of the incarnation had become the crux in the fight against false belief within the community. That false belief might well represent a continuation of tendencies which were apparent in the "Hellenist" editing of the hymn and this might have provided the evangelist with additional reasons for replacing Wisdom with λόγος.[52]

6. Christology and the Cross

From this perspective it might appear that for the evangelist also the coming of the revealer was all that was necessary to break the power of darkness, at least for the few who become believers. Much depends on what the evangelist intended by inserting σάρξ ἐγένετο when he exchanged λόγος for σοφία. Did his understanding of "becoming flesh" involve the inevitability of death?[53] I suspect that it did. Further, in addition to references to the "unique sonship" of the revealer in 14d, 18b,[54] which are characteristically Johannine (see 3.16,18), the evangelist added ὁ ὢν εἰς τὸν κόλπον τοῦ πατρός which is written from the perspective of the revealer's return to be with God.[55] His relation with the Father is a return to the situation with which the Prologue began,[56] see 17.5,11,13f. The use of κόλπῳ in 13.23 confirms that this is a Johannine addition and probably indicates that the evangelist intends to portray the relation of the

---

constructed on the basis of the Jewish Word tradition (see J. Sanders, *The New Testament Christological Hymns*, 43-57). Sanders draws on the work of Lorenz Dürr and Helmer Ringgren but overlooks the way the Prologue is made up of a patchwork of statements in praise of Wisdom. While Wisdom and Word can be identified (Wisdom 9.1) it was the evangelist who chose to use λόγος to express the self-revelation of God in his creating and revealing activity.

[52]See chapter 13, "The Farewell of the Messiah" below.

[53]There is a pervasive tradition that understands "flesh" predominantly in terms of the inevitability of death and corruption, Isa 40.6.

[54]An alternative reading of 18b is "only begotten God" (μονογενὴς θεός) which has strong textual support and might be original. Just as it is said "The λόγος was God" (1.1) now it is affirmed that the "only begotten" (Son implied) is God. Son is not only implied by the use of "only begotten" but also by the relation to "the Father" in both 14 and 18. It could be that "Son" has been introduced into the text by a scribe because of 3.16,18. If so, it is not a misleading gloss.

[55]Contrary to the thesis of F. J. Moloney, *The Johannine Son of Man* and my review in *ABR* 25 (1977), 43f.

[56]The same "exaltation" perspective is given in the saying in John 3.13.

BD to Jesus on the basis of the model of Jesus' relation to the Father and this analogy is extended to the disciples as a whole, see 17.20-23; 20.21. Thus from the evangelist's point of view the Prologue is written from the perspective of the departure or exaltation of the revealer and this finds expression in 18c. This perspective is also presupposed in 12c-13. In Johannine terms to be born of God is to be born of the Spirit and the coming of the Spirit is a consequence of the departure of the revealer. The believers who are born of God were designated $\tau\acute{\epsilon}\kappa\nu\alpha$ $\theta\epsilon o\hat{\upsilon}$ in the source. It was probably for this reason that the evangelist *twice* added $\mu o\nu o\gamma\epsilon\nu\acute{\eta}s$ in 14d and 18b, and also used $\upsilon\acute{\iota}\acute{o}s$ (see 3.16,18) to make clear the unique nature of Jesus' sonship. This might suggest that there was a tendency (by those who supported the Hellenist version of the hymn) to understand that the revealer and the believers stood in the same relation to God. The evangelist's distinction makes clear that this is not the case by speaking of believers as $\tau\acute{\epsilon}\kappa\nu\alpha$ $\theta\epsilon o\hat{\upsilon}$ and Jesus as $\acute{o}$ $\mu o\nu o\gamma\epsilon\nu\acute{\eta}s$ $\upsilon\acute{\iota}\acute{o}s$ and by making the revealer the intermediary between God and believers.

7. John's Witness Again

John's witness now interrupts the the confession of the believing community to the activity of the $\lambda\acute{o}\gamma os$. His witness is in the imperfect tense ($o\hat{\upsilon}\tau os$ $\mathring{\eta}\nu$, indicating that the perspective is retrospective in the light of the cross/exaltation, not from the context of Jesus' ministry, which is true of the later reference ($o\hat{\upsilon}\tau os$ $\acute{\epsilon}\sigma\tau\iota\nu$) in 1.30.[57] The words of John affirm that his disciple ($\acute{o}$ $\acute{o}\pi\acute{\iota}\sigma\omega$ $\mu o\upsilon$ $\acute{\epsilon}\rho\chi\acute{o}\mu\epsilon\nu os$) has taken precedence over him ($\acute{\epsilon}\mu\pi\rho o\sigma\theta\epsilon\nu$ $\mu o\upsilon$ $\gamma\acute{\epsilon}\gamma o\nu\epsilon\nu$). No doubt the evangelist uses the words of John (the Baptist) to legitimate what otherwise might have been seen as a leadership challenge. The legitimating reason given by John himself is $\acute{o}\tau\iota$ $\pi\rho\hat{\omega}\tau os$ $\mu o\upsilon$ $\mathring{\eta}\nu$. In this way the Baptist is made a witness to the incarnation of the eternal $\lambda\acute{o}\gamma os$ in Jesus.

8. The Unique Revealer

That the evangelist concludes the Prologue on a polemical note suggests that with it we encounter a problem contemporary with his interpretation of the hymn. The affirmation that no one has ever seen God has support in both Jewish tradition and Greek thought. On the other hand there was also

---

[57]In both 1.15 ($o\hat{\upsilon}\tau os$ $\mathring{\eta}\nu$ $\acute{o}\nu$ $\epsilon\hat{\iota}\pi o\nu$) and 1.30 ($o\hat{\upsilon}\tau\acute{o}s$ $\acute{\epsilon}\sigma\tau\iota\nu$ $\acute{\upsilon}\pi\grave{\epsilon}\rho$ $o\hat{\upsilon}$ $\acute{\epsilon}\gamma\grave{\omega}$ $\epsilon\hat{\iota}\pi o\nu$) there is reference back to an earlier occasion upon which this saying was made. While 1.30 refers back to 1.15 (allowing for a variation of wording, $\acute{\epsilon}\rho\chi\epsilon\tau\alpha\iota$ $\acute{\alpha}\nu\acute{\eta}\rho$ for $\acute{o}...\acute{\epsilon}\rho\chi\acute{o}\mu\epsilon\nu os$ in 1.15) there is no earlier saying to which 1.15 could refer. This suggests that it has been modelled on 1.30 and may refer back to the witness referred to in 1.6-8 though the words are not reported there. The use of $o\hat{\upsilon}\tau os$ $\mathring{\eta}\nu$ in 1.15 implies a post resurrection/glorification perspective.

the tradition that Moses had seen God. Given the antithesis of Law and grace it could be thought that it is this tradition that is opposed by the evangelist.[58] While it is likely that a Jewish tradition is opposed, given the lateness of the Prologue and the place of 1.18 in it, this was probably developed by the Hellenist Christians who understood their own relation to God to be analogous to the relation of Jesus to God. Against this position the evangelist affirmed that Jesus is the unique revealer of God and the intermediary between God and believers. Hence Jn affirms that the believers' relation to Jesus is analogous to Jesus' relation to God (the Father).

VI. CONCLUSION

Whatever source the evangelist might have used, the Prologue now stands as the introduction to his Gospel. By designating God, in his creative role, as the λόγος the evangelist gives expression to his understanding of God as "the God who speaks" in his works, as the God who reveals himself in all that he does. The evangelist asserts (3b) that "all things", without exception, have their being through the creative Word of God, excluding any thought of cosmological dualism. Paradoxically the world that exists through the λόγος is in darkness and, though the λόγος is the light for men, the light which always shines, the world of darkness did not receive or understand the light. Neither could it extinguish it. There is no attempt to explain the origin of the darkness but it constitutes an essential element of the evangelist's *Weltanschauung* which is the framework within which his antithetical/dualistic language operates. In all probability it is also a clue to the social factors shaping the evangelist's view of reality.

The announcement of the failure of the light of the eternal λόγος is the dramatic signal for the proclamation of the appearance of the historical revealer. The witness who proclaims his appearance is named John, a man sent from God, whose witness is contrasted with the light of the eternal λόγος. Though the light of the eternal λόγος was not received, in fact it has always shone in judgement upon every man. The entry of the λόγος into the world marked a new stage in the history of the revelation. Rejected by the world at large, and even by his own people (the Jews) in general, at his coming he was received by a few who came to believe in him. Given that this picture of the believers is the picture of a marginalized group we rightly call it sectarian. Through faith they received the gift of the life of the children of God, realized through the power of the

---

[58] It may be that 1.18 opposes the same tradition that is opposed in 3.13, "No one has ascended into heaven except the one who descended from heaven, the Son of Man".

Spirit of God.

The new possibility of eternal life is understood to have come about through the incarnation of the eternal λόγος. His coming made possible the revelation of the glory of God as Father in his Son, and that glory is confessed by believers. Paradoxically that glory is revealed in the cross in which the self-giving love of God as Father was seen. The cross is implied by the flesh assumed by the λόγος and the perspective of the exaltation which is assumed by John the Baptist (15) and the evangelist's conclusion (18). In this way the reader is reminded that the cross is an event in which the eternal λόγος was active, an event seen in opposition to the Law of Moses in which Jesus, the unique Son of the Father, is proclaimed as the revealer of God, who is confessed in the light of his exaltation and return to the Father.

The Johannine form of the Prologue raises important questions. What led the evangelist to characterize the world as darkness providing a context for the antithesis of light and darkness which dominates the Gospel? While the Wisdom literature provides the linguistic and conceptual resources made use of in the Prologue and there is in this literature a tradition of the rejection of Wisdom, except by the "few", there is no precedent here for the portrayal of the world dominated by the darkness. The evidence of Qumran is important here as is the Gnostic portrayal of the world of darkness. But John did not surrender his understanding of creation by the λόγος. Nevertheless he has taken over the understanding of the world of darkness from the source and radicalized the power of darkness by asserting its domination until the coming of the historical revealer. Even with his coming the world lies in the power of darkness and only a few believers leave the darkness for the light.

Cosmological speculation was a popular form for the proclamation of a message.[59] In the Prologue the cosmology provides the necessary framework for proclaiming the pre-existence of the revealer whose revealing work could only be grasped in and through an understanding of his coming and going, his descent and ascent. In spite of the strong teaching about the creation of all things by the λόγος the Prologue provides an explicitly dualistic *Weltanschauung*. It is extraordinary that Jn gave expression to the christology of the incarnation of the λόγος in this dualistic framework though his attitude to the world of darkness is intelligible in the context of the conflict with the synagogue which had, by the time the Prologue was added, hardened into an antagonistic separation.[60] Nor had the Johannine

---

[59]See Poimandres Tractate; 1 QS III.13–IV.26; Hebrews 1; Colossians 1.

[60]This could provide a context for the evangelist's change of attitude concerning the *effectiveness* of the revelation prior to the appearance of the

community found the relation to the Gentile world to be any more comfortable. Thus, for the evangelist, the believers are seen as a small point of light in the world of darkness.

The Johannine Prologue is an unusual introduction to the quest for the Messiah and provides a fundamental dimension of the christology of the Gospel. The starting point is not the messianic expectations of Judaism before 70 CE, as it is in Jn 1.19-51 and much of the rest of the Gospel. Rather the Prologue assumes the conflict between those who affirm that the Law is the Wisdom of God and those who proclaim Jesus as the Wisdom of God, and the evangelist's interpretation in the Prologue belongs to the period subsequent to the breach with the synagogue. Consequently attention is not focused on the affirmation that Jesus is the Messiah. The issues that emerge concern a correct christology in the context of a debate between rival positions amongst those who believe in Jesus. Both groups had progressed beyond messianic views to distinctive Christian christologies. The evangelist opposed a christology that did not take the humanity of Jesus seriously and did not sufficiently distinguish Jesus from those who were children of God by faith. In this context Jn affirmed the unique incarnation of the λόγος in Jesus and the revelation of God in and through him alone.

The Prologue provides the *Weltanschauung* within which the Johannine story in its finished form finally makes sense. The view set out is broadly apocalyptic.[61] The world is God's creation, created by his Word as a means of communicating his revelation. "Created by the *Logos*" is a way of indicating the intended purpose or function of the creation. Paradoxically the world is dominated by the darkness and, although the light of the eternal creative λόγος has always shone in it, the darkness has persisted and dominated the world. The dualistic language of Jn, especially the light/darkness antithesis, confirms that this problem persists *throughout the Gospel story*.

From this perspective it is surprising that, at least at a superficial reading, the Prologue can be read as if it taught that the incarnation of the λόγος was by itself the sufficient action of God to break the power of darkness and shed abroad the light of the λόγος. Everything seems to lead

---

incarnate revealer. Previously Israel and the Old Testament were viewed as evidence of the light shining in the darkness. But in the Prologue the light of the eternal *Logos* is not received, οὐ κατέλαβεν. The evangelist's interpretation of his source in John 1.10-12 is consistent with this. Those who received the revealer are the believers, in response to his historic incarnation/appearance.

[61] See my "Theology, Eschatology and the Prologue of John" in *SJT* 46 (1993), 27–42 for a more detailed treatment.

up to the triumphant confession, "and we beheld his glory". Everything now appears to signal that the light of the incarnate λόγος will dispel the darkness. Such optimism might have characterized the hymn used by Jn. But the evangelist has modified the hymn, introducing the entry of the incarnate λόγος, heralded by the Baptist (1.6-8) at 1.9. Thus the reader who understands the changes made by Jn knows that even the incarnate revealer was rejected by the majority and received by only a few. This can only mean that the incarnation is not the final act in the story because even after his coming the conflict with the darkness remains unresolved. The Prologue does not explicitly deal with the ongoing story though there are intimations of what is to come.

In the story itself Jesus confronts the prevailing darkness and the signs he performs are another aspect of his onslaught on the darkness. The healing of the man born blind in Jn 9 is a particularly important sign dealing with the confrontation of the darkness by the light, 9.39-41 and cf. 3.19-21.[62] In spite of the signs the power of darkness continues to hold sway in the world and the arrest/trial/crucifixion of Jesus can be seen as a triumph of the power of darkness.[63] But in Jn the dominant emphasis on these events is in terms of the lifting up/glorification of the Son of Man/himself, signifying that through this event "the prince of this world" will be cast out, 12.31. It is the event through which the revelation is completed and Jesus returns to the Father/is exalted to heaven and sends, as a consequence, the Spirit of Truth/Paraclete to believers.

While the Prologue leads the reader to expect that the coming of Jesus as the incarnate λόγος would dispel the darkness, there are intimations in the reference to the flesh that the incarnate λόγος is man born to die and the perspective of the exaltation is assumed in reference to the one who is "in the bosom of the Father", an exaltation perspective that is also assumed in the notion of those who are born of God, which in Jn's terms is born of the Spirit. When the coming and going of Jesus was complete then it seems that the real shift in the balance of power would take place.

The failure of the shift to eventuate would have been one crisis through which the Johannine community had to travel. Dealing with this problem

---

[62]See chapter 8, "The Son of Man : The Light of the World" below.

[63]In Lk 22.53 Jesus interprets his arrest in these terms, "This is your hour and the power of darkness". Those who arrest him are aligned with the power of darkness. The language is Johannine-like but the perspective is different because Jn perceives this event as another moment in the triumph of the light over the darkness. Yet even in Jn there is the acknowledgement that in the totality of the event that constitutes the exaltation/glorification there is a moment in which the light is withdrawn and this is the time of the power of darkness, 9.4-5; 12.35-36.

is at the heart of the development of the Farewell Discourses. There, as in a few other places in Jn, future eschatological expectations surface. These are not relics or fossils from some source. They are essential elements of Jn's point of view. The conflict with the darkness remains unresolved even if some progress has been made through the coming and going of Jesus with its consequences. The dualistic framework presupposes resolution in the future.

4

Quest Stories in John 1–4

The purpose of this chapter[1] is to relate work done on pronouncement stories in the Synoptic tradition to the study of the Gospel of Jn and to introduce the theme of the quest for the Messiah. When Vincent Taylor[2] coined the term "pronouncement story" he was building on the pioneering work of Martin Dibelius and Rudolf Bultmann who used the terms *paradigm* and *apophthegm*. More recently the *genre* has been related to the *chreia* discussed by ancient scholars. Taylor's descriptive title has the advantage of drawing attention to the way a pronouncement gives climactic focus to a story which has been told for the sake of that pronouncement. Yet it should be noted that such stories are closely related to others without a distinctive pronouncement in Greek literature. Earlier work on the Gospels was concerned with the history of the forms of the oral (pre-Gospel) tradition. More recently the *SBL* work group on *Pronouncement Stories* has produced a set of studies, edited by Robert C. Tannehill,[3] which takes the rhetorical function of the stories to be the key issue. From this perspective it is recognized that the stories might have been shaped at various stages of the transmission of the tradition both oral and written.[4]

The Synoptic pronouncement stories are similar to the *chreiai*[5] of the Graeco-Roman biographies and rhetorical texts,[6] here illustrated by the following examples:[7]

> (i) Once when Diogenes was having lunch in the marketplace and invited him to lunch, Plato said, Diogenes, how charming your unpretentiousness would be, if it were not so pretentious." (85)

---

[1]Which incorporates three papers now published in *JSNT* 36 (1989) 17-46; *JSNT* 41 (1991) 33-70; and *John and the Synoptics,* Leuven (1992), 498-506.
[2]*The Formation of the Gospel Tradition.*
[3]*Pronouncement Stories, Semeia* 20 (1981). This volume also provides bibliographical details of other essays on the subject.
[4]See R. Tannehill, point 0.2 on 102.
[5]A *chreia* can be described as the account of a significant saying or action set in a specific context.
[6]See Plutarch's *Lives* and *Moralia*; the *Lives* of Diogenes Laertius; Philostratus, *The Life of Apollonius of Tyana*; as well as the *Progymnasmata* of Theon of Alexandria.
[7]The following examples of *chreiai* are from R. F. Hock and E. N. O'Neil (eds), *The Chreia in Ancient Rhetoric*: vol. 1, *The Progymnasmata* (Texts and Translations 27)

(ii) Diogenes, on seeing a youth misbehaving, beat the paedagogus and said, "Why were you teaching such things?" (175)

(iii) Alexander the Macedonian king stood over Diogenes as he slept and said, "To sleep all night ill-suits a counsellor." And Diogenes responded, "On whom the folk rely, whose cares are many." (87)

Similar brief *chreiai* appear in the Synoptics:

(i) Now after John was arrested Jesus came into Galilee preaching the gospel of God and saying, "The time is fulfilled, the kingdom of God is at hand; repent, and believe the gospel." (Mk 1.14-15)

(ii) And passing by the Sea of Galilee he (Jesus) saw Simon and Andrew casting a net in the sea; for they were fishermen. And Jesus said to them, "Follow me and I will make you fishers of men." (Mk 1.16-17)

(iii) And the multitude asked him (John the Baptist), "What then shall we do?" And he answered them, "He who has two coats, let him share with him who has none; and he who has food, let him do likewise." (Lk 3.10-11)

Tannehill has analysed pronouncement stories into six sub-types, "correction", "commendation", "objection", "quest", "inquiry", and "description" stories as well as hybrids which have mixed the "types".[8] His analysis draws attention to the fact that the stories have two parts, the setting and the pronouncement response. Emphasis is laid on the interaction between the two parts, noting that the name relates more directly to one part than the other. Thus the names "correction" and "commendation" relate directly to the pronouncement while "inquiry" and "quest" relate directly to the setting. But the interaction between the two parts means that each part is appropriately formed in relation to the other. Thus the names are appropriate to the whole story, setting and response.

In this chapter we are concerned with only two types of pronouncement story, the "quest" story and "inquiry" story. In the following chapter we will be concerned with "rejection" stories. "Rejection" is preferred to "objection" because this more adequately describes the Johannine story where objection inevitably leads to rejection and better fits the place of these stories in the structure of the Gospel.[9] Both objection and correction

---

[8]*Pronouncement Stories*, 1–11.

[9]Chapters 5–12 deal with the conflict provoked by the coming of the revelation. That conflict can be expressed in terms of the encounter of the light with the darkness where the darkness is understood to be in mortal combat with the light. It is not possible that there should be peaceful co-existence. Naturally this is foreshadowed in chapters 1–4 (especially 1.5,10; 3.19-21). But the actual rejection of Jesus finds expression first in

are essential elements in the Johannine quest stories, though these objections are raised by Jesus and not by his opponents, as in rejection stories.[10] Objections or obstacles are characteristically raised concerning the quest and corrections are made to the quester's approach in order to show that, if the quest is to be fulfilled, it will be in a way quite different from that envisaged. This is part of the evangelist's strategy of modifying the quester's (and also the reader's) christology.

That it was the evangelist who shaped the tradition into quest and rejection stories is to be seen by the way he has reshaped traditional call stories into quest stories (1.35-2.11); a rejection story into a quest story (2.13-22); a pair of miracles into a quest story (6.1-35) and has modified his own quest story into a rejection story (6.1-71). Jn 3.1-15, which is, at this point, an unfulfilled quest story, appears to be based on a traditional quest story, the only unfulfilled quest story in the Synoptics (Mk 10.17-22).[11] In 4.46-54 a quest story has been formed from a miracle story, which might have been a traditional miracle quest story. The quest story of 12.20-(26)36 could well be a Johannine formulation of unfulfilled quest while at the same time foreshadowing universal fulfilment.

In the Synoptics pronouncement stories are concentrated in Mk and especially Lk. Relative absence of these stories from Jewish literature of the period as well as other early Christian and Gnostic literature is significant. It is in the Greek literature concerning the philosophers and politicians that significant examples are found.[12] Pronouncement stories are an expression of the rhetoric of persuasion related to the literary milieu of Graeco-Roman biography. The pronouncement stories inform us of the evangelist's rhetorical intentions and, as examples of a more widespread literary phenomenon, they draw attention to the struggle between conflicting values in the ancient world. The evangelist was intent to persuade and produce attitudinal shifts by means other than straight rational argument, appealing instead to the will and imagination.[13]

5.16,18. It is this rejection which dominates chapters 5–12 and leads to the crucifixion of Jesus.

[10] In the rejection stories a position opposed to Jesus is brought into confrontation with him. The action of the story does nothing to change the position of the opponent. Its purpose is to justify the alienation of the reader because of the action taken by those represented by the opponent(s).

[11] In Jn the story remains "open" rather than reaching a negative result, as it does in Mk. The evangelist takes up this story again in later scenes in the Gospel. Hence it is better to describe the result as "open".

[12] Tannehill, 9, 103, 111.

[13] Tannehill, 9-10, 111-4.

I. INQUIRY STORIES IN JOHN AND THE SYNOPTICS

Many of the Synoptic pronouncement stories are lengthy and our study is concerned to elucidate Jn's deployment of the quest story *genre* in writing his Gospel. Closely related to the quest story (though there are important differences) is the inquiry story, which is quite common in the *Lives* and in the Gospels. Here the inquiry and answer remain central and the outcome for the inquirers is irrelevant. The following inquiry stories come from Philostratus, *The Life of Apollonius of Tyana* I.37 and Plutarch's *Moralia* 6.504A.

> When the king asked him (Apollonius) how he could rule with stability and security, he said, "Honouring many but trusting few".

> And when a certain man at Athens was entertaining envoys from the king, at their earnest request he made every effort to gather the philosophers to meet them; and while the rest took part in general conversation and made their contribution to it, but Zeno kept silent, the strangers, pledging courteously, said, "And what are we to tell the king about you, Zeno?" "Nothing," said he. "except that there is an old man at Athens who can hold his tongue at a drinking party."

The first of these shows how brief an inquiry story can be. There are some brief Synoptic inquiry stories which move in the direction of quest stories. The first of these is Lk 3.10-11, which is Synoptic *chreia* (iii) above. The way an inquiry story may function almost as a quest story is important for our study of Jn.[14] In this Gospel there is a rich fund of quest stories to be added to the meagre supply from the *Lives* and the Synoptic Gospels. Before looking at these it will be useful to see how the evangelist has used a group of inquiries to build up expectation of the quest for the Messiah. Here he was building on traditional material.

The quest for the Messiah in Jn 1.19-51 can be seen in relation to a complex of traditions now found in Lk. In Jn elements from traditions concerning the questioning of the Baptist (Jn 1.19-25 and Lk 3.10-15),[15]

---

[14]Though the distinction is artificial because it was not recognized by ancient scholars, it is their practice that has enabled modern scholars to analyze the material in this way. It would be wrong, however, to regard the distinction as absolute.

[15]The Lukan parallels are used because Lk 3.10-15 is peculiar to Lk and Jn follows Matt and Lk in separating the two parts of the Markan saying about the two baptisms (Mk 1.7-8 and Lk 3.16). Because Lk 3.10-15 is adjacent to the preaching of the Baptist, which is common to Matt and Lk (Q), and the saying about the two baptisms is split in the same way by Matt and Lk (against Mk), it could be that all of this material was derived from Q and that Jn has some relation to the tradition in this source. The alternative

the quotation of Isa 40.3 (Jn 1.23 and Lk 3.4), the Baptist's witness to the coming one (Jn 1.26-27,33 and Lk 3.16), the descent of the Spirit and the declaration of the voice at the baptism of Jesus (Jn 1.32-34 and Lk 3.22), and the quest/call of the disciples (Jn 1.35-51 and Lk 5.1-11,27-32; 6.14a)[16] have been taken up in distinctive Johannine fashion. Distinctive to Jn is the way the Baptist himself bears witness, identifying himself as "the voice crying in the wilderness" (Jn 1.23), describing the descent and abiding of the Spirit on Jesus as the sign revealing the coming one (Jn 1.32-33) and declaring "This is the Son of God" (Jn 1.34). The narrator and the voice from heaven make these proclamations in the Synoptics.[17]

The questioning of the Baptist in Lk is presented as a series of "inquiry" stories which move in the direction of "quest" stories. In what follows it is argued that Jn has used tradition known to us in Lk 3.10-14; and 3.4 (Jn 1.19-23) and Lk 3.15-16,22 (Jn 1.24-27) to form a doublet of inquiry stories. The tradition is then reused in two further scenes[18] to portray the Baptist himself as a quester and to identify the coming one (Jn 1.29-34), thus creating a link between Jesus and the Baptist's questing disciples (Jn 1.35ff.). Though much of the tradition drawn on by Jn is known to us only in Lk, it is proximate to Q material and was probably known to Lk in Q. While generally following the Lukan narrative, agreements in detail with Matt or Mk against Lk suggest the possibility of a Mk Q overlap and Jn's knowledge of Q. Agreement in wording is not close and we are dealing with scenes that are likely to have been transmitted in variant

---

appears to be the evangelist's free use of Matt, Mk and Lk. The likelihood of this hypothesis depends on perceived modes of composition and the comparative dating of the four Gospels.

[16]Evidence of contact with the Synoptic tradition in Jn 1.35-51 is sparse. This would be consistent with Jn's use of Q, from which accounts of the call of the disciples might have been largely absent.

[17]Jn is closer to Matt ("this is my beloved Son") than Mk or Lk ("you are my beloved Son"). This could be a case of Mk Q overlap where Mt has followed Q while Lk has followed Mk. That the Baptist (in Jn 1.34) should use the 3rd person "This" rather than "You" is strange because there is no audience but Jesus in 1.29-34. It could be that the audience in 1.29-34 is the reader(s). But the idiom of address is normally determined by the audience *within* the text except where the *narrator* addresses the reader directly.

[18]Lk 3.16a ("I baptize you with water") is used in Jn 1.26a and again in 1.31,33. Lk 3.16b ("he comes..") is used in Jn 1.27 and again in 1.30 (cf. Jn 1.15). Distinctive Johannine sayings are repeated ("Behold the lamb of God") Jn 1.29,35; and ("And I did not know him...") 1.31,33. In 1.31 the purpose of John's baptism is stated as if it were his own initiative ("For this reason I came...") but 1.33 makes clear that his mission was initiated by another.

traditions. Consequently it is more likely that Jn has integrated Synoptic-like inquiry stories into his theme of the quest for the Messiah. The importance of the Synoptic parallels at this point is that they show that Jn was working with tradition.

Each of the following sections examines two scenes. 1. The Lukan inquiry stories; 2. Jn's inquiry stories; 3. Reworking the tradition of the inquiry stories.

1. The Lukan Inquiry Stories (Lk 3.10-16)

The stories are in two scenes. The first scene is made up of a set of three questions asked separately by three groups of questioners. These questions lead up to the second scene where a single question is asked by all. This signals a movement to the climactic question the answer to which enables the Baptist to announce "the coming one".

Scene one: the inquiry concerning "salvation" (3.10-14)

First questioners:

> And the multitude asked him (John the Baptist), "What then shall
> we do?" And he answered them, "He who has two coats, let him
> share with him who has none; and he who has food, let him do
> likewise." (Lk 3.10-11)

The inquiry of the multitude expresses the quest for "salvation" and the answer of the Baptist constitutes an obstacle to be overcome, though it is a direct answer to the question. But the evangelist does not (as is essential to the quest story *genre*) tell us the outcome of the inquiry. Without any indication of the outcome the focus falls on the content of the inquiry and the evangelist moves on to the inquiry of the next group.

Second questioners:

> Tax collectors also came to be baptized, and said to him (the
> Baptist), "Teacher, what shall we do?" And he said to them,
> "Collect no more than is appointed you." (Lk 3.12-13)

Again the inquiry concerns "salvation" and there is, in the answer, a stated obstacle to be overcome. But there is no stated outcome, only a move to yet another group.

Third questioners:

> Soldiers also asked him, "And we, what shall we do?" And he said
> to them, "Rob no one by violence or by false accusation, and be
> content with your wages." (Lk 3.14)

This accumulation of inquirers (all asking, "What shall we do?") gives the impression of a great ferment amongst the people generally (the multitude, tax collectors, soldiers), expressing a widespread quest for "salvation" and this, as we shall see, is bound up with the quest for the Messiah.

Scene two: the inquiry concerning the Christ (3.15-16)

As the people were in expectation, and all men questioned in their
hearts concerning John, whether perhaps he were the Christ. (Lk
3.15, cf. Acts 13.25)

The various groups are no longer the specific focus. Rather Lk now
reveals the hidden, underlying question of all.[19] Though the inquiry as to
whether the Baptist was the Christ was "in their hearts", the Baptist
responded contrasting his own form of baptism with the baptism of the
coming one.

"I baptize you with water; but he who is mightier than I is coming,
the thong of whose sandals I am not worthy to untie; he will
baptize you with the Holy Spirit and with fire." (Lk 3.16)[20]

This response is picked up in a similar inquiry context in Jn 1.26-27.

2. The Johannine Inquiry Stories (Jn 1.19-27)

While the groups of inquirers and the wording of the inquiries are quite
different from Lk, Jn and Lk each has two inquiry scenes followed by the
common use of traditional material in the same order. Jn's use of Isa 40.3
is in an order and context different from each of the Synoptics but in an
inquiry context which Jn shares with Lk. This material now enables the
evangelist to portray the beginning of the activity of the first believer and
original and ideal witness, whose work is narrated in a series of five scenes
over three days.[21]

The first *two scenes* are portrayed on the *first day* of the sequence:

Scene one: the inquiry, "Who are you?" (1.19-23)

And this is the witness of John when the Jews of Jerusalem sent to
him priests and levites to ask him, "Who are you?" And he
confessed and did not deny, and he confessed, "I am not the Christ."

---

[19]Lk 3.15 might bear the marks of Lukan redaction but the question of
whether the Baptist was the Christ appears to have been derived from
tradition (cf. Acts 13.25). The suggestion that Lk 3.10-14 are also
redactional is not persuasive unless all material peculiar to Lk is attributed
to Lukan redaction. Jn's relationship to tradition here is suggested by
common theme and the inquiry story *genre*, not by specific agreements with
Lk's wording.

[20]The preaching of the Baptist continues (Lk 3.17-18=Matt 3.12) though no
outcome is indicated.

[21]In the fifth scene centre stage passes from the witness to the subject of
the witness and that transition is marked by the movement of two of the
disciples of the Baptist to become the first disciples of Jesus. Two further
scenes follow in this sequence. Thus the story exhibits two forms of
sequence, narrative sequence marked by scenes and temporal sequence marked
by days and signalled by τῇ ἐπαύριον (1.29,35,43) and τῇ ἡμέρᾳ τῇ τρίτῃ
(2.1).

And they asked him, "What therefore?' are you Elias?" And he said,
"I am not." "Are you the prophet?" And he answered, "No."
Therefore they said to him, "Who are you? That we may give an
answer to those who sent us; what do you say concerning yourself?"
He said, "I am a voice crying in the wilderness; make straight the
way of the Lord, as said the prophet Isaiah." (Jn 1.19-23)

This scene involves a series of inquiries similar in function to those of Lk
3.10-14 except that the inquiries are all made by the same group (a formal
delegation from the Jews of Jerusalem) and the inquiries concern the
identity of the Baptist (cf. Lk 3.15) not the way of salvation as in Lk
3.10-14. Consequently the Baptist's responses in Lk 3.10-14 cannot be
used and because the response to Lk's second inquiry scene (Lk 3.16) is
used in Jn's second inquiry scene (Jn 1.26-27) a new response must be
found. The quotation of Isa 40.3 (Lk 3.4) is an impressive
pronouncement, now used in a new order and on the lips of the Baptist,
providing an answer to the repeated question of Jn 1.19,22, "Who are
you?" The Baptist's opening denial, "I am not the Christ", indicates that
the initial question, "Who are you?" is understood to mean, "Are you the
Christ?" (cf. Lk 3.15). Following the negative answers to the questions as
to whether he is Elijah or the prophet the delegation repeats the question,
"Who are you?" and the Baptist identifies himself with "the voice" of Isa
40.3. In all four Gospels this quotation is used in relation to the Baptist
in almost identical wording.[22] Only Jn places the quotation on the lips of

---

[22]Only the use of $\epsilon \dot{\upsilon} \theta \dot{\upsilon} \nu \alpha \tau \epsilon$ instead of $\dot{\epsilon} \tau o \iota \mu \dot{\alpha} \sigma \alpha \tau \epsilon$ distinguishes the
common wording of Jn from the Synoptics. But Jn does not have the
parallel clause, *"make straight his paths"*. In the Synoptics the quotation
formula naming Isa the prophet is given before the quotation. It follows
the quotation in Jn. In Mk the narrator quotes Isa before introducing the
Baptist. There the Isa quotation follows Mal 3.1 although the quotation
formula mentions only Isa. In Matt and Lk the Isa quotation is not
combined with Mal, though this quotation is used elsewhere (Matt 11.10
and Lk 7.27) with identical quotation formula ($O \dot{\upsilon} \tau \dot{o} s \dot{\epsilon} \sigma \tau \iota \nu \pi \epsilon \rho \dot{\iota} o \dot{\upsilon}$
$\gamma \dot{\epsilon} \gamma \rho \alpha \pi \tau \alpha \iota$), suggesting the separate use of the quotation was derived from
Q. Lk, like Mk, has the narrator quote from Isa. In Mt it could be part of
the Baptist's preaching because the quotation carries on from the summary
quotation of his preaching, though it probably should be understood as the
narrator's comment on that summary. In Jn the quotation was certainly
made by the Baptist who identified himself with the voice, $\dot{\epsilon} \gamma \dot{\omega} \phi \omega \nu \dot{\eta}$
$\beta o \hat{\omega} \nu \tau o s \dot{\epsilon} \nu \tau \hat{\eta} \dot{\epsilon} \rho \dot{\eta} \mu \omega$. Jn's quotation formula, like Mk's, begins with $\kappa \alpha \theta \dot{\omega} s$,
but differs from each of the Synoptics in minor ways for the rest.

the Baptist in response to the question, "Who are you?"[23] Nothing in his witness so far identifies the sought for Christ.

Scene two: the inquiry, "Why do you baptize?" (1.24-27)

This constitutes a second scene, the first with priests and levites (1.19-23) and the second with the inquirers freshly introduced as of or from the Pharisees (1.24-27).[24] It continues in order to link the Baptist's negative witness (1.19-23) to a more positive witness to the coming one (Jesus),[25] and make explicit the questioners' assumption that the Baptist's activity implied that he was the Christ, Elijah, or the prophet.

The question "Why do you baptize?" is a more appropriate introduction to the saying concerning the two baptisms than the first question,"Who are you?" which is Jn's equivalent to the inquiry of Lk 3.15 which there is the basis of the saying about baptism in Lk 3.16 for which Jn has developed the specific question, "Why do you baptize?", Jn 1.25. To this question the Baptist responds:

> "I baptize in (with) water: he stands in the midst of you whom you
> do not know, the one who comes after me, of whom I am not
> worthy to loose the strap of his sandal." (Jn 1.26-27)[26]

But these words do not explicitly answer the question "Why do you baptize?" (1.25) For this we must wait until 1.31.

The Baptist's response (1.26-27), found in the second of the Lukan inquiries (3.15-16), is used in each of the Synoptics. In Mk there are two distinct sayings, first about the coming one (Mk 1.7), the second concerning the two baptisms (Mk 1.8). In Matt 3.11 and Lk 3.16 the

---

[23]This involves the amplification. "*I am* the voice..." It may be this that encourages Jn to have the Baptist proclaim, "This is the Son of God", which the voice from heaven proclaims (with slight variation) in the Synoptics.

[24]The inquirers here are closer to the Pharisees and Sadducees of Matt 3.7 than the crowds of Lk 3.10-15. Given that Jn assumes that the two groups are the same, this involves an identification of the Jews of Jerusalem with the Pharisees.

[25]C.H. Dodd perceptively notes that 1.19-34 falls into two parts which correspond to the negative and positive clauses of 1.8 in the Prologue. *Historical Tradition in the Fourth Gospel*, 251. Thus the story now gives substance to the in principle statements of the Prologue.

[26]See chapter 7, "The Hidden Messiah in John 7-8" below. Especially relevant is Justin's dialogue with Trypho where Trypho says, "Even if the Messiah is already born and in existence somewhere, he is nevertheless unknown; even he himself does not know about himself, nor does he have any kind of power until Elijah comes and anoints him and reveals him to all." (*Dial* 8.4; cf. 110.1) Though John the Baptist denies that he is Elijah (in Jn), he fulfils the role of Elijah as set out by Justin.

saying about the coming one is inserted between the sayings concerning the two baptisms, suggesting a Mk/Q overlap.[27] Jn also splits the saying concerning the two baptisms suggesting that he knew it in a form similar to that of Q. The second part of the saying is held back until the next day (1.33). Thus all of the material between Jn 1.26 and 33 is framed by the two parts of the saying, "I baptize...this is the one who baptizes..."[28] Jn inserted a good deal more between the two parts of the saying than do Matt and Lk in order to make the first part a response to the inquiry of 1.25 and to bind scenes two (1.24-27), three (1.29-31) and four (1.32-34) together. The second scene concludes after the Baptist has spoken only of his own baptism and the presence of the disciple more worthy than his master. As in Lk 3.10-16, the inquirers simply vanish without trace leaving the focus on the inquiries and revealing to the reader the widespread quest for the Messiah as the context into which Jesus, who has not yet appeared, is about to be introduced. Jn 1.28 is a characteristic concluding summary (like 2.11 and 4.54):

---

[27]That Matt and Lk preserve Q material here is confirmed by their common variations and additional (to Mk) common account of the preaching of the Baptist. In the saying about the baptism of the coming one both add "and fire" and this is followed by a common characterization of the ministry of the coming one, Matt 3.12; Lk 3.17.

[28]The wording of the opening frame, ($\dot{\epsilon}\gamma\grave{\omega}$ $\beta\alpha\pi\tau\acute{\iota}\zeta\omega$ $\dot{\epsilon}\nu$ $\ddot{\upsilon}\delta\alpha\tau\iota$) is closer to Matt than Mk or Lk though there are minor variations between all four Gospels. Following this Jn alone adds, "In the midst of you stands [one] whom you do not know", giving expression to the theme of the hidden Messiah. See chapter 7, "The Hidden Messiah in John 7-8" below. What follows (1.27) is common to the Synoptics but is sometimes closer to Matt or to Mk or Lk.

*$\dot{o}$ $\dot{o}\pi\acute{\iota}\sigma\omega$ $\mu o\upsilon$ $\dot{\epsilon}\rho\chi\acute{o}\mu\epsilon\nu o\varsigma$ is as in Matt, apart from the absence of $\delta\epsilon$ from Jn. Only Lk does not have $\dot{o}\pi\acute{\iota}\sigma\omega$ $\mu o\upsilon$. Very likely the idiom, "coming after" denotes being a disciple.

*Like the Synoptics Jn has $o\dot{\upsilon}$ $o\dot{\upsilon}\kappa$ $\epsilon\dot{\iota}\mu\iota$, though $\dot{\epsilon}\gamma\grave{\omega}$ is added for emphasis.

*Jn uses $\ddot{\iota}\nu\alpha$ $\lambda\acute{\upsilon}\sigma\omega$ for $\lambda\hat{\upsilon}\sigma\alpha\iota$ in Mk and Lk/Acts and $\beta\alpha\sigma\tau\acute{\alpha}\sigma\alpha\iota$ in Mt.

*Like Mk and Lk, Jn has $\tau\grave{o}\nu$ $\dot{\iota}\mu\acute{\alpha}\nu\tau\alpha$, but preceded, not followed, by $\alpha\dot{\upsilon}\tau o\hat{\upsilon}$.

*The relation of Jn to Acts 13.25 in contrast to the Synoptics suggests that at points Lk follows Mk in the Gospel and Q in Acts and that Jn follows an independently transmitted Q tradition. See C.H. Dodd, *Tradition*, 253-4.

+In neither Jn nor Acts 13.25 does the Baptist say of the coming one "he is stronger than me". Contrast Matt 3.11=Mk 1.7=Lk 3.16.

+Jn and Acts 13.25 have $\dot{\alpha}\xi\iota o\varsigma$ (cf. C.H. Dodd, *Tradition*,255-6) for $\dot{\iota}\kappa\alpha\nu\grave{o}\varsigma$ in the Synoptics.

+Jn and Acts 13.25 use the singular though Jn has the genitive (not accusative) singular $\tauo\hat{\upsilon}$ $\dot{\upsilon}\pi o\delta\acute{\eta}\mu\alpha\tau o\varsigma$, not the genitive plural ($\tau\hat{\omega}\nu$ $\dot{\upsilon}\pi o\delta\eta\mu\acute{\alpha}\tau\omega\nu$) as in Mk and Lk or the accusative plural ($\tau\grave{\alpha}$ $\dot{\upsilon}\pi o\delta\acute{\eta}\mu\alpha\tau\alpha$) as in Matt.

"These things took place in Bethany beyond Jordan, where John was baptizing."

3. Reworking the Tradition from the Inquiry Stories
Scenes three and *four* are portrayed on the *second day.*

Scene three: the purpose of the water baptism (1.29-31)
In spite of the concluding summary of 1.28 the reader soon discovers that the sequence of events has not yet concluded. This is signalled by time references linking days together (1.29,35,43; 2.1 and cf. 6.22; 12.12)[29] and other linking material.[30] The use and reuse of traditional material is a Johannine characteristic which is evident in scenes 3 and 4.[31] A distinctive Johannine saying from the third scene (1.29, "Behold the lamb of God who takes away the sin of the world") is repeated in summary form in the fifth scene (1.36), connecting the events of the third day to the second. Twice the Baptist says, "And I did not know him" (1.31,33) connecting scenes three and four (1.29-31 and 1.32-34). Jn 1.29-31 continues to interpret the Baptist's role, "I baptize with water". Jn 1.31 now gives a specific answer to the inquiry of 1.25, thus linking scenes two and three, though there is now no sign of those who asked "Why do you baptize?" The answer is, "But because of this I came baptizing with water (see 1.26) that he might be revealed to Israel" (see 1.7). The Baptist's role was to identify the coming one. Not only is his preaching exclusively interpreted as witness to Jesus, it is specifically asserted that his activity of baptizing with water has this same purpose. Consequently scenes two and three (1.24-27 and 29-31), which contain references to the first half of the saying ("I baptize with water" 1.26), and its reiteration (1.31) definitively interpret the role of the Baptist. His mission was to reveal the coming one (the Messiah for whom all are searching) to Israel.

Scene four: the identity of the Spirit baptizer (1.32-34)
The narrator then (1.32) interjects to introduce the witness of the Baptist, although he was the speaker in 1.31, thus signalling a fourth scene. The focus now turns from the baptism of John to the coming one. Tradition concerning the baptism of Jesus underlies the narrative, though the baptism

---

[29]Contrast time notes separating events (2.12; 3.22; 4.43; 5.1; 6.1; 7.1; 21.1).

[30]Jn 1.29 leads to an inexact reference back (1.30) to a saying from the previous day (1.27), modified in the direction of the Prologue (1.15), and with other minor variations. "This was..." of the Prologue becomes "This is...", the simple accusative $\delta\nu$ becomes $\upsilon\pi\grave{\epsilon}\rho\ o\tilde{\upsilon}$ and $\grave{\epsilon}\gamma\acute{\omega}$ is added. $\acute{o}...\grave{\epsilon}\rho\chi\acute{o}\mu\epsilon\nu o\varsigma$ has become $\grave{\epsilon}\rho\chi\epsilon\tau\alpha\iota\ \grave{\alpha}\nu\grave{\eta}\rho\ \delta\varsigma$. $\grave{\epsilon}\rho\chi\epsilon\tau\alpha\iota$ is used in Mk 1.7=Lk 3.16.

[31]See note 18 above.

itself is not mentioned.[32] The Baptist speaks of the event as he witnessed it:

> "I have seen the Spirit descending as a dove from heaven and it remained upon him". (1.32; Lk 3.22).

In the repetition, "And I did not know him" (1.31,33), the Baptist signals the disclosure of the sign to reveal the coming one:

> "But he who sent me to baptize with water said to me, 'Upon whomsoever you see the Spirit descending and remaining, this is the one who baptizes with the Holy Spirit.'"[33]

This formally closes the contrast, "I baptize...he is the one baptizing..." (1.26,33), binding the intervening witness into a unity, although it takes place in three scenes over the course of two days.

In the Synoptics the narrator simply describes the descent of the Spirit.[34] In Jn the event is first narrated by the Baptist who then speaks of it as a sign foretold by God. This double account in the space of three verses makes a strong emphasis.[35] The point is to identify the one who baptizes with (the) Holy Spirit. Reference by the Baptist to his own water baptism is made subservient to the revelation of the one baptizing with (the) Holy Spirit (1.33). Then the Baptist affirms, "I have seen and borne witness, 'This is the Son of God'" (1.34) thus fulfilling the role of the voice from heaven in the Synoptics (see 1.23 and Isa 40.3). There the voice proclaims Jesus to be "my beloved Son", though Matt is closer to Jn in that the voice addresses Jesus in Mk and Lk but speaks about him in Matt and Jn, "This is..."

---

[32]It is a moot point whether this has been suppressed or is assumed.

[33]The common word order in Matt and Lk (against Mk) and the addition of καὶ πυρί suggests a Mk-Q overlap.

[34]In Matt 3.16=Mk 1.10 it is not clear whether the subject of "he saw" (εἶδεν) is Jesus or the Baptist. Jn may have interpreted such tradition as referring to the Baptist and turned the narrative into a first person account using τεθέαμαι for εἶδεν. τὸ πνεῦμα καταβαῖνον ὡς περιστεράν, apart from word order, agrees with Mk. To this Jn has added ἐξ οὐρανοῦ, probably from the reference to the voice from heaven (Lk 3.22. Matt and Mk have the plural with article τῶν οὐρανῶν) which he has replaced by the voice of the Baptist (Jn 1.34). Jn adds the reference to the Spirit abiding and, against Mk who uses εἰς, Jn like Matt and Lk (Q) uses ἐπ'.

[35]Variations in Jn's two accounts appear to be coincidental. The variation of ἔμεινεν and μένον is simply a change appropriate to narration and prediction and the use of ὡς περιστερὰν ἐξ οὐρανοῦ in the first is assumed in the second. Repetition may take the form of a summary because the reader needs no more to recall the meaning, see Jn 1.29,36.

4. Conclusion

That Jn has made use of tradition in constructing these scenes is clear but differences from each of the Synoptics in Jn and the probability of variant traditions suggest that he was making use of Synoptic-like tradition (Q?). What is clear is that the evangelist has systematically developed the fragments of tradition that we are able to isolate, developing from these a sequence of scenes in which the fragments of tradition are used and reused. The scenes are skilfully constructed to portray the theme of the quest for the Messiah. Each scene makes its own specific contribution to the overall theme. The opening inquiries make the reader aware that the quest for the Messiah is a live issue and by the last scene the Messiah has been identified and found.

Just as 1.19-23 has a doublet in 1.24-27, so 1.29-31 has 1.32-34. These double scenes have been created by the evangelist. While they make use of common material, there is a different focus in each scene. In the first sequence (1.19-27) the focus moves from the question (a) "Who are you?" (19-23) to (b) "Why do you baptize?" (24-27). In the second sequence (1.29-34) the focus moves from (a) the purpose or function of the water baptism revealing the coming one (29-31), to (b) the actual revelation of the one who baptizes with the Spirit, the Son of God (32-34). This sequence of scenes bears witness to the artistic and dramatic qualities of so much of the Gospel. The sequence has been constructed carefully to carry the plot forward while introducing and developing a variety of important themes. The opening scene reveals a ferment of expectation concerning the coming Messiah. In the second and third scenes it becomes clear that the Baptist himself was a seeker. The sign given to him enabled him to recognize and identify the coming one. This he does in the fourth scene. Then, in the fifth scene that follows on the third day of the sequence (1.35ff), the Baptist identified the coming one for two of his own disciples who were seeking him also, as is evident from the repeated refrain, "We have found..." (1.41,45).

The witness of John was given in response to a series of inquiries (1.19-27) which tend to express quest. Because the inquiries are made by a formal delegation from Jerusalem there is possibly a sinister note conveying a sense of "inquisition". The trial has already begun and John (the Baptist) is the first witness to be called. In this instance the witness is himself on trial. Through his witness it becomes clear that "they have got the wrong man". Consequently the inquiry serves a double purpose. It introduces the characteristic opponents of Jesus (the Jews from Jerusalem/Pharisees) while at the same time announcing the theme of the quest for the Messiah.

To read a note of hostility into the text at this point could be a mistake arising from re-reading the Gospel in the light of the hostile role in which the Jews/Pharisees will ultimately emerge. It is perhaps more likely at this stage that Jn is suggesting that the Jews of Jerusalem, priests, levites/Pharisees, were also in quest of the Messiah. In the course of the story these groups would be divided by their response to Jesus and in due course the Jews emerge as Jesus' implacable opponents. Even though Jn's use of "the Jews" has been shaped by his experience of rejection by the synagogue, it is a term that he has projected back into the story of Jesus where his use of it must take on board the complex responses to Jesus required by the telling of the story. Consequently we should expect a variety of meanings and even development in its use in the progress of the story. From this perspective we can review the delegation from the Jews in Jerusalem.

Coming to John (the Baptist) was an expression of the widespread quest for the Messiah which provided John with the opportunity of bearing witness to "the coming one", first to the priests and levites/Pharisees (1.19-28) and then, the next day, in the presence of Jesus (1.29-34). Finally (1.35-37), John's witness of 1.29-34 is repeated in summary form for the sake of two of his disciples.[36] In this way the response of John to the inquiry of whether he was the Christ has been extended to form five distinct but related scenes over the course of three days.

In each scene John is present as the witness. His words of witness, initiated by inquiry, overlap the scenes on each day so that an element of the witness from the first day (1.19-28) is repeated on the second (1.29-34); and an element from the second on the third (1.35-37). The audience on each day is different: the embassy from Jerusalem in the first; no stated audience except Jesus in the second; and the two disciples in the third. Given that no audience is specified on the second day the focus falls on the content of the witness and it is here that the fullest form of the words is given. Because there is no audience the words of the Baptist are addressed directly to the reader (see 1.15f.) and function like words of the narrator. At the same time the witness is himself revealed as one in quest of the Messiah, looking for the sign that would reveal him (1.31-34). The first scene functions to demonstrate the widespread quest for the Messiah, a theme which explicitly appears again in Jn 4.25,29. But no outcome of any quest is indicated. The scene is preparatory, providing a context for the third day on which the quest of the disciples is portrayed and the outcome of that quest is clearly narrated. The outcome, the gathering of a group of disciples, is a crucial element in the development of the story.

---

[36]The summary repetition (1.36) presupposes the full statement of 1.29-34.

Thus the scene on the third day demonstrates the quest of the disciples for the Messiah and the witness of the Baptist is given in summary form only so that the emphasis falls on the quest. The episodes on the three days commence with inquiry and conclude with a witness who enables two others to fulfil their quest for the Messiah. In turn this leads on to a series of quest and fulfilment episodes.

II. QUEST STORIES

Tannehill notes that, although quest stories are common in the Synoptics, they are not common elsewhere. Reference should be made, however, to the quest stories in Jn of which there are perhaps eleven. Further, while the self-contained quest story, as a type of pronouncement story, might not be common outside the Gospels, the theme of the quest is quite common and is prominent in works like Apuleius, *Metamorphoses*. Consequently we need to be aware of the influence of the theme of the quest even where the pronouncement story form is not present. The approach of this chapter gives precedence to discrete quest stories in the Gospel while noting evidence of the wider influence of the quest theme which has deeply influenced the narrative structure of the Gospel.

The anatomy of the quest story can be set out as follows:

1. A quester approaches with an implied or explicit request for help;
2. The quest dominates the story, holding the episodes together;
3. The quester is important and not a mere foil for Jesus as the opponent frequently is in objection/rejection stories;
4. The quest story is longer than other pronouncement stories because there are difficulties that must be overcome. These difficulties or objections are important because it is by means of them that the storyteller may wish to change the audience's attitudes. This is certainly true of the quest story of Jn 6, see especially 6.27,32.
5. The quest story, unlike the traditional story of Jn 6, focuses attention on the quest of the *individual* and emphasizes the need for individual response, 6.35. Though Jesus was speaking to the crowd he called for individual response, "the one who comes to me...the one who believes in me..." This accentuates the way the corporate quest has been reinterpreted in individual terms. The stress on the individual might well be intended by Tannehill when he says, "The story concerns a person in quest of something important to human well-being".[37]
6. In Jn what is important to human well-being at a physical level becomes the symbol of well-being at a spiritual level, see 4.10; 6.27. The quest is transformed by redirection from ordinary water and bread to

---

[37]*Pronouncement Stories*, 9.

life-giving water and bread, indeed, bread from heaven. It is fundamental to John's symbolic discourse that the material world, with its sources of life, cannot satisfy the human quest for life though it can and does point beyond itself to the transcendent source of all life.

7. The pronouncement by Jesus holds the key to the resolution of the quest, see 6.35;

8. The result of the quest is indicated, see 6.36.[38]

This chapter concentrates on the quest stories of Jn 1–4. It seeks to be precise in identifying quest stories while recognizing their relation to the extensive development of the quest theme for which the structure of Jn 1.19–4.54 is significant. The evangelist has developed quest stories from traditional material and has structured 1.19–4.54 on the theme of the quest. According to Tannehill quest stories are common in the Synoptics, but are rarely found elsewhere. There are nine quest stories in the Synoptics of which eight are to be found in Lk and four of these are found in Lk alone.[39] Only four quest stories were found in the Graeco-Roman Lives. Three were found in the *Lives* of Diogenes Laertius:

(i.) Someone wanted to study philosophy under him. Diogenes gave him a tuna to carry and told him to follow him. And when for shame the man threw it away and departed, some time later on meeting him, he (Diogenes) laughed and said, "The friendship between you and me was broken for a tuna." (6.36)

(ii.) A second similar unfulfilled quest story follows in which a cheese is substituted for a tuna. (6.36)

(iii.) She (Hipparchia) fell in love with the discourse and life of Crates, and would not pay attention to any of her suitors, their wealth, their high birth or their beauty. But to her Crates was everything. She used even to threaten her parents she would make away with herself, unless she were given in marriage to him. Crates was therefore implored by her parents to dissuade the girl, and did all he could, and at last, failing to persuade her, got up, took off his clothes before her face and said, "This is the bridegroom, here are his possessions; make your choice accordingly; for you will be no helpmeet of mine, unless you share my pursuits." The girl chose

---

[38]In his review of the first edition of *Quest* K. Grayston wrote *"Quest* corresponds to the frequent Johannine use of *zetein" (Epworth Review* [May 1993], 111). This totally ignores the literary analysis of the quest story and partially ignores the thematic complex of "following", "seeking" and "finding" which signals quest in Jn.

[39]See Mk 2.1-12=Matt 9.1-8=Lk 5.17-26; Mk 7.24-30=Matt,15.21-28; Mk 10.17-31=Matt 19.16-30=Lk 18.18-30; Mk 12.28-34=Matt 22.34-40=Lk 10.25-28; Matt 8.5-13=Lk 7.1-10; Lk 7.36-50; 17.12-19; 19.1-10; 23.39-43.

and, adopting the same dress, went about with her husband... (6.96-97)

There is another quest story in Plutarch's *Moralia*:

(iv.) For this reason they usually appoint as priest rather old men. By exception, only a few years ago, a young man, not at all bad, but ambitious, who was in love with a girl, gained the office. At first he was able to control himself, and succeeded in keeping out of her way; but when she suddenly came in upon him as he was resting after drinking and dancing, he did the forbidden thing. Frightened and perturbed in consequence, he resorted at once to the oracle and asked the god about his sin, whether there were any way to obtain forgiveness or to expiate it; and he received this response: "All things that must be doth the god condone". (5.403F-404A)

The quest story is longer than the other pronouncement stories[40] because a difficulty is posed for the quester and this must be overcome if the quest is to be successful. The success or failure of the quest must also be indicated. The distinction between the brief self-contained story and the extended development of the motif might well provide evidence of the difference between the story as a unit of oral tradition and the creative use of the theme in more extensive written works.[41] Consequently we need to be aware of the influence of the theme of the quest even where the concise and discrete pronouncement story form is absent.

1. From Call to Quest Stories

The evangelist has transformed the traditional stories of the "call" of the disciples into a series of episodes (not discrete quest stories) expressing quest (Jn 1.19-51). I take the Synoptic call stories as a good indication of the form in which the tradition came to Jn.[42] The evangelist's modifications are the clue to his interpretation even if he has retained one episode (1.43) as a call story. Here I take a view different from that of J. L. Martyn,[43] who thinks that the source contained a series of episodes moving from traditional expectation to discovered fulfilment and that this was modified by the evangelist. Martyn's case rests on the "first" ($\pi\rho\hat{\omega}\tau o\nu$) of 1.41, which is not followed by any obvious "second", and the difficulties of 1.43. He argues that, because it is said that Andrew *first*

---

[40]This is evident in the Synoptic quest stories. See, for example, Mk 2.1-12.

[41]See Apuleius, *Metamorphoses*.

[42]See Mk 1.16-20; 2.13-17; 3.13-19 and Lk 5.1-11.27-32; 6.14a. Because Synoptic-like tradition underlies Jn 1.19-34 it is likely that Jn has transformed "call" stories in 1.35-51.

[43]"We have found Elijah", in *The Gospel of John in Christian History*, 29-54.

finds Peter, it is implied that he next finds someone else. Originally this followed in the source (1.43). The sequence was disrupted when the evangelist introduced the travel narrative, "On the next day he wished to go out into Galilee".

Following R. E. Brown, Martyn thinks that, because the evangelist would hardly have bothered to remark that Andrew (or Peter)[44] wished to depart into Galilee, this must apply to Jesus although he is not mentioned by name until after the third verb in the verse (καὶ λέγει ὁ Ἰησοῦς). Thus (according to Martyn) it is Jesus who wished to depart into Galilee. The awkwardness of 1.43 is taken by Martyn to indicate that the evangelist was here editing his source which portrayed a passive Jesus. Andrew first found Peter and said, "We have found the Messiah". He (or Peter) then found Philip and said, "We have found Elijah". Philip found Nathanael and said, "We have found the one of whom Moses and the prophets wrote". It follows (according to Martyn) that the evangelist was responsible for transforming the scene with Philip into a call story, making Jesus the one who finds Philip (1.43). This change has two consequences:

> it alters the otherwise remarkably passive portrait of Jesus, showing him in *this* instance to take the initiative in finding a disciple; and it breaks the chain of witness-discovery so fundamental to the source's christological trajectory, which arches from traditional expectations to discovered fulfilment... – there are passages elsewhere in the Gospel which would seem to indicate considerable reservations on the part of the evangelist towards precisely the source's traditional christological trajectory.(49)[45]

---

[44]Given that Peter is mentioned at the end of 1.42 he could be the subject of the verb "he finds" at the beginning of 1.43. Alternatively Andrew, who first found Peter (1.41) may next find Philip. That Jn notes that these three come from Bethsaida (1.44) makes either suggestion plausible. Other less likely possibilities are that it was the second unnamed disciple (1.40) who found Philip, or that Philip was the second disciple and that Jesus found him *again*, or that Jesus found Philip for the first time in 1.43. Given that Jesus is introduced only in the second half of 1.43 as the one who told Philip to follow it is unlikely that he is the subject of the first half of the verse. See F. Neirynck, "The Anonymous Disciple in John 1", *Ephemerides Theologicae Lovanienses* LXVI/1 (April 1990), 7-12.

[45]Martyn refers to 5.14; 6.44, 65; 9.35; 15.16, all of which stress the initiative of God or Jesus. But all of these references fall outside the *inclusio* on the theme of the quest (1.19–4.54). The emphasis on the necessity of the divine initiative falls in those sections dealing with the rejection of Jesus. The example dealt with in some detail by Martin (6.44) occurs after the transformation of the quest story (6.1-35) into a rejection story (6.36-40). See chapter 6, "The Messiah and the Bread of Life" below.

It would seem, however, that, having decided to edit the verse for other reasons, the evangelist was happy also to seize the opportunity to reveal the gracious line which finds its beginning not in traditional expectation, but rather in God's sovereign election through Jesus Christ. (51)

The evangelist also rejected the identification of Jesus with Elijah, which he had found in the source. Martyn finds evidence for this identification in the underlying source in that John (the Baptist) denies that he is the Christ, Elijah or the prophet (1.19-21,25) and the disciples affirm "We have found the Messiah" (1.41) and "We have found the one of whom the law and prophets wrote" (1.45).[46] Hence only the identification of Jesus with Elijah is lacking. This is supplied by an ingenious attempt to reconstruct the source underlying 1.43.[47]

Certainly Martyn has identified real problems in the text. But it is doubtful that they can be overcome in the way suggested. If, for theological reasons, the evangelist transformed 1.43 into a "call" story, why did he not transform the other episodes also?[48] While Martyn argues that this transformation was a consequence of the introduction of the travel narrative and, in a sense, accidental, he also argues that the evangelist wished to *correct* the theology of the source.

Other problems in Jn 1 cast doubt on Martyn's hypothesis. John's denial, "I am not the Christ" ($X\rho\iota\sigma\tau\acute{o}\varsigma$, 1.20,25) and Andrew's affirmation, "We have found the Messiah" ($M\epsilon\sigma\sigma\acute{\iota}\alpha\nu$), to which an interpretative note is added (1.41), form a strange sequence. Are we to think that, in the source, John (the Baptist) used $X\rho\iota\sigma\tau\acute{o}\nu$ while Andrew used $M\epsilon\sigma\sigma\acute{\iota}\alpha\nu$? Logically we would expect the author of the source to have used $M\epsilon\sigma\sigma\acute{\iota}\alpha\nu$ with the explanatory note in the first instance of use. If the evangelist were to replace $M\epsilon\sigma\sigma\acute{\iota}\alpha\nu$ with $X\rho\iota\sigma\tau\acute{o}\nu$ we would expect him to do so consistently, either by noting he was doing so on the first occasion, in the manner of 1.41, or simply by straightforward replacement.

---

[46]Martyn (44 n75) thinks that the reference to the prophets (1.45b) might have been added to the source by the evangelist, to "round out the picture" but without specific reference to Elijah. He took the reference to the one of whom Moses wrote to be "the prophet".

[47]Martyn thinks that 1.43 originally contained the confession, "We have found Elijah".

[48]Robert Fortna, *Predecessor,* 6-10, 56 especially n119, argues that the evangelist's respect for his source (or awareness that his readers respected it?) influenced him to retain the source in its entirety and virtually unchanged. Yet Fortna and Martyn show that the evangelist has radically transformed the source, both formally and theologically. Thus "respect for the source" is not a persuasive argument to justify the evangelist's failure to transform the other episodes into "call" stories.

But this is not what we find. Rather the questioning of John appears to be based on tradition (see Lk 3.15-17) while the theme of the searching and finding disciples appears to be a Johannine development. There the Semitic term Μεσσίαν is introduced in the first reference to Jesus as Messiah to ensure that readers do not mistake Χριστός for a personal name.[49] It is more likely that John's source was a series of Synoptic-like call stories[50] which he interpreted in distinctive fashion than that he edited a distinctive source in a way that harmonized it with the Synoptics.

Following R. T. Fortna, Martyn (48 n79) recognized the temporal connectors (1.29,35,43) as the work of the evangelist, supporting his view that the evangelist was responsible for the travel narrative of 1.43. But in each of the other temporal notes Jesus is not the active agent or subject in the sentence in which the note occurs.[51] In 1.29 it is John who sees and speaks. In 1.35 it is again John who stands, but now with two of his disciples. In this way the author has subtly indicated that the scene of action is passing from John to his two disciples. It makes sense if it is Andrew (or Peter) who wished to go into Galilee to find Philip (1.43). Consequently the sequence is that Andrew first finds Peter and then he (or Peter) finds Philip. Whether Philip was the second of John's two disciples (1.35) it is impossible to say with certainty. It would be consistent with the clue (given in 1.44) that Philip was from the same town as Andrew and Peter. Thus 1.43 in no way breaks the sequence because Jesus' word, "Follow me" (peculiar to this incident) is his response to being introduced to Philip. The purpose of the saying is to identify the evangelist's sequence of events with the traditional call stories and, if Philip was the second of the two disciples, it does not break the quest pattern because he had already become a follower of Jesus. Contrary to Martyn it is argued here that the evangelist has reinterpreted traditional call stories so that they have become quest episodes in a more complex sequence of quest scenes.

2. The Quest for the Messiah (1.19-51)

The quest sequence begins with 1.19. In the following episodes the evangelist was clearly making use of traditional material. The clues show that the initiative was taken first by the embassy, then by the Baptist and finally by the would be disciples, not by Jesus. The embassy was

---

[49]This note, and others like it, were probably introduced in a late edition of the Gospel (probably by the hand or hands that added chapter 21) when it was prepared for a wider readership which was not familiar with Jewish culture.

[50]This is confirmed by the Synoptic-like character of the tradition underlying Jn's treatment of the Baptist's witness.

[51]See also τῇ ἡμέρᾳ τῇ τρίτῃ in 2.1 where the subject is the mother of Jesus.

inquiring about the Christ. The Baptist was searching for "the coming one" and, on the basis of his witness, the next group of seekers was introduced.

Scene five: the quest for the Messiah (1.35-42).[52] The quest stories of 1.35-51 take the place of the call of the disciples and the appointment of the "twelve" in the Synoptics. Scene five is set on the *third day*. Now the witness of the Baptist from the fourth scene is repeated in the presence of two of his disciples. Thus the Johannine stories are distinguished from the Synoptics by the association of Jesus' first disciples with the Baptist who was instrumental in redirecting the quest of two of his own disciples. They then *followed* (ἀκολουθοῦντας) Jesus. The initiative of *following* is stressed three times (1.37,38,40). The narrator not only says that they *followed* Jesus but also informs the reader that Jesus saw them *following*, and again, that Andrew was one of the two who *followed* Jesus. The initiative of one of these (Andrew) in bringing his brother Simon (Peter) to Jesus, and of Philip in bringing Nathanael to Jesus emphasizes the perspective of the quest.

The quest of the first two disciples is expressed in their action of following Jesus and is recognized in his question to them, "What are you seeking?"(τί ζητεῖτε, 1.38).[53] They responded, Ῥαββί, ποῦ μένεις. The use of the word abide (μένεις), an important Johannine term (see 15.1-10), probably signals a double meaning. The question not only concerns where Jesus intended to spend the night, it also refers to his abiding relation to the Father.[54] Jesus responded with a pronouncement, a command with a promise attached; Ἔρχεσθε καὶ ὄψεσθε. "Come" is imperative, "you will see" is future and conveys a promise, as does ὄψῃ in

---

[52]The first four scenes were discussed as the Johannine Inquiry Stories and their reworking above. Scene five is set on the third day of the temporal sequence.

[53]ζητεῖν is used 34 times in Jn, 14 times in Matt, 10 times in Mk, 25 times in Lk, 10 times in Acts and a total of 117 times in the NT. The use of the verb ζητεῖν is significant in Jn. The most frequent use concerns seeking Jesus, which signals the *quest* theme, 1.38; 6.24,26; 7.11,34,36; 8.21; 11.56; 13.33; 18.4,7,8; 20.15. Next are the references to the attempts (seeking) to kill Jesus, 5.18; 7.1,19,20,25,30; 8.37,40; 10.39; 11.8. In the Synoptics there is the seeking for a sign (Mk 8.11-12; seeking to arrest or kill Jesus, Mk 11.18; 12.12; 14.1,11. Also important is the Q saying, "seek and you will find" (Matt 7.7-8; Lk 11.9-10). The quest for the pearl of great price also uses the verb to seek, Matt 13.45. The theme of the quest is illustrated here and its prominence cannot be doubted in Jn.

[54]See Jn 1.18; 10.30, 37-38; 17.5,21,23.

the pronouncement of 1.50.[55] This necessity to "come" constitutes the obstacle that must be overcome if their quest is to succeed. We are then told ἦλθαν οὖν καὶ εἶδαν ποῦ μένει. What is more καὶ παρ'αὐτῷ ἔμειναν, 1.39. That is, their relation to Jesus is analogous to his relation to the Father.[56] Thus we have a successfully completed quest. But the sequence of quest episodes has just begun. What the two disciples saw led Andrew to find (εὑρίσκει) his brother Simon (Peter) and to announce to him, "we have found (εὑρήκαμεν)[57] the Messiah".[58] He then led him to Jesus in a way that suggests that Simon (Peter) was also searching for the Messiah. This situation allows Jesus to rename Simon as Peter.[59] Two sayings, in this sequence of stories, constitute pronouncements: "come and you will see" (1.39) and "you are Simon son of John; you will be called Kephas (Peter)", 1.42. The resolution of Andrew's quest is borne out by his own actions in his declaration "we have found..." and in bringing Kephas to Jesus. The resolution of Kephas' quest is borne out by Jesus' words to him in which he is given the name by which he becomes familiar as the disciple of Jesus.[60]

Scene six: the quest for the one of whom Moses and the prophets wrote (1.43-51). The sequence of events continues on the fourth day (1.19,29,35,43). Either Andrew or Peter finds Philip who was called directly by Jesus, apparently in a manner similar to the calling of the disciples in Mk. It is possible that Philip was the second of the two

---

[55]Contrast the use of the two imperatives in 1.46 and 11.34. No promise is involved in these sayings. The two imperatives convey the meaning, "Come and look for yourself".

[56]This theme is central in Jn 17, especially verses 16-19, 22-26.

[57]This saying declares the success of the quest in what is to become a refrain, "we have found...". The use of the verb εὑρίσκω in Jn 1.41,43,45 is significant. The verb is used a total of 19 times in Jn, elsewhere in 2.14; 5.14; 6.25; 7.34-36; 9.35; 10.9; 11.17; 12.14; 18.38; 19.4,6; 21.6, of which 6.25; 7.34-36; 10.9 and 21.6 are important for this theme. The complex of motifs (following, seeking, finding) is a clue to the Johannine development of the quest theme. It is especially important in the evangelist's treatment of the quest of the crowd in Jn 6.

[58] The saying reveals the nature of the quest. It is the quest for the Messiah. In the New Testament only in Jn is the Semitic Messiah used. Its use is a clue to the identity of author and intended readers, as is the supply of the Greek translation Χριστός, which is probably a late addition to prepare the Gospel for non-Jewish readers.

[59] Strangely he has already been introduced as Simon Peter in 1.40.

[60]It is a moot point whether the evangelist expects the reader to know the tradition of the naming of Peter in its Matthaean form (16.18) or in the simple Lukan form (6.14), "Simon whom he named Peter". The wording of Jn presupposes no more than Lk 6.14.

disciples who followed Jesus on the previous day.[61] After all we are told that he was of the same city as Andrew and Peter, 1.44. Philip then took the initiative in leading Nathanael to Jesus in a way that confirms that we should regard both of them as questers. What Philip said to Nathanael was, "We have found ($\epsilon\dot{\upsilon}\rho\dot{\eta}\kappa\alpha\mu\epsilon\nu$) the one of whom Moses wrote in the Law and (of whom also) the prophets (wrote)", Jn 1.45. If he was the second disciple of 1.35-40 his actions mirror those of Andrew. Just as Andrew *finds* Simon so Philip *finds* Nathanael and each announces "We have found" ($\epsilon\dot{\upsilon}\rho\dot{\eta}\kappa\alpha\mu\epsilon\nu$), which implies the fulfilment of the search/quest.[62] Nathanael now only needs to be convinced that Jesus is indeed the one for whom they have been searching. Jesus' supposed origin in Nazareth here constitutes the obstacle to the fulfilment of Nathanael's quest. If this obstacle is to be overcome Nathanael must come and see for himself.[63] Though still sceptical Nathanael does this and encounters Jesus whose mysterious insight convinces Nathanael that Philip was right and he confesses, "Rabbi, you are the Son of God, you are king of Israel" (1.49). This confession announces the fulfilment of his quest. Thus, while the Synoptics give the impression that Jesus called his disciples out of their self-satisfied lives, disturbing their equilibrium, in Jn they are depicted as already searching before they encounter Jesus. Nathanael's confession announces the successful completion of his quest and Jesus responds acknowledging Nathanael's faith and promising "You will see greater things than these."[64]

3. Quest and Fulfilment (1.19–2.11)

With the promise "you will see" (1.50 and compare 1.39) the quest is promised greater fulfilment which was at first supplied by 2.1-11. That the sequence of events from 1.19–2.11 is a continuing story is indicated by the temporal markers in 1.29,35,43; 2.1.[65]

---

[61]Thus Schnackenburg, *John* I, 310.

[62]The evangelist's portrayal of the Samaritan woman, herself an implied quester, leading others to the Messiah, follows the same pattern. Her confession ("Could it be that he is the Christ?" 4.29) was more tentative than those of Jn 1. But the tentativeness is more than compensated for in 4.42.

[63]Here $\dot{\epsilon}\rho\chi o\upsilon\,\kappa\alpha\dot{\iota}\,\dot{\iota}\delta\epsilon$ are both imperatives setting the tasks to be achieved if the quest is to succeed.

[64]$\mu\epsilon\dot{\iota}\zeta\omega\,\tau o\dot{\upsilon}\tau\omega\nu\,\dot{o}\psi\eta$, 1.50.

[65]On the first day the Baptist was questioned (1.19-28); on the second he bore witness (1.29-34); on the third his witness was repeated for the two disciples (1.35-43); on the fourth Philip and Nathanael met Jesus (1.43-51). Following that sequence the wedding took place on the third day (2.1). Counting the fourth day as the first in the new sequence, this indicates six

Scene seven: fulfilment (2.1-11). The wedding took place on the sixth day in the sequence. The evangelist was responsible for linking this temporal sequence but the story of the turning of the water to wine appears to be traditional. The evidence for this is the conciseness and simplicity of the story itself which leads up to the climactic concluding pronouncement by the ἀρχιτρίκλινος in 2.10, which is the longest of the dialogues.[66] The traditional story continues only as far as verse 10. The evangelist's addition of 2.11 integrates the story into the opening quest complex (1.19–2.11). We are told that Jesus manifested his glory and his disciples believed in him, implying that the disciples saw his glory and that, because of this, they believed in him. This fulfils the cumulative promise "you will see" from 1.50, which gathers up the promise of 1.39 as well. Yet the disciples are only mentioned coincidentally in 2.2 in the story itself. That reference has the appearance of an addition,[67] introducing them into a story from which they were originally absent. In the story only the mother of Jesus (perhaps) and the servants know what has happened to the water. But no conclusion is drawn concerning their response. Rather it is the ἀρχιτρίκλινος who pronounces the success of the miracle (2.10). There is nothing to suggest that the disciples "overhear". The pronouncement is meaningful only to the hearer/reader of the story. In spite of this, 2.11 turns the focus of the story on to the disciples by means of a comment by the narrator. It is as if the miracle had been worked for their sake so that they would see the greater things promised in 1.50 and consequently believe on this basis.

The evangelist has modified the traditional story by the addition of 2.11[68] in order to make 2.1-11 the climax and fulfilment of 1.19-50 and to

---

days in all, the fifth day being allowed for travel to Cana. The temporal markers show that the evangelist wished to bind together the sequence of events from 1.19–2.11.

[66]Birger Olsson (*Structure and Meaning in the Fourth Gospel*, 57-61, esp. n85) shows that the story leads up to the speech by the "steward" in 2.10 (57). He notes, "If we ignore the comment in v.11, the narrative...ends with a speech, the sixth and longest in the text."(61).

[67]The verb ἐκλήθη (in 2.2) is third person singular, indicating that Jesus was invited. Either καὶ οἱ μαθηταὶ αὐτοῦ is an "afterthought" reference or actually was added with 2.11 when the point of the story was made to be for their sake. The evangelist does use the third person singular in similar constructions (1.35; 3.22). This means that the introduction of καὶ οἱ μαθηταὶ αὐτοῦ would be quite straightforward and difficult to detect as an addition.

[68]The identification of this miracle as the first Cana sign is the work of the evangelist as might well be the identification of the location in Cana in 2.1.

prepare the way for an *inclusio* with 4.46-54. It follows that 2.11 is the evangelist's conclusion to the sequence 1.19–2.11.[69] The addition has the effect of making the sign function for the benefit of the disciples who are notable by their absence from the action of the story itself. Consequently 1.19–2.11 forms a unit portraying the successful fulfilment of the quest for the Messiah. The conclusion is clearly marked by 2.11. The μετά τοῦτο of 2.12 is a separating, not a connecting formula. It marks out a new beginning.[70]

4. Ultimate Fulfilment (1.51)

Into this literary creation the evangelist has subsequently (in a second edition) introduced the traditional Son of Man saying, 1.51.[71] That it is introduced is indicated by the introductory καὶ λέγει αὐτῷ, though Jesus is the continuing speaker from 1.50, and by the change from the singular ὄψῃ in 1.50 to the plural ὄψεσθε of 1.51. Thus with the introduction of 1.51 the miracle (sign) of 2.1–11 can no longer be seen as the fulfilment of the promise (of 1.50). What is promised in 1.51 is a vision of the heavenly Son of Man whose exaltation to heaven by way of the cross is in

---

[69]Contrary to R. Bultmann and R. Fortna and in agreement with M. Dibelius. Verse 11 is commentary by the narrator/evangelist speaking directly to the readers. The commentary fits the evangelist's own perspective. For Fortna all but the reference to the revelation of the glory, which is attributed to the evangelist, is assigned to the source, see *The Gospel of Signs*, 236. Yet Fortna now agrees that "the story culminates in the steward's declaration...2.10)" (*Predecessor*, 253) and that the steward's proverbial saying could have provided the concluding attestation to the miracle in the oral tradition and that the author of the Signs Gospel had added 2.11c (*Predecessor*, 50-1).

[70]Jn 2.12 is a characteristic travel narrative such as we find in 1.43; 2.1; 3.22; 4.3-4,43,46; 5.1; 6.1; 7.1. But 2.12 is distinctive in that it does not link scenes as do 1.43; 2.1, nor does it bring Jesus to the situation of the next episode of the story as do 3.11; 4.3-4,43; 5.1; 6.1; 7.1. Rather it introduces a brief interlude (καὶ ἔμειναν οὐ πολλὰς ἡμέρας). This brief interlude brings together for the first time in the story Jesus, his mother, his brothers and his disciples. Jesus, his mother and his disciples were together in Cana. Now the brothers are included. Through this association the reader is led to expect that they also believe in Jesus which makes more shocking the revelation (in 7.5) that his brothers did not believe in him. This seems to be the narrative purpose of 2.12 in addition to marking the new beginning after the concluding statement of 2.11.

[71]See R. E. Brown, *John* I, 88ff. Jn has transformed a traditional *parousia* saying into a saying concerning the exalted Son of Man by setting the scene in heaven. On this see my "The Church and Israel in the Gospel of John", *NTS* 25 (1978) 109-10.

focus in this Gospel,[72] but finds fulfilment in no single event such as 2.1–11. Yet 2.1-11 was allowed to stand so that the revelation of glory in that miracle story remains a fulfilment to the promise of 1.50, though it is now shown to be a preliminary fulfilment. Alternatively it could be said that the post-exaltation glory has been projected back into this miracle story. Whichever way we look at it, the focus has moved from a miracle-worker christology to an exalted Son of Man christology. To account for this we need to recognize the dialogue/conflict with the synagogue and the consequences of the conflict reaching a climax. The first edition reflects the time of dialogue with the synagogue while the second edition reflects the breach with the synagogue. Through that breach the distinctive Johannine christology emerged.[73]

III. MESSIANIC QUEST (1.19–4.54)

Jn 2.1-11 is the conclusion to the section begun with 1.19. It also forms an *inclusio* with 4.46-54. This *inclusio* is of the evangelist's making. He mentions the location of the marriage in Cana of Galilee (2.1), and the conclusion (2.11) notes "this beginning of signs", again mentioning Cana of Galilee. The second Cana sign is introduced by reference to Jesus' return "to Cana of Galilee where he made the water into wine" (4.46), and concludes (4.54) by referring to "the second sign Jesus did coming out of Judaea into Galilee". Thus the two Cana signs are explicitly linked by the evangelist. The *inclusio* is reinforced by the recognition that in these two stories we have the only two concise and discrete miracle quest stories in Jn.[74] In each the miracle is initiated by an

---

[72]That Jn 1.51 concerns the vision of the heavenly Son of Man is indicated by the opening "you will see the heavens opened". The Son of Man and the angels converging on him will be seen in heaven. On this see my "Christ and the Church in John 1.45-51" in *L'Evangile de Jean*, 359-62.

[73]R.T. Fortna, "Source and Redaction in the Fourth Gospel's Portrayal of Jesus' Signs", *JBL* 89 (1970) 152, who treats Signs Gospel as the major source of the Fourth Gospel, argues that the evangelist did not contradict his source, "he nowhere contradicts it", rather he reinterprets and deepens what he found there. These statements obscure, to some extent, how radical was the interpretation that he has suggested. In this study some attempt is made to distinguish the tradition from this overall narrative development of what we called the first edition and to examine evidence of the modification of this in subsequent editions.

[74]See 208–10 below. Tannehill recognized the miracle quest story as a sub-type of quest story, noting that a minority of Synoptic quest stories fall into this category. The raising of Lazarus is a miracle quest story in which the miracle was initiated by the sisters of Lazarus sending a message to Jesus which constituted an implied request (compare 2.3). But that story is neither concise nor discrete. It bears all the marks of extensive Johannine

implied or explicit request to Jesus. They are the only two miracle stories in Jn without any dialogues or discourse attached such as we find in Jn 5; 6; 9 and 11.[75] The evangelist has incorporated these miracle quest stories into an overarching framework by explicitly relating them to each other as the first and second Cana signs. In this way the whole of 1.19–4.54 has been made into a unified section dealing with the quest for the Messiah (1.26-27,29-34,45; 4.25-36,39-42) and the life that he brings (3.1-15; 4.10-11,13-14,50-54).[76] The next task is to see how the material from 2.1-11 to 4.46-54 has been interpreted in terms of the theme of the quest. The dominant theme of the quest for the Messiah has been overlaid by the muted harmony of the Messiah's quest for true worshippers (2.13-22 and 4.16-26, 31-38) which is an expression of God's own quest (4.23). Thus the relation of Jesus to the Father manifests the nuanced Johannine christology. Jesus seeks and the Father seeks. Yet there are not two seekers, but one.

1. The Quest of the Mother of Jesus (2.1-11)

The reader is told (by the narrator) that "the mother of Jesus was there".[77] This signals that she has a central part to play in the story. Indeed, she is portrayed as a quester. Her presence led to Jesus being called.[78] That she was a known and authoritative figure in the household is implied by her instructions to the servants (2.5) and, by implication, the authority of Jesus was not known to them.

Again (as in 1.35-51) Jesus' action is depicted as responsive. His mother took the initiative. Her quest is depicted in her coming to Jesus with the report of the shortage of wine (2.3). The report is to be

---

been overlaid with the theme of rejection. See chapter 11, "The Quests Continue" below. Indeed, in Jn, it was the raising of Lazarus, as much as anything, that led to the final rejection and crucifixion of Jesus.

[75]Those dialogue and discourse developments are the evangelist's trademark to signal conflict and rejection scenes. The dialogues between Jesus and Nicodemus and Jesus and the Samaritans are not based on *miracle stories* and do not lead to conflict and rejection.

[76]There are quest stories subsequent to 4.54 but these have been subjected to the theme of rejection, probably at a second level of the evangelist's interpretation. See chapter 5, "The Paradigm of Rejection", chapter 6, "The Messiah and the Bread of Life" and chapter 11, "The Quests Continue" below.

[77]The narrator introduces factual information of this sort when it is crucial for the reader if the significance of the narrative is to be grasped. Compare 2.13; 4.6; 5.1; 6.4; 7.2; 10.22; 13.30.

[78]That she was first mentioned suggests that she was responsible for the invitation to Jesus (and his disciples). ἐκλήθη has the sense here of "he was invited".

understood as an implied request. It implies the expectation that Jesus will act to provide a remedy, as do her instructions to the servants (2.5). In response to the request Jesus expressed two objections that had to be overcome if the quest was to be successful.

1. "What is there between us (τί ἐμοί καί σοί)[79], woman (γύναι)?"[80]
2. "My hour has not yet come".[81]

Thus, though we have been told that it is the mother of Jesus who makes the request,[82] Jesus failed to acknowledge the relationship and asserted that it was not his time to act. The point is clear if we recognize that his mother was responsible for his invitation and his response demonstrates his rejection of family obligations. As in Mk 3.31-35 Jesus here implies that the the eschatological family of believers has displaced the biological family. Yet in the crucifixion scene, though Jesus again addresses his mother as "woman", he takes thought for her care and well being in the future, Jn 19.25-27. He does so, however, in terms of her relationship within the eschatological family where she stands as mother in relation to the BD and he to her as son.

Although Jesus disassociated himself from his mother's claim on him, he does act to solve the problem. The objections were overcome in that, in spite of them, Jesus' mother tells the servants to do as instructed by

---

[79] On the use of this Semitic idiom see Mk 1.24 where it is used by the man with the unclean spirit (demon possessed) and A.H. Maynard, "TI EMOI KAI SOI", *NTS* 31 (1985), 582-586. The use of this formula is a repudiation of the implied relationship and constitutes an objection raised by Jesus, 2.4. Compare the enigmatic objection in Jn 4.48.

[80] And again in 19.25-27. The address is not in itself abrupt or rude; see 4.21 where Jesus addressed the Samaritan woman in this way. But it is not the form of address expected of a son to his mother. It thus distances Jesus from his mother by failing to acknowledge the relationship.

[81] The theme of Jesus' hour (ὥρα) is frequent in Jn. The word can indicate a particular hour of the day (1.39; 4.6,52,53; 11.9; 19.14,27), a point of time marked off from what precedes or follows it (5.35; 16.2,4,21,32), or the eschatological hour (4.21,23; 5.25,28). Many of the references are linked to Jesus much in the way of 2.4 (see 7.30; 8.20; 12.23,27; 13.1; 17.1). But these refer to Jesus' imminent death/exaltation/glorification. It is difficult to see how this is relevant to 2.4. Rather 7.6 appears to be more relevant although the term used there is καιρός not ὥρα which, in this instance, is used without distinction. Thus Jesus is here referring to the time to act. His time to act has not yet come. But the wording of 2.4 shades over into a suggested second level of meaning.

[82] It is notable that on both of her appearances in this Gospel she is not called by her name "Mary" but referred to as "the mother of Jesus" yet on both occasions Jesus refers to her as "woman" in a way that fails to acknowledge the relationship. This is all the more pointed because the narrator has referred to her as "the mother of Jesus".

Jesus. In this there is the assumption that Jesus will act and the action of Jesus resolved the dilemma at the wedding. The pronouncement was not made by Jesus[83] but by the ἀρχιτρίκλινος who asserts that, contrary to normal practice, the best wine has been kept until last, literally "until now" (ἕως ἄρτι), 2.10. Because, as is pointedly noted by the narrator, the ἀρχιτρίκλινος did not know the source of the wine, his evidence is the more impressive. In the independent story his pronouncement gave expression to the point of the story, symbolically asserting the dawning of the superior eschatological age.[84] The theme of the superior wine of the age inaugurated by Jesus' ministry is traditional and the evangelist was content to take it and use it. But he adds his own distinctive perspectives, especially the theme of quest and fulfilment. At the level of traditional themes Jn 2.1-10 introduces a series of episodes illustrating the superiority of the new age: New wine (2.1-10); New Temple (2.13-22); New birth (2.23–3.15); New worshippers (4.4-42); New life (4.46-54). In each case, though he has accepted and used these themes, the evangelist has interpreted the tradition along his own distinctive lines.

At the same time the quest of Jesus' mother, specifically fulfilled through the miraculous supply of wine, is left open because she disappears from the scene and does not explicitly witness the miracle. Her story is again taken up in 19.25-27. Thus the theme of her quest spills over this discrete quest story into the fabric of the Gospel,[85] suggesting that the evangelist was responsible for this development. The miracle quest story has also been woven into a larger complex, 1.19–2.11. Because of this the focus is no longer on the quest of Mary nor even on the pronouncement of 2.10, but on the fulfilled quest of the disciples. The evangelist has seen to this by the addition of the overpowering and impressive comment by the narrator in 2.11. But the adequacy of the faith of the disciples at this stage was to be put into question at the second edition by the insertion of 1.51 and, as we shall see, by the relocation of the narrative of "the cleansing of the Temple" so that it also becomes a comment on the faith of the disciples.

---

[83]This is consistent with the quest episodes of 1.19-50 where the pronouncements were made by the Baptist and the disciples, though there the pronouncements have a christological orientation, 1.34, 41, 45. See also the pronouncement of 4.42.

[84]See Mk 2.22 for an example of the way wine was used as a symbol of the new age.

[85]This is true also of the story of the quest of Nicodemus in 2.23–3.15, which spills over into 7.45-52; 12.42; 19.38-42.

An appended note on Jn 2.12.

Jn 2.12 formally marks a break in the sequence begun in 1.19 and signalled throughout by temporal connectors (1.29,25,43; 2.1) linking a series of scenes. But the verse does more than this. It signals the itinerant ministry of Jesus and indicates that his disciples (gathered in 1.35-51) travel with him (see 2.2), as does his mother. Thus the incident of 2.1-11 should not be understood as a family visit.

For a reader reading Jn for a second time, Jn 2.12 is surprising in that it indicates that the brothers of Jesus were with him. While some mss omit reference to the disciples, all evidence supports the presence of the bothers. It is surprising because the re-reader will have Jn 7.5 in mind where the narrator tells us that "his brothers did not believe in him". Alternatively we could say that in 2.12 the narrator has set up the first time reader for a shock when coming to learn in 7.5 that "his brothers did not believe in him." For the first time reader 2.12 suggests that Jesus' supporters included his disciples, his mother and his brothers, all of whom travelled with him. Indeed 7.5 confirms that Jesus' brothers travelled with him, though they are there declared to be unbelievers.

If Jn 2.12 formally breaks the sequence begun in 1.19, the specific links between 2.1,11 with 4.46,54, setting both signs in Cana of Galilee and naming them the first and second signs suggest that the signs of 2.1-11 and 4.46–54 form an inclusion. Thus 2.1-11 forms a bridge passage belonging both to 1.19–2.11 and 2.1–4.54.

2. The Quest for True Worshippers (2.13-22)

Jn has placed the story of "the cleansing of the Temple" at the beginning of Jesus' ministry,[86] following immediately after the first Cana sign. In so doing he has incorporated this incident into the series of episodes dealing with the disciples, their coming to Jesus (1.35-50) and their coming to believe in him (2.11; 2.22). That the placing of 2.13-22 in its present position took place in the second edition is probable.[87] Whereas the faith of the disciples (in 2.11) was an immediate response to the first Cana sign, the faith response mentioned in 2.22 did not take place at the time of the narrated incident but only when Jesus was risen from the dead. Consequently the perspective of this story, as it is narrated in Jn, is similar to that of 1.51. The first Cana sign is now set within the frame of 1.51 and 2.13-22, both of which put in question the adequacy of the faith

---

[86]If the Synoptics are right in their placement of the story it would seem that the evangelist has transformed a rejection story into a quest story. We should note however that there is also a demand for a sign (6.30) in the the quest story of 6.1-36, which has become the basis of rejection stories.
[87]See B. Lindars, *John*, 50.

of the disciples prior to the exaltation (1.51) or resurrection (2.22) of Jesus.

The event that provoked Jesus' arrest, focussing on the reaction of the chief priests and scribes (Mk and Lk), has been transformed (by Jn) into the theme of Jesus as quester (2.13-14; cf. 4.7,23) in search of true worshippers with the focus on the response of the disciples (2.22). Jesus' *coming* to the Temple (*ἱερῷ*) as the Passover[88] drew near signals his quest, which is apparently successful in that we are told that he found (*εὗρεν*), 2.14. But what he found was not what he sought. Clearly his words "Do not make my father's house a house of trade" (*ἐμπορίου*) show a rejection of what he found. He found only a marketplace. That the quest had failed is evident in that he cast them out (*ἐξέβαλεν*).[89] What then did he seek in the Temple? He was seeking true worshippers of God. If he did not find them in the Temple the focus of attention on the disciples suggests that we should turn our attention to them.

The narrator twice interjects (2.17,22) to inform the reader of the response of the disciples. At the time of the event, the disciples remembered (*ἐμνήσθησαν*) the scripture[90] (Ps 69.9), which provided one interpretative framework within which to understand the event. Jesus' action was understood as an expression of consuming zeal for the house (*οἶκος*) of God, which is consistent with Jesus' words in 2.16. This response does not yet mark them out as true worshippers.

Jn has incorporated into this story the questioning of Jesus' authority and the demand for a sign to justify his shocking action, Jn 2.18. The demand for a sign suggests a rejection rather than a quest story. Here the demand for a sign is made by the Jews but exhibits no extreme hostility. They take no action against Jesus but ask a sign by means of which he could authenticate his authority. It may be that Jesus is here perceived in terms of Malachi 3.1ff. His action is perceived to involve broadly messianic claims and what the Jews ask is an authenticating sign[91] and this request/demand constitutes the first objection to Jesus' quest.

---

[88]Passover is described as "the Passover of the Jews" (2.13), just as "the purification of the Jews" is mentioned earlier (2.6). Such comments by the narrator are a trademark of the evangelist, though "of the Jews" probably belongs to a late edition of the Gospel.

[89]On *ἐξέβαλεν* see 6.37; 9.22,34; 12.42; 16.2. While he cast out of the Temple those who had made it into a marketplace, "the one who comes to me I will certainly not cast out (*οὐ μὴ ἐκβάλω ἔξω*)" 6.37. On the other side, those who confessed Christ were cast out of the Synagogue (9.22,34; 12.42; 16.2) but *found* by Jesus, 9.35.

[90]This is indicated by the quotation formula *γεγραμμένον ἐστίν*.

[91]Compare the demand for a sign by the *crowd* in Jn 6.30. Following Jn 5.16,18 the Jews emerge in a more sinister role, hence it is the crowd that

The demand for a sign (2.18) introduces an objection to Jesus' quest. This objection had to be overcome if the quest was to succeed. In a saying which constitutes the pronouncement in the story Jesus promised a sign, "You destroy ($\lambda \acute{\upsilon} \sigma a \tau \epsilon$) this temple ($\nu a \grave{o} \nu$) and in three days I will raise ($\acute{\epsilon} \gamma \epsilon \rho \tilde{\omega}$) it" (2.19). The Jews did not pick up the reference to their part in the destruction. What attracted their attention was the fact that Jesus apparently said that he will raise in three days what had already been in the process of building for forty-six years (2.20). Consequently Jesus did offer a sign in response to their demand.[92] But it was a sign for which the Jews would have to wait. Only when they had destroyed his body would the sign of raising it up be given.[93]

Naturally the Jews, failing to understand that Jesus was not talking about the Jerusalem Temple, raised a second serious objection, 2.20.[94] The narrator again interjects (see 2.17), this time to inform the reader of

---

requests the sign in 6.30. When the Jews emerge in 6.41 they are cast as Jesus' opponents who murmur against him as the people of Israel murmured against God and Moses in the wilderness. Whatever problems we may have with 2.18 and 6.30, these texts confirm the expectation that messianic claims would be confirmed by signs. Because the reader is expected to perceive this without explicit explanation by the narrator it seems likely that this is not simply a Johannine construction.

[92] It is therefore correct to designate the resurrection of Jesus as the greatest sign in Jn, given in response to the demand of 2.18. The cleansing of the Temple is not portrayed as a sign but provides the context in which Jesus can predict his greatest sign.

[93] Here (2.19), and in 10.17-18, it is apparently Jesus who raises himself from the dead. Generally in the early Christian proclamation it is God who raised Jesus from the dead, see Acts 2.24, 32; 1 Cor 15.4 and cf. $\acute{\eta} \gamma \acute{\epsilon} \rho \theta \eta$ in 2:22. But it is unclear whether this is theologically significant. In 2.19 the saying is a response to a demand that Jesus should give a sign. In 10.17-18 the saying is intended to demonstrate Jesus' authority. This could explain the alternative idiom. Further, in terms of Johannine christology, what Jesus does the Father does also. It is this christology that enables the evangelist to affirm that it is Jesus who raises himself. Further, in 10.18 Jesus affirms that he received authority to do this from the Father.

[94] Objections to the quest are raised in various quest stories, see 2.4,18,20; 3.4; 4.9,11,48; 6.15,26-27. Objections are raised to the specific manner of the quest. While it is frequently Jesus who objects to various quests for the Messiah, here it is the Jews who object to his quest for true worshippers, 2.18. It is this that gives the story the look of a cross between a quest story and a rejection story which is characterized by various objections to Jesus' origin, word, or action. Here in Jn 1-4 the Jews have not yet taken on the role of the hardened opponents to Jesus. The placing of this story at the beginning rather than the end of Jesus' ministry necessitates a softer role for the Jews than we find in response to the same action in the Synoptics.

the Jews' misunderstanding, because Jesus was actually talking about the Temple of his body (2.21)[95] and by going on to speak of the response of the disciples (2.22) he shows that he is not really interested in the effect of this event on the unbelieving Jews. The disciples remembered, understood, and believed only when Jesus was risen from the dead. They remembered the word of Jesus concerning the Jews destroying the Temple and his own raising of it.

Through the attachment of the saying of Jesus, which identifies a sign of authority to his opponents, it has become a basis for the subsequent belief of the disciples[96] and obviously for the readers also. Consequently the disciples *subsequently* become the true worshippers sought by Jesus, the aspect of conflict is in the background and the effect on the disciples is brought into sharp focus through the narrator's conclusion in 2.22.

It is now said that "they believed the scripture" (Ps 69.9) and to this is added, "and the word of Jesus". What distinguishes this from 2.17, where it is said that the disciples remembered the Scripture, is not the replacement of "remembered" by "believed",[97] but the addition of "the word of Jesus". This belief has implications that go beyond the specifically defined content of belief to designate genuine believing, which is explicitly signalled by the reference to the post-resurrection context. The quest, that has been shown to have failed, is left open, to be fulfilled in a later episode of the Gospel. The narrator has signalled that the success was an outcome of the resurrection of Jesus, 2.22. The incident in Samaria (4.20-24,42) prefigures this, but the real fulfilment came only with the resurrection of Jesus, and this is again signalled by the quest story of 12.20-36.[98] The focus on the crucifixion and resurrection of Jesus in the narrator's comments signals that this interpretation belongs to the second edition of the Gospel as does the portrayal of Jesus as quester.

3. The Quest for the Kingdom (2.23-3.15)

While Nicodemus is a character peculiar to Jn, aspects of his story find echoes in the Synoptics. His *quest* (2.23-3.15) finds its closest parallel in

---

[95]In this story three different words are used to speak of the Temple, $\iota\epsilon\rho\hat{\omega}$ (2.14), $o\hat{\iota}\kappa o\varsigma$ (2.16-17), $\nu\alpha\acute{o}\varsigma$ (2.19-21). The changes are characteristic of the evangelist. The first word is customary for the Temple, the second, a quotation from scripture, and the third appropriate to the ambiguity of the Temple/body imagery.

[96]Jn (through the narrator) introduced the belief of the disciples into this incident just as he did in 2.2,11.

[97]For John, remembrance of the scripture in relation to Jesus' action implies belief.

[98]See the quest of the Greeks in chapter 11, "The Quests Continue" below.

the quest of "the rich young ruler" (Mk 10.17-22=Matt 19.16-22=Lk 18.18-23). While the quest of the rich young ruler failed, the quest of Nicodemus is left open, to be fulfilled in later episodes in the Gospel. In another similar story Jesus is tested by a scribe/lawyer (Mk 12.28-34=Matt 22.34-40=Lk 10.25-38). From the point of view of *genre*, the quest story provides a closer parallel. The Lukan version (18.18) designates the quester a ruler ($\dot{\alpha}\rho\chi\omega\nu$) and Nicodemus is also a ruler of the Jews. Two further detailed comparisons are worthy of comment:

1. The complimentary form of address used by Nicodemus is formally like the address in the conflict story (Mk 12.13-17=Matt 22.15-22=Lk 20.20-26). The title of address is similar, the Greek equivalent of the Jewish Rabbi is teacher. This is followed by a compliment that is justified by some evidence:

John	Mark/Luke
Rabbi,	Teacher
We know that you are teacher come from God	We know that you are true and do not care for any one,
for no one is able to do the signs that you do unless God is with him.	for you do not regard the status of men but teach the way of God in truth:

That the Nicodemus story is a quest, not a conflict story (like Mk 12.13-17), is apparent when the connection with 2.23-25 is recognized. Nicodemus is one of those who believed on the basis of signs and came seeking Jesus, though the nature of his quest is implied not explicit. The complimentary approach is also found in the "Good teacher" of Mk 10.17=Lk 18.18, but without the fulness of the form noted above. Although full parallels are not easy to find[99] it is not sufficient evidence to prove John's dependence on the Synoptic story, especially as the complimentary approach was a recognized element of classical rhetoric.[100]

2. The saying (3.3) and the variant (3.5) should be compared with Mk 10.15=Lk 18.17=Matt 18.3. Jesus in Jn (as distinct from the Synoptics) characteristically uses the double *amen*, addresses Nicodemus using the singular "you" and speaks of being begotten from above/by water and spirit. In some small details Jn is closer to Matt, but with reference to the kingdom of *God* Jn stands with Mk and Lk. The use of *amen* and the theme of "entering the kingdom of God" are not confined to particular sayings and the Johannine concept of divine begetting is quite distinct from anything in the Synoptics. The overall evidence shows that Jn's contact with the Synoptics is in terms of general characteristics suggesting

---

[99]*Pap Eg* 2 is almost certainly dependent on Jn.
[100]See C.H. Dodd, *Historical Tradition in the Fourth Gospel*, 329 n1.

that Jn has constructed the quest of Nicodemus making use of traditional *genre,* themes and motifs.

With the story of Nicodemus we return to the first edition with the dominant theme of the quest for the Messiah and the life that he brings. The narrative may be based on a traditional unsuccessful quest story known to us elsewhere in Mk 10.17-22. If this is the case Jn has incorporated other themes and motifs in writing his story. It is a concise story with a memorable pronouncement, reiterated with variation, as is characteristic of Jn. But it is not a discrete story because Nicodemus fades out without any stated outcome of his quest. Perhaps, for this reason, it should be classified as an inquiry story. But in an inquiry story we would expect a clear inquiry to be the focus of attention. Here, as is common in quest stories, the quest is not explicit but implied and it can be argued that the quest is not so much a failure (like the Markan story) as left open to future events. The story of Nicodemus is taken up in later incidents in the Gospel.

Nicodemus is portrayed as one of those who believed on the basis of signs (2.23; 3.2),[101] such a man as Jesus knows.[102] His quest is expressed in his *coming* to Jesus who interpreted his coming as a quest for the kingdom of God. The indication that Nicodemus came to Jesus by night signifies the furtive nature of the visit and the desire to keep it secret. Jesus' knowledge of what was in the mind of Nicodemus brought the quest to light and his words disclosed the solution to the quest. No clue is given in this narrative to show if the quester was successful. Indeed the narrative exists in its present form so that the quest of the reader may be successful. It carries a pronouncement of Jesus which is reiterated in varied form, "Amen, amen I say to you, except a person be born from above (or "by water and spirit")[103] he is not able to see (enter) the Kingdom of God", 3.3,5. The pronouncement presents an obstacle which must be overcome if Nicodemus' quest is to succeed. Nicodemus reveals his lack of comprehension in the questions he raised, 3.4,9.

Misunderstanding should not be understood as rejection because by means of the misunderstanding of characters in the story Jesus clarifies his position. Thus the misunderstanding of Nicodemus allows Jesus to

---

[101]In 3.2 and 9.31-32 Jesus' relation to God is inferred from the signs he performed. In Jn 6 the crowd's quest was also based on seeing the signs Jesus performed (6.2).

[102]Note the repetition of $\mathring{\alpha}\nu\theta\rho\omega\pi\sigma\varsigma$ in 2.25 and 3.1.

[103]Water here stands for the baptism of John (see Jn 1.26) so that Nicodemus was challenged to make his commitment public as a condition of receiving the baptism of the Spirit through Jesus (see Jn 1.33) which is the subject of Jn 3.5-15.

respond to specific difficulties and although the story does not recount the success of his quest, neither does it announce its failure. Rather we should see that the quest of Nicodemus progresses through future episodes until final success is narrated, 19.38-42.[104]

The second question by Nicodemus (3.9) is the cue for the evangelist, through a pronouncement of Jesus, to affirm the necessity of the lifting up of the Son of Man with the consequence of life for those who believe in him, 3.13-15. Thus, as in 1.51, the exalted Son of Man is the object of faith. By this stage Nicodemus has disappeared from the scene and the point of 3.13-15 is directed to the reader. That the narrator is speaking directly to the reader becomes increasingly clear in 3.16-21. From this point of view Jesus and Nicodemus, as participants in the drama, have disappeared from the scene and the narrator addresses the reader directly.[105] The narrator's comments and this christology probably belong to the second edition.

In 3.16-21 the narrator continues the theme begun with the response to the "How?" of Nicodemus. The contrast of salvation and condemnation (3.17-18) leads into an exposition of the nature of the judgement of the world (3.19-21) which is necessary if the quest for salvation is to succeed. Following this the witness of the Baptist is reintroduced (3.22-36) with a comparison of his baptism with that of Jesus (cf.1.26,33) to form a transition to the incident in Samaria (4.1-3).[106]

But the evangelist was not unmindful of the outcome of the quest of Nicodemus, and his story resurfaces at various points in the Gospel, 7.45-52; 12.42-43; 19.38-42. So that the reader will not miss the continuation of that story the narrator adds the reminder, in the subsequent episodes, that this Nicodemus is the person who came to Jesus formerly by night (7.50; 19.39). In the end his quest was successful. The subsequent episodes chronicle a growing openness and willingness to be identified with Jesus. Unlike the twelve, who had fled at the arrest of Jesus, Nicodemus, with Joseph of Arimathea, was responsible for the burial of Jesus, an act of

---

[104]The misunderstandings of the Samaritan woman (4.15) and the crowd (6.34) should also be understood in this manner.

[105]Naturally the whole Gospel is directed to the reader. But when characters in the story speak, they speak to the reader indirectly. Directly they address other characters in the story. But there are parts of Jn where Jesus (3.16-21), or some other character (John the Baptist in 3.31-36) cease to speak to any character in the story but address the reader directly. Then we should say that the narrator has intervened and is speaking although no directions are explicitly given to say that this is so. See also 1.15-18.

[106]Compare Jn 4.43-45 which forms a transition to the miracle quest story of 4.46-52.

openness and faith. While this action does not display true comprehension of the significance of Jesus it does show a growth in open commitment to Jesus in the face of intimidation. Again we note that the theme of the quest is woven into the fabric and structure of the Gospel and does not only appear in isolated stories.

4. Two Questers: Jesus and the Samaritan Woman (4.4-42)

Jn 4 is closely connected with the preceding material. The chapter opens with the comparison with John (the Baptist), a theme carried over from 3.22-36. This comparison apparently provides the basis for Jesus' journey to Samaria. The theme of baptism also looks back to 3.3,5 while the water pots, water and drawing of water (ὑδρίαι, ὕδατος, Ἀντλήσατε) of 2.1-11 are linked thematically with Jn 4 (ὑδρίαν, ὕδωρ ζῶν, ἄντλημα, ἀντλεῖν). The second set of dialogues (4.16-26) about the legitimate place of worship reopens the theme first introduced in 2.13-22. Further, in Jn 4, as in Jn 6, the evangelist has used a collection of traditional sayings to move the focus from one group to another.[107]

Various motifs have influenced the weaving of the fabric of the story. In Jn 1-3 the dominant motif is the quest for the Messiah. The muted theme of Jesus' quest for true worshippers also appears. Both themes are taken up in Jn 4 together with new themes related to the Samaritans. The lack of Synoptic parallels and the complexity of the story suggest that the evangelist has himself developed the episodes dealing with Jesus and the Samaritans. The story shows that Jesus was not restricted by the conventions of his time but freely initiated this relationship with a Samaritan woman, 4.9.

When the disciples returned they did not know the subject under discussion and they marvelled that he was speaking with a woman (rather than that he had asked for a drink from a Samaritan), 4.27. But the woman (4.9) had questioned how it could be that Jesus as a Jew could ask a drink from a Samaritan woman. The narrator adds the explanation, οὐ γὰρ συγχρῶνται Ἰουδαῖοι Σαμαρίταις. Obviously Jews and Samaritans did associate at certain levels. The disciples themselves had undertaken to purchase food. It has been argued by David Daube that συγχρῶνται might have some reference to the sharing of drinking vessels. It is clear from the *context* that what was unusual was that Jesus initiated a particular kind of relation with a Samaritan. Consequently the story highlights conventions concerning the relationships between both men and women and Jews and Samaritans.

---

[107] See 4.31-38 and 6.36-40.

Jn 4 tells the story of an encounter at a well. Such stories apparently were common in the ancient world, a number being found in the OT (Genesis 24.1-67; 29.1-30; Exodus 2.15b-22).[108] Robert Alter has called these stories, which are presented in order of decreasing length and detail, "the betrothal type scene". The future bridegroom, or his representative, journeys to a foreign land where, at a well, he encounters a maiden, identified as the daughter of so and so. Water is drawn and given, either by the man or the maiden. The maiden then rushes home with news of the stranger who is invited to stay and finally a betrothal is negotiated. Within this framework many variations occur to adapt the pattern to the particular needs of the overall story.

In the *first* of these "betrothal stories" we are given some important social data. It is in the evening when "women" go out to draw water from the well (Genesis 24.11). It is also said that "the daughters of the men of the city" come out to draw water (24.13). Hence it seems that both married and unmarried women came to the well to draw water. The servant plans to speak to a maiden (24.14) and indeed speaks to Rebekah. No other visitors to the well are mentioned in this story.

In the *second* story, concerning Jacob's meeting with Rachel at the well, there is a reference to time in Jacob's comment, "It is still high day, it is not time for the animals to be gathered together; water the sheep, and go, pasture them" (29.7). Further, the gathering of the shepherds at the well is mentioned (29.3). The shepherds are men (Jacob addresses them as "My brothers"), though it is mentioned that Rachel was bringing the sheep of Laban to the well. The well was covered by a stone that was removed only when all the flocks were gathered. When the flocks had been watered the stone was replaced. When Rachel arrived Jacob rolled the stone away and watered Laban's flock. This suggests an unusual gathering together of the flocks in the middle of the day. The meeting between Jacob and Rachel occurs in unlikely circumstances confirming that God has brought them together. Further, whereas it is normally the woman who gives drink to the "stranger", here it is Jacob who waters the flock of Laban.

In the *third* story Moses sat by a well. The seven daughters of Ruel came to water the flock of their father but were driven away by the shepherds. Moses enabled them to water their flock (Exodus 2.15b-17). Here it seems certain that the shepherds were men.

Certain points of comparison can be made between Jn 4 and these stories. Like Jacob Jesus is depicted at the well in the middle of the day (4.6), but although he asked for a drink he did not receive water from the woman. She mentions the flocks that are watered at the well (4.12),

---

[108]See Robert Alter, *The Art of Biblical Narrative*, 52-8.

which is in harmony with the mention of the shepherds and their flocks in the earlier stories. Like Moses Jesus sat at the well (4.6) and, as in the first story, Jesus' encounter with the woman occurs without mention of any bystanders. But none of this suggests that we have a betrothal story in Jn 4. Jesus did not come seeking a wife, asylum or refuge. Nor was the woman a marriageable maiden, and in the end the water pot was forgotten (4.28). It is fanciful to suggest that the accepted invitation and the stay of two days signifies a betrothal.[109]

Given the centrality of the oasis for the traveller it seems unlikely that all stories of encounters at the well would be betrothal stories. Not all who came to draw water were women and the women were not always unmarried. Other motifs besides betrothal were present in these stories. The motif of hospitality is fundamental. Thus recognition of the influence of the patriarchal well stories need not imply the theme of betrothal. The reader is told by the woman that the well had been given to them by the patriarch Jacob, suggesting that his story has shaped the telling of this story. But this falls short of asserting that what we have here is a betrothal story. Indeed it is possible to see those stories as incipient quest stories. Although they do not fit the precise form, they bear many of the marks and give expression to the motif of quest.

Like those stories, Jn's account of Jesus' encounter with the Samaritans does not appear as a discrete quest story,[110] but is more like the extended series of quest scenes of 1.19-51 and even more like the complex narrative of 11.1–12.11. In addition Jesus himself is presented as a quester, continuing the theme first introduced in 2.13-22. The drama progresses through six scenes:

1). Introduction including Jesus and the disciples, 4.1-6;
2). Jesus and the woman, 4.7-26;
   a). The gift of God: the life giving water, 2.7-15
   b). The mysterious give of the gift of God, 2.16-26
3). The disciples, 4.27;
4). The woman and the men of the city, 4.28-30;
5). Jesus and the disciples, 4.31-38;
6). The Samaritans and Jesus, 4.39-42.

Jesus is situated in Samaria (4.4), though only in 4.5-6 is he brought to the well outside the city of Sychar where the encounter occurs. Three points of significance are conveyed in this preparation.

1. Jesus "must" pass through Samaria, 4.4. While the normal route from Judaea to Galilee was through Samaria, it can hardly be said that

---

[109]Cf. Paul Duke, *Irony in the Fourth Gospel*, 101-3.
[110]Such as 2.1-11; (3.1-15) or 4.46-52.

there was a geographical necessity for Jesus to go through Samaria.[111] The necessity must therefore be of another order: the necessity of the meeting with the Samaritan woman, the necessity of the Samaritan mission, the divine necessity, of Jesus doing what the Father wills.

2. It is straightforwardly mentioned that "The well of Jacob was there." The observant reader will detect in this casual comment the narrator's technique of providing an essential element for the story of the encounter which is to follow.[112]

3.) In the same way the narrator tells us, "It was the sixth hour", 4.6.[113] Being noon it was not the hour to expect a woman to come to draw water. But the meeting was destined.[114] Thus she comes and finds Jesus sitting at, or on the well.[115]

The role of the disciples in this drama is even more superficial than in Jn 2.1-11; 2.13-22. There, at least, although they have no part in the action of the story, the narrator reports their response of faith as a consequence of the events reported. They are not mentioned in the narrative concerning Nicodemus and their role here is minimal. Mention of them serves to build up an understanding of the growing momentum of the Jesus movement, 4.1.

The *second scene* (4.7-26) is in *two parts*, the *first* focussing on water and introduced by Jesus' request, "Give me a drink", 4.7-15. His request already signals his quest although it is yet to be openly announced in the second part of the scene, 4.21-24. The first part is focussed on the quest of the Samaritan woman. She did not intentionally seek Jesus, but she came to the well seeking water and, in the context of the symbolic interpretation of water, this is an expression of her quest for life. The reader is alerted to symbolic dimension by Jesus' response to the woman's objection to his quest, an objection which complicates the story of her quest by interacting with the quest of Jesus. Her objection was that he, as a Jew was out of order requesting a drink from a Samaritan woman, a view the social force of which is reinforced by the narrator, 4.9. Jesus' response was to draw attention to the woman's ignorance of the gift of God (that which the water

---

[111]See Josephus, *Life*, 269; *Antiquities*, 20.118.

[112]Compare 2.1, "and the mother of Jesus was there".

[113]Compare 1.39; 4.52; 19.14. The significance of the statement of time is clear in 13.30 where, at the departure of Judas to betray Jesus, the narrator notes, "and it was night".

[114]Cf. Jacob's meeting with Rachel (Genesis 29.7)

[115]Cf. Moses' meeting with the daughters of Ruel (Exodus 2.15b-22).

symbolized, which was the source of true life)[116] and the identity of the mysterious dispenser of the gift of God, 4.10.

While the question of the identity of the giver (and his quest also) does surface in the first part, it is the main focus of the second part. The focus of the first part is on the gift of God, the life giving water and the quest of the woman, which Jesus has uncovered. Difficulties and objections to her quest were raised by Jesus (4.10,13-14). These challenged her understanding and her attitude progresses from skepticism (4.11) to the point where she requests the life-giving water (4.15). Such a request implies that she has accepted Jesus as the mysterious giver of the life giving water, little as she understands the full significance of this as yet.

In the dialogue with Jesus the woman, like Nicodemus, is shown to be lacking in understanding (3.4,9; 4.11-12). Just as Nicodemus misunderstood Jesus' words about birth $\check{\alpha}\nu\omega\theta\epsilon\nu$, so the woman thought of Jesus' offer of water in a way that failed to grasp his symbolism.[117] Correction was necessary and is provided by Jesus' words of clarification (3.10-15; 4.13-14). Whereas Nicodemus simply disappears, the woman responded positively to the pronouncement of Jesus in 4.13-14:

> "whoever drinks of the water which I will give to *him*,[118] will not thirst for ever, but the water which I will give to him shall be in him a well of water springing up to eternal life."

To this the woman responded with the request, $\kappa\acute{\upsilon}\rho\iota\epsilon$, $\delta\acute{o}\varsigma$ $\mu\iota$ $\tauo\hat{\upsilon}\tauo$ $\tau\acute{o}$ $\ddot{\upsilon}\delta\omega\rho$. As in the quest story of chapter 6, this request gives all the appearance of a a quest on the way to successful fulfilment even though misunderstandings must be clarified, 4.15; 6.34.[119]

In spite of this there is a trend to group the response of the Samaritan woman with those who do not believe, like the Jews of 2.13-23 "She is presented to the readers as a model of the absence of faith."[120] But this

---

[116]Almost certainly here we have reference to Jesus as the one who gives the Spirit, see Jn 1.12,13,26,33; 3.3,5; 7.37-39. While the reader has not yet read Jn 7.37-39 that reading serves to confirm what will already be suspected.

[117]See also 6.27 and the following discourse.

[118]The saying appears to have been inserted into this context because, although Jesus is talking to the woman, the saying is not addressed to the woman in the second person "you" but in the the third person masculine "him".

[119]Compare the request of the crowd to Jesus in 6.34, asking him $K\acute{\upsilon}\rho\iota\epsilon$, $\pi\acute{\alpha}\nu\tauo\tau\epsilon$ $\delta\acute{o}\varsigma$ $\acute{\eta}\mu\hat{\iota}\nu$ $\tau\grave{o}\nu$ $\check{\alpha}\rho\tauo\nu$ $\tauo\hat{\upsilon}\tauo\nu$ with the request of the woman $K\acute{\upsilon}\rho\iota\epsilon$, $\delta\acute{o}\varsigma$ $\mu\iota$ $\tauo\hat{\upsilon}\tauo$ $\tau\grave{o}$ $\ddot{\upsilon}\delta\omega\rho$. These requests have been given their literary form by the evangelist.

[120]F.J. Moloney, *Belief in the Word*, 145. See also H. Boers, *Neither on the Mountain*, 7-22,36-49.

fails to take account of the positive nature of the response which bears no marks of intended irony or sarcasm on the part of the woman even though it does involve misunderstanding. But misunderstanding is clarified in what follows. In the case of Nicodemus the misunderstanding remains when he disappears from the scene of Jn 3 because he is to reappear in later scenes in the Gospel where his story is further clarified. The story of the Samaritan woman is played out in Jn 4 and Jn 4.15 should be understood as a positive response on the way to the fulfillment of the woman's implicit quest for life.

The theme of Jesus as quester is reintroduced in the *second part* of the scene (4.16-26) and in 4.34 he reveals himself as the emissary of God whose food (and drink) is to do the will of the one who sent him and thus to fulfil his quest. Consequently the evangelist has a more complex development in view. First Jesus reveals his prophetic insight, which provokes the question from the woman that provides the opportunity for an answer in which there is a further revealing pronouncement made by Jesus in response to a question concerning the right place to worship.

"Believe me, woman, the hour is coming when neither in this mountain nor in Jerusalem will you worship the Father. You worship what you do not know; we worship what we know, because salvation is of the Jews. But the hour comes and now is, when the true worshippers shall worship the Father in Spirit and truth; For the Father *seeks* such as these to worship him. God is Spirit, and those who worship him must worship him in Spirit and truth." (4.21-24)

The transition is to the Father's (and Jesus') quest for true worshippers. In 2.13-22 Jesus came seeking true worshippers but found only a market-place. Here, in his request for a drink Jesus is presented as a quester. The woman's objections can be understood in terms of his quest for true worshippers, apparently putting in question a mission beyond strictly Jewish boundaries. Having asked for a drink, and having introduced the theme of the life-giving water, the transition to the second part of the scene, which returns to the theme of Jesus' quest, was made by an instruction of Jesus which allowed him to manifest his supernatural knowledge.[121] Jesus, now perceived to be a prophet, was asked about the right place to worship God. In 4.22-23 it becomes apparent that what Jesus sought was true worshippers which he had not found in the Temple (2.13-22). It is the true worshippers that the Father seeks ($\zeta\eta\tau\epsilon\hat{\iota}$) through the sending of his emissary (4.23).[122]

---

[121]Compare Jn 4.16-18 with 1.47-50.

[122]It is the coming of the emissary that signals the dawning of the eschatological hour, $\dot{a}\lambda\lambda\dot{a}$ $\ddot{\epsilon}\rho\chi\epsilon\tau\alpha\iota$ $\ddot{\omega}\rho\alpha,$ $\kappa\alpha\grave{\iota}$ $\nu\hat{\nu}\nu$ $\dot{\epsilon}\sigma\tau\iota\nu,$ 4.23.

The woman's acknowledgement that she is waiting for the Messiah allows Jesus to make a final (for this episode) self-revealing pronouncement, ἐγώ εἰμι, ὁ λαλῶν σοι (4.26). That the woman understands this as Jesus' self identification as the Messiah/Christ is confirmed by 4.29-30. In spite of this meaning, which is obvious in the context of the dialogue with the woman, the assertion is made that the ἐγώ εἰμι here is a divine self-revelation formula.[123] To justify this reading appeal is made to Exod 3.14; Isa 43.10; 45.18. But none of these passages provides a parallel with the Johannine use because in all of them it is obvious that God is the speaker and Exod 3.14 is not a formal parallel in that the verb "to be" is repeated. In none of them is there an assertion of divinity by an ungodlike figure such as a weary traveller at a well who asks for a drink. Given this context, and the woman's mention of the Messiah, the obvious meaning is that Jesus identifies himself as the Messiah and it is difficult to see how the woman or the reader could be expected to understand anything else. That the suggestion is quite untenable in relation to 4.26 is shown by the comparison with 9.9. In each case a speaker (or speakers) is referring to a known figure, the Messiah/Christ in 4.25 and the blind man in 9.8-9. The use of ἐγώ εἰμι is a self identification with the one spoken of. Had the evangelist taken these words to be a divine self-revelation they would not have been placed on the lips of the once blind man.

Given the context of the meeting at the well even the claim to be the Messiah would stretch credulity but the woman evidently accepts it with some hesitancy because of the impression the stranger's words have made upon her. This acceptance becomes the basis of another scene with the woman leading many from her village to Jesus suggesting to them that he is the Christ and the narrator tells us that they came to him (4.29-30).

The woman's role in leading others to Jesus follows the pattern of Jn 1, where one new disciple brings another to Jesus. Whereas Andrew declared boldly, "We have found the Messiah", her words should be understood as a hesitant suggestion, "Can it be that he is the Christ?" The woman spoke of Μεσσίας in 4.25, the narrator adding ὁ λεγόμενος Χριστός. This forms another link with Jn 1 where Andrew also spoke of the Μεσσίαν with the narrator adding, ὅ ἐστιν μεθερμηνευόμενον Χριστός, 1.41. In her report to her compatriots the woman spoke of ὁ Χριστός, 4.29. Naturally the evangelist knows that the latter is the Greek form of the Semitic former (see 1.20, 41). But the change from one to the other on the lips of one of the characters is unusual. It is also unusual that the

---

[123]Thus F.J. Moloney, *Belief in the Word*, 155. See also the discussion of Jn 6.20 in chapter six below.

Samaritan woman should use the Jewish title for the hoped for coming deliverer. But that is the sort of licence you would expect to be taken by a Jewish author writing for Jewish readers and subsequently making his meaning clear to non-Jewish readers.

What of the meaning of Jesus' response in 4.26 for the reader? Could Jesus' answer be understood as both an affirmation that he was the Messiah and as a divine self-revelation at the same time from this perspective?[124] We have already argued that the use of the ἐγώ εἰμι is not a divine self-revelation. Thus Jesus' affirmation is exclusively an assertion of messiahship, even for the reader. But the reader, unlike the characters in the story, has had the benefit of having read the Prologue and knows, through the ensuing narrative, that Jesus is the incarnate divine λόγος. While others had identified him with the Messiah/Christ prior to this episode (1.41), Jesus himself now makes this identification confirming that it is correct (4.26). Thus between the narrators revelation in the Prologue and the ensuing narrative we learn that Jesus is the incarnate λόγος, the Messiah/Christ. This the reader knows, not because of the use of ἐγώ εἰμι but because of having read the Gospel to this point. Only through the outworking of the events narrated in the completed Gospel (especially the glorification/exaltation of Jesus) will this meaning become evident to the believing characters within the drama.

Between Jesus' encounter with the woman and the coming of the villagers Jn has introduced the dialogue between Jesus and his disciples (4.27, 31-38). As in 2.1-11 they are largely absent from this incident also.[125] By introducing them here the evangelist has created a context in which the narrative can be understood in terms of the early Christian mission. In so doing he has made use of a complex of traditions and proverbial sayings.

By the end of the story Jesus has found true worshippers in the woman and her compatriots. Though they had previously worshipped in ignorance, this has been dispelled by the self-revelation of Jesus as the giver of the life-giving water, the saviour of the world. Thus it has

---

[124] To suggest that we have an instance of double meaning (double *entendre*) such as Jesus' use of ἄνωθεν in Jn 3.3 is not convincing. There is nothing to suggest that the woman has misunderstood Jesus.and the plain meaning of his response in 4.26 is a self identification with the Messiah/Christ who has just been mentioned. What is more, the Gospel was written to promote the belief that Jesus is the Christ (20.30-31), even if the meaning of the Christ is redefined in the process.

[125] In this case it could be that the absence of the disciples is simply a consequence of dramatic technique whereby only two parties are on stage at any given moment.

become evident that the woman's visit to the well was an expression of her search for life. Significantly, when the woman (who had come to the well for water) left, she even forgot her water pot (4.28). No doubt it was forgotten, not only by her but also by Jesus who is no longer hungry (4.31-34) or thirsty. The narrator has not forgotten and ensures that the reader is aware that Jesus and the woman have forgotten, reinforcing the point that the subject has really changed for both of them.

By the end of the story it is clear that the woman's quest for life has been satisfied beyond her expectation. Thus Jesus' words are shown to have been successful in correcting the woman's understanding and, through her witness, the villagers came to believe and hear Jesus for themselves. Consequently they confessed Jesus to be the saviour of the world (4.42). This confession is the final and climactic pronouncement of the story. It announces the successful outcome of the quest, not only for the woman and the villagers, but also for Jesus in his quest for true worshippers.

Jn 2.13-22; 3.1-15 preserve the temporal distinction between the "now" of Jesus' ministry and the eschatological moment of fulfillment in the resurrection/exaltation/glorification of Jesus so that the defective responses of the disciples and Nicodemus in the "now" look forward to fulfillment in the future. But in Jn 4 the "now" and the eschatological moment have come together, 4.23 and the expression of faith in 4,42 is portrayed in terms appropriate to the time of fulfillment. The story of the Samaritans does not spill over Jn 4 and the evangelist has taken it to completion by telescoping the "now" with the eschatological fulfillment. Perhaps another reason for doing this is because the perspective of this incident is the mission of believers beyond Jewish boundaries, a perspective evident in 4.9 and especially in the discussion between Jesus and the disciples in 4,31-38. The confession of 4.42 also brings the faith of the Samaritans to challenge the response of the reader in terms which the evangelist wrote to promote, 20.30-31. Jesus' encounter with the Samaritans confirms that the quest for the Messiah involves more than identifying Jesus as the Messiah. It also involves a reinterpretation of his messiahship.

Jn 4.43-45 forms a transition from Samaria to Galilee. It contains traditional material that has been used by the evangelist in a puzzling fashion. The problem concerns the identification of Jesus' own country where he has no honour (see Jn 4.44; Matt 13.57; Mk 6.4; Lk 4.24). It cannot be Samaria, from whence he has come, because the Samaritans received him. Nor can it be Galilee because we are told that the Galileans also received him. It seems therefore to be Judaea (Jerusalem) where the signs mentioned in 4.45 (cf. 2.23) had been performed. This could pick up the identification of Jesus as a Jew (Judaean?) in 4.9, 22.[126] In the Synoptics the tradition is associated with the rejection of Jesus in Nazareth of Galilee. In Jn it is associated with the acceptance of Jesus by the Galileans. The tradition seems to have been used to provide a transition into Galilee but at the same time implies that Jesus' home country is Judaea.[127]

5. The Quest for Life in the Second Cana Sign (4.46-54)

In many ways this is a typical miracle story.[128] The circumstances of the boy are noted. He was at the point of death. The means of healing is specified. Jesus' life-giving word, "Go, your son lives!", is portrayed as the instrument of healing (4.50). The evidence of the healing is given in some detail and there is a stress on the resulting belief consequent on the miracle.[129] But it is not a straightforward miracle story. This is noted by F.J. Moloney[130] who (following Bultmann) sets out the shape of the typical miracle story and his own analysis of the two Johannine Cana stories. The typical miracle story is set out as follows:

1. Problem stated; 2. Request made; 3. Manner of miracle is described;
4. Successful outcome announced; 5. Response of wonder described.

Moloney also gives a five point structure for the two Johannine stories:

1. Problem (2.3; 4.46); 2. Request (2.3; 4.47); 3. Rebuke (2.4; 4.48)
4. Reaction (2.5; 4.50); 5. Consequences (2.6-11; 4.51-53).

In particular what distinguishes the stories in Jn from the "normal" pattern is the rebuke of Jesus. This constitutes the objection which is essential to the structure of the quest story. The fourth part of Moloney's analysis (Reaction) is also flawed. He notes the reaction of the mother of Jesus (2.5) to the rebuke (2.4) but fails to note the reaction of the βασιλικός (4.49). In each case the "reaction" is a reaffirmation of the original quest.

---

[126]J.W. Pryor, "Jn 4.44 and the Patris of Jesus" (*CBQ* 42/2 (1987) 254-63) argues that, even in Jn, the tradition refers specifically to Galilee though it has secondary application to the whole of Israel. But this can hardly be the case in the light of the indication of the acceptance of Jesus by the Galileans in 4.45, 53. It remains an open question whether the tradition was known to Jn (as in *P Oxy* 1 and *Gos. Thom* 31) free of narrative context or whether, consciously contrary to the Synoptic tradition, he wished to show the acceptance of Jesus by the Galileans.

[127]Thus correctly Wayne Meeks, "Galilee and Judaea in the Fourth Gospel", *JBL* 85 (1966), 159-69.

[128]See R. Bultmann, *The History of the Synoptic Tradition*, 209-43.

[129]Having returned home and having discovered and made known the exact correspondence in time of the word of Jesus and the actual healing of his son, he and all the members of his household also came to believe.

[130]*Belief in the Word*, 90, 189-90.

which had been challenged by Jesus' objection. Jesus' life-giving word to the βασιλικὸς is noted (4.50) but his word to the servants is ignored (2.7), thus putting the instruction by the mother of Jesus to the servants on a level with Jesus' word, though Moloney notes that she refers to what Jesus will say. Moloney rightly notes the confirmation of the miracles leads to the faith of others, which is an important Johannine motif.

The miracle quest story is a sub-type of the quest story and Jn 4.46-54 belongs to this sub-type. The story has Synoptic parallels and the conciseness and simplicity of this story suggest that it has been taken over, more or less in the same form, from the tradition. It may have some relation to the miracle quest story of Matt 8.5-13=Lk 7.1-10 (Q?). Both stories are associated with Capernaum but in the Synoptics the quester is a centurion, in Jn a nobleman (βασιλικὸς).[131] In Matt the patient is the centurion's παῖς, in Lk his δοῦλος, in Jn the nobleman's son (υἱὸς).[132] In the Synoptics Jesus commends the centurion's faith whereas he reprimands the nobleman in Jn (4.48). While the reprimand does not fit the narrative naturally, an indication that it was so placed by the evangelist, it functions as an objection to the nobleman's quest, an objection that must be overcome if his quest is to succeed.[133] In this respect Jn 4.46-54 is a model miracle quest story. But there is insufficient evidence to show that it was derived from Matt or Lk. It is more likely that Jn has made use of Synoptic-like tradition, perhaps from Q.

The quest is expressed in the nobleman's purposeful visit to Jesus and his request. This story also conveys an important pronouncement of Jesus in 4.48. The saying tends to imply conflict, at least a critical attitude in relation to the request/demand for signs. It constitutes an objection to be overcome (compare 2.4). "Except you see signs and wonders, you will not believe." That objection was overcome by the nobleman's persistence, and Jesus responded affirmatively to the request. Indeed, as is commonly noted, the objection is strange in that the coming of the nobleman already signifies a degree of faith. This suggests that the saying of 4.48 has been inserted into a miracle story which now exists to give a context for the saying. The saying does put in question faith based on signs. It does so by using the expression "signs and wonders" (σημεῖα καὶ τέρατα), found

---

[131] Josephus uses this term to refer to soldiers of the emperor or of Herod. See U. Wegner, *Der Hauptmann von Kafarnaum*, 59 n 8. Thus the question of whether reference is to a Jew or a Gentile is not resolved.

[132] If the original reading was παῖς, both δοῦλος and υἱὸς might have been derived from it because παῖς may mean "child" or "servant".

[133] Compare the similarly inappropriate objection in the first of the pair of miracle quest stories (2.4) of which 4.46-54 is the second.

only here in Jn.[134] In the gospel tradition the expression is used of false Christs and false prophets who will perform "signs and wonders" to lead astray, if possible, the elect (Mk 13.22 and Matt 24.24). It may be that this critique concerns the "sign prophets" of whom Josephus was also critical.[135] Given this tradition, and the context of a demand in Jn, implied by the words "except you see...", it is clear that the saying is critical of faith which *demands* to see signs and wonders. Miracles are not an adequate criterion for identifying the Messiah.

Objections or problems to be overcome are an essential part of the quest story. The nobleman's persistence was rewarded by Jesus' life-giving word. The reader is then told that the nobleman believed Jesus' life-giving word, "go your way, your son lives", indicating a positive result to his quest. The faith of his household[136] was based on the successful healing coincident with the word of Jesus. Reference to the conversion of the "household" might evidence the mission situation of the early church surfacing in the narrative. If this is the situation, reference to the household might indicate a Roman context. But the evangelist makes nothing of this matter so that it does not appear to be significant for the narrative. Further, the narrator has ensured that the reader is aware that this sign was performed when Jesus had returned to Cana of Galilee. Thus the attempt to show a progress of Jesus' mission from Jewish territory (1.19-3.36) to Samaria (4.1-42) and finally to Gentiles (4.46-54) appears to be misguided. Rather the excursion into Samaria is emphatically made to look exceptional (4.9) and following this Jesus returns to Jewish territory.

Although critical of the demand for signs the miracle quest story was used apologetically to appeal to those within the synagogue who were open to the messianic claims of Jesus. The evangelist's strategy was to narrate and interpret a selection of signs with a view to leading the readers to authentic faith in Jesus, a true understanding of his messiahship (20.30-31). The disciples are entirely absent from this incident and no attempt has been made to introduce them.[137]

---

[134]It is found frequently in the LXX, for example, in Exodus 7.3 and in Josephus.

[135]*AJ* xix.162; xx.97-99, 167-172, 188; *BJ* ii.258-263; vi.285-286.

[136]Jn 4.53 and see Acts 18.8 and compare Acts 10.2; 11.14; 16.15.

[137]They are also absent from 2.23-3.15. Contrast 2.1-11; 2.13-22; 4.4-42 though even here their presence has no influence on the outcome of the events in the narrative.

IV. CONCLUSION

The *inclusio* formed by the linking of the two miracle stories (2.1-11; 4.46-54) in 4.46, 54 is commonly noted.[138] But recognition that the two Cana miracles have been presented formally as miracle quest stories needs to be stressed. Thus we have an *inclusio* on the theme of the quest. Further, 2.1-11 is a bridge passage, forming the conclusion to the quest episodes beginning at 1.19. Thus 1.19–4.54 finds its focus on the theme of the quest and this is important for the theology of the Gospel. Dominantly the theme is the quest for the Messiah and the life that he brings. In this quest and its fulfilment there is evidence of a developing christological perception. It is, in chapter 1, the quest for the Messiah, in which the questers proclaim, "We have found the Messiah". That messianic categories are too restrictive is already suggested in chapter 3 and by the insertion of 1.51 into chapter 1. In Jn 3 Jesus responds to the tentative approach by Nicodemus, in which he acknowledged Jesus as a teacher come from God, by turning his attention to the kingdom of God and the Son of Man (3.3,5,13-14). In chapter 4 messianic categories are again shown to be inadequate. The woman raised the question of the Messiah, with whom Jesus identified himself, and the woman tentatively confessed Jesus as such to her compatriots. But in the end they confess him as the saviour of the world.

In the final miracle quest story no christological categories are used. Instead, upon learning of the efficacy of Jesus' life-giving word it is said of the nobleman that "he believed and his whole house" (4.53). When, in the narrative, Jesus' life-giving word was pronounced, the narrator indicated that "the man believed Jesus' word" (4.50). Believing Jesus' word, in Jn, is significant belief.[139] But the concluding belief is absolute; no object is specified. Reference to the whole house believing is indication of the conversion of the household (see Acts 11.14; 16.14-15,31). Consequently the *inclusio* on quest finishes on a high note. This is true also of the quest of Jesus for true worshippers. Whereas he had not found them in the Temple in Jerusalem, he did find them in Samaria, where once they worshipped in ignorance, because they were willing to receive the new revelation, they now worshipped God in Spirit and Truth. In this context Jesus equates his quest for true worshippers with the Father's quest, foreshadowing the christology of Jn 5.17. This confirms the suspicion that the portrayal of Jesus as quester belongs to the second edition of the Gospel.

---

[138]See for example F.J. Moloney, "From Cana to Cana", *Salesianum* 40 (1978) 817-43.
[139]See 10.34-38.

It is difficult to overestimate the importance of quest stories in Jn. The evangelist himself was responsible for the development of many of the traditions into quest stories. He has transformed the traditional stories into quest stories because he perceived the turmoil of human life as a quest and Jesus as the fulfilment of the quest of all who were searching. The impression of the widespread searching could also be taken as an historical and cultural comment relating to the time and place of the evangelist. Such searching was common in the great Hellenistic urban centres.[140] It was especially true of urban *diaspora* Judaism after 70 CE which was in search of an identity. At the same time the evangelist depicts the quest as a consequence of the unfulfilled nature of human life apart from the revelation of God brought by Jesus. According to Rudolf Bultmann, it is a fundamental assumption of the evangelist that the universal quest for life has God as its goal, and that the quester meets the goal of the search in the revealer. Because of this the revealer presents himself in the ἐγώ εἰμι revelatory formula in which he identifies himself with whatever it is for which the people are searching. If this perception is true to the evangelist's point of view it is significant that quest stories should be an important feature of the Gospel.[141] Because human life is unfulfilled Jesus was able to present himself as the fulfilment of the human quest. This is the force of the ἐγώ εἰμι sayings. Naturally it is the evangelist who presents Jesus in this way even when he does so using the words of Jesus. The diversity of questers portrayed (the Baptist; disciples of the Baptist and their associates; the mother of Jesus; Nicodemus, a Pharisee, a ruler; Samaritans; a nobleman; a Galilean crowd; Mary and Martha; Greeks, Mary Magdalene)[142] seeking Jesus reveals the universality of the quest, that all are questers until they come to Jesus. On the other side of this issue, those who seek and find discover that they have been the object of the quest of Jesus and that in him God is in the quest for true worshippers.

---

[140]The Hellenistic philosophies of the market place fit this pattern along with the new religions of the Hellenistic age as evidenced, for example, in the *Corpus Hermeticum*.

[141] On this theme see R. Bultmann, *The Gospel of John*, 61-2, 182, 378-80, 530-2 and J. Painter, *Theology as Hermeneutics: Rudolf Bultmann's Interpretation of the History of Jesus*,120-6.

[142]The quest stories of Jn 6-20 will be discussed in subsequent chapters.

5

The Paradigm of Rejection[1]

The quest stories after chapter 4 (apart from 20.1-18, which is a special case, coming in the context of the resurrection narrative) have all been overlaid with the theme of rejection. For this reason they belong to the section of the Gospel which builds up to the final rejection of Jesus.[2] In a way there is no progress in Jn 5-12 beyond 5.16,18, though chapters 11 and 12 do introduce a formal plot to arrest Jesus and to bring about his death.[3] Even though the theme of rejection is dominant in this section it has been possible to identify underlying quest stories.

The category "rejection" is used in preference to Tannehill's "objection" because objections/obstacles to be overcome by the quester are an essential part of quest stories.[4] In rejection stories objections express entrenched opposition/rejection which nothing can change.[5] If these objections are answered they are exchanged for new objections because they express definitive opposition. Tannehill's analysis of the form and function of objection stories holds good for rejection stories.[6] The story has three parts:[7]

1. Cause of the objection;
2. Expression of the objection;
3. Response to the objection.

To this I would add, as is implied by Tannehill:

4. The final rejection of Jesus.

---

[1]This chapter is a much expanded version of my article "Text and Context in John 5".

[2]Rejection stories dominate Jn 5-19 so that even the quest stories of this section have been overlaid with the theme of rejection.

[3]Previous formal attempts had been made to arrest Jesus (7.32) but there no mention is made of the intention to kill him. Elsewhere attempts to stone/kill Jesus are mentioned (5.18; 10.36). But these look more like spontaneous (though repeated) reactions to particular events. After the raising of Lazarus a formal, calculated plan emerges and it is, in the end, successful, 11.45-57.

[4]Thus in quest stories it is normally Jesus who raises some objection to the particular form of the quest for the Messiah. His objection is aimed at the redirection of the quest.

[5]In rejection stories the opponents of Jesus object to some aspect of Jesus' origin, life, words, or works.

[6]See *Pronouncement Stories*, 8.

[7]Parts 1 and 2 may be combined.

Rejection was implicit in the story from the beginning but is expressed definitively in some subsequent word or action. It is the entrenched rejection that dominates the story. There is no chance that the protagonists might change position, whatever happens in the story. Objection leads inevitably to rejection.

On the whole the rejection stories are based on miracle stories, 5.1-18; 6.1-71; 9.1-41. The rejection element is introduced by the evangelist noting that the miracle was performed on the Sabbath (5.9; 9.14) or by the enunciation of a distinctive Johannine christology, 5.17,19-30; 6.41,52. Thus the law was used as a basis for rejecting Jesus even though the action which proved to be objectionable was a miracle of healing. It is to accentuate the inevitability of rejection that these stories often develop on the basis of miracle stories. Rejection occurs in spite of the miracle.

Rejection stories have also been built upon the basis of some quest stories in such a way that the the theme of rejection has come to dominate them. What this suggests is that rejection stories belong to a later situation when the Johannine Christians had been excluded from the synagogue. At this stage Jn came to argue that the quest for the Messiah could only be fulfilled when Jesus had been rejected.

Both Jn 6 and Jn 9 present hybrids[8] in that, in Jn 9 the behaviour of the once blind man is commended while the behaviour of the Pharisees/Jews is condemned for rejecting him and, by implication, Jesus as well. Jn 6. 1-36 was a quest story, but was developed into a rejection story. Even the latter is probably a hybrid in which the response of "the twelve" is commended[9] while the rejection by the Jews and the mass of disciples is condemned.

I. THE PARADIGM OF REJECTION (5.1-18)

Jn 5 is made up of three main parts:

1. The story (5.1-9b);
2. The disputation (5.9c-18);
3. The discourse, which is in two parts (5.19-30 and 31-47).

The miracle of Jn 5 is not done in response to any request. In rejection stories the initiative is regularly taken by Jesus. It is Jesus who sees the man and, knowing[10] his condition asks if he would be made *whole*. The serious nature of the man's illness is emphasized by indicating the length of time he has been ill and his inability to get into the pool unaided. The word of healing was spoken by Jesus, "Arise take your bed and walk",

---

[8]They mix the *genres* of rejection and commendation stories.
[9]There is no specific commendation, as there is in Matt 16.17.
[10]No doubt supernatural knowledge is implied, 5.6.

5.8. That word was enough and the readers are informed of the instantaneous nature of the healing which is evidenced by the man carrying off his bed. Thus far what we have fits the pattern of a straightforward miracle story.[11] The conditions of the problem are set out, the action of Jesus described, and the evidence of the healing verified.

Only when the healing has been completed and evidenced does the narrator inform the readers that it was the Sabbath on the day that Jesus healed the man, 5.9c.[12] The healed man then plays no further part in the story, except to identify Jesus as the Sabbath-breaker. Focus in this story falls squarely on Jesus and his developing conflict with the Jews.[13] Through the development of dialogues in the context of conflict Jesus is made to justify his action with a *pronouncement*: "My Father is working until now, and I am working", 5.17. The saying does not resolve the situation. Indeed it involves a claim more controversial than the Sabbath-breaking action which might perhaps have been justified using a different kind of argument. What follows is the first account of an attempt to kill Jesus (5.18).

The narrator reports this attempt as a response to Jesus' saying of 5.17, indicating that the Jews sought "all the more" ($\mu\hat{\alpha}\lambda\lambda o\nu$) to kill Jesus. But this is the first specifically recorded attempt! This means that the persecution mentioned in 5.16 is understood as an attempt to kill Jesus. A. E. Harvey[14] has argued that $\dot{\epsilon}\delta\dot{\iota}\omega\kappa o\nu\ \alpha\dot{\upsilon}\tau\dot{o}\nu$ means "they sought to bring a charge against him". If so the narrator (in 5.18) implies that it was a capital charge, though it is possible that what is in view is a move from legal action to direct action. The implication of ($\mu\hat{\alpha}\lambda\lambda o\nu$) is that both involved an attempt to kill Jesus. More likely, however, is the view that 5.16,18 imply less formal actions, expressed first in general terms and then specifically naming the quest of the Jews as a quest to kill Jesus. In this way the narrator builds the sense of conflict rapidly and dramatically. This reading is also supported by noting that the first formal attempt to arrest Jesus is expressed in 7.32-36 while the formal plan to have him put to death emerges only in 11.45-53. Thus in terms of Jn's

---

[11]See R.Bultmann, *The History of the Synoptic Tradition*, 209-243.

[12]See also 9.14. This suggests that two miracle stories have been transformed into rejection stories by the insertion of the Sabbath motif which has led to the development of controversial dialogues and discourses.

[13]Contrast the rejection story of chapter 9 in which focus falls on the once blind man until 9.39. Whereas in Jn 5 action was taken against Jesus, in Jn 9 it was the once blind man who was thrown out of the synagogue, not Jesus.

[14]*Jesus on Trial*, 50ff.

story there appears to be a progress from the informal hostile actions of 5.16,18 to the formal plots of 7.32-36; 11.45-53.

Jn 5.18 concludes the rejection story, though the evangelist has developed a lengthy discourse setting out the basis and meaning of the pronouncement (5.17), which is the text of the discourse, 5.19-47. But 5.1-18 is the paradigmatic rejection story. It provides the dual'bases for the Jewish rejection of Jesus, as a Law-breaker (Sabbath) and blasphemer (5.17; 10.33) and describes the rejection in terms of persecution and the attempt ($\dot{\epsilon}\zeta\dot{\eta}\tau o \upsilon \nu$) to kill Jesus, 5.18. Here, for the first time, $\zeta \eta \tau \epsilon \hat{\iota} \nu$ is used in the strong negative sense of the quest to kill (or arrest) Jesus. In this subtle way Jn again shows that the true quest can only be fulfilled when Jesus has been rejected. Thus his opponents inadvertently contributed to the fulfilment of the quest.

The four parts of the rejection story are clear. 1.) The cause of the objection is the Sabbath healing which became public when the man was observed carrying his bed. 2.) The objection was expressed in the questioning of the man and then in the persecution of Jesus (5.16). 3.) His response is given in the pronouncement of 5.17 which becomes the text of the later discourse. 4.) The response did nothing to overcome the objection but led to a more intense expression of rejection (5.18).

The traditional miracle story of Jn 5.1-9b appears to have been free of conflict motifs. Conflict was introduced only in 5.9c, after the miracle story had already concluded. This suggests that the evangelist was responsible for reworking a miracle story into a rejection story and did so by the addition of the subsequent dialogues. While the introduced note that it was the Sabbath comes as a surprise to the reader, it has great dramatic force. It changes everything that has happened. By holding back this information to the end, the miracle has been brought forcefully into conflict with the attitude to the Sabbath expressed by the Jews. The rejection of Jesus is certain from 5.9c-10. The rejection story has not been told to persuade those who have rejected Jesus to accept him. Rather it has been told to confirm the resolve of the Johannine community in facing the rejection which Jesus had faced before them.

II. TEXT AND CONTEXT IN JOHN 5

Jn 5.16-18 provides us with a text in context. The text is 5.17, "My Father is working until now and I am working". The context is the persecution of Jesus for breaking the Sabbath and for asserting that God was his own Father. This context gives a particular resonance to the idea of work/works (ἔργον/ἔργα) which is a key concept in the Gospel.[15] It is, to some extent, the equivalent of sign/signs (σημεῖον/σημεῖα).[16] Jn 5.17 introduces the first extensive treatment of the theme of Jesus' works.[17] Jesus' action on the Sabbath was an ideal context in which to assert the identification of his work with the work of God. This term (work) suggests the Sabbath controversy and the principal line of justification in the text (5.17) and its exposition (5.19-47). For what follows it is crucial that the healing miracle should have occurred on the Sabbath and that it should have been viewed as a Sabbath-breaking work. Why this should be so is made clear, at one level, by the place of Jn 5 in the structure of the Gospel.

1. The Context

Jn 5[18] presents the first discourse based on a miracle story.[19] It is the first of a number found in Jn 5-11.[20] Chapters 5-12 form an important section of the Gospel but there is evidence that suggests that the conflict section once concluded at 10.42.[21] The focus of this section is on the conflict

---

[15]In the controversy Jesus is set over against Moses and the Law. Perhaps the portrayal of the signs performed by Moses in Exodus 3.12–13.16 suggested the use of the term sign for Jesus' miracles as persuasive displays of power. See Robert Houston Smith, "Exodus Typology in the Fourth Gospel", *JBL* 81 (1962), 329. In Jn the force of Jesus' signs is made to modify the demand of the Law of Moses. See Jn 9.16 and my *JWT*, 19-24. In this controversy the ethical quality of Jesus' works is at least as important as the miraculous nature of the signs, Jn 10.32. This is also true in the healing of the man with a withered hand in Mk 3.1-6, especially verse 4. Perhaps the emphasis in Jn 9.16 on "such signs" also makes this point which is drawn out in the dialogue of Jn 9.24-34, especially verses 25,30-33. The choice of the term works is significant in the context of the Sabbath controversy in that it is work that is prohibited on the Sabbath.

[16]In 6.30 the crowd asked Jesus, "What sign do you do...what do you work (ἐργάζῃ)?" In Jn the works are part of the manifold witness to Jesus, 5. 36; 10. 25. See my *JWT*, 10-11, 23, 52-53, 72, 73, 75.

[17]See earlier only 3.21; 4.34.

[18]Jn 5 is marked as a new beginning by the opening words, "After these things" (Μετὰ ταῦτα), see 3.22, 5.1,14; 6.1; 7.1; 13.7; 19.38; 21.1.

[19]There are earlier discourses in Jn 3 and 4, but neither of these is based on a miracle story. There are earlier miracle stories, notably the two referred to as the first and second Cana *Signs* (2.1-11; 4.46-54), but neither of these is made the basis of a discourse.

[20]See also the feeding miracle of Jn 6; the healing of Jn 9 and the raising of Lazarus in Jn 11.

[21]Jn 10.40-42 is a summary transition duplicated by 12.37-50. But 11.1–12.50 also includes conflict material which could have been added to a later edition of the Gospel. On this see B. Lindars, *John*, 378-82 and especially Moody Smith, *Johannine Christianity*, 75 n 45. The narrative of the death

with "the Jews"[22] and it is in these chapters that the great debates and disputes take place. Jn 5 introduces the first attempts to persecute (arrest?) (5.16) and to kill (5.18; cf. Mk 3.6) Jesus;[23] a theme which recurs throughout this section, 7.1,11,19,20,25,30,32,44; 8.20,59;10.31ff.,39; 11.50,57; 12.9-11. What ties chapters 5 and 10 together in particular is the development of the theme of the Father/Son relationship. That relationship is set out at length in 5.17-47; and in 10.14-18,29-39. Because it is, to some extent a repetition, the theme is somewhat briefer in chapter 10. It reaffirms the Father's love for the Son, 5.20; 10.17; see also 3.35.

Although chapter 5 characteristically speaks of the Father and the Son in the discourse, Jesus also speaks of "my Father", 5.17; 10.25,29. In chapter 5 speaking of God as his Father was understood as a claim to equality with God, 5.18,[24] and in 10.30 Jesus himself drew out the implications in the words, "I and the Father are one" (see also 10.38) thus reiterating and extending the theme of chapter 5. In both chapters the relationship is made the basis for the claim that Jesus' works ($\xi\rho\gamma a$) are the works of God, 5.17,19ff.,30,36; 10.32,37f.; see 7.21-24; and this is expressed in terms of his mission from the Father, 5.23f.,36-38; 10.36; and see 7.16,18,28,33; 8.16,26,29.

The attempt to arrest or stone Jesus appears in chapter 5 and recurs in the following chapters, 5.16,18; 7.19,20,25,32,44; 8.20,59; 10.31ff.,39. In chapter 10 the charge of 5.18 is explicitly spelt out as blasphemy, 10.33; see 19.7. The charge of demon-possession recurs in 7.20; 8.48-52; 10.20-21. There is also an emphasis on the schism ($\sigma\chi\iota\sigma\mu a$) caused by Jesus and his words, 7.43; 9.16; 10.19. This theme is more pervasive in chapters 5-10 than the actual use of the term. It is indicated by the murmuring ($\gamma o\gamma\gamma\upsilon\sigma\mu\delta s$, $\gamma o\gamma\gamma\upsilon\zeta o\nu\tau os$) in the crowd (7.12ff.,32). Fear of the Jews (7.13; 9.22) inhibited open confession of faith. In spite of this a

---

and raising to life of Lazarus not only provides material parallel to the passion and resurrection of Jesus, the notable sign of the raising of Lazarus becomes an added provocation to the Jewish authorities who determined to kill Jesus, 11.53.

[22]Sometimes termed simply "the Jews" (5.10,15,16,18), or "the Pharisees", or "the chief Priests and Pharisees". In 9.13-17,40-41 the Pharisees are not distinguished from "the Jews" in Jn 9.18-22(34); 10.19-21. Both Jews and Pharisees can be viewed in unified opposition to Jesus or as divided by the response to him.

[23]In 5.16,18 both $\xi\delta\iota\omega\kappa o\nu$ and $\xi\zeta\eta\tau o\upsilon\nu$ should probably be understood as *inceptive* imperfects indicating the commencement of attempts to persecute and kill Jesus. The use of the imperfect tense in Jn 7 is probably *iterative*, indicating repeated action. See note 2 in chapter 7 below.

[24]Cf. Phil 2.6.

running theme is that many believed in him, 6.68f.; 7.31; 8.30; 10.42; and see 2.23; 11.45,47f.; 12.42.

The great festivals of Judaism provide the occasion for the conflicts.[25] But it is the conflicts rather than the festivals that are in focus. In the conflict Jesus' words, appealing to his relation to the Father (5.17ff.), justify his *works*, while in Jn 10 he appealed to his *works* as evidence to justify his words, 10.37-38. The argument about the relation of words and works turns full circle in chapters 5 and 10. The paradox is an example of the Johannine hermeneutical circle in that the words justify the works and the works justify the words. But there is a "correct" or easier point of *entry* into the circle and that is the works, 10.37-38;14.10-11. It is for this reason that the discourse of Jn 5 is developed on the basis of a miracle story. Thus, we have a miracle story which, through the insertion of a Sabbath context, has become the basis of a brief set of controversial dialogues. What follows the dialogues is formally a discourse (5.19-47) based on a text (5.17) in a context of persecution, 5.16,18.

i From miracle story to rejection story. *The miracle story* is the entry point to the discourse. The story itself is told with great economy 5.2-3a,5-9b.[26] It is introduced by a note indicating the reason for Jesus' presence in Jerusalem, 5.1. The note bears the imprint of the evangelist's hand in the style of the general time reference[27] and the note concerning "the feast of the Jews"[28] which provided the occasion for Jesus

---

[25]"Going up to Jerusalem" is a traditional idiom, Jn 2.13; 5.1; 7.8,10; 11.55. In each case a Jewish feast was involved; Passover, 2.13,23 (6.4);11.55; (12.1; 13.1; 18.28,39; 19.14), unspecified, 5.1; Tabernacles, 7.8,10. In Jn 5-12 the controversies are set in the context of the Jewish festivals. Reference to "the feast of the Jews" indicates the adaptation of the Gospel to a non-Jewish audience. See 2.13, though the absence of the name of the feast appears to have led to some textual confusion here ("a feast of the Jews", or "the feast of the Jews" which would have led to scribal attempts to identify the feast).

[26]Jn 5.3b-4 are omitted from the best mss.

[27]See 2.12; 3.22; 4.43; 5.14; 6.1; 7.1.

[28]Reference to the feast *of the Jews* indicates the adaptation of the Gospel to a non-Jewish audience, cf. 2.13; 3.1; 6.4; 7.2. The use of "the Jews" generally in the Gospel is complex. For example, it is acknowledged that Jesus is a Jew, 4.9; and salvation is of the Jews 4.22. On this see my "The Church and Israel in the Gospel of John", *NTS* 25, 103–12. In addition to the notes concerning the Jewish festivals there is the refrain of "your Law" in the conversation between Jesus and the Jews, 8.17;10.34; and "their Law", 15.25 which sets the Jews apart from the Johannine Christians. It is likely that we should understand that what Jn means by "the Jews" progresses in the telling of the story and that where the impact on his own

"going up to Jerusalem". The evangelist joined his editorial introduction to a traditional miracle story in such a way that the voice of the narrator is heard in 5.1-3a,5-6b. The narrator sets the scene, the feast being the occasion for Jesus being in Jerusalem, the place being a pool with five porticoes[29] where all manner of sick people gathered. One of these had been there 38 years. We learn this from the omniscient narrator who also informs us that Jesus knew the man's situation. The omniscience of Jesus is more significant in that this is supernatural whereas the omniscience of the narrator is simply the perspective of the storyteller.

The miracle story is completed by the first of a series of dialogues (5.6c-8) leaving the narrator to inform us of the immediacy of the cure which is evidenced by the man who, in response to the command of Jesus, took his bed and walked away, 5.9a-b. Only then is the reader informed by the narrator: "But it was the Sabbath on that day", 5.9c. The focus is on the Sabbath throughout the remainder of the dialogues, 5.9,10,16,18.

The miracle story itself is similar in form and content to many of the Synoptic miracle stories, especially Mk 2.1-12.[30] Mk's story is not located on the Sabbath, though the healing of the man with the withered hand is, Mk 3.1-6; Matt 12.9-14; Lk 6.6-11.[31] Mk 2.1-12 opens the conflict section (Mk 2.1-3.30) as does Jn 5.[32] The conflict in Mk 2.1-12

---

community is most obtrusive in the telling of the story of Jesus the hostility of the Jews is most pronounced.

[29]Textual variants concerning the Hebrew name of the pool are not significant because they do not help to locate it. The description of the five porticoes is more assistance here. See J. Jeremias, *Jerusalem,* 9-26. The porticoes were constructed by Herod and "housed" a number of pools.

[30]Compare especially Jn 5.8,9 with Mk 2.9,11. The wording of Jesus' command "Arise take your bed and walk" is exactly the same in Jn 5.8 and Mk 2.9,11, including the use of, κράβαττόν for bed, except that Mk has "Arise and (καί) take...". But there is evidence that the Johannine story is more developed in the stress on Jesus' omniscience, his sovereign control and the absence of any show of faith by the sick man.

[31]In addition to the controversial Sabbath setting this Synoptic tradition shares with the Johannine story the command of Jesus to the man to "arise" (ἔγειρε), Mk 3.3; reference to the man's hand being made whole (ὑγιής) Matt 12.13; Jn 5.6,9,11,14,15; and the justification that to do good (ἀγαθόν), to save life is permitted on the Sabbath, Mk 3.4. This form of justification is not used in Jn 5, though it is in 7.23; and perhaps 10.32. While 7.23 retrospectively attempts to justify Jesus' action of making the man whole on the Sabbath, no attempt to do this is made in Jn 5. The scandal of Jesus' Sabbath-breaking work is thus not reduced.

[32]In general Jn 1-12 follows the thematic order of Mk: (1) Prologue and call of disciples, Mk 1.1-20; Jn 1.1-51; (2) the revelation of Jesus through word and action, Mk 1.21-45; Jn 2.1-4.54; (3) Conflict Stories and disputations, Mk 2.1-3.30; Jn 5.1-10.39 (12.50).

concerns Jesus' claim to have the power to forgive sins and is expressed in the form of a *Pronouncement Story*, which is the form appropriate to conflict in Mk. Jn 5.1-18 is a more complex pronouncement story because the evangelist has transformed a simple miracle story into a rejection story. The memorable pronouncement comes at the conclusion of a set of dialogues followed only by the narrator's indication of the rejection of Jesus by the Jews who sought (ἐζήτουν) to kill him. The grounds for that rejection are clearly stated:

> not only because he broke the Sabbath, but also because he called God his own Father making himself equal with God. (Jn 5.18)

John Ashton[33] is formally correct in questioning why the Jews thought (wrongly?) Jesus "to be claiming equality with God simply because he calls him father". The answer is that in this summary the narrator assumes that in 5.17 Jesus signals the identification of his Sabbath-breaking work with the work of God implying equality in the sense, "my work is my Father's work". Hence the use of Father/Son language here is offensive because of the context of the Sabbath-breaking work that Jesus claims is the work of God.

ii The dialogues. In Jn dialogue often signals disputation. The dialogues, not as elaborate as those of Jn 9, nonetheless follow the same dramatic pattern where only two characters or groups appear on "stage" at a time, heightening the dramatic effect and emphasizing the force of the conflicts. Only the voice of the narrator intrudes, supplying essential information to the reader. The dialogues can be set out as follows:[34]

First Encounters

i. Jesus and the man (=AB): the healing, 5.6-8.

ii. The Jews and the man (CB): the question, "who is the Sabbath breaker?", 5.10-13.

Reprise

i. Jesus and the man (AB): the warning, "sin no more!" 5.14.

ii. The man and the Jews (BC): the answer, "Jesus is the man" 5.15.

New encounter

iii. The Jews and Jesus (CA): persecution and response, 5.16ff.

The dialogical development leads to the confrontation of Jesus with the Jews. On the way, the man Jesus has healed becomes an informer (5.15) and then disappears from the scene, unlike the healed man of Jn 9

---

[33]*Understanding*, 137.

[34]The letters (A, B, C) are used to indicate the characters in their order of appearance: Jesus, the man, the Jews. Compare the pattern is Jn 9 below.

who there plays the main role. Here in Jn 5 it is Jesus who holds centre stage and the dialogues soon return the spotlight of attention to him. The last of the dialogues provides the opportunity for Jesus to give the text (5.17) upon which the discourse of 5.19-47 is based.

The miracle story, which once was used to demonstrate Jesus' sovereign knowledge,[35] control[36] and power,[37] in an attempt to win other Jews to faith in Jesus, came to be used in the conflict with the synagogue. Then the Mosaic Law, especially Sabbath Law, was the principal focus. The dialogues evidence the use of the miracle story in that controversial context in which the synagogue demanded the choice between Jesus or Moses. Initially the evangelist responded that no choice was necessary because acceptance of Moses' words leads to belief in Jesus, 5.39-40,45-47. Such a position antedates the exclusion of believers in Jesus from the synagogue, 9.22,34; 12.42; 16.2.

In the dialogues two aspects of the miracle story are featured, one explicitly and the other implicitly. Explicit is the emphasis on the fact that the man was made whole ($\dot{v}\gamma\iota\dot{\eta}\varsigma$), in Jesus' question (5.6), the narration of the event (5.9), the question of the Jews (5.11), the statement of Jesus (5.14) and the answer of the healed man (5.15). What is more the incident is recalled in 7.23 where it is argued that making a person "whole" on the Sabbath should be permitted. This is not argued in chapter 5. Certainly it is emphatically and repeatedly stated that what Jesus had done, on the Sabbath, was to make the man whole.[38] But as yet there is no attempt to justify what he had done by appeal to the character of the act which will, in due course, be described as a *work,* that is, what is forbidden on the Sabbath. Rather, in Jn 5, what justifies the work is Jesus' appeal to his relation to the Father. This point would have been obscured if the argument, known to the evangelist and the Synoptics, that "good works" or "healings" were not prohibited by the Sabbath Law, had been introduced. Thus no debate arises here about the legitimacy of healing on the Sabbath.[39] To have taken this direction would not have served the purpose

---

[35]He knows the situation of the man without asking, Jn 5.6.

[36]He takes the initiative without any show of faith from the man, unlike Mk 2.5.

[37]He heals the man immediately; at his command, his word, the man became ($\dot{\epsilon}\gamma\dot{\epsilon}\nu\epsilon\tau o$) whole. Compare creation by the word in Jn 1.3 ($\pi\dot{a}\nu\tau a \delta\iota$ '$a\dot{v}\tauo\hat{v}$ $\dot{\epsilon}\gamma\dot{\epsilon}\nu\epsilon\tau o$).

[38]In 10.32 Jesus appeals to his many good works ($\pi o\lambda\lambda\dot{a}$ $\dot{\epsilon}\rho\gamma a \kappa a\lambda\dot{a}$) stressing there the character of his works. It is this, at least as much as the miraculous nature of the works that is important for the evangelist. See also 9.16; 10.21.

[39]Contrast Jn 7.23 which refers back to this event as well as 10.32 and see Mk 3.4.

of evangelist in developing his christology in terms of Jesus' relation to the Father.

An interesting comparison can be made between aspects of the healings in Jn 5 and 9.[40] It is noteworthy that, in Jn 5, the healing involved no action of Jesus such as making clay, nor did the man have to perform any task *in order to be healed* (9.6). The healing was instantaneous, at the word of Jesus. Just as all things came to be (ἐγένετο) by the λόγος, so now the man became (ἐγένετο) whole at the command of Jesus, 5.9. This suggests the comparison between this healing and the creative work of God pointing in the direction of the identification of Jesus' work with the work of God, which is the point of the text in which Jesus provocatively affirmed his own continuing *work* on the Sabbath arguing also that God ("My Father") continues to work.

Further, only the man breaks the Sabbath by carrying his bed and it was this act that caught the attention of the Jews. Yet , in Jn 5, it is Jesus, not the man (as in Jn 9) who is accused of breaking the Sabbath. Indeed, the narrator's statement of the charges concerning Sabbath-breaking uses the imperfect tense (ἐποίει, 5.16 and ἔλυεν, 5.18) suggesting that Jesus habitually broke the Sabbath. Nothing in the story justifies this charge unless Jesus' command to the man to carry his bed was taken to make him responsible for the act. But the evangelist is not concerned to defend Jesus against the claim. The fact that the charge, in generalized form, is stated by the narrator without any indication of irony or disagreement indicates that this charge is taken as proved. What the evangelist seeks to do is to set Jesus' Sabbath-breaking work in a different context. This context is revealed in the text and the meaning of this is expounded in the following discourse.

In Jn 9 the healed man holds centre stage for the bulk of the chapter. It is he who takes the brunt of the punishment meted out by the Pharisees/Jews. In Jn 5.15 the healed man becomes an informer, reporting to the Jews, through the narrator, that "Jesus is the man who made him whole". This report enabled the Jews to persecute Jesus for breaking the Sabbath. The saying of Jesus in 5.17, the text for the following discourse, is a strange response to persecution. It could be argued that it is an attempt to win over his protagonists. If so it is an ill-judged attempt because it only succeeded in provoking more violent

---

[40]Both chapters narrate miracle stories which become the basis of rejection stories through the introduction of a note indicating the miracle was performed on the Sabbath (5.9c; 9.14); both associate sin and sickness (5.14; 9.2). The chapters provide a paradigm for rejection, first of Jesus (Jn 5) and then of the Johannine Christians represented by the once blind man (Jn 9).

persecution with the first reported attempt (ἐζήτουν) to kill Jesus.[41] If the text is a strange response to persecution, the extended discourse of 5.19-47 hardly seems likely in the face of an even more determined attempt to kill him, 5.18. Here we must assume that the evangelist allows the narrative time to stand still while Jesus expounds the meaning of his text. By the end of the discourse there is no sign of those who were seeking to kill Jesus. The story with the dialogue has been used to explore the full extent of the conflict between Jesus and the Jews and the nature of their rejection of him. Likewise the evangelist has used the occasion to expound his own distinctive christology making clear the link between the rejection of Jesus and the fulfilment of the quest for true christological understanding.

2. The Text

In order to develop his position the evangelist has used the saying of Jn 5.17 as the text upon which the following discourse is based, at least 5.19-30.[42] The text is introduced by a quotation formula, "But Jesus answered them ..." Here only, and in 5.19, does Jn use the aorist, indicative, middle ἀπεκρίνατο. Elsewhere he uses the passive ἀπεκρίθη. The reason for this could be to draw attention to the connection between the text (5.17) and the discourse beginning with 5.19. The saying which follows (in 5.17) is a defence of Jesus' Sabbath-breaking action and is characteristically Johannine.[43] The assertion, "My Father is working until now and I am working", is formally in opposition to the idea that, after the six days of creation, God rested from his work. But the real issue concerns the institution of the Sabbath upon which all should cease from work, Gen 2.2-3; Exod 20.8-11.

The dispute is not about God working on the Sabbath. The Jewish sources recognize that God may and does work on the Sabbath, though the

---

[41]ἐζήτουν is probably an inceptive imperfect indicating the first of a series of attempts to kill Jesus. See chapter 7, "The Hidden Messiah in Jn 7-8" below.

[42]What follows in 5.31-47 is, by way of a concession to unbelief, an appeal to verifying witnesses. In fact the way those testimonies are presented only returns the reader to the scandal of Jesus' own claims.

[43]Jesus speaks of God as "my Father" and asserts the unity of the Father and Son (by implication of "my Father") in their works, see 5.17-18 and compare 10.30-38; 14.10-11. It is notable that the text (5.17) is not introduced by the Ἀμὴν ἀμὴν formula though the following discourse contains three such sayings (5.19, 24, 25).

nature of this work is sometimes qualified.[44] The dispute concerns Jesus' work on the Sabbath and it was initiated by Jesus' command to the man publicly to carry a "burden" in plain disregard for the Sabbath Law 5.8. Jer 17.21f. expressly forbids the carrying of burdens on the Sabbath. No attempt is made to argue that the κράβαττον is not a "burden" or that what Jesus had done was not work, either of which might have been acceptable to the Jews as a form of defence. This evidence suggests that the evangelist was not concerned to defend Jesus against the charge of Sabbath-breaking. Naturally the main reason for this is the intent to place Jesus and his action on the same level as God.[45] It may well be that the Johannine Christians did not keep the Sabbath, though this is not the point of the discourse which is to reveal Jesus' relation to God. The Sabbath controversy provided the opportunity for the evangelist to assert Jesus' unity with the Father. Once this has been done both the man[46] and the Sabbath controversy vanish. We are left with the text upon which the following discourse is based. It is expressed in the words of Jesus.

In the text (5.17) Jesus justified his work with the appeal: "My Father is working until now[47] . . .", assuming that the Father in question is God, which the Jews perceived, 5.18. This affirmation about God implicitly includes his continuing work on the Sabbath. As we have noted, this, in itself, was not controversial. What was controversial was the use of "*My Father* is working" in conjunction with the statement "and I am working". In other words, Jesus' work is in some sense being identified with God's work thus justifying Jesus' work on the Sabbath. This was perceived correctly to involve the claim to be equal (in some sense) with God.[48]

Jesus claimed an identity of action with the action of God while calling God his Father. The controversy that this provoked may well reflect the rabbinic rejection of two powers in heaven.[49] While this was certainly designed to exclude the Gnostic idea of two sources for good and evil, it was probably also aimed at what was perceived as ditheism in Jn.

---

[44]On this see the major commentaries, e.g. C.K. Barrett, *The Gospel According to St. John*, 255f.; E. Haenchen, *John 1*, 248-9; B. Lindars, *The Gospel of John*, 218f.; W. Rordorf, *Sunday*, 47.

[45]See my *JWT*,10,23,52f.,72,73,75.

[46]In Jn 5.5 the man is referred to quite specifically as "a certain man"(τις ἄνθρωπος) unlike Jn 9.1 where the man is at first representative of every man, and remains central to the ensuing dialogue where he has become representative of the ideal believer or the Johannine community.

[47]On "until now" (ἕως ἄρτι) see Willi Rordorf, *Sunday*, 98-100.

[48] Cf. Philippians 2.6.

[49]See Alan F. Segal, *Two Powers in Heaven*.

Thus it seems that the controversy in Jn 5 reflects the charge of ditheism brought by the Jews against the Johannine believers.[50]

It is the irony of Jn that the charge of 5.18 was formally correct but did not involve the blasphemy of ditheism. The charge was true but equality did not involve an assertion of independence from God; it implied dependence. The Father/Son relationship is portrayed as the Son's absolute dependence on the Father. Only because he did the Father's will was it the work of the Father that he did. This point is to be made in the discourse (5.19-30)[51] and in the assertion "I and the Father are one", 10.30. The immediate reaction to this claim was an intensification of the persecution of 5.16 in that now it is said that the Jews sought to kill him, 5.18. In 10.33 the charge is formalized as blasphemy. Paradoxically the charge there arose from the assertion "I and the Father are one" (10.30), which was supported by an appeal to "many good works" ($\xi\rho\gamma\alpha$ $\kappa\alpha\lambda\dot{\alpha}$) shown to the Jews from the Father. The paradox is that the claim to be one with the Father is understood in terms of ditheism, two powers. Several questions arise: What is meant by "one" in "I and the Father are one"? What is meant by "My Father" (5.17)? How is the work of the Father related to the work of the Son?

III. THE DISCOURSE

The discourse as a whole is in two main parts:
1. The works of the Father and the Son, 5.17,19-30 and
2. The function of the witnesses, 5.31-47.
The two parts are discerned on the basis of form and content.

In the first part Jesus continues to defend his work as the work of God while in the second he defends his own witness and in so doing appeals to other witnesses.

In the first part we find a group of three sayings each introduced by $\dot{\alpha}\mu\dot{\eta}\nu$ $\dot{\alpha}\mu\dot{\eta}\nu$[52] and the change, when referring to the emissary, from first to

---

[50]See J.L. Martyn, *Christian History*, 104f.

[51]The argument was acceptable in rabbinic terms because what was excluded by the rejection of two powers was a second power independent of God. While the text is open to this interpretation, the discourse excludes it.

[52]Jn 5.19,24,25. The formula emphasizes the solemnity/importance of the following saying. There are 25 *amen* sayings in Jn (see also 1.51; 3.3,5,11; 6.26,32,47,53; 8.34,51,58; 10.1,7; 12.24, 13.16,20,21,38, 14.12; 16.20,23; 21.18). These sayings, always doubled in Jn, are only found on the lips of Jesus as is the single form in the Synoptics. It has been argued (by Klaus Berger and Barnabas Lindars) that sayings so introduced come from the old tradition, perhaps going back to Jesus. Many of the sayings, however, are clearly Johannine constructions making use of traditional themes and motifs.

third person, to first person, to third person and back to first person again. This changing form of reference throughout 5.19-30 is noticeable because, on returning to the first person reference in 5.30 this is continued throughout the following part of the discourse, 5.31-47.[53] In 5.19-30 we have an intricate interweaving of the emissary christology with the christology of the Father/Son relation.[54] The interweaving is not only done by laying down the sequence of sayings but within particular sayings. The sayings about sending are mixed with language of the Father in first and third person, "my Father" and "the Father who sent him". It is also notable that there are two variant understandings of eschatology in the third $\dot{\alpha}\mu\dot{\eta}\nu$-saying, 5.25,28-29. It may be that the evangelist is here making use of traditional material but the variations appear to be expressly intended and further the evangelist's argument.

1. The Works of the Father and the Son (5.19-30)

The Jews assumed that Jesus' assertion (in 5.17) was an expression of his independence of the Father,[55] as if there were two sets of works, of the Father and of the Son. The text (5.17) is open to that interpretation. It asserts the equality of his action with the action of the Father. But the *main line* of exposition in the ensuing discourse is that the Son does only the works of the Father, that there is an identity of his own action with the action of the Father because of his dependence on the Father 5.19-21,23-27. Even in the *minor* theme, which attributes the work of judgement not to the Father but only to the Son (5.22) because he is Son of Man (5.28), that activity and authority is said to have been given to him by the Father. Thus the Son of Man mediates the judgement of God and in the discourse as a whole Jesus' relation of dependence on the Father is expounded. Here Jesus' claim to Sonship, implicit in 5.17, is made explicit by a change

---

[53]With the exception of 5.38b, "the one whom he sent", which reverts to the reference to the emissary in the third person.

[54]This interweaving is not simply taken over from tradition as is frequently assumed. It is also to be found in the second part of the discourse, 5.36,37,38,43. Here Jesus asserts "the Father has sent ($\dot{\alpha}\pi\dot{\epsilon}\sigma\tau\alpha\lambda\kappa\epsilon\nu$) me" and refers to him as "the Father who sent me" ($\dot{o}\ \pi\dot{\epsilon}\mu\psi\alpha\varsigma\ \mu\epsilon\ \pi\alpha\tau\dot{\epsilon}\rho$), though he refers to "the one whom he sent" ($\dot{\alpha}\pi\dot{\epsilon}\sigma\tau\epsilon\iota\lambda\alpha\nu$). The language returns to the idiom of the text when Jesus asserts "I have come in the name of my Father and you do not receive me". See part IV, "The Christology of the Discourse" pp. 244–49 below.

[55]Jn 5.18 indicates that calling God his own Father was taken to be a claim of equality to God ($\dot{\iota}\sigma ov\ \dot{\epsilon}\alpha\upsilon\tau\dot{o}\nu\ \pi oi\hat{\omega}\nu\ \tau\hat{\omega}\ \theta\epsilon\hat{\omega}$). In Johannine terms the conclusion drawn by the Jews is both right and wrong. In relation to the world, the Jews, the crowd, the disciples, Jesus was to them as God; but in relation to the Father he was subordinate, sent by the Father to do his works, see 9.5; 10.36-38.

from the first person (my Father) to the third person (the Son, 5.19; Son of God, 5.25).

Some scholars attempt to give Son and Son of God different meanings in Jn and to derive them from different traditions. Son of God is said to denote the Davidic Messiah while Son has a more profound sense and is used in the Father/Son relationship. But Jn does not distinguish the two.[56] Rather his aim is to deepen the messianic sense through the development of the Father/Son relationship. Consequently we find Son, Son of God, and Son of Man in Jn 5. These idioms are interwoven with the intent of embedding assertions of equality within the recognition of the dependence of the Son on the Father. It is tempting to analyse this part of the discourse into the two idioms (implied or explicit first person and third person self-reference):

i. The text is expressed in the first person ("My Father...I..."), 5.17;

ii. The first *amen*-saying is in the third person, speaking of "the Father", "the Son" and "the Father who sent *him*", 5.19-23;

iii The second *amen*-saying returns to the first person, speaking of "my words" and "the one who sent me", 5.24;

iv. The third *amen*-saying returns to the third person, speaking of "the Son of God", "the Father" and "the Son", "Son of Man", and "his voice", 5.25-29.[57]

v. Jn 5.30 returns to the first person, "I", "myself","the one who sent me", forming a stylistic *inclusio* with 5.17. What is more, this saying makes Jesus' work of judgement dependent on the one from whom he hears, whose will he does, "the will of the one who sent me."

If 5.19 tied the actions of the Son to what he saw the Father doing, in 5.30 his judgment is bound to what he hears from the Father. It is an expression of the will of the Father. The work of judgement committed to the Son (5.22), because he is Son of Man (5.27), is now affirmed by Jesus in 5.30 in the final"I" statement which ties his authority to the one who sent him and implies, through the connections between the five sayings, that the one who sent him is the Father. Yet the formula, "The Father who sent me" is not used here (5.30). The full formula appears only in the

---

[56]To note that only Son and not Son of God is used in the idiom of the Father/Son relation is hardly reasonable. If the Father in question is known to be God to talk of the Father and the Son of God would be strange.

[57]The evidence of the Synoptics suggests that the third person idiom might go back to Jesus in the use of Son of Man and the Q passage (Matt 11.27=Lk 10.22) may suggest the same for the use of "the Father" and "the Son". But the same passage (Matt 11.25-26=Lk 10.21-22) indicates that Jesus also addressed God as "Father" "my Father".

third person "the Father who sent *him*" in 5.23.[58] The *inclusio* formed by the text (5.17) and the saying of 5.30 is reinforced stylistically by Jesus' use of the first person identification of himself with the emissary in both verses.

The three *amen*-sayings introduce the note of judgement (κρίνειν, κρίσις), 5.22,24,27-30. In 5.22, contrary to the rest of the first saying, Jesus' work is distinguished from the Father's. The Father does not judge, the Son judges. In the third saying judgement is committed to him because he is Son of Man and his activity is expressed in terms of the general resurrection, at the end of the age, when some are to be raised to life and others to judgement (κρίσεως here implies condemnation). Some commentators have seen the hand of a redactor in these verses.[59] But the same sense of κρίσις is found in 5.24 also. More likely is it that the evangelist has taken over these themes from the tradition in which judgement was *delegated* to the Son of Man (5.27) but it is the voice of the Son of God that the dead will hear (5.25) and the Son who has life in himself. The tradition was taken up and used in relation to the evangelist's distinctive christology. To some extent it sits side by side with his own distinctive understanding, though this has also been modified by the tradition in 5.24. Further, by making Jesus dependent on the Father in his work of judgement the evangelist has adapted the tradition to fit into his own distinctive treatment of the theme.

The first *amen*-saying gives expression to the distinctive Johannine sense of the *dependence*[60] of the *Son* on the *Father*. The Son can do nothing of himself but only what he sees the Father doing,[61] just as Jesus will assert of himself as judge, "I can do nothing from myself; I judge according to what I hear (from the Father)", 5.30. These sayings exclude the possibility of two works, one of the Father and the other of the Son. The work of the Father is the work of the Son. There is an equality and

---

[58]But see 5.37 in the second part of the discourse and cf. 5.36.

[59]See for example E. Haenchen, *John* I, on these verses.

[60]Note the stress in Jn on "the sending Father" and on Jesus the Son as the one sent in this saying in Jn 5.23; and in the next, 5.24. Though ὁ πέμψας με πατήρ is not used here (cf. 5.37), it is implied by the third person response of 5.23 ("the Father who sent him") with the first person reference of 5.24 ("him who sent me").

[61]B. Lindars (*John*, 221) referring to the work of C.H. Dodd, argues that the definite article in 5.19 is to be understood in a generic sense and translated "a son can do nothing...". The parabolic saying upon which Jn was dependent would mean something like "like father, like son". If this was the original meaning it hardly does justice to its meaning in Jn. Given the text (5.17) the Father in question is God and Jesus is the Son. The point is that this Son does only what he sees the Father doing.

identity of action because of the total dependence of the Son on the Father. If 5.19 makes clear that the Son does only what the Father does, 5.20 goes further in stressing that he does all that the Father does.[62] This means that there is no action of the Father that the Son does not do. That his works should be seen as coterminous with the works of God is affirmed in terms of an emissary/envoy christology. But 5.20 goes further in expressing the intimate relation between Father and Son as a basis for a complete revelation (see 1.18) and total adequacy of action.

The purpose of the argument so far has been to justify Jesus' works on the Sabbath by identifying them with the works of God. Perhaps it is more accurate to say that the Sabbath-breaking works are used to bring to light that Jesus does the works of God. The remainder of this section turns attention to the future eschatological works of raising the dead and executing judgement. The reason for this may be that the evangelist wishes to show that Jesus performs the works that are peculiarly the works of God. Jn 5.20b-23 continues the image of the Son doing what he sees the Father doing, but now the action is in the future. The Father will show greater works than these to the Son, thus providing the basis for greater works to be done by the Son. Those greater works are spelt out in terms of the eschatological action of God raising the dead, giving life and judging. The purpose of these future works is said to be, "so that you may marvel ($\ell\nu\alpha$ $\dot{\nu}\mu\epsilon\hat{\iota}\varsigma$ $\theta\alpha\nu\mu\dot{\alpha}\zeta\eta\tau\epsilon$[63])", "that all may honour the Son ($\ell\nu\alpha$ $\pi\dot{\alpha}\nu\tau\epsilon\varsigma$ $\tau\iota\mu\hat{\omega}\sigma\iota$) even as they honour the Father", 5.20,23.

Jn 5.21 emphasizes the identical works of Father and Son. That the works are identical is made clear by the way what is said of each, Father and Son, is introduced ($\ddot{\omega}\sigma\pi\epsilon\rho...o\ddot{\upsilon}\tau\omega\varsigma...$). "For even as the Father...so also the Son..." Thus the assertion that the Son makes alive whomsoever he wills implies that the Father does also though, surprisingly, it is the will of the Son that is emphasized. Yet Jesus does not do his own will, but the will of the Father, 4.34; 5.19,30; 6.38,40.[64] What follows in

---

[62]Because the Father loves ($\phi\iota\lambda\epsilon\hat{\iota}$) the Son he shows him all that he does (5.20) and the Son does whatever he sees the Father doing (5.19). Compare Jn 5.20 with 3.35, "The Father loves ($\dot{\alpha}\gamma\alpha\pi\hat{q}$) the Son and has given all things in(to) his hand." See also 3.11-13,31ff.; 8.38. This use of the love terminology is an example of the evangelist's love of synonyms. The emphasis on the Father "showing all that he does" to the Son highlights the theme of revelation in the Gospel. Characteristically it is mediated revelation, the revelation of the Father through the Son, cf. Jn 1.18. In the same way the works of the Father are mediated through the Son.

[63]See 5.20b,28; 7.21; cf. 3.7; 4.27; 7.15; 9.30.

[64]Jn nowhere uses the language of "obedience" ($\dot{\upsilon}\pi\alpha\kappa\omega\dot{\eta}$, $\dot{\upsilon}\pi\alpha\kappa\omega\dot{\upsilon}\omega$). This may be for idiomatic rather than theological reasons though it may be that the

5.22 is also unexpected. We are told that the Father judges (κρίνει) no one but has given judgement (κρίσιν) to the Son.[65] This judgement is apparently condemnation, in contrast to the work of making alive which the Father shares with the Son.

That the Son, but not the Father judges, puts in question the notion that he does only what he has seen the Father doing. This suggests that the evangelist is already being influenced by the traditional view of the Son of Man which he has incorporated in Jn 5.26-27. The incorporation of the tradition is evidenced by the un-Johannine use of Father / Son in terms of the notion of judgement being delegated to the Son (Jn 5.22-23) which is in apparent opposition to Jn 3.16-18 where it is asserted the Son did not come to judge but to save the world. In spite of this, the coming of the Son, there depicted as the light, is said to be the judgement of the world, 3.19-21. But that judgement is depicted as the division caused by the coming of the light, involving both faith and unbelief, life and death, salvation and condemnation. In Jn 5 judgement is opposed to life-giving. Yet it can be understood in relation to 3.16-18 because the work of condemnation lies in the future and was not the purpose of his historical coming.

The giving of all judgement to the Son was for the purpose that all may honour (τιμῶσι) the Son as they honour the Father, 5.23.[66] This is the second stated purpose of the Father in his relation to the Son. The two purposes can be stated succinctly as follows:

1. He will show him greater works that all may marvel (ἵνα + the subjunctive θαυμάζητε), 5.20.

2. He has delegated all judgement to the Son that all may honour the Son (ἵνα + the subjunctive τιμῶσι), 5.23.

It is assumed that all do honour the Father. Delegation implies that the authority for judgement belongs to the Father and that it is delegated to the Son so that the Son is to be honoured as the Father is honoured. Here in Jn 5.23 we encounter the emissary christology[67] which the evangelist

---

language of obedience does not sufficiently recognize the freedom with which the Son does the will of the Father.

[65] On the theme of judgement see 3.19-21 and also 3.17-18; 5.24,27-29; 12.31,47-48; 16.8,11.

[66] The use of καθώς indicates an equality of honour in every way, quality and manner, implying an equality of status and action.

[67] On the sending Father (τὸν πατέρα τὸν πέμψαντα αὐτόν) in 5.23 see 4.34; 5.24,30,37; 6.38,39,44; 7.16,18,28,33; 8.16,18,26,29; 9.4; 12.44,45,49; 13.20; 14.24(26); 15.21(26); 16.5. The motif of the sending of the Son is also expressed using the verb ἀποστέλλω, Jn 3.17,34; 5.36,38; 6.29,57; 7.29; 8.42; 10.36; 11.42; 17.3,8,18,21,23,25; 20.21. This emissary Christology has its roots in the Synoptic tradition (see Mk 9.37; 12.6 and

combines with a more essential Father/Son relation. He speaks of the Father and the Son. The usage has two sources: Jesus' address of God as Father and the early Christian designation of Jesus as Son of God. Even so, the Johannine language concerning "the Father and the Son" is distinctively part of the emissary christology. Thus both Father and Son raise[68] the dead and give life with the view that all may honour the Son who honour the Father. But the total adequacy of the emissary to represent the sender presupposes the Father/Son relation.

The second *amen*-saying (5.24)[69] continues the emphasis on the emissary christology and brings out the theme of his life-giving word. The focus, as in Jn generally, is on the life-giving power of Jesus' word to the believer in the present time. This is a theme illustrated, at a symbolic level, in Jesus' word to the man in 5.8. In the story his restored physical life has become a symbol for the giving of life which is manifest in faith even though he himself failed to believe in Jesus. This inconsistency could be a consequence of the use of the miracle story, which had been used to proclaim the power of Jesus' life-giving word, in the dialogue with the synagogue. In this context new dialogues were constructed that prepared the way for the rejection of Jesus. In this process the healed man becomes part of the opposition to Jesus. Hearing the word of the emissary leads to belief[70] in the one who sent him. Such belief is the way to receive the gift of life. The imagery is that of passing out of one realm (death) into the realm of life. But the future judgement is not denied. Rather, in believing in the emissary there is escape from the future judgement. Evidently the realm of death is conceived as the judgement, the condemnation ($\kappa\rho i\sigma\iota\varsigma$). It is as if all are under the dominion of death until the voice of the Son of God is heard and then those who believe pass from death to life while those who do not believe are irrevocably condemned to death, see 3.19,21; 9.39-41. The saying proclaims what the coming of the emissary has achieved and does so in words in which Jesus speaks of himself, his words, and the

---

parallels) but it has been systematically developed and featured in Jn. On this see my Durham PhD thesis, *The Idea of Knowledge in the Gospel and Epistles of John*, 124-8. On the way response to the one sent is understood as response to the sender see 5.23; 12.44; 13.20; Matt 10.40; Lk 10.16. Jn 13.20 and Matt.10.40 speak of the sender being received in the one sent (δ $\delta\epsilon$ $\dot\epsilon\mu\dot\epsilon$ $\lambda\alpha\mu\beta\dot\alpha\nu\omega\nu$ $\lambda\alpha\mu\beta\dot\alpha\nu\epsilon\iota$ $\tau\dot\omicron\nu$ $\pi\dot\epsilon\mu\psi\alpha\nu\tau\alpha$ $\mu\epsilon$ in Jn and $\kappa\alpha\dot\iota$ $\dot o$ $\dot\epsilon\mu\dot\epsilon$ $\delta\epsilon\chi\dot o\mu\epsilon\nu\omicron\varsigma$ $\delta\dot\epsilon\chi\epsilon\tau\alpha\iota$ $\tau\dot o\nu$ $\dot\alpha\pi\omicron\sigma\tau\epsilon i\lambda\alpha\nu\tau\dot\alpha$ $\mu\epsilon$ in Matt).

[68] The use of $\dot\epsilon\gamma\epsilon i\rho\epsilon\iota$ here looks back to Jesus' command in 5.8.

[69] On the form $\dot\alpha\mu\dot\eta\nu$ $\dot\alpha\mu\dot\eta\nu$ $\lambda\dot\epsilon\gamma\omega$ $\dot\upsilon\mu\hat\iota\nu$ $\delta\tau\iota$... see also Jn 5.25;10.7.

[70] Jn 5.24. The verb $\pi\iota\sigma\tau\epsilon\dot\upsilon\epsilon\iota\nu$ is used 98 times in Jn. The noun is not used.

one who sent him, not of the Father and the Son as in the first saying nor of the Son of God and the Son of Man as in the third saying.

The third *amen*-saying (5.25-29)[71] develops the theme of the eschatological fulfillment brought about by the mission of the Son of God.[72] Here the eschatological fulfilment is divided into two moments. The eschatological moment (ὥρα) is coming and now is when the life-giving word of the Son of God will ring out and those (figuratively spoken of as dead) who hear/believe, will live, 5.25. The future tense (ζήσουσιν) is immediately prospective. This is made clear by the addition of "and now is" to the proclamation of the coming hour (ὥρα). Because the hour has arrived the voice of the Son of God, with its life-giving power, can already be heard.[73] This happens because the word of the Son is the word of the Father and his life-giving power is the life-giving power of the Father.

Jn 5.26 returns to "the Father and the Son" idiom. Here it is clear that "the Father" is the source of life but the form of the saying brings out the identity of life in the Father and the Son.[74] What is meant here by life cannot be simply "to be alive", it involves the possession of life-giving power.[75] The subordination of the Son to the Father is brought out also by asserting that the Father has given this life-giving power to the Son and it is because of this that those who hear his voice will live. The Father's gift of life is mediated through the Son to those who believe. This gift of life is the eschatological life of the Kingdom of God, or, in more characteristic Johannine terms, it is the life of the new age, eternal life. The first aspect of the emissary christology is expressed in terms of the Father's gift of life-giving power to the Son.

None of this need exclude the theme about future judgement which the evangelist made use of from the tradition, 5.27-29. Indeed, in the face of the physical death of believers (given a date for the Gospel towards the end of the century) we must assume that the theme would have remained essential to him. Consequently the second moment is still coming (ἔρχεται ὥρα) and the second aspect of the emissary christology is expressed in terms of the gift to the emissary of the authority (ἐξουσίαν)

---

[71]On 5.25-30 see G. Richter (*Studien*, 346-82) and A.J. Mathill, "Johannine Communities", 308.

[72]This continues the dominant "realized eschatology" of the second saying. See also Jn 4.21,23. Jn 5.25,28 reverses the order of 4.21,23 in that the saying about present fulfilment (5.25) precedes the saying about the future (5.28).

[73]No doubt the evangelist envisages the voice of the Son of God ringing out through the Gospel he had penned.

[74]The identity is expressed in the terms ὥσπερ...οὕτως...

[75]See Jn 1.4.

to make judgement (κρίσιν) because he is Son of Man.[76] Yet earlier (5.22) it has been said that all judgement has been delegated to the Son. Naturally, the evangelist sees both designations referring to Jesus,[77] hence there can be fluidity in his use of titles with their associated themes. In the tradition it appears that judgement (κρίσις) was the function of (the) Son of Man. This time there is no indication that the time is now. Rather the moment yet lies in the future when all in the tombs will hear the voice of the Son of Man (5.27-28). There is now no question of hearing or not hearing. All will hear and come forth out of the tombs. Now the point of division is not the Johannine understanding of the hearing response to the word of Jesus but the traditional understanding of judgement on the basis of works.[78] Those who have done good things proceed to the resurrection[79] which is life (eternal life) and those who have practised foul deeds proceed to the resurrection which is condemnation. The basis of this future judgement is similar to the grounds of the judgement caused by the coming of the light, 3.19-21. Those who do the truth (good works?) come to the light. Those who practice foul deeds (evil works) hate the light, reject it. Consequently a future judgement on the basis of works is not un-Johannine.

The delegation of judgement to the Son, or Son of Man has been emphasized in 5.27-29 but Jn 5.30 returns to the theme of doing what he hears from the Father. In this "I" saying, which forms an *inclusio* with the text (5.17), the theme of judgement is continued. His enactment of judgement is on the basis of this hearing. In this way Jesus affirms his total dependence on the one who sent him Jn 5.30. He speaks of himself, "I" and of "the one who sent me", thus returning to the idiom of Jn 5.24. It is because of his dependence in seeking the will of the one who sent him[80] that Jesus affirms it is righteous judgement (ἡ κρίσις ἡ ἐμὴ

---

[76]Here only in Jn 5.27 "Son of Man" is without "the", as in Dan 7.13-14. It is apparently evidence of a traditional Son of Man saying, now used by the evangelist. For a fuller discussion see chapter 9, "The Enigmatic Son of Man" below.

[77]In Jn, as in the NT generally, there has been a merging of all messianic titles in their application to Jesus. It may be that the merging of the distinctive messianic roles had already begun in first century Judaism but the evidence of this is indecisive. Of course it is also true that Jn has his preferred titles and uses them in characteristic fashion and these contribute to his christology rather than being indicators of rival christologies in the Gospel.

[78]See Dan 12.2.

[79]On resurrection see 2.22; 11.23-26; 21.14.

[80]Cf. Jn 4.34.

δικαία ἐστίν).[81] It is not judgement on the basis of appearances (7.24) but judgement in accordance with reality (8.16). True and righteous judgement correspond and reflect the underlying influence of the Hebrew *emunah* which is translated by both of these terms in Greek.

From this discussion it can be seen that Jn is here handling a traditional theme. His emphasis, however, lay on the recognition that Jesus was the revelation and action of God in relation to his world. Because of this it was crucial that Jesus' works should be identified with the works of God and that his whole life and mission be gathered up under the heading of his work, 17.4. Only because he did the Father's will could he make the Father known, and in so doing he worked the works of the one who sent him. Could it be that it is this perspective which accounts for the Johannine development of the theme of the *works* of Jesus?

In Jn *works* can be the equivalent of *signs*, see 6.30. But works is the characteristically Johannine term, the noun and verb being used 34 times compared with a total of 16 in the Synoptics. Jn's use of signs (17 times) is more or less comparable with Matt's (13 times). In Jn Jesus normally talks of his "works" while signs represent the view of his works by others who concentrate on the spectacle. Those who do not believe demand a sign, and faith based on signs is often shown to be shallow. But the works witness to Jesus' unity with the Father (5.36; 10.25), nowhere more pointedly than his Sabbath work which is the work of God, 9.5. Thus, out of the rejection of Jesus (5.18) comes the exposition of the authentic perception of the Johannine christology as the expression of the true fulfilment of the quest for the Messiah.

2. The Function of the Witnesses (5.31-47)[82]
The discourse continues in 5.31 using the first person idiom. The appeal to witnesses is relevant because Jesus' defence so far has been his own testimony and the validity of this witness was questionable.[83] With the focus now falling on the theme of witness the reader is reminded of the setting of the trial within which the evangelist has told the story of Jesus.[84] It is ironical that the one who has been revealed as the judge (Jn

---

[81] In Jn there is an interesting variation between true judgement and righteous judgement. Cf. Jn 5.30; 7.24 and 8.16. It is righteous because it corresponds to God's reality.

[82] See especially Johannes Beutler, *Martyria*, 237-76.

[83] Jesus' defense has been compared with the defence against false gods in Isaiah 42.8; 43.8-13; 44.6-23.

[84] See A.E. Harvey, *Jesus on Trial: A Study in the Fourth Gospel.* The verb (μαρτυρεῖν), "to bear witness", is used 33 times and the noun (μαρτυρία) "witness", is used 14 times in Jn. Contrast the use in the Synoptics 2 and 4

5.22,27,29), who carries out the judgement of God, should himself have to face trial before men. This irony has its roots in the Johannine double perspective of heavenly and earthly. The heavenly perspective reveals Jesus as the judge though on earth he is found to be on trial, condemned and executed.

i On self-witness (5.31-32). The legal situation of Deuteronomy 19.15 is reflected in 5.31, though a broadening of the legal principle was involved as reflected in the Mishnaic Tractate *Kethuboth* 2.9. Self-witness is not acceptable. Thus Jesus says that if he bears witness concerning himself his witness is not true ($\dot{\alpha}\lambda\eta\theta\eta\varsigma$).[85] This denial of self-witness is formally contradicted by 8.13-14. There, following the self-witness of Jesus in 8.12, in a characteristic "I am..." saying, he is accused of self-witness which is self-evidently not true. Jesus' response was to indicate that even if he did witness to himself, nevertheless his witness was true. The language is almost identical word for word, with 5.31 except for the negative, "not true" in 5.31, "is true" in 8.14. Here we have to question whether the formal contradiction is an indication of unresolved tensions in the evangelist's editing of his sources/traditions[86] or if we have here more evidence of the literary sophistication of the evangelist in self-conscious paradox and irony. The latter view is supported in this study. The language of the two statements is almost identical but for the negative in 5.31 and the absence of it in 8.14. Hence the statements are not to be attributed to different traditions. They are an expression of the evangelist's own views and the language suggests that both positive and negative statements were made self-consciously in different contexts.

In 8.14 it is claimed that this witness is an exception because Jesus, unlike his interrogators, knows his origin and destination. It is different also because the Father who sent him is present in his witness (8.16). Consequently Jesus argues that his witness complies with the requirement of two witnesses (8.17-18). The failure of the Pharisees to recognize the witness of the Father was a consequence of their failure to recognize Jesus as the Son (8.19). Had they recognized this they would have known the witness of the Father in the witness of the Son just as they would have

---

times respectively. The Synoptics (but not Jn) also make use of $\mu\alpha\rho\tau\dot{\upsilon}\rho\iota o\nu$ 9 times. The greater emphasis on witness in Jn is apparent.

[85]In Jn's usage "...$\dot{\alpha}\lambda\eta\theta\eta\varsigma$ is applied only to opinions and statements, and those who hold or make them..." Barrett, *John*, 160. Consequently it does not have the potential meanings of $\dot{\alpha}\lambda\eta\theta\epsilon\iota\alpha$ and $\dot{\alpha}\lambda\eta\theta\iota\nu\dot{o}\varsigma$ which go beyond this.

[86]Thus Robert Kysar, *John*, 85. The contradiction is noted by C. K. Barrett, *John*, 264 as evidence implying that the evangelist might not have "fully revised his work". See also R. E. Brown, *John* I, 224.

recognized the work of the Father in the work of the Son (5.17). The paradox of the two witnesses implies Jesus' affirmation, "I and the Father are one" (10.30).

It is a matter of two perspectives, heavenly and earthly, or flesh and spirit. Hence (in 5.31-32) the irony is of self-witness that is no self-witness. In the light of 5.17,19-30 the denial of self-witness is not straightforwardly convincing. The denial is made to allow Jesus to redefine the status of his own testimony and to introduce other witnesses. A list of witnesses follows in 5.32ff.

ii The witness of another ($\text{\it{ἄλλος}}$) (5.32).[87] This additional witness is not however perceived apart from Jesus and his activity because the witness is one with him in bearing witness to him. This witness is the Father who is reintroduced in 5.37 following the *discursus* on John the Baptist in 5.33-35, and the witness of the works, 5.36. Of this other witness Jesus says "I know[88] that the witness which he witnesses is true".[89] While Jesus claims to know the witness of the Father, this witness is mediated to others via Jesus' works and words and through the witness of others. Recognition that it was the Father who bore witness in Jesus' words and works was not dependent simply on accepting Jesus' claims. The character of the words and works themselves was vital evidence. Thus Jesus has begun to redefine his own witness.

iii The witness of John (5.33-35). It was not Jesus but the Jews who sent an embassy to John to gain evidence from him, 5.33 and see 1.19ff. Whereas Jesus affirmed that the Father's witness was true, he asserts that John has borne[90] witness to the truth ($\text{\it{ἀλήθεια}}$). Of course this means that his witness was true. Beyond this, as witness to Jesus it was witness to the truth, 14.6, just as it was witness to the light 1.8, which is Jesus, 8.12. Here we have an example of another type of double

---

[87] In Greek there are two words that might be translated "other", $\text{\it{ἄλλος}}$ and $\text{\it{ἕτερος}}$. If the terms were used with precise distinctions $\text{\it{ἕτερος}}$ would indicate another kind of witness while $\text{\it{ἄλλος}}$ could indicate another witness like the first. Certainly Jn excludes the use of $\text{\it{ἕτερος}}$ in a precise sense in this context.

[88] Though some texts read "you know" or "we know", the correct reading is "I know". It is attested by the best textual evidence and fits the context. The Son knows the truth of the Father's witness. Certainly the Jews of 5.18 do not know this.

[89] The idiom "the witness which he witnesses" ($\text{\it{ἡ μαρτυρία ἥν μαρτυρεῖ}}$) is possibly a Semitism.

[90] Perfect tense indicates that the witness was borne in the past (see 1.19ff.), though it is the significance of that witness in the present for Jesus' hearers that is now in view.

meaning employed by the evangelist. Yet Jesus asserts (5.34) that he does not receive the witness from a man, even if it is true, to the truth. What does this mean? It is not as if Jesus needed the witness of John to confirm his messianic awareness, as some might have argued on the basis of the tradition of Jesus' baptism by John. Jesus had the witness of the Father which he alone knew. Yet the witness of John is of value to the Jews. Hence Jesus speaks of it so that they may be saved ($\emph{lva}...\sigma\omega\theta\hat{\eta}\tau\epsilon$) because it is through John's witness that all may come to believe, 1.7. Consequently the purpose of Jesus' words about John was to keep his witness in view for those who needed it as a means of coming to faith.

Jesus referred to John as "the burning and shining lamp" ($\dot{o}\,\lambda\acute{v}\chi\nu o\varsigma$ $\dot{o}\,\kappa a\iota\acute{o}\mu\epsilon\nu o\varsigma\,\kappa a\grave{\iota}\,\phi a\acute{\iota}\nu\omega\nu$) 5.35. Thus, though John was not the light ($\tau\grave{o}\,\phi\hat{\omega}\varsigma$, 1.8), that is, the true light ($\tau\grave{o}\,\phi\hat{\omega}\varsigma\,\tau\grave{o}\,\dot{a}\lambda\eta\theta\iota\nu\grave{o}\nu$, 1.9), he was a derivative luminary ($\lambda\acute{v}\chi\nu o\varsigma$). The evangelist terms John as the shining lamp, giving him a significance beyond that of other human witnesses. This is in keeping with 1.7 which states that through the witness of John "all may come to believe". John is presented as the primordial witness through whom all would come to believe, 1.6-8. That this was to be the case is borne out in the narrative of 1.19ff. where we see that it was through the witness of John that the first disciples of Jesus *sought* him out and *followed* him. The portrayal of John as the foundational witness is reinforced by the language used to describe his mission both by the narrator and in his own words. In the Prologue the narrator describes him as a man "sent from God" ($\dot{a}\pi\epsilon\sigma\tau a\lambda\mu\acute{\epsilon}\nu o\varsigma\,\pi a\rho\dot{a}\,\theta\epsilon o\hat{v}$). He himself refers to God as "the one who sent me" ($\dot{o}\,\pi\acute{\epsilon}\mu\psi a\varsigma\,\mu\epsilon$)[91], 1.33. Thus both the narrator and John himself refer to him using the characteristic language used to portray Jesus as the emissary of God. Surprisingly the narrator uses this language of John before applying it to Jesus and John uses the pregnant formula $\dot{o}\,\pi\acute{\epsilon}\mu\psi a\varsigma\,\mu\epsilon$ to speak of God and himself as God's emissary before Jesus takes this language on his own lips and it becomes his own "signature theme". That it was used first of the Baptist giving prominence to his mission and his words is a puzzle. One can only ask why the evangelist allows the Baptist to initiate this language. Certainly it makes clear that both he and Jesus come from the same sender. But the Prologue has already set up a contrast. Though sent from God the Baptist appears only in the course of history but in Jesus the eternal $\lambda\acute{o}\gamma o\varsigma$ is present. For this reason Jesus not only speaks of $\dot{o}\,\pi\acute{\epsilon}\mu\psi a\varsigma\,\mu\epsilon$ but of $\dot{o}$ $\pi\acute{\epsilon}\mu\psi a\varsigma\,\mu\epsilon\,\pi a\tau\acute{\eta}\rho$. The language of the Baptist moves in this direction because he is the ideal, primordial witness.

---

[91]The full reference is $\dot{o}\,\pi\acute{\epsilon}\mu\psi a\varsigma\,\mu\epsilon\,\beta a\pi\tau\acute{\iota}\zeta\epsilon\iota\nu$....

In a few cases the words of Jesus and the Baptist are initially directed to a specific audience in the text but that audience seems to disappear so that Jesus and the Baptist address the reader directly (see Jn 1.15f.;3.11-21;3.28-36).[92] Indeed Jn 3.28-36 is extraordinary because the Baptist's words are characteristically Johannine, giving expression to the most profound form of Johannine christology.[93] Other confessions of faith prior to the resurrection of Jesus are shown to have limitations. This is not the case with the Baptist. His words, like the words of Jesus himself, are addressed by the narrator directly to the reader because Jesus, the Baptist and the narrator alike express the views of the author and all speak the sonorous tones of the Johannine language. The Baptist is not only portrayed as the ideal witness but also as the ideal believer who perceives the mystery of the person of Jesus and confesses this in Johannine terms.

Surprisingly, Jesus says "you were willing ($\eta\theta\epsilon\lambda\eta\sigma\alpha\tau\epsilon$) to rejoice for a while in his light ($\phi\omega\tau\iota$)", 5.35.[94] The audience is apparently "the Jews of Jerusalem" who sent the embassy to John, Jn 1.19; 5.33.[95] Temporary willingness indicates that they are no longer willing to listen to his witness. The comment reflects a situation of conflict, though perhaps prior to the breach with the synagogue.

iv The witness of the works (5.36). The first witness to which Jesus appeals is the works ($\tau\alpha$ $\epsilon\rho\gamma\alpha$) which the Father has given him to complete.[96] This witness is greater than John. Indirectly it is the witness of the Father because the works done are those commissioned and authorized by the Father. It is the works done by the Son which he sees the Father doing, 5.19-20. Because the works of the Son are the works of the Father they bear witness "that the Father has sent me" (cf. 14.11). The use of the present tense $\mu\alpha\rho\tau\upsilon\rho\epsilon\iota$ indicates the ongoing witness of the works of God in the ministry of Jesus, ongoing even on the Sabbath, 5.17. Thus like 5.19-20 which is in the idiom of Father/Son, Jesus' talk

---

[92]Here it may be appropriate to say that the voice of the Baptist has merged into the voice of the narrator just as the voice of Jesus merges into the voice of the narrator in 3.11-21.

[93]For example he speaks of Jesus as the one whom God sent ($\alpha\pi\epsilon\sigma\tau\epsilon\iota\lambda\epsilon\nu$) who speaks the words of God. He affirms that "the Father loves the Son and has given all things in(to) his hand. He who believes in the Son has eternal life;" 3.34-36. This language is comparable to Jesus' own third person self-reference in 5.19-30 and has the same message as the first person self-reference found there.

[94]On Jn's popularity see Josephus, *AJ* 18.2.

[95]The "Jews" having a changing role in Jn, moving from openness to hardened rejection of Jesus and the Johannine community.

[96]$\iota\nu\alpha$ $\tau\epsilon\lambda\epsilon\iota\omega\sigma\omega$. Cf. 14.34; 17.4.

of "the Father" in 5.36 implies his identity as "the Son" and the Father/Son relation is expressed in the context of an emissary christology. The works testify "that the Father has sent me" (ὅτι ὁ πατήρ με ἀπέσταλκεν).

v The witness of the Father (5.37-38). The Witness of the Father in 5.37-38 names and develops the witness of the "other" of 5.32. The works given by the Father to Jesus "testify...that the Father has sent me", 5.36. Now, in 5.37, Jesus appealed to the witness of "the Father who sent me" (ὁ πέμψας με πατήρ ἐκεῖνος μεμαρτύρηκεν περὶ ἐμοῦ). In each case (5.36,37) reference is made to Jesus as sent by the Father, but using slightly different idioms. Two different verbs (ἀποστέλλω and πέμπω) are used without distinction of meaning. Πέμπω is used in the formula "the Father who sent me".[97] In this formulation the focus is on the Father as the sender. Thus 5.36-37 has emphasized that *Jesus* was sent by the Father and that the *Father* sent Jesus. The witness of the Father occurred in Jesus' works and is possibly also to be found in the Scriptures (5.39), though it is less than certain that Jn thought of God speaking in the Scriptures, 5.46. Rather it is Moses who wrote what is written there.

That the evangelist does not think of Scripture as the expression of the Father's witness is implied in the denial that the Jews had ever heard the Father's voice or seen his form. Thus it is unlikely that the perfect tense (μεμαρτύρηκεν) refers back to the Sinai witness.[98] The Scriptures claimed that God had been heard (Deut 4.12,15) and seen (Exodus 19.11). It is more likely that the evangelist has in mind the witness of the Father borne to John (the Baptist) enabling him to bear witness to Jesus as Son of God, 1.31-34. In this way the witness of the Baptist is made subordinate to the prior witness of the Father. The evidence that the Jews do not know God is that they do not believe[99] the one whom God sent. This demonstrates that God's word (λόγος) does not abide (μένοντα) in

---

[97] In this formula πέμψας is an aorist active participle, a form which is not found with ἀποστέλλω in Jn. See the analysis of the use of these two verbs in Jn below.

[98] That tradition (e.g. Deut 4.12,15) is not only denied in relation to the Jews in Jesus' audience (5.37), the evangelist denies that anyone has seen God, 1.18; 6.46. In spite of a Scriptural tradition narrating encounters with God, there developed the view that God was directly unknown, unseen and unheard but that the knowledge of God could be mediated, for example, by the λόγος. The evangelist and Philo reflect this development.

[99] Here (5.38) it is a failure to believe Jesus (indicated by the dative τούτῳ), though no self-witness is overtly claimed. Yet believing Jesus involves believing in him because his word draws attention to himself as the emissary of the Father. Thus we should not force the distinction between the dative and εἰς with the accusative to indicate the object of belief.

them, 5.38. Here it is not clear whether the ὅτι indicates the cause of the lack of knowledge or the evidence of it. Possibly this is a false alternative. That (ὅτι) they do not believe in the one sent is both cause and evidence of their failure to know the sender.[100] Here again the status of Jesus' self-witness is addressed.

vi The witness of the Scriptures (5.39-40). It is not clear whether Jesus calls on the Jews to search (ἐραυνᾶτε) (imperative) or acknowledges that they do search (indicative) the Scriptures. It is probably the latter. This searching implies the study of the Torah as in the Qumran community and rabbinic Judaism. Such study is pursued because it is considered (δοκεῖτε) to be the way to "eternal life", though this is the Johannine term. But, for the evangelist, the searching is to be taken as a misguided expression of the quest for the Messiah, the one sent by God to bring life to the world. Hence the hope that they possessed life in the Scriptures apart from Jesus is shown to be false. It is shown to be false by those Scriptures which bear witness to Jesus. It is false because he is the giver of life. Hence it is ironical that the Jews, who seek eternal life in the Scriptures, will not[101] come to Jesus, that is believe in him (cf. 6.35,37; 7.37).[102] Indeed, the opinion that they already possessed (in the Scriptures) the means to have eternal life was a hindrance to finding that life in Jesus.

vii Self-witness which is not self-witness (5.41-47). Jesus' words continue, "I do not receive glory[103] from men". Glory here has the sense of praise. Jesus does not seek acclaim from men. He seeks rather the "glory" of God, that is, praise from God and praise for God (see 7.18). There is possibly also the sense of the glory of God as the revelation of God (see 1.14) It is because of this that his witness to himself as the emissary of the Father is really witness to the Father and not self-witness.

---

[100]The identity of the word of Jesus with the word of God is also in view in 3.33; 8.14-18.

[101]They were willing, for a short time, to rejoice in the light of Jn (5.35). They were not willing to come to Jesus.

[102]Coming to Jesus is common as a symbol for believing in Jn 1.47; 3.2; 4.30,40,47. See my *JWT*, 77f.

[103]"Glory" (δόξα) is a key Johannine term. See 1.14; 2.11; 5.41,44; 7.18; 8.50,54; 9.24; 11.4,40; 12.41,43; 17.5,22,24 and the related verb (δοξάζω) 8.54; 11.4; 12.16,23,28; 13.31,32; 14.13; 18.8; 16.14; 17.1,4,5,10; 21.19.

Just as Jesus had said that the word of God was not abiding in the Jews who rejected him, now he says "I know[104] you, that you do not have the love of God in yourselves". Here we are not to think of Jesus exhibiting supernatural knowledge, as in 1.48. Rather Jesus' knowledge was based on the Jewish rejection of himself, the one whom the Father had sent. "The love of God" could mean "God's love" or "man's love for God". The parallel with "the word of God" in 5.38 confirms that it is "God's love" that is in view and this is the sense found in the rest of the Gospel.[105] That it is love for God is sometimes argued on the basis of Jn 3.19-21. But here we should note that it is the verbs (not the noun) to love and to hate that are used; love and hate are used in the Hebraic sense, common in Jn, for to choose and to reject (cf. 12.43); it is love for the darkness or the light; there is no reference to the love of God being in anyone or not. It is this idiom which suggests that it is God's love that is in view. Compare Jn 17.26 where Jesus prayed that "the love with which you love me may be in them (the disciples)". The idiom here is comparable to 5.42 and confirms that it is God's love for them which is in view.

Jesus' assertion "I have come in the name of my Father" gives expression again to the emissary christology. It is equivalent to the appeal to the Father who sent him.[106] It is for this reason that witness to himself as the sent one who comes in the name of the Father is really not witness to himself but to the Father. To come in the name of the Father is to come as the revealer of the Father, to come as the one in whom the Father is present and acting. He has come as having no independent and rival significance. He is what he is only for the Father. Jesus reported "you do not receive me" as the one in whom the Father is present and active. That comment reflects the rejection of Jesus. The acceptance of another who comes in his own name does not have anyone in particular in view. Rather it reflects the values of those who reject Jesus. The values of the Father, whom Jesus reveals, are contrary to the values of the world which

---

[104]ἔγνωκα is perfect tense indicating the completed acquisition of knowledge so that the verb is rightly translated as indicating a state of knowledge, "I know".

[105]In the Gospel and Epistles of Jn, only in 1 Jn 4.20ff. is there any clear reference to man's love for God and there the discussion is in response to what the author considered to be the false claim, "I love God". On this see my *JWT*, 92-8, 121-5 and chapter 14, "The 'Opponents' in 1 John"below.

[106]The mission of Jesus, expressed in the verbs of sending and in Jesus' claim to have come, so prominent in Jn, has its roots in the Synoptic tradition. Using ἀποστέλλω and πέμπω see Mk 9.37; 12.6 and parallels, as well as Matt 15.24; Lk 4.18,43; 10.16; and using ἦλθον see Mk 2.17; Matt 5.17; 10.34-35; 11.3 and parallels.

is self-seeking. Given this opposition of values it was inevitable that they would not accept, receive, believe in Jesus -- they were not able to believe. Those values were reflected in seeking praise ($\delta\delta\xi\alpha$) from men rather than praise ($\delta\delta\xi\alpha$) from the only God.[107] Thus the question "How are you able to believe?" implies the negative answer. They, whose values are such, are not able to believe. All of this is a consequence of the perversion of the quest. They do not seek ($o\dot{v}\,\zeta\eta\tau\epsilon\hat{\imath}\tau\epsilon$) the glory/praise from the only God. When God falls out of the focus of the human quest all values go awry.

In 5.39 Jesus indicates that the Jews were of the opinion ($\delta o\kappa\epsilon\hat{\imath}\tau\epsilon$) that they had eternal life in the Scriptures. Now (5.45) he says to the Jews,"Do not think ($\mu\dot{\eta}\,\delta o\kappa\epsilon\hat{\imath}\tau\epsilon$) that I will accuse ($\kappa\alpha\tau\eta\gamma o\rho\dot{\eta}\sigma\omega$) you to the Father." Thus Jesus is not the accuser.[108] Rather Moses, in whom the Jews have placed their hope,[109] is the accuser ($\dot{o}\,\kappa\alpha\tau\eta\gamma o\rho\hat{\omega}\nu$). Yet the Father has committed all judgement to the Son, Jn 5.22. Here is another paradox because the judgement performed by the Son is unlike judgement practised and recognized by the world. It is the division caused by the light coming into the darkness, Jn 3.19-21. This leaves out of account the judgement which lies in the future at the resurrection of the dead from the tombs, 5.28-29. Is it because that judgement is on the basis of works that it can be said that Moses will be the judge? But then the division caused by the coming of the light is also on the basis of works, 3.19-21. Thus the present and future judgements form two complementary parts of the overall work of judgement.

The witness of Moses to Jesus is the witness of the Scriptures. To believe Moses implies believing Jesus. Failure to believe Jesus shows that Moses has not been believed. The form of the sentence "For if you had A you would have B" makes B the test of A. Failure to believe Jesus, which has been apparent from Jn 5.16ff., proves that the Jews have not believed Moses. How it comes about that believing Moses involves believing Jesus is then explained. "He wrote of me". But where did Moses write of Jesus? What text or texts are in view? Although Deut

---

[107]On the phrase "the only God" ($\tau o\hat{v}\,\mu\acute{o}\nu o\upsilon\,\theta\epsilon o\hat{v}$) see Jn 17.3 "the only true God" ($\tau\acute{o}\nu\,\mu\acute{o}\nu o\nu\,\dot{\alpha}\lambda\eta\theta\iota\nu\acute{o}\nu\,\theta\epsilon\acute{o}\nu$). There Jesus Christ is also mentioned as the sent one ($\dot{o}\nu\,\dot{\alpha}\pi\acute{\epsilon}\sigma\tau\epsilon\iota\lambda\alpha\varsigma$).

[108]Cf. Jn 3.15.

[109]$\dot{\eta}\lambda\pi\acute{\iota}\kappa\alpha\tau\epsilon$, the perfect indicative active appears to have been used here in the sense of believed though this belief in Moses is bound up with the hope of "eternal life", Jn 5.39. Belief in Jesus is also bound up with the hope of eternal life but neither the noun nor the verb "hope" are used of Jesus in Jn. To believe in or know are the key terms in Jn.

18.15,18 may be in view, as is his custom, the evangelist alludes to the Old Testament generally rather than quoting texts.

Next Jesus compares the Jewish failure to believe the written words (γράμμασιν) of Moses with their failure to believe his oral words (ῥήμασιν). It could be that the suggestion is that the written words are easier to believe than the oral. More likely the point is that the Jews claim to be disciples of Moses yet failed to believe his words. Those words would have led them to believe in Jesus. Given that unbelief, the rejection of Jesus is to be expected. There is in then a propensity to unbelief.

Here, in Jn 5.39,45-47, it is clear that the evangelist has a positive view of the Jewish Scriptures, seen as a witness to Jesus as the one sent from the Father. How that view is to be related to the question of observance of "the Law of Moses" is less clear. The Sabbath controversy has already emerged in Jn 5, and will resurface again in Jn 9. It is indicative of a problem of which the reader is made aware without ever being given enough information to be able to resolve it. It is notable that only in Jn 1.17 is the Law/grace antithesis expressly stated and the circumcision problem is not mentioned. Hence Jn appears distinct from the Pauline mission with its attendant controversies. Nevertheless the Johannine form of Christianity appears to have confronted the problem of the Jewish Law in its own way. Paul addressed this more directly and systematically, perhaps because of his relation to the Gentile mission. The different conceptual worlds of Jn and Paul suggest that, however close their theologies may be at times, they arrived at them via quite different routes.

IV. THE CHRISTOLOGY OF THE DISCOURSE

The discourse (including the text) challenges the Jews to come to a new understanding of Jesus. Indeed, while making use of traditional material, it develops the distinctively Johannine understanding of Jesus. Yet there are peculiarities about this discourse. The idiom constantly switches from first person to third person discourse and back again. By contrast the discourse on the witnesses (5.31-47) maintains a first person idiom throughout. It could be argued that the changes of idiom are a consequence of working with sources in 5.17-30 while working more freely in 5.31-47. Certainly traditional material does appear to surface in 5.17-30. Within this complex we find three groups of sayings each introduced by the double-*amen* formula. While it has been argued (by Berger and Lindars) that sayings introduced in this way are traditional, the recognition that such sayings are often the most distinctively Johannine puts such an hypothesis in question.[110]

There is other evidence that could be taken to indicate the use of distinctive sources. In the text (5.17) Jesus speaks of God as "My Father" and implies that he is "Son". The first *amen*-saying is carried through using the third person idiom of "the Father" and "the Son"[111]. In contrast, in the second *amen*-saying (5.24) and in the final saying (5.30) Jesus speaks of "the one who sent me", implying that he is himself "the sent one" or emissary.[112] The third *amen*-saying uses the third person idiom but combines the use of Son of God, Father/Son and Son of Man. Here, as when used elsewhere, the Father/Son idiom denotes the emissary of God and Son of God and Son of Man both refer to the one who judges. Does this provide us with evidence of an emissary (Son) christology alongside a Son of God (5.25) christology?

Building on the work of S. Schulz, J. Becker and J.-A. Bühner,[113] John Ashton[114] argues that in Jn "Son" is to be distinguished from "Son of God", which is a messianic designation. "Son" is to be understood in the context of the juridical conventions of the time as "the son of the house" (בן בית) who represents the landowner with full authority over the estate. He is υἱός not νήπιος. His sending is a formal commissioning so that the Son is the emissary. Thus Jn found ready made language to express his conviction that Jesus is the emissary of God.

If that is the case the evangelist has produced a significant synthesis in this discourse (5.19-30) where dominant Father/Son language has been used in conjunction with Son of God (5.25) and Son of Man (5.27) and third person sayings (about the Father/Son, Son of God and Son of Man) have been used with first person "I" sayings of Jesus. In this discourse what Jesus says of the Father/Son he also says in "I" sayings. Elsewhere what Jesus says in characteristic Son of Man sayings is repeated in an "I" saying (12.32) and he says "I am Son of God" (10.36). Given that the latter is not understood in a messianic but divine sense an argument for a distinction between the meaning of Son of God and Son language in Jn is fragile. Rather, when Father/Son language is used the "of God" is

---

[110]See the discussion of the double-$\dot{a}\mu\dot{\eta}\nu$ sayings in chapter 10, "The Messiah as the Good Shepherd" below.

[111]There is the fine distinction between "my Father" in the text (5.17) and third person "the Father and the Son" idiom of the first *amen*-saying. But is this more than a change of idiom?

[112]The text also uses the first person idiom and in addition there Jesus refers to God as "My Father...".

[113]*Gesandte*, 195-198.

[114]*Understanding*, 322-9, 357-68.

245

redundant when the Father in question is known to be God. It remains true that Father/Son is used in conjunction with the "sending" motif to announce unambiguously that Jesus is the emissary of God while Son of God remains ambiguous because it can be understood messianically as well as in divine terms.

The evangelist was quite capable of mixing the idioms. Thus Jesus speaks of "my Father" (5.17), "the Father" and "the Son" (5.19-23,26),[115] "the Father who sent him" (τὸν πατέρα τὸν πέμψαντα αὐτόν, 5.23), "the one who sent me" (5.30) and "the Father who sent me" (ὁ πέμψας με πατήρ, 5.37). In all of these references to the one who sends, the construction is the aorist active participle of πέμπω, used with the definite article (e.g. ὁ πέμψας). Elsewhere Jesus speaks of his mission using the verb ἀποστέλλω. But the evidence does not suggest that this is a consequence of the evangelist making use of a distinctive source or sources.

The idea of prophetic mission is suggested by the language of sending in the Synoptics, see for example Mk 9.37 and parallels; Mk 12.6 and parallels; Matt 15.24; Lk 4.18, 43; 10.16. Of special note is Mk 12.6 and parallels. Matt and Mk use ἀποστέλλω but Lk (20.13), changing the idiom, uses πέμπω. Here the change of tense appears to have determined the verb form used. The use of both verbs in the Synoptics alerts us to the roots of the evangelist's emissary christology in the Synoptic tradition. The theme has, however, become much more prominent in Jn who uses ἀποστέλλω 28 times,[116] 17 of which refer to the sending of Jesus by the

---

[115] J. H. Charlesworth, "Jesus Research: A Paradigm Shift for New Testament Scholars" (*ABR* 38 (1990), 27ff.) attempts to argue that the use of "the Father" and "the Son" in Jewish sources contemporary with Jesus provides a basis for the use of these terms by Jesus in describing his relation to God. But none of the examples he gives uses the definite article. The indefinite "son of God" is vastly different from "the Son of God" and the use of Father/Son language where the Father is known to be God. Consequently much of what Charlesworth says at this point is not relevant. Rather "the Father" and "the Son" language applied to Jesus in his relation to God is Christian and distinctively Johannine though it may well grow out of Jesus' custom of addressing God as Father. A Denaux, "The Q-Logion Mt 11.27 = Lk 10.22 and the Gospel of John" (Leuven Colloquium 1990) argues that Jn's use is dependent on the Q passage. This passage shows only that this use was wider than the Johannine literature though what we have there is a single *pericope* compared with the rich use in Jn.

[116] Compared with 42 times in Matt; 2 in Mk; and 25 in Lk. There is not the same concentration of christological uses in the Synoptics. Hence Matt's relatively high use of ἀποστέλλω needs qualification. J.-A. Bühner, *Der Gesandte und sein Weg*, has explored in impressive detail the relevance of the background of the mission of the prophet and heavenly (Son of Man)

Father. The same verb is used to indicate the sending of the Baptist by God; the sending of the disciples by Jesus; and the sending of various other individuals and groups. Hence no technically christological meaning is conveyed by the word itself. It is the concentration of use, in Jn, in relation to the sending of the Son by the Father, that makes the term important. Of course, as a secondary motif, Jesus also sends his disciples.

Statistically even more important is the evangelist's use of πέμπω, 32 times,[117] 24 times on the lips of Jesus using the formula ὁ πέμψας με (πατήρ).[118] The Baptist also uses this formula of God (ὁ πέμψας με βαπτίζειν), though without πατήρ. It is used in generalizations (7.18; 13.16) and in plural form the messengers sent (ἀπέστειλαν) by the Jews refer to their senders as τοῖς πέμψασιν ἡμᾶς (1.19,22). It is used of the sending of the disciples by Jesus twice in the indicative active, once in the present tense and once in the future tense,13.20; 20.21; and three times of the sending of the Spirit by Jesus and the Father in the future indicative active, 14.26; 15.26; 16.7. The comparative use of the two verbs in Jn can be summarized as follows:

1. Both verbs are used of the sending of Jesus by the Father and of the disciples by Jesus.
2. In Jn 13.20; 17.18 the Father who sent (ἀπέστειλας, 17.18) Jesus is described as τὸν πέμψαντά με (13.20; see also 1.6 and 33; 1.19 and 22).
3. In Jn 20.21 the synonymous nature of the sending described by both verbs is made clear by the use of καθώς and κἀγώ.
4. Of the 32 uses of πέμπω 27 use the formula of the aorist participle with the article; there are four uses of the future indicative active and one present indicative active.
5. Only πέμπω is used of the promise of the sending of the Spirit, in the future tense.
6. In Jn, unlike the Synoptics, ἀποστέλλω is not used as an aorist active participle with the article though it is so used with the passive participle. The aorist active participle is used only with πέμπω.
7. The majority of uses of ἀποστέλλω are aorist indicative active, though there are a few uses of the perfect indicative active and of the passive participle.

---

messenger in Jewish mission literature. The portrayal of Jesus in Jn can be exemplified here. In this way Bühner has provided an alternative (to the Gnostic emissary) background but one which highlights the emissary model with similar interpretative consequences.

[117] Compared with 4 in Matt; 1 in Mk; 10 in Lk. Jn's use is even more remarkable when it is noted that ἀποστέλλω is used over 700 times in the LXX while πέμπω is used only 26 times. The change comes because of Jn's placing of the formula to describe God as the sending father on the lips of Jesus.

[118] See 4.34; 5.23,24,30,37; 6.38,39,44; 7.16,(18),28,33; 8.16,18,26,29; 9.4; 12.44,45,49; 13.20; 14.24,26; 15.21; 16.5.

Jn's use of these two verbs probably arises from the tradition as is suggested by a comparison with the Synoptics. His choice of one or other appears to be based on preference for grammatical form:[119] Πέμπω supplies the present and future indicative active and the aorist active participle while ἀποστέλλω supplies the aorist and perfect indicative active and the passive participle. No doubt we also need to recognize the evangelist's love of the use of synonyms. What this use of language does is to focus attention on Jesus as the one sent. This is especially the case where the verb ἀποστέλλω is used. When the formula using the article and the aorist active participle (πέμπω) is used, the focus is on the one who sent Jesus. Thus God is characterized as the sending[120] Father in Jn and Jesus is the the "sent one". Naturally the significance of Jesus as the sent one is determined by the significance of the sender. The evangelist has combined the language of the emissary with the language of God as Father and Jesus as Son (Son of God).

It is likely that the language of sending has its origin in the conception of the prophetic mission. Comparison with the language of the mission of the Baptist, which is also described using both ἀποστέλλω and the formula ὁ πέμψας με, confirms this. This concept has been transformed by the notion of being sent "into the world".[121] It may be that here some tradition of the heavenly messenger has been laid over that of the prophetic messenger. But the status and role of the messenger finds its true Johannine focus in the language concerning the Father and the Son, and in Jesus' reference to the sender as "the Father who sent me".[122]

---

[119]Thus contrary to Calvin Mercer, "ΑΠΟΣΤΕΛΛΕΙΝ and ΠΕΜΠΕΙΝ in John" who thinks that ἀποστέλλω implies an act of commissioning not present in πέμπω.

[120]The two verbs are used 45 times of God as sender out of a total of 59 uses in Jn.

[121]J.-A. Bühner (Der Gesandte und sein Weg, 427) has argued "Die ursprünglich jüdisch-esoterische und rabbinisch nachwirkende Verbindung von 'Prophet' und 'Engel' ist damit die grundlegende religionsgeschitliche Voraussetzung der johanneischen Christologie vom 'Weg des Gesandten';" and is closer to Jn than the Hellenistic vision of God or the image of the Gnostic redeemer.

[122]While Bühner can rightly object to the inclination to interpret all christological motifs in Jn in the light of the affirmation of the incarnation of the λόγος in the Prologue, he has himself failed to give due weight to the way the evangelist has interwoven the portrayal of the emissary, the Father/Son relation, Son of God, Son of Man , and I sayings by Jesus. Due consideration of this intricate interweaving is essential to a precise understanding of the christology of the Gospel and would modify Bühner's view of a prophet/angel model for Jn's christology. Here Peder Borgen, who has examined Jewish views of agency as the background to Jn's

This formula used by Jesus, sometimes without the use of "Father", is concentrated in chapters 5-12. Before Jn 5 it is used only in 4.34 and after chapter 12 only in 13.20;[123] 14.24,26;[124] 15.21; 16.5. Surprisingly, given the concentration of use in Jn 5, the formula is absent from Jn 10 which continues the theme of the relation of the Son to the Father.[125] It is also absent from Jn 11.[126] The formula is clearly concentrated in Jn 5-12 which focus on Jesus' conflict with the Jewish authorities, and to a lesser extent, in the Farewell Discourses where Jesus prepares the disciples for conflict. This pattern is borne out by the use of $\dot{a}\pi o\sigma\tau\dot{\epsilon}\lambda\lambda\omega$. It is used of Jesus as the one sent by God prior to Jn 5 only in 3.17,34 and after Jn 11[127] only in Jn 17[128] (from which the formula with $\pi\dot{\epsilon}\mu\pi\omega$ is absent) in the Farewell Discourses and in 20.21[129] in Jesus' commission to the disciples.

V. JOHN AND APOCALYPTIC IDEOLOGY

The nature of apocalyptic is complex. Jn is clearly a very different book from *Revelation* which, because of its opening words, suggested the name for the *genre* of literature that was to be recognized in relation to it. Jn clearly does not belong to that literary *genre* but with those works called Gospels. But even from a literary point of view Gospels can share apocalyptic features. Here Mk 13 stands out as an important example, but one that has no parallel in Jn. Thus the conclusion can easily be drawn,

---

christology, hold views similar to Bühner's except he sees the messenger as "the divine and royal Son of Man". See his "Some Jewish Exegetical Traditions as Background for Son of Man Sayings in John's Gospel (Jn 3.13-14 and context)", 246 and *Logos was the Tue Light*, 121-32 for a discussion of the language of agency in a Jewish context.

[123]Here the focus has moved from Jesus to those whom he sends, who stand in the same relation to him as he does to the Father. See also the use of $\dot{a}\pi o\sigma\tau\dot{\epsilon}\lambda\lambda\omega$ in Jn 17 and 20.21.

[124]This use does not quite fit the formula but promises that the Father will send the Spirit "in my name". See 15.26.

[125]But the sending of the Son by the Father is asserted using $\dot{a}\pi\dot{\epsilon}\sigma\tau\epsilon\iota\lambda\epsilon\nu$ in 10.36.

[126]But $\dot{a}\pi o\sigma\tau\dot{\epsilon}\lambda\lambda\omega$ is used twice in Jn 11, once where Jesus explains (to the reader!) that his action was done "that they may believe that you (Father) sent ($\dot{a}\pi\dot{\epsilon}\sigma\tau\epsilon\iota\lambda\alpha\varsigma$) me, 11.42.

[127]In Jn 5-11 see 5.36,38; 6.29,57; 7.29; 8.42; 10.36; 11.42.

[128]Jn 17.3,8,18,21,23,25. Here, and in 20.21, the sending of Jesus by the Father is made the basis and pattern for the sending of the disciples into the world by Jesus. Thus in these passages it is the status of the disciples that is in view rather than the status of Jesus as in Jn 5-12.

[129]Compare Jn 17.18 for the mission of the disciples from Jesus based on the pattern of the mission of Jesus from the Father.

and often is, that Jn has nothing in common with apocalyptic ideology.[130] The drawing of such a conclusion is the consequence of a superficial grasp of the nature of apocalyptic ideology.

The antithetical language which is characteristic of Jn (and some of the Texts from Qumran) manifests an underlying dualistic *Weltanschauung* characteristic of apocalyptic writings. While some scholars argue that the antithetical language is not dualistic, being qualified by the clear affirmation that all things were created by God (through the λόγος), this is true of Jewish apocalyptic works generally and does not exclude a real if limited dualism. Jn asserts that the world is in darkness, having rejected the light of the eternal λόγος. Thus the whole world lies in the power of the evil one and human agencies are powerless to break free. In Jn the antithetical language has spatial, temporal and ethical dimensions.[131] Precisely because the world created by the λόγος lies in the power of the evil one, the λόγος became flesh and in his ministry brought an assault on the darkness. Although there are no exorcisms (so common in Mk) in Jn,[132] the portrayal of the conflict with the power of evil manifests an apocalyptic dimension and Jesus' exaltation/glorification is portrayed as the judgement of the world through which the prince of this world is cast out (ἐκβληθήσεται ἔξω), that is, as an eschatological cosmic exorcism.

This understanding of the world shows why it was necessary for the λόγος to become flesh. But neither his coming nor his ministry brought an end to the reign of darkness. For Jn it was necessary for the Son of Man to descend and be exalted to heaven by way of the cross in order that the prince of this world might be cast out. In Jn the prince of this world is clearly identified with the devil and the opponents of Jesus are called (by the Johannine Jesus) "children of the devil". When Judas goes out into the night (the darkness) to betray Jesus the narrator informs the reader that Satan had entered into Judas. Thus in some ways the Gospel looks to the coming and going (exaltation/glorification) as a completed event as if this will overcome the darkness. But the Farewell Discourses look to the continuing struggle of the believers with the darkness into the foreseeable future. Thus, while not central to the perspective of the Gospel, a future

---

[130]"The non-apocalyptic nature of John's vision of truth suggests that he would not have found the Danielic apocalypse particularly congenial." D.R.A. Hare, *The Son of Man Tradition*, 92.

[131]See the discussion of dualism in chapter 2, "Johannine Christianity" above.

[132]As in the Synoptics Jesus is himself accused of (being a Samaritan and) demon possession in response to his charge that the Jews are children of the devil (Jn 8.41,44,48).

resolution (judgement) is assumed and comes to light from time to time as in 5.27-29.

VI. CONCLUSION

Jn 5 is a definitive presentation of the rejection of Jesus. The rejection is stated definitively in 5.16,18. The basis for the rejection is Jesus' Sabbath-breaking work and his justification of this on the basis of his relation to the Father, 5.17. Nothing in the discourse that follows suggests that the Jews might change their opinion. Even though 5.19-30 does remove the most extreme basis of the objection to Jesus' words of 5.17, as if he claimed independent equality with God, his claimed relation to the Father remains objectionable. Thus Jn 5 sets out the rejection in the face of the miracle (work) of making the man whole ($\dot{v}\gamma\iota\dot{\eta}s$), and in spite of Jesus' claim to be dependent on the Father. Naturally the fact that Jesus, as the unique messenger from God, had to assert his own position presents something of a problem. If self-assertion was to become an admissible form of evidence, what criteria could there be to discern truth from megalomania? The criterion offered here is that the true messenger from God did not seek his own glory, nor did he seek praise from men but only praise from and for the sender. Yet to be recognized as the messenger of God was, inevitably, to be given a position of great authority. Even the stress of the dependence of the Son on the Father and the assertions that he does only what he sees the Father doing, that he bears witness only to what he has seen, that he speaks what he has been taught by the Father, what he has seen from the Father (3.32; 5.19,30; 8.28,38), that he does the will of the one who sent him (5.30) only serve to highlight Jesus' authority as the one who does God's work and speaks his word. Thus it is the argument that the Son is subordinate to the Father that establishes his equality and this is the purpose of the arguments.

It may be because of this that Jesus appeals to other corroborating witnesses, Jn 5.31-47. The claim not to be offering self-witness but to witness to the one who sent him is, as we have seen, paradoxical. Given that the witness of John the Baptist is not appealed to by Jesus (5.34,36) it is surprising that it is given first. Perhaps this is because it is the only witness that can be seen as independent from his own. It may be also that we are to understand the assessment of it in terms of its necessity for the Jews, if they are to believe, though Jesus himself does not need it. Jesus reminds the Jews that they sent an embassy to John to hear his witness and it may be for this reason that it is given first. More important, from the point of view of Jn 5 (especially 5.17), is the witness of Jesus' works. It is asserted that the nature of his works points to the fact that the Father is the author of these works. "If this man were not from God he could do nothing", 9.33. The appeal to the witness of the sending Father would, of course, have included the witness of the works. But it is possible that the sign given to John is taken to be the special witness of the Father, 1.31-34. The appeal to the witness of the Scriptures would add more weight here if accepted, though the evangelist's reading of Scripture was open to Jewish objections. This is implicitly recognized (5.39) but in a way that assumed that alternative readings were incorrect although no argument is given in favour of the Johannine reading. The witness of Scripture is simply laid alongside the other witnesses to Jesus.

The purpose of laying down the evidence in favour of recognizing the truth of the Johannine perception of Jesus is not to provide the Jews in the story with the opportunity of revising their judgement of Jesus (5.16,18). Rather it is to show how implacable their rejection of him was. No evidence that could be supplied would change their views. The reason for this is, according to Jn, that the whole direction of their lives was wrong. They assumed they had life in their possession and therefore did not seek it. In refusing to seek for life they also refused to seek for God. Rejection of Jesus thus, according to Jn, flows from the perversion of the quest for the Messiah and the life that he brings which, as becomes clear in Jn 5, is the quest for the only true God. In this account of the implacability of unbelief the readers, as believers in Jesus, could find comfort, encouragement and confirmation of their own belief in Jesus.

6

The Messiah and the Bread of Life

That Jn 6 was intended as a self-contained unit is clearly signalled by the evangelist, who has commenced chapters 5,6, and 7 with Μετὰ ταῦτα,[1] a formula that marks a new beginning. Yet there has long been controversy regarding the unity and integrity of the chapter and its present place in the Gospel. Here it is argued that, though independent of the Synoptics, Jn has made use of Synoptic-like tradition and that Jn 6 provides evidence of a developing and yet unified interpretation of that tradition. The tradition was the basis of successive editions of the chapter.

Recognition and characterization of the tradition is an important beginning in the attempt to understand Jn 6. A second step is to note the signals indicating changes of time, place and audience which coincide with changes of literary *genre*. Changes are signalled from the crowd at Capernaum (6.22-40) to the Jews in the synagogue at Capernaum (6.41-59) to the mass of disciples and "the twelve" at some unspecified location (6.60-71). There are two references to each audience in the narrative of these sections (6.22,24,41,52,60,66,67,71) and a Son of Man saying in each of Jesus' responses, to the crowd (6.27), the Jews (6.53), and the disciples (6.62). Changes of *genre* from quest (6.1-35) to rejection (6.41-59 and 6.60-66) to commendation (6.67-71) stories confirm these divisions. There is also a transition from the emphasis on the emissary christology in the quest story to the soteriology of the rejection stories. These changes, brought about by the evangelist's developing interpretation, led to the relocation of the chapter, which once followed Jn 4. Relocation was relatively easy (though some *aporiai* can be recognized) because chapters 5 and 6 are more or less self-contained and Jn 7 marks a new beginning.

The transition from quest to rejection stories is evidenced by a change of dialogical pattern which can be detected by the quotation formulae:

1. In the feeding story (6.1-15) there is dialogue between Jesus and his disciples. Three saying of Jesus to the disciples are introduced (6.5,10,12) and two sayings of the disciples to Jesus (6.7,8). Jesus initiated the dialogue to test Philip, who fails the test. But Andrew, who is again introduced as the brother of Simon Peter (6.8 and see 1.40) to remind the reader of the initial quest of Andrew, shows a glimmer of comprehension. Those (οἱ ἄνθρωποι) who saw the sign also make a confession *about* Jesus.

---

[1]See 3.22; 5.1,14; 6.1; 7.1; 13.7; 19.38; 21.1, in all eight times. The slightly more specific μετὰ τοῦτο is used four times in 2.12; 11.7,11; 19.28.

But this is apparently done in his absence and manifests their misunderstanding. As in 1.47-49 Jesus displays supernatural knowledge, this time to escape from the misguided attempt to make him king, 6.15. Interestingly, in 1.50 Nathanael mistakenly confesses Jesus as king, a confession that Jesus corrects with a saying about the exalted Son of Man.

2. In the narrative of the sea-crossing (6.16-21) only one saying of Jesus is introduced though the story is told from the perspective of the disciples. The specific reference to their fear (6.19) and their failure to speak to Jesus further manifests their lack of comprehension.

3. In the dialogues between Jesus and the crowd (6.22-35) there are four sayings of the crowd to Jesus (6.25,28,30,34) and four *responses* by Jesus to the crowd (6.26,29,32,35). This makes clear the initiative of the crowd and the responsive nature of Jesus' sayings.

4. The ultimatum of Jesus in 6.36-40 is formally addressed to the crowd, though there is no indication of their response to these pronouncements on their unbelief. The request of the crowd (6.34) and the self-revelation of Jesus (6.35) have not prepared the reader for this devastating verdict. The crowd is given no opportunity to reply to the stern pronouncement of their fate by Jesus in words that have the appearance of a collection of sayings on the subject of unbelief.

5. Neither the Jews (6.41-59) nor the mass of disciples (6.60-66) speak to Jesus though Jesus does react in two stages (6.43,53 and 6.61,65) to what he knows they are saying about him (6.43,53 and 6.61,65). It may be that here also we are meant to think in terms of Jesus' supernatural knowledge.

6. In the dialogue between Jesus and the twelve two sayings of Jesus are introduced (6.67,70) and one by Peter speaking for the twelve (6.68).

Neither the Jews (6.41-59) nor the mass of disciples (6.60-66) speak to Jesus though he does know what was being said about him and reacts with pronouncements in the form of ultimatums which bring out the lack of genuine dialogue. There are dialogues between Jesus and the disciples (the twelve) and the crowd, portrayed as potential disciples. Indeed the dialogical pattern is strongest in 6.22-35 dealing with Jesus and the crowd. This section stresses the initiative of the crowd and the responsiveness of Jesus to their approach. The Jews and the mass of disciples move towards the inevitable rejection of Jesus. Yet surely the crowd ought not to be portrayed more positively than the mass of disciples! This suggests that the story of the crowd is earlier than the story of the mass of disciples, the latter reflecting the period subsequent to 70 CE, probably from the time of crisis for Jewish believers within the synagogue. The evidence in Jn 6 suggests that a series of editions expanded the Gospel in various ways. In the end the evangelist has made use of these expansions to produce a narrative development so that the resulting chapter is a literary unity. What enables the critic to penetrate beneath this surface unity is the evangelist's failure to introduce the changing groups in his normal fashion and the resulting *aporiai*.

I. TRADITION

1. John 6 and the Synoptics

Evidence that Jn was dependent on the Synoptics is often found in the overall agreement of order between Jn and Mk within which close verbal parallels occur.[2] When allowance is made for the duplicate feedings in Mk the evidence of Jn 6 provides as strong a case for this point of view as anything in the Gospel.

	John	Mark
Multiplication for 5000	6.1-15	6.30-44
Walking on the Sea	6.16-24	6.45-54
Request for a sign	6.25-34	8.11-13
Remarks on bread	6.35-59	8.14-21
Faith of Peter	6.60-69	8.27-30
Passion theme: betrayal	6.70-71	8.31-33[3]

As in Mk, the feeding is followed by the sea crossing, with Jesus walking on the water. Further agreements with the Markan order include the demand for a sign, elements of the discourse on bread, the confession of Peter and the passion theme. Hence a tradition with something like the Markan order underlies Jn 6. But there is evidence that suggests that a theory of Synoptic dependence involves serious problems.

i. Much of the evidence of the relation of Jn 6 to the Synoptics concerns tradition that, at first glance, could be attributed to dependence on Mk. The evidence, however, turns out to be more complex because Jn is sometimes closer to Matt or Lk than to Mk and some differences from all of them are not easily explained in terms of redactional tendencies.

a. Tradition common to Matt, Mk and Lk:

Jn 6.9 (Matt 14.17; Mk 6.38; Lk 9.13). But Jn, exactly as Matt, has πέντε ἄρτους and where the Synoptics use ἰχθύες Jn uses ὀψάρια. The latter

---

[2]See C.K. Barrett, *John*, 43 for "a list, which is certainly not complete, of corresponding passages which occur *in the same order* in both Mark and John". Barrett notes in particular that the sequence of the feeding and the walking on the lake "is not readily explicable except on the hypothesis of literary relationships". One may ask, however, whether the dependence is direct or indirect, because Mark could have taken over the sequence from his tradition. To this view Barrett can respond, "Anyone who after an interval of nineteen centuries feels himself in a position to distinguish nicely between 'Mark' and 'something much like Mark' is at liberty to do so." *John*, 45.

[3]See R.E. Brown, *John* I, 238.

could be due to Johannine editing (see Jn 21.13). Although Jn 21 is an appendix, it probably contains tradition from the Johannine school.

Jn 6.13 (Matt 14.20; Mk 6.43; Lk 9.17) though δώδεκα κοφίνους is exactly as Matt.

Jn 6.30 σημεῖον (and Matt 16.1; Mk 8.11; Lk 11.16).

b. Tradition common to Matt and Mk:

Jn 6.5, though Jn has θεασάμενος ὅτι πολὺς ὄχλος while Matt 14.14 and Mk 6.34 have εἶδεν πολὺν ὄχλον.

Jn's use of πόθεν relates to the second feeding of Matt 15.33; Mk 8.4.

Jn uses ἀγοράσωμεν while Matt 14.15; Mk 6.36 use ἀγοράσωσιν.

Jn 6.10 uses χόρτος; Matt 14.18 (χόρτου) Mk 6.39 (χόρτῳ).

Jn uses ἀνέπεσαν as in Mk 6.40, but see the second feeding Matt 15.35 and Mk 8.6.

Jn uses ἄνδρες πεντακισχίλιοι as in Matt 14.21; Mk 6.44.

Jn 6.11 and Matt 15.36; Mk 8.6 (the second feeding) use εὐχαριστήσας but εὐλόγησεν is used by Matt 14.19; Mk 6.41; Lk 9.16 in the first feeding.

Jn 6.15 and Matt 14.23; Mk 6.46 use εἰς τὸ ὄρος but Jn "adds" αὐτὸς μόνος and Matt has κατ' ἰδίαν and both Matt and Mk "add" προσεύξασθαι.

Jn 6.17 has ἐμβάντες εἰς πλοῖον ἤρχοντο πέραν τῆς θαλάσσης εἰς Καφαρναούμ. Compare Matt 14.22; Mk 6.45 which use ἐμβῆναι εἰς τὸ πλοῖον καὶ (αὐτὸν, Matt only) εἰς τὸ πέραν (πρὸς Βηθσαϊδάν, Mk only). Both Matt and Mk go on (with minor variations) to indicate that the disciples did this while Jesus dismissed the crowd. This differs from Jn, where it is Jesus who withdrew from the crowd. The destinations of Jn and Mk also differ. Minor variations in wording are more serious obstacles to a theory of Synoptic dependence in the light of these observations.

Jn 6.19, θεωροῦσιν τὸν Ἰησοῦν περιπατοῦντα ἐπὶ τῆς θαλάσσης and see Matt 14.26; Mk 6.49.

Jn 6.20, ἐγώ εἰμι·μὴ φοβεῖσθε and see Matt 14.27; Mk 6.50 both of which add θαρσεῖτε. Mk, like Jn, uses the introductory formula λέγει αὐτοῖς.

Jn 6.21, εἰς τὸν πλοῖον as Matt 14.32; Mk 6.51.

Jn 6.24, ἀνέβησαν (or ἐνέβησαν), see Matt 14.22 and Mk 6.45.

c. In the few cases where Jn is related to Mk alone the evidence remains complex.

Jn 6.1, ἀπῆλθεν and Mk 6.32 ἀπῆλθον and see Jn 6.27.

Jn 6.2, πολύς and Mk 6.33 πολλοί.

Jn 6.5, and Mk 6.36 φάγωσιν.

Jn 6.7, διακοσίων δηναρίων ἄρτοι and Mk 6.37 δηναρίων διακοσίων ἄρτους.

Jn 6.10 and Mk 6.40 ἀνέπεσαν and see Mk 8.6 and Matt 15.35.

Jn 6.20 and Mk 6.50 λέγει αὐτοῖς.

d. Dependence on Mk will not explain those cases where:

1. Only Jn and Matt agree:

Jn 6.10, οἱ ἄνδρες τὸν ἀριθμὸν ὡς πεντακισχίλιοι and Matt 14.21 ἄνδρες ὡσεὶ πεντακισχίλιοι.

Jn 6.13 and Matt 14.20 δώδεκα κοφίνους.

Jn 6.19 and Matt 14.24 σταδίους.

Jn 6.19, ἐφοβήθησαν and Matt τοῦ φόβου, and later of Peter, ἐφοβήθη, Matt 14.30.

Jn 6.68 and Matt 16.16 Σίμων Πέτρος. See also the references to Jn 6.9,13 in a. above.

2. Jn has tradition common to Matt and Lk:

Jn 6.2, ἠκολούθει δὲ αὐτῷ ὄχλος πολύς and Compare Matt 14.13; Lk 9.11 which introduce the theme of the crowds following Jesus οἱ [δὲ] ὄχλοι ἠκολούθησαν αὐτῷ whereas Mk mentions πολλοί and does not refer to following, though this might be implied. It could be argued that Jn's ὄχλος πολύς is a combination of Mk's πολλοί and Matt's and Lk's ὄχλοι. Alternatively it might derive from a variant tradition. See also Jn 6.69 ὁ ἅγιος τοῦ θεοῦ and Matt 16.16 ὁ Χριστὸς ὁ υἱὸς τοῦ θεοῦ and Lk 9.20 τὸν Χριστὸν τοῦ θεοῦ and Mk 8.29 has simply ὁ Χριστός.

3. Jn agrees with Lk alone:

Jn 6.1. Neither Jn nor Lk mentions a boat at this point. While Lk does not recount the return sea-crossing Jn does and has to introduce the boat at that point suggesting that the two stories were once separate but had become joined in the tradition used by Jn yet without introducing the first sea-crossing as do Mk and Matt.

Jn 6.5, ἐπάρας οὖν τοὺς ὀφθαλμοὺς is a Lukanism, see Lk 6.20; 16.23; 18.13. This however might be a case of Johannine editing rather than Lukan dependence, see Jn 4.35; 17.1.

Jn 6.42, οὐχ οὗτός ἐστιν Ἰησοῦς ὁ υἱὸς Ἰωσήφ; and Lk 4.22 οὐχὶ υἱός ἐστιν Ἰωσὴφ οὗτος;

While some of these points of contact might be a result of coincidental editing, the obvious implication is that, if Jn is to be understood on the basis of dependence on the Synoptics, it must be dependent on the three of them and, given the creative kind of composition Jn is, this does not seem likely.[4]

That the theory requires dependence on Matt, Mk and Lk is surely less credible than if Jn could be understood on the basis of Mk alone. For example, I would judge that Matt dates from about the same time as Jn. Jn itself bears the marks of a long process of composition. Given the completion of Jn around the same time as Matt, a theory of substantial

---

[4]See now Moody Smith, *John Among the Synoptics*, 180

dependence on Matt is hardly credible.[5] Further, the differences between Jn and the Synoptics need to be noted. Though many of these could be due to Johannine editing, it is likely that Jn has made use of a variant source of the feeding and other traditions now recorded in Jn 6. Other evidence can be given to support this view.

ii. There were several variant traditions of the feeding story and the subsequent sea-crossing. Two of these were known to Mk and agreements between Matt and Lk against Mk suggest that they knew yet another version of the feeding story. Jn's account of the feeding story resembles aspects of both of Mk's accounts as well as the variant in Matt and Lk. At no point do Jn's agreements occur where we have demonstrable Markan, Matthaean or Lukan redaction. It is more likely that Jn made use of a Synoptic-like variant of the traditions than a patchwork from all that is now found in Matt, Mk and Lk.

iii. While some of the variations from the Synoptics in Jn's feeding story are a consequence of the evangelist's editing,[6] there are others which are derived from the tradition. Both Matt and Lk, like Jn, refer to the crowd *following* Jesus to the desert place. Only Jn explains why.[7] They followed him seeing the signs he did on the sick, 6.2. Jn also tells of the crowd's response to the feeding miracle, 6.14-15. They confessed him to be the prophet and attempted to make him king, a political motif not likely to have been added by Jn. It was to escape from this that Jesus withdrew, not to pray (as in Matt 14.23; Mk 6.46). In Matt and Mk, following the feeding and at Jesus' command, the disciples embarked in the boat leaving Jesus. But no-one asked him how he would follow them. Only then did he dismiss the crowd and go further up the mountain to pray, an apologetic motif emphasizing Jesus' piety. In Jn Jesus fled from the crowd, leaving the disciples at the same time. When evening came the abandoned disciples attempted to make their way back across the lake. This is a more natural

---

[5]This judgement need not be based on the two document hypothesis though that is the assumption of this chapter. The early stages of Jn (perhaps even earlier than Mk) already made use of the feeding story as the evidence of the expansion and modification of it shows.

[6]Touches of the evangelist's hand are to be noted in the telling of the story itself: the time reference (μετὰ ταῦτα); the note indicating that the Passover is the feast of the Jews; the dialogues with Philip and Andrew; the direct commands by Jesus and his distribution of the food. The account of the sea-crossing also has some differences from the Synoptics for which the evangelist might be responsible; the account is more compressed and instead of the stilling of the storm there is a miraculous arrival at the destination.

[7]That Jesus should flee to a desert place at the execution of John the Baptist (see Mk 6.14-29 and parallel) is reasonable enough. This does not explain why the crowd followed him.

sequence of events and without apologetic motif or evidence of Johannine themes. Here Jn appears to have preserved primitive elements of the tradition.

iv. The Synoptics cannot account for a number of the *traditions* used in Jn, notably the healings of Jn 4.46-54; 5.1-9; 9.1-11. In addition Jn 2.1-11 and the underlying tradition of 11.1-44 should perhaps be added. It is enough to show that a number of important Synoptic-like stories cannot have been derived from the Synoptics and are unlikely to be Johannine creations but have probably been drawn from another source[8] from which have come also the basic traditions now in Jn 6. According to Moody Smith, "The distinctive character of the Johannine narrative material within the Gospel strongly suggests a principal source (or sources) and one independent of the Synoptics."[9] There is, however, need to distinguish the distinctive character of the Gospel, which is, at least in part, a result of the evangelist's interpretation of tradition, from the Synoptic-like character of that tradition.

2. The Traditional Stories in John 6.1-21

Synoptic parallels make quite clear that Jn 6 has been developed on the basis of a sequence of traditional material. The appropriate approach for the detection and identification of the underlying tradition begins by noting agreements with the Synoptics. But it is unlikely that the tradition was confined to this material. Departures from the Synoptics should be examined with a view to ascertaining whether these have arisen in the tradition or are due to the evangelist's handling of his material. Without the control of the Synoptic comparison, this task, though necessary if we are to appreciate the evangelist's achievement, is hazardous.

i The miraculous feeding (6.1-15). Unlike Matt and Mk neither Jn nor Lk mentions the departure of Jesus in a boat, though Jn, in agreement with Matt and Mk, introduces the boat for the return journey. This probably indicates that the feeding and the sea-crossing were once independent stories that had come to form a sequence in the traditions used by Mk and Jn.[10] It is unlikely that Mk and Jn independently created the

---

[8]C.H. Dodd (*Historical Tradition in the Fourth Gospel*) argued, in case after case, that the traditions he had isolated were not derived from Matt, Mk and Lk though they were Synoptic-like.

[9]D.M. Smith, "Johannine Christianity", *NTS* 21/2 (1975) 229.

[10]That neither Lk nor Jn mention the departure in a boat and Lk does not follow the sequence of the miraculous feeding with the miraculous sea crossing support this view. The tradition used by Jn stands between Mk and Lk. Jn makes no attempt to explain from whence the boat comes.

sequence. In Jn the general directions imply a desert place,[11] which is explicit in Matt and Mk. Given that Jn has reproduced, from the tradition, the account of the political response of the crowd, it may be that he has de-emphasized the desert place because Jesus' decision to lead the crowd there might imply complicity with their political intentions. Matt and Lk indicate that the crowd followed Jesus, implied in Mk and explicit in Jn who alone indicates the reason, ὅτι ἐθεώρουν τὰ σημεῖα ἃ ἐποίει ἐπὶ τῶν ἀσθενούντων.[12] The reason was probably given in Jn's source and might have been suppressed in the Synoptics. In Matt and Mk Jesus' flight to the desert place followed the execution of John the Baptist. This does not explain why the crowds should have followed him. Jn's source answers this question.

Whatever the crowd expected, in the wilderness Jesus performed a *sign of deliverance*.[13] Paul Barnett[14] has argued that in Josephus there is evidence of a class of "sign prophets" and that the pattern of the prophet, sign (Exodus motif), wilderness location, crowd as audience, is significant, suggesting some relation between Jesus and the sign prophets.[15] While each intended the sign to show that he was "the prophet", because the promised deliverance was not achieved we find a class of failed sign prophets. Of special importance, for an understanding of Jesus' miracle in

---

[11]This is complicated by verses 22-24, which are not part of the tradition used by Jn and probably contain an interpolation. See R. Schnackenburg, *The Gospel according to St John* II, 33.

[12]This use of τὰ σημεῖα ἃ ἐποίει ἐπὶ τῶν ἀσθενούντων has the specialized sense of "miracles of healing" which appears to be derived from the source. R. T. Fortna, "Source and Redaction in the Fourth Gospel's portrayal of Jesus' Signs", *JBL* 89 (1970) 160, has argued that the source did not speak of "seeing" signs. Such reference, he thinks, was introduced by the evangelist. It is uncertain whether the correct reading in 6.2 is ἑώρων or ἐθεώρουν. It is argued that the latter is an assimilation to 2.23. If that is the case ἐθεώρουν is used in 2.23; ἑώρων is used in 6.2; and ἰδόντες in 6.14. According to Ed Freed, this variation of vocabulary is characteristic of the evangelist and not the tradition, see "Fortna's Signs-source in John", *JBL* 94 (1975) 563-79. But if Fortna is correct the source may have indicated that the crowd followed Jesus "because of the signs he performed on the sick". These distinctions are less convincing if a loose collection of tradition is in view rather than a complex signs source or Gospel.

[13]See Josephus, *AJ* xx.168,188, and especially *BJ* ii. 259; vi.285.

[14]"The Jewish Sign Prophets", *NTS* 27/5 (1981) 679-97.

[15]*AJ* xix.162; xx.167-172,188; *BJ* ii.258-263; vi.285-286. In *BJ* vi.286 Josephus mentions a multitude of such prophets. That they were perceived to be prophets by the masses is clear from his reluctant naming them as such though he himself uses the term γόης of them.

the wilderness is Theudas,[16] who, according to Josephus, promised to part the Jordan, allowing his followers safe passage, thus re-enacting the Exodus:

> During the period when Fadus was procurator of Judaea, a certain impostor (γόης) named Theudas persuaded the majority of the crowd (τὸν πλεῖστον ὄχλον) to take up their possessions and to follow him to the Jordan River. He stated that he was a prophet and that at his command the river would be parted and would provide them an easy passage. With this talk he deceived many. Fadus, however, did not permit them to reap the fruit of their folly, but sent against them a squadron of cavalry. (Josephus, AJ xx.97-99)

Because Jesus was the first of those known to us (only John the Baptist was earlier, and he did no sign, Jn 10.41), Barnett suggests that Jesus himself, and the proclamation of his signs, might have "set this pattern". But it is hardly likely that later Jewish movements would have patterned themselves on Jesus or that Josephus was influenced by the Jesus movement in his portrayal of them.

R.A.Horsley has responded critically to Barnett's article.[17] He rightly asserts that the accounts of both Josephus and Jn must be treated critically in the awareness that they are not straightforward accounts of what happened. His analysis of Josephus leads to the conclusion that the first century prophets were of two kinds: the individual oracle prophets and those who led popular prophetic movements. The latter, he thinks, arose from among the common people and were concerned with the deliverance of the the common people from the socio-economic oppression of the day. He stresses that the association with deliverance is essential to this movement though signs are not. Here Horsley's own summary account (8-9) hardly bears out his insistence that deliverance was essential while signs were not. True, the prophets were perceived as deliverers. But how were they recognized in the first place? The accounts in Josephus suggest that Exodus type signs played some part in this,[18] but Horsley fails to note that the promised parting of the Jordan river and the promise that the walls of Jerusalem would fall down constitute signs even if they are not so called by Josephus. That he does not use the terminology there suggests that

---

[16]See D. Aune (*Prophecy in Early Christianity*, 127-8) who argues that Theudas saw himself as "the prophet like Moses".

[17]"Popular Prophetic Movements", especially 4-10, 15.

[18]*AJ* xx.97, 169-71; *BJ* ii.261-2. See also *AJ* xviii.85-86; and *BJ* ii.259; *AJ* xx.167-8. The final reference describes a number of "deceivers and imposters" (obviously the evaluation of Josephus rather than their followers) who led their followers out into the wilderness anticipating that God would give them "signs of liberation". This generalized account makes explicit what is implicit in the other accounts.

Josephus has no particular reason for introducing the view but that it represents the popular perception of the movement.[19] If Horsley is only concerned to show that the descriptive title "sign prophets" is not the most apt for this movement he has gone too far in his attempt to break the link with signs because, even though these prophets were concerned with deliverance, they were recognized through the promise or performance of Exodus-type signs.[20]

According to Jn, the crowd which followed Jesus into the desert place responded to him in a way consistent with the perception of him in these terms (6.2,14-15). Because it is a position rejected both by the evangelist and the tradition used by him it is likely that it represents a pre-crucifixion response. Indeed it is unlikely that such an overtly political motif would have been added. This suggests a known Jewish tradition which led to the recognition of Jesus as a sign prophet, that is, *the* prophet legitimated by sign(s). Recognition that there was a *group* of such prophets only reveals those who failed to be legitimated. That is, they failed to deliver. This would account for the disparaging view of the movements that we find in Josephus.

Rabbinic statements affirm that just as the first redeemer (Moses) brought down the manna, so also will the latter redeemer. While these references are somewhat later than Jn, 2 Baruch 29.8, which is more or less contemporary with Jn, tells that the manna will come again at the dawning of the new age.[21] The narrative of the feeding miracle in Jn, but not those in the Synoptics, reflects this expectation which appears to be related to the expectation concerning the sign prophet.[22] That would not be surprising if that expectation were based on Deut 18.15,18.[23] It would make sense of the response of the crowd in the Johannine account. According to the story, the crowd followed Jesus out into the desert because of the signs he was performing. In the desert Jesus replicated the giving of

---

[19]Contrary to Horsley 25 n22

[20]See Schürer, *History* II, 603-6.

[21]See C.K. Barrett, *St. John*, 288f. and R. Schnackenburg, *The Gospel according to St. John* II, 449 n110 for references.

[22]Such figures are referred to as "millennial prophets" by J.D. Crossan (*The Historical Jesus*, 158).

[23]At Qumran the expectation concerning the eschatological prophet was based on this text. See 4 *Q test* 5-8 and 1 *QS* 9.11. The relation of this figure to the Teacher of Righteousness is a question open to speculation. Horsley (15-17) rightly insists that the Teacher from Qumran is another example of the popular prophet with his movement. This recognition is important because it shows that, for the Qumran Community, the Teacher was not just one prophet amongst many and indeed may have been identified with the coming Prophet.

the manna by Moses. It is not surprising that the people[24] should perceive Jesus to be *the* prophet (6.14) and that they should attempt to make him king.[25] Moses was the prophet-king.[26] That Jesus was the prophet-king is the view of those who witnessed the sign, 6.14-15.[27] Thus we are warned against insisting that the categories of eschatological prophet and messianic king were always viewed separately. Clearly they are closely related by those depicted in Jn 6.14-15 and this should not be seen as as a Johannine or early Christian construction but as a popular perception of Jesus in response to his signs and the the feeding sign in particular.

 Horsley wishes to distinguish the popular prophetic movements from overtly political movements (Sicarii and Zealots) and popular messianic movements. The distinction between those who sought deliverance by armed uprising and those who waited to participate in the deliverance wrought by God is probably clearer in theory than actuality. The War Scroll of Qumran suggests that with the dawning of God's deliverance the children of light would be engaged in the battle as an essential part of the forces of God.[28] The key was to know when was God's time to act. Certainly the Romans would have found difficulty in distinguishing the two types of prophet deliverers, as is indicated by the case of the self-styled

---

[24]Here Jn does not speak of the crowd but of the $\check{\alpha}\nu\theta\rho\omega\pi\sigma\iota$. Jn's use of οἱ $\check{\alpha}\nu\theta\rho\omega\pi\sigma\iota$ (the people) is probably intended to indicate that not all of the crowd saw the sign (see 6.26) and specifies those who did, 6.14. While the Synoptics have no equivalent to Jn 6.14-15 both Matt and Mk refer to the $\check{\alpha}\nu\delta\rho\epsilon\varsigma$ who were fed, and in this they are followed by Jn 6.10. Matt adds $\chi\omega\rho\grave{\iota}\varsigma\ \gamma\upsilon\nu\alpha\iota\kappa\hat{\omega}\nu\ \kappa\alpha\grave{\iota}\ \pi\alpha\iota\delta\acute{\iota}\omega\nu$.

[25]See J.L. Martyn, *History and Theology in the Fourth Gospel*, 98-101.

[26]See Wayne Meeks, *The Prophet-King*.

[27]The vast majority of mss read $\sigma\eta\mu\epsilon\hat{\iota}o\nu$, but $\mathfrak{P}^{75}$ B a boh read $\sigma\eta\mu\epsilon\hat{\iota}\alpha$, which is probably an assimilation to Jn 6.2. Thus the singular should be read. It refers specifically to the feeding and does not include the healings. If, as argued, the confession of Jesus as the prophet-king is inadequate (according to Jn) the illuminating study of that name by Wayne Meeks does not penetrate the depths of the Johannine mystery. See now John Ashton, *Understanding*, 100 n76.

[28]Yigael Yadin (*The Scroll of the War of the Sons of Light against the Sons of Darkness*, 15) says that the purpose of the scroll "was to supply an urgent and immediate need, a guide for the problems of the long predicted war, which according to the sect would take place in the near future". The association of zealot tendencies with heavenly and earthly messianic figures at Qumran is argued by R. Eisenman and M.Wise, *The Dead Sea Scrolls Uncovered*, especially on the basis of materials until recently unpublished.

prophet in the time of Fadus.[29] Horsley (5) rightly stresses that we do not have access to the intentions of the various prophets. Nor do we have access to their actions but only to the perception of their actions as reported.[30] That Jesus was perceived by the masses as the prophet is inherently probable. It is also probable that, in popular perception, the prophet was not sharply distinguished from the Messiah.[31]

Horsley's distinctions might correspond more precisely with the intentions of the leaders of various movements. The problem, acknowledge by Horsley, is that we do not have direct access to the evidence of those intentions but only to the perception of the movements by others. While differences do emerge it is clear that various leaders had to struggle against a generalizing interpretation of their roles and movements. Both Horsley and Crossan acknowledge that the Romans tended to interpret the various movements in socio-political terms and to suppress them even where, on the evidence of Josephus, that suppression does not appear to be justified.[32] In reading Josephus critically or "against himself" the evidence confirms that in popular perception traditions were assimilated. Jn 6.14-15 confirms this while emphasizing that both Jesus and Jn reject this popular perception.

Reference to "the feast of the Jews", has all the hallmarks of the evangelist's hand,[33] but the Passover theme itself probably belonged to the traditional story giving force to Jesus' sign of feeding the crowd in the wilderness. The evangelist has not simply taken over the reference to the Passover. Birger Olsson referred to the Sinai screen of 1.19–2.11.[34] In Jn 6 the evangelist has interpreted the traditional material through a

---

[29]See the quotation of *AJ* xx.87-99 above. Gerd Theissen, *The Shadow of the Galilean*, reconstructs the story of Jesus to show that although Jesus did not lead a revolutionary movement against the Romans they *perceived* him as a political threat and executed him.

[30]In the case of Jesus we also have access to the perception of his words and the significance of this should not be minimized. As G. Vermes has frequently noted, the significance of Jesus' teaching sets him apart from other popular prophetic movements in his day.

[31]See Schürer, *History* II, 598-606.

[32]See Crossan, *The Historical Jesus*, 159ff.

[33]See 2.13,23; 6.4; 11.55; 12.1. On each of the three occasions the Passover is described as a feast of the Jews.

[34]*Structure and Meaning in the Fourth Gospel*, 102-9. There he says, "I use 'screen' and not 'pattern' or 'structure' or 'motif' because of its dynamic character and its usefulness in the semantic structure of a text and postsemantic processes behind a text." (102 n29). "The Sinai screen explains the composition and many of the details...[and] confirms the total interpretation."..."The narrator saw in his material an equivalent of the events that once took place at Sinai,..." (109).

Passover/Exodus screen. The Synoptics tell of Jesus' early Galilean popularity but they mention no attempt to take him by force ($\dot{a}\rho\pi\dot{a}\zeta\epsilon\iota\nu$) and to make him king. This attempt explains Jesus' withdrawal into the mountainous region alone. Matt 14.23 and Mk 6.46 explain this withdrawal as being $\pi\rho\sigma\sigma\epsilon\dot{v}\xi a\sigma\theta a\iota$, which might be the implied purpose of the original withdrawal, according to Matt and Mk. In Jn Jesus' calculated withdrawal itself shows his rejection of the attempt to make him king.[35] While we would not expect an actual crowd, intent on making Jesus king, to take his refusal so easily, it is important to remember that, from the point of view of the story, Jesus' rejection was both clear and final. There is nothing to be gained by telling that the crowd persisted in its intent. Indeed, it was the evangelist's purpose to proceed to the next scene.

It is unclear what christological perception was communicated in the traditional story as distinct from the christology of the crowd which it reported. It is possible that the story was intended to proclaim Jesus as the eschatological deliverer. Fragments of this position are to be found in 6.27,39,40,44,54. The emphasis is on the food ($\beta\rho\hat{\omega}\sigma\iota\varsigma$) which the Son of Man[36] will give ($\delta\dot{\omega}\sigma\epsilon\iota$) and the resurrection on the last day. It seems that the tradition proclaimed Jesus as a man approved of God by signs and wonders,[37] exalted to God's right hand as the judge elect of all the world. Both christologies (that of the crowd[38] and that of the traditional story[39]) proposed corporate solutions to the envisaged problem. The crowd looked for a political resolution to the Roman occupation, while the traditional story looked for an apocalyptic solution to the ills of the world. Because, as we shall see, the traditional story has become absorbed into the evangelist's quest story development (6.1-40) the apocalyptic eschatology remains only as a relic alongside the christology of the quest story. This suggests that the evangelist did not reject that eschatology but made an

---

[35]In 6.15 the use of $\pi\dot{a}\lambda\iota\nu$ indicates a further movement into the deserted mountainous region.

[36]The first Son of Man saying (6.27) is in the quest story (1-35); the second (6.53) in the controversy with the Jews (6.41-59); and the third (6.62) in the controversy with the disciples (6.60-66). Traditional third person Son of Man sayings and third person Father/Son sayings are reworked with characteristically Johannine "I" sayings in the first person, or "my Father" sayings. This reworking is a Johannine characteristic. See also the discussion of 5.19-30 in chapter 5, "The Paradigm of Rejection" above.

[37]See Acts 2.22-36; 3.19-21.

[38]Synoptic parallels show that reference to the crowd is traditional.

[39]Clearly the crowd in the story and the story as a whole give expression to rival christologies. Thus political messiahship was already rejected in the tradition used by Jn.

emissary christology the focus of the quest story. This christology made Jesus the source of life for the believer in the present.

ii The miraculous sea-crossing (6.16-21). The evangelist agrees with Mk (and Matt) in telling the story of the miraculous sea-crossing following the feeding story because it was already attached to his story of the feeding, though the evidence suggests that the stories were originally independent. His account of the miraculous sea crossing is much briefer than those of Matt and Mk which, apart from Matt's addition of Peter's walking on the water, are quite similar. They differ from Jn in that, according to their accounts, Jesus enters the boat and the storm ceased whereas, in Jn, Jesus' appearance and self-identification miraculously coincides with the boat reaching its destination.[40]

In all three accounts Jesus identifies himself with the words ἐγώ εἰμι· μὴ φοβεῖσθε.[41] It is sometimes argued that this is used by the evangelist as a theophany formula.[42] Against this view: 1.) The evangelist has simply taken this over from the tradition and has made nothing of it. 2.) Mk portrays the amazement of the disciples, and notes their lack of understanding (Mk 6.51-52), and Matt (14.33) has the disciples proclaim "Truly you are Son of God", though this response is to the miracle rather than Jesus' words. But Jn has no confession from the disciples, which would be expected if this were a revelation formula. In Jn it is only noted that the disciples wished to take Jesus into the boat, having identified who it was. Whether this happened remains unstated. Instead we are told that immediately the boat reached its destination. 3.) While the frequent use of ἐγώ εἰμι in Jn suggests something significant, appeals to various examples where God himself as speaker reveals himself using *ani hu* (Exod 12.12; Isa 45, especially verses 5-8, 18-22) do not provide a basis for interpreting the Johannine use because in all of these instances it is clear that God is the speaker, "I am the Lord, and there is no other". Here in Jn 6.20 the "I am" is simply an identification, "It is I/me".[43]

All of this suggests that the evangelist is not narrating a theophany through his telling of the sea crossing. He tells the story because it was already attached to the feeding story. But he has used the story to good effect. This story dramatically separates Jesus from the crowd which had followed him into the desert. Separation could have been achieved simply

---

[40]See Psalm 107.29-30. In the Psalm the stilling of the storm and the arrival at the desired destination occur together and perhaps this is also presupposed in Jn.

[41]In both Matt and Mk this saying is prefixed by θαρσεῖτε.

[42]See B. Gärtner, *John 6 and the Jewish Passover*, 17-18, 28 and P. Borgen, *Bread from Heaven*, 180.

[43]Thus C. K. Barrett, *St John*, 281.

by Jesus' withdrawal into the wilderness of the mountain. But that would have been an ambiguous action in relation to the political affirmation for which the desert was the legitimate milieu. The story of the sea-crossing was used because it lay ready at hand to make the point of Jesus' rejection of the political role while, at the same time, separating Jesus from the crowd. That separation was then used to emphasize the renewed seeking of Jesus by the crowd "on the next day".

II. INTERPRETING THE TRADITION

It is notable that in the narrative description: in 6.22-35 there are two references to the crowd (6.22,24); in 6.41-59 there are two references to the Jews (6.41,52); in 6.60-66 there are two references to the disciples (6.60,66); and in 6.67-71 there are two references to the twelve (6.67,71).[44] This balance does not seem to be accidental. Rather the evangelist appears to have developed further discourses on the basis of the quest story of 6.1-35 of the first edition. Verses 36-40 are based on the concluding pronouncement of the quest story. In this section (36-40) we also find remnants of the eschatological messiahship[45] which the tradition used by the evangelist had offered as an alternative to the rejected political messiahship of 6.15. But the primary function of this section is to form a transition to the rejection of Jesus by the Jews and the mass of disciples in 6.41-66. Of course this also means that the quest of the crowd has ended in failure and it is said that they have seen and not believed, 6.1-40. The function of verses 67-71 is less clear. It could be that they make a hybrid of the rejection story by introducing an element of commendation, the twelve, through Peter, being commended for exemplary faith.

1. The Quest Story of 6.1-40: First Edition

i **Quest stories in John.** The case for recognizing a quest story in Jn 6 is facilitated by the recognition of the *genre* and its use in earlier parts of the Gospel.[46] Here a pattern emerges that is recognizable elsewhere,

---

[44]Jesus also refers to the twelve in 6.70.

[45]See the reference to the Son of Man (in 6.27) and the use of the future δώσει. This future tense is later taken up in an "I" saying by Jesus in 6.51 ἐγώ δώσω and see 4.14. The future tenses in chapter 6 appear to point forward to a future event while in 4.14 Jesus was referring to a present possibility, see 4.10. There are traces of a continuing future eschatological dimension in Jn 6; see 6.27,39,40,44,54.

[46]See chapter 4, "Quest Stories in John 1-4" above.

including Jn 6.[47] The transformation of the opening series of quest stories by the insertion of 1.51 is also relevant to Jn 6 where the focus has been moved from a miracle worker christology to an exalted Son of Man christology. See 6.62.

ii The quest story of 6.1-40. Reading 6.1-15 from the perspective of the quest story we note the initiative of the crowd which followed Jesus (ἠκολούθει δὲ αὐτῷ) seeing the σημεῖα he performed. The crowd was rewarded and they were fed by Jesus. This suggests a successful quest. But the story is not yet finished. The crowd's quest to make Jesus king was frustrated by his premature withdrawal. Here an action provides the objection to the quest which now appears to have failed. But the story still continues and is taken further by 6.16-21 which dramatizes Jesus' separation of himself from the crowd. Had the wilderness withdrawal been used for this purpose the crowd, renewing its seeking of Jesus, would have come again to him in the desert place, the location associated with the sign prophet, which role Jesus had rejected. Instead of this it was necessary for the crowd to come seeking him in Capernaum.

The use of τῇ ἐπαύριον in 6.22[48] ties the following events, dialogues, and discourses, to the sea-crossing, which is integrally related to the feeding story, 6.1-21. Thus, "on the next day" the story of the crowd that commenced in 6.2 is taken up again with all the appearances of a successfully completed quest. The crowd which had followed (ἠκολούθει) Jesus to the place of the feeding miracle (6.2) now comes again seeking Jesus (ζητοῦντες τὸν Ἰησοῦν), 6.24.[49]; and indeed finds him (εὑρόντες αὐτόν) 6.25. Yet again what follows shows that the quest failed. Jesus' response (6.26) is provided with characteristic Johannine quotation

---

[47]See especially the motifs of "following", "seeking" and "finding" in 1.37,38,40,41,43,45; 6.2, 24-26 and the connection of events by the use of τῇ ἐπαύριον, 1.29,35,43; 6.22.

[48]See 1.29,35,43; 6.22; 12.12. The expression is used elsewhere in the NT only in Matt 27.62; Mk 11.12; and Acts 10.9,23,24; 14.20; 20.7; 21.8; 22.30; 23.32; 25.6,23. Its use appears to be characteristic of Jn and Acts but it is notably absent from Lk!

[49]It is not likely that the evangelist intended his readers to understand that there were two crowds, one which had seen the feeding miracle and the other which had not, though this is advocated by M.E. Boismard and adopted by R.E. Brown, *John* I, 259.

formula,[50] and introduced by a solemn double *amen*-saying.[51] In this saying Jesus acknowledged the crowd's quest, ζητεῖτέ με. But it is no longer the quest of 6.1-15, οὐχ ὅτι εἴδετε σημεῖα. Note especially 6.2,14. While the crowd had followed Jesus because they saw the signs he was performing in healing the sick, only some of the crowd (οἱ ἄνθρωποι) saw the sign of the feeding. All were fed, but only some saw the sign and they sought to make Jesus king, 6.14-15.

Jesus' departure from the desert place left no doubt that he had rejected the perception of him as a sign prophet (prophet-king). Yet the crowd still sought him because they had eaten of the loaves and were satisfied.[52] This saying of Jesus (6.26) is not a reproach. Rather it draws attention to the christological vacuum left by the rejection of the political role. The crowd no longer sought him as one who had given a sign of liberation. They sought him because he satisfies the hungry ("you ate of the loaves and were satisfied"). It is this theme of satisfying the hungry that the discourse develops. But to do this a distinction must be made (in verse 27) between the loaves that have been eaten, that is, the food (βρῶσις) which perishes, and the food (βρῶσις)[53] which gives eternal life. Through the dialogues of 6.25-36 we are led, with increasing expectation, to the request of the crowd, κύριε, πάντοτε δὸς ἡμῖν τὸν ἄρτον τοῦτον (6.34)[54] and finally to the pronouncement of 6.35.

Yet surprisingly, in the end we are told that the crowd's quest ended in failure, 6.36. The surprise is heightened by the expectation of success given by the request of 6.34 which resonates with the sound of the request of the Samaritan woman (4.15) which foreshadowed a successful quest, not only for the woman, but also for the people of her town. Both the

---

[50]"Jesus answered them and said". The same formula is used with an *amen*-saying in 3.3; 6.26 and introducing other sayings of Jesus in 1.48,50; 3.10,13; 6.29,43; 7.16,21; 8.14.. Other quotation formulae are used in another ten *amen*-sayings while the remaining thirteen *amen*-sayings are without quotation formulae as they do not commence a Jesus -saying.

[51]See 1.51; 3.3,5,10,11; 5.19,24,25; 6.26,32,47,53; 8.34,51,58; 10.1,7; 12.24; 13.16,20,21,38; 14.12; 16.20,23; 21.18. Nothing can be deduced concerning the authenticity of the sayings from the use of this formula. In Jn 6 two *amen*-sayings occur in the quest story and two in the story of conflict with the Jews.

[52]For the use of ἐχορτάσθητε see Mk 8.8.

[53]The term is used in 6.27 in the quest story and 6.55 in the story of Jewish rejection. In the latter it is used to introduce the idea of the true food and drink, the flesh and blood of Jesus, symbols of the giving of his life in death.

[54]See 4.15 κύριε, δός μοι τοῦτο τὸ ὕδωρ,... The reader is obviously expected to recognize the echo of this request in 6.34.

269

Samaritan woman and the crowd in Jn 6 misunderstood the nature of the water/bread that Jesus offered. Misunderstanding is a common means by which clarification is made on the way to understanding and belief. Because this was the case with the Samaritan woman the reader has every reason to expect that the crowd that has resolutely followed Jesus across the lake and back to Capernaum will also succeed in its quest now redefined by Jesus. Thus the pronouncement of their unbelief (6.36) comes as a shocking announcement. Further, 6.36-40 is made up of a collection of isolated sayings which form a transition to the rejection story of 6.41ff. and was probably added when the quest was transformed into rejection. The collection of sayings is quite different from the set of short dialogues between Jesus and the crowd up to this point.

In the quest story 6.27 should be seen as a new objection to the renewed quest of the crowd. Their quest is now for the perishable food. They are told that it does not satisfy, that it does not give eternal life. For this they need the food which the Son of Man will give to them. In 6.27 we have the first in a string of what were unrelated traditional sayings linked by the association of works ($\xi\rho\gamma\alpha$) and sign ($\sigma\eta\mu\epsilon\hat{\iota}o\nu$).[55] In this first saying the crowd is exhorted to "work..." ($\dot{\epsilon}\rho\gamma\dot{a}\zeta\epsilon\sigma\theta\epsilon$). The term $\beta\rho\hat{\omega}\sigma\iota\varsigma$ is used rather than $\dot{a}\rho\tau o\varsigma$. The food which perishes is distinguished from the food which abides to eternal life. The Son of Man is named as the giver. It is said that he will give ($\delta\dot{\omega}\sigma\epsilon\iota$) the food which abides. What is essential to well-being at a physical level has become symbolic of the source of spiritual well-being.

The theme of working (6.27) is thematically related to 5.17[56] and linguistically linked to working the works of God (6.28), which is probably to be understood in the sense of signs. But this is redefined by Jesus in terms of believing in the one sent by God, 6.29. To believe Jesus (6.30) is to believe in the one whom he (God) sent (6.29) which, in the dialogue, it is assumed, refers to Jesus, which the crowd understood. Because of this the crowd demanded a sign. The demand, as Synoptic parallels show, is from the tradition. It may be that Jn has added the purpose "that we may see and believe you", and the interpretation of the demand in terms of $\tau\dot{\iota}$ $\dot{\epsilon}\rho\gamma\dot{a}\zeta\eta$, 6.30. Thus, in the demand by the crowd, signs and works are here equated. For the evangelist Jesus' works included

---

[55]That 6.27-30 is based on tradition is shown by Synoptic parallels and the linking of unrelated sayings by common words.
[56]"Work" involves the expending of effort to produce an effect. In 5.17 the question concerns the expending of such effort on the Sabbath. The specific work on the Sabbath to which reference was made in 5.17 was indeed a $\sigma\eta\mu\epsilon\hat{\iota}o\nu$. But what was prohibited on the Sabbath was the expending of effort to produce an effect whether or not a miracle was involved.

the signs he worked because the whole mission of Jesus is summed up as his work, 4.34. But the crowd demanded to see a sign that would authenticate that Jesus was the one sent by God.

The demand for a sign is strange in the context of this chapter in which the performance of a notable sign has been recognized, 6.14. Even stranger is the nature of the demanded sign, 6.31. The crowd appealed to "our fathers", a term used of the generation that came out of Egypt.[57] They appealed to the fathers because they ate manna in the desert. This becomes a crucial issue in the subsequent conflict with the Jews, 6.49,58. There Jesus recalls the assertion of 6.31a (not the text of 6.31b), but adds "your (the) fathers" who ate the manna are dead, proving conclusively that the manna was not the life-giving bread from heaven, a distinction dependent on 6.27 and 6.32-33. Nor did Jesus' feeding miracle provide the true bread from heaven, and this is the point of 6.27. Only in 6.35 is the true bread from heaven identified.

What did the crowd seek in asking for a legitimating sign (6.30)? It was not to the repetition of the sign that the appeal to Scripture[58] refers but to the original event. By analogy this reference could be understood as the call for a new feeding miracle such as Jesus had recently performed. This would imply that the crowd was blind to that sign but 6.14-15 hardly confirms this.

For the text of 6.31b appeal is generally made to Neh 9.15; Ps 78(77).24; and Exodus 16. Here it is appropriate to discuss the important and influential thesis of Peder Borgen.[59] Borgen thinks that both Jn and Philo[60] made use of midrashic techniques that provide a pattern for dealing with the manna tradition. The pattern involves the use of a text from the *torah* (Exod 16.15) in 6.31b followed by a text from the prophets (Isa 54.13) in 6.45a. The primary text is interpreted by breaking it up and substituting new words for words that appear in the text thus bringing new

---

[57]See further in 6.49,58 and 1 Cor 10.1. In 6.49 Jesus refers to "your fathers" distinguishing himself from those for whom they are "our fathers". In 6.58 Jesus refers to "the fathers" which is more neutral. In the rabbinic literature *aboth* (fathers) is used of the ancestors of the nation. The term is used by the Samaritan woman of the ancestors of the Samaritans in 4.20 and specifically of the patriarch Jacob in 4.12.

[58]The quotation formula $\kappa\alpha\theta\acute{\omega}\varsigma\ \acute{\epsilon}\sigma\tau\iota\nu\ \gamma\epsilon\gamma\rho\alpha\mu\mu\acute{\epsilon}\nu o\nu$ occurs here and at 12.14. It appears to be the Johannine variation of the very common $\kappa\alpha\theta\grave{\omega}\varsigma\ \gamma\acute{\epsilon}\gamma\rho\alpha\pi\tau\alpha\iota$. Jn 6.45 has the variation $\acute{\epsilon}\sigma\tau\iota\nu\ \gamma\epsilon\gamma\rho\alpha\mu\mu\acute{\epsilon}\nu o\nu\ \acute{\epsilon}\nu\ \tauo\hat{\iota}\varsigma\ \pi\rho o\phi\acute{\eta}\tau\alpha\iota\varsigma$. See also 7.38. On the quotation formulae see E. D. Freed, *Old Testament Quotations in the Gospel of John*.

[59]*Bread from Heaven*.

[60]See *Leg. all.* iii.162-168; *Mut.* 253-263.

insights to the text. Persuasive as some aspects of this thesis are there are certain problems that need to be addressed.

1. The first Scripture quotation (6.31b) is closer to Ps 78(77).24 than Exod 16.15 even if this is combined with 16.4. Precise identification of the Scripture quoted has not been possible.[61] Georg Richter suggests that the quotation is not from the *OT* but from a Jewish manna tradition.[62] The quotation formula must cast some doubt on this suggestion but the difficulty of identifying the text with a specific citation from the *torah* must cast doubt on Borgen's hypothesis.

2. Borgen's hypothesis disregards the narrative context of the discourse. Indeed he suggests that the feeding miracle is merely the excuse for the discourse. If this were the case the complex narrative elements of the chapter would be inexplicable. Rather they are to be seen as decisive indications of transformation in the discourse.

3. Borgen sets the discourse as a whole in the context of the Johannine struggle with a form of docetism similar to that which is illustrated in the writings of Ignatius. How this correlates with the use of techniques of Palestinian midrashim is difficult to assess. It also fails to do justice to much of the material which seems to have been shaped in the dialogue and conflict with the synagogue. That does not exclude the possibility that late elements in the discourse reflect the conflict with docetism within the Johannine community. Borgen's hypothesis fails to take account of the layers in the discourse though these should not be attributed to different authors.

4. The text upon which the discourse as a whole is based is 6.35 not 6.31b though 6.31 *as a whole* is used (with 6.27) in leading up to the pronouncement of 6.35. Thus Borgen's thesis need not be rejected but it should be modified so that the midrash of Jn 6 is seen to have its basis in the authoritative (for the evangelist) words of Jesus which come to light in the structure of the quest story.

The crowd's appeal to the manna tradition (6.31b) provided Jesus with the position against which he could pit his own. Here (6.32-33) the words of Jesus make certain modifications to what was asserted by the crowd.

1. It is said that the giver is "my Father" not Moses,[63] though previously (6.27) it has been asserted that the Son of Man *will give* the abiding food ($\beta\rho\tilde{\omega}\sigma\iota\nu$).

2. The gift is to the crowd ($\dot{\upsilon}\mu\hat{\iota}\nu$) not to those who came out of Egypt ($\alpha\dot{\upsilon}\tauo\hat{\iota}s$).

3. Jesus asserts *gives* ($\delta\dot{\iota}\delta\omega\sigma\iota\nu$) not gave ($\check{\epsilon}\delta\omega\kappa\epsilon\nu$) or will give ($\delta\dot{\omega}\sigma\epsilon\iota$), 6.27.

4. He refers to the true bread from heaven.

---

[61]See also 7.38. Freed thinks that the evangelist modified the quotations to suit his own purpose.

[62]*Studien zum Johannesevangelium*, 211-29.

[63]This assumes that the "he" who "gave" ($\check{\epsilon}\delta\omega\kappa\epsilon\nu$) was understood to be Moses. Naturally this is not clear.

5. The true bread from heaven is designated the bread of God.

6. It is identified with he (or that which)[64] who comes down from heaven giving life to the world, 6.33.

7. That which/the one who comes down from heaven gives ($\delta\iota\delta o\acute{v}s$) life to the world, 6.33.[65] It is because it/he gives life to the world that it/he is called "the bread of God".

The crowd obviously assumed that $\acute{o}\ \kappa\alpha\tau\alpha\beta\alpha\acute{\iota}\nu\omega\nu$ referred to the bread. But why should they think of Jesus as the giver if he has said that it is his Father who gives this bread? (6.32). This can only mean that the crowd, provisionally at least, has accepted Jesus as the emissary of God (6.29), that is, the Son of Man whom, he has said, "will give" the food that abides to eternal life (6.27). This food is the true bread from heaven so that what Jesus says the Son of Man "will give" is identical with what he says "my Father gives" (6.32). Apparently there are two givers but only one giving and one gift.[66] That this point was perceived is implied in that after Jesus has spoken of the Father the crowd requests, "Lord, always give us this bread". This implies that the crowd now perceives Jesus as the Son of Man, the emissary of God who will give the bread of God.[67] What persuaded them of this? Jesus performed no further sign such as was demanded in 6.30. Jesus in Jn allows that belief on the basis of his signs/works is a valid starting point, 5.36; 10.25,38; 14.11, but here it is Jesus' words that overcome the demand for a sign and lead to the request of 6.34, $\kappa\acute{v}\rho\iota\epsilon,\ \pi\acute{a}\nu\tau o\tau\epsilon\ \delta\acute{o}s\ \acute{\eta}\mu\hat{\iota}\nu\ \tau\grave{o}\nu\ \acute{a}\rho\tau o\nu\ \tau o\hat{v}\tau o\nu$. At this point the quest appears to be on the threshold of success.

The ambiguity of $\acute{o}\ \kappa\alpha\tau\alpha\beta\alpha\acute{\iota}\nu\omega\nu$ in 6.33 is then clarified by the climactic concluding pronouncement of Jesus in 6.35: $\acute{\epsilon}\gamma\acute{\omega}\ \epsilon\acute{\iota}\mu\iota\ \acute{o}\ \acute{a}\rho\tau o s$ $\tau\hat{\eta}s\ \zeta\omega\hat{\eta}s\cdot\ \acute{o}\ \acute{\epsilon}\rho\chi\acute{o}\mu\epsilon\nu o s\ \pi\rho\grave{o}s\ \acute{\epsilon}\mu\grave{\epsilon}\ o\grave{v}\ \mu\grave{\eta}\ \pi\epsilon\iota\nu\acute{a}\sigma\eta,\ldots$ The self-

---

[64]Because $\acute{a}\rho\tau o s$ is masculine it is unclear whether $\acute{o}\ \kappa\alpha\tau\alpha\beta\alpha\acute{\iota}\nu\omega\nu$ should be translated as "he who" or "that which".

[65]In 6.33 "descending" ($\kappa\alpha\tau\alpha\beta\alpha\acute{\iota}\nu\omega\nu$) and giving ($\delta\iota\delta o\acute{v}s$) are present participles, see also 6.50. The aorist participle ($\kappa\alpha\tau\alpha\beta\acute{a}s$) is used in 6.41,51,58 and 3.13. The aorist participles indicates the specific, historic nature of the descent while the present participles signify the characteristic action of the redeemer. With both the aorist and present participles Jesus speaks in the third person either of "he" or "it" (the bread). The perfect tense $\kappa\alpha\tau\alpha\beta\acute{\epsilon}\beta\eta\kappa\alpha$ is used by Jesus in "I" sayings in 6.38,42. The other side of the descent is the ascent of the Son of Man, 6.62, see also the use of $\acute{v}\psi\omega\sigma\epsilon\nu$ in 3.14 which is the equivalent of $\acute{a}\nu\alpha\beta\acute{\epsilon}\beta\eta\kappa\epsilon\nu$ in 3.13. The Son of Man who descended from heaven is the only one to have ascended ("to heaven" is implied).

[66]Compare the discussion of 5.17 in the previous chapter II.2. "The Text".

[67]The request marks real progress towards the recognition of Jesus' relation to God even if residual misunderstandings remain.

identification of Jesus with the life-giving bread is both a new objection to the quest of the crowd, which has progressed to recognize Jesus as the emissary of God, and a clarification of their misunderstanding of the nature of the bread. At this point Jn's symbolic use of bread brings out the soteriological implications of his christology over against the Jewish symbolic use with reference to the *Torah*. At this point a real choice has to be made.[68]

Given that the stress is on the crowd's quest, and that they have appealed to the manna, the bread from heaven, Jesus is saying that he, not the manna is the bread from heaven,[69] just as he has said that his father, not Moses, gives the true bread from heaven, 6.32. In 6.35 bread from heaven, which could mean bread rained down from the sky like the manna (6.33), is interpreted as the life-giving bread. Hence, the fact that those who ate the manna are dead is evidence that the manna was not the true life-giving bread, as will be argued in 6.49,58. Thus "from heaven" no longer simply indicates the origin of the bread. Rather it is an indication of the quality of the life given by this bread. It is the life of the age to come that is offered by Jesus in the present.[70] He has offered it in such a way that it is clear that individual response to Jesus is necessary if the life of the age to come is to be enjoyed. Thus the quest story focuses attention on the person of Jesus as the fulfilment of the quest.

The implied contrast with Jesus is the Law of Moses, represented by the symbol of the manna, the bread from heaven.[71] Naturally this contrast, inherent in the quest story, belongs to the dialogue between the Johannine Christians and those Jews who, though not yet believers, were open to the appeal of Jesus.[72] At this stage it is belief in Jesus as the emissary[73] from

---

[68]To complete the quest story all that now remains to be done is for the narrator to announce the success or failure of the quest. The surprising failure of the quest is announced in the words of Jesus in 6.36.

[69]See R. Bultmann, *John*, 225 n3. Bultmann argues that 6.35 (as well as 6.41,48,51) is an example of ' *recognition formulae*. "This formula is also found in sacred language, sometimes in such a way that by the ἐγώ εἰμι something which men are looking at or already know is given a new interpretation"..."It is used as a revelation formula proper (i.e. where the speaker, being present, reveals himself by the ἐγώ εἰμι as the one whom people were waiting for or looking for)."

[70]In rabbinic statements the manna has become the symbol of the new age, Ecclesiastes R. 1.128. See Barrett, *St. John*, 288.

[71]See Proverbs 9.5; Genesis R. 70.5; Str.B. II. 483f.

[72]It would become a basic tool in the struggle with the synagogue reflected in later parts of the discourse.

[73]The emphasis on the emissary is made through the use of ἀπέστειλεν, 6.29,57; πέμψαντος, 6.38; ὁ πατήρ ὁ πέμψας με, 6.44; and indirectly ὁ ὤν

heaven (from God) that is held out as the fulfilment of the quest. A definite individual response is called for if the life Jesus offered is to be enjoyed. The story concludes with Jesus' proclamation of the failure of the crowd's quest (6.36), forming a transition to the rejection stories.

It is likely that the conclusion to the quest story in the first edition was more open than this. But as the story now stands the note of rejection is sounded for the first time in 6.36 which now marks the failure of the quest. Yet at no point in the dialogues between 6.22-36 does the crowd reject Jesus or his words though (as is expected in a quest story) Jesus does offer objections to their understanding and in this way the crowd is led to request of Jesus, "Κύριε, always give us this bread", a request that resonates with the successful request of 4.15. An expectation of success for this quest is thus established. Jesus then identifies himself with the bread of life (6.35) which clarifies the nature of the bread that he offers. Without any further response from the crowd Jesus pronounces that they have not believed. The reader has not been prepared for this negative evaluation of the crowd's quest.

The movement of the story suggests, as we have seen, that the negative conclusion was not original. This observation is made probable by the transitional nature of verses 36-40 which appear to be a collection of traditional sayings. The saying introduced by "But I told you..." has no precise earlier reference,[74] though 6.26 could be in view. If so, then a new negative interpretation is given to that saying and this supports the suggestion that a new negative conclusion was given to the story in the second edition. The point of the saying (6.36) is now to introduce the theme of unbelief. Jesus proclaims the failure of the crowd's quest thus providing a transition to the rejection stories. When the audience is next identified (6.41) it is no longer described as "the crowd", but as "the Jews" and the theme of the possibility of coming to Jesus being dependent on the Father (6.37) is now stated in negative terms. No one is able to come unless he is drawn by the Father, 6.44. The theme of raising up on the last day those who come is also repeated, 6.39,44. Thus 6.36-40 belongs with 6.41ff. and the transformation of the quest story into a rejection story.

παρὰ τοῦ θεοῦ', 6.46 and reference to the Son of Man as τοῦτον γὰρ ὁ πατὴρ ἐσφράγισεν ὁ θεός, 6.27.

[74]It is characteristic of Jesus in Jn that he quotes his own earlier sayings, sometimes exactly, sometimes with less than clear reference. Thus 3.7 refers to 3.3; 3.28 to 1.20; 4.53 to 4.50; 5.11 to 5.8; 6.36 possibly to 6.26; 6.41 to a combination of 6.33 and 35; 6.65 to 6.37 etc.

The importance of the quest story *genre* in Jn is difficult to overestimate.[75] The use of the first of the great symbolic "I am" sayings as the climactic pronouncement of the quest story of Jn 6 alerts us to the theological significance of this particular quest story. The use of the symbolism of bread within this quest story suggests that, although the context implies a contrast is being made between Jesus' understanding of bread and the Jewish understanding of the *manna* as a symbol for the Law, a more universal application is in order. That the crowd was fed by Jesus and comes again seeking bread confirms this. Bread was for them the means of sustaining life. It was for this reason that bread, the *manna*, became a symbol for the Law. The logic of the symbolism is dependent on the perception that "the life is more than food".[76] The great religions of the world have all recognized that physical existence does not exhaust the meaning and purpose of human life. The contrast is not between bare existence and the desired quality of life which today is often invoked in discussions of *euthanasia*.[77] In such discussions bread is not a symbol but the desired reality. In other words, physical life is the reality and bread is the means of supporting this. But for the life of which Jesus speaks he is himself the bread, that is, the source, the means of supporting that life. The viability of this use of language arises from the fact that material possessions do not satisfy the human quest/thirst/hunger for life. Death, which terminates physical life is one reason for this. More significant, however, is the human quest for some meaning in the context of a world that so often seems meaningless and purposeless. In the midst of competing ideologies, one of which was the Jewish understanding of the Law, Jn proclaimed Jesus as the bread of life, the source of true life.

2. The Rejection Stories of 6.36-71: Subsequent Editions

i **Transition (6.36-40).** The whole of this section appears to be a transitional addition. Indeed, it was this addition that gave the negative conclusion to the quest story. While the dialogues of 6.26-35 arise from the feeding story of 6.1-15, find focus in 6.31, and reach their climax in the pronouncement of 6.35, the sayings of Jesus in 6.36-40 are an elaboration of the "believing"/"coming" idea of 6.35. They also introduce the theme of being cast out (cf. 9.34). Unlike the Jewish authorities of 9.22,34, Jesus will not cast out those who come to him. This theme signals

---

[75] See the conclusion to chapter 4, "Quest Stories in John 1-4" for a statement concerning the relevance of Jn's use of quest stories to an understanding of the social context and theological message of the Gospel.
[76] See Matt 6.25ff.
[77] Here, when the desired quality of life is irrevocably lost it is sometimes argued that the self-determined termination of life is justifiable.

coming conflict. The subsequent discourse is, as a whole, developed on the basis of the saying of Jesus in 6.35.[78]   Neither of the Scripture texts quoted in 6.31 and 6.45 deals with the question of "coming" to Jesus. This is a central theme of the Jesus saying in 6.35 and it is the recurrent theme of 6.36-71.[79]

Picking up the negative conclusion of 6.36,"You have seen and you have not believed",[80] 6.36-40 provides a transition to 6.41-59 by giving an explanation, in predestinarian terms, for the relative failure of the mission to the synagogue while, at the same time, proclaiming the benefits for believers.[81] Jesus said that everything[82] the Father gives him comes to him and he does not cast them out because he has come down from heaven[83] to do the will of the Father, the one who sent him. Those who come to him, who see him and believe, he will raise up on the last

---

[78]Jn 5.17 is another text with the discourse of 5,19-30 based on it. On this see chapter 5, "The Paradigm of Rejection" above.

[79]See 6.37,44,45,65. If we add to this the parallel theme of 6.35, "believing", the dependence of 6.36-71 on 6.35 becomes even more obvious. See 6.40,47,64,69. Then there is the reiteration of the basic affirmation of 6.35 in 6.48, and with slight variation in 6.51. The themes of eating and drinking in 6.50-58 also arise from the affirmation of 6.35 which indicates the satisfaction of hunger and quenching of thirst.

[80]Although $\mu\epsilon$ is well attested by the majority of mss including $\mathfrak{P}^{66}$ and probably $\mathfrak{P}^{75}$ as well as B D K L, it should probably be omitted along with $\aleph$ A it $^{a\ b\ e\ q}$ syr$^{c\ s}$. The introduction of "me" is more easily accounted for than its omission. The point is that they have seen the sign of the giving of the bread from heaven and yet have failed to believe in the one who is himself the bread of heaven.

[81]The combination of first and third person self-references in Jesus' description of his relation to the Father so characteristic of 5.17-30 is also characteristic of 6.37-40,43-51. In the majority of cases in Jn 6 Jesus speaks of himself in the first person but the use of "the Father" in 6.37 (not "my Father") implies "the Son" which we find in 6.40 and there Jesus refers to "the Son" as "him". In 6.44 Jesus refers to "the Father who sent me" mixing implied third person with first person. The third person combination of "the Father" with "the one who is from God" is found in 6.46. The third person "This is the bread coming down out of heaven" (6.6.50) is combined with first person "I am the living bread which came down out of heaven" (6.51). In this case the third person self-references are more appropriate because of the use of the bread symbolism.

[82]"Everything" ($\pi\hat{\alpha}\nu$) 6.37,39, becomes "everyone" ($\pi\hat{\alpha}\varsigma$) 6.40, and see 6.45.

[83]See 6.38 and 6.33.

day.[84] The assertions concerning his Father and his descent from heaven provide the basis for the murmuring[85] rejection by the Jews in 6.41-59.

ii **Rejection by the Jews (6.41-59).** This phase is signalled by the indication of the changed audience. The audience is specifically "the Jews" and the location for the discourse the synagogue, 6.59. Two things are clear:

1. The evangelist does not normally alternate between "the crowd" and "the Jews" when referring to the same group.[86] The Jews of 6.41,52 can hardly be identified with the many disciples of 6.60,66 or "the twelve" of 6.67,71. If these terms distinguish different groups it seems clear that the crowd is to be distinguished from the Jews also.

2. The evangelist can hardly have intended to suggest that the dialogues and discourses between Jesus and the crowd as well as between Jesus and the Jews, had taken place in the synagogue at Capernaum.[87] That is the venue for Jesus' debate with the Jews (Jewish experts on the Law).

It is argued here that the change of terminology from the crowd to the Jews indicates a change of audience and a change of time, and that the note concerning the synagogue in 6.59 indicates a change of location. 6.41-59 reflects the struggle between the Johannine Christians and the synagogue. For this context "the Jews" is the appropriate term of reference. They do not represent the Galilean crowd which had followed and subsequently come seeking Jesus. They are the Jews of the synagogue.

---

[84]See 6.39,40,44,54.

[85]The reference to murmuring is an echo of the murmuring of the fathers in the wilderness, Exod 16.2,8f. Such murmuring was regarded as unbelief, Ps 105.24-25 LXX. In Jn the murmuring of the Jews is mentioned in 6.41,43 and the murmuring of the disciples in 6.61. We have here evidence of the Passover/Exodus screen through which this tradition has been interpreted.

[86]Discussions of the evangelist's use of "the Jews" tend to isolate 6.41 and 6.52 as a special case. The assumption is that the evangelist has used the term of the Galilean crowd, hence it cannot here mean the Judaeans as it does in 7.1. See U. C. von Wahlde, "The Johannine 'Jews': A Critical Survey", *NTS* 28/1 (1982) 33-60. While he has suggested that "the Jews", on the one hand, and the "Pharisees", "chief priests" and "rulers" on the other, belong to two different strata or sources (see U. C. von Wahlde, "The Terms for Religious Authorities in the Fourth Gospel: A Key to Literary-Strata?", *JBL* 98/2 (1979) 231-53) this has not been argued concerning the use of "the crowd" in 6.22,24, which is presumably the audience as far as 6.35(40), and "the Jews" of 6.41,52, are presumably the audience until 6.59. The evangelist indicates by this change that there are in fact two different audiences, times and places.

[87]C. K. Barrett (*John,* 300) notes that "the discourse with its interruptions suggests a less formal occasion than a synagogue sermon".

There is no suggestion that the "murmuring" of 6.41 and "fighting" of 6.52 caused a division amongst the Jews such as is to be noted in 10.19 and in relation to the Pharisees in 9.16, to which 10.19 probably refers. Rather these references to *murmuring* (6.41,43,61) recall the murmuring of the Israelites against God and Moses (Exod 15.24; 16.2,7,8,9,12; Num 14.2,27,29,36; 16.11,41; 17.5,10) which is interpreted as unbelief (Ps 105.24-25 LXX). Consequently the Jews now repeat the unbelief of the *fathers* in the wilderness. Even though they ate the manna they died. Given that the Exodus context is explicit in the dialogues (6.31,49,58) it is extraordinary that John Ashton suggests that "their murmuring (γογγυσμός v.41) is prompted more by bewilderment than real antagonism".[88] On the contrary, the murmuring is to be understood as unbelief and the rejection of God and his messenger, not now Moses but Jesus.

The alternation between Pharisees (9.13-17,40) and the Jews (9.18-23; 10.19-20) and the indication that both groups were divided with regard to their attitude to Jesus, the majority in each case being against him, suggests that we have there reference to the same group by different names. The same cannot be said concerning the references to the crowd and those to the Jews in Jn 6.[89] The crowd, though it has misunderstood Jesus, requests that Jesus should always give them the bread of which he has been speaking, 6.34. The clarification of misunderstanding is a standard way in which characters within the story (Nicodemus, the Samaritan woman) are led to a more adequate understanding of Jesus. This expectation is raised as Jesus progressively corrects and clarifies the expectations of the crowd leading up to the final clarification of 6.35.[90] On the other hand the Jews do nothing but raise *objections* to what Jesus has said. They represent the hardening attitude of the synagogue to the Johannine Christians and this part of the discourse gives us the response of the Johannine Christians at this stage of the conflict with the synagogue. It is based on the text given by Jesus in 6.35.

The *objection* of the Jews in 6.41-42 is to the christology of the quest story. They objected to Jesus' claim to be the emissary of God, the bread which comes down (6.33,50) or came down (6.41,51a) or has come down (6.38,42) from heaven.[91] Jesus responded by asserting that only those drawn and taught by the Father could come to him (6.44-45), taking up the

---

[88]*Understanding*, 200.

[89]Jn 7.12,40-44 attest the σχίσμα in the crowd but there is no identification with the Jews who were feared by the crowd, 7.13.

[90]Of course the reader is also led in a progressive process of understanding and this is the real purpose of the telling of the story.

[91]ὁ καταβαίνων, 6.33,50; ὁ καταβάς, 6.41,51a; καταβέβηκα, 6.38,42.

theme of 6.35,37-38 and providing a rationale for the rejection that the Johannine community was experiencing. Their rejection sealed their election by God while those who rejected them revealed only that they were not drawn and taught by the Father. The unique role of the emissary is emphasized in 6.46[92] and the necessity of believing in him is stressed in 6.47. All of this only repeats, in more provocative and confrontational terms, what has already been asserted. But it leads on to a more scandalous assertion, that the bread which must be eaten is Jesus' flesh which he says "I will give ($\delta\dot{\omega}\sigma\omega$)[93] for the life of the world", 6.51b. This assertion only antagonizes the Jews who then ask amongst themselves "how can this man give us his flesh to eat?"(6.52). Jesus then asserted the necessity of eating the flesh of the Son of Man and drinking his blood (6.53), which is even more scandalous and provocative. While this language is influenced by the Eucharistic practice of the early church,[94] and the controversy reflects Jewish accusations concerning cannibalism,[95] that is hardly the point of the statement. Just as eating and drinking are symbols of coming and believing in Jesus' person in 6.35, so now in 6.51 what is intended is belief in the life-giving function of the giving of Jesus' life for the world.[96]

Far from answering the objection of 6.41-42, this assertion only heightens the problem, 6.52. What is more, Jesus does not attempt to minimize the scandal but goes on to assert that "unless you eat the flesh of the Son of Man and drink his blood you do not have life in yourselves", 6.53. As in the earlier statement, eating and drinking are symbols for coming and believing, not now simply in the person of Jesus, as the use of flesh and blood indicates, but belief in the efficacy of his death. Characteristically for Jn, Jesus' language moves from the third person idiom of 6.53 (Son of Man) to the first person language of 6.54-57. At the heart of this development is a passion prediction concerning the Son of Man which is based on tradition. Thus in the rejection story attention has moved from the call to belief in the person of Jesus as the emissary of God

---

[92]Compare ὁ ὢν παρὰ τοῦ θεοῦ, 6.46 with ὁ ὢν τὸν κόλπον τοῦ πατρός, 1.18.

[93]See 6.27. Hans Weder, "Die Menschwerdung Gottes: Überlegungen zur Auslegungsproblematik des Johannesevangeliums am Beispiel von Joh 6", *ZTK* 82 (1985) 325-360, especially 352-5 rightly stresses the centrality of the incarnational theology. Thus, without importing the specific reference to Jn 1.14 into Jn 6, if Jn uses the language of an emissary christology it is also clear that the emissary comes from God and has become flesh.

[94]This view finds support in the Madrid SNTS seminar paper by Maarten J.J. Menken, "John 6.51c-58: Eucharist or Christology" (1992).

[95]See Origen, *Celsus*, VI.27, *GCS* 3.97.

[96]From this perspective it is unnecessary to propose a redactional addition in 6.51c-58.

(in the quest story) to belief in the saving efficacy of his death. No doubt is left that the Jews rejected this call.

iii Rejection by the disciples (6.60-66). Next we have the change from the synagogue, where the Jews formed the audience, to an unspecified situation where disciples constitute the audience. Jn 6.59 indicates the synagogue location up to that point ($\tau a\hat{v}\tau a$ $\epsilon\hat{\iota}\pi\epsilon\nu$) and implies a new context for what follows. Indeed 6.60 is the first indication of a large number of disciples. It does not fit easily with earlier references to the disciples in 6.3,8,12 where, almost certainly, the twelve are in view as reference to the twelve baskets probably confirms, 6.13.[97] Now it is a large number ($\pi o\lambda\lambda o\acute{\iota}$) of disciples who find Jesus' word hard ($\Sigma\kappa\lambda\eta\rho\acute{o}s$ $\acute{\epsilon}\sigma\tau\iota\nu$ $\acute{o}$ $\lambda\acute{o}\gamma os$), and are scandalized ($\sigma\kappa a\nu\delta a\lambda\acute{\iota}\zeta\epsilon\iota$) by it, so that it causes them to murmur ($\gamma o\gamma\gamma\acute{v}\zeta o\upsilon\sigma\iota\nu$), and ultimately to defect, 6.60-61,66.

There is no indication that the murmuring indicates a division. The many, who are here mentioned, all defect. Because Jn now deals specifically with the defection of disciples it is improbable that 6.41-59 should be interpreted in terms of dissension within the Johannine community. But the murmuring of the disciples arose on the same grounds as that of the Jews of 6.52-59. While this confirms that two different groups were in view the problem remained the same. That problem concerned the developing Johannine christology, explicitly in relation to the death and exaltation of Jesus. Apparently these were Jewish believers within the synagogue who were unable to follow the evangelist in the development of a more exalted christology. They may have been secret believers within the synagogue who, when a crisis arose in confrontation with the synagogue, fell away from faith. At least, that was their position as perceived by Jn.

Evidently what scandalized the disciples was Jesus' discourse (6.53-58) about eating his (or the Son of Man's) flesh and drinking his blood.[98] In response to the murmuring Jesus asked (6.62) "What if you see the Son of

---

[97]Each basket represents one of the disciples collecting the fragments left-over. Reference to "the twelve" is specific in 6.67-71. The "twelve" also seem to be assumed in the story of the sea-crossing (6.16-21) because a large crowd of disciples would not have fitted into a small boat. The earliest edition of the story included only Jesus, the small group of disciples and the crowd. It is the addition of the Jews and the mass of disciples that has produced untidy transitions in the narrative. But these additions were made necessary by the course of history and the evangelist's interpretation of the tradition in relation to this.

[98]$\acute{a}\kappa o\acute{v}\sigma a\nu\tau\epsilon s$ refers to a specific conversation as does the $\Sigma\kappa\lambda\eta\rho\acute{o}s$ $\lambda\acute{o}\gamma os$, 6.60. The question of how this was overheard need not be raised because 6.60-66 is a literary development on the basis of the previous story.

Man ascending (ἀναβαίνοντα) where he was formerly?"[99] That ascent, or being lifted up (ὕψωσεν, see 3.13-14), refers to Jesus death on the cross by means of which he is exalted in saving efficacy, 12.32. The interpretation of the saving efficacy of Jesus' death probably emerged in the struggle with the synagogue and many believers found the view unacceptable. That the words about eating Jesus' (or the Son of Man's) flesh and drinking his blood were not meant in a materialistic sense is clear from the quest story itself (6.35) and further clarified by 6.63. Set in the narrative context of Jesus' ministry the words should have been free from that misunderstanding. Even so it was the words of 6.53-58 that scandalized the many disciples and this scandal was not removed by the provoking words of 6.62-63. It was this provocation[100] which led to the apostasy of the "many disciples", 6.66. This passage might well reveal the conflict with the synagogue when many of those who believed either defected or became secret believers. It reflects a time of division amongst the Johannine Christians, a schism that left the evangelist and his supporters in the minority. It is unlikely that this defection reflects the schism of 1 Jn 2.19[101] because the grounds of apostasy are the same as those for the rejection of Jesus by the Jews.

In terms of the rejection story, the pronouncement remains that of the the quest story, that is, 6.35. It is elaborated in various ways in both stories of rejection, by the Jews and the mass of disciples. No new definitive pronouncement emerges in either of these stories. This alerts us to the fact that we do not have here self-contained rejection stories but adaptations on the basis of a quest story. It is the pronouncement of 6.35 and elaborations of it to which both the Jews and the mass of disciples object. The elaborations in what follows do not lessen, but in fact heighten their grounds for rejecting Jesus. The actual rejection of Jesus by the Jews is implied and the rejection by the mass of disciples is clearly stated, 6.66. While rejection stories are polemically spoken against the Jews and apostates, they are addressed to the Johannine community as an assurance to those rejected by men that they are chosen by God.[102]

---

[99]While we may ask whether this (ἀναβαίνοντα)) is perceived as a possible aid or a greater problem, no direct answer is given. The question produces no positive response from the disciples but rather accentuates or brings out the difficulty and leads to the defection of the mass of disciples.

[100]This is the force of the ἐκ τούτου which probably means both "from this time" and "for this reason".

[101]Pace R. Schnackenburg, John II,3ff.

[102]This is especially clear in the rejection story of Jn 9 where the once blind man, cast out from the synagogue, was received by Jesus, 9.34-38.

iv The twelve: commendation or condemnation? (6.67-71). That leaves only "the twelve", represented by Peter. Tradition provided the basis for the confession of Peter as the spokesman for the faith of the disciples,[103] in Jn, for "the twelve". This suggests that we have a contrast between the rejection story of 6.60-66 and the commendation story of 6.67-71.[104] The behaviour of the many is not to be followed; the confession of Peter is to be emulated. If this reading is persuasive we should perhaps attribute this part of chapter 6 to the latest edition of the Gospel along with chapter 21. There we find evidence of an attempt to reconcile the beloved disciple and his tradition with Peter (and "the twelve"?).[105]

It is notable, however, that Jesus in no way commends Peter for his confession, as he does in Matt 16.17. The form of the confession in Jn, "you are the holy one of God", differs from the Synoptics, "you are the Christ", Mk 8.29; "you are the Christ the son of the living God", Matt 16.16; "the Christ of God", Lk 9.20 and in Jn Jesus does not refer to his death, as he does in the Synoptics.[106] In Matt and Mk the confession of Peter is followed by Jesus' passion prediction, Peter's objection and Jesus' rebuke, "Get behind me Satan, you are a scandal to me, because you do not think the thoughts of God but of men", Matt 16.23; Mk 8.33. In Jn there is no rebuke to Peter. Instead Jesus refers to Judas Iscariot, the betrayer, as a devil, 6.70-71. That looks like a transfer of the rebuke from Peter to Judas. It could be, however, a way of casting doubt on the credibility of "the twelve" as a group, including Peter as spokesman. The episode concludes by noting that Judas was εἷς ἐκ τῶν δώδεκα, 6.71. In the light of this conclusion the words of Peter's confession need to be re-examined.

The title "holy one of God" is known to us nowhere else in Jn and in the Synoptics only on the lips of the demon-possessed, Mk 1.24; Lk 4.34. The use of this title in Peter's confession has been something of a puzzle. Because it is a *hapax legomenon* in Jn it is not likely that it represents an important Johannine title. Nor does it seem to have a discernible nuance arising from the context of Peter's confession. Given the Synoptic accounts of Peter's confession it is unlikely that it was derived from the tradition. It may be that the use of the title confessed by the demon possessed is no coincidence but places Peter in the role of the Satan. Alternatively, the point of the use of the title, "holy one of God", might be

---

[103]See Mk 8.29 and parallels.

[104]In both Jn 6 and 9 rejection stories are combined with commendation stories.

[105]There is first the reinstatement of Peter, 21.15-19 followed by the statement of the relative roles of Peter and the BD, 21.20-23.

[106]See Mk 8.31 and parallels.

to draw attention to the revelation involved in the confession. Just as the demons confessed by supernatural knowledge, so now Peter's confession is a result of divine revelation, see Matt 16.17. Given that "the twelve" are contrasted with "the many" it seems right to understand 6.67-71 as a commendation story aimed to reconcile the community of the BD with the tradition of Peter, but there are some puzzling and conflicting signals that disturb this reading of the story.

III. CONCLUSION

The traditional feeding story dramatized Jesus' rejection of the political role of the sign prophet proclaiming him instead as the eschatological judge. The evangelist himself transformed the tradition, turning it into a quest story. The quest story depicts the crowd seeking Jesus. Just as the Samaritan woman sought water at Jacob's well, so now the crowd seeks bread. Just as Jesus distinguished the water of the well from the water which he gives, so in chapter 6 he distinguished the bread which perishes from the bread which abides. The request of the woman (4.15) is remarkably like the request of the crowd (6.34). The similarities suggest that the two chapters originally belonged together. In one there is the offer of the life-giving water and in the other there is the offer of the life-giving bread. Here we have the two fundamental and universal symbols of the sources of life which have universal appeal. The symbols also have a particular resonance for Judaism. The well is the Law,[107] though the well actually represents the water which it contains and this is apparent also in Jn 4. Bread, the manna, also became a symbol for the Law.[108] In using these symbols the Jesus of Jn set himself in opposition to Moses and the Law as the giver/mediator of life. Here the evangelist has used a Passover/Exodus screen to interpret the tradition and this screen provided a resource for use in the conflict with the synagogue.

The quest of the crowd itself provides evidence of the failure of the Law to bring life. The quest story, developed on the basis of the traditional story, leads through the request of the crowd to the climactic pronouncement of Jesus in 6.35. This saying is not only the climax of the quest story, it is the text upon which the dialogues and discourses which follow are developed. These follow because of the reaction of the synagogue to the success of the Johannine Christians. That reaction created conflict and what follows in 6.36-71 is in response to conflict. The placing of chapter 6 immediately after chapter 4 belongs to the first edition

---

[107]See *CD* VI.4. Jesus also is the spring/well from which issues the life-giving water, 7.37-39. He is the giver of the life-giving water, 4.10,13-14.
[108]See *Str.B.* II, 483f. noting Proverbs 9.5; Genesis R. 70.5.

and constitutes an appeal to sympathizers and secret believers within the synagogue.

In the light of 6.36-71 it is easy to see that Jn 6 has become predominantly concerned with rejection. The quest story has now been modified so that the theme of rejection by the crowd, the Jews and the mass of disciples becomes dominant. The use of the term rejection here draws attention to the way objections raised lead to the rejection of Jesus and ultimately to his execution. This theme demands that the chapter be placed in the conflict section of the Gospel after chapter 5. This new position has caused problems for the itinerary of Jesus' ministry, leaving rough seams between chapters 4 and 5, 5 and 6, 6 and 7. Evidently the evangelist considered the thematic structure of the Gospel to be more important than a straightforward description of Jesus' itinerary. It is, however, perplexing to find evidence of sophisticated literary developments alongside poorly integrated material. Three basic responses have been made to this problem:

1. Literary sophistication is attributed to the source (thus Haenchen) alongside the ineptness of the evangelist;
2. Disruptions are explained by some accident to the completed Gospel (Bultmann);
3. Disruptions are explained as a result of the death of the evangelist prior to the completion and publication of the Gospel (see 21.20-25).

In this study the third response is accepted along with the recognition that the order of the text, as it is, suggests the priority of thematic structure over geographic itinerary. Thus Jn 6 has become predominantly focused on rejection and the appropriate place for this chapter is in chapters 5-12. Chapter 5 is the appropriate introduction to the rejection section because it introduces the two specific objections to Jesus: as a Law (Sabbath) breaker and a blasphemer, a man claiming divine status for himself. It also sets the pattern of the response of Jewish rejection, 5.16,18.

In the rejection section of Jn 6 there is a development in christological perception. Whereas the crowd that followed Jesus into the desert perceived him to be a sign prophet, a messianic political deliverer, the traditional story proclaimed Jesus as the future eschatological judge/deliverer. But in the quest story of the first edition there is an emphasis on Jesus, not Moses as the emissary of God, as the life-giver and that Jesus not the Law is the life-giving bread, This interpretation developed in the period of dialogue and apologetic approach to the synagogue. There are two stages in this development. In the first Jesus is understood to be the Messiah/Son of Man, the *giver* of the eschatological bread from heaven, 6.27,34. But there is a significant development of the Jewish expectation because Jesus is himself the life-giving bread, 6.35. In the conflict that develops the stress falls on the necessity of Jesus' death in order that, as the bread of life, he should bring life to the world, 6.51. To some extent this development merely made explicit what was implicit in the symbolism of the bread of life, 6.35. Just as bread sustains physical life, so Jesus gives eternal life. But whereas 6.33 seemed to imply that the bread gave life to the world by coming down from heaven, now it becomes clear that the bread must be eaten. At this point, by introducing the symbols of hunger and thirst the evangelist has transformed the notion of bread into food and drink that sustain life. Eating and drinking are symbols of coming to Jesus and believing in him, 6.35. While coming is symbolic of believing, the point of this set of symbols (as it is developed in 6.51-58) is that belief in Jesus takes account of his death for the life of the world.

Robert Fortna is right in seeing the development from christology to soteriology.[109] In this chapter we have traced a development from the belief in the eschatological deliverer and judge of the traditional story and belief in the heavenly emissary of the quest story to the theme of the saviour whose death brings life to those who believe in him, the glorified, exalted Son of Man, glorified and exalted by way of the cross. This theme emerged in the conflict with the synagogue. Reference to the death of Jesus could not but draw attention to the Jewish involvement in the execution of Jesus. But while this polemic is spoken against the Jews and apostates from within the community, it is spoken to the community to assure them that though they have been rejected by men they are the chosen of God. The development represents another stage in the evangelist's quest for the Messiah, now a Messiah who brings life through giving up his own life. Indeed we can say that in the quest for the Messiah Jn has developed his own distinctive christology and with this has produced his characteristic understanding of salvation.

In Jn 6 the quest for the Messiah turns out to be an expression of the universal quest for life. For Jn this quest finds its fulfilment in Jesus as the emissary from God who not only reveals God but in his life, death/resurrection/exaltation/glorification is the action of God bringing life to the world. This emphasis not only produced conflict with the Jews, it was to bring conflict within the Johannine community, first as in 6.60-66, then in a conflict over the role and significance of Jesus' earthly life which was to be manifest in a schism specifically mentioned in 1 Jn 2.19.

---

[109]See R. T. Fortna, "From Christology to Soteriology", *Interpretation* 27 (1973) 31-47. Fortna rightly recognizes that christological belief has soteriological consequences.

7

The Hidden Messiah in John 7–8

The dialogues of chapters 7 and 8 are not tied to miracle stories and it is difficult to isolate the underlying tradition or to plot something like the course of the evangelist's development of the material. Jn 7–8 present the reader/interpreter with numerous problems. Nevertheless they maintain the conflict initiated by chapter 5.[1] Jn 7 begins with an indication that the Jews of Judaea were *seeking*[2] to kill Jesus, recalling the situation of 5.18. The imperfect tenses also feature in 5.16. There it is said "Because of this (διὰ τοῦτο refers to the healing of the man on the Sabbath) the Jews were persecuting Jesus", thus making the persecution of Jesus their characteristic response to him though the cause is said to be a specific action. What follows shows that the specific action of Jesus was also characteristic of him, "because he was doing these things on the Sabbath". This point is reinforced by 5.18 which announces that the Jews "were seeking to kill Jesus not only because he was breaking (ἔλυεν) the Sabbath" but also because he was claiming (ἔλεγεν) a special relation to God as his Father. This theme of continuing attempts to kill Jesus runs through chapters 7 and 8 (7.1(11),19-20,25,44; 8.37,40, 59; see also the attempts to arrest Jesus, 7.30,32,44-45). In both 5.18 and 7.1 the evangelist has written "the Jews were seeking to kill him" (ἐζήτουν αὐτὸν οἱ Ἰουδαῖοι ἀποκτεῖναι). Given that we have here the first and second references to the quest of the Jews to kill Jesus the exact repetition of wording is significant. It signals a resumption. Narrative time has stood still between 5.18 and 7.1. Now (7.1) Jesus' evasive action takes account of the continuing attempt to kill him.

The use of ζητεῖν in the formulation of the quest to kill Jesus is no accident.[3] The verbs ζητεῖν and εὑρίσκειν are frequently used in Jn and often in conjunction. The quest of the first two disciples is signalled by Jesus' question Τί ζητεῖτε; (1.38) and the success of the quest is announced by the refrain Εὑρήκαμεν τὸν Μεσσίαν, 1.41 and see 1.45 and 6.24-25. Given that in the dialogues of Jn 7–8 Jesus takes up the theme

---

[1] Like Jn 5 and 6, Jn 7 commences with the vague temporal reference (μετὰ ταῦτα) which might signal the evangelist's rearrangement of these chapters.
[2] Verbs in the imperfect tense are concentrated in Jn 7.1,5,11,12,13,15,25,30,31,40,41,44. Characteristic (repeated) responses to Jesus in word or action are introduced by the imperfect tense. "They were saying" or "they were seeking to arrest" or "to kill" Jesus.
[3] See 5.18; 7.1,19,20,25,30; 8.37,40; 10.39; 11.8.

of seeking and finding,[4] it is certain that the theme is significant when it occurs in the narrative. Consequently we should be alert to the twin motifs of seeking and finding which are concentrated in Jn 7 and 8, especially Jn 7.[5]

I. JESUS' DIALOGUE PARTNERS

The presentation of the roles of the crowd, the Jews and the Pharisees and chief-priests in Jn 7–8 is confusing. Just who the Jews are is not always clear. The names (crowd, Jews, Pharisees, chief-priests) appear to represent different groups but those within the groups overlap in some ways with those in other groups. This at times give the impression that the groups are not distinct. Nevertheless the names depict different social and power groups which play a role in the conflict with Jesus and his followers. It is possible that confusion exists also because the groups are used as types and that the evangelist wished to show that there were exceptions in each group with respect to the response to Jesus. The coming of Jesus brought division amongst the crowd, the Jews and the Pharisees. But this is not the case with the chief-priests, none of whom are depicted in a positive relation to Jesus. The Jews are the opponents of Jesus in Jn 7–8 even if momentarily some of them can be said to have believed Jesus and, because he had been speaking of his relation to the Father, this involved believing in him, 8.30-31.[6] But they are soon shown to be children of the devil who seek to kill/stone Jesus, 8.31-59. Thus after 7.1 when it is said in 7.11 that the Jews were seeking Jesus at the feast there is the superficial possibility of a positive quest. But this is really excluded by the wording which resumes 7.1. The ambiguity arises from the absence (from 7.11) of ἀποκτεῖναι. The sense that this might be significant is a result of the various views expressed in 7.12-13. But

---

[4]See 7.17-18,34-36; 8.21-22,50,54.

[5]ζητεῖν is used 11 times in Jn 7 and 5 times in Jn 8 and εὑρίσκειν is used 3 times in Jn 7. Though εὑρίσκειν is not used in Jn 8.21-22 it is implied that the Jews who will seek Jesus and cannot go where he is going will not find him, especially as this is a repeated theme from 7.34-36 where εὑρίσκειν is used.

[6]In 8.30 we are told "many believed in him" (πολλοὶ ἐπίστευσαν εἰς αὐτόν) and in 8.31 the many are identified with the Jews who are now said to have believed him (τοὺς πεπιστευκότας αὐτῷ Ἰουδαίους). In 8.30 belief in Jesus is in response to what he was saying and thus appropriately described also as believing him.

this is to ignore the introduction of the crowd[7] in 7.12a. It would be a mistake simply to identify the Jews with the crowd.[8]

Certainly the crowd's response to Jesus was not uniform, 7.12-13,20,32,40-43. Thus the crowd was divided. Some said, "he is a good man". Others said "No! but he leads the crowd astray ($\pi\lambda\alpha\nu\hat{\alpha}$)" (7.12). In the latter comment the speakers, though formally part of the crowd, distance themselves from it.[9] Later (7.40-44) when it is said that there was a schism ($\sigma\chi\iota\sigma\mu\alpha$) in the crowd it is evident that there were more than two views. Some were saying "This man is truly the prophet"; others were saying "This man is the Christ"; but they were also saying "Surely the Christ does not come from Galilee". Others unsuccessfully attempted to arrest Jesus.[10] In these responses to Jesus the opinions of the Jews would be included. But the crowd is viewed as distinct from the Jews in that fear of the Jews inhibited open debate about Jesus, 7.13.[11] Perhaps the matter can be put this way. The Jews infiltrated the crowd so that their views were represented there. But in their own evaluation of the crowd and in the crowd's fear of them they remained a distinct group. Probably it is right to say that the Jews are made up of the Pharisees, the chief-priests

---

[7]The textual evidence is neatly balanced between the singular ($\tau\hat{\omega}\ \delta\chi\lambda\omega$) and plural ($\tauo\hat{\iota}s\ \delta\chi\lambda o\iota s$) readings. The plural could be said to be the more difficult reading for two reasons. 1. The singular is used regularly in what follows, 7.12c,20,31,40,43,49. 2. Indeed 7.12a would be the only use of the plural in Jn. Here we need to take account of the preference of different authors. Mk, like Jn prefers the use of the singular but Matt uses both the singular and plural. See the variation from singular to plural in Matt 14-15 where the singular and plural forms are each used 8 times. Though the plural is the more difficult reading from the point of view of Johannine use, it could be said to be suggested by the context. The murmuring ($\gamma o\gamma\gamma\upsilon\sigma\mu\delta s$) concerning Jesus may have implied a plurality of views to an editor and could have led to the plural reading "crowds".

[8]Scholars sometimes mistakenly argue that the Jews of Jn 6.41 are simply to be identified with the crowd which had been Jesus' dialogue partner from 6.25 (see 6.24). Thus U.C. von Wahlde, *The Earliest Version of John's Gospel*, 37 who attributes the demand for a sign in Jn 6.30 to the Jews.

[9]Does this indicate that the Jews, though formally part of the crowd, distance themselves from it? Compare the way the Pharisees also distance themselves from the crowd in 7.47-49. It is notable that they ask the servants "Surely you have not also been led astray ($\pi\epsilon\pi\lambda\delta\nu\eta\sigma\theta\epsilon$)?" and they pronounce the crowd to be accursed, "But this crowd which does not know the Law is accursed", which is to identify the crowd with "the people of the land", a term frequently used by the rabbis and used in Ezra 4.4 to refer to those opposed to the building of the Temple.

[10]See 7.30; 8.20.

[11]See also 9.22; 12.42; 19.38; 20.19.

and their servants. That there is some ambivalence amongst this group appears for first time with the return of the servants (7.45-46) and then with Nicodemus (7.50-51 and see 12.42).

II. THE IMPLICATIONS OF HIDDENNESS

The theme of seeking to kill or arrest Jesus runs through these chapters, 7.1,11,20,25,30,32,44; 8.37,40,59. It is in the context of the plot to kill Jesus that the theme of hiddenness and openness/revelation is developed, 7.4,10,26-27,28-29. It was first introduced in 1.26 and reiterated in 1.31,33. There the Baptist stresses that "the coming one" remains hidden, although he is already present. He remains unknown until he is revealed by a prearranged sign. This theme is illuminated by a tradition made known to us by Justin[12] where Trypho says:

> Even if the Messiah is already born and in existence somewhere, he is nevertheless unknown; even he himself does not know about himself nor does he have any kind of power until Elijah comes and anoints him and reveals him to all.

Against this background the Baptist's denial that he is Elijah is strange and might suggest that Jn knew the tradition in another form but because Jn narrates the role of the Baptist in revealing Jesus this seems unlikely. The readers probably understood the sign to have taken place in the context of the baptism of Jesus (understood as an anointing), an event not specifically mentioned in Jn. Trypho says that even the Messiah does not know himself until he is revealed. This might seem to run contrary to the contrast Jesus makes in 7.25-29 where he compares the supposed knowledge the Jerusalemites claim to have of his origin with their ignorance of his relation to and mission from the Father, of which he knows himself. But[13] it is not this that distinguishes the portrayal of Jesus in Jn from the tradition in Justin because (according to Jn 1.26,31,33) Jesus had already been anointed and revealed to all. The Baptist thus fulfills the role of Elijah and it is through him that all may believe, 1.6-7. Where Jn differs from the tradition in Justin is that even after Jesus has been revealed he remains hidden because the witness (the Baptist) was rejected. The theme of hiddenness re-emerges in the context of the theme of rejection of Jesus and his witness.

Initially Jesus' unbelieving brothers interpreted the withdrawal of Jesus from Judaea as secretive activity inconsistent with one who performs

---

[12]*Dialogue with Trypho*, 8.4 and cf. 110.1.
[13]Contrary to Ashton, *Understanding*, 305.

mighty works. We could understand this as a failure to believe that Jesus actually performed mighty works.

> Therefore his brothers said to him, "Come down from here and go into Judaea, that your disciples may see the works[14] that you are doing; for no one does anything in secret and seeks ($\zeta \eta \tau \epsilon \hat{\iota}$) to be known publicly. If you do these things reveal ($\phi a \nu \epsilon \rho \omega \sigma o \nu$) yourself to the world.." For his brothers did not believe ($o \dot{\upsilon} \delta \dot{\epsilon} \ldots \dot{\epsilon} \pi \iota \sigma \tau \epsilon \upsilon o \nu$)[15] in him. Jn 7.3-5.

The incident is open to other interpretations. It confirms the understanding the reader has formed from Jn 2.12 that the brothers of Jesus travelled with him as part of his retinue though, surprisingly, neither the disciples nor the mother of Jesus were present on this occasion. The request or challenge by the brothers seems to assume that Jesus' disciples were in Judaea or may only imply that Judaea was the place for open actions. "If you do these things" (7.4), in conjunction with the unfulfilled condition, implies that the brothers did not believe that Jesus performed such works and the narrator appears to confirm this, 7.5.[16] The narrator, however, says that "they did not believe in him", not that they did not believe that he performed signs. The narrator's comment in 7.5 is intended to be shocking but perhaps in a more subtle way.than seems obvious.

It may be that what the narrator implies is that the brothers, as part of the retinue of Jesus, wished Jesus to precipitate a mass response to his signs in Judaea, a response of which the narrator has shown suspicion, 2.23-25. But there the response to Jesus' signs is described as "many believed in his name", whereas here it is said that the brothers did not believe in him. Certainly this again distances Jesus from his biological family but this may imply no more than the statement in Jn 12.16 concerning the disciples of whom it is said that "they did not know (understand) these things" until Jesus was glorified. More in the idiom of Jn 7.5 is Jesus' response to the disciples' affirmation, "we believe" (16.30). Jesus then asked, "Do you now believe?" implying that he did not think that they did as yet. Understood in these terms the brothers did

---

[14]It is somewhat surprising that the "unbelieving" brothers should use the term "works" ($\dot{\epsilon} \rho \gamma a$) rather than "signs" ($\sigma \eta \mu \epsilon \hat{\iota} a$), see 2.23-25. Perhaps "works" is used because it carries on in the language of the controversy from Jn 5.

[15]The use of the imperfect rather than the aorist tense indicates that this was not a momentary failure to believe but was characteristic of them, at least at this stage though it not to be understood as definitive and final either.

[16]"See also 9.18.

not aspire to Johannine expectation of real faith even though they formed a part of the retinue of Jesus.[17]

Jesus met the request of his brothers with the same objection given to his mother.[18] Yet in each case he did what he was asked to do, but in his own time. His words also introduce the theme of the hidden and manifest Messiah. Because his time has not yet come to manifest himself Jesus sends his brothers off to the feast and only later and secretly (οὐ φανερῶς ἀλλ' ἐν κρυπτῷ) does he go up himself. Ἀνέβη is used here (as also in 5.1) to indicate the traditional "going up" to the festivals in Jerusalem. It is also a word associated with the Son of Man in Jn 1.51; 3.13; 6.62. From the retrospective perspective of Jn the Son of Man is the one who has ascended into heaven. That too is a secret ascent. Indeed it is by going up to Jerusalem that the Son of Man will return to where he was formerly, in heaven with the Father.

The secrecy motif no longer simply indicates that it is unsafe for Jesus to be in Judaea. The Jews were seeking him and saying, "Where is he?" When Jesus appears in the middle of the feast, publicly teaching in the Temple, it is a public manifestation, 7.14.[19] Yet having revealed himself and his teaching openly in the Temple Jesus and his teaching remain a mystery to the Jews because they do not know his relation to the Father, 7.15-18. The irony of the situation is noted by some of the Jerusalemites.

---

[17]It is unjustifiable, on the basis of Jn 7.5, to assume that James and the other brothers and sisters of Jesus did not believe in him during his life time. The other evidence must be read independently, especially in the light of lack of clarity concerning the meaning of 7.5 and its obvious place as an aspect of Johannine redaction rather than primitive tradition.

[18]See 7.6-9. Here Jesus says ὁ καιρὸς ὁ ἐμὸς οὔπω πάρεστιν and ὁ ἐμὸς καιρὸς οὔπω πεπλήρωται. Compare 2.4 (οὔπω ἥκει ἡ ὥρα μου) where what is in view appears to be the time for Jesus to act though this is not unrelated to the eschatological moment as the resulting belief of the disciples shows, 2.11. It is however a typological relation in that Jesus' revelation of his glory through the sign at Cana pointed to the ultimate manifestation of glory in the exaltation of the Son of Man which can be understood as the revelation of the Son of Man, 8.28. The difference between 2.4 and 7.6,8 does not arise from the use of ὥρα in 2.4 and καιρός in 7.6,8. Indeed the eschatological moment is directly in view in 4.21,23; 5.25,28; 7.30 all of which use the term ὥρα.

[19]The public nature of Jesus' teaching was an important aspect of his defence before the High Priest, see 18.19-20. "I have spoken openly (παρρησίᾳ) to the world, I always taught in synagogue and in the Temple, where all the Jews gather, and in secret (ἐν κρυπτῷ) I have said nothing." This language of openness and secrecy looks back to Jn 7 where Jesus taught openly in the Temple.

They recognize Jesus as the one "they are seeking to kill" (7.25), though the crowd, speaking with a single voice had denied that any one was seeking to kill Jesus, 7.19-20. At the same time some of the Jerusalemites noted that Jesus was speaking openly, without any interjection or opposition (7.26a). Because of this they raised the question, though incredulously:

> "Surely it cannot be true that the chief-priests know that this man is the Christ? But we know from whence ($\pi\delta\theta\epsilon\nu$)[20] this man is; whenever the Christ comes no one knows from whence he is." (7.26b-27)

It is unclear whether this represents two positions amongst the Jerusalemites or whether it is an incredulous question with the reason given for the incredulity. It is probably the latter though the possibility that the Jerusalemites were divided on the issue is suggested by the introduction "certain of the Jerusalemites".[21] Yet if this is so there is no indication that two different groups form these assessments. Consequently it is best taken as a rejection of Jesus' messiahship on the grounds of the criterion of the hidden Messiah. Jesus responded, admitting that they know him and his origin ($\pi\delta\theta\epsilon\nu$) but asserting that they do not know the one who sent him. This means that their assertion is superficially correct but profoundly untrue. The consequence of this was another failed expression of the continuing quest to arrest Jesus, 7.30. There is no indication of who made this attempt so that it is probably right to assume that it was the same Jerusalemites who questioned why no action was taken against Jesus though manifestly he failed the test of hiddenness. This is obviously an important context for the discussion of the hiddenness of Jesus and his words and works.

---

[20] In Jn $\pi\delta\theta\epsilon\nu$ carries an important meaning. See it use in 1.48; 2.9; 3.8; 4.11; 6.5; 7.27[2],28; 8.14[2]; 9.29,30; 19.9. The use of this term in Jn 7-9 is concentrated on the origin of Jesus or the Messiah.

[21] Compare similar references to "Some of the crowd...($\dot{\epsilon}\kappa$ $\tauο\hat{υ}$ $\dot{ο}\chi\lambdaου$)" in 7.31,40. In 7.31 we are told that many of the crowd believed and it is apparently what they were saying that is reported. In 7.40-44 we are told not only what some of the crowd were saying (7.40), but also about others (7.41a), and others again (7.41b). In 7.25 (cf. 7.31) we are told only what some of the Jerusalemites were saying with a response which may be given to their own rhetorical question or may be given by others.

III. A DIVIDED RESPONSE TO JESUS' SIGNS

The explicit discussion of the hidden Messiah[22] takes place in order to exclude Jesus because they say of him, "We know where this man is from (πόθεν)", 7.27. Here Jesus admits that both he and his origin (πόθεν) are known, 7.28. Superficially this is true. Rather than argue with this view the evangelist has chosen to have Jesus appeal to the one who sent him whom, Jesus asserts, "you do not know; but I know him, because I am from him and he sent me", 7.28-29. Here, using both the formula ὁ πέμψας με and ἀπέστειλεν Jesus affirms his relation to God which constitutes his origin in the most significant sense. As in Jn 5, where this theme appeared in response to the charge of having committed a Sabbath-breaking work, this response led to a renewed attempt to take action against Jesus, 7.30 and cf. 5,16,18. But in Jn 7 the crowd is introduced at this point with a view to asserting that

> Many of the crowd believed in him and were saying, "When the
> Christ comes will he perform more signs that this man did?" (7.31)

The effect of this is to show a divided response to Jesus but it is not the Jerusalemites that are divided. Many of the crowd express the expectation of the Messiah as a worker of signs.[23] According to the Gospels (Matt 11.2ff.; Lk 7.18ff.)[24] when the Messiah comes he will prove his identity by means of miracles. This view, consistent with Jn 7.31, is absent from the rabbinic texts.[25] It may be that the rabbinic texts have suppressed this tradition in the light of the two disastrous wars and the Christian tradition

---

[22]The tradition of the hidden Messiah assumes his hiddenness only until the moment that he is revealed. See Marinus de Jonge, *Jesus Stranger from Heaven and Son of God*, 88-9 and 109 n28.

[23]So far in Jn 7 the brothers of Jesus have referred incredulously to his works (7.3) and Jesus has referred to his one work (7.21) evidently referring back to the healing of Jn 5. Consequently the reference to *signs*, especially stressing their quantity and the many who consequently believed may signal the evangelist's critical attitude to this response as in 2.23-25.

[24]Especially significant here is the reference to "the works of the Christ (Messiah)", which seems to be a Matthaean gloss on a Q *pericope*, Matt.11.2. The works of the Christ are the miracles of healing Jesus has been performing (Lk 7.1-17) and the preaching of the good news (Matt 11.1), which is assumed by Jesus' answer in both Matt (11.4-6) and Lk (7.22-23) using terms reminiscent of Isa 35.5-6; 61.1 which were apparently understood as messianic texts by Matt and Lk and probably in Q before them also.

[25]See Schürer, II, 525 and Joseph Klausner, *The Messianic Idea in Israel from its Beginning to the Completion of the Mishnah*, 506.

of the signs of Jesus. It would be risky to assume that the tradition was a Christian invention.

Next the evangelist informs the reader that when the Pharisees heard the murmuring of the crowd (τοῦ ὄχλου γογγύζοντος) they and the chief priests sent (ἀπέστειλαν)[26] servants to arrest Jesus, 7.32. The narrative sequence is puzzling. The Jerusalemites unsuccessfully attempted to arrest Jesus (7.30). Was that an unofficial attempt and is the mission of the servants (7.32) seen as an official attempt to arrest Jesus? Many of the crowd believed in Jesus, 7.31 and apparently were asking "Whenever the Christ comes will he do more signs than this man did?" While no other view is expressed we may take it that although the question is posed in a form that suggests a negative answer (μὴ πλείονα σημεῖα ποιήσει), it was debated. This would provide a basis for the narrator's use of γογγύζοντος in 7.32. Perhaps the Jerusalemites are considered to be part of the crowd. Differences between those who were seeking to arrest Jesus and those who believed in him on the basis of signs would certainly justify the use of γογγύζοντος. Otherwise it refers back to the use of γογγυσμὸς in 7.12. In both instances the context makes clear that what is in view is a murmuring dispute within the crowd concerning Jesus.[27]

In the discussion of the hidden Messiah Jesus responded to the criticism that his origin was known by appealing to his relation to the one who sent him and affirming that he himself was sent.[28] For some of the crowd this affirmation drew attention to the signs of Jesus. Certainly in Jn 5 Jesus' appeal to his relation with the Father was a response to the criticism of his Sabbath-breaking work. So there is an association between Jesus' appeal to his relation to the Father and his work. Both his appeal and his work point to his hidden origin. This stage of the debate concludes with a divided response to Jesus' signs.

---

[26]Cf. 1.19.

[27]Here the Exodus context does not influence the interpretation of the language as it does in Jn 6 where the language is influenced also by the hardened opposition to Jesus. In Jn 7-8 the opposition is growing but there are yet voices of dissent, even in high places, 7.40-52.

[28]This is the meaning to be construed from the use of both ὁ πέμψας με and κἀκεῖνός μ ε ἀπέστειλεν. The use of the formula (7.18,28,33; 8.16,18,26,29) and the appeal by Jesus to himself as the one sent (7.29; 8.42) are concentrated in Jn 7-8 so that it is clear that Jesus' relation to God is the key to the whole of Jn 7-8 as it is to Jn 5.

IV. A DIVIDED RESPONSE TO JESUS' WORDS

Clearly the crowd had earlier been divided concerning Jesus, 7.12-13. Then when Jesus revealed himself in the middle of the feast he taught in the Temple and the Jews marvelled:[29]

"How does this man know letters never having learned?" (7.15)

Here the Jews acknowledge that they do not know the origin of Jesus because they do not know the origin of his teaching. This is precisely Jesus' response:

"My teaching is not my own but comes from him who sent me (τοῦ πέμψαντός με)".

Just as in 5.17, 19ff. Jesus now formally gives testimony in support of his own case and was equally sensitive to the charge that this was invalid, see 5.31ff. Consequently certain criteria are offered to test his teaching. 1.) The person who wills to do God's will, will know the origin of the teaching, 7.17. It is now clear that the sender to whom Jesus appeals is God.[30] 2.) Apparently more constructive is the criterion of whether Jesus seeks his own or the Father's glory. This criterion is stated in the impersonal third person but the principle is intended to apply to Jesus' claim to be sent by God. It provides us with another example (see Jn 5) of Jesus' reference to himself first in the first person then in the third person, here using the same formula (τοῦ πέμψαντός με and τοῦ πέμψαντος αὐτόν). But the problem with this criterion is that the glory of the one sent is intimately bound up with the recognition of the glory of the sender.[31]

The divided crowd is again in view in 7.40-44. What divided them was the words of Jesus, this time the impressive saying made on the last, the great day of the feast, 7.37-38. So impressive was this saying that it

---

[29]ἐθαύμαζον, 7.15 and see 7.21 where Jesus said "I did one work and you all marvelled (θαυμάζετε)". See also 5.20. The implication is that the one work which Jesus did was shown to him by the Father.

[30]This test does not escape ambiguity. As a criterion it is open to the objection that anyone who disagrees with the desired answer can be said to be seeking their own and not God's will.

[31]The theme recurs in 8.50,54 because, like the charge of bearing witness to himself as the unique revealer who comes from God, his justification is dependent on the recognition of his relation to God. This makes sensitive the charge that Jesus is seeking his own glory or bearing witness to himself and the evangelist returns to it again and again.

warrants an explanatory note by the narrator.[32] Some of the crowd were saying:

> "Truly this is the prophet!" Others were saying "This is the Christ!" Again others were saying "Surely the Christ does not come from Galilee? Did not the scripture say that the Christ comes of the seed of David, and from Bethlehem the village of David?" (7.40-42)

The result was a $\sigma\chi\iota\sigma\mu\alpha$ in the crowd because of Jesus and some attempted unsuccessfully to arrest him (7.43-44). Consequently here it is the words of Jesus that cause division and lead to an unsuccessful attempt to arrest him, just as it was the works of Jesus that caused division and an unsuccessful attempt to arrest him (7.30) in 7.25-31. The stress on Jesus' words is continued in 7.45-52. The servants, returning to report to the chief-priests and Pharisees explain their failure to arrest Jesus by saying,

> "Never did man speak ($\dot{\epsilon}\lambda\dot{\alpha}\lambda\eta\sigma\epsilon\nu$) as this man!" (7.46)

The response of the Pharisees was to assert that none of the rulers or Pharisees had believed in Jesus and to class the servants with the crowd which, because it was ignorant of the Law was accursed and had consequently been led astray by Jesus.[33] The double irony of the situation is brought out by the role of Nicodemus at this point. His objection shows that in condemning Jesus without a hearing the Pharisees were acting contrary to the Law and in this sense they do not "know" it because knowing and doing are inseparable.[34] Further, Nicodemus is both a ruler and a Pharisee (Jn 3.1) and the narrator reminds us it is he who formerly came to Jesus by night.[35] Though it is not said here the reader is meant to remember that Nicodemus there confessed Jesus to be a teacher come from God. Here in Jn 7 his interjection on behalf of Jesus is meant to reveal him as a disciple of Jesus, and a fearful one at that.[36] Apparently the only recourse left to the Pharisees was to reiterate the objection raised by some of the crowd concerning the Christ, [37] extending it to refer also to any prophet, and mocking any who might disagree.

---

[32]Jn 7.39. See 2.21-22 for a similar note explaining the impressive saying of 2.19.

[33]See 7.12,47-49. The crowd is here evaluated in terms that indicate that they are viewed as the ignorant people of the land.

[34]This presupposes a Semitic understanding of knowledge.

[35]On each of the two reappearances the narrator reminds the reader that Nicodemus was the one who formerly came to Jesus by night, 7.50; 19.39.

[36]See also 12.42.

[37]See 7.41 and 1.46.

"Surely you are not also from Galilee? Search[38] and see that a prophet does not arise out of Galilee." (7.52)

The works/signs of Jesus raised the question as to whether he was the Christ, 7.31. Now it is the words of Jesus that raise the question as to whether he is the prophet or even a prophet, 7.40,52. The official response is that his Galilean origin excludes him. It is also held to exclude his messianic claim. Thus, even if the Messiah's origin is unknown or hidden, he is not hidden in Galilee.[39] Alternatively we find the popular identification of the Messiah as the seed of David and from the village of David. Paradoxically this was to assert the known origin of the Messiah. Hence we may have to allow for different messianic traditions. It may be that the unknown Messiah is to be thought of as a heavenly figure, hidden away until the time of his manifestation.[40] In Jn, however, the evangelist has thrown up the two traditions of known (Davidic) and unknown origin in order to show confusion and lack of sound reason in the rejection of Jesus, whose origin with the Father satisfies the criterion of the unknown Messiah.[41] It is also probable that he expects his readers to know the tradition of Jesus' birth in Bethlehem. If this is the the case then Jesus satisfies these (apparently contradictory) criteria. The reader implied by this argument appears to possess some knowledge of the gospel tradition, if not in its Johannine form.

V. SELF-WITNESS

Just as Jesus returns to the theme that he seeks not his own but the Father's glory (see Jn 5.41-44; 7.17-18; 8.50,54) so he returns to theme of self-witness (5.31; 8.13-19).[42] Jn 8 provides a justification for Jesus' self-witness, the charge concerning which arose from his saying: "I am the light of the world...", Jn 8.12. In its form it is clearly self-testimony.

---

[38]See 5.39.

[39]It may be that Galilean uprisings have something to do with the emergence of this position.

[40]See 1 Enoch 48.6-7; 62.7; 2 Apoc Bar 29.3; 39.7; 73.1; 4 Ezra 7.28; 12.32; 13.26,32,52; 14.9.

[41]Indeed the notion of the Messiah hidden away in heaven is not the only motif. Sometimes the idea of the Messiah incognito appears. In other words, the Messiah is a known person but until he is revealed as Messiah his messiahship is not recognized (see Justin, *Dialogue with Trypho*, 8.3-4; 49.1; 110.1). It seems that, according to his own teaching, Jesus satisfies both of these expectations. See Erik Sjöberg, *Der verborgene Menchensohn in der Evangelien*, esp. 41-98.

[42]See the discussion of Jn 5.31 in chapter 5, "The Paradigm of Rejection" above.

Thus Jesus does not here, as in 5.31,[43] deny that he bears witness to himself. The charge that the Pharisees brought against him (8.13) was formally correct. But Jesus asserts that his witness is nevertheless true because uniquely he knows his origin and destination (8.14) which are not known by the Pharisees, invalidating their judgement. Appeal to Jesus' origin (πόθεν) is an appeal to his relation to the Father, to his mission from the Father. Appeal to his destination is less obvious. It is an appeal to the way the Son returns to the Father, his glorification or exaltation, see 8.28. This leads on to Jesus' discussion of seeking and not finding. The failure of the Pharisees to know Jesus' origin and destination arose because "You judge according to the flesh" (8.15), that is, according to appearances.[44] In this way Jesus returns to the theme that, contrary to appearances, the Father who sent him is present with him and confirming his witness, 8.16-18. Of course this claim was open to challenge and Jesus could only reply that the refusal to acknowledge him as the one sent arose from the failure to know the Father who sent him, 8.19. From the point of view of the Pharisees this was an inadequate defence and it led to another unsuccessful attempt to arrest Jesus, 8.20.

VI. A FAILED QUEST

When the Pharisees and chief-priests sent servants to arrest Jesus (7.32) he responded by announcing (Jn 7.33-34):

Ἔτι χρόνον μικρὸν μεθ' ὑμῶν εἰμι καὶ ὑπάγω πρὸς τὸν πέμψαντά με.	"Yet a little while I am with you and I go to the one who sent me.
ζητήσετέ με καὶ οὐχ εὑρήσετε (με),	You will seek me and will not find (me),
καὶ ὅπου εἰμὶ ἐγὼ ὑμεῖς οὐ δύνασθε ἐλθεῖν.	and where I am you are not able to come."

In what follows (7.35-36) the Jews question the meaning of Jesus' words, especially "you will seek me and will not find me". The one possible meaning that they can see in his words is that he is about to go into the

---

[43]In 5.33 Jesus simply raises the question of self-witness in order to dismiss it. In 8.13 it is the Pharisees who charge Jesus with bearing witness to himself and pronounce that his witness is not true.

[44]Jesus responded to their judgement by saying that he judged no one, 8.15. This is in formal contradiction with 5.22,27 but in agreement with 3.17. To some extent these apparent contradictions are to be reconciled by saying that the historic mission of the Son into the world was to save, but that coming produced division, belief and unbelief, a kind of judgement, 3.19-21. Nevertheless judgement according to works will be carried out in the future by the Son (of Man).

diaspora and teach the Greeks.[45] In this way the failed quest of the Jews is stated emphatically though they will not be able to find him because he is going to the Father and inadvertently they will provide the means by which he returns to the Father.

Following another failed attempt to arrest him, this time by the Pharisees (8.13,20), Jesus reiterates the theme of seeking but not finding him, 8.21.[46]

Ἐγὼ ὑπάγω καὶ ζητήσετέ με,
καὶ ἐν τῇ ἁμαρτίᾳ ὑμῶν ἀποθανεῖσθε·
ὅπου ἐγὼ ὑπάγω ὑμεῖς οὐ δύνασθε
ἐλθεῖν.

"I go away and you will seek me, and you will die in your sins; where I go you are not able to come."

There is now a slight variation from the wording of 7.33-34.[47] Again his words are repeated (not by the Pharisees but by the Jews, 8.22). In the place of the denial "and you will not find me", Jesus says "and you will die in your sins". It is because they do not find him that they will die in their sins. Those who seek to arrest or kill Jesus will not find him. Thus this variation does add a new dimension to the theme. This theme suggests that the Pharisees/Jews will seek Jesus too late; they will die in their sins.

VII. CHRISTOLOGY AND THE JOHANNINE DUALISM

When the theme of Jesus' departure was first addressed the question of where he was going was tentatively[48] answered with the suggestion that he might be going to the *diaspora*. It is now suggested, with equal tentativeness, "Surely he is not about to kill himself?" This is their response to the saying "Where I am going you are not able to come". But Jesus focuses attention on the new theme introduced in 8.21, the theme

---

[45]Here the association of the Greeks with the *diaspora* suggests that it is Greek-speaking Jews that are in view. What is envisaged is the expansion of Jesus' mission to the *diaspora*.

[46]The narrator says that "He (Jesus) said to them again (πάλιν)". Thus the reiteration is announced by the narrator and not simply left for the reader to note.

[47]Where Jesus had said (7.34) "where I am (εἰμί) you are unable to come", he now says "where I am going (ὑπάγω) you are not able to come." The theme of going is present in 7.33 as well as 8.21-22. Thus the motif of going to the one who sent him is present in both sayings and this variation adds nothing to the reiteration. Rather the use of the single word (ὑπάγω) in 8.21 recalls the whole theme (ὑπάγω πρὸς τὸν πέμψαντά με) from 7.33.

[48]In fact the question of where Jesus is going is (in both 7.35 and 8.22) answered by another question introduced by μή (or μήτι). Rather than saying that the question expects a "no" answer it seems that we should say that it is uncertain, tentative.

"you will die in your sins". He now gives his reason for making this assertion. It is because

"You are from below ($\kappa\acute{\alpha}\tau\omega$), I am from above($\acute{\alpha}\nu\omega$);
you are of this world, I am not of this world.
Therefore I told you, 'you will die in your sins.'" (8.23-24)

This situation appears to be irrevocable, inevitable. But Jesus continues, now with a conditional statement, "Except that you believe that I am ($\acute{\epsilon}\gamma\acute{\omega}$ $\epsilon\grave{\iota}\mu\iota$) you will die in your sins", 8.24. The dialogue continues with the Jews asking "who are you?" There is certainly no indication that the Jews understood the $\acute{\epsilon}\gamma\acute{\omega}$ $\epsilon\grave{\iota}\mu\iota$ as a claim to divine status. Had they understood the meaning along these lines they would have charged Jesus with blasphemy and attempted to stone/kill him as ultimately they will do in 8.59 and see 10.30-31. Nor does Jesus suggest that the $\acute{\epsilon}\gamma\acute{\omega}$ $\epsilon\grave{\iota}\mu\iota$ should be understood as a claim to divine status. Instead Jesus appeals to what he has been telling the Jews from the beginning. He goes on to affirm:

"the one who sent me is true, and what I have heard from him these
things I speak to the world." (8.26)

The narrator interjects that "they (the Jews) did not know that he was speaking to them of the Father", 8.27. In response to this ignorance Jesus said:

"When you have lifted up the Son of Man, then you will know that I
am ($\acute{\epsilon}\gamma\acute{\omega}$ $\epsilon\grave{\iota}\mu\iota$), and I do nothing from myself, but even as ($\kappa\alpha\theta\acute{\omega}s$)
the Father taught me these things I speak. And the one who sent
me ($\acute{o}$ $\pi\acute{\epsilon}\mu\psi\alpha s$ $\mu\epsilon$) is with me; he has not left me alone, because I
always do what is pleasing to him." (8.28-29)

It is commonly suggested that here the "I am" is short for "I am the Son of Man". But the overall context indicates that Jesus is here appealing to his earlier teaching (5.17,19-30 and Jn 7) about the relation of the Son to the Father as the one sent by the Father. That Jesus does the works of the Father and speaks the words of the Father reveal that the Father sent him. Thus the meaning is: "When you have lifted up the Son of Man you will know that I am the one sent by the Father, that is, the emissary of God." Surprisingly this stage of the dialogue does not conclude with another attempt to arrest or kill Jesus. Rather we are told that "While Jesus was speaking these (words) many believed in him", 8.30.

Does this mean that they have believed in a way that satisfies the condition stated in 8.24 and thus will not die in their sins? In support of this view we might note that the belief is in response to what Jesus was saying, not a response to the signs. Nevertheless the statement that *many* believed (see 2.23; 7.31) alerts the reader to the possibility that there is a problem with this belief. The problematic nature of the belief is also suggested by Jesus' accusation that "your are from below...,you are of this world...." Thus it is no real surprise that these believers turn out to be the Jews (8.31) and that discipleship is conditional on abiding in Jesus' word. This condition was not satisfied and Jesus refers to them as children of the devil, 8.38,41,44,47. That this is the case is revealed by the attempts to kill Jesus (8.40) and the refusal to hear his words as the words of God (8.47). Thus we have returned again to the theme of Jesus' relation to the Father. It is summed up in the words:

"I speak what I have seen from the (my) father
and you therefore do what you have heard from the (your) father."
(8.38)[49]

The two fathers in question are God and the devil and this is understood by the Jews who responded in kind by accusing Jesus of being a Samaritan and demon-possessed, 8.48-49.[50] To this accusation Jesus replied again in terms of his relation to the one who sent him and of seeking glory. This recalls the theme of 7.17-18. Jesus does not seek ($o\dot{v} \zeta\eta\tau\hat{\omega}$) his own glory, he does not glorify himself but "my Father glorifies me", 8.50,54. The distinctive nature of the glorification of Jesus finds focus in Jn 17.1.

The final scene of this act is precipitated by Jesus' affirmation

"Before Abraham was ($\gamma\epsilon\nu\acute{\epsilon}\sigma\theta\alpha\iota$) I am ($\dot{\epsilon}\gamma\acute{\omega}\ \epsilon\dot{\iota}\mu\iota$)". (8.58)

Here the "I am" takes its significance from the context, "Before Abraham". The Jews rightly understood this to be a claim to be older than Abraham. Though this is not the pronouncement of the divine name the implication of a claim to be older than Abraham does move in the direction of a divine claim and this is understood also. That is why this act ends with another attempt to stone Jesus, which perhaps implies the charge of blasphemy (8.59 and see 10.31; 11.8). Jesus' response was to withdraw secretly from the Temple[51] just as he had secretly come in the first place, 7.10. Thus the hidden Messiah, who has revealed himself in the Temple, remains hidden at the end of Jn 8. The reason for this is that that the ultimate

---

[49] While the textual evidence suggests that "my" and "your" are editorial additions, the editor has correctly interpreted the evangelist's intention with these glosses.

[50] The bitter terms of mutual abuse which appear in this dialogue should be understood in the context of the early Christian debate with Judaism where Jesus was charged with demon-possession (Mk 3.22; Matt 12.24; Lk 11.15) and the use of magic and Jewish believers in Jesus were excluded from the synagogue. They in turn responded by naming (through Jesus) the Jews as the children of the devil.

[51] Thus Jn 7-8 are focused on the Temple. In the middle of the feast Jesus revealed himself in the Temple, 7.14. On the last, the great day of the festival Jesus made an impressive announcement, 7.37ff. Finally Jesus withdrew from the Temple, 8.59.

revelation of the Messiah did not take place to John the Baptist (1.33-34) nor in the Temple, but was to await the uplifting of the Son of Man. When this was done they would know, 8.28. The Messiah remained hidden because the Jews regarded his interpretation of and claim to messiahship as blasphemy. This was the cause of the attempt to stone him.

Why then did the Jews fail to recognize Jesus' words as words from God? Why did they fail to recognize his works as the works of God? Already we have noted the answer in terms of differing origins and different fathers. This dualistic understanding is set in the context of the Jewish and Johannine teaching of creation. Against this background Jn 12.36b-43 is significant. There the narrator is concerned to ask about the cause of unbelief in the face of Jesus' signs. He concludes that "they were not able to believe" and quotes Is 6.10 as an explanation, 12.39-40. Jn's quotation of this text follows neither the Hebrew or the LXX. The consequence of the changes is that the one who has blinded their eyes is spoken of in the third person while the one who would heal them is spoken of in the first person. Thus the one who would heal is distinguished from the one who has blinded. The one who has blinded them is the devil[52] and his blinding work has prevented Jesus from healing them. In this sense they are children of the devil and under the sway of his power. That this limits the power of Jesus as the emissary of God must be acknowledged. But what appears to be an ontological situation is qualified through the conditional "Unless you believe that I am you will die in your sins", 8.24. While this qualification appears to offer opportunity for belief, the tone of threat returns. "When you have lifted up the Son of Man you will know that I am", 8.28. In this context the words are threatening, suggesting that, only when it is too late will they come to know. Yet there is another level of meaning because only through the uplifting of the Son of Man could the prince of this world be cast out (12.31-33) and the power of darkness broken. This theme, first stated in Jn 1.4,8-10 is reiterated in 3.19-21 and 8.12 before being taken up systematically in Jn 9.

The negative implications of the dualism may appear scandalous in an age that has rightly become sensitive to anti-semitism. We should keep in mind that these views were formed in a bitter struggle with the synagogue and that equally serious charges were laid by both sides. Indeed the

---

[52]See "Eschatological Faith Redefining Messiahship" below. The dualistic interpretation continues in 1 Jn where the false confession of faith is attributed to the influence of the Antichrist |and the Spirit of Error, 1 Jn 4.3.6.

Johannine Christians were excluded from the synagogue by the Jews. They were excluded from participation in the people of God. Their own response was to exclude the Jews asserting that they were children of the devil. But even for Jn this accusation has no validity outside the synagogue struggle. It is also allowed that the protagonists may change sides through coming to belief in Jesus as the Messiah (or through apostasy!). It also needs to be remembered that the Johannine Christians were themselves of Jewish descent.

The Son of Man: The Light of the World

In recent studies Jn 9 has been used as a crux for the interpretation of the Gospel.[1] In this chapter, it has been argued, we find important indications of the context in which the Gospel was formed and that awareness of this context enables the reader to perceive the evangelist's intention. What is more, the chapter has been used as an example of the evangelist's compositional method.[2] Recently Ernst Haenchen has challenged this position, arguing that most of ch. 9 is derived from a source which gives expression to views antithetical to those of the evangelist, who was responsible only for 9.4-5, 39-41.[3] He contends that the attitude to signs reflected in the chapter (apart from 9.4-5, 39-41) is that of the source, not of the evangelist. In the source signs are used to demonstrate/prove that Jesus is the Messiah whereas, for the evangelist, the signs point beyond themselves.[4] Consequently Haenchen argues that the literary compositional characteristics of ch. 9 are derived from the source and are not an indication of the evangelist's literary skills.[5]

Haenchen's characterization of the theology of the source might be correct, but I doubt that his delineation of the scope of the source in ch. 9 is. The source seems to be much more restricted than Haenchen has argued and thus the evangelist's contribution is far greater than he allows. While the miracle story is used as a proof, Haenchen overlooks the evangelist's symbolism in 9.8-38 where sight and blindness are interpreted in terms of the healed man's growing perception, while the hardening opposition of Jews/Pharisees is treated as a developing blindness.

The dialogue (in 9.8-38) brings out the way the man who had been blind grows in his perception of Jesus. He refers to Jesus as: the man called Jesus (9.11); a prophet (9.17); from God (9.33); until, in the conclusion, he *worships* Jesus as *Son of Man*. The understanding of the Son of Man as a figure to be worshipped is distinctively Johannine.[6] The designation, "from God", is open to two levels of interpretation, as a man

---

[1] See for example, J. L. Martyn, *History and Theology in the Fourth Gospel*.
[2] *Ibid.*, 4ff.
[3] Ernst Haenchen, *John* II, 41. "In chapter 9, an artfully constructed source is reproduced virtually without editorial insertion; only verses 4f. stem from the Evangelist, and he has probably added verses 39-41."
[4] *Ibid.*, 41ff.
[5] *Ibid.*
[6] See my "Christ and the Church in John 1.45-51", in *L'Evangile de Jean*, ed. M. de Jonge, 359-62.

of God (cf 3.2), which is little or no advance on "a prophet", and in the full Johannine sense, which perceives Jesus as "the stranger from heaven", from God. In this sense it is more or less the equivalent of Son of Man. Hence, the ambiguity of the term makes it an ideal transition from prophet to Son of Man. While the growing perception of the blind man is dramatically described, the evangelist graphically depicts the growing opposition of the Pharisees who were progressively hardened in blindness (9.15-17,18-23,27,29,34,39,41). Also, the judgement of the light is portrayed in Johannine terms in the way the Jews are divided in their response to Jesus' sign (9.16). Both aspects (the division and the growth in perception and blindness) are essential to the interpretation of 9.39.[7] This suggests that 9.39 is in fact the evangelist's conclusion to 9.13-38 because it is 9.39, in conjunction with 9.3-5, which alerts the reader to the symbolic development of the themes of sight and blindness in 9.13-38.

Haenchen is right in seeing the evangelist's interpretative layer in 9.39-41 and linking this with 9.4-5 [8] Because of this he attributed the remainder of the chapter to the source and concluded that the literary skills ought *not* be attributed to the evangelist. However, the evidence suggests that the evangelist himself was responsible for more than 9.4-5,39-41. Nor does it necessarily follow that different layers must be attributed to different hands.

We can agree with Haenchen that the evangelist used a source as the basis of this chapter and that verses 4-5, 39-41 are not part of the source. But these verses might not comprise the extent of the evangelist's interpretative comment on his source.[9] Rather there is a case for recognizing two layers of interpretative comment by the evangelist. The miracle is narrated in vv. 1-7 (apart from 2-5) with 8-11 providing "proof" of the miracle. Verses 12-39 are largely the work of the evangelist. That does not mean that vv. 40-41 are to be attributed to another hand, that of the redactor, even though they provide a second interpretation. Rather they (vv. 40-41) constitute a second level of interpretation by the evangelist, as

---

[7]The emphasis on the division ($\sigma\chi\ell\sigma\mu\alpha$) caused by Jesus (by the coming of the light) is Johannine (9.16). Cf 7.43;10.19 for the use of $\sigma\chi\ell\sigma\mu\alpha$ and 3.19-21 for the dividing power of the light. Haenchen attributes the use of Son of Man and dividing activity of the light in 3.14,19-21 to the redactor (*John* I, 207), but there is no mention of the redactor in ch. 9. What is absolutely clear is that the characteristics under discussion do not belong to the source.

[8]*John* II, 41.

[9]Such a view tends to turn the Gospel into "a scrap book" and the evangelist into a "collector" who contributes only "captions" to his material.

is shown by the way they develop out of the interpretation of 9.13-39, applying the theme of judgement to the situation where relations between the Johannine community and the synagogue have completely broken down. The new theme of judgement (no longer the division caused by the coming of the light) is now the definitive condemnation brought by the coming of the light. From this point of view we need to understand Jn 9 as a whole and its place in the Gospel.

Given the attempts to arrest or kill Jesus in Jn 7-8, Jn 9 opens surprisingly with Jesus walking openly in Jerusalem with his disciples, 9.1-2.[10] Jn 9 commences without any apparent break following Jesus' secret withdrawal from the Temple (8.59). When he withdrew he was alone and Jn 9 commences with the narrator informing the reader that as he passed by he saw a man blind from birth. But we are then told that the disciples are now present and ask the question which leads on to Jesus' healing action. How they came to be present is not explained. It is likely that the evangelist has introduced the disciples into this story in order to provide a basis for the imposing saying of Jesus in 9.3-5 which he wishes to use at this point. That the evangelist has done this is suggested by the fact that, having asked the question the disciples play no further part in the story.[11] Their question (9.2) fits naturally enough in the context as do the sayings of Jesus in response. The sayings conclude with the words:

"While I am in the world,   ὅταν ἐν τῷ κόσμῳ ὦ,
I am the light of the world".   φῶς εἰμι τοῦ κόσμου.

which is the resumption of the theme first announce and in full form in 8.12.

"I am the light of the world;   Ἐγώ εἰμι τὸ φῶς τοῦ κόσμου·
the one who follows me shall   ὁ ἀκολουθῶν μοι οὐ μὴ περιπατήσῃ ἐν
not walk in darkness,   σκοτίᾳ,
but will have the light of life."   ἀλλ' ἕξει τὸ φῶς τῆς ζωῆς.

Recognition of this resumption suggests that Jn 9 is a narrative exposition of the theme of 8.12. It also implies that the Pharisees, who object to the saying and charge Jesus with false witness (8.13), are in view

---

[10] One of the puzzles of the presentation of the conflict from Jn 5.18 on is that at one moment we are told of the attempt to arrest or kill Jesus and in the next we are told that he is walking openly and without any apparent cause for fear. In Jn 7-8 Jesus, having kept away from open appearances in Jerusalem, reveals himself by teaching openly in the Temple. The evangelist makes a point of having the Jerusalemites note the irony of the situation (7.25-26). They were clearly puzzled by it and the evangelist intended the reader to be aware of this.

[11] Compare Jn 2.2. There they appear to have been introduced into the traditional story so that in the end they may be the beneficiaries of the sign, 2.11.

in the narrative exposition in Jn 9 and they emerge in 9.40-41. Their appearance there is somewhat surprising in that they overhear the words of 9.39 which in the narrative appear to have been spoken to the once blind man who says nothing in response to these words. He disappears from the scene and it is the Pharisees who respond allowing Jesus to pronounce his final (for this scene) word of judgement upon them.

The association of the themes of light and judgement with the Son of Man in Jn 9 is significant. Jn 9 begins with Jesus revealing himself as the light of the world, a theme expounded in the chapter, and concludes when he reveals himself as the Son of Man and is worshipped as such, 6.35-38. All that remains to be done is for Jesus to announce the judgement brought about by his (the light/Son of Man) coming into the world (3.19-21; 9.39). In 9.39-41 sight and blindness have a harmonic relationship with light and darkness. In Jn both the Son of Man and the coming of the light bring about the judgement of the world. This association of the Son of Man, the coming of the light and judgement is to be found in 3.13-21 (see also 12.34-36) and justifies the title of the present chapter, The Son of Man: The Light of the World.

Though the miracle story has been thoroughly integrated into the context there is decisive evidence of the use of a discrete miracle story as the basis of Jn 9. Not only is there the clue which arises from the introduction of the disciples (9.2) with the question that allows for the significant sayings of Jesus to be used (9.3-5),[12] it is only in what follows the miracle story that the healed man is led to the Pharisees and the narrator informs the reader that it was the sabbath when Jesus performed the healing, 9.14 and see 5.9. The controversial dialogues of 9.13-41 are clearly not part of the original miracle story but have been introduced by inserting the reference to the sabbath controversy.

I. THE MIRACLE STORY (9.1, 6-11)

Isolating the underlying miracle story is relatively straightforward. The introduction sets out the serious circumstances of the case (9.1). The man was blind from birth. Originally there may have been a request for healing making the story a miracle quest story like 4.46-54. If that was the case it has been removed by the evangelist when making the miracle story the

---

[12]The evangelist's characteristic emphasis on "the works of God" ($\xi\rho\gamma\alpha$) rather than "signs", his reference to God as $\tauο\hat{υ}\ \pi\acute{ε}\mu\psi\alpha\nu\tauο\varsigma\ \mu\ \epsilon$, the night/day, light/darkness "dualism" and the formulaic designation $\phi\hat{ω}\varsigma$ $\epsilon\iota\mu\iota\ \tauο\hat{υ}\ \kappaό\sigma\muου$, all in the space of three verses, betray the evangelist's hand. In this way the reader of the story is prepared for the symbolic interpretation which is to follow in 9.13-39.

basis of a rejection story.[13] In these stories the healings are performed at the initiative of Jesus. Following the description of the circumstances of the man the miracle itself is vividly and briefly described (9.6-7).[14] The story concludes with an account of the evidence that demonstrates the reality of the healing (9.8-11). Thus we have a neatly recognizable "miracle story" setting out the problem, describing the healing, and attesting the reality of the miracle. Verse 12 is an editorial link to relate the story to the dialogue/controversy which follows in 9.13-39.

1. The Source of the Miracle Story

No miracles of the giving of sight to the blind are known to us in the Old Testament but the restoration of sight to the blind seems to have been an aspect of messianic expectation (Isa 29.18; 35.5; 42.7; 61.1-2; see Matt 11.5 = Lk 7.22; Lk 4.18). While it is possible that the expectation gave rise to stories of the healing of the blind by Jesus, the widespread attestation of this activity in the gospel tradition, and the absence of messianic overtones from many of these stories, suggest that some, at least, are derived from the healing ministry of Jesus (see Mk 8.22-26;10.46-52). Thus the evidence that the evangelist made use of a traditional miracle story in Jn 9 allows for the possibility that the tradition might go back to the healing ministry of Jesus. Our concern, however, is the means by which the tradition came to be known and used by the evangelist.

Jn's story corresponds to no single Synoptic story but it is possible that he drew on various accounts to produce a story in which the chief differences from the Synoptic stories are:
1. the extended review of the evidence demonstrating the reality of the miracle and
2. the interrogations and debates which follow the miracle.

This material tends to serve the Johannine theological interests[15] and is a consequence of the evangelist's writing up of the incident. These differences belong to the dialogue/controversy section which has (to say

---

[13]Compare 5.1-9a.

[14] Reference to the use of spittle and the making of clay to anoint the eyes is reminiscent of the healing of the blind man in Mk 8.22-26. The use of such "crudely physical means of healing" is often taken as a sign of primitive tradition and of contact with Hellenistic means of healing.

[15]See R.E. Brown, *John* I, 378-9. "Of course, these strikingly different details are often the very points that serve the Johannine theological interests, and therefore one is hard put to prove scientifically that they were not invented for the sake of pedagogy." This point is noted by Brown who argues in favour of the "primitive and authentic character of the Johannine story . . . "

the least) been heavily edited by the evangelist. It is likely that the dialogues in 13-41 are largely his creation. But what of the characteristics of the miracle story itself?

The use of spittle in Jn 9.6 links the story with Mk 8.23, but differences in the details of the stories preclude the identification of the Markan account as the source of Jn's use of this motif.[16] It is, however, a "primitive" feature of the Johannine story. The Markan spittle miracles seem to have been deliberately omitted by Matt and Lk. The use of spittle was part of the primitive tradition about Jesus but left him open to a charge of engaging in magical practice.[17] Other aspects of Jn's story indicate that the tradition has undergone greater literary development than the Synoptic tradition. This can be seen in the emphases which tend to "heighten" the miraculous nature of the healing.

1. The man was blind "from birth" (9.1). The healing of the blind was remarkable enough in itself but the giving of sight to one blind from birth was incredible (9.32). Development is also to be seen in the language "blind from birth", which is Hellenistic, rather than the Semitic, "blind from the mother's womb".[18]

2. The emphasis is on the initiative of Jesus and no mention is made of the man's faith (9.3ff.).

3. There is an extended account of the evidence to demonstrate the reality, extent and nature of the miracle,[19] though most of this probably does not come from the source, and should not be used to characterize the source.

While it is *possible* that the evangelist drew on Synoptic miracle stories, the differences (after allowing for the evangelist's editing) make it *probable* that the story in Jn 9 was part of a miracle tradition which surfaces again at 2.1-10; 4.46-54; 5.1-9a; 6.1-21; 11.[20]

2. The *Sitz im Leben* of the Miracle Story

The Form historians suggested that the miracle story genre had its *Sitz im Leben* in the missionary preaching of the early church and it seems probable that such a collection of miracle stories was developed as an evangelistic resource. Bultmann argued that the signs source was the

---

[16]Bultmann reversed his earlier view that the motif of the use of spittle was taken from Mk 8.23. See his *John*, 330 n1.

[17]Brown, *John* I, 372.

[18]Brown, John.I, 371 and Bultmann, *John*., 330 n6.

[19]See Martyn, *History and Theology in the Fourth Gospel*, 4ff

[20]See Bultmann, *John*,111f, etc. On Bultmann's Semeia Source hypothesis see D.M. Smith Jr, *The Composition and Order of the Fourth Gospel*, 35-44. On the Signs Source see also Robert Fortna, *The Gospel of Signs*; W. Nicol, *The Semeia in the Fourth Gospel* and the survey in Robert Kysar, *The Fourth Evangelist and his Gospel*, 17-37. See the discussion of the signs source in chapter 2, "Johannine Christianity" above.

product of converts from the Baptist sect and was used by them in their efforts to win those who remained in the sect to faith in Jesus.[21] He attributes the theme of faith on the basis of signs to the signs source and argues that the evangelist was critical of this theme. As evidence of this he draws attention to the evangelist's criticism of faith on the basis of signs (2.23ff.; 4.48). Haenchen also argues that the evangelist was critical of the presentation of the signs (in the signs source)[22] as proof that Jesus is "from God". However, neither Bultmann nor Haenchen has done justice to the fact that the evangelist *chose* to use the source. Haenchen acknowledged that the evangelist did not question the reality of the miracles but understood them symbolically (that is my word)[23] rather than as proof, which is the view he discerns in 9.1-3,6-7,8-38, and therefore he attributes these verses to the source.

While the original use of the miracle story in relation to the Baptist sect cannot be excluded, the literary context suggests that it (and others like it in Jn) was used in the synagogue. It could be that the synagogue in question included a number of those who still considered themselves to be disciples of the Baptist. The miracle story itself is free from the overtones of controversy which are to be found in vv. 13-41. It presents Jesus as the one who opens the eyes of the blind, emphasizing the miraculous nature of the event in a way suitable for the missionary preaching of the early church and may have been in the form of a miracle quest story. In the attempt to win members of the synagogue to faith, Jesus was presented as "a man attested to you by God with mighty works and wonders and signs" (Acts 2.22 and see Jn 9.11).[24] Judged in its own terms it seems that this mission was successful. Whether the evangelist was, at that time, *completely* satisfied with this approach it is difficult to say. While he makes use of the signs there are indications that he does not regard faith *based on signs alone* to be altogether adequate, both in terms of durability and in terms of the perception of the true nature of Jesus. Indeed, he might have linked the failure to endure with an inadequate recognition of Jesus,

---

[21]Bultmann, *John*, 108 n6.

[22]Haenchen, *John* II, 41f.

[23]*Ibid*. Haenchen says that the signs point beyond themselves.

[24]In fact the response of the man who had been blind in Jn 9.11, 16-17, 33 fits well with the christology of the early Christian preaching of Acts 2.22 where signs are used to prove that God was with Jesus, a view to be found also in Jn 3.2. However, in both Jn 3 and Jn 9 that christology is shown to be inadequate. Not wrong, but inadequate. That inadequacy becomes clear in what follows in each case, in Jn 9 in vv. 35-38. In the light of these verses some progress can be seen in the perception of the blind man. Likewise the Pharisees became progressively blind.

an inadequate christology.

These comments might suggest that the evangelist was at odds with his source. Two observations are important. The evangelistic use of the source occurred at an early stage in the composition of the Gospel. Further, though the evangelist was critical of faith based on signs *alone* and the approach that made signs *necessary* for faith (20.29), he allowed signs some place in the *development* of faith (10.37-38). Faith based on signs was a real beginning, even if only a beginning. Moreover, it appears to have been in the later controversies with the synagogue that the faith *based only on signs* proved to be inadequate.

II. THE DIALOGUES-CONTROVERSY (9.2-5,12-39)

Unlike the signs of Jn 5 and Jn 6, the sign of Jn 9 is not followed by a lengthy discourse but by a series of dialogues which constitute a controversy. The touch of the evangelist's hand is evident in the symbolic interpretation of the growth of sight (the blind man) and of blindness (the Pharisees) and the division caused by the presence of the light.

The question of the disciples, whom the evangelist frequently introduces into the narrative, provides the opportunity for the use of the key sayings of Jesus in 9.3-5. At the same time this raises the problem, in a Jewish context, of the relation between sin and sickness.[25] While Jesus did not deny the connection, he asserted that, in this instance, the man's blindness was to serve the purpose of God, linking the themes of sight and blindness with the symbols light and darkness.[26] The evangelist's editorial comments, adapting the story to the situation for which he was writing, are clearly visible in 9.3-5 and in the light of this that situation becomes evident in 9.13-39.

From 9.13-34 there are controversial dialogues between the man and the Pharisees (Jews) and other witnesses. The dialogues lead to action being taken against the healed man. Because he refused to affirm that Jesus was a sinner he was thrown out of the synagogue, 9.34, and see 9.22. No attempt was made to take action against Jesus. That is surely surprising unless the story is understood in terms of the situation of the Johannine Christians. In 9.35-41 the outcast man was received by Jesus and a word of judgement was pronounced on the unbelieving Pharisees. Thus 9.39 is

---

[25] Jn 9.2-3. In the miracle story of Jn 5 the problem of the relation of sin and sickness is featured in a later dialogue between Jesus and the healed man, 5.14. Having found the man in the Temple Jesus said to him, "Behold you have become whole, sin no more lest something worse befall you." This saying, like the question of 9.2, assumes the connection between sin and sickness.

[26] Compare 9.3-5 with 11.9-10,15.

the impressive final pronouncement and the outcome of the conflict for the Pharisees is stated in 9.40-41. Whereas in Jn 5 it was Jesus who was rejected, in Jn 9 the once blind man was rejected by the Jews/Pharisees. He was, however, received by Jesus, who condemned the Pharisees. Thus this story is a hybrid. It is a rejection story, telling of the rejection of the once blind man (and, by implication, of the Johannine Christians) and it is a commendation story, commending his courageous response. His example is set out as a model to be followed by the secret believers within the synagogue.

The literary skills of the evangelist are revealed in the arrangement of the chapter which (as in Jn 5 but more elaborately) fits the following schema in which two characters or groups appear in each scene leading on to Jesus' final confrontation with the Pharisees.

First Encounters:
1. Jesus and his disciples (2-5); the problem of sin and suffering.
2. Jesus and the man (6-7); the account of the miracle.
3. The man and his neighbours (8-12); the proof of the miracle.
4. The man and the Pharisees (13-17); the controversy over the Law (sabbath).
5. The Jews and the parents (18-23); the threat of excommunication.

Reprise (partial):
6. The man and the Jews (24-34); faith overcomes fear of excommunication.
7. Jesus and the man (35-38[39]); Jesus reveals himself as the heavenly Son of Man. Verse 39 is both the conclusion of this dialogue and the bridge to the one that follows.

New Encounter:
8. Jesus and the Pharisees (39-41); unbelief is condemned.

Jn 9 reveals the literary skills of the evangelist who has made use of a simple miracle story in such a way that it has become a dramatic masterpiece. In common with drama in the ancient world, only two characters/groups appear on "the stage" at any given time, heightening the dramatic effect and, in these dialogues, emphasizing the force of the conflicts. The narrator supplies the information essential to the reader if he is to understand the conflict. The narrator informs the reader that the sign was performed on the sabbath (9.14),[27] a point not mentioned in the story itself. He also reveals the decision to cast out of the synagogue any one who should *confess Christ* (9.22). Thus it is the narrator who sets the scene of the conflict and indicates its terms. It is a conflict where the "wonder-worker" is set over against Moses and the Law, and anyone who

---

[27]See also 5.9-10. The introduction of the Sabbath issue marks the transition from the evangelistic use of the miracle story to a use in controversy with the synagogue.

sides with the "wonder-worker" is excluded from the synagogue. In this situation it is no longer possible to choose both Moses and Jesus. In the formulation of 9.22 the "wonder-worker" is designated "Christ", indicating that the decision described relates to the general conflict between Jews and *Christian Jews* (within the synagogue) and not simply to the conflict described in Jn 9 over the healing of the blind man. Part of the evidence for this is that, in the story and in the dialogues, "Christ" is used only in the prohibited *confession*.

If, in the dialogues, no one suggests that "Jesus is the Christ", the prohibition in those terms does not fit the context of the story but that of the narrator/evangelist. Further, as "Christ" is not the evangelist's own chosen designation (in this story the blind man is led to faith in the Son of Man) we must suppose that it is the christology of the "secret believers" for whom it is probably to be understood in terms of "traditional Davidic Messiahship". It was the evangelist's purpose to reinterpret this christology, which he considered to be inadequate.[28] In the synagogue controversy this christology proved to be inadequate and those who held it were unable to cope with the opposition of Moses and the Law. The evangelist's reinterpretation was therefore crucial for the "secret believers" in their conflict with the synagogue.

The Jewish situation is indicated by the controversies which concern the sabbath, the Law of Moses and the Christ. At first the believers were simply members of the Jewish community and the miracle stories were used to win members of the synagogue to faith in Jesus as "a man attested by God" by the signs and wonders which he worked (cf. 2.23ff.; 3.1f). Even after "persecution" had begun, some "believers" continued to live within the Jewish community as "secret believers" (cf. 3.1f; 7.50ff.; 9.22;12.42;19.38f; 20.19). Evangelism on the basis of the miracle stories had been successful enough to bring about a synagogue reaction which led to the *excommunication* of those who *confessed Christ* (9.22,34; 12.42; 16.2; especially 9.22). In the New Testament the terminology of "excommunication" occurs only in Jn. The formula in 9.22, "to confess Christ", is formal and belongs, not to the time of the ministry of Jesus, but to a later stage of church development.

The situation of persecution by the synagogue is the clue to the chronological placing of this layer. It was shaped by the evangelist in the

---

[28] See Jn 1.49-51; 20.30f, where traditional Davidic Messiahship is reinterpreted in terms of the Johannine understanding of *Son of Man* and *Son of God*. On this see my "The Church and Israel in the Gospel of John", *NTS* 25 (1978), 103-12, and "Christ and the Church", in *L'Evangile de Jean*, ed. M. de Jonge, 359-62.

period of growing tension with the synagogue which culminated in the expulsion from the synagogue of those who confessed Jesus to be the Christ. The conflict does *not* concern the entry of Gentiles but is focused simply on the *confession of Christ* (see 9.22;12.42). This situation seems to have been formative, not only for Jn 9.13-41, but for much of the Gospel. The conflict appears to have had two stages. The first culminates in the *introduction* of the "ban" which is relevant to 9.13-39. At first "secret believers" found it possible to remain within the synagogue. That time passed and in the second stage the relationship between the Johannine community and the synagogue had completely broken down. That is the situation of 15.1–16.4a and of 9.40-41. When the believers were excluded from the synagogue the Johannine community was born. In the new community the evangelist exerted his influence reinterpreting the tradition for his own situation. In the face of the growing Jewish hostility the need for an adequate christological basis for faith was highlighted. The evangelist saw his understanding (reinterpretation) of Christ as the basis of a courageous confession of faith in these circumstances.

The evangelist's christology is expressed, in this section (vv. 13-39), in terms of *the heavenly Son of Man*. While the designation is itself traditional, and *some aspects* of the traditional use are retained by Jn (e.g. the designation occurs only on the lips of Jesus,[29] and the apocalyptic association is retained in Jn 5.27-29), the overall treatment of Son of Man is distinctive in the Fourth Gospel. He is the descending and ascending Son of Man who ascends (is glorified) by way of the cross. What emerges in 9.13-39 is that the growing perception of Jesus culminates in his self-revelation as Son of Man and as Son of Man he was worshipped by the once blind man, 9.35-38. Consequently the dialogues with the man are bounded by Jesus' revelation of himself as the light of the world in 9.5 and as Son of Man in 9.35-38. Given that 9.5 resumes 8.12 we concluded that Jn 9 is a narrative exposition of the theme of 8.12. In Jn 9 the judging power of the light of the world is in view and that judgement is understood in terms of the division brought by the light (9.16) which is exemplified especially by story of the man, cast out from the synagogue but received by Jesus. At the end of this sequence Jesus' self-revelation as Son of Man implies that it is as Son of Man that he is the light of the world, giving light and life to those who follow him but condemning the rest to darkness.

The development of the dialogue section reflects the situation of conflict with the synagogue. It seems to be addressed to those who remained

---

[29]Jn 12.34 is no real exception as the use by the crowd is a question in response to Jesus' use of the "title".

sympathetic within the synagogue, the secret believers. It has two purposes in relation to them: to draw out *the implied* christology of the sign; and, on the basis of that christology, to encourage those who remained within the synagogue to confess their faith courageously, to face excommunication, and to join the Johannine community. These purposes are fulfilled in the dialogue section when the man faces persecution and is subsequently led to faith in Jesus as Son of Man and worships him. His example was intended to encourage timid, fearful believers within the synagogue to confess their faith, face excommunication and to join the Johannine community.

The giving of sight to the man has been interpreted as the giving of the light of a growing perception of the mystery of the person of Jesus so that in the end he worships him as Son of Man. In this way the quest for the Messiah is taken a step further. That Son of Man is to be understood in the context of the messianic question is clear from 9.22. Messiahship is conceptually modified by the manifestation of the Son of Man as the light of the world in Jn 9.

III. THE EXECRATION (9.39-41)

The next section brings Jesus and the Pharisees together for the first time. Prior to this Jesus has been involved only with his disciples, who vanished after asking their question, and with the man who also vanishes so that the Pharisees may occupy centre stage with Jesus. The introduction of Jesus with the Pharisees marks a new phase in the development of the tradition in this chapter. This new phase is linked to the previous one by verse 39, which is appropriate to both. However, while, in the previous section, sight and blindness are seen to be possibilities created by the coming of the (Son of Man) light, in 9.40-41 the blindness of the Pharisees is pronounced definitively and permanently.

Verse 39 appears to have been the original conclusion to the evangelist's interpretation of the miracle story in the crisis of conflict with the synagogue. With 9.3-5 it provides the clue to the evangelist's symbolic interpretation. The climax is reached when the man (who, because of his confession of faith, was excluded from the synagogue) was found by Jesus who revealed himself to the man as *Son of Man*, and the narrator informs us that the man worshipped him. After that encounter the evangelist concludes with a summary statement through the words of Jesus. These words are a conclusion though, if they are spoken to anyone, they are spoken to the man who had been blind. Had the chapter concluded with 9.39 we would see the verse as a summary *conclusion following* the dialogues. The addition of 9.40-41 implies an audience for 9.39 (apart from the reader and the man). The hearers, according to 9.40-41, were the Pharisees, although there is no indication how they came to "overhear" this conversation. Given the careful staging of the dialogues in 9.12-39 (see how we are told of the way the man was brought before the Pharisees in 9.12-13), this must be taken as a clue indicating that 9.40-41 has been added to the evangelist's completed interpretation in 9.1-39 so that 9.40-41 constitutes a second interpretation.

The situation of 9.40-41 reflects the hardening of the breach between the synagogue and the Johannine community. There is no attempt, in this section, to win the synagogue over to faith in Jesus. Rather, the community, which has been rejected by the synagogue, pronounces its own rejection of the synagogue in the authoritative words of Jesus. The condemnation (9.41) implies that the breach with the synagogue is final. It tells the secret believers that there is no future in the synagogue and confirms that those who have faced the breach are in the light, that they truly see. The transition from the situation of conflict to one of mutual execration might have been quite rapid, though a protracted conflict seems to be implied by the pervasive influence it has had on the tradition in the Gospel, the extensive treatment of the theme of "secret believers" (cf. 9.13-39) and the attempt to win them from the synagogue into the Johannine community.

This layer of the Gospel (vv. 40-41) justifies the separation which had taken place, Jn 9.39-41;15.1-16.4a. Those who had been rejected by the synagogue now respond by rejecting the synagogue. Here the theme of light versus darkness is important. The light/darkness dualism was prominent in the Qumran texts.[30] There the dualism was an expression of the community's separation from the world in general and from the rest of Judaism in particular. The Qumran Covenanters viewed themselves as the sons of light and "the rest" as the sons of darkness. The light/darkness dualism in Jn serves the same purpose. The Johannine Christians were the sons of light while synagogue Judaism is condemned to the darkness (9.39-41). For this reason also the Johannine Christians claimed to be members of the *true vine* while unbelieving Jews were cast off.[31] Thus, in its final form, the story legitimates the separation of the Johannine Christians from the synagogue and portrays those who rejected them as

---

[30]On this theme at Qumran see chapter 2, "Johannine Christianity" above and J.H. Charlesworth (ed.), *John and Qumran*, especially 76-106.

[31]See my "The Church and Israel in the Gospel of John", *NTS* 25 (1978), 103-12, especially 112, and chapter 13, "The Farewell of the Messiah" below. It was while writing the paper that forms the basis of that chapter (delivered at the *SNTS* meeting in Toronto, 1980) that I became convinced of the evangelist's double interpretation of the miracle story in Jn 9.

under the judgement of God. Indeed it is as the Son of Man, to whom judgement has been committed, that Jesus pronounces that judgement.

IV. IN THE CONTEXT OF THE QUEST FOR THE MESSIAH

In Jn 9 it becomes apparent that the struggle with the synagogue concerned the quest for the Messiah. The synagogue excluded those who confessed Jesus to be the Messiah (9.22). Messianic claims concerning him were ruled out on the basis of the Mosaic Law.[32] Jesus was a Law-breaker and (according to the synagogue) certainly not the Messiah. But the evangelist called on all to confess Jesus as the Messiah and in so doing transformed the meaning of messiahship. An alternative image in this transformation was the identification of Jesus with the Son of Man. This provided an aspect of his reinterpretation of Jesus the Messiah now spoken of also as Son of God (Jn 20.30-31).[33] It is hardly surprising that this understanding encountered Jewish opposition and rejection. In the conflict Jn portrayed the judgement of the world in terms of the light coming into the world and emphasized Jesus as Son of Man in his role as eschatological judge.

---

[32] From the perspective of the synagogue the Law was a more solid foundation on which to build than some concept of messiahship. The application of the criterion of the Law to exclude Jesus' messianic claims supports the view that Jn 9 was shaped in the conflict with the synagogue after the Jewish war (after 74CE).

[33] It is for this reason that the evangelist has written not simply "that you may believe that Jesus is the Christ" but has added "the Son of God" thereby transforming the meaning of messiahship in terms of his distinctive interpretation of the Father/Son relation.

9

The Enigmatic Son of Man[1]

The Johannine Son of Man is an enigma, though one thing is clear: the enigma is relevant to the theme of the quest for the Messiah. Outside the Gospels only Acts 7.56 provides a comparable use of Son of Man. Jn is in touch with the gospel tradition in maintaining the use of Son of Man only on the lips of Jesus[2] and that, as in the Synoptics, Son of Man is used as a self-designation by Jesus in passion predictions,[3] and as a corrective to inadequate perceptions of Jesus and confessions of faith in him.[4] We are left with the impression that the earliest church did not find the designation significant although the evidence suggests that it might well have been Jesus' own preferred use of language. This leaves open the question of whether, in Jesus' use, Son of Man was a self-designation and whether his use covered the various perspectives found in the Gospels.

Recent studies tend to deny the titular use of Son of Man by Jesus.[5] Vermes thinks that Son of Man reflects the Aramaic idiom where *bar nasha* could be used as a circumlocution for a self-reference. According to Ragnar Leivestad in the Gospels the case is different only in Jn 9.35 where Son of Man "has become a pregnant christological term"[6] which was not derived from Judaism, but had taken on specific meaning in early Christianity. Now Mogens Müller has argued that Jn 9.35 is also a circumlocution, a

---

[1] An earlier version of this chapter appeared in *The Four Gospels 1992* vol 3, 1869-87.

[2] Jn 12.34, for all its problems, is no real exception because the crowd was responding to what it conceived to be Jesus' claims concerning the Son of Man.

[3] See Mk 8.31; 9.31; 10.33f. (45) and John 3.14; 8.28; 12.32-34. It is true that the passion predictions in John have been "Johannized" through the use of ὑψοῦν, which means "to exalt", but which the narrator explains (12.33) as a *signifier* of crucifixion, the manner of Jesus' death.

[4] See Mk 8.27-33 and John 1.43-51; 3.1-15; 6.14-15,27,53,62; 12.23-36. J.L.Martyn (*History and Theology in the Fourth Gospel*, 134) argued that the evangelist used Son of Man to correct the perception of Jesus as the Mosaic prophet-Messiah. See also F.J. Moloney, *The Johannine Son of Man*, 33-38,181,185,214 and in the Appendix to the second edition (1978) 237 n53 and my *John Witness and Theologian*, 54-55 and "Christ and the Church in John 1.45-51", 359-362, especially 360-1.

[5] See G. Vermes, *Jesus the Jew*, 160ff.

[6] "Exit the Apocalyptic Son of Man", *NTS* 18 (1971-72), 251.

non-titular use of Son of Man.[7] The question "Have you faith in the Son of Man?" enables Jesus to identify himself as the one who had restored the man's sight. To add weight to this argument Müller asserts that none of the remaining eleven uses of Son of Man is titular suggesting that 9.35 is non-titular also.

Certainly Jesus' use of Son of Man in Jn is intended as a self-reference. But this need not be understood as a circumlocution. In Jn 9.35ff. Jesus is revealed as Son of Man in his work of judgement which is also spoken of in terms of the coming of the light into the world, bringing separation/division (cf. 3.19-21; 8.12; 9.5,39-41). In 9.35-39 that separation is seen in relation to the once blind man who leaves the darkness for the light whereas in 9.39-41 Jesus' words are pronounced on the unbelieving Pharisees, condemning them to the darkness. Those who argue for a non-titular use of Son of Man in Jn pay too little attention to the context of judgement in the distinctive Johannine development which grows out of Jewish Apocalyptic traditions as interpreted in early Christianity. The Johannine use has developed its own distinctive nuances while retaining a traditional eschatological orientation.

The view of a non-titular use of Son of Man as a circumlocution for a self-reference (Müller) is to be distinguished from the recognition of a titular use that finds its focus on the humanity of Jesus (F. J. Moloney; D.R.A Hare; M. Pamment),[8] though both the circumlocution and this titular use focus on the human Jesus. Hare and Moloney focus on the incarnate, human Jesus while Pamment sees the Son of Man as something like the ideal human being, the fulfillment of human potential. But in the non-titular use there is no particular view. It is simply a self-reference. The view expressed in *Quest* is that the Son of Man is the eschatological judge who represents the point of view of heaven to earth and as such he is the heavenly judge who is worshipped by the once blind man, 9.38.

I. THE ISSUES

The following theses are argued though they will not be considered in this order but more or less as they appear in the sequence of the sayings:
1). The significance of the placing of the thirteen Son of Man sayings[9] in Jn 1-13 is that they assert and define the nature of Jesus' kingship. The sayings provide a corrective to inadequate christological views.
2). The distinctive motifs of the Son of Man sayings (exaltation) and Father/Son sayings (the Father's love[10] for and sending of the Son) are

---

[7]"Have you Faith in the Son of Man?", *NTS* 37 (1991), 291-94.
[8]See chapter 5.V "John and Apocalyptic Ideology" above.
[9]Jn 1.51; 3.13,14; 5.17; 6.27,53,62; 8.28; 9.35; 12.23,34(twice); 13.31.
[10]See Jn 3.35 and 10.17.

united in the "I" sayings of Jesus but glorification is a common motif in both Son of Man and Son traditions as well as "I" sayings. Thus there is no Son of Man christology though the Son of Man motifs are a constituent part of Jn's christology. But Son of Man is not simply a stylistic variant on Son and Son of God.

3). The use of Son of Man draws attention to Jesus as a heavenly being first descending and then ascending to heaven again. Ascent also carries something of the meaning of enthronement. This does not mean that Jn denies the humanity of Jesus. The humanity of Jesus is not questioned in the Gospel. What is questioned is the validity of a man claiming divine status (5.18; 10.33).

4). Ascent and glorification are defined in relation to the cross. These two terms are used to emphasize the event of revelation. In relation to the Son of Man the revelation functions as an act of judgement.

5). Revelation and judgement are featured in the association of the Son of Man (and his coming/descent and ascent) with the coming and going of the light.

6). The motifs associated with the heavenly Son of Man and the revelation and judgement that he brings belong to the second edition of the Gospel and the polemical context of the struggle with the Synagogue.

II. THE SIGNIFICANCE OF THE SON OF MAN TRADITION

Clearly the traditional Son of Man motif has been Johannized. It is this that makes it impossible to ascertain whether Jn is making use of Synoptic tradition or is utilizing traditional themes and motifs without any direct dependence on particular literary traditions, Synoptic or otherwise. As with the Synoptics, there is a case for recognizing that Jn has made use of the Danielic Son of Man. The influence of Dan chapters 7 and 12 is relevant though what is important here is not the scientific exegesis of Dan but the first century interpretation in traditions that might have influenced the evangelist and his own reading of Dan. John Ashton considers Jn 5.27 to be "an unambiguous allusion to Dan's vision"[11] and J.L Martyn describes this verse as in some respects "the most 'traditional' Son of Man saying in the New Testament".[12]

In Jn 5.27-29 recognizable apocalyptic tradition surfaces but many scholars think Jn has nothing in common with apocalyptic ideas and either attribute these verses to a redactor or suggest that they are a vestige of an earlier tradition that the evangelist has failed to assimilate.[13] Thus it is generally recognized that apocalyptic elements are evident in the text as it has come down to us. A sustained critique of Jn shows that these features are not alien bodies within it but essential to the framework of the Gospel.

---

[11]*Understanding the Fourth Gospel*, 361.

[12]*History and Theology*, 139.

[13]See also Jn 6.40,44,54; 11.24.

That Jn 5.27 builds on Dan 7.13-14 is generally recognized because of the anarthrous use of "Son of Man" (without the definite article) and the terms in which the judgement is portrayed are reminiscent of Dan 12.1-2.

The connection with the Danielic Son of Man is not, however, universally recognized.[14] It has been challenged by scholars who take the second century understanding of Son of Man as the point of departure for understanding the New Testament. For these scholars all "Son of Man" sayings refer to the human, incarnate one.[15] D. R. A Hare notes that "Higgins and Borsch have quite properly attacked this proposal (concerning dependence on Dan 7.13-14), pointing out how very weak is the evidence for conscious allusion in this case." He goes on to say, "The non-apocalyptic nature of John's vision of truth suggests that he would not have found the Danielic apocalypse particularly congenial."[16] Hare's view is based on his rejection of the anarthrous $v\iota\dot{o}\varsigma$ $\dot{\alpha}\nu\theta\rho\dot{\omega}\pi o\nu$ as evidence of the influence of Dan 7.13 and his judgement that Jn "would not have found the Danielic apocalypse particularly congenial." This latter judgement is superficial, taking no account of apocalyptic dimensions in Jn.[17]

Borsch bases his rejection of the influence of the Danielic Son of Man in Jn on his critique of the work of Sigfried Schulz. He recognized that Schulz argued that Jn 5.27-29 is a traditional unit[18] but limited his

---

[14]D. Burkett (Son of Man) now argues that the anarthrous use in Jn 5.27 means "a human being" and has no reference to Dan 7.13 or any apocalyptic association. He argues that with the article "the Son of Man" is dependent on a variety of scriptural texts: Jn 3.13 is dependent on Prov 30.14; Jn 1.51 on Gen 28.12; references to the lifting up of the Son of Man on Isa 52.13; Jn 6.27,53,62 with Isa 55.1-3,10-11; Jn 8.28 with Isa 46.16; Jn 9.35 with Gen 1.5. While the influence of these scriptural passages need not be denied it hardly explains Jn's use of Son of Man.

[15]See M. Pamment, "The Son of Man in the Fourth Gospel"; D.R.A. Hare, The Son of Man Tradition, 79-111. Hare concludes (111) that Son of Man refers to the incarnational existence of the Logos, the unique humanity of the incarnate one. He (like Moloney, The Johannine Son of Man) emphasizes the concentration on the death of Jesus in the Son of Man sayings, though Moloney recognizes the titular use with Danielic reference.

[16]The Son of Man Tradition, 92. See A.J.B. Higgins, Jesus and the Son of Man, 166 and F.H. Borsch, The Son of man in Myth and History, 294. Günter Reim (Studien zum alttestamentlichen Hintergrund des Johannesevangeliums, SNTS MS 22, 186) finds no evidence of dependence on Dan in John at all.

[17]See my "Theology, Eschatology and the Prologue of John", SJT 46 (1993) The apocalyptic character of the Johannine world view is best seen in terms of the Johannine dualism which is local, temporal and ethical. See the discussion of dualism in chapter 2 above.

[18]Untersuchungen zur Menschensohn-Christologie im Johannesevangelium, 113f.

discussion to the Son of Man saying in 5.27. Certainly it is not enough to argue that the anarthrous use of Son of Man in Dan 7.13 and Jn 5.27 makes the link with Dan 7.13 clear, especially because in Jn 5.27 "Son of Man" is the object placed before the verb ἐστίν.[19] There is, however, also the agreement in the wording of the LXX text of Dan 7.13 (καὶ ἐδόθη αὐτῷ ἐξουσία) and Jn 5.27 (καὶ ἐξουσίαν ἔδωκεν αὐτῷ). Borsch objects that ἐξουσία is only one of a number of powers given to the Son of Man in Dan. But this ignores the agreement in the wording of Jn and the LXX text. Though Borsch asserts that the judicial function of the Son of Man is not specifically mentioned in Dan 7 he admits that it is implied and it is prominent in the first century tradition of interpretation (1 Enoch).

It is at this point that the importance of considering Jn 5.27-29 as a unit becomes apparent. The judgement of the Son of Man is expressed in terms of the resurrection of the dead, those doing good to the resurrection of life and those practicing evil to the resurrection of condemnation, 5.29. This double resurrection echoes Dan 12.2 where there is a resurrection to everlasting life and a resurrection to shame and everlasting contempt. The order of life and punishment in both texts is significant. Though the Son of Man is not mentioned in Dan 12 2 the tradition of interpretation implied his role in this context and Jn 5.27-29 interprets the judgement of the Son of Man of Dan 7.13 along the lines of Dan 12.2. Dan has influenced the Son of Man sayings in the Synoptic tradition and there is evidence of the direct influence of Dan on the evangelist in his construction of 5.27-29 suggesting that Jn was reading Dan from the perspective of first century interpretation illustrated by the Gospels, 1 Enoch, 4 Ezra; 2 Baruch.[20]

III. THE HEAVENLY SON OF MAN IN JOHANNINE CONTEXT

For Jn, the Son of Man is a heavenly messianic figure whose revelation brings judgement on earth. What then are the implications for the other twelve Son of Man sayings in Jn? Given that the Son of Man is introduced for the first time at the end of chapter one we might expect 1.51

---

[19]The literature consistently refers to the article by E. C. Colwell, "A Definite Rule for the use of the Article in the Greek New Testament", *JBL* 52 (1933), 12-21. Colwell shows that definite objects placed before the verb frequently appear without the definite article.

[20]From these texts it is clear that the Son of Man figure of Dan 7.13 had come to be understood as an individual, pre-existent heavenly, messianic figure. See the paper delivered by J. J. Collins at the 1991 Meeting of *SNTS* at Bethel entitled "The 'Son of Man' in First Century Judaism" now in *NTS* 38/3 (1992) 448-66, especially 464-6. Jn 5.27-29 belongs to this tradition of interpretation. See also J. D. Crossan, *The Historical Jesus*, 238–59.

to provide a key to the way the evangelist uses this term. First we note that Son of Man is Jesus' own designation coming at the end of a string of other confessional titles. It is right to say that, in this instance, Son of Man is used to correct the other confessions, not because they were wrong, but they were inadequate. This might seem to confirm the conclusion that Son of Man was the evangelist's preferred christology and the christology of the Johannine community.[21] This need not be the case. It may be the title used in the context of conflict and it is likely that it was introduced at what I have called the second edition of the Gospel. Conflict with the Jews over the Law is clear enough in the context in which 5.27 occurs and also in the context of 9.35. In 5.27 the Son of Man is revealed as the one through whom God enacts his judgement. Consequently the Jewish judgement of Jesus on the basis of the Law of Moses is met with Jesus' reference to the judgement of God through the Son of Man.

There has been something of a consensus that in the incident with Nathanael Jesus identifies Nathanael as the true Israelite (Jacob) and that 1.51 builds on the interpretation of Gen 28.12.[22] For a number of reasons I doubt this approach to 1.51.[23] If, for the moment, it is allowed, it would seem that (in Jn 1.51) the Son of Man replaces the ladder rather than Jacob, with whom Nathanael has supposedly been identified.[24] But differences from the Jacob story should be taken into account. Most importantly, in Gen the ladder is set up *from the earth* and the scene takes place there while in Jn the focus is turned to the heavens, "You will see the heavens opened". Christopher Rowland has entitled his work on apocalyptic literature "The Open Heaven". This title marks an apocalyptic

---

[21] As is sometimes asserted in relation to the call for belief in the Son of Man in 9.35 which also comes as the conclusion to a series of confessional titles. See Higgins, *Son of Man*, 155.

[22] The work of H. Odeberg (*The Fourth Gospel*, 33-42) has been seminal in this development. Odeberg noted that Rabbinic interpretation allowed that the angels were ascending and descending either on the ladder or in some sense on Jacob. It is the latter that he thinks lies behind Jn 1.51. For Odeberg the angelic traffic was between the heavenly image of Jacob and the sleeping Jacob on earth. He is followed in this interpretation by F.H. Borsch (*Son of Man*, 280) amongst others.

[23] See my "Christ and the Church in John 1.45-51" and also my "The Church and Israel in the Gospel of John", *NTS* 25 (1978) 103-12.

[24] Joachim Jeremias ("Die Berufung des Nathanael", *Angelos* 3 (1928) 2-5) suggests that the Son of Man is to be identified with the Bethel stone as the symbol of the gateway to heaven (Gen 28.17). But the Bethel stone is not mentioned in John and this approach makes no sense of the angels *ascending and descending*, which in Gen is on the ladder and in Rabbinic speculation could be upon Jacob but not on the stone.

theme dealing with revelation.[25] In Jn 1.51 revelation is signalled also by the "You will see". Given its association with the open heavens this has a character quite different from the promise of 1.50 where the "greater things" probably had its initial fulfillment in the sign of Jn 2.1-11. But the promise of 1.51 finds fulfillment in no single event such as is described in 2.1-11.[26]

It is, however, specifically fulfilled in the "exaltation" or "glorification" of the Son of Man (3.13-21; 6.62; 8.28; 12.23-36; 13.31-35) and in the light of this can be seen (by the reader) unfolded in the whole of the Gospel. Further, the exaltation/glorification[27] is not to be understood as a single event. Indeed only one aspect of this complex event can be described by Jn in narrative form. The other aspects provide a depth to the meaning of the event which is visible to the naked eye. When the evangelist explains the meaning of ὑψωθῶ (12.32) it is in terms of signifying the manner of Jesus' death by crucifixion (12.33). This explicit explanation and the focus of the Son of Man sayings on the necessity of being lifted up, which find a parallel in the Synoptic sayings on the necessity of the suffering of the Son of Man, confirms for some scholars that Son of Man is the evangelist's way of signifying the humanity of

---

[25]F.J. Moloney (*The Son of Man*, 36 n67) notes, "The theme of the opening of the heavens and a subsequent revelation of the truth is frequent in the apocalyptic literature. See, for example, Rev. 4.1; 19.11; Test. Levi 18.1-14; Test Judah 29.1-6."

[26]F.J. Moloney (*Son of Man*[2], 237 n53) gives a rather confused account of my position. See my *John*, 55. His summary ("the communication of the heavenly in the human Jesus is never fulfilled in the rest of the Gospel") of what is supposedly denied in my article misses the mark. My point is that while the promise of 1.50 could be understood in terms of the events of 2.1-11 and the like, this is not the case with 1.51. Moloney himself recognized something of this problem when he says (38), "The saying does not seem to point to any particular historical fulfillment. There is no scene in the life of the Johannine Jesus where angels ascend and descend upon him." He goes on to assert that (37 and cf. 237 n53) "The whole Gospel will be a gradual unfolding of the promise of 1.51." I agree with this position with the *proviso* that we question to whom it is unfolded. Surely the answer is, "the reader", and then we understand that "gradual" allows that although the Prologue, in a sense, reveals all, there is still room for detailed unfolding. Indeed it is only in the light of the end that the Prologue reveals all and this gives the impression that the Prologue provides the key to the true understanding of the story. This is true for those who already know it!

[27]It is possible that the connection of glorification and exaltation reflects the influence of Isaianic servant theology and in particular of Isa 52.13.

Jesus,[28] thus finding agreement with second century patristic interpretation.[29]

For Moloney Son of Man is the title[30] Jn uses only during his account of the earthly ministry of Jesus to refer specifically to the incarnate one.[31] From this perspective he denies that Son of Man has any reference to the pre-existence or ascension of Jesus. "In his pre-existent state he is called the Logos, but as man he is sometimes referred to as 'the Son' and sometimes as 'the Son of Man'."[32] For Moloney the ὑψωθῆναι of the Son of Man must refer to an event of Jesus' earthly life. "The whole of the passion and elevation to glory of the Son of Man must be regarded as a single event."[33] Thus all the references to the ὑψωθῆναι of the Son of Man concern the crucifixion and have no reference to the ascension of Jesus.[34] But Moloney fails to ask why it is that Jn chose to use ὑψωθῆναι to refer to the crucifixion of Jesus when it means "to be exalted", not "to be crucified". His argument fails to take account of the function of Jesus' death as his departure[35] and return to his former glory (Jn 17.5).

Moloney also denies that Jn 1.51 has any reference to the ascension of Jesus. In 1.51 it is the angels "ascending and descending, not the Son of Man". But the case for the heavenly Son of Man does not depend on the use of these words in 1.51, though they are words that become associated with the Son of Man in 3.13 and 6.62.[36] The case begins with the

---

[28]The strength of this position is the strong emphasis on the death of Jesus in the Son of Man sayings (3.14; 6.53; 8.28; 12.23,34; 13.31).

[29]See E.M. Sidebottom, *The Christ of the Fourth Gospel in the Light of First Century Thought*; E. Ruckstuhl, "Die johannische Menschensohnforschung 1957-1969" and "Abstieg und Niedergang des johanneischen Menschensohnes"; F.J. Moloney, *Son of Man*; M. Pamment, "Son of Man"; D.R.A. Hare, *The Son of Man Tradition*.

[30]*Son of Man*, 81. But the title, he argues, refers to the humanity of Jesus.

[31]*Son of Man*, 11,178,201.

[32]*Son of Man*, 122.

[33]*Son of Man*, 195.

[34]*Son of Man*, 61,66, "When John speaks of the human event of the cross he speaks of the Son of Man...and never of the Son (of God)."

[35]See G.C. Nicholson, *Death as Departure*.

[36]In 1.51 the order "ascending and descending" is part of the evidence that suggests that John is building on Gen 28.12. It appears also in 3.13 and is implied in 6.62 where ὅπου ἦν τὸ πρότερον implies descent which, though mentioned second is an event prior to the ascent (as it is in 3.13 also) which is yet to take place. The order of ascending and descending in 1.51 is strange if the starting place of the angels is thought to be heaven. Whereas the priority of movement is clear in 3.13 and 6.62 (first descent then ascent), there is no indication of priority in 1.51 and contemporaneous

recognition that in Jn, unlike Gen, our attention is directed to heaven. Heaven is opened and it is there that the vision of the Son of Man is revealed. We have noted that the opened heaven is an apocalyptic theme. Here, as in Dan 7, the Son of Man is presented as a heavenly figure associated with other heavenly figures. If it is argued that heaven is opened to let the angels down we note the order is first ascent then descent. Whereas Gen 28.12 has a ladder set up on earth, Jn 1.51 has the heaven opened.[37] The focus of the one scene is earth and the other is heaven. A second difference from Gen is that in Jn 1.51 the evangelist uses $\dot{\epsilon}\pi\iota$ with the accusative not the genitive case.[38] Consequently 1.51 turns our attention to the heavenly Son of Man upon whom angels converge from above and below, they come "towards" him. Jn 1.51 is an extraordinary reference to the exaltation/glorification/enthronement of the Son of Man as heavenly king. The heavenly character of the event is directly in view. Subsequently in 3.14; 6.62; 8.28; 12.23,34; 13.31 this event is referred to paradoxically in relation to the crucifixion. The Johannine perspective, is that the humiliation *is* the glorification/exaltation, or at least the beginning of it, not the precursor, as in Acts 2.33; 5.31; Phil 2.9. That is to say that, in Jn, the crucifixion is given revelatory value and is caught up

---

actions may be in view thus giving the impression of convergence on the Son of Man.

[37] Those who wish to keep the focus on earth appeal to the tradition of the baptism of Jesus where the heavens were rent/opened and the Spirit descended like a dove upon Jesus. Evidence concerning the relation to the Synoptic tradition at this point is complex. Jn is closer to Matt and Lk who both use some form of $\dot{\alpha}\nuo\iota\gamma\omega$ but not $\dot{\alpha}\nu\epsilon\omega\gamma\dot{o}\tau\alpha$. Mk has $\sigma\chi\iota\zeta o\mu\dot{\epsilon}\nuo\upsilon\varsigma$. In other respects Jn is closer to Matt and/or Mk who both indicate some one saw, in Matt it was Jesus, in Mk it was Jesus or John the Baptist; closer to Mk in that there he saw the heavens rent and the Spirit descending whereas in Matt only the latter was said to be seen; closer to Mk in using two participles $\dot{\alpha}\nu\alpha\beta\alpha\iota\nu\omega\nu \ldots \kappa\alpha\tau\alpha\beta\alpha\dot{\iota}\nuo\nu$ whereas Matt uses $\dot{\alpha}\nu\dot{\epsilon}\beta\eta \ldots \kappa\alpha\tau\alpha\beta\alpha\dot{\iota}\nuo\nu$ (Lk does not mention the ascent). Naturally it should be remembered that although this provides the correct order of ascent and descent it is Jesus who ascends (from the water) and the Spirit that descends from heaven. That Jn 1.51 should be thought of as a Johannine version of the baptismal sign is hardly likely in the light of the use of it already in 1.33. Jn 1.51 looks forward to a future event and in this regard Acts 7.56 provides a more useful comparison. There Stephen says, "Behold I see the heavens opened ($\delta\iota\eta\nuo\iota\gamma\mu\dot{\epsilon}\nuo\upsilon\varsigma$) and the Son of Man standing at the right hand of God."

[38] This point is missed by Moloney (*Son of Man*, 237 n5) who argues that my translation of $\dot{\epsilon}\pi\iota$ as "towards" "is to force the Greek, which reads $\dot{\alpha}\nu\alpha\beta\alpha\iota\nuo\nu\tau\alpha\varsigma \kappa\alpha\iota \kappa\alpha\tau\alpha\beta\alpha\iota\nuo\nu\tau\alpha\varsigma \dot{\epsilon}\pi\iota$: 'ascending and coming down *upon*'."

into the glorification/exaltation of Jesus.[39] The initial reference to the
Son of Man identifies him as an enthroned heavenly figure, but only in the
subsequent references does it become apparent that he is enthroned by way
of the cross.

The first appearance of the Son of Man in Jn establishes him as a
mysterious heavenly figure, though perhaps more mysterious to us than to
the first readers if, as we think, there was in first century Judaism a
tradition of the Son of Man as a heavenly messianic figure. The *Sitz-im-
Leben* of this use of Son of Man (in what I have called the second edition
of the Gospel) was the conflict with the synagogue in which the divinity
(5.17-18; 10.30,33) or heavenly origin of Jesus was contested (6.41-42,51-
58).

IV. DESCENT AND ASCENT

The second appearance of the Son of Man in Jn 3.13 is as enigmatic as the
first. It comes towards the end of Jesus' dialogue with Nicodemus.
Though there is no formal break until 3.22, there is a case for seeing 3.13-
21 as commentary by the narrator/evangelist in the same way as the words
of the Baptist formally continue until 3.36, and many scholars see 3.31-36
as commentary by the narrator/evangelist.[40] By verse 13 Nicodemus has
disappeared from the scene and much of 13-21 seems to have little

---

[39]I first argued this case in my doctoral thesis (Durham,1965-67) and briefly
alluded to it in my 1975 book on *John*, 53-5. A similar point of view has
been argued by Robert Maddox, "The Function of the Son of Man in the
Gospel of John" in Robert Banks (ed.), *Reconciliation and Hope*, 186-204,
especially 190, and more recently William Loader has given a paper (*SBL*,
Rome, July 1991) setting out the various interpretations of 1.51 and the
evidence in favour of the understanding of it as a vision of the enthroned
Son of Man.

[40]See, R. Schnackenburg, *The Gospel according to St. John* I, 361;
Moloney, *Son of Man*, 50,65; Ashton, *Understanding*, 374. Indeed
Schnackenburg argues that 3.13-21,31-36 originally belonged to a
kerygmatic homily composed by the evangelist. Consequently he, with
Bultmann, Bernard, and others rearranges the order of the material in this
chapter. Moloney, correctly identifies 3.31-36 as commentary by the
evangelist. He may include 3.11-21 in this category though this is not clear
from his comments. Rather than speak of commentary by the evangelist I
prefer to assign 3.13-21 and 3.31-36 to the narrator because these words are
addressed directly to the reader and the dialogue partners in the narrative have
dropped from view. This material belongs to the second edition in which
the Gospel was made relevant to the conflict with the synagogue. The
heavenly origin and divinity of Jesus are emphasized (cf. Jn 5) and the
judgement of the world brought about by his coming into the world is in
view (cf.Jn 5;9;12).

relevance to his situation. It is certainly relevant to the reader for whom a number of important associations are made. The sequence of ascent and descent, established in 1.51, is repeated but only to assert that the only one to have ascended into heaven first descended. Giving life and judgement are associated in a paradoxical fashion and the coming of the Son of Man is analogous to the coming of the light into the world (3.19-21). This theme is picked up quite specifically in Jn 9 where the conflict with the synagogue is quite explicit (9.22,34,35-41 and cf. 9.4-5).

With Jn 3.13 a number of important problems must be addressed. The first is the authentic wording of the text, then its meaning and finally the question of its polemical context. At the end of 3.13 some texts add "who is (ὢν) in heaven", others "who was (ἦν) in heaven", and others "who is from (ἐκ) heaven". In the first edition of the UBS *The Greek New Testament*[41] the editors gave an [A] rating to the omission of all of these readings and concluded the verse with the reference to the Son of Man. But in the third edition[42] that reading is given only a [C] rating. The [A] rating was based principally on the evidence of $p^{66,75}$. No new textual evidence has come to light and the shorter reading is still retained but the reduced confidence in it reflects the recognition that "who is in heaven" is the most difficult reading from which the others are explicable as attempts to overcome the difficulty.[43] Given that Jesus is the speaker, reference to "the Son of Man who is in heaven" is puzzling. The easiest solution is simply to omit "who is in heaven". Alternatively "who was in heaven" or "who is from heaven" also overcome the problem by becoming references to his pre-existence. Given that the text refers to his descent from heaven these readings fit well. Recognizing "who is in heaven" as the most difficult reading from which all variants could be derived we conclude that it is probably original.

There is also contention about the meaning of the uncontested words of 3.13. The majority of scholars translate the verse to read, "and no one has ascended into heaven except the one who first descended from heaven, the Son of Man . . . " Understood in this way the longer reading, "who is in heaven", fits quite well. It implies that the words are spoken from the perspective of the ascension of Jesus. But apparently Jesus is himself the speaker here, in his conversation with Nicodemus. To overcome this difficulty some scholars have suggested reading "and no one has ascended

---

[41] Stuttgart, 1966.
[42] Stuttgart, 1983.
[43] See *A Textual Commentary on the Greek New Testament*, edited by B.M. Metzger, London, UBS, 1971.

into heaven, but one has descended from heaven, . . . "[44] But as Ashton says, this translation "places an unbearable strain on the Greek".[45] Consequently we must face the difficulty of the asserted ascension of Jesus while he is still on earth. The preferred longer reading ("who is in heaven") understands the assertion from the perspective of the resurrection/ascension. If the earthly Jesus is the speaker this is indeed strange and has given rise to the variants. But we have argued that 3.13-21,31-36 are to be understood as words of the narrator[46] where an ascension perspective is not surprising.

Jn 3.13 is to be understood polemically against the claim that someone has ascended into heaven and come back with heavenly knowledge. The most obvious candidate to be opposed is Moses.[47] Against the view that Moses ascended and then descended with revelation Jn asserts that the Son of Man first descended with revelation and then reascended. The revealer (Son of Man) is then a heavenly figure.[48] This is the straightforward sense

---

[44] See E.M. Sidebottom, *The Christ of the Fourth Gospel* ; E. Ruckstuhl, "Die johannische Menschensohnforschung 1957-1969" and "Abstieg und Niedergang des johanneischen Menschensohnes"; F.J. Moloney, *Son of Man*; D.R.A. Hare, *Son of Man*.

[45] *Understanding*, 350. See my review of Moloney's book in *ABR* 25 (1977), 43. Like Ashton I noted that appeal to Rev 21.27 actually undermines his position. In the appendix to the second edition (245 n84) Moloney appeals to added support for his position and names Ronald Knox who argues that a Hebrew idiom underlies both Rev 21.27 and Jn 3.13. This is a desperate attempt to get around what he recognizes to be the meaning of the Greek of which Knox says, "Verse 13 runs literally 'No one has ever gone up to heaven except he who came down from heaven', but this is an eccentricity of Hebrew idiom". Given that the text is in Greek, and perfectly good Greek, this comment is not relevant. See now Delbert Burkett, *Son of Man*.

[46] Compare Jn 1.16-18 which apparently continues witness of the Baptist from 1.15 but should be understood as witness of the narrator.

[47] In Jn 5 and 9 Moses is opposed to Jesus. See on this the work of Peder Borgen, "Some Jewish Exegetical Traditions as Background for Son of Man Sayings in John's Gospel" in M. de Jonge (ed.), *L'Evangile de Jean*, 243-58. Borgen notes, Philo, *Vita Moses*, I.158f.; Josephus, *AJ* III.96; Ps Philo *Ant Bib* 12.1 etc.

[48] On the descent of a heavenly figure see the work of Charles Talbert, "The Myth of a Descending-Ascending Redeemer in Mediterranean Antiquity", NTS 22 (1975/76), 418-43. Ashton (*Understanding*, 355) strangely thinks that Jn, in his christological development, has fused the two mythical patterns identified by Borgen and Talbert. But it seems truer to say that Jn's christology is closer to one and is opposed to the other. The Johannine christological/revelation pattern is not up then down but first down and then up again.

of 6.62 also. The Son of Man is the one from above, from heaven.[49] This is the central controversy with the Jewish opponents.

In 3.13 the ascent ($\dot{\alpha}\nu\alpha\beta\acute{\epsilon}\beta\eta\kappa\epsilon\nu$) and descent ($\kappa\alpha\tau\alpha\beta\acute{\alpha}\varsigma$)[50] of the Son of Man are spoken of and 6.62 uses the same term to describe the ascent ($\dot{\alpha}\nu\alpha\beta\alpha\acute{\iota}\nu o\nu\tau\alpha$), now viewed prospectively rather than in retrospect. In 6.62 the prior descent is implied ($\ddot{o}\pi o\upsilon\ \ddot{\eta}\nu\ \tau\dot{o}\ \pi\rho\acute{o}\tau\epsilon\rho o\nu$). Characteristic of Jn is the view of Jesus as the Son of Man who has descended from heaven and has returned to his former glory (6.62). Indeed the Gospel can speak in retrospective terms as if Jesus had already returned to the glory of

---

[49]Although Moloney rejects this interpretation of 3.13 and 6.62 and asserts (*Son of Man*, 66) that "'The Son of Man' only appears in one context – that of Jesus as the unique revealer who is 'lifted up'", he also speaks of "the descent of the Son of Man as the revealer of heavenly things" (59) and asserts that the Son of man is from above (66), once dwelt with God (180), that Son of Man was used by Jesus "because he was the only man ever to come down from God". These statements seem to say that Son of Man relates to the heavenly pre-existent one as well as the human Jesus. Moloney, however, seeks to make a fine distinction, "he has descended in the incarnation and become the Son of Man (3.13), . . . " (180-1). Consequently Moloney thinks he can refer to the descent of the Son of Man while asserting that the title does not refer to the pre-existent one. But this distinction is too fine and artificial. The fact that Son of Man is not used to give detailed comment on the state of the pre-existent one reflects the perspective of the the Gospel with its concentration on the earthly ministry of Jesus. For John, that ministry can only be properly understood when it is recognized that the central character of the story is from above, from heaven, from God. Ashton (*Understanding*, 353 n51) complains that both Moloney and J. D. G. Dunn ("Let John be John: A Gospel for its Time", in P. Stuhlmacher (ed.), *Das Evangelium und die Evangelien*, 309-39) have presupposed the perspective of the Prologue as the starting-point. Given that "Son of Man" does not occur in the Prologue and, I would argue, that the Prologue is a later stratum of the Gospel providing a later perspective, it is methodologically wrong to *introduce* the notion of the incarnation in explaining Jn's use of Son of Man as Moloney does (181-2). In spite of this Ashton's fundamental criticism misses the mark because, for Jn, the Son of Man is the one from above. Only because Moloney has attempted to obscure this has he needed to appeal to the Prologue. In fact the heavenly origin of the Son of Man runs parallel to the pre-existence of the *Logos* and the descent of the Son of Man runs parallel to the incarnation of the *Logos*. Also, given that the evangelist knew what he was doing, we may assume that this connection was intentional and that the reader of the completed work has not misunderstood it when grasping this connection.

[50]For other uses of $\kappa\alpha\tau\alpha\beta\alpha\acute{\iota}\nu\omega$ to refer to the descent (of Jesus) from heaven see 6.33,38,41,42,50,51,58. The descent of the Spirit is also spoken of in 1.32,33.

the Father (1.18; 3.13).[51] Hare rejects the notion of the pre-existence of the Son of Man because he thinks that it implies that he must be understood as an angelic being, a view that is clearly not Johannine. This need not follow from an understanding of pre-existence. Hare has confused this issue of the status of the Son of Man with the question of whether Son of Man refers specifically and exclusively to the incarnate one *without reference to pre-existence or exaltation*. He also thinks that acceptance of the pre-existent Son of Man involves wrongly assuming that *Jesus* pre-existed his earthly appearance. But this problem is not tied to the use of one or other titles. If pre-existence is asserted by Jn the problem cannot be solved by using a variety of names for the different states, pre-existent, incarnate and exalted.

Naturally for Jn the flesh of Jesus was not pre-existent but assumed at the incarnation. But the λόγος encountered in Jesus did pre-exist the incarnation. Perhaps with hindsight we can say that it is the *identity* of the incarnate λόγος that is encountered in Jesus and this identity is in view in Jn's use of Son of Man. It can also be affirmed that for Jn the Son of Man is pre-existent, incarnate and exalted (via the cross) without implying angelic status even if Son of Man was an angelic figure in the tradition influencing the use in the Gospels. Further, Jn like the Synoptics speaks of the eschatological judgement to be performed by the Son of Man on the last day and in terms more Danielic than the Synoptics. Jn however has transformed traditional apocalyptic motifs in order to emphasize the role of the Son of man as revealer in between his descent and ascent (3.11-13). Naturally revealers are characteristic of apocalyptic writings but Jesus as the unique revealer has been given a distinctive stamp in Jn. As the revealer, those who receive his words live (5.24). Nevertheless the dualistic framework allows for, even demands, the role of the Son of Man in the resurrection on the last day. Thus for Jn, the Son of Man is an apocalyptic figure of heavenly dignity portrayed in terms of his descent and ascent as well as his role in the end time judgement.

Apart from various conventional references to going up to Jerusalem/Temple/feasts, ἀναβαίνω is used in 1.51 (where it does not refer to Jesus); 6.62 and 20.17. In the latter (as in 6.62) it is used prospectively of the imminent ascension of Jesus to the Father. In Jn 3.14 ὑψωθῆναι is used and Moloney argues that this verb is to be distinguished

---

[51] Both Borgen and Bühner think that the ascent affirmed in Jn 3.13 occurred prior to the descent. For Borgen "this pre-existent ascent means installation 'in office'..." "Some Jewish Exegetical Traditions", 245.

from ἀναβαίνω and that it refers exclusively to the crucifixion.[52] But Jn saw the crucifixion as an essential stage of Jesus' exaltation to heaven as heavenly king and not as humiliation subsequently overcome by exaltation as in Acts 2.33; 5.31; Phil 2.9. Naturally, for Jn, it is only believers who see in the crucified Jesus the Son of Man exalted to his reign in heaven and this is brought out in 3.15 by the implied interpretation of looking at the exalted Son of Man in terms of believing in him.[53]

V. THIRD PERSON AND FIRST PERSON SAYINGS

With the use of ὑψωθῆναι our attention is drawn to the way what is said of the Son of Man in third person sayings (3.14; 8.28; 12.34) Jesus affirms of himself in a first person "I" saying (12.32). Son of Man is used with studied intent along side Father/Son, Son of God, sender and sent one language. Naturally this means that there is some overlap in meaning but it would be wrong to conclude that the titles are synonyms.[54] Naturally the Father/Son language highlights relationship, the formula speaking of the Father as sender emphasizes his authority while the focus on Jesus as the one sent by the Father bases his dignity in the Father. In 5.27 the use of Son of Man brings to light the eschatological role of the Son of Man as judge. The importance of these observations is the obvious conclusion that the christology of Jn cannot be read out of the titles unless they are interpreted in the overall context of the Gospel. Here again we have evidence that Jn was intent to develop a nuanced christological interpretation that can be seen neither as the expression of Jewish messianic expectations nor as the common early Christian confession though it builds on both. For Jn both Jewish questers after the Messiah and many believers in Jesus were still in search for the truth which was to be found in him.

The Son of Man tradition supplies only part of Jn's christology, being taken up into "I" sayings by Jesus. This is true also of the "Son", "Son of God" traditions. The distinctive notion of the Father sending the Son is taken up by Jesus who characteristically speaks of God as "the Father who sent me". Thus, while the Son of Man is not sent and it is not said that

---

[52]See 3.14; 8.28; 12.32,34 and see Moloney, *Son of Man*, 61. As we have seen, Moloney does not think that the ἀναβέβηκεν of 3.13 implies the ascension of the Son of Man/Jesus though the same verb is used of the ascension of Jesus in 20.17.

[53]In the text in Num 21.9 it was those who looked on the uplifted serpent who lived while in Jn it is those who believe in the exalted Son of man who have eternal life.

[54]*Pace* E. D. Freed, "The Son of Man in the Fourth Gospel", *JBL* 86 (1967), 402-9

the Son or the Son of God is exalted, it is a feature of the discourses in Jn that the motifs are united in Jesus' sayings about himself which change from third person idiom to first person idiom. The theme of glorification appears to be more ubiquitous being used of the Son of Man, Son (of God) and by Jesus in self-reference. See Jn 7.39; 8.54; 11.4; 12.16,23; 13.31f.; 14.13; 16.14; 17.1,5.

In the Son of Man sayings of 3.14; 12.34 it is said that the Son of Man *must* (δεῖ) be lifted up, whereas in 12.32 Jesus says of himself, "I if I am lifted up . . . " Consequently it seems that 12.34 looks back to the δεῖ of 3.14.[55] The conversation (in 12.32-34) grows out Jesus' declaration that the hour had come for the Son of Man to be glorified (12.23), his subsequent affirmation that the hour of judgement had come (12.31) and in first person he says, "if I am lifted up". The narrator then informs the reader that Jesus was signifying the manner of his death (12.33) just as 12.24-25 shows that the glorification of the Son of Man also refers to his death *and its consequences.*

VI. KING AND JUDGE

The Son of Man motif draws attention to the nature of Jesus' kingship as heavenly king.[56] This becomes even clearer when the place of the Son of Man sayings in the structure of the Gospel is noted. The phrase "the kingdom of God" occurs only in 3.3,5 and Jesus is referred to as king in Jn 1-12 only in 1.49; 6.15; 12.13,15. But Son of Man is used of Jesus thirteen times in Jn 1-13 and nowhere after this. In Jn 18-19 Jesus is referred to as king twelve times and in 18.16 Jesus spoke of "my kingdom" three times making clear that it was not a political kingdom belonging to this world. Only when Jesus' death was imminent did he accept the kingship ascription. Prior to this the nature of his kinship was revealed in the Son of Man sayings. In doing this Jn was developing further motifs that were fundamental to the Son of Man tradition.[57]

In 5.22 it is said that the Father has given judgement to the Son but the focus is on life-giving and raising the dead, 5.21. The negative judgement of condemnation is not mentioned in the context of Jesus' ministry, cf. 3.17. What is in focus in all of this is the relation of the Father to the Son. However, both the Son and the Son of Man perform the peculiar *works* of God. In Jn 5.27 the Son of Man is depicted as king and judge. Judgement is given to him because he is Son of Man. The

---

[55]It is probable that these sayings have some relation to the Synoptic passion predictions (Mk 8.31 and see also 9.31; 10.33) where the divine necessity is also implied by the use of δεῖ with the passive voice.
[56]See my *John*, .53-8.
[57]For a brief summary of this position see my *John*, 54.

focus is on judgement but it involves life as well as condemnation. Consequently what is in view here is an exposition of the theme of 5.17 (Jesus does the works of God) though 5.27-29 has a more apocalyptic eschatology than 5.20-26 which projects the works of God into the activity of Jesus' ministry. Here it is as Son that the activity in Jesus' ministry is spoken of but as Son of Man that the end-time judgement is depicted including the judgement of condemnation. It is as Son of Man that Jesus performs the eschatological works of God.

VII. FROM GIVER TO GIFT

The three Son of Man sayings of Jn 6 form an interesting complex. The distribution (6.27,53,62) is interesting in that the first occurs in Jesus' discourse to the crowd, the second in the controversy with the Jews, and the third in the controversy with the mass of disciples. Transitions in the discourse are signalled by indications of the change of audience, time and place and *genre* as well as the function of each of the three Son of Man sayings.[58] In 6.27 there is a contrast between the food ($\beta\rho\hat{\omega}\sigma\iota\nu$) that perishes and that which the Son of Man *will give* which abides to eternal life.[59] Who is it that gives the bread that perishes? At one level it is Jesus himself (6.1-13) and the crowd had come seeking a repeat performance of the feeding miracle. Some of the crowd had seen this feeding as evidence that Jesus was the prophet (like Moses), 6.14-15. Moses, and Jesus after him, had given food which did not issue in eternal life. That food had sustained physical life for a short time. Now Jesus appeals to the Son of Man, a title signifying heavenly origin, and the bread that he will give is bread from heaven (6.33) that sustains life at another level (6.35) and this bread ($\check{\alpha}\rho\tau\sigma\varsigma$) is identified with Jesus himself, though not in a Son of Man saying. The Son of Man saying (6.27) only makes the point of the heavenly origin/nature of the food ($\beta\rho\hat{\omega}\sigma\iota\varsigma$) that the Son of Man *will give*. Jesus identifies himself with the life-giving bread ($\check{\alpha}\rho\tau\sigma\varsigma$) in a characteristically Johannine "I am" saying, 6.35. In 6.27,35 the focus moves from the giver to the gift.

Jn 6.53 falls in the middle of the discourse (6.48-58) where, in an "I" saying, Jesus *again* identifies himself as the life-giving bread that came down from heaven (6.48,50) and asserts that the bread is his flesh that he *will give* for the life of the world, 6.51, recalling 6.27. But here (picking up 6.35) there is the added identification of Jesus with the bread, now

---

[58] See chapter 6, "The Messiah and the Bread of Life" above.

[59] The use of $\beta\rho\hat{\omega}\sigma\iota\varsigma$ in this saying rather than $\check{\alpha}\rho\tau\sigma\varsigma$ perhaps indicates that Jn is drawing on traditional material not related to the feeding miracle. Alternatively Jn may have chosen to use $\beta\rho\hat{\omega}\sigma\iota\varsigma$ because it is associated with the food of eternal life in mythology.

ἄρτος (as in 6.35) not βρῶσις (as in 6.27), and it is further specified that
the bread is his flesh. This saying leads to specific controversy with the
Jews who contest the possibility of what Jesus has here offered, 6.52. The
controversial context is matched by the form of the Son of Man saying
which follows. The *content* of the previous "I" saying is repeated now in a
Son of Man saying. But whereas the "I" saying made a statement offering
life to those who eat, asserting that the giving of Jesus' flesh would give
life to the world, the Son of Man saying has a more negative and
threatening tone in stating conditionally, "Except you eat the flesh of the
Son of Man and drink his blood ...". Jn 6.54 returns to the positive tone
and idiom of the "I" sayings in which Jesus offers his flesh and blood and
the life in view here is resurrection on the last day.[60] The discourse
continues, returning to the idiom of 6.27 using βρῶσις rather than
ἄρτος,[61] with Jesus appealing to his relation to the Father as the one who
sent him. Here we see how "I" sayings draw on Son of Man sayings with
their distinctive themes and Father/Son sayings with their distinctive
themes bringing them together although the Son of Man sayings remain
distinct from the Father/Son sayings.

Jn 6.60-65 deals with a controversy between Jesus and many who were
considered disciples, demonstrating the controversial context of the Son of
Man sayings. Whereas the stress had been on the coming down from
heaven of the Son of Man/bread and the identification of the the bread with
his flesh, Jesus now appeals to the possibility of seeing the Son of Man
ascending (ἀναβαίνοντα) to where he was formerly. This is an
hypothetical question expressed formally in a conditional clause lacking an
apodosis where ἀναβαίνοντα refers prospectively to the ascension of the
Son of Man whereas the same word signals the same event retrospectively
in 3.13.[62] Reference to "where he was formerly" also asserts the pre-
existence of the Son of Man and implies his descent. Descent and ascent
imply the heavenly character of the Son of Man and it is this that
scandalizes the disciples.

---

[60]Compare the Son of Man saying in 5.27-29.

[61]Here Jn wishes to use the idiom of food and drink for which the pair of
words βρῶσις and πόσις is suitable.

[62]*Pace* Moloney, *Son of Man*, 120-3. Thus Jn uses both ἀναβαίνω and
ὑψόω to speak of the ascension of Jesus. But only ὑψόω is used to refer to
the crucifixion also because it has the sense of "exalt" and not simply to go
up. For John Jesus was not simply being lifted up on the cross, he was
being exalted/glorified.

VIII. EXALTATION AND GLORIFICATION AS
CRUCIFIXION PLUS

Jn 8.28 might seem to prove that ὑψωθῆναι cannot refer to the ascension but only to the crucifixion, especially in the light of the explanation of the term in 12.33. Jn's identification of Jesus with the heavenly Son of Man had to take account of the passion and death of Jesus. John Ashton[63] appeals to the work of Morna Hooker on Mk, who notes that, although the Son of Man in Dan 7 is predominantly a triumphant figure, he will suffer when God's authority is denied. He also notes the work of John Bowker who associates "son of man" with "man born to die". These suggestions do not fit easily with the recognition of the first century view of the Danielic Son of Man as an individual, pre-existent, heavenly, messianic figure. The solution to the problem of how a heavenly figure could be thought to suffer and die seems to be more straightforward. If Jesus came to be identified with the heavenly Son of Man the fact that he was actually crucified meant either that the concept of the Son of Man had to be adjusted to take account of this event or the identification of Jesus with this figure had to be given up. What the figure of the heavenly Son of Man does is to help us understand how the death of Jesus came to be associated with exaltation. Belief in the risen Jesus also contributed to this development.

In 8.28 ὑψώσητε refers to what the Jews are about to do. According to Jn they are responsible for the crucifixion of Jesus. But can they be said to be responsible for his ascension? The answer must be, "Yes!" By crucifying Jesus they were causing him to be exalted to heaven because this was the means by which he would depart from this earthly scene. Thus in the language of Jn the Jews will exalt[64] Jesus. Here it is said of the Jews, "when you have lifted up the Son of Man you will know that I am". Many commentators think what they will know is that Jesus is the Son of Man.[65] But the context shows that Jesus was appealing to his relation to the Father as the one sent (8.27-29) and has brought together the motifs associated with Son of Man and Father/Son in an I saying. What the Son of Man motifs contribute here is the sense of revelation ("you will know") which perhaps foreshadows the Scripture quoted in the passion narrative, "they will look on him whom they pierced" (19.37 and see Zech 12.10). But in Jn 8.28 the context implies that the knowledge

---

[63]*Understanding*, 369f.

[64]In 8.28 ὅταν followed by the aorist subjunctive active ὑψώσητε signifies a specific act to be *done by the Jews* to the Son of Man sometime in the indefinite future.

[65]There is no case for assuming that Jesus is here claiming the divine name for himself.

that comes when they have lifted up the Son of Man is too late. Hence the revelation in the Son of Man takes the form of judgement.

When it is said that Jesus/the Son of Man must be exalted (passive), a divine action is in view, especially where the passive is used with δεῖ, indicating divine necessity, 3.14; 12.34. This also could be the case in 12.32 where ἐάν followed by the aorist subjunctive passive ὑψωθῶ indicates the possibility of an act in the future to be *done to Jesus* ("if I am lifted up")[66] and forms the first part of a conditional sentence which is followed by a statement in which Jesus affirms what he will do if the condition is fulfilled, "I will draw all men to myself." But in 12.34 the crowd questions why Jesus says that the Son of Man *must* be lifted up (δεῖ plus the aorist passive infinitive ὑψωθῆναι), evidently harking back to the wording of 3.14. Thus the crowd fails to perceive the divine plan, revealing that their perception of the Son of Man/Messiah needs to be transformed.

IX. KINGSHIP TRANSFORMED

The context of two Son of Man sayings of Jn 12 (12.23,34) introduces the kingship theme. It is asserted in the narrative of Jesus' entry into Jerusalem (12.12-19) especially in the quotation of Zech 9.9 (12.15). The indication that the disciples did not understand (οὐκ ἔγνωσαν) at the time but when Jesus was glorified (ἐδοξάσθη) they remembered that these things were written of him and they did these things to him(12.16)[67] implies a reinterpreted kingship from the later perspective. This event is linked to the raising of Lazarus by the indication that the crowd that went out to meet Jesus heard the witness of the crowd that had been with him when he called Lazarus from the tomb, 12.17-18 and see 12.9. It is not, however, the response of the crowd that interests Jn but the response of the disciples with a view to contrasting response before and after the glorification of Jesus. The glorification transforms the disciples' understanding of Jesus' kingship.

This incident prepares the way for Jesus' prediction of the imminent glorification of the Son of Man in 12.23, marked by the coming of the Greeks seeking to see Jesus. The glorification is shown to entail his death and its consequences (12.24-25) just as the the idiom of "exaltation" (12.32) is explained in terms of the manner of Jesus' death (12.33). Together 12.16 (in an "I" saying) and 12.23 (in a Son of Man saying) point to the idea of revelation involved in glorification and 7.39; 16.7

---

[66]The passive, even without δεῖ could signal the divine action and could be signalled by the positive outcome of the event expressed in the apodosis, "I will draw...".

[67]Compare Jn 2.22 and note the relation to 7.39; 16.7.

suggest that the revelation involves the activity of the Spirit. The substance of the revelation involved Jesus' death which, as revelation, is concerned with the character of God. The passion of Jesus/Son of Man is understood as the revelation of the self-giving of God which can also be spoken of as the love of God in giving his Son, 3.16. It is through this event that all men come under his loving rule.

X. MESSIAHSHIP TRANSFORMED

The Son of Man saying is followed by analogies throwing light on the meaning of glorification (12.23-25). The idiom again changes to first person "I" sayings focused on glorification (12.26-28). The narrator then tells of the voice from heaven concerning glorification past and future (12.28) and the response of the crowd (12.29) before returning to the first person idiom of the sayings of Jesus in 12.30-33. The glorification is related to the "now" of the judgement of this world and the casting out of the prince of this world (12.31). What follows (12.32) is not a Son of Man saying but an "I" saying using $\dot{v}\psi\omega\theta\hat{\omega}$ which, in the third person, is used in relation to the Son of Man. Jesus here speaks conditionally, "if I am lifted up from the earth", not of the necessity as in 3.14 and 12.34 concerning the Son of Man. The narrator indicates that this image signifies the manner of Jesus' death (12.33). Jesus' death is so symbolized to show that the death is the means by which his authority is realized and revealed, bringing about the judgement of the world, which is the distinctive work of the Son of Man.

It is something of a puzzle that the "I" saying of 12.32 becomes the basis for the crowd to respond as if Jesus had spoken of the Son of Man, which they have understood as a messianic designation (12.34). It could be said that the crowd used Son of Man because of the use of the title by Jesus in 12.23. But there the saying concerns the hour of the *glorification* of the Son of Man. In 12.32 Jesus speaks of his exaltation in an "I" saying. What is more, it is a conditional "if I am lifted up. . . " saying, not an assertion of the necessity ($\delta\epsilon\hat{\iota}$) of the exaltation of the Son of Man assumed in 12.34. The nearest reference to the exaltation of the Son of Man is 8.28, but there the reference is to some indefinite time in the future ($\delta\tau\alpha\nu$) when the Jews would lift up the Son of Man. Only in 3.14 (prior to 12.34) are we told that the Son of Man *must ($\delta\epsilon\hat{\iota}$) be lifted up/exalted*. It strains credulity to suggest that the crowd of 12.34 is "recalling" the saying of 3.14. But the author of a literary work can take liberties so that it is the memory of the *reader* that is important.

The asides of the narrator such as 12.33 are generally for the reader alone so that the understanding of the crowd in 12.34 is surprising. Jn 12.34 apparently assumes that the crowd understands the meaning of ὑψωθῆναι as explained by the narrator. The "death" of the Son of Man, by whatever means, is in conflict with the received wisdom from the Law that the Christ abides for ever though some other understanding of "exalt" need not be. Apparently the meaning of the crowd's first question, "How can you say that the Son of Man must be exalted?" is, "Given that the Son of Man is Messiah who abides for ever, how can you say that the Son of Man must die?" The crowd assumes, therefore, that *this* Son of Man cannot be the Messiah and asks, "Who then is *this* Son of Man?"

Jesus' response to the crowd's question was to speak of the short time the light would be present and to call for belief in the light, 12.35-36. Here Jesus apparently equates the light with the Son of Man by answering the question about the Son of Man in terms of the light. This justifies interpreting the Son of Man as the light of the world and using 3.19-21; 9.4-5,39-41 as resources for understanding the Son of Man in Jn, reinforcing the interpretation of the Son of Man as revealer and judge coming into the world and departing from it. The sayings about being present for a little while takes up an earlier "I" saying of Jesus, 7.33-34; 13.33.

XI. GLORIFICATION PAST AND FUTURE

Jn 13.31 also concerns the glorification of the Son of Man. This saying is precipitated by the departure of Judas to betray Jesus at which point the evangelist, with a fine sense of drama, informs the reader, "and it was night". The light was present only for a little while. What follows is reminiscent of 12.23,28,34. The departure of Judas heralds the glorification of the Son of Man. The arrival of the hour (12.23) has as its equivalent the "Now" of 13.31. The betrayal of Judas is the clue to the interpretation of the glorification of the Son of Man in the crucifixion of Jesus. The crucifixion is a revelatory event. This saying goes further by asserting "and God is glorified in him". The self-giving of the Son of Man is the revelation of the self-giving of God. But 13.32 also speaks of the immediate prospect of glorification. Thus we have the paradox that 13.31 asserts: "Now the Son of Man is glorified (aorist passive) and God is glorified (aorist passive) in him. But in 13.32 two future tenses (δοξάσει) are used. How can glorification be past and future? One approach is to break glorification into two moments, the first stage being the lifting up of the Son of Man in the passion (3.14; 8.28; 12.32; 13.31) and the second being the return of the Son to the Father, to the glory of his pre-existence (13.32; 17.1-5).[68] But this distinction cannot be justified because 13.32 does not introduce the Father/Son relationship. It is the Son of Man who was glorified and will be. Perhaps it could be said that the glorification of of the Son of Man has two moments that together constitute the exaltation of the Son of Man. Alternatively the aorist tenses of 13.31 could be taken as inceptive aorists so that the glorification is set in motion by the departure of Judas. Jesus continues in 13.33 with an "I" saying to the disciples that takes up the theme which was first addressed to the Jews (7.33-34 and cf 12.35-36). The passage concludes with the assurance of the revelation of the love of Jesus in his disciples which is the manifestation of the love of God.

XII. CONCLUSION

It is the achievement of Jn that he has brought together what he has to say about the glorification of the Son of Man (13.31-32) and the Son (17.1-5) with the distinctive elements related to these titles and has united them in the "I" sayings of Jesus. What this means is that there is no Son or Son of Man christology in Jn but that motifs from these traditions have contributed to his christology and it is in grasping the way these have come together that the quest for the Messiah finally reaches fulfillment.

---

[68] See Moloney, *Son of Man*, 197-8. Moloney's intent is to preserve his understanding of Son of Man as relating exclusively to the earthly life of the human Jesus.

10

The Messiah as the Good Shepherd

Jn 10 is a complex chapter. Problems arise for the interpreter because of questions about the relation of the chapter to the rest of the Gospel as well as doubts about the order of the chapter itself. Special features, such as the ἀμήν-sayings, the παροιμία and the ἐγώ εἰμι-sayings, also complicate the task of interpretation.

It has been argued that chapters 5-10 form an important section of the Gospel in which the great debates and disputes take place. These chapters focus on conflict with "the Jews" and are bound together by a common treatment of certain themes[1] which constitute an *inclusio*. The interlocking themes of these chapters are all related to the conflict with "the Jews"[2] and recognition of this provides a key for interpreting Jn 10.[3]

Jn 10, like chapter 15, with which it shares a number of characteristics, follows a chapter that appears to have concluded its theme, yet the new chapter does not signal a new beginning. There is no note indicating a new time, place, or audience for the discourse. Chapter 10 opens with a characteristic Johannine double ἀμήν-saying.[4] Most of these sayings have an introductory quotation-formula such as, "Jesus said to them". In six instances the ἀμήν-saying is a continuation of Jesus' discourse and does not require a quotation formula. Thus 10.1, being without introductory

---

[1] In both chapters 5 and 10 Jesus speaks of the Father/Son relation in the third person as well as the first; "my father" (5.17; 10.25,29); the Father's love for the Son (5.20; 10.17); and of his own works (ἔργα) as the works of God (5.17,19-21,30,36; 10.32-33,37-38, and see 7.21-24). The works demonstrate that he has been sent by the Father (5.23-24,36-38; 10.36; and see 7.16,18,28,33; 8.16,26,29). See chapter 5.II.1 "The Context" above.

[2] Conflict is expressed in the murmuring (γογγυσμός), 6.41-43,61; 7.12-13; division (σχίσμα) caused by Jesus' word, 7.43; 9.16; 10.19; the charge of demon-possession brought against Jesus, 7.20; 8.48-52; 10.20-21; and fear of the Jews,7.13; 9.22, which inhibited open confession of faith. In spite of this, many believed, 6.14-15; 7.31; 8.30; 10.42, and see 2.23; 11.45,47-48; 12.42.

[3] In this regard Jn follows the general order of Mk: Prologue and call of the disciples (Mk 1.1-20; Jn 1.1-51); the revelation of Jesus through word and action (Mk 1.21-45; Jn 2.1–4.54); conflict stories and disputations (Mk 2.1-3.30; Jn 5.1–10.39). In both Mk 3 and Jn 10 Jesus is accused of demon-possession.

[4] The ἀμήν-sayings in Jn, of which there are twenty five, always double, are to be found in (1.51; 3.3,5,11; 5.19,24,25; 6.26,32,47,53; 8.34,51,58; 10.1,7; 12.24; 13.16, 20,21,38; 14.12; 16.20,23; 21.18. They are always placed on the lips of Jesus.

formula, is formally a continuation of the words of Jesus begun in 9.41. The tension between the formal continuity of chapters 9 and 10 and the apparent change of subject in the παροιμία has led to a widely held view that the text of chapter 10 has been disrupted. This is supported by the view that the σχίσμα[5] caused by the words of Jesus (10.19-21) fits well as the conclusion to 9.39-41, especially as 10.21 refers back to the healing of the blind man. Jn 10.22-29 is then seen as the introduction to the new section, providing a temporal and geographical note, to the effect that the incident about to be narrated took place in Solomon's porch in the Temple, during the feast of Dedication in mid-winter. In this situation "the Jews" were provoked to demand that Jesus tell them plainly whether or not he is the Christ. Verses 1-18 would then follow 10.22-29. The order suggested by Bernard, and followed by others, is 10.19-21,22-29,1-18,30-42. But there are problems with this suggestion quite apart from the lack of textual evidence for the disruption. The schism of 10.19-21 does not fit the unbelieving Pharisees of 9.40-41 but implies a broader group such as is referred to in 9. 16. The words of Jesus in 10.26-30[6] presuppose at least the παροιμία of 10.1-5. Consequently this case for rearrangement breaks down.

An alternative to a disruption theory, for which, as we have seen, there is no textual evidence, no convincing explanatory hypothesis or textual reconstruction, can be developed on the basis of the hypothesis that the Gospel was not written at a single sitting. Without denying that the evangelist made use of sources or that his work might have been subjected to later redaction, the evidence suggests that the evangelist's compositional work was a process taking place over a number of years. It is sometimes possible to discern the tradition with which the evangelist was working and to uncover layers of interpretation applicable to various stages of the history of the Johannine Christians. This evidence is consistent with a process of composition and need not imply that a different hand was responsible for each layer.

---

[5]Reference to a σχίσμα also occurs in 9.16. There it is the Pharisees who are divided, whereas in 10.19-21 it is the Jews. In 9.40 reference is again made to the Pharisees so that it can be asked if the group in 9.16 and 9.40 is the same and whether reference to "the Jews" (in 10.19-21) is simply a variation without distinction. But there is no σχίσμα amongst the Pharisees of 9.40. The dialogue of 9.39-41 indicates that this group contains only those who have rejected Jesus.

[6]Jesus answered the Jews, "You are not able to believe because you are not my sheep". Jeremias (*TDNT*, VI, 494-5) rightly concludes that the rearrangement is unconvincing.

For the evangelist, 10.1 is a continuation of the words of Jesus begun in 9.41. The παροιμία is addressed to the unbelieving Pharisees of 9.40-41. The words of 9.41, and hence 10.1-6 also, are addressed to "those of the Pharisees" (ἐκ τῶν Φαρισαίων, 9.40, and see 9.16). In 9.16 it is said that certain of the Pharisees (ἐκ τῶν Φαρισαίων τινές) concluded, "This man is not from God because he does not keep the sabbath". But 9.13-17 makes clear that this was not the view of all of the Pharisees. In fact, others (ἄλλοι) concentrated on the σημεῖα Jesus did. Hence there was a σχίσμα amongst the Pharisees (9. 16). The Pharisees in 9.13-17 should be compared with the Jews of 10.19-21, which begins with the reference to the σχίσμα amongst the Jews. The majority (πολλοί) accused Jesus of being mad, in the theological terms of the day, demon-possessed. The minority (ἄλλοι) rejected this view, drawing attention to Jesus' work of opening the eyes of the blind. Thus in Jn 9-10 there is no distinction in Jn's use of "Pharisees" and "Jews". Indeed, he refers alternatively to the Jews and Pharisees in Jn 9.1-10.21. In both groups there is a σχίσμα because of Jesus' words and actions. It is the unbelieving "Jews" who cast out the man from the synagogue (9.22,34), and it is upon the unbelieving Pharisees that Jesus pronounced judgement (9.39,41; 10.1-5).

I. THE *ΠΑΡΟΙΜΙΑ* (10.1-5)

Jn 10.1-18 can fruitfully be compared with 15.1-11. These passages recount what, for Jn, most closely resemble the parables and allegories of the Synoptics. In Jn there are other short parabolic sayings, such as Jn 5.19-20; 12.24, but no other extended parables or allegories. We may ask whether the isolation of such sayings puts us in touch with ancient traditions, perhaps authentic Jesus traditions. Jn 15.1-11 contains an allegorizing interpretation (of an implied parable) in the form of an extended "I am" saying. The παροιμία of Jn 10.1-5 is, however, allegorized only through the "I am" sayings which follow in the interpretations (10.7-18).[7] In the allegories of both chapters the relation between Jesus, the Father, and

---

[7]Naturally parable and allegory are not alien: categories, so there could be "mixed forms". In Jn 10 the παροιμία is separated from the allegorical interpretation by an editorial note (10. 6), as is the parable of "the soils" (Mk 4.11-12). Since preparing the paper (which forms the basis of this chapter) for *SNTS* Atlanta (1986), Richard Bauckham's "Rediscovering a Lost Parable of Jesus" has appeared, *NTS* 33 (1987) 84-101. There Bauckham compares Jn 10 and 15 noting similarities and the implied parable of 15.1-11. In both Jn 10 and Mk 4 the "parable" requires interpretation if it is to be understood and is like an apocalyptic riddle. The difference is that Jesus is the interpreter in Jn but because he is the heavenly revealer the difference from the angelic revealer of apocalyptic is not great at this point.

believers is set out. Unlike Jn 15, however, chapter 10 begins with a παροιμία which is introduced by a solemn double ἀμήν-saying. This saying, and the one following in 10.7, bring this discourse into relation with the recurrent use of the formula throughout the Gospel.

1. The Double Ἀμήν-Sayings

This formula, peculiar to Jn, is always placed on the lips of Jesus. It is the equivalent of the single ἀμήν-formula of the Synoptics, there also always on the lips of Jesus.[8] It could be that the evangelist has portrayed a characteristic mode of Jesus' speech, simply doubling the ἀμήν for the sake of solemnity. While Barnabas Lindars recognizes that the double ἀμήν-formula is no part of the saying that it introduces, he argues that the evangelist has used it to signal that authentic material from the Jesus tradition follows.[9] It may be that the evangelist does sometimes introduce old and even authentic traditions with this formula, but an analysis of the twenty-five ἀμήν-sayings does not confirm Lindars' view, because many of these sayings are distinctively Johannine. Given the difficulty in distinguishing the evangelist's reinterpretation of traditional sayings from his creation of sayings using traditional themes, it is not justifiable to take the παροιμία as a traditional saying of Jesus simply because it is introduced by the ἀμήν-formula.

2. The Παροιμία

Nothing can be concluded concerning the tradition used in the παροιμία of 10.1-5 on the basis of the use of the introductory double ἀμήν-saying. Nor do Synoptic parallels throw much light on the situation. The παροιμία was not derived from the Synoptic tradition, though elements of it might have been. See Mk 6.34 (= Matt 9.36) and the Q parable of the lost sheep (Matt 18.12-14 = Lk 15.3-7) and possibly also Mk 14.27(= Matt.26.31) in which Zech 13.7, ("I will smite the shepherd and the sheep will be scattered") is quoted by Jesus to foretell the way the disciples would be scattered by his arrest and execution. On this see Jn 16.32. That tradition (Zech 13.7) is not mentioned in Jn 10.1-5. Reference to the scattering of the sheep does occur in the second interpretation (10.12, σκορπίζει) and their regathering is in view in 10.16. All of this is consistent with the evangelist's reworking of traditional themes.

---

[8] See Matt 5. 18. Lk sometimes translates ἀμήν (in his source) as ἀληθῶς, Lk 9. 27; Mk 9.1.

[9] *The Gospel of John* , 355. Lindars has made use of the work of Klaus Berger, *Die Amen-Worte Jesu.*

There is widespread agreement that the παροιμία has been developed making use of traditions from the Old Testament[10] in which God is depicted as the shepherd of Israel[11] and the leaders of the people as true or false shepherds.[12] The question is, was the παροιμία created by Jesus, introduced into the tradition, or constructed by the evangelist? By isolating the parable in 10.1-5 and demonstrating its Synoptic-like character some scholars hope to show that the evangelist has derived it from the tradition.[13] The problem is more complex because the evangelist could have created this parable by using traditional themes and motifs. What is needed is an overall view of the evangelist's compositional method. This can, however, only be built up by a detailed examination of each part of the Gospel where the problems we have noted in 10.1-5 also appear. Only in certain narratives, where there are Synoptic parallels (the cleansing of the Temple, 2.13-22; the healing of the nobleman's son, 4.46-54; the feeding miracle, 6.1-15; the walking on the water, 6.16-21; and elements of the passion narrative) can we be certain that the evangelist is using traditional material. In all of this there is evidence of Johannine interpretation but there can be no doubt that there is underlying tradition. In some other instances (the healing of the paralytic, 5.2-9a; the healing of the blind man, 9.1-12) although there is no Synoptic parallel we may feel confident that the evangelist is working with traditional stories. The situation is quite different when we turn to the discourse and sayings material.[14]

In an attempt to isolate the tradition more precisely J. A. T. Robinson argued that the παροιμία of 10.1-5 is a merging of the remnants of two independent parables.[15] In the first (10.1-3a) Jesus challenges the "watchmen" of Israel (represented in the parable by the θυρωρός) to

---

[10]C. H. Dodd (*Interpretation of the Fourth Gospel*, 358-9) rightly stresses the importance of Ezek 34. See also C.K. Barrett, *The Gospel according to St. John*, 373-5; and the chapters by Beutler and Turner in *The Shepherd Discourse of John 10* edited by Johannes Beutler and R.T Fortna.

[11]Especially in Pss 23.1; 80.2 and implied in 74.1; 79.13; 95.7; 100.3. See also Isa 40.11; Jer 31.9.

[12]Ps 78.70-72; Jer 2.8; 10.20; 12.10; Ezek 34; 37.24; Micah 5.3; Pss of Solomon 17.45. See also Num 27.17.

[13]This is true of J.A.T. Robinson, C. H. Dodd, and B. Lindars. Even if it could be shown that the παροιμία was traditional, it need not follow that it goes back to Jesus.

[14]In classical historiography a degree of freedom was often taken in placing speeches on the lips of the actors.

[15]"The Parable of the Shepherd", *ZNW* 46 (1955) 233-40. Both Dodd and Lindars accepted Robinson's argument about the merging of two parables. More recently Robert Kysar, *John*, 159 has argued that the evangelist wove together as many as four distinct allegories in Jn 10.1-16.

recognize his authority, while the second (10.3b-5) affirms that Jesus' authority cannot be proved by signs. The interpretation of the first parable is implausible because that would make Jesus' authority dependent on his recognition by the Jewish authorities, "to him (the shepherd) the θυρωρός opens the door", and the interpretation of the second is more appropriate to the evangelist than the Jesus tradition. There is a double interpretation of the παροιμία of 10.1-5 in 10.7-18. But need this imply two parables? That 10.1-5 does not provide an adequate basis for the following discourse is perhaps the strongest evidence that the evangelist was here drawing on tradition, a view supported by the Synoptic-like material of 10.1-5. But if the double interpretation manifests the underlying parables, why did the evangelist merge them? The duality is evident only in the interpretation. The theory of two conflated parables is, therefore, unconvincing. The inadequacy of the actual παροιμία as a basis for the double interpretation strongly argues against the theory that the evangelist conflated two parables.

An alternative to this is to see 10.1-6 as a stratum of the Gospel to which 10.7-18 was added later. The point of the παροιμία, and to a lesser extent the first allegorical interpretation (10.7-10), was to judge the Jewish leaders by their attitude to Jesus. For this, the tradition of Ezek 34 was important, and perhaps also Jer 7.11. In Jn 10.11-18 however, the unique authority of Jesus appears to be asserted in the context of an internal conflict within the Johannine community. Probably the first interpretation (10.7-10) was slightly modified to take account of the addition of 10.11-18.[16] Consequently, it is especially the second layer of interpretation, which introduces figures not to be found in the παροιμία, that has given the impression of a double parable.

Tradition suggests the identification of Jesus with the shepherd (Lk 15.1-7=Matt 18.1-12). Certainly in Jn 9 Jesus has acted as the shepherd. He has found the once blind man, who in turn has recognized his voice and followed him. But he would not listen to the voice of others (the Jews and the Pharisees, 9.13-34, especially verses 25,30-33; and see 10.3b-5). The question then is, who is the θυρωρός upon whose recognition the shepherd depends? In the παροιμία it seems that the Baptist is thought of in this role (1.6-7,29-34), though the παροιμία can be interpreted so that Jesus is

---

[16]By the addition of πρὸ ἐμοῦ (v. 8) and of ἐγὼ ἦλθον ἵνα ζωὴν ἔχωσιν καὶ περισσὸν ἔχωσιν (10b). Hence the πρὸ ἐμοῦ (v. 8) is original, though omitted by some subsequent editors because it does not fit the affirmation identifying Jesus with the door. The implications of πρὸ ἐμοῦ are taken up again and more fully in 10b. These additions were made by the evangelist to prepare the way for the second interpretation and are part of the completed Gospel.

identified with the θυρωρός.[17] From this (later) perspective the shepherd is the leader of the Johannine community who comes to the sheep, being admitted by Jesus. The key for the identification of the shepherd is that he is admitted by the θυρωρός. Those who are not so admitted are thieves and robbers.[18] The thieves and robbers are to be identified with the Jewish leaders who rejected the once blind man (and Jesus as well as the Johannine community). Jn's Gospel can be understood at two levels. Straightforwardly it is the story of Jesus. At a second level we discern the story of the Johannine community. The story of Jesus is best portrayed if the Baptist is understood as the θυρωρός and Jesus is the shepherd. This was probably the original Johannine meaning of the παροιμία which is confirmed by the reintroduction of the witness of the Baptist in 10.40-42. Thus in the παροιμία itself Jesus is understood to be the shepherd while the Baptist is the θυρωρός and the Jewish leaders are the thieves and robbers.

3. On Recognizing True and False Shepherds

In the παροιμία of 10.1-5 the authority of the recognized shepherds of Israel is challenged. They have not come into the sheepfold by the door. They are thieves and robbers. The sheep (the Johannine community) do not listen to them. In chapter 9 action is taken against those who confess Jesus to be the Christ, not against Jesus himself as in Jn 5; 7; 8 and later in chapter 10. This clue suggests that the conflict with the false shepherds (10.1-5) does not directly involve Jesus, but the Johannine community (represented by the once blind man) and the unbelieving Jewish leaders in the synagogue who had cast them out. In the παροιμία the position of the believers is authenticated by the evidence that they hear the shepherd's voice and follow him (10.3b-5). The theme is characteristic of a sect, which justifies its rejection and lack of recognition by those outside in such terms. In condemning the leaders of the synagogue the evangelist intended to reassure the members of his own community, who were the readers or hearers of his Gospel, that they were in the right and to ground this reassurance in his appeal to the evidence that listening to his voice (the

---

[17]The saying in 10.7-10 is dependent on the παροιμία for the use of θύρα as a symbol. If Jesus came to be identified with the θυρωρός this might have determined the evangelist's choice of θύρα rather than πύλη. The two words are used as alternatives in the Q tradition (Lk 13.24=Matt 7.13-14).

[18]Reference to thieves and robbers might have arisen from the use of Jer 7.11 in the gospel tradition of the cleansing of the Temple (Mk 11.17 and parallels). Jn does not refer to this tradition in his account though οἶκον ἐμπορίου (2.16) might be a Johannine interpretation, assuming the identification of the Jewish leaders with the robbers.

voice of Jesus as it is heard in Jn) proved they were genuine members of the flock.

II. THE INTERPRETATION OF THE ΠΑΡΟΙΜΙΑ (10.7-18)

The παροιμία of 10.1-5 shares certain features with the parable of "the soils" in Mk 4. Both follow a series of conflicts with the Jews. In each case an editorial note follows, indicating that the hearers did not understand (Mk 4.10-12; Jn 10.6).[19] An explanation of the parable to "the twelve" then follows in Mk 4.10,13-20. In Jn 10.7-18 there is no indication of a change of audience,[20] though the introduction of the editorial note in 10.6 might imply such a change if it were thought that Mk 4 influenced Jn at this point. Rudolf Schnackenburg argues that in 10.7 there is "With πάλιν the beginning of a fresh discourse by Jesus (cf. 8.12,21)", which is addressed neither to the Pharisees of 9.40 nor the Jews of 10.19, but to the believing readers.[21] Indeed, the whole Gospel is addressed to believing readers, but the words spoken by the actors in the drama imply an audience within the narrative of the Gospel. The case is different in a few situations where the words of the actor fade into the words of the narrator as in 3.13-21 and 3.31-36. Those instances differ from 10.7-18 because here we are told that Jesus is the speaker and his words presuppose the same audience as 10.6, which can only be the unbelieving Pharisees. On the other hand, 10.19-21 indicates a broader audience, including, alongside the majority which rejected Jesus, a minority which was impressed by the opening of the eyes of the blind. This is the audience of the preceding verses. But is the implied audience of 10.6-7 the same as that of 10.19-21 and is 10.7-18 a single stratum of the Gospel?

---

[19]"This παροιμία Jesus spoke to them (αὐτοῖς) but they did not know what it was he spoke to them (αὐτοῖς)" (Jn 10.6). Presumably "them" refers to the unbelieving group of Pharisees to whom 9.39,41 were addressed.

[20]Concerning the quotation formula of 10.7 Brown (*John* I, 386) notes that "The manuscript tradition on the inclusion, omission, and order of these words [to them again] is very confused." They are probably original since it is easier to explain their omission than their addition. The πάλιν may have been omitted by an overly literalistic scribe who noted that this was in fact the first time Jesus had solemnly affirmed "I am the door". The αὐτοῖς may have been omitted because it obviously referred to the unbelieving Pharisees, to whom the αὐτοῖς of 10.6 also refers, while the scribe thought that the words of Jesus in 10.7-18 were more appropriately addressed to believers. The original order of the words is more problematical.

[21]*John* II, 288.

Jn 10.7-18 contains four "I am" sayings,[22] the first being introduced by an $d\mu\dot{\eta}\nu$-saying with quotation formula, indicating some sort of new beginning after the editorial note. The use of the $d\mu\dot{\eta}\nu$-saying in 10.7-10 repeats and takes up the double $d\mu\dot{\eta}\nu$ of the introduction to the $\pi a\rho o\iota\mu\dot{l}a$ in 10.1.[23] The "I am" sayings are characteristically Johannine but the identification of Jesus with the door in verses 7-10 does not fit the context of the $\pi a\rho o\iota\mu\dot{l}a$ where Jesus is thought to be the shepherd (perhaps the $\theta\nu\rho\omega\rho\dot{o}s$ at a second level). Verses 11-18 appear to be a later stratum of interpretation again which neither fits the $\pi a\rho o\iota\mu\dot{l}a$ nor the first level of interpretation in 10.7-10. The addition of this section probably led to minor modifications of verses 7-10. It is 10.11-18 which presupposes the audience of 10.19-21. The words of Jesus in 10.11-18 make an appeal to the hearers of a broader audience, whereas the $\pi a\rho o\iota\mu\dot{l}a$ and 10.7-10 condemn the false shepherds whom Jesus addresses in 9.41. Naturally, in reality the evangelist was addressing the completed Gospel to the members of his own community. Consequently, the other side, implied by the words of condemnation, is the assurance to the members of the community that they have found life, salvation. It is confirmed to them in that they recognize the shepherd's voice (10.4-5, 8), and is emphasized in the interpretation of Jesus as the door to salvation (10.7-10).

---

[22]On the formal parallel between the first two and second two sayings see Schnackenburg, *John* II, 289-90, 294-5; also the chapter by Johannes Beutler, in *The Shepherd Discourse of John 10*.

[23] The double $d\mu\dot{\eta}\nu$ of 10.7 is followed by $\delta\tau\iota$ and an $\dot{\epsilon}\gamma\omega\ \epsilon\dot{l}\mu\iota$ saying. The $\delta\tau\iota$ clause following the double $d\mu\dot{\eta}\nu$ is unusual in Jn and is sometimes taken to indicate that the saying, as it stands, is not the work of the evangelist. This argument is often combined with the view that the door symbol is not original but has displaced the shepherd motif. But a $\delta\tau\iota$ clause does follow the double $d\mu\dot{\eta}\nu$ in 8.34 and 13.21. More unusual is the use of a symbolic $\dot{\epsilon}\gamma\omega\ \epsilon\dot{l}\mu\iota$ saying following $\delta\tau\iota$. These peculiarities are not sufficient ground for questioning the authenticity of the reading, especially as the door motif is reintroduced in 10.9, where it is characteristic of a number of symbolic "I am" sayings, especially "I am the way...", 14.6. On the relation to 14.6 see J. Jeremias, *TDNT* III, 179-80. It could be that 14.6 influenced the evangelist in his choice of the symbol of the door. More of a problem is the change of use from 10.7 to 10.9. In the former it is "the door of the sheep", which is consistent with the meaning in the $\pi a\rho o\iota\mu\dot{l}a$ if the "of" is taken to mean "to the sheep". But in the latter it is the door to life or salvation which the sheep enter, a meaning which can also be conveyed by the first statement of the theme in 10.7.

1. First Interpretation (10.7-10)

While the general theme of 10.7-10 arises from the παροιμία of 10.1-5, surprising new ideas are also introduced. The "I am" saying of 10.7 surprisingly identifies Jesus with the door not the θυρωρός or the shepherd,[24] and with the door "*of* the sheep" not *to* the sheep, as might be expected on the basis of the παροιμία, implying that it is the sheep, not the shepherd, who are to enter, as confirmed by 10.9. This modification may have been influenced by the evangelist's characteristic christocentric treatment of a theme from the gospel tradition (Q, Lk 13.24=Matt 7.13-14) concerning entering the door to life/salvation,[25] a development reflected in Jn 14.6, which may have influenced the interpretation of Jesus as the door in 10.7, 9. The declaration of verse 8, that "all who came before me are thieves and robbers", fits the παροιμία, implying that Jesus alone is the shepherd. But in 10.9 the "I am" straightforwardly identifies Jesus with the door and what follows shows that it is the sheep who go in and out, not the shepherd. Verse 10 fits the παροιμία in filling out in a little detail what thieves do and identifies Jesus with the shepherd by having him affirm his life-giving purpose. Thus, what originally identified Jesus with the shepherd, hence showing the self-styled shepherds of Israel to be thieves and robbers, was subsequently modified to present Jesus as the door to life and finally modified to prepare the way for the presentation of Jesus as the good shepherd who gives his life for the sheep. This interpretation, though formally addressed to the unbelieving Pharisees, was aimed at waverers in the synagogue, affirming that only by facing excommunication and entering the Johannine community could they have life. Naturally it was also addressed to the Johannine community to assure them that they had eternal life and this was the purpose of the completed Gospel.

2. Second Interpretation (10.11-18)

Whereas the contrast in the παροιμία (and 10.7-10), was between the shepherd and thieves and robbers, in 10.11-18 two new figures are introduced, the μισθωτός and the λύκος.[26] The dominant contrast is

---

[24] This unexpected identification gave rise to the variant reading, "I am the shepherd of the sheep" in 𝔓[75] and the Sahidic version.

[25] That the Matthaean form has influenced Jn is perhaps indicated by the association of false prophets with "ravening wolves" in 7.15. But Matt uses πύλη rather than θύρα (which is used in Lk 13.24). Consequently we can assume only a general influence of the gospel tradition (perhaps Q) on Jn at this point.

[26] In the standard literature there is a lack of attention to the question why the evangelist has introduced the figures of the μισθωτός and the λύκος into his interpretation of the παροιμία.

between the shepherd, now designated as ὁ ποιμὴν ὁ καλός,[27] with whom Jesus identified himself, and the "hireling". The exclusiveness of the door in 10.7-10 is now matched by the exclusive role of the good shepherd, a role already implied in 10.3b-5,8,10, which is now spelt out in the contrast with the "hireling". The shepherd is the one to whom the sheep belong[28] and he gives his life for the sheep. The sheep do not belong to the hireling, who flees in the time of danger. Since the figure of the hireling has been introduced into the discourse, without any basis in the παροιμία, we are probably right in seeing the figure as representative of a problem in the life of the Johannine Christians.[29] What clues has the evangelist left to help us identify the figure?

The insistence that Jesus alone is the good shepherd suggests that the figure of the hireling[30] is representative of the claim of some other to be the legitimate shepherd. The claim is not identified with the problem of the thieves and robbers, that is, the unbelieving Jewish authorities. The hireling has a legitimate role, though it is relativized by comparison with the shepherd, to whom the sheep belong. Hence it seems likely that 10.11-18 reflects an internal Jewish Christian conflict concerning leadership in the community. The evangelist argued that no leader in the community replaced Jesus. In support of this he set out the differing behaviour, in the face of danger, of the shepherd and the hireling. The good shepherd gives

---

[27]The precise meaning of καλός in this phrase is debated. In Jn the term is used also of the "good wine", 2.10; and Jesus' "good work(s)", 10.32,33. Matt's use of "good tree" using both καλός and ἀγαθός (Matt 7.17-18) suggests that "good" is the correct rendering, but there are arguments for relating the term to Jn's use of ἀληθῶς, ἀληθινός, which would bring the saying into line with Jn 15. 1 ("I am the true vine..."), etc.

[28]This emphasis has already been foreshadowed by 10.3b-4a in the παροιμία.

[29]The figures of the hireling and the wolf are not necessary for the evangelist to develop the role of the good shepherd in giving his life for his sheep. This was already possible in relation to the thieves and robbers who have no other purpose than κλέψῃ καὶ θύσῃ καὶ ἀπολέσῃ. Indeed, as Jn attributes the responsibility for Jesus' death to the Jewish authorities, it would have been appropriate for the thieves and robbers to be responsible for the death of the good shepherd. Thus, the introduction of the hireling and the wolf requires explanation.

[30]While the term μισθωτός refers to a hired worker (compare Mk 1.20 with Jn 10.12-13), it is not the emphasis on payment that is in view in Jn 10. Those who are paid are not those to whom the sheep belong. Hence it is unlikely that the figure of the hireling signals a conflict between Christian leaders who were paid and the unpaid leaders of the Johannine community. The word has no different meaning than μίσθιος, which is used only in Lk 15.17,19,21. More interesting is the fact that the μισθωτός is contrasted with the θεῖος ἡγεμών in Plut., Mor., 37E.

his life for the sheep.[31] On the other hand, the hireling flees in the face of danger. In Mk 14.27-31 (and parallels) Jesus predicts the scattering of the the sheep, quoting Zech 13.7, "I will smite the shepherd and the sheep will be scattered ($\delta\iota\alpha\sigma\kappa\sigma\rho\pi\iota\sigma\theta\acute{\eta}\sigma\sigma\nu\tau\alpha\iota$)." In what follows Peter argued this would not be true of him and Jesus predicted his threefold denial. The tradition was known to Jn (see 13. 36-38 and 21.15-19). Indeed, in Jn 21 Peter's reinstatement is portrayed in terms suggesting the role of an hireling. The point is made after each of Peter's affirmations of devotion when Jesus called on him to "feed my sheep". In each case it is clear that the sheep are the flock of Jesus.[32]

The scattering of the flock (referred to in Mk 14.27, from Zech 13.7) strikes a chord with the description of what happens when the hireling flees before the wolf (Jn 10.12). The wolf ravages the flock and scatters ($\sigma\kappa\sigma\rho\pi\acute{\iota}\zeta\epsilon\iota$) it. This happens because the hireling does not care for the sheep. In the New Testament $\lambda\acute{\nu}\kappa\sigma\varsigma$ is used only six times, two of which are in Jn 10.12, and two from the Q mission charge (Matt 10.16=Lk 10.3). But perhaps the most important reference is in Paul's farewell address to the Ephesian church leaders in Acts 20.28. They are called on to shepherd ($\pi\sigma\iota\mu\alpha\acute{\iota}\nu\epsilon\iota\nu$) the flock ($\pi\sigma\iota\mu\nu\acute{\iota}\omega$),[33] the church of God, and are warned of the coming of ravening wolves. The wolves here represent those who bring heresy and schism within the flock, and it is said that some of the leaders present will do this. Also important is the portrayal of the "false prophets" as "ravening wolves" ($\lambda\acute{\nu}\kappa\sigma\iota$ $\acute{\alpha}\rho\pi\alpha\gamma\epsilon\varsigma$) in Matt 7.15 (compare Jn 10.28-29). Such false prophets shatter the unity of the community. Their appearance in the Johannine community is referred to in 1 Jn 4.1. They caused a schism in the community (1 Jn 2.19), and there is a good case for seeing the wolf in Jn 10 as representative of those who have rent the community by their false teaching.

The wolf took his opportunity in the neglect of the hireling. Once the situation of confusion had arisen, the hireling, claiming to be the shepherd,

---

[31]Here again we find evidence that the evangelist saw Jesus' saving work as involving his death for "his own". See also 1.29,36. Hence it is not correct to say that Jn portrays Jesus simply as the revealer, even if it is not clear how the death of Jesus is thought to be a saving act.

[32]It might be objected that in the dialogue of Jn 21.15-17, Peter is instructed not only to feed ($B\acute{\sigma}\sigma\kappa\epsilon$, 21.15,17), but also to shepherd the sheep ($\Pi\sigma\acute{\iota}\mu\alpha\iota\nu\epsilon$, 21.16), implying that he is portrayed as a shepherd. But those who are hired to look after the sheep also shepherd them. Further, in each of the three instances it is emphasized in the words of Jesus, "Feed (or shepherd) my sheep". Since it is emphasized that the sheep belong to Jesus, Peter is a hireling (see 10.12).

[33]See Jn 10.16, in which the work of the good shepherd leads to the creation of one flock ($\mu\acute{\iota}\alpha$ $\pi\sigma\acute{\iota}\mu\nu\eta$).

sought to assert his authority. The evangelist, however, argues that the scattering of the flock is a result of the flight of the hireling and that the confusion cannot be remedied by an appeal to authority. The use of Peter as a representative figure, as the hireling, needs further clarification. Naturally it is not Peter himself who is in view. He had long been dead by the time of this crisis in the Johannine community. Jn 10.11-13 appears to have been formed in the internal struggle within the Johannine community, which the evangelist thinks was a result of the appearance of heretical teachers. In that crisis appeal was made for the recognition of a more formal institutional authority, such as Peter represents. While the evangelist recognizes the need of leadership within the community, he did not accept the claim that the leaders hold an institutionalized authority over the community. Absolute authority belongs to the shepherd, the leaders are hirelings.[34]

Jn 10.14-18 further develops the role of the good shepherd. Initially this is rooted in the $\pi\alpha\rho\omicron\iota\mu\iota\alpha$, where it is said that the shepherd knows his sheep by name and they know his voice. This is now expressed, in words placed on the lips of Jesus, in a mutuality formula which is extended christologically to express not only Jesus' relation to his own but also his relation to the Father.

> "I am the good shepherd, and I know mine and mine know me, even
> as the Father knows me and I know the Father." (10.14-15a).

While this relation is implicit throughout the Gospel, the expression of it in these terms is unique and, according to Bultmann, signals the influence of a mystical tradition such as occurs in the Gnostic literature,[35] where it describes "the mutual determination of the elements which have been combined together into a single whole". It is true that the formula admirably fits the Gnostic schema. Alternatively, it can be seen as an expression of sectarian consciousness[36] and it is helpful to see the evangelist's image of the community as the mirror image of his christology. It should also be seen in relation to the Q tradition (Matt 11.25-27 = Lk 10.21-22). Here again we find that one of the most distinctive of Johannine themes has roots going back into the Synoptic tradition.[37] Of course it also needs to be noted that this particular Q

---

[34]The question now to be answered is, Where and how is the voice of the good shepherd to be heard?

[35] *The Gospel of John*, 380-1.

[36]By this I mean the consciousness of those who have been rejected by, and have rejected the world and who think of themselves and the world in terms that justify this separation.

[37]See A. Denaux, "The Q-Logion Mt 11.27/Lk10.22 and the Gospel of John", in *John and the Synoptics*, Leuven Colloquium1990.

passage is quite unique in the Synoptics. It is not part of a common Synoptic theme, though it could be seen as an elaboration of the Father/Son relation in the Synoptic tradition along lines that were taken up more systematically by Jn.

The clue to what the evangelist means by this mutual knowledge is to be found in the παροιμία, as far as the relation between Jesus and his own is concerned, and in 10.15b, as far as his relation with the Father is concerned. Jesus, as the good shepherd, knows his sheep, he calls them by name. The sheep know him and his voice and they follow him. Jesus' relation to the Father is expressed in laying down his life for the sheep and taking it again (10.15b,17-18). This he does at the command of the Father. Hence the Father's knowledge of the Son is expressed in sending him, commanding him, and the Son's knowledge of the Father is expressed in obedient fulfillment of the Father's will. Because of this they are one. The Son's knowledge of his own is expressed in calling them, and that call is expressed in his giving of his life for them, while their knowledge of him is expressed in obedience to his call.[38]

In both of the "I am" sayings of 10.11-13 and 10.14-18 the role of the good shepherd is spelt out in terms of his giving his life for "*the* sheep". It is given for "the sheep", not "*my* sheep", which might have been expected in 10.15, following the mutuality formula.[39] In the first saying his life-giving action is contrasted with the action of the hireling. In the second it is portrayed as the appropriate action expressing the mutuality of knowledge (10.14-15). In it he fulfills the will of the Father. Consequently it is important to stress the voluntary nature of the act (10.17-18). He has the authority and responsibility to give his life and take it up again. Thus the image of the good shepherd goes beyond that of the door because it is interpreted in terms of Jesus' death, and also, to some extent, in terms of his resurrection. 1 Jn also focuses attention on the significance of Jesus' death, perhaps in opposition to those who saw him

---

[38] On this see my *JWT*, 98-100. It should be noted that the mutuality formula is also expressed in terms of love, the love of the Father for the Son and the Son for the Father; and the love of the Son for his own and his own for him and for one another. Both sides of the relation are not, however, expressed in the same text. The emphasis is on a descending order of love, of the Father for the Son, of the Son for his own, and of the disciples for each other.

[39] By definition "the sheep" are his sheep. The sheep belong to the shepherd. But saying that the good shepherd gives his life for *the* sheep has a less exclusive ring about it than saying that he gives his life for *his* sheep. That this impression is intended is borne out by 10.16. There are other sheep which must be brought into the one fold.

only as the way of initiation into knowledge.[40] Against such teachers the evangelist asserts that Jesus is the good shepherd who gives his life for the sheep.

The shepherd also looks to the task of bringing other sheep, not of the Johannine community ($\tau\hat{\eta}\varsigma$ $\alpha\dot{\upsilon}\lambda\hat{\eta}\varsigma$ $\tau\alpha\dot{\upsilon}\tau\eta\varsigma$), to constitute one flock under one shepherd (10.16). It could be that this is the counter-strategy of the evangelist against the attempt to bring the Johannine community under the authority of the one he designates a hireling. Those who are scattered need to be united in one flock under the one shepherd, Jesus. His authority depends on the sheep hearing his voice, and the evangelist conceives of his Gospel as the means by which the voice of Jesus would call his sheep into one flock. More likely than the view that the Gentiles are intended is the suggestion that the evangelist has other Jewish Christians in mind, or perhaps the regathering of his own community, scattered through the emergence of rival teachers and false teachings evidenced in 1 Jn (compare especially 1 Jn 4.1 and Matt 7.15).[41]

III. THE RESPONSE (10.19-21)

With these words (10.19-21) the narrative context of the life of Jesus returns to the surface. The evangelist announces the $\sigma\chi\acute{\iota}\sigma\mu\alpha$ among the Jews as a result of hearing the words[42] of Jesus. It is said that a $\sigma\chi\acute{\iota}\sigma\mu\alpha$ occurred again,[43] referring to 7.43. There (in 7.37-39) the $\sigma\chi\acute{\iota}\sigma\mu\alpha$ is also a consequence of hearing Jesus' words ($\tau\hat{\omega}$ $\lambda\acute{o}\gamma\omega\nu$ $\tau o\acute{\upsilon}\tau\omega\nu$), and, as in 9.16, a variety of views is expressed before concluding that there was a $\sigma\chi\acute{\iota}\sigma\mu\alpha$. In 10.19 the schism is first stated, before indicating the variety of views in response to Jesus' revelation of himself as the good shepherd in which he predicted his passion and resurrection.[44] Yet there is no specific reference to this discourse by either side in the schism. The majority ($\pi o\lambda\lambda o\acute{\iota}$)

---

[40] On this see chapter 14, "The Opponents in 1 John" below.

[41] The hope of regathering the scattered might indicate that this discourse is earlier than 1 Jn where the scattering appears to have hardened into a schism with no hope of a reconstituted unity (1 Jn 2.19).

[42] Interestingly it is $\delta\iota\grave{\alpha}$ $\tau o\grave{\upsilon}\varsigma$ $\lambda\acute{o}\gamma o\upsilon\varsigma$ $\tau o\acute{\upsilon}\tau o\upsilon\varsigma$ that the schism occurred (10.19), while those who reject the view that Jesus was demon-possessed asserted $\tau\alpha\hat{\upsilon}\tau\alpha$ $\tau\grave{\alpha}$ $\acute{\rho}\acute{\eta}\mu\alpha\tau\alpha$ $o\grave{\upsilon}\kappa$ $\acute{\epsilon}\sigma\tau\iota\nu$ $\delta\alpha\iota\mu o\nu\iota\zeta o\mu\acute{\epsilon}\nu o\upsilon$ (10.21). Consequently it seems unlikely that the evangelist distinguished between $\lambda\acute{o}\gamma o\varsigma$ and $\acute{\rho}\hat{\eta}\mu\alpha$.

[43] Reference to the $\sigma\chi\acute{\iota}\sigma\mu\alpha$ occurs in 9.16 and 7.43. In 9.16 the $\sigma\chi\acute{\iota}\sigma\mu\alpha$ is in response to the word of the healed man. He represents the Johannine Christians who have been ejected from the synagogue because of their witness to Jesus. The focus in 10.19 and 7.43 is on the $\sigma\chi\acute{\iota}\sigma\mu\alpha$ resulting from Jesus' words.

[44] Jn 10.18 is the equivalent of Mk 8.31, etc. See also Jn 6.51-59.

357

conclude that Jesus has a demon and is raving,[45] and this might be intended as a reference to the content of the discourse. The minority (ἄλλοι) reject this view, appealing to Jesus' work of opening the eyes of the blind.[46] The majority demand of them, "Why do you hear him?" The defence does not appeal to Jesus' words, but defends them by appeal to his works, in this case the healing of the blind (10.20). This prepares the way for the subsequent charge of blasphemy against which Jesus defends his words by appeal to his works (10.31-39) though it was his words, explicitly christological, that caused the schism.

Verses 19-21 are the narrator's summary. Unlike 9.16, which is also a summary statement, 10.19-21 is appended to the preceding section. It is not an integral part of it as is 9.16 in the dialogues of that chapter. In this regard it is more like 7.40-44, to which πάλιν (of 10.19) refers. Given that 10.19-21 is a loose addition, what are we to make of it in the context of the Gospel? In chapter 9, the decision of the Jews to cast out from the synagogue anyone who confessed that Jesus is the Christ was executed on the healed man, and at the end of the chapter Jesus pronounced judgement on the unbelieving Pharisees. The situation of broken relations is also presupposed by 10.1-18. But such a situation implies that Jesus no longer walks freely amongst the Jews. Yet in the narrative of the Gospel Jesus' final conflict with the Jews remains in the future, and this summary statement brings the reader back to that perspective. Naturally the schism within the Jewish community can also be read at a second level to indicate the schism within the Christian community over the question of leadership. In the narrative of the Gospel, however, 10.19-21 reintroduces the situation of disputation, not now between the healed man and the Jews, but between Jesus and the Jews directly, thus preparing the way for what is to follow.

---

[45] It seems that "demon-possession" was a theological diagnosis and madness a popular diagnosis; see also 7.20; 8.48-53 and Mk 3.22-30. It is possible that the charge of demon-possession is intended to recall the context in which it was first made in 7.20. There it was a consequence of Jesus' asking why the Jews sought to kill him. Though they deny the charge, it is accepted as true in 7.25; see also 5.18.

[46] The reference is a generalization, using the plural τυφλῶν, hence making the case in chapter 9 typical. As such the response seems to be a reflection of the early Christian preaching rather than a response to the event narrated in chapter 9. Interestingly, in the schism of chapter 9, those who defended Jesus did so by an appeal to his signs (σημεῖα, 9.16). Again it is a generalization, not referring specifically to the healing of the man in question.

IV. THE DISPUTATION (10.22-39)

The disputation (10.22-39) has direct links with the situation of chapter 5 (and 7). It is largely the composition of the evangelist using a few traditional themes and motifs. In both chapters 5 and 10 Jesus' words concerning his relation to the Father and his *works* are closely related, and the reported attempts to kill him in chapter 5 lead well into chapters 7-10. In this context it might seem that chapter 6 is something of a diversion, not only geographically, but also thematically. This view does not sufficiently take account of the disputational character of chapter 6 and the way it concludes with the rejection of Jesus by the Jews and the mass of disciples and by noting that Jesus knew that not all of the disciples were true believers and which of them was about to betray him (6.60-71).[47] Immediately following (in 7.1) the narrator indicates that Jesus could not move openly in Judaea "because the Jews sought to kill him". He does subsequently (at the feast of Tabernacles) go up to Jerusalem and reveal himself in the middle of the feast (7.14). From that point onwards there is an open disputation with the Jews seeking to arrest ($\pi\iota\acute{\alpha}\sigma\alpha\iota$, 7.30,32,44; 8.20; 10.39; 11.57) or to kill Jesus (7.19,20,25; 8.59; 10.31,33; 11.49-50). Only chapter 9 breaks this pattern. There the action is directed against the man rather than against Jesus himself. It is also notable that there is no indication of time and place in chapter 9.

That lack is now supplied in 10.22. It is now mid-winter, some two months after the last reference to time in 7.2,14,37. The occasion is the feast of Dedication, celebrating the purification of the Temple after its profanation by Antiochus Epiphanes. That Jesus should be walking in the Temple at the feast of Dedication is quite fitting, but perhaps surprising in the light of earlier attempts to arrest or stone him and reports of his own evasive action. Indeed, the narrative seems to presuppose a situation prior to any decision to take action against Jesus or his followers. The Jews are however presented as cohesively hostile (10.24), unlike the divided Jews of 10.19-21. That hostility is indicated by the way they surrounded ($\acute{\epsilon}\kappa\acute{\nu}\kappa\lambda\omega\sigma\alpha\nu$) Jesus, and by the nature of the question and its apparent tone. The question is really a demand that Jesus should tell them plainly if he is the Christ. It ignores the fact that, according to the dialogues of Jn 9, there are already those who confess "Jesus is the Christ", and that the decision had been made to cast them out of the synagogue (9.22). The tone of the demand in 10.24 reflects the evangelist's return to the situation of the story of Jesus.

---

[47] See chapter 6, "The Messiah and the Bread of Life" above.

There is, however, another perspective which impinges on the demand for an answer. In the traditional narrative of the trial of Jesus, the demand was made that he should answer whether or not he is the Christ (Mk 14.61 and parallels). In Mk 14.62, as in Jn 10.24-25, an unequivocal answer is given. This detail, absent from Jn's trial scene, has been introduced at this point because in Jn Jesus' christological claims are made openly almost from the beginning of the Gospel. All of the evangelists set their accounts of Jesus' life in the context of such claims, but only Jn places these claims directly on the lips of Jesus, for example, in the great "I am" sayings. Hence it is fitting that this question should be put to him prior to his trial. It is also important for the evangelist that Jesus himself should defend the christology proclaimed in his Gospel because it involves a reinterpretation of traditional messianic categories. There is, in these disputations, a defence, not only against the Jewish charge of ditheism, but also against the charge laid by Christian Jews that this christology is not true to Jesus' messianic status and role.[48]

The defence is given in the words of Jesus (10.25-30), making the following points:

a. He has already told them what they desire to know but they will not believe his words;
b. His works, done in his Father's name, support his claim;
c. They do not believe because they are not his sheep;
d. His sheep hear his voice and follow him;
e. He gives his own (sheep) eternal life: they will never perish; none can snatch (*ἁρπάσει*) them from him;
f. The Father, who has given them to him, is greater: none can snatch (*ἁρπάζειν*) them from him;
g. The climax is reached in the assertion, "I and the Father are one".

The theme of a.) and b.) is taken up again in 10.37-38. Here it is clear that the question of whether Jesus is the Christ has been answered in the affirmative but interpreted in terms of the Johannine understanding of Son of God (see also Jn 20.31). The disputation is not then about a Jewish concept of messiahship but about its Johannine interpretation. In c.), d.), and e.) we find the expression of a sectarian consciousness which explains why the mass of people do not believe and reassures the few of the correctness and security of their position. That security is dependent on the relation of Jesus to the Father which is expressed in f.) and g.).

Central to the expression of these points is a dependence on the *παροιμία* and its interpretations in 10.1-18, where the relation of the shepherd to his sheep is developed, and the role of the wolf is described

---

[48]The decision to cast out of the synagogue anyone who confessed Christ(="Jesus is the Christ", 9.22) was aimed at such Christian Jews.

using the verb ἁρπάζει (10.12, and see 10.28, 29, and λύκοι ἅρπαγες in Matt 7.14). None can snatch (ἁρπάσει) the sheep from Jesus' hand nor from the Father's. If the wolf is the symbol of the false teachers, these words are a guarantee to the faithful that they are safe against such onslaughts. What guarantees their safety is Jesus' hand which guards them. He guards them because the Father has given them to him.

Now comes the paradox that is essential to the Johannine christology. The Father is greater than the Son and his hand also protects the sheep. But there are not two protecting hands because the Son and the Father are one. Here we find, in enigmatic form, the argument based on the relation of the Son to the Father that was set out in 5.17,19-30. The truth is that Jesus does the will and work of God, which he was sent to do, so that what he does the Father does. There can be no distinction between the two agents in the action. Yet the Son is not the Father, who is greater than the Son, though the Son has come to make the Father known and to do his work. In the language of the emissary, applied to Jesus, and the affirmation that the Father is greater, we find evidence of subordination. But in the Father/Son relation and the language of unity (and equality, 5.18) there is evidence of an ontological equality. Perhaps the closest we can get to the formulation of Jn's view is that he proposed an ontological equality and a functional subordination because if Jesus did not do the Father's will he could not make the Father known.[49]

This christology was developed in the conflict with the synagogue; and the charge of blasphemy which follows in 10.31-39 was a natural response to it, with the indication that the Jews again (πάλιν) took up stones to stone Jesus.[50] Jesus' appeal to the many good works[51] which he had shown them from (ἐκ) the Father[52] (10.32 and see 10.25), like the appeals in 9.16 and 10.21, is a generalized appeal to works, though he then asks

---

[49]Jesus' words can be understood as a response to the charge of ditheism which was probably brought against the Johannine Christians. Jesus' response was to affirm "not two powers or authorities in heaven but one". On this matter see A. Segal, *Two Powers in Heaven.*

[50]Jn 10.31,33 and for a previous attempt to stone Jesus see 8.59. Attempts to arrest or kill Jesus occur frequently in chapters 5-11 (5.16,18; 7.19,20,25,30,32,44; 8.20; 10.39; 11.57).

[51]As in the designation "good shepherd" the evangelist uses the adjective καλός (here the neuter plural καλά) rather than ἀγαθός.

[52]In 10.25 Jesus refers to "the works I do in the name of my Father", and in 10.35 he answers, "Many good works I showed you from (ἐκ) the [or my] Father". In the former we have the language of agency, depicting Jesus as the emissary of the Father, while in the latter we find the language of ontological unity, asserting that the works done by Jesus originate in the Father.

which of these works is the basis for their decision to stone him. Here (10.32) there is an emphasis on the good works (ἔργα καλά) not made in 9.16 and 10.21, though it may be implied in the reference to such signs (τοιαῦτα σημεῖα), and in the assumption that opening the eyes of the blind (plural) is a good act. Here no room is left for ambiguity. Jesus asserts the goodness of his works. This is not contested. But it is not allowed (by the Jews) to have a bearing on the dispute. The reference to works (ἔργα), with the dispute which follows, indicate that we have returned to the theme of chapter 5, especially 5.16-30. Indeed, it may be that the charge of working on the sabbath suggested the appropriateness of the term "works" at this point.

In 5.17 Jesus justified his action on the sabbath by appeal to the accepted view that God works on the sabbath. In itself that was no justification for his own action. It would only justify him if he could show the identity of his action and the action of God. Calling God his own (ἴδιον) Father in this context was (according to the Jews) to make himself equal (ἴσον)[53] to God. In what follows in chapter 5 it is argued that equality does not imply independence but dependence. Only because the Son does the Father's will can he make the Father known and there can be an identity of action. In Jn 10 the Jews follow the same logic as they had expressed in chapter 5. Jesus' speaking of God as his Father is now formally called blasphemy because it is understood in terms of a man claiming to be God (10.33).

Jesus' defence here, unlike in chapter 5, takes the form of an appeal to the Jewish Torah.[54] The logic is simple and follows the pattern of rabbinic argument. If, in the Torah, those to whom the word of God came are called gods, how much more appropriate is the term for the one whom the Father sanctified and sent into the world. The precedent in Scripture justifies the ascription of the title "god" or "son of God" to the emissary of God.[55]

At the level of the language the ascription of the title "son of God" is said to be justified in that Jesus is demonstrably the emissary of God. The works are the evidence. The language of sonship and the works form a

---

[53] See Phil 2.6 and chapter 5, "The Paradigm of Rejection" above for a more extensive treatment of Jn 5.17.

[54] Is it not written in *your* Law (ἐν τῷ νόμῳ ὑμῶν)", and what follows is an appeal to Ps 82.6. On the significance of this see the articles by Anthony Hanson "John's Citation of Psalm 82", *NTS*, 11 (1964-65), 158-62 and "John's Citation of Psalm 82 Reconsidered", *NTS*, 13 (1966-67), 363-7. With these words, Jesus has distanced himself from the Jews by disavowing that it is also his Law.

[55] This form of argument may be dependent on tradition. It is similar to Mk 12.35-37 in the way it uses a scriptural precedent as justification.

unity. This emissary christology has its roots in the Synoptic tradition, for example in the Q passage found in Matt 10. 40 and Lk 10. 16 and in Mk 9.37 and parallels. There Jesus says that the disciples stand in the same relation to him as he does to the one who sent him (ἀποστείλαντα με), a saying to be compared with Jn 13.20, except that there the verb πέμπω is used (τὸν πέμψαντα με). Given that, in Jn, the two verbs are used more or less synonymously (of the sending of Jesus, and the disciples) the use of different verbs is not theologically significant.[56] The points of contact with the Synoptics show that the evangelist is drawing on tradition.

Characteristically, the evangelist has Jesus speak, not only of "the one who sent me", but of "the Father who sent me"(ὁ πέμψας με πατήρ). The emissary is not only sent, he is the one "whom the *Father* sanctified and sent into the world" (ὃν ὁ πατὴρ ἡγίασεν καὶ ἀπέστειλεν εἰς τὸν κόσμον, 10.36). The Father/Son relation is an essential ingredient, and the notion of being sent *into the world* implies more than an emissary christology. It implies that the emissary is not merely a human messenger but comes from the divine side of reality into the world. With the combination of functional and ontological sonship we find the distinctive Johannine christology, which is the result of a reinterpretation of the tradition.

The argument concludes (10.37-38) with an appeal to take account of the works. Perhaps that implies that even the provisional acceptance of emissary status is an acceptable beginning, though Jesus' own words call for the acceptance of an ontological sonship. The argument that follows shows that beginning with the works will lead on to understanding the ontological sonship of Jesus since, "the Father is in me and I in the Father" (10.38), which is a variation on the theme expressed in 10.30, "I and the Father are one". The form of the argument seems to be aimed at those who already acknowledge Jesus as Messiah rather than at outright Jewish opponents. It is likely that the Johannine christology appeared as blasphemy to early Christian Jews. What the evangelist does is to show the implications of believing that Jesus does the works of God and to argue that recognition of Jesus as a messenger of God implies recognizing him as Son of God, one with God, in whom God is present and acting. The consequence of the argument is that the Jews again (πάλιν) sought to arrest (πιάσαι) Jesus, but he evaded them (10.39).[57]

---

[56]On the place and importance of the language of sending in Jn see chapter 5, "The Paradigm of Rejection", part IV "The Christology of the Discourse" above.

[57]At this point we have returned to the situation of 8.59. There the Jews took up stones to stone Jesus but he withdrew secretly from the Temple.

V. TRANSITIONAL SUMMARY (10.40-42)

The transitional note, appropriately following 10.39 indicates Jesus' return to the place where John was first baptizing, and provides the context for the final contrast between John and Jesus (10.41). The role of John as witness is reiterated and, in denying that he performed any signs, the evangelist cleverly draws attention to the signs of Jesus and the many who believed because of them, suggesting that 10.40-42 was the original transition to the Passion story. Alternatively, the reference to the Baptist might have originally followed the $\pi\alpha\rho\omega\mu\dot{\iota}\alpha$, to draw out for the reader the identification of the Baptist as the $\theta\nu\rho\omega\rho\dot{o}\varsigma$. The emphasis on Jesus' signs continues the theme from chapter 10 while reaffirming the legitimacy of the Baptist as a witness to Jesus. The probability is that this material is developed on the basis of tradition, though it has been thoroughly reworked by the evangelist. Reference is made to the signs ($\sigma\eta\mu\epsilon\hat{\iota}\alpha$), not to the works ($\check{\epsilon}\rho\gamma\alpha$), which would have been more in keeping with the language and theme of chapter 10. But it could be a mistake to attribute this to the influence of a source because it is the Johannine Jesus who characteristically speaks of his works while the narrator indicates that the masses believe on the basis of the signs (2.23; 3.2; 6.2,14; 11.45,47-48; 12.18,37,42). In the words of the narrator the contrast of 10.41 implies that Jesus did many signs and that this is the basis of the belief of the many mentioned in 10.42 which is not unrelated to the witness of the Baptist (1.6-8) who himself did no signs.

In this place Jesus stayed ($\check{\epsilon}\mu\epsilon\iota\nu\epsilon\nu$),[58] and many came to him. Here the account is to be understood at the level of the story of Jesus. Whatever opposition he may have faced from the institutional leadership of the Jews, his popularity amongst "the masses" ($\pi\omega\lambda\lambda o\dot{\iota}$) seems clear. Consequently it is indicated that "many ($\pi\omega\lambda\lambda o\dot{\iota}$) believed in him there".[59] It is interesting and important to note that here the evangelist does not put in question the faith of the masses, as he does, for example, in 2.23 and 12.42. Obviously signs have their place in the process of the development of faith and the construction of the Johannine christology.

---

[58] Although this is a significant word for the evangelist it is unlikely that any overtone is intended here. Perhaps it was already to be found in the tradition used by the evangelist.

[59] On the use of this phrase see, 2.23; 7.31; 8.30; 11.45,47-48; 12.42. Another use of $\pi\omega\lambda\lambda o\dot{\iota}$ in the Gospel (10.20) indicates that "many" Jews reject Jesus. The evangelist's own perspective involves reserve about the mass response of belief in his signs.

VI. CONCLUDING REMARKS

In plotting the course of the history of Johannine christology the following points can tentatively be made: a.) Signs were used in the early stages of Johannine history to demonstrate Jesus' messianic status in the debate with the synagogue and it could be that, in relation to Baptist loyalists, the aim was to show that Jesus, not John, was the Messiah. b.) In the debate with the synagogue where Jesus' opposition to Moses and the Torah was stressed, the evangelist emphasized Jesus' status and role as the emissary from God. Here he was able to use traditional material which suited his purpose. c.) Given the logic of the evangelist's argument, Jesus' mission from God implies an ontological relation to God. Hence the traditional language is reinterpreted to develop a christology of functional and ontological sonship, an emissary and incarnational christology.

On the basis of our analysis of the παροιμία in Jn 10.1-5 and its subsequent interpretations, certain conclusions can be drawn about history and tradition in that chapter: a.) The basic contrast drawn in the παροιμία is between the shepherd and the thieves and robbers. It appears that (in the παροιμία) Jesus is to be identified with the shepherd and that the Baptist is the θυρωρός. b.) Only in the interpretation that follows (10.7-10) is he identified with the door to salvation. In the first interpretation, as in the παροιμία, the thieves and robbers are identified with the Jewish leaders who have rejected Jesus and his followers. c.) In the παροιμία the shepherd can only represent Jesus or, at a secondary level, the leader (the evangelist) or leaders of the Johannine community. It is possible that 10.1-5 is a traditional parable, though it is more likely a composition of the evangelist, using traditional themes and motifs. d.) In the second interpretation (10.11-18), Jesus is the good shepherd. The theme of recognizing his voice, which dominates the παροιμία (3b-5), and is important in chapter 9 (35-38), is now muted. In its place is the emphasis on the good shepherd laying down his life and taking it again, for which the παροιμία has not prepared the reader. The thieves and robbers have disappeared, and with them, it seems, the conflict with the synagogue. In their place we find two figures who have not appeared in the παροιμία, the "hireling" and the "wolf". The focus on the "hireling" reflects a leadership struggle within the community. The evangelist appeals to the direct relationship between the good shepherd and those who respond to his voice. The treatment of the denial and restoration of Peter suggests that we have here a reflection of a struggle with Petrine Christianity. That struggle might well have developed after the Johannine community was ravaged by a schism caused by what the evangelist perceived as false teaching.[60] The false teachers are portrayed as ravening wolves that scatter the flock. The shepherd's aim was to re-gather the flock. It is interesting that, in 1 Jn and in Jn 10.11-18, focus falls on the significance of Jesus' giving his life (soteriology), something which "the opponents" in 1 Jn either ignore or deny. Consequently, a case can be made for seeing the later strata of the Gospel as more or less contemporary with 1 Jn, though probably prior to the hardening of the schism of 1 Jn 2.19.

In Jn 10 the quest for the Messiah passes through various stages. There is first the debate within the synagogue about whether Jesus is the Messiah and an attempt to establish criteria for testing his claims. The proclamation of Jesus as the good shepherd in the context of a conflict with the Jewish leaders suggests that Jesus is being portrayed as the legitimate or ideal ruler and in Jewish terms this is the Messiah. For Jn this involves developing his distinctive christology which appears to have led to conflict with others who confessed Jesus to be the Messiah. There was conflict with Judaism because the work of the Messiah was interpreted as giving his life for the sheep, a suffering and dying Messiah, to be resurrected to be sure. This conflict with other believers can be seen in two stages. The first was in relation to conservative Jewish Christian belief in Jesus which held reservations concerning Jesus' divine sonship which is expressed in terms of the the mutual knowledge of the Father and the Son (Jn 10.14-15). The second was a response to the devaluing of the human life of Jesus and especially the saving quality of his death. Significantly the later strata of the Gospel and 1 Jn as a whole stress the importance of Jesus' saving death and this complex of material will be illuminated in the context of the discussion of 1 Jn. Thus the Johannine tradition develops from a focus on christology with an implied soteriology to an explicit soteriology in the later strata.

---

[60] On the relation of this stratum of the Gospel to the opponents in 1 Jn see chapter 14, "The Opponents in 1 John" below.

11

The Quests Continue

Like Jn 7 chapter 11 presupposes that the situation in Judaea no longer permits Jesus to move freely there. In 7.1 it is the narrator who tells us

> Jesus did not wish[1] to walk in Judaea, because the Jews were seeking (ἐζήτουν) to kill him.

In Jn 11 it is the disciples who, in an attempt to dissuade Jesus from going up to Jerusalem, remind (?) him:[2]

> "Rabbi, even now the Jews are seeking (ἐζήτουν) to stone you" (Jn 11.8)

While in Jn 7 Jesus had every intention of going up to Jerusalem, the suggestion that he should do so, which Jesus openly rejected, was made by his unbelieving brothers, 7.5. In Jn 11 the suggestion was made by way of the message from Mary and Martha and this, given that they expected Jesus to do something to save Lazarus, is to be understood as a believing request.[3] Nevertheless there is a degree of parallelism between Jn 7-8 and Jn 11.

I. THE QUEST OF MARY AND MARTHA (11.1-45)

The story of the raising of Lazarus raises special problems. Without Synoptic parallel it can be questioned whether the evangelist has constructed the story from Luke's mention of Martha and Mary (Lk 10.38-42) and the parable about the rich man and Lazarus (Lk 16.19-31)[4] or has access to an independent tradition. The question seems to be impossible to answer with any degree of probability. Recognition of traditions independent of the Synoptics in other parts of Jn leads to a reluctance to attribute to a Synoptic source traditions that show minor contact with the Synoptics but widely diverge from them. While it is possible that the evangelist is responsible for such differences, evidence that this was the

---

[1] A less likely reading is "he did not have authority" (εἶχεν ἐξουσίαν). This reading has much less impressive ms support and can be explained as an expression of reluctance to indicate that Jesus did not wish to go to Judaea when in the course of the narrative he would soon make the journey there (7.10).

[2] See 8.59; 10.31. The use of the imperfect (ἐζήτουν) in 11.8 indicates repeated attempts.

[3] Cf. Jn 2.3; 4.47.

[4] See Barrett, *John*, (1978²), 389-90.

case is difficult to establish.[5] Our concern is whether or not the evangelist was responsible for the quest story. The extent and complexity of this story suggest that the evangelist himself has developed the quest story which is shot through with Johannine features. As with chapter 6 the evangelist has subsequently over-laid the quest story with the theme of rejection.

There are similarities between the opening of this story and the introductions to the stories of Nicodemus and the "lame man" of Jn 5 who are introduced ἦν δὲ ἄνθρωπος and ἦν δὲ τις ἄνθρωπος. In Jn 11.1 it is ἦν δὲ τις ἀσθενῶν and in spite of the use of τις Lazarus is used as a representative figure.[6] But before he can become representative he must die. The death of Lazarus then symbolizes that all are dead and that those who hear the voice of the Son of God will live (Jn 5.25) and that those in the tombs will hear his voice and come forth (5.28-29). That a symbolic interpretation of the story is intended by the evangelist is clearly indicated by the profound pronouncement by Jesus to Martha:[7]

> "I am the resurrection and the life; he who believes in me even if he should die he will live, and every one living and believing in me shall certainly not die for ever. Do you believe this?" (Jn 11.25-26)

The story, told by the narrator who sets the scene and provides continuity, proceeds by means of a number of dialogues in which Jesus remains the central figure:

1. Jesus and the messenger(s) from the sisters, 11.3(4).
2. Jesus and his disciples, 11.7-16.
3. Jesus and Martha, 11.20-27.
4. Martha and Mary 11.28.
5. Mary and Jesus, 11.32.
6. Jesus and the Jews, 11.34-37,39.
7. Martha and Jesus, 11.39-40.
8. Jesus and the Father, 11.41-42.
9. Jesus and Lazarus, 11.43.
10. The Sanhedrin debate, 11.47-50.
11. Discussion amongst "the many" in Jerusalem, 11.56.

The story is introduced strangely. Lazarus, whose resurrection is about to be narrated, is identified as being from Bethany, the village of Mary and

---

[5] Here I am less optimistic than some scholars that it is possible to detect the redactional traits of Mk or even of Matt and Lk where we are dealing with the material found only in each of those Gospels.

[6] Compare the role of the blind man in Jn 9.

[7] Compare the reiterated pronouncement of Jn 9.5, cf.8. 12.

her sister Martha.[8] In other words, he was identified by reference to them. Mary is further identified by a note (11.2) indicating that she was the one who had anointed the Lord ($\tau \grave{o}\nu \, \kappa \acute{u}\rho \iota o\nu$)[9] and wiped Jesus' feet with her hair and Lazarus, who was sick, was her brother. Hence, an event that has not yet been narrated (see Jn 12.1-8) is used to identify Mary and she, as the known person, is the point of reference for the identification of Lazarus.[10] It could be suggested that the order of the two events should be reversed but then the anointing is prefixed by reference to the raising of Lazarus, 12.1.[11] A more likely solution is that the anointing was taken to be a widely known event to which reference could be made even before it had been narrated.[12] In 11.5 Martha is mentioned first, then her sister (but without name) and finally Lazarus without mentioning that he was the brother of Mary (and Martha, see 11.20). Here it is said that Jesus loved ($\acute{\eta}\gamma \acute{a}\pi a$) them, that is, Martha, Mary and Lazarus. In 11.19 it is said that many of the Jews had come to comfort Martha and Mary (in that order) and it is Martha who first goes out to meet Jesus (11.20). Her conversation with Jesus runs from 11.20-27 commencing with:

"$K\acute{u}\rho \iota \epsilon$, if you had been here my brother would not have died." (11.20)[13]

and concludes with her impressive confession of faith:

"Yes $K\acute{u}\rho \iota \epsilon$, I have believed that you are the Christ the Son of God who is coming into the world." (11.27)

Given that (in the first instance) Mary is introduced first and is given an impressive introduction it is strange that Martha should be Jesus' leading dialogue partner in this story. Not only is the scene between Jesus and Martha longer than the other dialogues, her scene concludes with the

---

[8]Mary is mentioned first and then Martha.

[9]This use of "the Lord" by the narrator is less ambiguous than the vocative ($\kappa \acute{u}\rho \iota \epsilon$) which can be translated as a polite "sir" and is used by the messengers (11.3) and by the disciple (11.12).

[10]That Lazarus needs such elaborate identification by itself excludes the possibility that he was the BD. Although it is first mentioned in the message to Jesus that Jesus loves Lazarus ($\kappa \acute{u}\rho \iota \epsilon$, $\mathit{l}\delta \epsilon \, \mathit{\delta}\nu \, \phi \iota \lambda \epsilon \hat{\iota}s \, \mathit{d}\sigma \theta \epsilon \nu \epsilon \hat{\iota}$, 11.3 and cf. 11.36) it follows soon after (11.5) that Jesus loved ($\acute{\eta}\gamma \acute{a}\pi a$) Martha and her sister and Lazarus. The two verbs for love are used in Jn without distinction of meaning. There is nothing here to suggest Lazarus is the BD.

[11]This should warn us against hasty rearrangements of Jn on the basis of what appear to us to be incongruous temporal links in the narrative.

[12]See Matt 26.13; Mk 14.3-9.

[13]Compare the repetition of this refrain by Mary (11.32) and the Jews (11.37). Apart from the placing of $\mu o\nu$ the wording used by Martha and Mary is identical.

impressive confession of 11.27. This suggests that she has penetrated the mystery surrounding Jesus' person and has given expression to it in characteristic Johannine terms. But in what follows it appears that Martha no more than the disciples has yet grasped this. She announces to Mary only that the teacher (διδάσκαλος) has come (11.28) and when Jesus orders the removal of the stone it is Martha who objects:

"Κύριε, already he stinks, for it is four days." (11.39)

These words certainly show no grasp of Jesus' assurance that Lazarus will rise from the dead because Jesus is the resurrection and the life. Consequently Jesus' words (of 11.25-26) appear to have escaped Martha and her understanding remains tied to the traditional belief about resurrection on the last day (11.24) in spite of the confession of 11.27.

The quest is expressed in the sending,[14] by Mary and Martha, of (a) messenger(s) to inform Jesus of the sickness of Lazarus, 11.3:

"Κύριε, the one you love (φιλεῖς) is sick."

The information obviously carries with it an implied request and this is understood, as Jesus' dialogue with the disciples[15] makes clear, 11.4-16.[16] The disciples object to Jesus' announcement that they are going again to Judaea saying (Jn 11.8):

"Rabbi, the Jews are now seeking (ἐζήτουν) to stone you, and are you going there again?

An attempt to stone Jesus was mentioned in 10.31 and more recently (10.39) that "they were seeking (ἐζήτουν) again to arrest him". In both 10.39 and 11.8 the imperfect tense (ἐζήτουν) indicates ongoing or repeated attempts. Thus two quests (for the resurrection and to kill Jesus) have come together in Jn 11 and eventually we will see that the two quests are one.

The first obstacle to be overcome if the quest of Mary and Martha is to succeed is the threat that the Jews of Judaea pose to Jesus, 11.8,16. This threat may have been overlaid on the quest story, preparing the way for the rejection of Jesus which becomes prominent in 11.46-57. Jesus' justification for going to Judaea in the face of the threat is comparable to

---

[14]Here ἀπέστειλαν recalls the sending of the messengers to question John in Jn 1.19.

[15]The role of the disciples in Jn 11 is restricted to the dialogue about whether to go up to Judaea or not (11.6-16) and the subsequent departure into the desert to a town called Ephraim, 11.54. There is no sign of the disciples in the dialogues between 11.17-53. The reason for this is probably the evangelist's approach to constructing dialogues between two parties. Introduction of the disciples into any of these scenes would have detracted from the focus of the dialogues.

[16]11.4,9-10 should be compared with 9.3-5.

Jn 9.4 and see 11.9-10. The reason for delay has already been stated in 11.4 and is explained more fully in 11.14-15. Jesus' delay was planned in order that Lazarus would die and be dead long enough for his death to be beyond doubt. Both Martha and Mary express a reproach to Jesus by asserting that, had he been present, Lazarus would be alive, 11.21,32.[17] The death of Lazarus then constitutes the second obstacle to be overcome and the seriousness of this is emphasized by the evidence that he had been dead for four days.[18] The perspective of the questers is that, though they consider that Jesus could have prevented the death of Lazarus, they do not conceive that there is anything he can do once Lazarus is dead (11.21,32). This also appears to be the position of the Jews who were present as mourners, 11.37. It is possible that Martha implied that with Jesus now present there was still hope, 11.22. But this appears to be ruled out by her response to Jesus' affirmation "your brother will rise from the dead" (11.23), which she understood as an event on the last day (11.24) in terms of traditional eschatology and by her response to Jesus' command to remove the grave stone (11.39). Thus the real obstacle to be overcome is the unbelief of Martha and Mary (11.40).

Certainly a level of belief is indicated in the message sent to Jesus by Mary and Martha. But since the sending of the message a new obstacle has arisen. The critically sick Lazarus has died. If this were not bad enough, four days have passed since his death and all hope of his recovery has now been lost. Jesus moves from a discussion of the traditional Jewish belief in the resurrection on the last day to the significant *pronouncement* of 11.25-26:

> "I am the resurrection and the life; he who believes in me even if he should die he will live, and everyone living and believing in me shall certainly not die for ever. Do you believe this?"

To this question Martha responds affirmatively:

> "Yes Lord (κύριε), I have believed that you are the Christ the Son of God who is coming into the world."

---

[17]Apart from word order in the second part of the saying the wording of the two sayings is identical so that the expectation and reproach becomes a refrain. The refrain is repeated, with variation, also by the Jewish mourners in 11.37. They made mention of the opening of the eyes of the blind man as precedent for the expectation that Jesus could have saved Lazarus from death. There is no suggestion that he might raise him from death.

[18]11.39. This suggests that Lazarus died soon after the messengers were sent. The four days allow one for the journey of the messengers, two for the intentional delay of Jesus (11.6) and one for the journey by Jesus and his disciples.

This affirmation is the climactic *confession* of faith in this chapter[19] and the reader might have expected to proceed directly to the account of the resurrection of Lazarus. But some further scenes must yet be narrated. In these Mary reiterates Martha's point of view (11.32) as do the Jews who were present, 11.37.[20]

At the tomb a further scene is described in terms which set up a contrast with the portrayal of Jesus' resurrection.[21] The stone remained sealing the tomb of Lazarus and Jesus commanded that it should be taken away. The objection of Martha (11.39) confirms that she had not comprehended Jesus' words (11.25-26). Yet Jesus persisted affirming

"Did I not tell you,'If you believe you will see the glory of God'?" (11.40)

Nowhere does the evangelist report Jesus speaking these words at an earlier stage and certainly not to the assembled group. Perhaps they are to be understood as a summary of Jesus' words to Martha (11.25-26) though the words are closer to Jesus explanation to the disciples:

"This sickness is not to death but for the glory of God, that the Son of God may be glorified through it." (Jn 11.4)

The action that follows Jesus' challenge to belief is to be understood as an affirmation of faith. They removed the stone from the tomb. According to the narrator the actions and words of Jesus that follow were for the benefit of the crowd that was present, "that they may believe that you sent me", 11.42. The manner of the raising of Lazarus was staged by Jesus to reveal his relation to the Father. Consequently Jesus' words were publicly addressed to God as "Father" and with eyes uplifted. Having established the relationship Jesus cried out with a loud voice, "Lazarus, come forth!" And he came out bound hand and foot in the grave clothes until Jesus told them to loose him and let him go.

---

[19]The confession that Jesus is the Christ is deepened by the addition of the Johannine understanding of the Son of God which is signalled by the words "who is coming into the world". The reinterpretation of the understanding of Jesus as the Christ (Messiah) is one of the significant accomplishments of Jn. Cf. 20.30-31.

[20]The Jews here accept that Jesus has given sight to the blind man (Jn 9) and ask if he could not have prevented the death of Lazarus. The implied answer is that he could have prevented it.

[21]At the resurrection of Jesus those who came to the tomb found the stone rolled away and the grave clothes lying but no body. Jesus was already risen.

The result of this is that many of the Jews who had come as mourners, when they saw what (the sign?)[22] Jesus did they believed in him, 11.45.[23] At this point the quest of Mary and Martha appears to have been successful and the resurrection of Lazarus is also the occasion for the confession of faith in the Johannine Christ by Martha (11.27) and the explicit revelation by Jesus (11.25-26,41-42). The result, many believed in Jesus. But within this quest story has been the trail of another quest, the quest to kill Jesus. Here the belief of the many is put in question because some of them inform the Pharisees of what Jesus did, 11.46.

The quest story is clearly implied by the sending of the messenger(s) with the implied request. Various objections arise which must be overcome if the quest is to be successful. First Jesus must overcome the threat posed by the Jews if he is to go to Bethany. More important is the death of Lazarus by the time Jesus arrived. The focus falls here because the narrator and Jesus make certain that the reader is aware of Jesus' intentional delay and its purpose (11.4,6). Then there is the threefold refrain expressing the view that had Jesus been present Lazarus need not have died. That the death of Lazarus is the chief obstacle to be overcome is confirmed by the significant pronouncement of Jesus (11.25-26). The length of time following Lazarus' death reinforces this point. While in one sense the death of Lazarus and the length of time that he had been dead posed problems for Jesus to overcome, in the mind of Jesus and the narrator this is no serious problem for Jesus. But a serious problem is thereby created for Mary and Martha. Can their faith rise above this? The sending of the messengers was an expression of faith in Jesus as a healer comparable to the request of the nobleman (4.47) who requested Jesus to come down and heal his son who was at the point of death. The actual death of Lazarus and the subsequent passage of four days sets the event in another class. The actual and certain death of Lazarus was necessary so that Jesus could develop the christological implications of the resurrection (11.25-26). While the narrative at first suggests that Martha has grasped this (11.27), what follows shows that she has not progressed past traditional eschatological belief. But there is a sufficient response of faith in the removal of the grave-stone to allow Jesus to act and raise Lazarus

---

[22]There is weak textual evidence indicating that what was seen was a sign. This is probably a correct scribal interpretation rather than the original reading.

[23]The formula that many believed on the basis of seeing signs, from its first appearance, is suggestive of a problematical belief, see 2.23-25; 7.31; 8.30. There is also a strong connection between the christology of Jn 11 and Jn 7-8.

from the dead. Consequently it is a successful quest story and this is graphically described[24] with Lazarus coming out of the tomb swathed in grave clothes. It is also confirmed by (11.45):

> many of the Jews who came to Mary and when they saw what he did
> they believed in him.

In what follows (11.46-57; 12.9-11) it becomes clear that the death and resurrection of Lazarus are intimately bound up with Jesus' own death and resurrection. The impressive pronouncement of Jesus (11.25-26) brings to light the symbolic character of the Lazarus story and in it he expounds the soteriological implications of the christology of the Gospel.

II. THE QUEST TO KILL LAZARUS AND JESUS
(11.46-57; 12.9-11)

The miracle quest story of the raising of Lazarus is subsequently made the basis of an attempt to kill Lazarus as well as Jesus. This occurs because some of those who witnessed the sign reported the event to the Pharisees. Implicit in this report is the evidence of the many who believed because of the sign, 11.45-46. The result was a gathering of the chief-priests and Pharisees in the Sanhedrin. They accepted that "This man does many signs". They saw this as a threat to the survival of the nation and the Temple. In response Caiaphas prophesied that

> "it is expedient that one man should die for the people so that the
> whole nation should not perish". (Jn 11.50)

Indeed the narrator indicates that, as High Priest, Caiaphas prophesied and spoke more truly than he knew because

> Jesus was about to die for the nation, and not for the nation only
> but that he may gather into one the scattered children of God.
> (11.51-52)

This was of course the object of Jesus' quest and means that in their quest to kill Jesus the Jews would inadvertently enable Jesus to fulfil his quest. This ironical situation was essential to the early Christian proclamation. Though crucified by the hands of lawless men Jesus gathers the scattered children of God.[25]

The formal decision to kill Jesus (11.53)[26] now meant that he could no longer move freely in Judaea, 11.47-54,57. Indeed, the plot was not now

---

[24]In stark contrast to the resurrection of Jesus which is announced but not actually described.

[25]Cf. Jn 12.31-33 and Acts 2.23-24. On the gathering of the scattered children of God see my "The Church and Israel in the Gospel of John". *NTS* 25 (1978), 103-12.

[26]Compare the less formal decisions, 5.18; 7.1, 25, 32, 44; 8.20,59; 10.31.

only against Jesus but against Lazarus also because his resurrection, more than any other sign, led to mass belief, 12.9-11. All of this has been embedded in a context of conflict (from 5.16,18 onwards) so that the incident narrated here is presented as the event which caused the definitive decision to arrest and execute Jesus. Even so, the quest for Jesus continues with a degree of ambiguity. Jn 11.55-56 indicates that many pilgrims going up to Jerusalem as the Passover (the feast of the Jews) drew near, were seeking Jesus (ἐζήτουν). The question on everyone's lips[27] at the Temple was "Surely he will not come to the feast will he?"[28] The reason for this view was the command from the chief-priests and Pharisees that anyone with knowledge of Jesus should inform on him so that they could arrest him, 11.57.

III. THE ANOINTING AT BETHANY (12.1-8)

The anointing at Bethany is set within the framework of the story of the raising of Lazarus and the stated outcome of that event. It is placed in about the same chronological order as an anointing story in Matt 26.6-13; Mk 14.3-9. There are some notable differences. In Jn the anointing takes place six days before the Passover, in the house of Lazarus, Martha and Mary (not Simon the leper). It is Mary who extravagantly anoints Jesus' *feet* in Jn not an unnamed woman who anoints his *head*. In Jn the criticism of Mary's action was made by Judas Iscariot (not the disciples). The important difference is the anointing of Jesus' *feet* by Mary. This action suggests a comparison with the washing of the disciples' feet by Jesus. At the final meal Jesus acted as servant to the disciples and washed their feet. This action was a parable of his life-giving work for them. At that meal Peter in particular revealed himself to be uncomprehending. But at Bethany Mary had perceived and extravagantly cared for Jesus' needs before the meal and at the same time had prepared his body for burial. It seems likely that some comparison between the two "footwashings" was intended. The sinister role of Judas is highlighted in both but the focus is on Mary in the first and Peter in the second suggesting that a comparison between the two is intended. If this is the case there can be no doubt that Mary comes out of the comparison viewed to advantage.

---

[27]The force of the imperfect ἔλεγον is repeated asking.
[28]This is the force of the question introduced by οὐ μή.

IV. THE QUEST OF THE CROWD (11.55-56; 12.12-19)[29]

It seems likely that the crowd that went up to Jerusalem for the feast, that went out to meet Jesus when they heard that he was coming to Jerusalem (12.12), are those who were seeking him in Jerusalem, 11.55-56 and cf. 12.17. They were seeking the Messiah, 12.13. But the Messiah they found was meek and lowly seated on the foal of an ass. The crowd did not perceive the transformation of their quest, nor did the disciples until Jesus was glorified, as the narrator carefully notes, 12.16. The narrative of this event, like that of the cleansing of the Temple, has been turned to focus on the disciples who are coincidental to the actual events. Through the interpretative role of the narrator the significance of these events is set out in terms of the disciples' reflection of faith from the perspective of the resurrection/glorification of Jesus, 2.22; 12.16.

V. THE QUEST OF THE GREEKS (12.20-(26)36a)

While the story of the coming of the Greeks is simple and self-contained it bears the marks of the evangelist's hand in its focus on the role of Philip and Andrew[30] and, though it makes use of some traditional sayings, the focus falls on the characteristically Johannine saying concerning the hour of the glorification of the Son of Man (12.23) which is elaborated in the following dialogues by Jesus with aid from "the Father" and the narrator (12.27-28,30-33,35-36a).[31] In this story the authentic goal of all quests is specifically identified in what is the last story of Jesus' public ministry.

Certain Greeks in Jerusalem at the Passover to worship at the feast approached Philip with the request, Κύριε, θέλομεν τὸν Ἰησοῦν ἰδεῖν. The request was taken, via Andrew, to Jesus. The quest story remains, technically, unfulfilled. The Greeks vanish without trace. But their coming signals the coming of Jesus' hour, which in 7.6 has not yet come. It is the time of his glorification when all men will be drawn to him. But this is to go beyond the formal quest story itself which has as its climactic pronouncement, "The hour has come for the Son of Man to be glorified', 12.23.[32] The theme is taken up again in 12.24-36, but the audience,

---

[29] Jn's account appears to be based on tradition independent of the Synoptics. See D. Moody Smith, "John 12.12ff. and the Question of John's use of the Synoptics" in *Johannine Christianity*, 97-105.

[30] See 1.40,43-46; 6.5,7; 14.8-9.

[31] See chapter 9, "The Enigmatic Son of Man" above.

[32] Like the quest story of chapter six this quest story is also followed by a series of miscellaneous sayings, here on the theme of life out of death. But in the sayings it is not the death of the Son of Man that is in view because the sayings are about discipleship. In this way, as in Mk, the sayings about

apparently from 12.27 is the crowd of 12.29. Nevertheless it is in 12.31-33 that the meaning of 12.23 becomes clear. Whereas Jesus had there spoken of the glorification of the Son of Man now, in an "I" saying, he says that if he is *lifted up* he will draw all men to himself. It is the narrator who informs us that this "being lifted up" is an image of the manner of Jesus' death. That is certainly the way 12.24 interprets the hour of the glorification of the Son of Man also. In 12.32 Jesus tells us that in this event he will draw all men to himself thus making possible the success of the quest of the Greeks. At this point quest and conflict have come together because the conflict must run its full course before the quest can be fulfilled. What is more, the promise to Nathanael (1.51), which, as the plural ὄψεσθε shows, was really a promise to all questers, is now about to be fulfilled. It is this that the quest of the Greeks signifies.

At this point it is the crowd that correctly understands that the lifting up of Jesus entails his death as a departure, as is confirmed by the narrator, 12.33-34. They had understood Jesus' identification of himself with the Son of Man to constitute a messianic claim. They considered this claim to be ruled out by the manner of his departure. If not messianic in meaning, they demanded to know what was the significance of this Son of Man of whom he spoke. Given that the rejection of the messianic understanding of Jesus' role was on the basis of his imminent death as a departure, Jesus' response was to address the significance of the departure. He did so with a change of imagery. The temporary presence of the Son of Man is now exchanged for the image of the temporary presence of the light, 12.35-36. The presence of the light constitutes the time of opportunity and the possibility of belief. The withdrawal of the light would allow the darkness to prevail as an act of judgement.

VI. THE ROOT OF UNBELIEF (12.36b-43)

Nevertheless we are told of the failure of Jesus' public ministry, 12.37. In spite of the many signs he had done publicly, they did not believe in him. That it was a hostile unbelief is signalled by the narrator who indicates that at the conclusion of the dialogue with the crowd, Jesus *hid* from them (12.36b), reintroducing the theme of the hidden Messiah. How then is the unbelief in the face of the presence of the light/Son of Man to be explained? The answer is, the overwhelming power of the darkness (σκοτία ὑμᾶς καταλάβῃ) for those who did not walk in the light, 8.12; 12.35. Even while the light is present the power of darkness cannot be

---

the suffering Son of Man are followed by sayings about the suffering of the disciples.

ignored. The signs failed to produce belief because of the power of the darkness, the ruler of this world (12.31) who blinded the eyes and hardened the hearts of those who should have believed.[33]

It is then surprising to read that many of the rulers believed in him, 12.42; cf. 7.45-52. Reference to the belief of "many" should alert the reader to the possibility that all is not quite as it seems at first, cf. 2.23-25. Nevertheless it is surprising to read that the rulers feared the Pharisees and did not confess (οὐχ ὡμολόγουν) their faith so that they would not be excommunicated from the synagogue. This decision showed, for the evangelist, the false values of these timid believers. "They loved (meaning valued or chose) the praise of men rather than the praise of God".

Jn 12.42 is closely connected to 9.22. There we are told that the Jews had decided to excommunicate from the synagogue any who confessed Jesus to be the Christ. Here it is the Pharisees who implement this policy.[34] What the rulers would not confess was that "Jesus is the Christ". Given that Jn 9 reflects the situation of the Johannine believers towards the end of the first century we conclude that the same is true of Jn 12.42. Consequently and paradoxically we have to take account of two aspects of the consequences of Jesus' death as departure. On the one hand this is understood as his exaltation/glorification, the judgement of this world and the prince of this world. On the other hand Jesus' departure left the world in darkness. That these two aspects represent two later phases of interpretation is possible with an awareness of the continuing power of darkness overshadowing an earlier hope of the judgement of the world brought about by the exaltation of the Son of Man.[35]

VII. THE QUEST TO ARREST JESUS (18.1-11)

In John the majority of uses of ζητεῖν concern the *seeking* of Jesus which signals a quest story theme, 1.38; 6.24,26; 7.11,34,36; 8.21; 11.56; 13.33; 18.4,7,8; 20.15. Next are the references to the attempts (*seeking*) to kill Jesus, 5.18; 7.1,19,20,25,30; 8.37,40; 10.39; 11.8. In this regard 18.4,7,8 overlap both categories. Though the story is from the tradition the evangelist has made his own interpretation by introducing a cohort (600) of Roman soldiers under a tribune led out by Judas along with the servants of the chief priests and Pharisees, 18.3. Twice Jesus asks τίνα

---

[33]See chapter 12 section VI, "The Judgement and Unbelief" below.

[34]Thus the Pharisees of 12.42 play the same hostile role as the Jews of Jn 9.22.

[35]See the third version of the discourse in chapter 13, "The Farewell of the Messiah" below.

ζητεῖτέ; (18.4,7), and having been informed that they seek Jesus of Nazareth the evangelist twice notes that Jesus identified himself, ἐγώ εἰμι, 18.5,8. The quest is again emphasized in verse 8 when Jesus directs, "If therefore you *seek* me, permit these to leave." In this way focus on Jesus alone as the object of the quest is emphasized as it is also in Jesus' double ἐγώ εἰμι response. This straightforwardly means only that Jesus has identified himself. But the use of the self-revelation formula itself and the response of of those who sought Jesus, falling to the ground, signals something more.[36] Given the use of the self-revelation formula in other quest stories (6.35; 11.25) it is possible that the evangelist is hinting that Jesus fulfils their quest in a way beyond all expectation.

VIII. THE QUEST FOR THE BODY (20.1-18)

The Johannine account is quite distinctive. The quest for the body is expressed by the coming of Mary Magdalene who then reported to Peter and another disciple that the body had been stolen. They in turn came seeking the body with the consequence that the other disciple believed. Then (in verse 11) the quest of Mary is taken up again, first in an encounter with two ἀγγέλους (20.13), then in an encounter with Jesus, 20.15. While both ask her, 'Woman (γύναι)[37] , why do you weep?', Jesus adds, τίνα ζητεῖς; thus making her quest explicit.[38] The problem to be overcome is Mary's failure to recognize Jesus. Her quest is then satisfied by Jesus revealing himself to her by the use of her name. The incident concludes with Mary reporting to the disciples, ἑώρακα τὸν κύριον. Thus the quest for the body concludes with the proclamation of the risen Lord and this constitutes the concluding pronouncement and Mary Magdalene is the first witness to the risen Lord.[39]

---

[36]Of course it was not to be expected that a "fugitive" would give himself up so easily, indeed as if he were himself in control of the situation.

[37]See 2.4; 4.21; 19.26.

[38]Compare Jesus' question to the two disciple of John, τί ζητεῖτε; 1.37.

[39]The notable role of women in Jn deserves close attention. The mother of Jesus appears as a notable disciple in 2.1-11; 19.25-27; the role of the Samaritan woman as a witness puts the disciples to shame in Jn 4; Mary and Martha have an intimate relation to Jesus (Jn 11) and Mary, by anointing Jesus' feet (12.1-8) exposes the blindness of the disciples, especially Peter, 13.1-11. Women are notably present at the crucifixion, 19.25-27. Then Mary Magdalene is the first witness to the risen Jesus, 20.18. It seems probable that the evangelist intends the narrative as a form of comment on the role of women

IX. CONCLUSION

The quest stories after chapter 4, apart from 20.1-18, which is a special case, have all been overlaid with the theme of rejection. For this reason they belong to the section of the Gospel which builds up to the final rejection of Jesus. In a way there is no progress in this section beyond 5.18, though chapters 11 and 12 do introduce a formal plot to arrest Jesus and to bring about his death. Even though the theme of rejection is dominant in this section it has been possible to identify underlying quest stories.[40]

It has already been suggested that the development of the quest stories belongs to the context of *diaspora* Judaism in some large urban centre such as Ephesus after the destruction of Jerusalem. The quest stories themselves display the emissary christology characteristic of John.[41] On the basis of some of these quest stories the evangelist has developed rejection stories. There are also some independent rejection stories. The way the rejection stories have come to dominate the Gospel from chapter 5 onwards suggests that a Gospel that once appealed more openly to Jews of the synagogue has been modified to take account of a synagogue reaction. The dominant theme from here on is the persecution of Jesus, the attempt to arrest or to kill him. Yet this does not easily fit in with the picture of Jesus moving freely amongst those who have recently been depicted as those who would arrest or kill him. This suggests that the rejection theme has been imposed on some of these stories. That is not to deny that the Gospel, even in its earliest stages of development, had to take account of the rejection and crucifixion of Jesus. That was a brute fact that could not be ignored. But it could be and probably was de-emphasized during the period when a strong appeal was being made to the synagogue. This could account for the reinterpretation of the cleansing of the Temple so that the story in John has become more concerned with Jesus' quest for true worshippers than the basis for his rejection by the Jews. The rejection stories of chapters 5-12 are presented in such a way as to hammer home the impression that the rejection was unreasonable. Time and again rejection occurs on a basis that should have led to belief. Thus we do not have an historical presentation of the events leading up to the decision to kill Jesus. Rather we have that decision made again and again and each time as if no previous decision had been made. Naturally the final decision

---

[40]On the significance of the quest stories in Jn see the Conclusion to chapter 4, "Quest Stories in John 1-4" above.

[41]See chapter 6, "The Messiah and the Bread of Life" above.

is presented in such a way that it sums up all previous decisions and does in fact lead to the arrest and execution of Jesus.

Rejection stories, such as chapter 9, appealed to secret believers within the synagogue, offering to them the once blind man as the model of the true and courageous confession of faith. There is also the example of Nicodemus, who, in fear and trepidation, moves slowly out of the darkness into the light. His story is told in progressive episodes, 3.1-15; 7.45-52; 12.42; 19.38-42. It is a story told to encourage other fearful believers. But the Gospel as a whole stands on the other side of a mutually constructed wall dividing the Johannine community from the synagogue. That wall represents the act, taken by the synagogue, of excluding the Johannine Christians, and the word of judgement spoken against the synagogue by the Johannine Christians, 9.39-41. In this situation dialogue is no longer possible. Under these conditions there is room only for bitter recriminations, 7.20; 8.44-59.

In this conflict with the synagogue the evangelist developed the characteristic soteriology of the Gospel. Emphasis falls no longer simply on Jesus as the emissary of God. He is now the one who must be lifted up, the Son of Man who must be glorified, the Good Shepherd who must give his life for his sheep. Whereas the coming of the emissary made saving faith in his person possible, now the saving action of the emissary is emphasized. Because his glorification or lifting up involved his death this focus naturally highlights the conflict with the Jews. Thus the soteriology of the Gospel has a polemical cutting edge while the christology itself is apologetic, appealing to Jewish beliefs. While belief in the person of the emissary led to salvation, the transition from focus on christology to soteriology brought out the necessity of the death of Jesus and justifies the claim that there is a transition from christology to soteriology in the later strata of the Gospel.[42]

---

[42]See R. T. Fortna, 'From Christology to Soteriology', *Interpretation* 27 (1973) 31-47.

12

Eschatological Faith
Redefining Messiahship[1]

Nowhere in the New Testament is the relation between history and interpretation or history and faith such an *obvious* problem as it is in the Gospel of Jn. Jn stands apart from the Synoptics with regard to chronology, content and style. None of the Gospels records bare history but in Jn theological *reflection* has progressed beyond the limits that we find in the Synoptics so that sources can no longer be detected with any certainty. The Gospel is a stylistic unity. Narrative and discourse passages are written in the same style and bear the impress of one mind. The language and style of the discourses differ greatly from the teaching of Jesus in the Synoptics. Certain words and phrases, frequently used in the Synoptics, rarely occur in Jn. "The kingdom of God", so important in the Synoptics, is to be found only in Jn 3.3,5. But there is a close theological relation because the seed of all the important Johannine themes can be found in the Synoptics, for example, Jesus as the new temple, the new birth, eternal life, the mission of Jesus, the glorification of Jesus and the faith of discipleship.

Jn develops the theme of believing, emphasizing the experience of salvation and the nature of the person of Christ. In doing this he becomes, with Paul, one of the leading theologians of the New Testament. Paul wrote of the permanent significance of the person and work of Christ showing little *evidence* of interest in the historical Jesus. By writing a Gospel Jn shows that the Jesus of history and the Christ of faith are one, and gives a detailed treatment of the eschatological nature of faith in relation to the historical revelation in Jesus.

I. THE VOCABULARY OF FAITH

Jn asserts that faith is the proper response to the revelation in Jesus. His understanding of the revelation has determined his understanding of faith. Statistical comparisons show the importance of believing in the Gospel. The following table gives a list of some of the words important in Jn, comparing the number of uses with other books in the New Testament. The different usage in discourse and narrative passages should also be noted as indicating the difference between the ideal and the actual.[2]

---

[1] An earlier form of this chapter appeared in the *Festschrift* for Dr. Leon Morris entitled *Reconciliation and Hope* edited by Robert Banks.
[2] See section III. below, "Symbolic Parallels to Believing".

	Jn 1-12	Jn 13-7	Jn 18-21	Jn total	Paul	Syn- optics	1 Jn	NT Total
πιστεύειν	76	15	7	98	54	30	9	239
πίστις	0	0	0	0	142	24	1	244
γινώσκειν	33	21	2	56	49	61	25	221
γνῶσις	0	0	0	0	23	2	0	29
εἰδέναι	54	15	16	85	102	72	15	230
ἀγαπᾶν	7	25	5	37	33	26	27	142
ἀγάπη	1	6	0	7	76	2	18	118
φιλεῖν	4	3	6	13	2	8	0	25
μαρτυρία	12	0	2	14	2	4	6	37
μαρτυρεῖν	26	3	4	33	8	2	6	76

Πιστεύειν is used in every chapter except 15, 18 and 21. In chapter 15 μένειν is used to express the abiding of faith in the allegory of the Vine. Πιστεύειν is used only once in the passion narrative (19.35), because this is the record of the rejection of Jesus. But it is used six times in chapter 20 plus ἄπιστος and πιστός in 20.27, drawing attention to the centrality of the resurrection for faith.

There is a concentration on believing in chapters 1-12 where Jesus confronts the world with the challenge to believe. In chapters 13-17 the confrontation is past and the nature of authentic faith is developed by the use of other words, such as μένειν, τηρεῖν, γινώσκειν and εἰδέναι. While εἰδέναι is used more frequently than γινώσκειν in narrative passages, both words seem to cover the same semantic area except that εἰδέναι is never used in the formula of mutual knowledge, nor of the Father's knowledge.[3] Jn's more frequent use of εἰδέναι than γινώσκειν stands with the use of Paul, the Synoptics and the New Testament in general. The use of these two verbs as equivalents points away from Gnosticism to the use in the LXX.

Jn uses neither πίστις nor γνῶσις. The absence of γνῶσις is not surprising. It is used only twice in the Synoptics[4] and 29 times in the New Testament, of which 23 occur in the Pauline Corpus. Γινώσκειν is used 221 times in the New Testament. The preference for the verb can hardly be regarded as an anti-Gnostic device. The books which reflect contact or conflict with Gnosticism are the ones in which γνῶσις is to be

---

[3]But as the formula is used only in 10.14-15, and the Father is the subject of the verb "to know" on only one occasion (10.15), this is hardly significant. That γινώσκειν is always used where the future realization of knowledge is in view is only of grammatical importance (7.17; 8.28,32; 10.38; 13.7,35; 14.20,31; 17.3,23).

[4]Lk 1.77; 11.52.

found, especially 1 and 2 Corinthians. If Jn was anti-Gnostic at this point we would have expected γνῶσις to have been used, but with an anti-Gnostic meaning.

The absence of πίστις is more difficult to explain in the light of its frequent use in Paul and the New Testament as a whole. The fact that πίστις is used only twice in the Corpus Hermeticum has been noted as evidence that Gnostic association had not prejudiced its use.[5] Had there been Gnostic associations that Jn was countering we would have expected him to have used the word in a redefined sense.

There is a clear preference for πίστις in the Pauline Corpus and there is a concentration of use in contexts dealing with the conflict between faith and works as the way of salvation.[6] It is also used 16 times in a similar conflict in James. Jn was not concerned with this conflict.[7] In the Pastoral epistles πίστις is used 33 times, often to express the content of faith. While Jn does not disregard the content of faith (expressed by πιστεύειν ὅτι), other elements are also prominent. He chose πιστεύειν because it suited his understanding of the proper response to the revelation, which is the primary theme of the Gospel and hence the concentration on πιστεύειν.

II. THE ΠΙΣΤΕΥΕΙΝ FORMULAE[8]

1. The verb followed by the dative of the person or object believed is used 18 times, and expresses the most important aspects of belief on the basis of witness.[9] Jn wrote to emphasize the possibility of belief on the basis of witness (20.31).[10] There is a multiple witness which has a single point of

---

[5] W. F. Howard, *Christianity According to St. John*, 155.

[6] In Romans 39 times, 26 in chapters 1-5; in Galatians 22 times, 14 in chapter 3.

[7] 6.28f. does not deal with this subject.

[8] In 2.24 Jesus is the subject, but the verb is used in a sense different from the rest of the Gospel. Neither Jesus nor the Father is said to believe, nor does Jn use the verb in the Old Testament sense of the faithfulness of God. In 9.18 the verb is followed by . . . περί . . . ὅτι. The Jews refused to believe that the man in question had been blind. By discarding the miracle one possible way of coming to believe in Jesus was rejected. The construction used in 9.18 is not a straightforward πιστεύειν ὅτι construction, which is used in Jn to express the content of Christian faith.

[9] These include Jesus: 4.21; 5.38,46; 6.30; 8.31,45,46; 10.37,38; 14.11; Jesus' words: 2.22; 4.50; 5.47; Jesus works: 10.38 (14.11); Him who sent Jesus: 5.24; the Scripture: 2.22; 5.46,47; 12.38.

[10] There is a tenfold witness to Jesus in the Gospel. (1)The Baptist: 1.7,8,15,32,34; 3.26; 5.33; (2) The woman of Samaria: 4.38; (3) Jesus: 5.31; 8.18; 18.37; (4) Jesus' works: 5.36; 10.25; (5) The Father: 5.37; 8.18; (6) The Scriptures: 5.39f; (7) The crowd: 12.17; (8) The Paraclete:

focus, Jesus. Jesus' self-testimony and the witness of the Father to Jesus in his works stand apart from the rest (5.31-39; 8.13-18). The witness of the works may provide a transition (10.38; 14.11), but ultimately the scandal of Jesus' self-testimony cannot be avoided.[11] All but one use of this construction (πιστεύειν followed by the dative case) fall in chapters 1–12 where there is also a concentration of the use of the vocabulary of witness. After the resurrection the testimony of the eyewitnesses takes on a new significance. Because of this Jn uses the individual cases in chapters 1–12 as illustrations of the effectiveness of witness and chapters 13–17 outline the possibility of all future belief on the basis of the apostolic testimony (15.26-27; 17.20f.).

2. There are two instances of the verb followed by ἐν (3.15; 20.31). In 3.15 the construction is in synonymous parallelism with the verb followed by εἰς in 3.16. The order of the words indicates that the meaning is "to believe in". There was a tendency in the New Testament period for εἰς and ἐν to overlap in meaning as in 3.15f.[12] Jn 20.31 is less clear because of the word order. But as believing in Jesus' name is elsewhere spoken of (1.12; 2.23; 3.18, using εἰς), and there is no other reference to having life in Jesus' name, it should be taken as "believing in. . .". This is borne out by the parallelism between believing followed by ὅτι. . . and believing followed by ἐν. . . Further, 1 Jn 5.13, which is modelled on Jn 20.31, refers to those who believe in (εἰς) the name of the Son of God.

3. There are 36 instances where the verb is followed by εἰς[13] out of 47 uses in the New Testament. Of these 3 *occur* in I Jn, 3 in Acts and no other book has more than 1 use of this construction, which is peculiar to the New Testament.[14] This construction indicates belief in Jesus, except in 12.44 and 14.1 where reference is made to believing in the Father who sent Jesus. It is usually used with a personal object, but 6.29; 8.30 and 1 Jn 5.10 are probable exceptions. In each case the verb with εἰς is followed by the use of the verb with the dative (Jn 6.30; 8.31; 1 Jn 5.10) suggesting

---

[11] In 4.21 and 14.11 Jesus' appeal to believe him is followed by a clause indicating that to believe Jesus' self-testimony is to believe certain things about him, i.e., his place in salvation history (4.21), and his relation to the Father (14.11).

15.26; (9) The apostles: 15.27; (10) The beloved disciple: 19.35; 21.24. Only those instances where the terminology of witness has been used are listed.

[12] See Moule, *Idiom,* 69,75,80f. This construction was used in the LXX and there is one clear instance of its use in Mk 1.15.

[13] 1.12; 2.11,23; 3.16,18[(2)],36; 4.39; 6.29,35,40; 7.5,31,38,39,48; 8.30; 9.35,36; 10.42; 11.25,26,45,48; 12.11,36,37,42,44[(2)],46; 14.1[(2)],12; 16.9; 17.20.

[14] Ecclus. 38.31 is not a parallel.

that believing Jesus' word is in view. Further, in Jn 5.24 the verb followed by the dative case has a personal object and has much the same meaning as the verb followed by $\epsilon\iota\varsigma$, for example in 14.1. Thus while there is a personal element in this faith other constructions can also express this.[15]

4. The verb is used absolutely 28 times,[16] but the contexts supply the objects of all but 16.[17] While 1.50 is a formal example of the absolute use, the context shows that only superficial faith in Jesus in current Messianic terms is involved. Such faith is challenged to reassess Jesus (1.51). The absolute use, like the verb followed by $\epsilon\iota\varsigma$ (2.23f.) or by the dative case (8.31), can be used to express superficial faith. But the truly absolute use, both uses with $\epsilon\nu$ and many uses with $\epsilon\iota\varsigma$ or followed by the dative case indicate authentic faith. These uses tend to fall in the discourses.

5. There are twelve instances where the verb followed by a $\delta\tau\iota$ clause indicates the significance of Jesus.[18] The use of this construction often occurs with verbs of knowing, with $\epsilon\iota\delta\epsilon\nu\alpha\iota$ (16.30) and with $\gamma\iota\nu\omega\sigma\kappa\epsilon\iota\nu$ (6.69; 10.38; 17.8, 21; cf. 17.23) and is used to express the *perception* of authentic faith. The Gospel paradoxically shows that confessions of faith made in these terms by individuals (6.69; 11.27; 16.30) were not authentic at the time of making (6.70f.; 13.36f.; 11.39; 16.31f.).

6. Twenty-five uses of $\pi\iota\sigma\tau\epsilon\nu\epsilon\iota\nu$ fall in narrative passages, where rejection and partial faith in Jesus are stated.[19] Expressions of faith are brought into question by their contexts. All of the constructions are used to express both partial and authentic faith and the verb followed by $\epsilon\iota\varsigma$ is used more frequently than any other construction to describe partial faith.

7. Four instances describe activities which have the purpose of provoking belief (1.7; 17.21; 19.35; 20.31). Authentic faith was not a

---

[15]Contrary to C. H. Dodd, *Interpretation of the Fourth Gospel* , 183 and L. L. Morris, *John*, 336. Morris is also wrong in suggesting that this construction indicates a sense of mystical abiding.

[16]1.7,50; 3.12[(2)],18; 4.41,42,48,53; 5.44; 6.36,47,64[(2)]; 9.38; 10.25,26; 11.15,40; 12.39; 14.11,29; 16.31; 19.35; 20.8,25,29[(2)].

[17]1.7; 4.48,53; 5.44; 6.36,47,64[(2)]; 11.15,40; 14.29; 19.35; and probably also 20.8,25,29[(2)], referring to belief in the risen Lord which is at the heart of the meaning of "believe" used absolutely.

[18]That Jesus is the Christ the Son of God: 6.69; 11.27; 20.31; that "I am": 8.24; 13.19; that the Father sent Jesus: 11 42; 17.8,21; that the Father is in Jesus and Jesus in the Father: 10.38; 14.10; that Jesus has come from God: 16.27, 30.

[19]Both 2.24 and 9.18 fall in narrative passages, as do two uses of the verb followed by the dative case, eleven uses followed by $\epsilon\iota\varsigma$, seven absolute uses, and three uses followed by $\delta\tau\iota$.

reality during Jesus' ministry, but the Gospel was written for a new situation when such faith had become possible.[20] Descriptions of those who came to partial faith during Jesus' ministry have become examples of the possibility of coming to authentic faith. Thus there is no difference in terminology in the narrative descriptions of partial faith and the descriptions of authentic faith that Jesus uses in his discourses.

III. SYMBOLIC PARALLELS TO BELIEVING

The idea of believing is also indicated by a number of symbolic parallels. The symbols do not have exactly the same meaning as πιστεύειν but focus on an aspect of what is a complex response to the revelation in Jesus. Most of the references occur in discourse passages and deal with an aspect of authentic faith, but in a few instances they occur in narrative passages and there are indications of the limitations involved. In other instances the narrative context indicates that the aspect in view is restricted to those who knew Jesus during the days of his ministry. The distinction between those who believed having seen Jesus and those who believed without having seen is also indicated using πιστεύειν (17.20; 20.29).

The symbols can be analyzed in terms of certain aspects of what it means to believe. Believing involves (1) Perception, recognition, understanding; (2) Decision; and (3) Dependence and obedience.

1. Believing as Perception, Recognition, Understanding

This aspect is emphasized when the verb is used with ὅτι and with verbs of knowing, as well as with the following symbolic descriptions.

	Narrative	Discourse
To see[21]	1.14	1.39,46,51; 6.40,62;
11.40;12.40;		14.7, 17.
To hear	4.42; 10.20	5.24,25,45; 8.43,47[(2)];
		10.3,8,16,27.
To remember	2.17,22; 12.16	14.26.

---

[20]Debate about the tense of the verb to believe in 20.31 is not relevant because Jn was concerned that faith should be authentic, perceive the true nature of Jesus and thus lead on to real decision and obedience. Hence it is not simply a matter of moving from unbelief to belief but of progressing to authentic faith.

[21]Bultmann is right in saying that the various verbs of seeing are used without any difference of meaning being intended (see *Das Evangelium des Johannes*, 54 n1. The difference of use is grammatical in that the different forms are used to supply different tenses.

2. Believing as Decision

To come	1.39,46	3.20,21; 6.35,37,45,65; 7.37; 14.6.
To receive or reject		1.5,11,12; 3.11,32,33; 5 43; 12.48(2); 13.20; 14.17; 17.8.
To love or hate	(21.15,16,17)	3.19,20; 8.42; 12.25,43; 14.15,21,23, 24, 28; 16.27.
To confess or deny	9.22; 12.42; 18.25,26.	13.38.
To follow	(1.37,38,40) 6.2	1 .43; 8.12; 10.4,5, 27; 12.26.

3. Believing as Dependence and Obedience.

To drink		4 13, 14 (6.35); 7 37.
To eat		(6.35); 6.51, 52.
To be a disciple	9.27	8 31; 13.35; 15 8-
To learn or be taught		6.45.
To keep		8.51(52); 14.15,21,23,24,28.
To abide	(1.39)	6.56; 8.31 (12.46); 15.4,5,6,9,10.
To serve		12.26.
To worship	9.38	4.23,24.

Some of the terms overlap from one group to another so that "to hear" and "to worship" can involve all three categories and "to follow" can involve obedience as well as decision. In the category of perception, seeing and remembering are restricted to the situation of Jesus' ministry. Only those who had actually seen him with their eyes could see him in this way i.e., remember with new understanding what their eyes had seen.[22]

IV. DRAMATIS PERSONAE

The object of the verbs of believing is Jesus except where belief in God is expressed and then it is God as the one who has sent Jesus, as revealed in Jesus. Thus one is called to believe (in) Jesus, his words, his works, and certain facts about him concerning his relation to the Father. But these are not ultimate distinctions. Because his words are self-testimony, to believe him is to believe in him. He is the content of his own message and

---

[22]Contrary to the views of most commentators. Both Bultmann and Dodd take this sight to be the vision of faith, open to all believers, though they differ on points of detail. But Dodd refuses to interpret Jn 19.35 in this way, saying that the evangelist was not the sort of person who could affirm the veracity of his evidence while offering only a suggestive symbol (*Historical Tradition in the Fourth Gospel*, 135). This comment is equally applicable to 1.14 (and 1 Jn 1.1ff.). Further, the Gospel clearly distinguishes seeing and believing, and believing without seeing (20.29).

because he is the emissary of the Father, to believe in him is to believe in the Father. For this reason Jn has designated Jesus as the Logos.

Neither Jesus nor the Father is the subject of the verb to believe.[23] Every other major and most other minor characters deny or affirm faith in the course of the Gospel. The disciples, as individuals (1.50; 6.69; 20.8,29) or as a group (2.11,22; 16.27,30; 17.18), are described as the believers more frequently than any one else. But there are indications that, in the context of Jesus' ministry, they did not really believe (2.22), and Jesus even questioned whether they believed at all (16.31). After the disciples "the many" are most frequently described as believers. This belief is normally in response to signs (2.23; 7.31; 8.30; 10.42; 11.45; 12.11) and is brought into question (2.23ff.). In 8.30 "the many" are identified with the Jews of 8.31, who, more frequently than any others, are those of whom it is said that they do not believe (5.38,47; 8.45-46; 9.18; 10.25, 26; 12.37).

V. THE JOHANNINE SITUATION

Jn brings out the stark contrast between believing in and rejecting Jesus, making decision a prominent element in what he understands as believing. Judaism forms the background to the Gospel, Judaism fragmented by sects, the sect of the Way being the one which most threatened its life and faith. The excommunication of those who confessed Jesus to be the Christ is to be understood in this context.[24]

The threat of excommunication encouraged those who believed in Jesus to remain within the fold of Judaism as secret believers. Nicodemus is treated as a typical example (3.1ff.; 7.5ff.; 19.38ff.). He is the typical *man* who believed on the basis of *signs* (2.23-25; 3.1-2).[25] He is the typical *ruler* who would not openly confess his faith for fear of excommunication (12.42). Even "the twelve" become secret believers because of fear of the Jews (20.19). The threat was also used to make timid believers recant. In Jn 9 the man who had been blind overcame intimidation and was ultimately excommunicated, becoming an example of the true believer in the Jewish situation.

The Gospel demonstrates that the revelation in Jesus justifies the cost of facing persecution. In the context of conflict between believing and

---

[23]Jn 2.24 is an exception where Jesus is the subject and the many ($\pi o \lambda \lambda o \ell$) who believed in his name (2.23) are the indirect object of the verb used with the negative ($o \dot{v} \kappa$) and in a different sense. Jesus did not trust them.

[24]See the discussion of "The Community and its History" in chapter 2 part III.2 above.

[25]Note the use of "man" and "signs" in both passages.

unbelieving Jews the Prologue asserts that the revelation in the incarnate Word supersedes the Law of Moses. The Jewish Scriptures, like the Baptist, are rightly understood only in terms of their witness to Jesus.[26] The Jewish religion as it had been known was surpassed by the new way (2.1-11).[27] The old Temple was made obsolete by the risen Jesus as the new Temple for the meeting of God and man (2.13-22). The automatic identification of Jews with the citizens of the Kingdom of God is denied. Those who believe in Jesus enter the Kingdom (3.1-15) and are the true worshippers who receive the Spirit through believing in Jesus (4.23-24). The coming of the Word made flesh in history brought about the judgement of the world, portrayed in terms of light coming into the darkness (3.19-21). The light was not conquered by the darkness, it overcame the darkness (1.5; 16.33). The judgement by the light causes division.[28] Those who believe, who come to the light, are divided off from those who reject Jesus.

VI. THE JUDGEMENT AND UNBELIEF

According to Jn unbelief is the rejection of Jesus and his place in salvation history. Jesus came offering life and freedom. The Jews claimed that they had life and that they had never been in bondage (5.39f.; 8.33). Because of this they *misunderstood* what Jesus offered and could not see the new possibility his coming had brought about. He came with knowledge of the unseen God. But the Jews claimed that they knew God and rejected the possibility of knowing him in Jesus. Their knowledge was based on the Scriptures (5.39,45) which they used in proof-text fashion to avoid facing the claim of Jesus' works and words. They ruled out the possibility that Jesus had a place in salvation history, on various grounds. There is a need to distinguish the intellectual arguments used to justify the rejection of Jesus from what Jn portrays as the moral and spiritual causes of unbelief.

The intellectual arguments form two groups. Firstly, there was the tendency to reject the reality of Jesus' miracles (7.4; 9.18). When the miracles could not be denied, their significance could be misconstrued. Secondly there are arguments from Scripture which were used to deny Jesus any place in salvation history:

1. His origin (family) was known but the origin of the Messiah was to

---

[26]1.7,8,15,32,34; 3.26; 5.33,39,46f; 8.56,58; 12.41.

[27]The best wine was kept until last. Compare Mk. 2.22.

[28]Jn uses σχίσμα in 7.43; 9.16; 10.19 to indicate the divisive effect of Jesus' words and works. But the theme is more pervasive than the word. See 3.19-21,36; 7.31,40-44,45-52; 8.30ff.; 9.16,39-41; 10.19-20,31-42; 11.45; 12.37-43.

be unknown (7.27; 6.42).[29]
2. His place of origin was wrong, Galilee not Bethlehem as foretold (7.41f., 52).
3. His origin was not known whereas it was known that Moses came from God (9.29).[30]
4. He broke the sabbath law (5.10ff.; 9.13ff.).

There are inconsistencies in these arguments because of the diversity of messianic expectation in this period. The notion of the hidden Messiah stands beside the expectation of the Messiah of the line of David. While these views could be reconciled it is likely that Jn wanted them to appear as rationalizations for the rejection of Jesus which occurred for other reasons. The real problem was that Jesus did not fit into the religious pattern of life which they claimed had come from God.

The conflict is best seen in relation to the charge of sabbath-breaking. But the Jewish Scriptures gave precedents for the performance of certain works on the sabbath (7.21ff.). Jesus also argued that he only did what God was doing. God's creative works continued on the sabbath (5.17f.), a point acknowledged in the Rabbinic literature and Philo. In this way Jesus challenged the Jews to see God's ultimate revelation and act in him. His claim was rejected because it went beyond the bounds of the Scriptures and it was assumed that if a man claimed to be God (whatever this might mean) he was a blasphemer. In the face of the scandal caused by his self-testimony Jesus appealed to the witness of the Father in his works (5.36; 10.31-39). If his words could not be accepted his works should show that he had some place in salvation history (9 16). Jesus argued that those who rejected both his words and works did so because their standard of judgement was perverted.[31]

Our attention is turned to *the moral cause* of unbelief, which can be described as false or perverted love. Love is directed to the wrong object, indicating wrong choice. The element of choice is prominent when love and hate are used together or when it is indicated that love is directed wrongly. Both characteristics appear in 3.19-21. The first false love is love of the darkness. The darkness is the world apart from God, which rejects God's approach in the revelation of the light. The light is rejected because the world apart from God is chosen. People prefer their own evil actions to the change that accepting the judgement of the light would

---

[29]See chapter 7, "The Hidden Messiah in John 7–8"; above.
[30]Johannine irony lies behind each of these three arguments. The Jews did not know his father; he did come from Bethlehem; he had come from God.
[31]It should be remembered that the evangelist's perspective was shaped by the bitter struggle with the synagogue.

bring.[32] The second false love is love for the glory of man rather than the glory of God (5.41-44; 7.18; 8.50; 12.43); the choice of self-advancement and self-exaltation, of false greatness, greatness apart from God and opposed to God. The third false love is love for one's own life (12.25), love for self as opposed to love for God or anyone else. The fact that this love leads to death indicates that it is opposed to faith which leads to life.[33] These three loves involve the claim to already possess life, which made the Jews hostile to anyone who threatened their possession or called it into question. Jesus opposed and condemned this self-assurance because it prevented them from acknowledging his works and hearing his words:

". . . because you say 'We see', your guilt remains" (9.41).

The Jews closed themselves against the revelation, willing self-preservation rather than knowledge of the origin of Jesus' doctrine. Contrary to this position Jesus taught that those who seek to do God's will, who seek to honour God and honour from God, will know the origin of his doctrine (7.17).

According to Jn the rejection of Jesus resulted from a moral failure. False standards produced false judgements and false moral standards have a *spiritual cause*. They have arisen because some people ("the Jews") are children of the devil (8.43ff.); are not Jesus' sheep (10.26f.); are not of the truth (18.37). These statement have suggested to some scholars that Jn's language reflects Gnostic dualism or that the Gospel teaches a deterministic doctrine of predestination whereby people are fixed in two groups, the good and the bad, the saved and the damned, according to the fixed purpose of God. But (contrary to the Gnostic view) it is not that some people are saved by nature, for all, including "the twelve", were once in the darkness, in the world (15.19; 17.6,9f.,24). It is only through believing that one leaves the darkness and becomes a son of light (8.12; 12.35-36). Yet this could still allow that those who believe were given to Jesus by the Father in such a way that they automatically believe (cf. 6.37-65 esp. 37,44,45,65) and those who do not believe are prevented from doing so by God (12.37-41). This understanding of the spiritual cause of unbelief undermines Jn's critique of the moral culpability of those who do not believe. If it is divinely determined that those who do not believe should belong to the darkness and not the light they had no real opportunity to believe. While this view undermines any real moral responsibility this

---

[32]Love of the darkness may also be described as love of the world, 1 Jn 2.15f.

[33]Eternal life is the gift of God to those who believe (3.15ff.). Life is no more to be equated with knowledge than it is with faith, contrary to Bultmann on Jn 17.3. The meaning is that those who know God in Jesus receive eternal life as a consequence just as believers are given eternal life.

alone does not show that Jn did not hold it together (inconsistently or paradoxically) with a recognition of moral accountability.

An alternative to the deterministic predestinarian view is to be found in the context of the very passages in Jn which seem to suggest it. Jn 6.36-40, for example, should be seen as providing a transition from the quest story of Jn 6.1-35 to the rejection of 6.36-66.[34] This material reflects the reality of conflict with the synagogue, the growing rift between it and the Johannine believers. But while verses 36-40 reflect on the reality of unbelief (6.36), the central purpose of this section is to reassure the believers. Thus the point of 6.37 is to stress that those who come to Jesus, who are given to him by the Father, will certainly not be cast out by Jesus. This point is forcefully made (οὐ μὴ ἐκβάλω ἔξω). The language foreshadows the fate of the once blind man who is to be cast out of the synagogue because of his belief in Jesus (καὶ ἐξέβαλον αὐτὸν ἔξω 9.34). It is those who come to him that Jesus will not cast out. The theme of "coming" looks back to the universal appeal of 6.35.

That those who come to him are given by the Father is not to be understood in such a way as to override the universal opportunity of belief. Rather in this way the ultimate ground of security for the believer is revealed. Similarly 6.39, which also refers to those given to Jesus by the Father, provides the ultimate basis for confidence that not one of these will be lost. Thus the security of the believer is grounded not only in Jesus who will not cast out or inadvertently lose any, but in the Father who has given believers to Jesus. Just as 6.37 is balanced by 6.35 so 6.39 is balanced by 6.40, indicating that the Father gives Jesus those who believe in him. Those given by the Father, that is, those who believe in Jesus, he will raise up on the last day. The shift of focus from experiencing eternal life in the present to focus on the resurrection on the last day may well provide evidence of a later interpretative layer dealing with the problem caused by the death of believers.[35]

The theme is continued in 6.44 where Jesus responds to the objections raised by the Jews who have been introduced in 6.41 as a signal that we are now dealing with the theme of rejection. In the face of their rejection Jesus tells them:

"No one is able to come to me unless the Father who sent me draws (ἑλκύσῃ) him, and I will raise him up on the last day." (6.44)

It is the eschatological role of Jesus to which the Jews continue to object. But whereas the giving by the Father of those who come to Jesus had

---

[34]See chapter 6 "The Messiah and the Bread of Life" above.
[35]See chapter 5, "The Paradigm of Rejection" above.

previously been stated in positive terms (6.37,39),[36] the matter is now stated negatively.[37] The purpose of this saying is clearly to retain the focus on the necessity of coming to Jesus in a context where objections have been raised to his role. Because of these objections Jesus maintains (in the discourse) that his role is grounded in the will and the work of the Father who sent him. That God is spoken of in these terms is clearly understood. Consequently coming to Jesus is made dependent on hearing and learning from the Father, 6.45.[38] The context suggests that 6.44 should not be understood in a deterministic sense. What is more 6.44 does not indicate *how* the Father *draws* (ἐλκύσῃ) men.

Jn 12.32 indicates that *all* people are to be *drawn* (ἐλκύσω) by the uplifted Son of Man. The same verb is used in 6.44; 12.32 and in Jer 38(31).3 (LXX)[39] where it is the love of God that *draws* people. The universal scope of the love of God is asserted in Jn 3.16; 12.32. The lifting up of the Son of Man is the necessary condition to make effective the love of God in drawing all people because the power of darkness prevents belief. Some people believed as a result of the coming of the light of the world, breaking the power of darkness.[40] For John that coming implies the fulfillment of Jesus' mission and his return to the Father via his exaltation.

An alternative description of the blinding power of darkness was given by Jesus when he told the Jews who had refused his offer of freedom that they did so on the basis of the false standards which they had derived from listening to their father, the devil (8.38-44). They had false standards of truth, freedom, life, and God. Because of this they rejected the truth of the knowledge of God in Jesus and the freedom from sin, eternal life, which he came to bring. They rejected his words and his works. Had they given

---

[36]That all who are given come does not rule out that others may come also.

[37]Now it is said quite exclusively that only those drawn by the Father can come. Thus the theme of "coming to Jesus" introduced in 6.35 is continued in 6.44. It is interesting to note that in 6.37 Jesus refers to "the Father", in 6.39 "the one who sent me", and in 6.44 "the Father who sent me" providing a comprehensive reference encompassing the previous two formulae. In this way the sayings are bound together warning against interpreting them outside their literary context which draws attention to the historical context.

[38]The matter is again stated positively. "Every one who has heard from the Father and has learned from him comes to me". The point then is to show that those who do not come to Jesus have not heard and learned from the Father.

[39]κύριος πόρρωθεν ὤφθη αὐτῷ 'Αγάπησιν αἰωνίαν ἠγάπησά σε, διὰ τοῦτο εἵλκυσά σε εἰς οἰκτίρημα. See also the theme in Hosea 11.4.

[40]Compare Matt 12.28ff.

heed to his works their standards would have been changed. The transparently good nature of his works would have led to the conclusion that he had come from God (9.16). However, the majority of people failed to draw this conclusion. The Jews did not believe because they failed to see the glory revealed in Jesus (12.40-41), primarily in his signs (12.37).

Though the Jewish authorities tended to be sceptical (9.18), they could acknowledge that Jesus performed (miracles) signs (11.47), as did the crowd which failed to take adequate account of the feeding sign (6.26) and demanded one immediately after the feeding miracle (6.30). The repeated demand for a sign indicates the failure to see Jesus' miracles as signs of his authority (2.18; 4.48; 6.30). The Jews did not believe because they did not take Jesus' signs into account in their assessment of him (9.16). They denied his claims, the meaning of his miracles and the witness of those who believed in him. But those who believed insisted on taking the signs into account (9.16,25,30ff.; 10.19-21). The failure to *see* the glory manifest in the signs, which witnessed to Jesus' authority, prevented faith. The question is, "Who or what is the source of the blinding power which prevents faith?"

The answer to this question is given in Jn 12.37-43. The long prevailing interpretation of this passage is that it expresses the view that unbelief was predestined by God.[41] This can be combined with the view that the signs performed by Jesus are the actual instrument used by God to cause blindness and unbelief.[42] Certainly this would account for Jn's use of the third person singulars $\tau \epsilon \tau \acute{v} \phi \lambda \omega \kappa \epsilon \nu$ and $\acute{\epsilon} \pi \acute{\omega} \rho \omega \sigma \epsilon \nu$ in 12.40 because the neuter plural $\sigma \eta \mu \epsilon \hat{\iota} a$ takes a singular verb. But if 12.39 raises the question why they did not believe *in spite of the signs*, it hardly seems to be an answer to say that the signs are the cause of the unbelief. Rather, because they have seen the signs their unbelief is the more reprehensible.

Scholars who adopt the view that unbelief was predestined by God frequently go on to qualify their understanding of predestination as expressed by Jn. Thus Schnackenburg says that it is a puzzle that the divine decree "does not remove the obscurity of human guilt".[43] Barrett warns:

> That on the other hand his (the evangelist's) words were not the cut and dried statement of a philosophical theology appears at once from the exceptions immediately introduced at v.42 ($\delta \mu \omega s \mu \acute{\epsilon} \nu \tau o \iota$), and indeed the existence of Jewish Christians, such as Peter and the

[41]See for example, C. K. Barrett, *John*, 430-431; R. Schnackenburg, *John* II, 259-74 especially 264,271,274; Craig Evans, *To See*, 130,132-35; E. D. Freed, *Quotations*, 84-8,122.
[42]See Evans, *To See*, 135.
[43]*John* II, 274 and see 263-264.

beloved disciple.[44]

Thus there is within the interpretation of some of those who read Jn 12.39-40 in terms of divine predestination a serious qualification. Predestination normally means that there is no anterior cause motivating the divine decree. The qualifications of both Schnackenburg and Barrett show that they are unwilling to accept this position. James Charlesworth seems to go even further though his overall position may not be very different. He writes:

> We conclude, therefore, that no doctrine of predestination is put forward in this Gospel, nor is there any strong emphasis on determinism. Man's destiny is balanced between God's sovereign initiative and man's response.[45]

Charlesworth's stress here could be a consequence of his contrast of Jn with what he perceives to be the rigorous determinism of Qumran. This differs from Schnackenburg's recognition of the place of freedom at Qumran[46] and probably accounts for Charlesworth's more extreme language in the comparison with Jn.

Although Barrett adopted the language of predestination in relation to unbelief we have seen that this was done in a qualified manner. Further, he quotes Hoskyns to the effect that the deliberate changes to the quotation of Isa 6.10 in Jn 12.40 "are best explained by the intention of the writer of the gospel to emphasize the judgement as the action of God".[47] This means that the action of God is to be seen as the judgement of God and it is implied that human sin is the cause of that judgement. Consequently the divine decree is not without anterior motivation. Much as there is to commend this view it is not a totally persuasive interpretation of Jn 12.39-40. Perhaps we should say that it is the judgement of God to leave those who choose the darkness in the grip of its power, but this does not yet account for the role of the power of darkness itself.

The case for seeing the cause of unbelief in response to the signs of Jesus to be the power of darkness has not been given adequate attention. For example, Schnackenburg argues that John

> attributes the blinding and hardening to God directly and without disguise. Of a reference to the devil as agent there is no sign at all.[48]

This is hardly an adequate exploration, but at least Schnackenburg

---

[44] John, 431.

[45] John and Qumran, 95.

[46] John II, 268.

[47] John, 431.

[48] John II, 416. The position is now also mentioned dismissively by Bruce G. Schuchard, Scripture within Scripture", 99-100 and Ronald L. Tyler, "The Source and Function of Isaiah 6.9-10 in John 12.40", 207 n4.

mentioned this possibility, if only to dismiss it instantly. It is not considered at all by most commentators. There are several lines of evidence *in support* of this view not considered by Schnackenburg:

1). The context in John.
2). The evangelist's changes:
   '   to the tense, person and voice of the verbs in the text quoted.
        by omission or use of alternative language.
3). The comparative relevance of the dualistic worldview of First Century Judaism.
4). The support of Origen and Cyril of Alexandria.

1. The Context in John

i Macro-context. The quotations (12.38,40) fall in a passage (Jn 12.36b-43) dealing with unbelief which provides a summary conclusion to the "public ministry" of Jesus (Jn 1-12). The summary passage, understood in isolation, gives the impression of the failure of Jesus' mission even though this is qualified in a somewhat paradoxical way. The qualification puts in question the impression of failure as does a study of the context. It is then apparent that the summary is a transition to the passion narrative.

The more immediate context is Jn 11-12. Jn 11 features the sign of the raising of Lazarus and its consequences. The immediate consequence of the raising of Lazarus is stated in 11.45-46:

> Therefore many of the Jews coming to Mary and seeing what he did believed in him; but certain of them went to the Pharisees and told them what Jesus did.

What is described here is a divided response[49] to the sign of the raising of Lazarus though the stress is on the consequent belief which is stated first, is the response of "many" ($\pi o\lambda\lambda o\iota$) and is re-emphasized by restatement in 12.11. Overwhelming belief in response to the signs of Jesus, especially the raising of Lazarus, is stressed in what follows. But if many believed, some of the Jews who saw what Jesus did reported this to the Pharisees and a council meeting was convened to respond to the question:

> "What shall we do because this man does many signs? If we permit him (to go on in) this way all will believe in him". (11.47-48)[50]

---

[49] While the "some of them" ($\tau\iota\nu\grave{\epsilon}\varsigma$ $\delta\grave{\epsilon}$ $\grave{\epsilon}\xi$ $\alpha\dot{\upsilon}\tau\hat{\omega}\nu$), who went to the Pharisees in 11.46, could refer to those who believed out of the Jews, that is, some of those who believed, it is more likely that it refers directly to the Jews. Many of the Jews who saw what he did believed; some of the Jews who saw what he did (an implied minority) went to the Pharisees.

[50] It could be argued that recognition of the signs performed by Jesus without acknowledging belief in him turns the signs into signs of judgement. But Jesus' opponents were also capable of denying the actuality of his signs, 9.18.

The result was a "plot" to put Jesus to death, 11.53. Consequently Jesus was not able to go about openly though the crowd going up to Jerusalem for Passover were seeking (ejzhvtoun) him and questioned whether he would appear at the feast in the light of the decision to arrest him, 11.54-57. The impression is of overwhelming belief in Jesus in response to the sign of the raising of Lazarus but of a determined plot to arrest and execute him by the powerful minority associated with the Sanhedrin. These opponents were blind to the significance of the signs except that they saw in the one who performed them a threat to the survival of the nation as it was.

In the account of the anointing at Bethany (12.1-8) many of the features of the Synoptic accounts appear. What was an independent tradition (see Matt 26.6-13 and Mk 14.3-9) has been caught up into the saga concerning Lazarus by locating the event in the presence (perhaps at the house of) Lazarus, Martha and Mary and by naming Mary as the the woman who anointed Jesus. The anointing keeps Lazarus in the picture and the narrator reminds the readers that the great crowd of the Jews had come out not only on account of Jesus but also to see Lazarus and that through him many of the Jews believed in Jesus. Consequently the plot was not only to kill Jesus but Lazarus also, 12.9-11, cf. 11.53,57. Again overwhelming belief is portrayed as the response to the sign of the raising of Lazarus but with a powerful minority determined to kill not only Jesus but Lazarus also.

Apparently the anointing was followed ("on the next day") by Jesus' entry into Jerusalem, 12.12-19. The great crowd (12.9,12) that came out from Jerusalem is thus portrayed as those who have come to believe, especially through hearing of the *sign* of the raising of Lazarus from the crowd that had been present at the time and had borne witness to it, 12.17-18. The incident returns to the perspective of the crowd and the assessment of the Pharisees that, "the world has gone out after him", 12.17-19. That assessment recalls the basis of the decision to arrest and kill Jesus. Unless he is prevented from continuing as he is, all will believe in him with catastrophic consequences, 11.48.

The assessment that "the world has gone out after him", already evidenced in the crowd that went out to meet him, is further verified by the coming of the Greeks seeking Jesus, 12.20-26. In what follows (12.27-36a) Jesus (and the narrator) explore the significance of the hour that has now arrived. It is the hour of death and glorification at the same time (12.27-28). It is also the hour of the judgement of this world and the casting out of the prince of this world, 12.31. Having spoken of his death in terms of glorification and judgement Jesus now speaks conditionally, "if I am lifted up (ἐὰν ὑψωθῶ) I will draw all people to myself" (12.32). The narrator informs the readers that this is an image of the manner of Jesus' death, 12.33. At this point the crowd is reintroduced and they note that Jesus has referred to his death as a departure. This is used as an objection to the messianic interpretation of Son of Man.[51] Jesus' response was to change the idiom to the transitory presence of the light which creates the possibility of leaving the darkness and, by believing in the light, to become sons of light, 12.35-36a. Thus, in the passage immediately preceding the use of the quotations dealing with unbelief, Jesus has spoken of:

1). The coming of the hour as the time of the judgement of this world and the casting out of the prince of this world;

2). The consequence of his own being lifted up as the moment of drawing all people to himself;

3). The presence of the light as the time of the opportunity for belief.

To this we add the reiterated motif running through Jn 11-12 that the majority openly believed on the basis of the sign of the raising of Lazarus and it is this widespread open belief which causes the powerful minority to plot the death of Jesus and of Lazarus as well.

The public ministry of Jesus concludes (Jn 12.44-50) with his solemn call (ἔκραξεν καὶ εἶπεν) to believe in him as the one sent by the Father. He returns to the image of the light coming into the world so that every one who believes in him should not remain in the darkness. Consequently 12.36b-43 is framed on either side by the call to believe in Jesus as the light and as the only way to be delivered from the darkness, 12.35-36a,44-46. Thus 12.36b-43 occurs in the context of the theme of the conflict of the light and the darkness.

ii Micro-context. When Jesus called on his hearers to believe in the light that they may become sons of light the narrator surprisingly indicates (12.36b) that Jesus hid himself from them. Those from whom he hid seem to be the many who believed through the sign of the raising of Lazarus (11.45,47-48; 12.11,17-18) and the Greeks who came seeking him (12.20-26). In the background is the plot to arrest and put Jesus to death (11.46-53,55-57). The motif of Jesus hiding himself must recall this,as is confirmed by Jn 12.37 which asserts:

But although he had done so many signs (τοσαῦτα δὲ αὐτοῦ σημεῖα)
in their presence they did not believe in him

---

[51]The crowd assumes that Jesus' "I" saying can be transposed into a Son of Man saying, that Son of Man is a messianic designation, and that "lifting up" refers to Jesus' death as departure. The last point is particularly surprising because the reader has to be informed of this meaning by the narrator who does not normally supply information that is known to the characters in the story (apart from Jesus).

ignoring the dominant motif running through Jn 11.1–12.36a which is the belief of the many. Now it is asserted that unbelief was the response to Jesus' ministry *in spite of the signs*. The quotations from Isaiah are then given to support this conclusion.

First Isa 53.1 is introduced by a fulfillment quotation formula:[52]

In order that the word of Isaiah the prophet might be fulfilled which he said, "Lord, who has believed our report? And to whom is the arm of the Lord revealed?"

It is sometimes argued that the "report" is to be understood as the teaching of Jesus and that "the arm of the Lord" refers to the divine action in the signs of Jesus.[53] But appeal to the words of Jesus makes little sense at this point as it is clear that they constitute a more serious stumbling block for belief than the signs (or *works* as Jesus refers to them, 10.38), and the quotation formula identifies this saying as the word of the prophet Isaiah who refers to "our report". Consequently it is more likely that here reference is only to the signs of Jesus, specifically referred to in Jn 12.37, and indirectly in 12.38 as "the arm of the Lord". While the saying is introduced by a fulfillment quotation formula there is nothing to be fulfilled in the question of 12.38. It has been used because it specifically raises the question of "who has *believed?*" The subject under discussion, introduced in 12.37, is the failure to *believe* in spite of the signs. The question, "and to whom is the arm of the Lord revealed?" understood in relation to the signs, asks who has perceived the signs as the saving acts of God. Failure to perceive them as such is the basis of unbelief. But how could they fail to perceive in the signs of Jesus, done before their very eyes, the arm of the Lord in action?

Jn 12.39-41 goes further than 12.37, which simply states that "they did not believe". Now it is said

Because of this (διὰ τοῦτο) they *could not* believe, because (ὅτι) again Isaiah said, ...

The initial "Because of this" may seem to look back to the quotation of Isaiah 53.1 but we have seen that this quotation gives no explanation for the unbelief in the face of Jesus' signs. Rather the διὰ τοῦτο is taken up in the ὅτι-clause, "because again Isaiah said". Thus the failure to believe is actually taken up in the quotation of Isa 6.10 (in Jn 12.40) which

---

[52]The fulness of this formula should be compared with Jn 15.25. Barnabas Lindars, *New Testament Apologetic* (1961) rightly notes the application of this text from the past to what was for John the events of the present as *pesher* interpretation now commonly know to us in the texts from Qumran.

[53]Thus C. K. Barrett, *John*, 431 and E. D. Freed, *Quotations*, 84-5.

provides the reason why they could not.[54] At this point John was wrestling with the reality of the unbelief of the Jews. Some consolation may be found in the recognition that Isaiah provides evidence that they could not believe. Isaiah 6.10 does not, however, refer to belief. Rather, as we have seen, John introduces the theme of belief by quoting Isa 53.1 in association with Isa 6.10. Blind eyes and hardened heart made it impossible to see the signs and consequently made belief impossible. The narrator asserts (12.41) that the glory of the pre-existent Jesus (λόγος) was seen by Isa (cf. Abraham in Jn 8.56) who thus bore witness to Jesus. Thus the context of Isaiah is important as the paradigm for understanding what was happening in the evangelist's day. Just as the witness of the prophet to the glory of the eternal λόγος was met with unbelief, so was the witness of the evangelist to the glory of the incarnate λόγος. Unbelief in the evangelist's day is interwoven with the theme of unbelief in response to the signs of Jesus giving the impression that this was the pervasive response in Jesus' day.

In spite of this[55] John goes on to assert that "many of the rulers believed in" Jesus (12.42), apparently contradicting, or at least qualifying 12.37,39. The qualification reflects a return to the perspective of Jesus' ministry where the response of belief was common. Even this is qualified by the shadow of the later situation and it is noted that they did not *confess* that belief openly because they did not wish to be cast out of the synagogue, putting in question the validity of that belief, though John does not hesitate to say of these rulers that "they believed in him (Jesus)". Here fear (cf. Jn 9.22) is not said to inhibit the confession of faith but love of the praise of men rather than praise from God (Jn 12.43). In a way we are here presenting an artificial alternative because the rulers who had believed feared the power of the Pharisees who could have them cast out of the synagogue. The explanation that they preferred the praise of men gives the basis for their unmentioned fear. They feared the loss of praise from men. These rulers are said to have believed but the evangelist qualified this by indicating they were unwilling to confess their belief openly. There is not doubt that they are presented as believers because they are made an exception (ὅμως μέντοι) to the assertion that "they were not able to believe".

iii Qualifying the obvious. Some qualifications must be made to the assertion that "they were not able to believe":

---

[54]Thus the fulfillment formula of Jn 12.38 applies more to the quotation of 12.40 than 12.38.
[55]The exceptional nature is brought out by the use of ὅμως μέντοι.

1. The disciples, who were Jews, are depicted in the process of coming to authentic faith towards which they move after the passion and resurrection of Jesus.

2. Immediately before and after this announcement of unbelief Jesus called for belief (Jn 12.35-36a,44ff) apparently with the expectation that such belief remained a possibility.

3. Belief appears to be the mass and open response to Jesus as a consequence of the sign of the raising of Lazarus, Jn 11.45-46,47-48; 12.9-11,12-19.

4. Jn 12.42 introduces a heavily qualified ($\delta\mu\omega\varsigma\,\mu\acute{e}\nu\tau o\iota\,\kappa a\acute{\iota}$) exception to the assertion that "they were not able to believe". "Nevertheless however even from among the rulers many believed in him". True, this belief is then qualified by the indication that these rulers would not confess their faith openly because they preferred praise from men rather than praise from God. But the evangelist does not hesitate to say that they "believed" and he sets out this belief as an exception to the assertion, "they were not able to believe".

5. John was combining two sets of data: tradition from the ministry of Jesus in which he openly gained a large popular following and the reality of the situation of his own time in which the Jews not only were not believers but active opponents of those who were. Intimidation was one reason for the reluctance of many to believe openly, 9.22; 12.42; 16.2.

If Jesus' activity was aimed at calling forth belief, what, according to John, was it that prevented that belief? In Isa 6.10 God is thought to be the speaker, but in Jn 12.41 the revelation is thought to be of the pre-existent Jesus.[56] Given that the pre-existent Jesus is the speaker in Jn 12.40 it is he who would heal them though this was prevented by their failure to be turned to him as a consequence of being blinded and hardened. On this reading it could be God who has blinded and hardened them so that Jesus may not heal them.[57] While this reading has some appeal, and support for a predestinarian view can be found in other parts of the Gospel, the world of thought that surfaces in the Gospel, the immediate and broader

---

[56]The two uses of $a\mathit{\dot{v}\tauo\hat{v}}$ do not clearly refer to Jesus, but the $a\mathit{\dot{v}\tau\acute{o}\nu}$ of 12.42 does and it is inconceivable that the person in view has changed. Jn nowhere calls the pre-existent one Jesus. It would be anachronistic to use the name of the incarnate $\lambda\acute{o}\gamma o\varsigma$ in this way though Jesus assumes a continuity in Jn 8.58.

[57]Thus R. Schnackenburg, *John*, II, 415.

literary contexts of the text,[58] and the modifications the evangelist has made to the text from Isaiah, all suggest an alternative view.

2. The Evangelist's Changes

i. Changes to the tense, person and voice of the verbs in the text quoted in Jn 12.41 draw attention to the opposition between the the one who has blinded and hardened and the one who would heal. Whether the evangelist has used the Hebrew, LXX, or some other version, or has quoted from memory, possibly influenced by Targumic interpretation, cannot be answered with certainty. It is sufficient to say that the quotation of Isaiah 6.10 in Jn 12.40 does not agree with the LXX, the Hebrew or any of the other New Testament quotations of the text. Like the LXX, John concludes the quotation with $\kappa\alpha\grave{\iota}$ $\acute{\iota}\acute{\alpha}\sigma o\mu\alpha\iota$ $\alpha\grave{\upsilon}\tau o\acute{\upsilon}\varsigma$,[59] thus using the verb in the first person singular future indicative active in place of the passive of the Hebrew. Given that in Isaiah God is understood to be the speaker, the use of the first person singular in the LXX is a correct interpretation of the divine passive in the Hebrew. John's view emerges in 12.41-42 which identify Jesus rather than God with the one revealed. Unique to John also are the changes to the verbs at the beginning of the quotation, from the imperative mood to the third person singular perfect indicative active, thus setting the action in the past (though the consequences remain) rather than the future and distinguishing the agent of the past action (blinding) from the action of Jesus who would heal them. Although most interpreters attribute these changes to the evangelist too little attention has been paid to them because it is assumed that the changes were not intended to make any material difference to the use of the quotation. Yet they necessitate the distinction of the one who has blinded from the one who would heal.

ii. Language introduced or excluded by the evangelist is a clue to the origin of the obduracy. First, it is regularly noted that John omits the reference to hearing. According to Evans, "Throughout the fourth gospel emphasis is placed on seeing rather than hearing,..."[60] This is hardly convincing when the concentration on discourse material is remembered and this perspective can be summed up in Jesus' words, "Truly truly I say to you, the one who hears my words and believes on the one who sent me has eternal life..." (Jn 5.24) More to the point, Evans draws attention to the significance of "the immediate context in which Jesus has healed a blind

---

[58] Associated themes that emerge from the consideration of the context should be taken into account, especially Jn 3.19-21; 9.39-41; 12.31-32,35-36a,46.

[59] For Hoskyns the use of these words confirmed that Jn was using the LXX.

[60] *To See*,.129

man". The use of τυφλός in Jn 9 may have suggested the use of the verb τετύφλωκεν in Jn 12.40. But this is not altogether convincing, given that three lengthy chapters lie between that chapter and the use of τετύφλωκεν.

Given that the issue at stake is the failure of the signs to lead to faith, the emphasis on blindness is appropriate. Does this mean that they failed to believe because, being blind, they were unable to see the signs? Certainly there were those who were sceptical of the actuality of the signs (Jn 9.18) and Jn 6.26 has been interpreted as if it denied that those who sought Jesus were able to see his signs and as a consequence they failed to believe in him:

"Truly truly I say to you, you seek me not because you saw signs,
but because you ate of the loaves and were satisfied."

But this is a mistaken reading. Jesus did not deny that the crowd that sought him had seen the signs (referred to 6.2,14). It is not a different crowd from the one that followed him and was fed by him. They had eaten of the loaves and been satisfied (6.26). If the people mentioned in 6.14 saw the sign (of the feeding) it is hardly likely that the evangelist intended the reader to think that the crowd as a whole knew nothing about it. The evangelist has a different point to make. The people in the crowd knew of the sign and were aware that they had benefited from it. They followed Jesus because they wished a repeat performance in which they would again benefit. They looked for another sign. Thus "sign" has various levels of meaning in John. It means first, "a mighty work" or, what we might call, a "miracle".[61] Clearly those who opposed Jesus recognized that he performed many signs (11.47), one of which was the raising of Lazarus, 12.9-11. For the evangelist, however, the signs were more than simply "mighty works" and some of those who saw them were aware of this.

Those who saw the sign of the feeding recognized that it signified something about Jesus. In this, according to the evangelist, they were right. But they were not right in what they thought was signified and this is shown by Jesus' rejection of the attempt to make him king (6.14-15). Thus, even for those who perceive that the signs point to the significance of Jesus, there is the question of whether the perception is right. Naturally, for Jn, the correct perception is believing perception which corresponds with his own view.

The evangelist has substituted the blinding of the people for the shutting of their eyes. Either way they do not see so that the change might

---

[61]Reluctance to use the term "miracle" is an indication that the term has no exact equivalent in the first century. The modern understanding of miracle owes much to the discussion of David Hume.

not seem significant. But blindness is a more serious problem because those who shut their eyes may open them. In the ancient world blindness normally refers to the total and permanent loss of sight. Blindness was generally considered to be incurable.[62] Blindness was a state over which the blind had no control. Given the parallel with the hardening of the heart it is clear that the language of blindness is used metaphorically even though the eyes are specifically mentioned. But because the evangelist has changed the language of closing the eyes to blinding, the purpose of doing this would seem to be to bring out the seriousness of the situation. Indeed, in normal terms, blindness was a hopeless condition.

In the Masoretic text the prophet is instructed to "shut" the people's eyes while in the LXX the people shut their own eyes thus portraying them as being responsible for their own failure to see. In John it is affirmed that "he has blinded their eyes" ($\tau\epsilon\tau\acute{u}\phi\lambda\omega\kappa\epsilon\nu\ a\dot{u}\tau\hat{\omega}\nu\ \tauo\grave{u}\varsigma$ $\dot{o}\phi\theta a\lambda\muo\grave{u}\varsigma$). If John is using the LXX he has moved from describing a voluntary action of the people to the portrayal of a destructive act committed upon them by a third party. The notion of being blinded is, as we have seen, much more negative than the shutting of eyes. Those who shut their eyes may open them again but those who are blind are not able to see. According to John, God's purpose in creation is not for eyes to be blind, an issue that almost surfaces in Jn 9.2. Rather, in John, it is God who makes the blind to see (Jn 9 and see Isa 35.4-6).

The notion of blinding is somewhat sinister and the rare use of $\tau\upsilon\phi\lambdao\hat{u}\nu$ in the LXX, where it is used only three times, suggests that we need to account for the introduction of the term at this point in John. This impression is confirmed by the rare use of $\tau\upsilon\phi\lambdao\hat{u}\nu$ in the New Testament. The verb is used only three times, in Jn 12.40; 2 Cor. 4.4 and 1 Jn 2.11 and these uses are mutually clarifying.

According to Paul in 2 Cor. 4.4:

... the god of this world has blinded the minds ($\dot{\epsilon}\tau\acute{u}\phi\lambda\omega\sigma\epsilon\nu\ \tau\acute{a}$ $\nuo\acute{\eta}\mu a\tau a$)[63] of the unbelievers, to keep them from seeing the light of the gospel of the glory of Christ, who is the image of God.

Here Paul addresses the problem of unbelief and concludes that the fault lies neither with the gospel, nor with those who preach it, but with Satan who has blinded those who, as a consequence, are unable to believe. They do not believe because Satan has blinded them.

In 1 Jn 2.11 the writer asserts that "the darkness blinded his eyes" ($\dot{\eta}$ $\sigma\kappao\tau\acute{\iota}a\ \dot{\epsilon}\tau\acute{u}\phi\lambda\omega\sigma\epsilon\nu\ \tauo\grave{u}\varsigma\ \dot{o}\phi\theta a\lambda\muo\grave{u}\varsigma\ a\dot{u}\tauo\hat{u}$):

---

[62]Schrage, *TDNT* VIII, 271, 273.
[63]In 2 Cor. 4.4 it is $\tau\acute{a}\ \nuo\acute{\eta}\mu a\tau a$ that are blinded while in Jn 12.40 the hardened heart is not able to perceive ($\nuo\acute{\eta}\sigma\omega\sigma\iota\nu$).

> The one hating his brother is in the darkness and walks in the
> darkness and does not know where he goes, because the darkness
> blinded his eyes.

The language of 1 Jn is closer to the Gospel than 2 Cor. though both 1 Jn
and 2 Cor. use the aorist tense while the Gospel uses the perfect tense. But
in both Jn and 1 Jn it is eyes that are blinded and both use the idiom of
"walking in the darkness". The notion of blinded eyes rather than minds is
more a difference of idiom than meaning because neither the Gospel nor 1
Jn is dealing with physical blindness at this point. In the Gospel this is
confirmed by the way, in the quotation of Isa. 6.10, blinded eyes are in
parallel with hardened heart and the failure to see with eyes with the failure
to perceive ($\nu o\acute{\eta}\sigma\omega\sigma\iota\nu$) with heart. Thus John is not far from the notion
of the blinding of the minds ($\nu o\acute{\eta}\mu a\tau a$) though his use of heart rather than
mind reveals a more Semitic train of thought.[64] What is clear is that God
is not the agent of blinding in either 2 Cor. or 1 Jn. In 2 Cor. the agent is
the god of this world and in 1 Jn the agent is the darkness.[65]

In the LXX $\dot{\epsilon}\pi a\chi\acute{u}\nu\theta\eta$ is used to signify the hardening of the heart of
the people but John uses $\dot{\epsilon}\pi\acute{\omega}\rho\omega\sigma\epsilon\nu$. In this instance the variation does
not seem to be significant because there is a group of terms, including
these two, rightly translated as "to harden". Schmidt draws attention to the
interchangeability of these terms in Luther's translation and confirms the
correctness of this through a study of interchangeable readings.[66] In this
instance it is not possible to show any intent in the change of term. Thus
the emphasis falls on the blinding which is clarified by the description of
the hardening of the heart which destroys the possibility of the perceiving
heart. What we are talking of here is a spiritual blindness of which eye and
heart have become symbols.

In John the god of this world (the prince of this world) is the power of
darkness, Jn 12.31; 14.30; 16.11. Having mentioned the prince of this
world in 12.31, attention is drawn to the blinding effect of walking in the
darkness (Jn 12.35-36a and see 1 Jn 2.11). In Jn 12.35-36a Jesus
announced that the light (he himself, 8.12; 9.5) was to be present for but a
short time and exhorted his hearers to walk in the light while it was with
them so that the darkness would not overtake them ($\H{\iota}\nu a\ \mu\acute{\eta}\ \ldots$
$\kappa a\tau a\lambda\acute{a}\beta\eta$). Those who refuse to believe in the light have been overcome
by the darkness. But the light has not been overcome by the darkness ($o\dot{\upsilon}$
$\kappa a\tau\acute{\epsilon}\lambda a\beta\epsilon\nu$, Jn 1.5), rather Jesus himself has overcome the world (Jn

---

[64]See *TDNT* IV, 950.
[65]Compare here Eph. 6.12; Col. 1.13; 1 Jn 5.19; Lk 8.12; and from Qumran
1 QM XIII–XIV.9; 1 QS III.13-26, especially III.20-24.
[66]*TDNT* V, 1023.

16.33). Consequently Jesus called on his hearers to believe in the light so that they may become sons of light (12.36a). But 12.36b-41 indicates that the power of darkness had its sway and they could not believe though, as we have seen, this is qualified. Following the announcement of the failure to believe, Jesus is depicted as again calling for belief (12.44) and announcing:

"I have come into the world as light, that every one believing in me should not remain in darkness." (12.47)

He goes on to speak of those who hear and keep his words, which is a characterization of those who have been rescued from the power of darkness. Thus immediately on either side of the reference to "He has blinded their eyes" the evangelist portrays Jesus speaking of himself in terms of the light in conflict with the power of darkness which overcomes those who walk in it and it is clear that the power of darkness is to be understood in terms of the prince of this world mentioned in 12.31.

3. The Comparative Relevance of First Century Judaism

Jn's affinity with Qumran is nowhere more significant than in relation to the expression of dualism. For this see the discussion of Dualism in relation to John and Qumran in chapter 2 above.

4. The Support of Origen and Cyril of Alexandria

The understanding of the devil as the agent of blinding and hardening in Jn 12.40 has the support of Origen[67] and Cyril of Alexandria[68] Given that Greek was their language and they were not dualists but believers in one God their reading of Jn 12.40 must carry considerable weight. Since Augustine, who emphasized the sovereignty of God in interpreting this verse, their line of interpretation has been overlooked. But the interpretation of Origen and Cyril has the support of a contextual reading and is consistent with a reading of the dualistic sections of the Qumran Texts. That Jn has the power of darkness in mind in Jn 12.40 is also suggested by the relationship of Jn 12 to the Gethsemane account in Lk. There, in response to the act of betrayal by Judas and and the actual arrest, Jesus is recorded as saying, "but this is your hour, and the power of darkness" (Lk 22.53). Although the arrest narrative does not come until Jn 18, Jn 12.27 is related to the Synoptic prayer in Gethsemane and in what follows in Jn 12.31-36 Jesus speaks of his conflict with the prince of this world and the conflict of the light with the darkness.

---

[67]Fragment XCII (*Die Griechischen Christlichen Schriftsteller der ersten drei jahrhundrerte*, 554ff.

[68]See the fragment on Jn 12.40 in *PG* 74, 96-97 ; W. Bauer, *John*, 165; J.

5. Conclusion

In common with Paul (2 Cor. 4.4), the first letter of John (2.11) and the sectarian writings of Qumran John recognized that, although God is in control of the whole of creation, the power of darkness and falsehood cannot be overlooked. It is likely that this viewpoint was reinforced by the bitter struggle between the Johannine community and the synagogue although the links between John and the Qumran Texts suggest that the language of dualism was integral to the evangelist's worldview.[69] The significance of the language should not be reduced to an indication of the social situation of the community signaling its sectarian consciousness. The sectarian conscious reinforced the validity of this language but the dualistic language makes clear that power of evil is real and is opposed to God.

This dualistic interpretation is reinforced by the evidence of the Qumran Texts.[70] The general affinity of the Gospel with the Qumran Texts makes this parallel the more significant, especially as the affinity is nowhere more pronounced than with regard to the Johannine "dualism". In Jn, the prince of this world is the power of darkness (12.31; 14.30; 16.11). Having mentioned him (12.31), attention is drawn to the blinding effect of walking in the darkness (12.35ff.).[71] Jesus, the light (8.12), was present for a short time (9.5). He exhorted his hearers to believe in the light that the darkness may not overwhelm them ($\kappa\alpha\tau\alpha\lambda\dot{\alpha}\beta\eta$). Jesus had not been overcome ($o\dot{v}$ $\kappa\alpha\tau\dot{\epsilon}\lambda\alpha\beta\epsilon\nu$) by the darkness (1.5). He had conquered the world (16.33). Those who refused to believe had been overcome by the darkness. The only way to overcome the darkness was to believe in the light. The power of darkness still had its sway (12.39), but there were some exceptions (12.42).

Jn, like Paul and the Qumran Sect, acknowledged God's rule over the whole creation, but the power of darkness is not overlooked. The coming of the Word made flesh made belief possible (3.19-21). During the ministry of Jesus the signs had a limited effect, producing a limited faith (2.23ff.), even among the leaders (12.42f.). When Jesus was lifted up the power of evil was broken (12.31f.) and faith on a universal scale became possible. The possibility is linked with Jesus' glorification (2.22; 12.16) and the coming of the Paraclete (14.26; 16.7). In the eschatological moment all men are called to believe (4.22ff.; 5.25) Those who refuse

---

Blank, *Krisis*, 304-5; M. Wiles, *The Spiritual Gospel*, 109.

[69] See chapter 2, "Johannine Christianity" above.

[70] QM XIII.1-XIV.9; 1 QS III 13-IV.26, especially 1 QS III.20, 24.

[71] Note I Jn 2.11 and the relation of Jn 12.27 to the Gethsemane prayer in which Lk (22.53) records Jesus' words, "but this is your hour and the power of darkness."

definitively choose the darkness and are finally and irrevocably in the darkness (3.19ff.; 9.39ff.). Those who believe leave the world of darkness for the light.

The Gospel presupposes the reality of the power of darkness. It is because of the pervasive power of darkness in the world created by the λόγος that the λόγος became flesh. But the "incarnation" by itself did not overcome the power of darkness. Consequently Jesus' ministry is portrayed as an assault on the power of darkness (3.19-21; 8.12; 9.5,39-41; 12.35-36a,46). That assault is portrayed as a struggle leading up to a cosmic exorcism (Jn 12.31-33).[72] Although the signs of Jesus play a significant role in the struggle, 12.36b-43 inform the reader that the signs failed to overcome the darkness. In spite of the many signs Jesus did before them they failed to believe in him. But how could this be? The evangelist's answer is that they were unable to believe because the prince of this world, the power of darkness, blinded their eyes and hardened their heart. This makes clear that the decisive conflict is yet to take place and, according to 12.31-33, in the immediate future. Jesus' ministry of signs was not without impact. Although the signs were not decisive, the evangelist indicates that "even of the rulers many believed" (12.42). But the character of this belief reminds the reader of the power of darkness because the values of these believers were corrupted by the darkness (1 Jn 2.11). Because they loved the glory of man rather than the glory of God (12.43) they were unwilling to confess their faith openly. Coming at the end of Jesus' ministry the concluding summary of 12.36b-43 serves to reinforce the critical nature of the lifting up of Jesus as the judgement of the world and exorcism of the prince of this world.[73]

There may be little appeal in a dualistic worldview in the twentieth century but the attraction of such a view for the evangelist is obvious. He needed to explain the rejection and crucifixion of Jesus and the rejection of believers by the synagogue. Such a mystery of evil confirmed his view of a limited dualism. Those who rejected Jesus and the believers were children of the devil whose eyes were blinded by the power of darkness. The evangelist and his community believed themselves to be children of God,

---

[72]See chapter 5 part V, "John and Apocalyptic Ideology" above and my "Theology and Eschatology in the Prologue of John", *SJT* 46/1(1993), 27-42.

[73]The finished Gospel recognizes that the power of darkness continues to confront the believers in the world even after the death and resurrection of Jesus. It is for this reason that the Farewell discourses look to the role of the Paraclete/Spirit of Truth to continue the judgement of the world (see 16.4b-11) and Jesus prays that the disciples, left in the world , will be kept from the corrupting power of darkness (Jn 17).

children of the light.

VII. REVELATION AND RESPONSE

Jn speaks of varying responses of faith, based on:

(1) signs (2.23f. *et al.*);

(2) the witness of Jesus' works (10.37f.; 14.10f.);

(3) Jesus' word (5.31; 8.18);

(4) the apostolic witness (15.26f.; 17.20ff.).

We may ask whether the varying responses are in any way related to the different bases of faith.

1. Superficial Faith

Faith expressed in the context of Jesus' ministry can only be understood as a partial faith. It expresses the attraction of people to Jesus as a miracle worker, teacher, prophet, or Messiah. The form of the statement in 2.23 reveals two characteristics of popular superficial faith:

i. $\Pi o\lambda\lambda o\grave{\iota}$ $\dot{\epsilon}\pi\acute{\iota}\sigma\tau\epsilon\upsilon\sigma\alpha\nu$ or variations using $\pi o\lambda\acute{\upsilon}s$ or $\pi\acute{\alpha}\nu\tau\epsilon s$[74] indicate popular, superficial faith. The aorist tense is normally used,[75] drawing attention to the specific situation which attracted the crowds. Nothing is indicated about the quality or duration of faith by the tense of the verb. But the contexts show that this faith had yet to face the scandal of Jesus' claims about himself. In many cases it proved transitory. But there were those who went on to believe authentically.

ii. This faith arose out of seeing Jesus' signs.[76] While this was a real turning to Jesus, Jn indicates that it was inadequate (2.24), because these believers wanted to find the fulfillment of their own purpose in Jesus (6.15; 12.13ff.).

Misunderstanding is also a mark of superficial faith. Those who are said to have believed are shown to have misunderstood Jesus' role and significance. This is an historical problem in that misunderstanding arose from the Jewish categories. Jesus was thought of as a prophet, miracle worker, or as the Messiah, understood as a political figure. Such faith had to meet the scandal of Jesus' self-testimony. The way Jn has used misunderstanding indicates the significance of a proper assessment of the person and work of Jesus for authentic faith.

The misunderstanding motif has been recognized as a pedagogical

---

[74]2.23; 4.39,41; (6.2) 7.31; 8.30; 10.42; 11.45,48; 12.11,42.

[75]In 6.2 and 12.11 the use of the imperfect tense anticipates rejection and in 11.48 the future tense is used in a prediction.

[76]2.23ff.; 3.2; 6.2,14,49f.; 7.31; 9.16; 10.41-42; 11.45,47f.; 12.18-19,37,42.

technique used by Jn.[77] But it is not merely a literary device. It has for Jn the same function as the messianic secret in Mark, and expresses an appreciation of the historical situation of Jesus' ministry. The problem is not merely that the Jews did not know that Jesus was the Messiah, nor that they understood the messianic role in terms of a conquering king rather than in terms of service and suffering. Jn emphasizes that Jesus is the one in whom God is present and active in his love for the world. Thus the misunderstanding motif is historically based, dramatically developed and has a pedagogical purpose in the structure of the Gospel which was written to remove inadequate attitudes to Jesus which would not be able to stand the test of Jewish persecution. The Gospel was written to bring about authentic faith which perceives Jesus' unique place in salvation history as the incarnate Word which Jn has made the basis for his interpretation of the messiahship of Jesus as Son of God (20.31). Misunderstanding is confronted by Jesus' self-testimony which scandalized his hearers and produced murmuring.[78] The murmuring indicates dissatisfaction with the one who has not measured up to expectations. Jesus indicated that he did not intend to fulfil these expectations and brought about a direct confrontation of his way with theirs (6.26ff.). This led to *division*, the rejection of faith by some of those who had originally believed (6.64-66) and the affirmation of faith by "the twelve" through Peter (6.68ff.; c£ Mk 9.27ff.).

2. Authentic Faith

Various statements suggest the realization of authentic faith during Jesus' ministry (1.14,49f.; 2.11; 4.42,53; 6.68-69; 9.35-38; 11.27; 16.29-30). But the fact that superficial faith cannot be distinguished from authentic faith by the formula used suggests that the contexts of these passages should be examined.

Jn 1.14 is part of the prologue and does not fit into the historical context of Jesus' ministry. It is a *reminiscence,* placed at the beginning of the Gospel to make the true nature of faith clear from the beginning.[79]

---

[77]Bultmann *op. cit., p.* 127, n1 etc. claims that this device was taken over from hellenistic revelation literature. He lists as examples of misunderstanding 2.20; 3.3f; 4.10ff,32f.; 6.32ff.; 7.34ff.; 14.4f,7f.,22ff.; 16.17f. A number of other examples could be added, 1.49ff.; 8.31ff.,38f.; 11.11ff.,23ff.; 13.8ff.; etc.

[78]γογγύζειν is used in 6.41,43,61;7.38, and this constitutes half of the uses of this verb in the New Testament. It is used twice in I Cor 10.10 to refer to the murmuring of the Israelites against Moses and Aaron, but ultimately against God, as in Exod 16.2; Num 14.2,36; 17.6-15 LXX.

[79]In 1.14 Jn asserts that the glory was visible to the eyewitnesses; that God was the origin of the glory; that the *nature* of the glory is the loving

The confession of 1.49, based on Jesus' miraculously acquired knowledge, is shown to be inadequate by 1.51. Jesus responded that the faith of Nathanael would ultimately be based on the assessment of him as the exalted Son of Man, worshipped by men and angels (1.51).[80] The certainty, "you shall see. . .", should be compared with the hypothetical, "What if you see. . ." (6.62). The certainty of the one and the uncertainty of the other distinguishes the faith of Nathanael from the superficial faith of the mass of disciples who would abandon Jesus. What distinguishes them at this stage is not greater perception, but the reality of Nathanael's decision to follow and his willingness to obey Jesus. The wording of his confession is capable of being understood at two levels, in terms of the Messiah of Jewish expectation or in terms of the unique, incarnate, Son of God of Johannine understanding.[81] This allows the reader to perceive more than was possible for Nathanael to know at the time.

The confessions of 4.42,53 and 9.35-38 are not modified by their contexts. Perhaps 4.42 looks forward to the fulfillment in the later Samaritan mission. In 4.53 the form of the statement should be compared with Acts 11.14 and 16.14-15,31, foreshadowing the Gentile mission. The man who had been blind becomes the example of the true believer in the Jewish situation who openly confessing his faith disregards the threat of excommunication (9.35-38).

The confession of Martha in 11.27 can also be understood at two levels. The words "who comes into the world" are Johannine and suggest the perception of authentic faith. But 11.39 indicates that this perception is lacking and that her understanding is as it was in 11.24, not having taken account of Jesus' self-testimony in 11.25f. Peter's confession in 6.68f., and the disciples' confession in 16.29-30 are both couched in the terminology of authentic faith. But the prediction of the disciples' defection brings this into question (6.70-71; 13.2,38; 16.31-32).

---

faithfulness of God seen in its fulfillment in Jesus.

[80]"You will see the heavens opened", and the Son of Man will be revealed as the central figure with the angels converging on him. Compare Acts 7.56. The scene is set in heaven as in Rev 4.1. The use of $d\nu\epsilon\omega\gamma\delta\tau a$ draws attention to the baptismal stories (Matt 3.16f.). But while the placing of 1.51 may suggest some relation to the baptism, the event spoken of is future, the lifting up of the Son of Man in his heavenly enthronement by the cross, receiving not only the worship of men (9.36-38), but also of angels (cf. Heb 1.6 and Mk 13.26; 14.62). His kingship does not await the future coming of the Son of Man but is revealed by his being lifted up to heaven by the cross.

[81]Understood in terms of Johannine irony the words "Rabbi, you are the Son of God. . ." express awareness of the incarnation, that the unique Son of God is to be known in a man, a mere Rabbi.

From the narrative confessions it is clear that authentic faith was not a reality during Jesus' ministry. These expressions, however, foreshadow the development of the fullness of faith and are an assessment in retrospect which recognizes an integrity lacking in the superficial faith of the multitudes. Faulty perception led to the defection of the disciples, but the integrity of their faith led to reinstatement. Because of this integrity Jesus prayed for his disciples in a way that he did not pray for the world, 17.9. The reason for stating faith in authentic terms in the context of Jesus' ministry is pedagogical. It is not an attempt to distort the historical perspective. There are many indications that this faith only came later and Jn develops, almost systematically, the reasons why it could only come later. The pedagogical purpose is based on the fact that the words and works of Jesus could not provoke authentic faith in the context of his ministry, but the reminiscence of them in the apostolic witness could. The difference between the situation of the ministry of Jesus and that of the apostolic witness is threefold and authentic faith presupposes:

1. The uplifting or glorification of the Son of Man (3.14ff.; 12.23,31f.; 13.31,32; (17.1)). The true glory of God in his love for the world was manifest in this event. Thus it was crucial for the coming of authentic faith. This event also brought about the effective judgement of the world by which Jesus overcame the blinding work of the power of darkness, making authentic faith possible.[82]

2. The coming of the Paraclete. This event is associated with the glorification of Jesus and the judgement of the world (7.37ff.; 16.7ff.).[83] The judgement began with the coming of Jesus, reached a critical stage at his glorification and continues to be made effective by the Paraclete whose coming Jesus' glorification made possible.[84]

3. The resurrection of Jesus. Great stress is laid on belief in the risen Lord (20.8,18,20,25,27-29). The resurrection is understood as an aspect of the glorification of Jesus. Through this event the disciples became aware

---

[82]No account is taken at this point of the sacrificial interpretation of Jesus' death in such passages as 1.29; 6.51; 10.11,17-18; 13; 17.19 etc.

[83]7.37f. deals with Jesus' offer of the Spirit. The appeal to Scripture is to be understood christologically as is usual in Jn. This is confirmed (in the explanation) by the clear statement concerning Jesus as the giver of the Spirit in 7.39. The same is true of 4.10 where the gift becomes the inexhaustible source of life in the believer (cf. 4.14). Jesus is the giver of the Spirit, the believer is the one who receives. See Schnackenburg, vol 1, 430f.

[84]While Jn emphasizes the eschatological fulfillment in Jesus' ministry (4.21,23; 5.25) and glorification (12.23; 13.1,31-32; 17.1), the complete fulfillment of the judgement on the last day remains in the future (5.25f; 6.39,44,54; 11.24).

of the true significance of Jesus and *remembered crucial* events in the life of Jesus so that they understood them in the perspective of salvation history, in relation to the Old Testament (2.22; 12.16). This *remembrance* is linked to the activity of the Paraclete (14.26).[85] While the events that were remembered were unchanged, the memory was modified by a new perspective, the resurrection of Jesus and the coming of the Paraclete (cf. Rom 1.4).

Because the Gospel was written for this new situation the narratives frequently have two levels of meaning. One has its roots in the situation of Jesus' ministry and the other takes account of the new situation. The distinction between the eyewitness believers and those who believe on the basis of their testimony (cf. 15.26-27; 17.20ff.; 20.29) is important because the Gospel is written eyewitness testimony. Thus there is a concentration on the terminology of witness and a complete absence of gospel and preaching terminology commonly found in the Synoptics, Acts and Paul. Because the Gospel purports to be written testimony for this new situation there is no distinction in terms between the professions of faith and the descriptions of authentic faith in Jesus' discourses. The record of his words and works, which were largely ineffective during his ministry, is offered as that which can provoke authentic faith (20.30f.).

VIII. CONCLUSION

Believing is an eschatological phenomenon because it is a response to the eschatological event. It involves a *perception* that was possible only after the glorification of Jesus. It is a gift of the eschatological age, made *possible* by the coming of Jesus, but made *actual* by the coming of the Paraclete.

The *decision* involved in believing is set against the background of Jewish persecution. The necessity of this decision is only clear when it is recognized that the eschatological revelation surpassed all previous revelations. It is the decision to follow Jesus no matter what the cost. The reality of the decision is worked out in *obedience* to Jesus' word, in the willingness to confess him openly no matter what the cost, and in loving service after the pattern of Jesus' own love (13.35). Both of these aspects of obedience are to be understood as the eschatological gifts of the Spirit to believers.

Faith is the eschatological gift to those who respond with integrity to the revelation in Jesus, whose coming potentially broke the grip of the power of darkness over men. To those who take advantage of the

---

[85]The accumulation of the terminology of remembrance is significant in 2.22; 12.16; 14.26.

opportunity created by his coming, the Paraclete brings the gift of authentic faith.

All people are the creation of the Word. Response to the Word is a possibility given in creation. The problem concerns the origin of the rejection of the Word. Jn explains this in terms of the power of darkness, the prince of this world, who has perverted people and blinded their eyes. The coming of the incarnate Word in judgement broke the grip of the power of darkness so that those who would could leave the darkness for the light that had confronted them in Jesus.[86] Those who came to him were given the Paraclete, through whom authentic *perception, decision, and obedience* became actual in the world. This is a phenomenon of the eschatological age of salvation. Given this perspective it is clear that the evangelist was aware that the arrival of the eschatological moment had led to the transformation of traditional messianic expectation in the christological understanding of eschatological faith. Expression of this faith is set out in terms that reflect the struggle of the believers with the synagogue. Thus Jesus, not the *Torah* is the light of the world and in this judging role he is confessed to be Son of Man.

---

[86]It is important to distinguish the power of the revelation event and the witness to or proclamation of it from the activity of the Spirit in the lives of the believers, those who have accepted the revelation. Jn affirms the power of the revelation just as Paul asserts the power of the proclamation (1 Cor 1.18; 2.4-5).

13

The Farewell of the Messiah

The fourth evangelist, like the other Gospel writers, has made use of a farewell scene. Each of the evangelists has set the farewell scene in the context of a farewell meal but Jn has developed a much more elaborate farewell discourse than the other evangelists. The focus on the farewell scene has precedent in both Jewish and Greek literature but there is probably no reason to look beyond the pattern in the literary *genre* of the *Testaments* of second Temple Judaism[1] which apparently has its precedent in the farewell scenes of Genesis. Here the central character calls together family and friends, recalls significant events, expresses foreboding and anticipation concerning the future and utters blessings, warnings and prayers. There is little doubt that Jn's farewell discourse and prayer have been shaped under the influence of this *genre*.

It is generally recognized that the farewell discourse and prayer represent a late stage in the development of the Gospel but those who adopt this approach tend not to consider whether that, like the Gospel as a whole, the farewell discourse contains several strata. The Gospel contains strata coming from different stages in the history of Johannine Christianity and in this chapter we hope to show that there are strata in the farewell discourse and that not all of these come from the later stages of development.

I. THE HYPOTHESIS

There is evidence to suggest that the evangelist composed not one but three versions of the farewell discourse: (l.) 13.31–14.31; (2.) 15.1–16.4a; (3.) 16.4b-33. He later added chapter 17 which is new material and not another version of the discourse. Originally 14.31, "Arise, let us be going" was followed by 18.1, ταῦτα εἰπὼν Ἰησοῦς ἐξῆλθεν σὺν τοῖς μαθηταῖς αὐτοῦ... At this point, and not before, they actually leave. In due course the second and third versions and chapter 17 were added. The second and third versions build on the first in a way that suggests that they are new versions of it. Each version reflects a particular situation of crisis in the history of the Johannine Christians. The crisis appears to be the occasion of the particular version of the discourse in which the evangelist makes his teaching response. This hypothesis of three versions explains why the Paraclete/Spirit of Truth material is not consolidated in one

---

[1] See especially *The Testament of the Twelve Patriarchs*.

block nor is it scattered at random. This material is the core of the evangelist's teaching response to each crisis. For completeness chapter 17 is included in this discussion but the main focus is on the versions of the farewell discourse of which chapter 17 forms no part. The form and *genre* of chapter 17 call for separate treatment though the prayer is an essential part of the farewell scene in its completed form.

II. EVIDENCE AND ARGUMENT

Four lines of evidence and argument are offered to support the hypothesis:
1. Apparent dislocations or breaks in the narrative;
2. Stylistic and word-thematic patterns of relationship and their bearing on the development of the discourse;
3. Historical reflections in the strata of the discourse;
4. Correspondingly reformulated teaching material.

For convenience points 3 and 4 will be dealt with together but they constitute two separate lines of evidence and argument. Points 1 and 2 will be discussed first, because they deal with *formal* aspects of the evidence, before turning to the *material* aspects of content.

1. Apparent Dislocations or Breaks

Recognition of the unity of the discourse need not prevent the detection of separable strata.[2] We are alerted to this, in the first instance by 14.31, "Arise, let us be going." It does not seem reasonable to suggest that the evangelist wrote this with the intention of continuing the discourse in 15.1 as if there had been no break. Nor does the suggestion that what follows in 15.1–16.33 was spoken "on the way", as Jesus walked with his disciples, solve the problems. There is no indication in 15.1ff. that they are "on the way". It is difficult to imagine chapter 17 as a prayer "on the way". But conclusively, 18.1 indicates that only then does Jesus leave with his disciples. How then can this apparent dislocation be accounted for?

Either, with Bultmann and others, we can rearrange the text on the assumption that, for whatever reasons, it is not now in the order intended by the author. Bultmann's reconstruction is as follows: 13.1-31a; 17.1-26;13.31b-35; 15.1-27; 16.1-33; 13.36–14.31; 18.1ff. Certainly this overcomes the problem of the dislocation but at the expense of the structure and development of the discourse as a whole.[3] There is an intelligible order of development in the discourse as it is. Here we need

---

[2]See George Johnston, *The Spirit Paraclete in the Gospel of John*, 70-4,162-71. But what he suggests is a "sequence of dramatic scenes" with "stage directions" such as 14.31.
[3]See Johnston, *The Spirit Paraclete*, 164.

note only that 14.16 appears to be the original introduction of the Paraclete/Spirit of Truth but this comes at the end in the reconstruction.

The problem of this apparent dislocation can be overcome while maintaining the existing order if it is recognized that the evangelist produced more than one version of the discourse. On the basis of the dislocation in 14.31, C. K. Barrett[4] suggested that two versions of the discourse were included in the Gospel: (1) Jn 14 (or 13.31–14.31) and (2) Jn 15-17 (or 15-16). That suggestion is now taken further at three points:
1. It postulates three versions;
2. It attempts to explain the need for three versions against the background of crisis situations reflected in the discourse;
3. It interprets the teaching of each version as the evangelist's response to the specific situations by reformulating the teaching about the Paraclete/Spirit of Truth.

The break between 14.31 and 15.1 is clear. That we have a new beginning in 16.4b is also generally recognized. The $\tau a \hat{v} \tau a$ of 16.1 is retrospective (as is shown by the use of $\lambda \epsilon \lambda \acute{a} \lambda \eta \kappa a$) linking 16.1-4a with chapter 15, while the $\tau a \hat{v} \tau a$ of 16.4b is prospective, referring to what Jesus is yet to say. The $\tau a \hat{v} \tau a$ of 16.6 refers to Jesus' announcement of his departure in 16.5 while 16.12 goes on to refer to what Jesus is as yet unable to tell the disciples, that which must await the coming of the Spirit of Truth. Our aim is to show that this literary seam (16.4a, 16.4b) marks the transition from the second to the third versions of the discourse.

2. Stylistic and Word-thematic Patterns of Relationship
This evidence, though complex, suggests the work of a single author[5] and the dependence of the second and third versions on the first.

i. *Data common to the three versions* includes the following expressions and themes:
"to ask in my name", 14.13-14; 15.7,16; 16.23f.;
"joy", 14.28; 15.11; 16.22,24;
$\tau a \hat{v} \tau a \lambda \epsilon \lambda \acute{a} \lambda \eta \kappa a$ and variations, 13.19; 14.25,29; 15.11; 16.1,4a,4b,6,25,33.

Each version makes use of the Paraclete/Spirit of Truth teaching, but in a developing fashion in which the second and third versions are closer to the first than to each other, suggesting that each of them was developed on the basis of the first. While it is only in the first version that there is reference to the $\check{a}\lambda\lambda o\nu$ Paraclete, linking him with Jesus (see 1 Jn

---

[4]*John* (1955), 379 and (1978[2]), 454f.
[5]C. K. Barrett, *John* (1978[2]), 455.

2.1), each version *introduces* the Paraclete and indicates the conditions of his coming, at Jesus' request, 14.16; sent by Jesus from the Father, 15.26; sent by Jesus who must first depart, 16.7. Such repetition makes good sense if what we have is the *introduction* of the Paraclete in each of three successive versions, though the reference to the Paraclete in 14.16 looks like the original introduction.

ii. *The first and second versions* share the following expressions and themes:
keeping Jesus' word/commandment, 13.34; 14.15,21,23,24; 15.12,17;
keeping and loving, 14.15,21-24; 15.9-10;
obedience and protection, 13.34f.; 14.21, 27; 15.1-17;
foretelling as a basis of belief through *remembrance*, 14.29; 16.4a.
Both versions use Paraclete and Spirit of Truth as synonyms, 14.16-17; 15.26-27, while the two titles are given distinct functions in the third version.

iii. *The first and the third versions* are connected by the stress on the abandonment of the disciples, 13.31-38; 14.1ff.,18ff. In the first version the initial sense of abandonment at the death of Jesus is overcome by the appearance of the risen one. When these appearances cease there is the hope of his coming again, 14.3. A new crisis emerged when it became clear that the promised return had been delayed. It is likely that the first version is a response to the problem of the "failure of the parousia". The Paraclete/Spirit of Truth is the new mode of Jesus' presence with his disciples.

Abandonment by Jesus was experienced with increased intensity when the believers were excommunicated from the synagogue. This accounts for the re-emergence of this theme in the third version with its stress on the overwhelming λύπη of the disciples, 16.6,20,22; brought about by the departure of Jesus, 16.5,16,28; cf. 13.33; 14.19.

The third version picks up the *ex eventu* "prophecy" of Peter's denial (13.38) and foretells the apostasy of the disciples, 16.32. The forced break from the synagogue probably led to the defection of a number of believers, leaving the community in disarray. The disconcerting effect could be overcome to some extent by showing that Jesus had foretold the defection and given his assurance of ultimate victory, 16.33.

In both versions the temporary nature of the crisis is stressed by the use of μικρὸν, 13.33; 14.19; 16.16,17,18,19, and there is great stress on the promised consolation, 14.1,3,18,23,27,28; 16.6,20-22,33. The coming consolation is not far distant (ἐν ἐκείνη τῇ ἡμέρᾳ) things will be changed, 14.20; 16.23,26. But the teaching of the third version goes beyond the first in the confident promise of victory over the world, 16.33, cf. 16.8-11, the victory of faith over unbelief. It seems that the situation reflected in each version is different; in the first it is the crisis of Jesus' absence, probably as a consequence of the growing awareness that his coming again was not to be in the near future; in the third the crisis is the renewed experience of Jesus' absence as a consequence of the believers' excommunication from the synagogue and experience of alienation in the world.

iv. *The second and third versions* share a stress not to be found in the first. The believers face trials and tribulations, the central theme in the second version, 15.18-20,23-25. and 16.1-4a where the tribulations spoken of generally in chapter 15 have become the persecution of the believers by the Jews. It is possible that 15.18-25 has been modified in the more general sense of worldly hostility in the light of the situation reflected in the third version, 16.25-33. Both versions conclude by foretelling disaster (ταῦτα λελάληκα) 16.1-4a; 16.32-33. But while the purpose of this in the second version is that faith might *survive*, in the third version the words are spoken as an assurance of victory already achieved in Jesus' victory over the world which continues to be manifest through the presence of the Paraclete with the believers, 16.8-11.

Our analysis suggests that the second and third versions have been developed on the basis of the first. Alone this evidence might merely indicate that the evangelist developed the discourse as a whole on the basis of the foundation laid in the first part, 13.31-14.31. That this is not the case is signalled by the clear break in 14.31, which alerts us to the less clear break between 16.4a and 16.4b. The case is further strengthened by taking account of the changing historical reflections and the corresponding teaching responses which have already been the subject for some discussion in this section.

3. Historical Reflections and Reformulated Teaching

Each version of the discourse reflects a particular crisis to which the evangelist responded with a reformulation of the teaching about the Paraclete/Spirit of Truth. It seems likely that, quite early in the history of Johannine Christianity, the evangelist began to use the Paraclete/Spirit of Truth teaching to justify his own distinctive position, in particular his "higher" christology. Thus the reader is able to understand Jesus more adequately than those who encountered him in the Gospel drama and to perceive the deeper meaning in the traditional confessions of Jesus' messiahship.[6] Through the teaching about the

---

[6]See my "The Church and Israel in the Gospel of John: A Response", *NTS* 25 (1978-79),109ff.

glorification of Jesus and the coming of the Paraclete/Spirit of Truth the evangelist justified these developments, perhaps against those who would not go beyond the terms used in the context of the ministry of Jesus. Without denying the validity of that tradition the evangelist reinterpreted it believing himself to be under the guidance of the Paraclete/ Spirit of Truth. Raymond Brown makes the point as follows:

> The sacred material from the tradition of the original community became the source of reflection and expanded teaching in a later period as the community moved towards a higher christology ... John uses the concept of the Paraclete to justify the audacity of the Johannine proclamation.[7]

This point is well made but I question two points of detail. I doubt that the community as a whole moved. Rather the evidence seems to suggest that the evangelist moved (and the Johannine school with him) and that the Gospel is intended to encourage a more widespread movement. The centrality of the christological presentation makes sense in a context where the readers needed to be persuaded of the truth of this position. Nor do I see why this process must have occurred in "a later period".[8] If the farewell discourse is viewed as a literary unity this is necessary.[9] But if 13.31–14.31 is the first of three successive versions there is no reason why it should not have been composed at a relatively early stage of Gospel development.

As the Paraclete/Spirit of Truth teaching is used to justify the "higher" christology of the Gospel as a whole it is hardly likely that this material is a later redactional insertion. But the origin of the evangelist's use of the Paraclete title remains a mystery.[10] The Qumran texts provide linguistic parallels for certain of the activities of the Paraclete[11] and certainly throw light on the use of "the Spirit of Truth" especially in 1 Jn 4.1-6 where the Spirit of Truth is opposed to the Spirit of Error, corresponding to the opposition of the Spirit of Truth and the Spirit of Falsehood in the texts.[12] In the New Testament "Paraclete" is not used

---

[7]*The Community of the Beloved Disciple* .28.

[8]Pauline christological development had already taken place by the middle of the first century.

[9]Jn 16.2 would make a later date necessary.

[10]The attempt by Eskil Franck (*Revelation Taught*) to uncover the background for the Johannine Paraclete in the function of the *Methurgeman* as midrashic interpreter in the Synagogue does no more than highlight some parallel functions.

[11]See O. Betz, *Der Paraklet*.

[12]The "dualism" of Spirits reflects schisms in the two communities; the Qumran sect from Judaism as a whole and the Johannine community from

outside the farewell discourse except in 1 Jn 2.1 where it refers to Jesus. The introduction of the Paraclete in Jn 14.16 refers to "another Paraclete" suggesting a familiarity with the tradition of 1 Jn 2.1. Here (in Jn 14.16) the Paraclete takes the place of the departed Jesus or, perhaps better expressed, is the means by which Jesus, though absent, is present with his disciples.[13] The Paraclete is the new mode of Jesus' presence which means, because Jesus was the mode of God's presence, the new mode of the presence of God, 14.19-24. But this is the *beginning* of an understanding which must be unravelled in the development of the discourse.[14]

The first version of the discourse is essential to the christological position of the Gospel as a whole, suggesting the relatively early formulation of this material. The successive versions appear to be later compositions. This is suggested by dislocation and *aporia*, and literary and word thematic relations between the three versions, which are related to the historical reflections and the corresponding teaching responses.

i The first version (13.31–14.31). The historical situation reflected is the scene of Jesus' departure leaving the disciples sorrowing, abandoned, orphaned, 13.31-38; 14.1ff.,18ff.,27. The crisis is depicted in emotional, psychological terms. The question is, how can the disciples overcome the trauma caused by the departure of Jesus? The evangelist's response is given in theological terms, and at two levels. The first level is that of the narrative situation which is prior to the crucifixion of Jesus. The sense of abandonment brought about by this event would be overcome by the appearance of the risen one to the believers, 14.18-20; cf. 20.1-29, especially 19-29. Perhaps 20.28 is to be seen as the fulfillment of 14.20. But this is a temporary solution as the risen one does not continue to be *seen*. At the second level, the post-resurrection situation, there is still the problem of the absence of Jesus. The evangelist's response is in terms of the coming of the Paraclete/Spirit of Truth. There are two Paraclete passages in the first version.

The first passage (14.15ff.), stresses the role of the Paraclete/Spirit

---

those who went out from them, 1 Jn 2.15. See also *Test. Judah* 20.1-3.

[13]R. E. Brown, *The Gospel According to John,* vol. 2, 1139, 1143, and see my *JWT,* 64-70. For this reason it is frequently noticed that the Paraclete is Jesus' "double" so that the functions ascribed to Jesus are also ascribed to the Paraclete.

[14]Here we can agree with Eskil Franck (*Revelation Taught*) that, because it is impossible to discover the origin of the evangelist's use of Paraclete, for us the Paraclete can only be "what he does". This is a methodological statement concerning discovering the role of the Paraclete in Jn and is not intended as a reductionist statement concerning the status of the Paraclete.

of Truth in overcoming the sorrow and sense of abandonment of the disciples. This is possible because the Paraclete is the new mode of Jesus' presence, of God's presence. So intimately does the evangelist link the Paraclete with Jesus that the language about the coming of the Paraclete is not clearly distinguished from the language concerning Jesus' coming to the disciples as the risen one. Perhaps that is because he thinks of them as different modes of the same presence because, like Jesus the Paraclete is the mode of God's presence, cf. 14.18-24. Because the Paraclete is with them the believers are to realize that they have not been abandoned.

In the *second passage* the Paraclete/Spirit of Truth is spoken of as the one who makes Jesus' teaching present and effective by *reminding* the believers of all that Jesus had taught them, 14.25ff. This appears to be an indication of *some form* of Christian prophecy in the Johannine community which was the recognizable form of the presence of the Paraclete. It is teaching by means of *reminding* the believers of all that Jesus had taught them. No doubt this *is memory* in the light of the *glorification* of Jesus which, the evangelist asserts, enabled him to understand Jesus in relation to the Jewish Scriptures and salvation history. Two examples of this style of memory have been given in the Gospel.

> Therefore when Jesus was risen from the dead his disciples *remembered* that he said this and they believed the Scripture and the word which he spoke." (Jn 2.22)

> At the time his disciples did not understand these things, but when Jesus was glorified they *remembered* that this had been written of him and they had done these things to him. (Jn 12.16)

Two things stand out about the nature of this teaching. Firstly, it is rooted in the historical tradition about Jesus, what he said, what was done to him. Secondly, the historical tradition is interpreted in the light of *a particular understanding* of the Old Testament. Thus the prophetic activity of the Paraclete is here portrayed in terms of the reinterpretation of the Jesus tradition to give expression to the evangelist's understanding of christology. Throughout the Gospel, traditional christological titles are reinterpreted to give expression to the so called "higher" Johannine christology[15] and this, it is claimed, is the work of the Paraclete.

The teaching of the first version in response to the sorrowing disciples was relevant to some extent as soon as Jesus had departed but especially

---

[15]See my "Christ and the Church in John 1.35-51" in M. de Jonge, ed. *L'Evangile de Jean.* David Hill (*New Testament Prophecy,* 149) rejects the association of the Gospel with a Christian prophet but immediately accepts the prophetic role of the Paraclete. But how was the activity of the Paraclete embodied or manifest if not in a Christian prophet or prophets?

when it became apparent that his promised return (14.3) had been "delayed". The christological development might also suggest that some time must have elapsed before this version could have been produced. Christological development needs, however, to be understood in relation to the dialogue with the synagogue and it should be noted that there is *no indication* of a critical situation in which relations might have been broken off by either side. The only crisis in view is the sense of abandonment by Jesus.

In terms of dating the first version much depends on how we assess christological development and eschatological reinterpretation. The "I am..." of 14.6 and "He who has seen me has seen the Father", 14.9, express a "high" christology, balanced, to be sure, by "the Father is greater than I", 14.29. Even so, Jesus is presented in a unique relation to the Father and as the only way to him. Given our awareness of christological development and eschatological reinterpretation in the letters of Paul, and the evangelist's special needs in the dialogue with the synagogue, there appears to be no good reason for dating the development later than the 50s. At this time, prior to the break from the synagogue, there was no separate Johannine community but simply *Christian Jews* of varying persuasions, amongst whom was the evangelist and in all probability, a small group associated with him which we call, for want of a better term, the *Johannine school*. Later they were to form the nucleus of the *Johannine community*.

ii The second version (15.1–16.4a). Talk of Jesus' departure has now disappeared. That crisis appears to have been overcome. The situation reflected in this version is the bitter conflict with the synagogue, 16.1-4a, especially 16.2,[16] cf. 9.22,34; 12.42. The synagogue had rejected and cast out those who confessed Christ,[17] or was in the process of doing

---

[16]The terms for excommunication from the synagogue are used only in Jn 9.22; 12.42; 16.2 in the whole of the NT. This is significant for the Johannine situation. See J. L. Martyn, *History and Theology in the Fourth Gospel*, chapter 2, 17ff. and C. K. Barrett, *John*, 361f.

[17]Brown, *The Community of the Beloved Disciple*, 123 notes that πιστεύειν is used 98 times in the Gospel and ὁμολογεῖν 3 (or 4) times while πιστεύειν is used 9 times in the Epistles and ὁμολογεῖν 6 times, a significant increase in proportionate use of ὁμολογεῖν over the Gospel. He concludes that the Gospel was not concerned with public confession. This might be true of early strata but the material formed in the conflict with the synagogue cannot be included in this assessment. Further, statistics are sometimes misleading. The importance of the occasion of use should be noted. If Martyn is right Jn 9 is of pivotal importance hence the use in 9.22 should be reassessed, as should 12.42, in the light of the importance of the treatment of the "secret believers" in the Gospel. Although ὁμολογεῖν is not used in 16.2 it is implied by the connection with 9.22 and 12.42 and the

so (ἀποσυναγώγους ποιήσουσιν ὑμᾶς), and was even causing the execution of believers. This action led to the formation of the Johannine community as a *Jewish Christian* community. Slight modifications seem to have been made to 15.18-25 to relate the theme of Jewish hostility to the later experience of the Johannine community, isolated from the synagogue and facing a hostile world, perhaps at the time of the third version. Only slight modifications need to have been made to 15.18-19 and the Jewish situation reappears in 15.25. The section in general lacks the specific and dramatic force of 16.1-4a which clearly deals with Jewish persecution, though the version as a whole deals with this problem.

While the synagogue had rejected the believers the evangelist responds with the rejection of those who do not abide in Jesus, the true vine, the true Israel of God, 15.1-10 and compare Hosea 10.1ff., Psalm 80.8-16. This excludes the unbelieving Jews but the real focus of the argument is the "secret believers" who were attempting to remain within the synagogue. This accounts for the absence of πιστεύειν from Jn 15, the only chapter prior to chapter 18 from which it is missing, because it is addressed primarily to those who in some sense could already be described as "believers". The situation finds a parallel in 8.31f. where the Jews who believed were challenged to *abide* in Jesus' word. The challenge to true discipleship in this situation of persecution focused on the enduring, abiding nature of faith and hence the stress on μένειν. Only those who abide belong to the vine. In this way the evangelist met the synagogue's rejection of those who confessed Christ (rejection from the people of God, 16.1-4a) and alternatively rejected those who did not abide in Jesus, who constitutes the true vine.

That the conflict with the synagogue was still in process in the formative stage of this version is confirmed by the fact that the teaching response of the evangelist is directed to this problem, first, as we have seen, in the "allegory" of the true vine, and then in his teaching about the Paraclete/Spirit of Truth. As in the first version, the Paraclete is simply identified with the Spirit of Truth. But now the activity of the Paraclete is seen in response to the crisis of believers being put on trial for their faith. Thus the Paraclete has become the Spirit of inspired Christian witness in the face of persecution. Put on trial before the synagogue the Spirit will speak through them in inspired *witness*, 15.26-27. The evangelist might well be interpreting the word of Jesus (in Q?), Matt 10.19-20 = Lk 12.11f.

---

understood μαρτυρεῖτε (περὶ ἐμοῦ) carried through from 15.26-27. The use of ὁμολογεῖν in this controversial context presupposes public confession as does the use in 1 Jn.

"When they bring you before the synagogues and rulers and authorities do not be anxious how you conduct your defence or what you will say. For the Holy Spirit will teach you in that hour what you must say." (Lk 12.11f.)

While it is generally recognized that Jn 15.26-27, which speaks of the witness of the Paraclete alongside the witness of the disciples, does not indicate two separate witnesses but rather indicates that the witness of the disciples is inspired by the Paraclete, this is not seen as related to the situation of trial depicted in 16.1-4a. But it is the witness of those who are on trial that is in view. This is an encouragement to those who might face the trial. They will not be left alone, though they might face death for their witness. Thus in 15.26f. we have precedent for the identification of the *witness* (μάρτυς) with the martyr, 16.2.

According to 16.1 Jesus' forewarning of persecution was given so that the disciples would not be taken by surprise in such a way that their faith would fail. In the crisis they will *remember* that Jesus had forewarned them, 16.4a. No mention is made of the Paraclete here, though 15.26f. is not far away, and the specific role of the Paraclete, according to the first version 14.26, is to *remind* the disciples of Jesus' words. This *remembrance* seems to be a reinterpretation of the role of the Paraclete according to the first version. It is now reinterpreted to take account of the situation of persecution. When the Paraclete comes he *reminds* the disciples of Jesus' forewarning and inspires their *witness* in the time of trial.

The situation of persecution by the synagogue is the clue to the chronological placing of this version. It is not sufficient to speak generally of conflict between Jewish believers and Judaism. Jn 15.1-16. 4a belongs to what we have called the *third wave of conflict*.[18] 15.1-10 should be compared with Romans 11. While the two "allegories" are similar it is the differences that highlight the different situations. In Jn 15 the evangelist makes the highly charged claim that Jesus (and by implication, not Israel) is the true vine. Participation in the vine depends on abiding in Jesus. Those who do not abide are cut off, i.e. unbelieving Israel. What is left is believing Israel. There is no suggestion of the grafting in of wild branches as Paul depicts in Romans 11. Thus the conflict does *not* concern the entry of Gentiles. The third wave of conflict is focused simply on the *confession of Christ*, see 9.22; 12.42. This situation seems to have been formative, not only for the second version, but for much of the Gospel. It seems probable that the bulk of the Gospel

---

[18]See "The Community and its History" pp.75–79 above.

was shaped in the formative periods represented by the first and second versions of the farewell discourse.

iii The third version (16.4b-33). The situation reflected here bears no traces of the struggle with the synagogue. The separation is now past and final and the community finds itself alienated from Judaism and in a hostile world. In this situation the believers experienced the abandonment by Jesus with increased intensity, 16.16-24. The evangelist again stresses that this grief would be short lived. It would be turned to joy and in the first instance (as in the first version) this is because of the appearance of the risen one. His return signals a new cause for joy, cf. 16.22 and 20.20. Whatever the believers ask the Father in Jesus' name will be given them and this is cause for complete joy. The break from the synagogue probably lies in the immediate past as the community does not yet appear to have come to terms with the world. It can only be apprehensive at the hostility of the unknown. Here the evangelist assures the believers of Jesus' victory over the world and appeals to that victory as the guarantee that the believers also will overcome the world. The situation seems to be that of a community in isolation and in danger of turning in on itself for protection. The evangelist sought to prevent that withdrawal by reformulating the teaching about the Paraclete, whose functions are now distinguished from those of the Spirit of Truth. The reason for this needs to be discussed.

In the first version Paraclete=Spirit of Truth and it is said that the world does not receive, see or know him, 14.16f. The problem with which that version was concerned was the disciples' experience of abandonment and the evangelist's teaching was a response to that problem. But the third version is concerned with the relation of the believers to the world. In extending the teaching about the Paraclete to relate to the world the evangelist followed a line of understanding already begun in the second version where the Paraclete/Spirit of Truth is said to inspire the witness of believers on trial for their faith. Thus the Paraclete has an indirect relation to the world. This is taken up in the third version where "Paraclete" is used in relation to the world and Spirit of Truth relates to the believing community where the world is not directly in view. The discussion of this teaching, after the pattern of the Johannine material, is divided into two parts:
1. Concerning the Paraclete and the world, 16.7-11;
2. Concerning the Spirit of Truth and the believing community 16.12-15.

1. *The Paraclete and the world* (16.7-11). Taking up the theme of the relation of the Paraclete to the world implied in 15.26f. the evangelist develops this theme in 16.7-11. The conflict with the unbelieving world goes on but there is now no critical threat in this encounter, as there was in

the conflict with the synagogue. It could be suggested that the community was experiencing "withdrawal symptoms", that is, isolating itself from the hostile world. In response to this problem the evangelist asserts that the community experiences Jesus' victory over the world in the reality of its own faith, 16.33, cf. 1 Jn 5.4. The life of the community, its faith and love, manifest Jesus' victory and evidence the activity of the Paraclete. From this perspective it turns out that the world, not the believing community, is on trial. What is said here of the Paraclete is parallel to what is said about Jesus as the judging revelation of God in Jn 1-12, especially in the use of the "light" symbolism of 3.19-21 and 9.4-5,39ff.

The Paraclete's role is to "convince", or "convict", or better, to "expose" ($\dot{\epsilon}\lambda\dot{\epsilon}\gamma\xi\epsilon\iota$) the world, Jn 16.8 and note 3.20.[19] In Jn 3.20, using the same word, describes the activity of Jesus in terms of the coming of the light:

> "This is the judgement,
> light has come into the world
> and men loved the darkness rather than the light,
> because their works were evil.
> Everyone practising evil works hates the light
> and does not come to the light,
> lest his works be *exposed* ($\dot{\epsilon}\lambda\epsilon\gamma\chi\theta\hat{\eta}$);
> but the person who does the truth comes to the light,
> that his works may be revealed ($\phi\alpha\nu\epsilon\rho\omega\theta\hat{\eta}$)
> because they are the works of God." (Jn 3.19-21)

Jn 9 also presents Jesus in terms of the light of judgement, exposing the sin of the world, condemning unbelief, and making belief possible. Jn 16.7-11 asserts that the judging activity of Jesus continues in the believing community through the presence of the Paraclete. Through his presence and activity the light continues to be active:

exposing the unbelief of the world as the epitome of sin;

revealing God's vindicating action in the resurrection of Jesus.[20]

It is the resurrection of Jesus that exposes unbelief as sin and at the same time vindicates Jesus and those who believe in him. For Jn the resurrection of Jesus is the basis of true faith, 20.8,19f. The very existence and the continuity of that faith are evidence of the vindication of Jesus whose presence, through the Paraclete, is manifest in that faith and in the brotherly love by which he lived and died (13.1) and which brings about

---

[19]The word is used elsewhere in Jn only in 8.46.

[20]In Jn 16.8 $\dot{\epsilon}\lambda\dot{\epsilon}\gamma\xi\epsilon\iota$ has a double meaning, the equivalent of $\dot{\epsilon}\lambda\epsilon\gamma\chi\theta\hat{\eta}$ and $\phi\alpha\nu\epsilon\rho\omega\theta\hat{\eta}$ in Jn 3.19-21. See B. Lindars, "$\Delta IKAIO\Sigma YNH$ in John 16.8 and 10" in *Festschrift für B. Rigaux* (Gembloux, 1970), 275-85 especially 280.

their recognition as his disciples, 13.35. The revelation of the light within the believing community is at the same time the revelation that judgement has taken place; the prince of this world has been judged and the power of darkness has been broken. The believing community itself is the evidence. The darkness no longer has power over them. They have left the darkness and come to the light and this is manifest in their faith and love. The event which made this possible was the uplifting of the Son of Man, his glorification, which was the moment of judgement for the power of darkness, shattering that power and enabling men to come to the light, 12.31f. It was also the event which brought about the coming of the Paraclete to the believing community, 16.7; cf. 7.37.

A glance at the commentaries[21] is sufficient to show the complexity of 16.7-11. In the outline given above $\grave{\epsilon}\lambda\acute{\epsilon}\gamma\xi\epsilon\iota$ is translated first as "he will expose", but this verb applies to three objects (sin, righteousness and judgement) and carries a different nuance in relation to each. Hence to do justice to the meaning in English this verb has to be translated more than once in this passage. The second sense of "revealing" is related positively (a good sense) while "exposing" is related negatively (a bad sense) to $\grave{\epsilon}\lambda\acute{\epsilon}\gamma\xi\epsilon\iota$. The argument can be set out as follows. The world is to be exposed concerning sin, righteousness and judgement. Jesus had been declared a sinner and judged guilty of death. The believers had also faced trial and been judged worthy of death, 16.2. The situation is reversed by the Paraclete. The world is now on trial. The sin of the world is exposed in its unbelief because Jesus' righteousness has been *revealed* through the vindication of his resurrection and exaltation to the Father. That reality is *revealed* in the coming of the Paraclete whose presence is manifest in the faith and life of the community. Thus the revelation of the vindication of Jesus exposes the claim of the world to righteousness as unrighteousness. Further, the world's claim to have judged Jesus is exposed by the revelation of the true judgement of which the believing community itself is the evidence demonstrating that the power of darkness is broken.

According to Jn 16.7-11 the Paraclete mediates the challenge of the revelation in Jesus to the world. The teaching is wholly optimistic about the outcome, possibly suggesting the rapid conversion of the world. It is the evangelist who expresses this optimism, probably in the face of the tendency of the community as a whole to withdraw from outside contacts. His teaching is a response to this problem. As yet the power and seduction of the world had not been felt with the impact that is evident in Jn 17 and 1 Jn. What the evangelist did see at this point was that, if the community

---

[21] See C. K. Barrett, *The Gospel According to St. John*, 405ff.

was to maintain the challenge of the revelation to the world, it would need to respond to new and changing situations. How could it face this task? It appears that he set out to inspire "mission" in this section.[22] But what could be offered in terms of guidance for the future?

2. *The Spirit of Truth and the believing community* (16.12-15). In describing the role of the Spirit of Truth the evangelist appears to be reinterpreting 14.26 which speaks of the Paraclete, the Holy Spirit. In the first version "Paraclete" and "Spirit of Truth" were used without distinction. But in the need to confront the world, "Paraclete" emerged as the reference to the Spirit in his "judicial" function in relation to the world of unbelief. In 16.12-15 the discussion of the role of the Spirit of Truth is restricted in scope to the believing community. The Spirit of Truth brings about a genuine understanding of the complete truth which is bound up with the confession of faith. There is as yet no problem concerning distinguishing the true from the false confession of faith which resulted in the antithesis between the Spirit of Truth and the Spirit of Error in I Jn 4.1-6. In Jn 16 the conflict is between the believing community and the unbelieving world and this is expressed in the use of "Paraclete", 16.7-11. "Spirit of Truth" is used exclusively in relation to the believing community in Jn 16.12-15 and appears in a conflict situation in I Jn only after the controversy concerning the true and false confession of faith had broken out *within* the community.

In the first version the teaching role of the Paraclete was described in terms of *reminding* the disciples of Jesus' teaching, 14.26. Thus the Paraclete's *interpretative* role was firmly tied to the Jesus tradition. But now it is said of the Spirit of Truth "he will guide you into the whole sphere of truth", 16.13. This is said in the context where Jesus asserts that the disciples cannot yet cope with all he has to say to them, 16.12. Thus the Spirit of Truth is to bring new truth which Jesus was not able to communicate to the disciples during his earthly ministry because of their limitations. But the evangelist asserts that this new communication remains the truth of Jesus:

"But when he comes, the Spirit of Truth,
he will lead you into the complete truth;
for he will not speak from himself,
but whatever he hears he will speak,
and he *will announce* to you the things that are coming.
He will *glorify* me,

---

[22]See Teresa Okure, *The Johannine Approach to Mission* and my review of this in *Pacifica* 3/3 (1990) 347-9.

because what he will receive from me he also will *announce* to you.
All that the Father has is mine;
because of this I said,
he receives from me and *will announce* to you." (Jn 16.13-15)

The threefold stress on *announcement* indicates the new orientation to the future and to new truth to be revealed. But the evangelist has not lost his christocentricity. All that the Father has belongs to Jesus, therefore the new truth for the future also belongs to him. The role of the Spirit is set out in terms of the significance of Jesus for future generations. His task is to glorify Jesus. That does not change. But the teaching does, as it is made relevant to the ever changing situations. In the new and bewildering situations the Spirit would guide the way, bound to Jesus but not bound to the past. Thus the truth of eternity is to be unveiled as the situations arise for which it is relevant. The new is bound to Jesus because, he asserts, "All that the Father has is mine". In this, however, there is no harking back to a fossilized tradition, rather there is the ministry of a living voice which speaks anew to each generation and situation. In fact, is this not what we have seen done in the successive versions of the farewell discourse?

While this interpretation has been set out in a fashion that could suggest that the evangelist created the Paraclete/Spirit of Truth to cope with the problems he encountered this is not what is intended. Rather the evangelist believed that he experienced the activity of the Paraclete/Spirit of Truth and set out to explain his experience in adequate terms. In the final version the role of the Spirit of Truth was presented in such a way that the truth revealed was no longer clearly bound to the Jesus *tradition*. New truth was to be revealed. No doubt this truth was believed to be uttered under the inspiration of the Spirit. But this raised the problem of recognizing true inspiration from the false. This problem had not emerged in the third version, rather it appears to have been encouraged by it.

iv **The community and the world (Jn 17).**[23] The situation reflected in this section appears to be slightly later than the third version and slightly earlier than I Jn. It is not a fourth version of the discourse as it presents quite different material. Certainly the break from the synagogue lies in the past and the community experiences its life in the "world". But the world is not now so much an aggressor as a seductive threat, 17 11-19. The hopes for the conversion of the world are still in view, 17.21,23, and

---

[23]See my *JWT*, 59ff.

the community probably already included some Gentiles. But the evangelist was aware that the community was in danger of falling away from the revelation that *had been given*, 17.6,8,14,17-19. The stress of the evangelist's teaching is to be seen in Jesus' requests.

The prayer can be analysed into three sections: for Jesus' glorification (1-5); for the disciples, that they may be kept from the corrupting power of evil (6-19); and for future generations of believers who believe on the basis of the word of the first believers, that the mission to the world may continue through them (20-26).[24]

The focus of the prayer is on the requests for the disciples and subsequent believers. It can be summarized in terms of keeping the disciples true to the revelation, of sanctifying them, that is, keeping them free from the corrupting power of the world, 17.11,15,17. There is also the repeated prayer for unity, 17.11,21-23. While the primary reference is to the unity of the believers with God through the revelation in Jesus there is obviously intended in the prayer a consequent unity of the believers in relation to each other. The threat to that unity might well have emerged in the situation of "second hand" believers (17.20-26). and we can suppose that their entry into the community brought about the threat of disunity. The "second hand" believers no longer had a direct link with the Jesus tradition and the third version of the discourse encouraged them to think of the revelation of new truth through the Spirit of Truth. Such "second-hand" believers, after the break from the synagogue, were probably predominantly Gentile with a tendency to interpret the activity of the Spirit in terms of "ecstatic utterance".[25] If this reconstruction is somewhere near the truth it helps to explain why there is no reference to the Spirit in chapter 17 but a return to the emphasis on the words of Jesus, the revelation that *had been given*. The repeated prayer for unity suggests that there was already a real threat of schism but that this had not yet occurred. The evangelist had hopes that this might be averted and that the revelation of the love of God seen in the community, whose life was grounded in the revelation in Jesus, would bring about the conversion of the world, 17.20-26.

The evidence of I Jn suggests that the evangelist's attempt to control the interpretation of the third version by reasserting the definitive nature of the revelation in Jesus failed and that a schism resulted, 1 Jn 2.19. There his "opponents" found his teaching about the Spirit to have an "elective

---

[24]More detailed analyses can be given but this is adequate for our purposes. See my *JWT*, 59ff.
[25]*Ibid.*, 123ff.

affinity" (Max Weber) with their developing Gnostic thrust. Spirit "enthusiasm" was not then just a danger threatening the mission, it threatened the survival of Johannine Christianity as such. By the time I Jn was written the author was wholly on the defensive. The stress is on the authoritative tradition and the theological interpretation of it. The vision of the role of the Spirit and world mission have fallen out of sight.

III. CONCLUSION

We have argued that the farewell discourse developed through a reworking of traditional material in successive versions. The hypothesis takes account of the time and events through which the evangelist and his community passed, through which the gospel tradition now in Jn also passed. It is not unreasonable to suggest that such processes as the ones outlined will have affected the gospel tradition as a whole.

In the case of the farewell discourse this process of development produced three chronologically consecutive versions of the discourse. This model of development is not suggested concerning the whole Gospel. There is good evidence for suggesting that elsewhere early tradition passed through a process of interpretation and reinterpretation, for example in Jn 9.[26] There a traditional miracle story, which had probably been used to win members of the synagogue to faith in Jesus, went through a double reinterpretation, first to encounter "secret believers" with the challenge to come to an open confession of faith in Jesus as the Christ as interpreted and understood by the evangelist, and then to justify and explain the problem of unbelief. Consequently, when it comes to the Gospel as a whole different processes must be taken into account. In Jn 9 traditional material has been reworked and expanded over a period of time; new material has probably been introduced late in the process of the development of the Gospel in the case of the Prologue (1.1-18) and 17.1-26; and a discourse has passed through double reinterpretation with the new versions following consecutively upon the original discourse in the case of 13.31–16.33 though it is possible that here also earlier versions were slightly modified in the light of the later situations (see 15.18-25). Because each version was addressed to a specific crisis it served the evangelist's purpose better to produce new versions rather than simply to revise the earlier version to take account of the new situations. Had he done this his response to each crisis would have been less clear and direct. For the same reason earlier versions were not discarded as they dealt with separate issues.

---

[26]See chapter 8, "The Son of Man: The Light of the World" above.

In the struggle with the synagogue and the debate with believers of more traditional christological views the farewell discourse provided the evangelist with a rationale for the transformation of traditional messianic expectation into his own distinctive christology. So distinctive was that christology that any connection with Jewish messianic views became perilously thin. Indeed in the farewell of the Messiah in Jn the evangelist set out a basis for farewelling Jewish messianic expectation in the interest of the development of a distinctive Christian christology. The function of each version of the discourse, whatever else it does, legitimates the Johannine christology. But there is a marked development in the understanding of the believing community and the role of the Spirit Paraclete. Here we find that the understanding has developed from that of the community conscious of the new mode of Jesus' presence in it to that of the community aware of its own "messianic" (in the new Johannine sense) destiny. The community is to be the mode of Jesus' continuing presence and mission in the world. Naturally this is what the evangelist taught and we can only assume that for the community that received the Gospel as their own this came to be their view also.

Given the distinctive understanding of Jesus and the believing community and its role in the world this Gospel clearly needed legitimating authority. This the evangelist found in the role of the BD and the teaching role of the Spirit of Truth. That the Gospel expresses the tradition coming from the BD is clearly attested. It is also implied that this tradition embodies the authentic witness of the Spirit of Truth. But it would be a mistake to conclude that the evangelist intended to restrict the role of the Spirit to the BD. Whatever problems were raised by the teaching, the finished Gospel proclaims the presence of the Spirit of Truth with all believers.

14

The "Opponents" in 1 John

The question of the "opponents" in I John has long been recognized as significant for the study of that "letter". The great commentaries by Theodor Häring, R. Law and Rudolf Schnackenburg make the conflict with the "schismatics" the key to their interpretations. Recently Raymond E. Brown[1] has presented a detailed account of the conflict in the context of the history of Johannine Christianity as the basis for his own commentary. I find myself in general agreement with the approach and position set out there. But I remain unconvinced on a number of important issues where I find that my views remain fundamentally unchanged.[2] These views need further elaboration and defence in due course. Before doing this certain preliminary matters need to be dealt with.

I have referred to the "opponents". An alternative nomenclature could have been used without prejudice to this study. Raymond Brown prefers the term "secessionists" (69, 70, 70 n156 etc.); he also refers to "adversaries" (415, 574, 618); "opponents" (x); "deceivers" (358f.); and "propagandists" (429). They could also be called "schismatics" or "heretics". None of these terms is used of them in the Johannine Epistles. Had they been used they would reflect the author's point of view.[3] Each of the terms can be justified as representative of his point of view. Certainly he wrote against those he viewed as adversaries. We conclude that the opposition was mutual. Clearly also he spoke of those who had broken away from his own group and hence, from his point of view, they were "schismatics" or "secessionists" (1 Jn 2.19). From his point of view also the schism was rooted in false practices, but more important, a false confession of faith. It is more important because the false confession gave

---

[1] *The Johannine Epistles.*

[2] See my *JWT*, 114-28.

[3] The author of 1 Jn, often called the Presbyter, does not refer to himself in this way (but see 2 Jn 1; 3 Jn 1) nor does he use the term anywhere, even where it might have been expected. Instead he speaks to those he calls πατέρες (1 Jn 2.14) in the sequence τεκνία, νεανίσκοι, πατέρες. He may have avoided the term πρεσβύτεροι because he rejected the authority structure it implied – see 2.20,27, or because his reference to the πατέρες was to an age group not to the tradition bearers. Brown (*Epistles*, 107ff.) rightly argues that attitude to ecclesiastical authority separated the author of 1 Jn from Diotrephes. Hence, if the Presbyter wrote 1 Jn, that title can only indicate one who was a tradition bearer. For him it was the tradition rather than the tradition bearer that was authoritative.

rise to the false practices. Hence, from his point of view they were "heretics". If such titles are pejorative that is no more than our author intended.

I. HYPOTHESIS

The Johannine tradition was decisively shaped in the dialogue/conflict with the synagogue and its themes and emphases are a response to the Jewish rejection of Jesus as the Revealer/Redeemer from God. As a consequence of this conflict the Johannine Christians were excluded from the synagogue and the later strata of the Gospel reflect this situation and take account of the presence of Gentile Christians in the community. The Jewish Christians of Jn did not keep the Mosaic Law. This is evident in those passages dealing with controversy about the sabbath, especially in Jn 9 where the Jews set Moses in opposition to Jesus. Because the Johannine tradition came to its present form in some large urban centre of the *diaspora*, such as Ephesus, the Johannine Christians would have come into closer contact with Gentiles when they were excluded from of the synagogue, Jn 9.22,34ff. Because the Johannine Christians did not demand circumcision and other ritual requirements of the Mosaic Law the way was open for Gentiles to enter the community. This they did in significant numbers. 1 Jn was written in this period. It is a response to the problems caused by those (Gentiles) who had entered the community and interpreted the Johannine tradition without reference to the Jewish conflict in which it had been formed. The perspective of the opponents led to an emphasis on a limited number of themes; a one-sided emphasis and an interpretation of the selected themes which amounted to a distortion of the Johannine tradition. It is not that the opponents blatantly "imported" foreign ideas and practices into the community. Rather what is argued here is that, lacking the perspective of the Jewish conflict, and bringing a perspective[4] formed by a predominantly Gentile background, the opponents developed ideas and

---

[4]It is not possible to be without a perspective. Lacking the perspective of the Jewish conflict they must have had another! Brown (*Epistles* 71, 97-9, 103, 111, 223) recognizes that the schism occurred after the separation from the synagogue. He also recognizes the presence of Gentiles but does not think that either of these issues was materially relevant to the schism. He admits that it was the Jewish conflict that explains the silences and emphases in Jn that allowed the "opponents", in their new context, to develop their position. But he rejects the view that they were importing "totally foreign ideas" (*Epistles*, 324 n20). What is argued here is that they imported ideas by reinterpreting the Johannine tradition *from their perspective*.

practices on the basis of their interpretation of the Johannine tradition. That interpretation was in fact, not only in the view of our author, a distortion of the Johannine tradition. This distortion made it necessary for our author to move from concentration on Jesus the revealer of God (the emphasis of the Gospel) to affirm his understanding of God which excluded his opponents' christology with its consequences.

II. METHODOLOGICAL CONSIDERATIONS[5]

The title of this paper takes into account that almost all of the evidence concerning the opponents is *in I Jn* and that our knowledge of them must be reconstructed on the basis of our author's polemical statements against them. Such a process is fraught with hazards. Because the position of the opponents is accessible only through the criticism of our author it must be asked whether the opponents are merely a literary creation. 1 Jn is a stylized book in which the author addresses his reader variously as ἀγαπητοί (cf. ἀδελφός), τεκνία, παιδία, πατέρες, νεανίσκοι,[6] suggesting that the opponents could be a literary sounding board against which the author could express his own views. Against this possibility is the evidence that those who broke away from the community were identified as "liars", "anti-christs" and "false prophets", 1 Jn 2.18-19 cf. 4.1-6. The reality of the conflict is evident beyond reasonable doubt.

If 1 Jn arose out of and addressed a particular crisis in the life of the Johannine community that crisis is not only part of the "supposed background", it is also the central subject matter addressed.[7] Once this is recognized the reader is aware that the presence of the opponents pervades the whole book. That presence would have been more obvious to the original readers for whom the schism of the opponents was a recent painful, traumatic experience. Because the meaning of the book is bound up with that situation some attempt must be made to reconstruct it if 1 Jn is to be understood.

---

[5]Brown's "methodological cautions" (*Epistles,* 72ff.) are well formulated and justified, though his refusal to acknowledge that the opponents distorted the Johannine tradition where this position makes best sense of the evidence is to take the cautions to a point where it must be assumed that the evidence is distorted.

[6]See 2.1,7,12,13,18,28. Brown (*Epistles,* 545) attempts to use the forms of address as a guide to the division of the book. See also *Epistles,* 300.

[7]It is therefore not possible to ignore the problem of the opponents, which was the historical context of 1 Jn, and to concentrate only on the literary context, because the opponents also appear in the literary context.

The position of the "opponents" is accessible to us only through the eyes of our author, their implacable opponent. It is possible that they evaluated his position in much the same way as he criticized theirs, as opposition based on false beliefs and practices. Such mutual opposition led to schism. But unless the author falsified his account it was his opponents who initiated the schism and broke away from his community. It might well be that the opponents were more numerous and prosperous than the community they left behind.[8] What marks them as the schismatics was their initiative in the schism, 1 Jn 2.19.

It can be questioned also whether the opponents were a single group or a variety of dissenting groups or individuals, a question discussed by most commentators. It is not easy to answer this question. Perhaps the only criterion that can be used is the question of the integrity of the position of the opponents reconstructed on the basis of the critique by our author. Hence the question can only be answered when that reconstruction is completed. However the treatment of the schism (1 Jn 2.19) predisposes the answer in terms of a specific group. The finding of a coherent position would also count against the notion that the opponents were simply a literary fiction to provide a sounding board for our author's views.

Reconstructing the position of the opponents from the polemics of our author is a task to be done with caution. It may be that he has not always done justice to their position. Hence a degree of sympathy in interpreting their position is called for. Both our author and his opponents were Johannine Christians interpreting the Johannine *tradition*. But here the question of what stage of the development of that tradition is presupposed by the opponents is vital. It is argued in this paper that the "opponents" were *not* interpreting the Gospel *in its present form* and that, for example, the Prologue was modified in response to their challenge.[9] Hence caution must be exercised in attempting to correct the presentation of the

---

[8]Brown (*Epistles*, 70) takes this view. Had the author's group left (separated from) the opponents this could easily have been expressed in terms of separation from the world. Thus we must take seriously the evidence that the opponents initiated the "schism".

[9]G. Richter ("Die Fleischwerdung des Logos im Johannesevangelium", *NT* 14 (1972) 265ff.) has argued that the author of 1 Jn was the anti-docetic redactor who added Jn 1.14-18. This is a suggestive line of thought, though not all of 1.14-18 is Johannine, as the uncharacteristic vocabulary indicates. But σὰρξ ἐγένετο was a Johannine addition and was anti-docetic. See chapter 3,"Christology and History in the Prologue" above. Brown (*Epistles*, 109f.) doubts that 1.14 is anti-docetic, appealing to Käsemann's view that "appeared" is a possible translation of σὰρξ ἐγένετο. Against this we note that the Gnostics did not adopt σὰρξ ἐγένετο as a docetic formula.

opponents' position in the polemics of the author on the basis of what is possible as an understanding of our Jn. A one sided interpretation, or even a distorted one, is also a possibility which should not be excluded.[10]

While recognizing the danger of reconstructing the position of the opponents from our author's criticisms it needs also to be remembered that, had he badly distorted their position in order to refute it, that distortion would have been evident to his readers. It is not as if he was dealing with a group remote in time and place from his own adherents. Had his refutation depended on a distorted picture, he would have allowed an easy avenue of response to his criticisms, especially if he was concerned with those amongst his adherents who were tempted to follow his opponents. Thus, while allowing that sympathy for the opponents' position is called for in the work of reconstruction, this should not go beyond the limits set by the criticisms. This comment needs to be related especially to the christological denial of the opponents and their failure to love the brethren (one another) as charged.

III. THE EVIDENCE

The evidence concerning the opponents is complex. Part of that complexity is the stylized form in which that evidence is expressed:

First of all there are the "boasts" which are recognizable by their form.[11] There are seven "boasts" in all; a threefold "if we say (boast)", 1.6, 8,10; a threefold "he who says (boasts)", 2.4,6,9; and a single "if anyone says (boasts)", 4.20. The various stylistic formulae used to introduce the "boasts" are a complication. What is implied by the variety? Do we have actual "boasts"? Or are the more definite sayings ("he who says") more

---

[10]Brown (*Epistles*, 73) recognized that the opponents were dependent on Johannine tradition, not Jn and argued that they were loyal to that tradition (*Epistles*, xi, 42f., 69-72). Hence they reveal the dangers inherent in Jn (*Epistles*, xi). Their position was defensible on the basis of Jn (*Epistles*, 79). They exploited the silences and one-sidedly emphasized certain themes (*Epistles*, 97). Yet Brown also suggests (*Epistles*, 164, 178, 181, 278) that the opponents "misinterpreted" Jn. What led to that misinterpretation? Our argument is that the opponents interpreted the Johannine tradition from a perspective different from the one in which it was formed. It is possible that Brown's references to "misinterpretation" are a concession to the point of view of the author whereas this paper argues that the opponents did in fact misinterpret Jn.

[11]The detection of the boasts of the "opponents" through these introductory formulae was highlighted in my 1967 Durham Ph.D. and found expression in *JWT* (1975), 118-21. It was subsequently taken up by J. Bogart, *Orthodox and Heretical Perfectionism* (1977).

precise quotations than the rest in which our author only attempts to capture the position of the opponents in his own words.[12] If the latter is the case, extreme caution would need to be used in relation to the "boasts" constructed by our author. Alternatively, the variations in the introductory formulae could be a stylistic device without prejudice to the veracity of the quotations. Given the stylized form of 1 Jn, this seems to be probable. Hence the "boasts" provide particularly valuable information concerning the position of the opponents. The emphasis on the seventh boast - it is treated at length before and after it is quoted - suggests that it was more central to the conflict than the other boasts.

Second, there is evidence of what the opponents denied. Having identified the schismatics with the anti-Christs (1 Jn 2.18-19) our author goes on to characterize them as false prophets who refuse to confess ($\delta \mu \dot{\eta}$ $\delta\mu o\lambda o\gamma\epsilon\hat{\iota}$) that Jesus Christ is come in the flesh, 1 Jn 4.1-6. These passages are important because they give expression to our author's eschatological views.[13] The opponents are treated as a phenomenon of the last days. As false prophets they manifest the Spirit of Error which, in the last days, takes the form of anti-Christs. The evaluation of the opponents as anti-Christs[14] and *false* prophets inspired by the Spirit of *Error is* an expression of our author's view. Probably they claimed to be prophets through whom the Spirit of Truth spoke. What is at stake at this point is the interpretation of the teaching in the Johannine Farewell Discourses[15] concerning the Spirit of Truth.

According to our author the opponents refused to confess that Jesus Christ had come in the flesh, which he understood to be the equivalent of denying that Jesus is the Son of God, that Jesus is the Christ. Given the context in which this argument is recorded it is probable that their position depended much more on the claim concerning the Spirit than on any Christological confession. They claimed to be begotten of God and that the $\sigma\pi\acute{\epsilon}\rho\mu a$ of God dwelt in them.

---

[12]Brown (*Epistles*, 232, 255f.) suggests that this may be the case.

[13]While Jn does not, in the conflict with Judaism, need to emphasize future eschatology (see Brown, *Epistles*, 98), 1 Jn re-emphasizes this theme against the opponents, see also 2.28; 3.2-3. The opponents, like the $\pi\nu\epsilon\nu\mu a\tau\iota\kappa o\acute{\iota}$ at Corinth, stressed present fulfillment to the exclusion of future eschatology. They believed that they had "arrived" already.

[14]They were anti-Christs because they would not confess that Jesus is the Christ, Jesus is Son of God, Jesus Christ is come in the flesh. Does a refusal to confess constitute a denial? This evaluation is comparable to Jesus' assessment of the Jews as "children of the devil" in Jn 8.39-47.

[15]See chapter 13, "The Farewell of the Messiah" above.

Third, there is the evidence concerning the opponents' view of and emphasis on the Spirit. In this context the lack of emphasis on the Spirit in 1 Jn is intelligible. There the Spirit is never designated Paraclete – though Jesus is – nor is the term Holy Spirit used, though it could be implied in the reference to the Holy One, 1 Jn 2.20. That reference occurs in the context of the discussion of the true and false confessions (1 Jn 2.18-25). The appeal to the anointing (χρῖσμα) from the Holy One is made against what appears to be an exclusive claim to knowledge made by the opponents. Against them our author assures his readers, as recipients of the anointing, "You all know".[16] The truth which they know is christological, "Jesus is the Christ", which is denied by the opponents who are here characterized as "the liar", "the anti-Christ". The context and argument is much the same as 1 Jn 4.1-6. Thus, where the Spirit is discussed it is with a view to laying down criteria for the distinction of the Spirit of Truth from the Spirit of Error. In such a situation all that could be hoped for was to set up criteria to limit the confusion caused by the claims of the opponents to speak prophetically in the Spirit.

Fourth, there is also the evidence of the so called antitheses. A number of stylistically antithetical statements provide evidence of the position of the opponents. Here our author opposes his own views to those of the opponents.

1. See 2.29b; 3.3a, 4a,6a,6b,9a,10b,15; 5.4,18[17] where πᾶς ὁ is followed by a participle in the present tense (except in 5.4). In this group of sayings our author, having declared that God (or Christ)[18] is righteous, goes on to distinguish those born (children) of God from the children of the devil who belong to the world. Those who do righteousness are born of God. By speaking of *"doing* righteousness" he stressed the active nature of righteousness which is incompatible with sin (= lawlessness). Doing righteousness is understood in terms of loving one another (the brother) while sin is portrayed as hating, murdering the brother.[19]

---

[16]An alternative reading asserts "you know all things", which could be justified on the basis of Jn 14.26; 16,13. See Brown (*Epistles,* 348) who accepts on contextual grounds "You all know" against the exclusive claims of the opponents and explains the reading "You know all things" as verbal harmonization with Jn 14.26.

[17]See my *JWT,* 118.

[18]In 2.29 where the theme is "born of God" probably God is in view though "Jesus Christ the righteous" is spoken of in 2.1.

[19]1 Jn uses the Johannine term ἀλλήλους and introduces ἀδελφός, possibly because of using the story of Cain who hated/murdered his brother, 3.12ff.

2. Taking up the same theme but using a different form is another group of sayings (3.7,8,10,14f.; 4.8) in which the form is "he who" (δ) + the present participle.

3. A third group of sayings concentrates attention on the witness of the Spirit to the "archaic confession" of Jesus Christ having come in the flesh (5.6,10,12). In 5.6 the article plus the aorist participle is used to state the author's view while another form is used to express the view rejected. In 5.10,12 the article is used with the present participle in both the statement of the author's position and in the negated position where the negation is indicated by the introduction of μή and oύ(κ).

4. In 5.19 the antithesis is expressed without the form. The author declares "We know that we are of God and the whole world lies in (the power/sphere) of the evil one."

5. In 2.23 πᾶς ό + the present participle is used to state the position of the opponents as interpreted by the author while ό + the present participle is used to set his own views against theirs. The opponents did not intend to deny the Father. They denied the Son. It is our author's conclusion that by denying the Son they deny the Father also. But what did denying the Son involve?

The conflict with the "opponents" runs throughout 1 Jn from the beginning, in the refutation of their boasts, to the end where our author opposes their position with antithetical statements. The focus of the conflict is on God[20] though the "opponents" view of God leads them to reject the author's christological confession. While the emphasis on being born of God has its roots in the Johannine tradition, the importance of the theme in 1 Jn seems to be a consequence of the emphasis of the opponents.[21] In the development of this theme they made use of the

---

[20]Especially in the boasts, see Brown (*Epistles*, 249) concerning 1.5–2.11. Brown does not sufficiently take account of 4.20 as the final boast which is treated at great length in 1 Jn. The theological focus comes out in the sayings "God is light" (1 Jn 1.5) and "God is love" (1 Jn 4.16). See my *JWT*.

[21]Brown (*Epistles*, 386) recognizes the use of this theme by the opponents and sees it as the common property of the Johannine community. However, it is probable that the Johannine treatment of this theme belongs to the later strata which already respond to the emerging problem of the opponents, see Jn 1.12-13; 3.3-5. In these sections Jn distinguishes Jesus as Son from the children of God and emphasizes his unique status with the term μονογενής, 1.14,17; 3.16,18. The opponents probably saw Jesus' sonship in the same terms as their own. Jn emphatically distinguishes the two. While Jn uses υἱός only of Jesus and τέκνα θεοῦ of the believers, both words are used of believers by Paul, Romans 8.14-17. Perhaps the

Johannine tradition concerning the Spirit/Paraclete. If they aimed to verify their claim to be born of God by giving evidence of their possession of the Spirit, this would explain why the author does not emphasize the role of the Spirit.[22] He does not deny that the opponents possess the Spirit. Rather he sets up criteria for the recognition of the Spirit of Truth and the Spirit of Error. Possession of (the) Spirit is ambiguous because such may be possession of the Spirit of Truth or the Spirit of Error.

Fifth, the lack of dependence on the Old Testament (there is only the reference to Cain who murdered his brother) is surprising given the prominence of the OT in the Johannine tradition. For Gentile Christians the OT could be an unconvincing basis for overcoming controversies. Rather than using the OT the author appeals to the "primitive" Johannine tradition, those aspects of the Johannine tradition which the opponents ignored or denied.[23] Finally, the author warns his readers "Little children, guard yourselves from idols". While other interpretations are possible, given other links with Gentile Christianity at Corinth as evidenced in 1 Corinthians, it is probable that we have here evidence that the opponents participated in idolatry, a practice abhorrent to our author. Some of this evidence will now need to be discussed at greater length.

IV. INTERPRETING THE EVIDENCE

1. The Slogans or Boasts

The position of the opponents is expressed positively in their boasts. But before this evidence is put to use in reconstructing their position some assessment must be made of the accuracy of these "quotations". The conditional form of groups 1 and 3 distinguishes them from the second group of boasts. The first group is distinguished from the others by the use of the first person plural. Could this mean that some of the author's own adherents were wavering in their resolve and were showing signs of following his opponents into schism? Perhaps they had taken up these slogans though it is probably only a stylistic variation.

Did our author quote his opponents or did he put the words together himself in a way that allowed him to bring out the problems in their position? R. E. Brown (*Epistles*, 252f.) suggests that the first three

---

opponents had been influenced by a misunderstanding of this position. See chapter 3, "Christology and History in the Prologue" above.
[22]Brown (*Epistles*, 216, 240) rightly recognizes this.
[23]Rightly recognized by Brown (*Epistles*, 97f.).

boasts, introduced hypothetically "If we say ...",[24] should be considered as more loosely constructed representations of their position than the second three which are introduced specifically "He who says ..." and quote more or less precisely the slogans of the opponents. In support of this position Brown (*Epistles*, 186,232) argues that κοινωνία was not a "secessionist" term but was introduced by our author. Hauck *(TDNT* III, 807) adds support to that view by asserting: "In 1 Jn κοινωνία is a favourite term to describe the living bond in which the Christian stands."

The first boast. "If we say 'we have κοινωνία with him (God)' ..." If κοινωνία was a "favourite" term for our author it would be more difficult to show from the evidence that it was also a term used, perhaps in a different sense, by his opponents, though that would not be impossible. Against that possibility Brown argues that κοινωνία was an ecclesiastical term by means of which the author affirms the importance of the relation to the tradition. The "secessionists" used the Gospel terms μένειν ἐν and εἶναι ἐν whereas the author used κοινωνία. If Brown is right at least the first of the boasts was constructed in our author's terms and the same could be true of the other two boasts introduced by "If we say...". However, against this position, it is argued here that the different introductory formulae are stylistic variations[25] which are not part of the quotation and do not indicate different levels of accuracy in quotation. Moreover, the term κοινωνία is not drawn from the Johannine tradition; it is not used at all in Jn. Nor is it reasonable to see it as some kind of equivalent to μένειν ἐν or εἶναι ἐν, neither of which is used of the believers' relation to one another. Further, if κοινωνία were the evangelist's interpretation of the opponents claim to "abide in God", why did our author also present the boast in the opponents' own terms in 2.6 where they boast that they abide in (μένειν ἐν) him?

Not only is κοινωνία not taken up from the Johannine tradition, it is by no means prominent in the Johannine epistles, appearing in neither 2 nor 3 Jn (nor in Rev) and only 4 times in 1 Jn, all in the section dealing with the boast of the opponents, "We have κοινωνία with him", 1.6; see

---

[24]The ἐὰν εἴπωμεν ὅτι formula is used in the three boasts of 1.6,8,10, and is an example of our author's liking of arrangements in threes. On the stylistic variations and arrangements into units of three and seven see Brown, *Epistles*, 116ff., 123. In 1.6,8 κοινωνίαν and ἁμαρτίαν are used with ἔχομεν, the latter negatively with οὐκ, but 1.10 negates the perfect tense οὐχ ἡμαρτήκαμεν. See note 36 below.

[25]Brown (*Epistles*, 116ff., 123) also notes our author's characteristic stylistic forms of arrangement but failed to ask if this might account for the variation of formulae introducing the boasts.

also 1.3,7. The evidence suggests that our author took up and used the term because his opponents were using it. However he modifies the meaning of the term as used in the boast. The opponents boast, "We have κοινωνία with him (God)". Our author makes the primary reference of κοινωνία to be μετ' ἀλλήλων (1.7) and this is dependent on κοινωνία μεθ' ἡμῶν which opens up κοινωνία with the Father and his Son Jesus Christ, 1.3.

In the opponents' boast of κοινωνία with God the term is not used in an ecclesiastical sense. It may be that Hellenistic religions provide some sort of clue to what was meant[26] by the opponents who seem to be claiming some kind of mystical union with God which had no relation to the lives of other believers. That is suggested by the way the theme of κοινωνία μετ' ἀλλήλων is introduced. The use of ἀλλήλων[27] suggests some relation to the love command in the Johannine tradition, ἀγαπᾶτε ἀλλήλους καθὼς ἠγάπησα ὑμᾶς ...[28] Jn 13.34. Indeed κοινωνία μετ' ἀλλήλων is ἀγαπᾶν ἀλλήλους. In this way our author has reoriented the theme from a direct relation with God to the believers' relation with each other.

Our author also took up his opponents' understanding of God. According to the message of the tradition bearers "God is light and there is no darkness in him at all", 1.5. This statement of the message does not come from the Johannine tradition. Rather it is our author's restatement in order to provide a basis for correcting the boasts of his opponents. It already foreshadows their boast claiming to be in the light, 2.9. If God is light, in whom there is no darkness at all, to have κοινωνία with him excludes the possibility of being in the darkness. Our author has interpreted being in the darkness as hating the brother while he who loves his brother abides in the light, 2.9-10 (ὁ ἀγαπῶν τὸν ἀδελφὸν αὐτοῦ ἐν

---

[26]See *TDNT* III, 799f.

[27]See 1 Jn 1.7; 4.7,12. Both themes in 1 Jn are treated in response to the opponents' claims to have fellowship with God and to love God. In both instances the claims are tested in terms of the relationship with one another and the reality of fellowship is tested in terms of love. Hence the view of E. Malatesta that 1 Jn is constructed around the theme of κοινωνία cannot be justified. Our author used this term only in response to the use of it by his opponents (4 times in 1.3,6,7). Characteristically and in common with the Johannine tradition he uses love terminology.

[28]The "new commandment" also provided our author with the model for his καθώς ethic (see 2.6; 3.3,23; 4.17), which is also implied in 1.7; 2.27; 4.11,19, and is expressed negatively in 3.12. It is based on Jn 13.34 but see also Jn 17.11,14,16,18,21,22; 20.21. Hence according to Jn the disciples of Jesus are to live (walk) as he lived. See Brown, *Epistles*, 97f.

τῷ φωτὶ μένει). Thus κοινωνία had no ecclesiastical sense when used by the opponents. But our author reinterpreted the term to assert dependence on the tradition bearers and the obligation to love one another. On the basis of his reinterpretation he declared his opponents to be liars when they claimed to have fellowship with God but failed to love the brethren, 1.6.[29] Thus, the first of the boasts appears to have been presented in the terms used by the opponents. Our author reinterpreted κοινωνία and developed criteria which would demonstrate that the opponents did not have κοινωνία with God.

The second boast of the opponents introduced by the formula "If we say ..." took the form of the affirmation "We have no sin". This was probably understood to be as a consequence of union with God (κοινωνία). Sinlessness was understood to be a state of being. In our author's view such an understanding was self-deception. For him the correct way to deal with sin was not to deny it but to confess it. The form of the boast, "If we say ...", is matched by the form in which the correct response is expressed, "If we confess ...". The result of such confession is forgiveness and cleansing. Such a situation might be described in terms of being free from sin, but not as a state of being. Rather it was understood in dynamic terms on the basis of the confession of sins and consequent forgiveness and cleansing.

The third boast, introduced again by the formula "If we say ...", went further to assert "we have never sinned". While the second boast asserted a state of sinlessness from the time of κοινωνία with God, the third boast assumes the absolute sinlessness of those who affirmed it. Perhaps this allowed that there were those who were sinless by nature while others only became sinless through union with God, presumably at their (χρῖσμα) initiation.[30]

While the claim to be sinless is said to be self-deception, the claim never to have sinned is said to make God a liar and to demonstrate that his Word is not abiding in them. This would seem to indicate that our author was more sure that he could *demonstrate* the error of those who claimed never to have sinned because this claim runs contrary to the message of

---

[29] The liar also denies that Jesus is the Christ and in so doing denies the Father and the Son; on the liar see 1.6; 2.22; 4.1 (false prophets); 4.20.

[30] See my *JWT*, 120. Brown (*Epistles*, 82) rejects this view because "children of God by nature" cannot be derived from Jn. But this use of the criterion that the position of the opponents must be derivable from Jn is too rigorous and inflexible. If the opponents made the heavenly origin of the "Son" the paradigm for their own "sonship", Jn could provide a basis for such a view though such a view would be a misinterpretation of Jn.

forgiveness and cleansing in the gospel, including the Johannine tradition, Jn 1.29; 13.10; 15.3; 17.17. However, the claim to be sinless consequent to believing in Jesus is not as easily demonstrated to be false. No clear statements in the Johannine tradition exclude the view. None the less our author was prepared to assert that those who claim such a state of being are deceiving themselves.

Our author's attitude to sin is complex. It should be confessed so that it may be forgiven and cleansed, 1.9; that cleansing takes place through walking in the light by means of which the effects of Christ's death cleanse the believer, 1.7. Yet he commands his readers, "Do not sin!" Yet again, the believer who sins has the assurance of the advocacy of Jesus Christ the righteous whose death *makes possible* the forgiveness and cleansing of the sins of every one in the world, 2.1-2. Such forgiveness is not automatic. It is dependent on the confession of sins and walking in the light. This suggests two levels of forgiveness and cleansing. There is the initial forgiveness and cleansing for the believer. There is also the recognition that the believer may slip and fall into sin which, if confessed, and if the believer returns to walk in the light, will be forgiven and the believer cleansed and reinstated to a dynamic sinlessness, 2.1-2; 5.16-17.

The subject is taken up again in the discussion of the children of God and children of the devil, 2.28f.; 3.1ff. In 2.29 the link between God, who is righteous, and his children, all those who do righteousness, is affirmed. The children of the devil are identified with those who commit sin, who act lawlessly. Further, righteousness is associated with loving the brother and sin is the negation of that. It is hating the brother, the murder of the brother. The characterization of the children of God and children of the devil in terms of their opposite behaviour is understandable in a situation where our author sought to distinguish himself and his adherents from his opponents. He goes on to assert that:

> Every one born of God does not sin[31] because his σπέρμα abides in him; and he is not able to sin, because he is born of God. This is how the children of God and the children of the devil are revealed (are to be recognized); everyone not doing righteousness is not of God, even (that is) he who does not love his brother. (1 Jn 3.9-10)

Our author's aim in this tortuous statement is clear enough. It was to provide a test to be passed by those who claimed to be God's children. That test was acting righteously, that is, loving the brother. Those who did not do this, and in his view his opponents did not, were not children of

---

[31]In English the sentence is translated better "no one who is born of God sins...".

God but children of the devil. What is more it is argued that God's σπέρμα abides in his children and they are not able to sin. How is this to be reconciled with our author's earlier rejection of his opponents' claim to be sinless?

Probably the opponents claimed that God's σπέρμα dwelt in them and *as a consequence they were sinless*. What our author does is to reverse the function of the argument by changing the question that the assertion answers. The question is not - as it was for the opponents - "who is sinless?"; answer - "those who possess God's σπέρμα!" Rather the question is, - "how do you know who possesses God's σπέρμα?"; answer - "the one who does righteousness, who loves his brother possesses God's σπέρμα!" However, by accepting the language of his opponents at this point he has adopted a form of words in 3.9 which is difficult to reconcile with 1.8,10.[32] Reconciliation is possible by seeing that the overall argument of the passage 2.28-3.24, especially 3.4-10, is about how to recognize the children of God. The *claim* to have the σπέρμα is not enough. Nor is the *claim* to have the Spirit, 4.1-6.

In none of the boasts except 2 and 3 (1.8,10) does our author reject the validity of the wording of the boasts. What he does elsewhere is to question whether the boasts are true of *his opponents*. On the basis of his understanding, the lives of his opponents demonstrate that the boasts were not true of them. In thinking that they were it is evident that they understood them in some way different from our author. Hence his criteria and critique are unlikely to have made any impression on them. In any case the critique was probably not aimed at them but at his own adherents who had been disturbed by the schism.[33]

Boasts 2 and 3 (1.8,10) are rejected outright. Boast 2, the claim to be sinless, is said to involve self-deception and boast 3 could only be held as true if God was a liar. There is no attempt to reinterpret them. For this reason 3.9 and 5.18[34] should not be understood in terms of the boasts

---

[32]The language of 3.9 is not drawn from Jn but is characteristic of the mystery religions, *TDNT* VII, 545. This, together with the apparent contradiction of 1.8,10 and the way our author has modified the assertion of 3.9 by setting up a test for the claim in the immediate context of the passage in which it has been embedded, indicates the claim to possess God's σπέρμα comes from the opponents.

[33]For this reason 1 Jn exhibits both polemical and paranetic characteristics because it was written to oppose the "heretics" and to encourage the author's adherents. It did this by transmitting and interpreting the Johannine tradition. See my *JWT*, 112f.

[34]Both 3.9 and 5.18 assert "everyone born of God does not sin". According to 3.9 it is because God's σπέρμα abides in him, whereas in 5.18 it is

denied in 1.8,10. Perhaps, having used the opponents' terms, our author was arguing that those born of God are not able *to live in sin*. This could be the subtle point of the present tenses rather than aorist, which would indicate a specific act of sin. The person born of God ἁμαρτίαν οὐ ποιεῖ because God's σπέρμα in him and οὐ δύναται ἁμαρτάνειν because he is born of God, 3.9. The same point is made in 5.18 where it is asserted that every one who is born of God οὐχ ἁμαρτάνει. Such a position does not preclude that a person born of God might lapse into sin and for such a person the community is urged to pray, 5.16f.[35]

The fourth boast (2.4) is introduced by the formula "He who says".[36] In this boast the opponents declared "I know him". To whom does this boast refer - to God or to Christ? Brown (*Epistles*, 253) considers that the reference is to God because of the parallelism (i) with 2.3a where the "him" most likely refers to God and (ii) with 2.6a where the "him" must be God. Further, in 1 Jn, "commandments" are always God's commandments. I find the idea that the opponents claimed to know God attractive because it fits what I perceive to be their position. However, I find Brown's arguments unconvincing. Jesus Christ is mentioned in 2.1-2 and if God (not Christ) is referred to in 2.3 the only indication of the change of subject is the plural "commandments", which the reader cannot be expected to know is always used in relation to God. Such a change would be too subtle, rather like the change sometimes suggested in the use of αὐτός and ἐκεῖνος.[37]

Determining whom the opponents claimed to know (2.4) is related to the question of in whom it is that they claimed to abide, 2.6a. Why must

---

because ὁ γεννηθεὶς ἐκ τοῦ θεοῦ τηρεῖ αὐτόν. God's σπέρμα is ὁ γεννηθεὶς ἐκ τοῦ θεοῦ in the thought of the opponents though our author may have identified ὁ γεννηθεὶς with Christ.

[35]In the conditional sentence of 5.16 the present participle is used of a particular sin. The specific act of sin is indicated by the use of the cognate accusative. The present participle indicates that the act was in process at the time of the action of the verb in the conditional clause. Given the proximity of 5.18 to this discussion it could be suggested that the οὐχ ἁμαρτάνει there implies πρὸς θάνατον. But 3.9 is too far away for this assumption to work there. For an alternative solution see J. Bogart, *Orthodox and Heretical Perfectionism*.

[36]The second group of three boasts, each of which is introduced ὁ λέγων (ὅτι)... The first uses ὅτι + the perfect tense ἔγνωκα αὐτόν. The second and third use ἐν + the dative + a present infinitive: ἐν αὐτῷ μένειν and ἐν τῷ φωτὶ εἶναι; 2.4,6,9. See note 24 above.

[37]See my *JWT*, 120 for a discussion of Bultmann's distinction (*Epistles*, 24 n2, 48 n22, 49 n24, 55 n51, 71) between αὐτός, which refers to God, while ἐκεῖνος refers to Christ. This change would be too subtle to be recognized.

the "him" of 2.6a refer to God not Christ? The possibility that it might refer to God is opened up by the reference to the love of God in 2.5. Hence the claim to know that we are in him could refer to God but need not because 2.5 speaks of "who ever keeps his word" as the one in whom the love of God is perfected. Surely the αὐτοῦ (his word) refers to Christ so that by keeping Christ's word "we know that we are in him" and the αὐτῷ could refer to God or to Christ. That being the case the fifth boast "to abide in him" could refer to God or to Christ. That our author has interpreted it in terms of Christ is indicated by the test he devised. The one who so boasts "ought to walk even as he walked". Here the αὐτός must refer to Christ. Hence I conclude that in the author's interpretation of boasts 4 and 5 the αὐτόν and αὐτῷ are both understood of Christ. If the opponents also understood the boasts in relation to Christ the tests added by our author would suggest that it was the heavenly Christ who was in view in their boasts. The tests draw attention to the need to keep Jesus' commandments, the ones he gave during his earthly life, and to live as he lived during his earthly life. Here we find an appeal to the καθώς ethic which has its roots in the Johannine tradition.

What would this claim to know (whether the object is God or Christ) involve? First, the use of the perfect tense implies definitive knowledge. The boast asserts that the one who makes it really has arrived at complete knowledge. What else could be required? Second, the claim to know ignored the earthly life of Jesus, words, commands and example. While I have no doubt that in the context of 1 Jn boasts 4 and 5 are interpreted in terms of Christ it could be that the opponents referred directly to God. If this were the case it would explain the resulting uncertainty about whether the 4th and 5th boasts referred to Christ or to God. If the opponents claimed to know God definitively, our author asserted that God was to be known only in Jesus Christ, the historical revealer, and that knowing was demonstrated by keeping his word, his commandments. By keeping his commandments the love of God was perfected in the believers who expressed love for one another, as Jesus had commanded. This understanding of knowing as obedience to commandments is Hebraic. To know is to obey[38] and to disobey is to demonstrate a failure to know. Such an understanding of knowledge betrays our author's Jewish

---

[38]*TDNT* I, 698. "...it is knowledge of His claim, whether present in direct commands or contained in His rule. It is this respectful and obedient acknowledgement... Knowledge...is possessed only in its exercise and actualization."

background/heritage (see Brown, *Epistles*, 97 n.224). His opponents did not share this view of knowledge and the conflict was a consequence.

If our author tested his opponents' claim to know God in terms of his own understanding of knowledge of Jesus Christ this is because, for him, God is to be known only in Jesus Christ, the historic revealer. Here he was true to the Johannine tradition though some parts of it might not have been as emphatically clear as the Prologue Jn 1.14-18.

It is probable that the opponents held the view that there were those who, because the divine σπέρμα dwelt in them, knew God fully and perfectly, and by virtue of the divine σπέρμα were sinless by nature. Yet there were others who came into this knowledge through initiation (χρῖσμα) in relation to Christ. Through initiation they claimed to have no sin but could not claim, as did those who claimed to possess the divine σπέρμα, that they had never sinned. Our author reinterpreted both σπέρμα and χρῖσμα by equating σπέρμα with χρῖσμα and claiming that all of his adherents had this "experience".[39] In this way σπέρμα is interpreted in terms of initiation and the opponents' understanding of initiation is reinterpreted.

In the fifth boast, introduced by the "He who says" formula, the opponents claimed "to abide in him", 2.6.[40] Evidently this boast is taken to be the equivalent of 2.5, which speaks of knowing "we are in him". Such union was probably thought of as the consequence of definitive knowledge. According to our author, the one who makes this boast "ought to walk[41] as he walked". The test suggests that the opponents failed to qualify at this point, indicating a different understanding of what it meant to "abide in him". The different understanding could be bound up with the question of in whom it is that the opponents claimed to abide (see above), though the opponents may have referred to both God and the heavenly Christ. But for them what was in view was a mystical abiding, a mystical

---

[39]R. Schnackenburg, *Die Johannesbriefe,* 152.

[40]Brown rightly recognizes that the opponents used the Johannine term μένειν. It is used 40 times in Jn, 17 times (as in the Synoptics) in relation to a locality and 23 times in a "spiritual" sense which might betray Gnostic influence though reinterpreted in terms of the revelation in Jn. The concentration of use is increased in 1 Jn (23 times) in response to the boast of the opponents in which the Gnostic sense re-emerges. Jn, 1 and 2 Jn account for 66 of the 113 uses of μένειν in the New Testament. These statistics would be more impressive if only "spiritual" uses were indicated.

[41]On the use of "walk" as a figure for living see *TDNT* V, 945. Here in 2.6, as often in Paul, under the influence of the LXX, the walk is qualified by a καθώς statement. See also Bultmann, *John,* 343 n1.

union, which involved no particular way of life in relation to the word and example of Jesus.

The sixth boast, also introduced by "He who says", makes the claim "to be in the light", 2.9.[42] This claim is tested by indicating that it is falsified by hatred of the brother. Such behaviour shows the person to be in the darkness. This interpretation is related to the teaching that God is light, in whom there is no darkness at all, 1.5. Hence the claim "to be in the light" is shown to be equivalent to the claim to have κοινωνία with God. To walk (be) in the darkness, i.e. to hate the brother, is the evidence which falsifies both the first and the sixth boasts. Our author believed that the opponents could not satisfy this test. Nor is it likely that they would have accepted the test because they had a different view of κοινωνία with God, a different view of being in the light. Probably they claimed mystical enlightenment which took no account of the historical revelation in Jesus with its ethical implications.

From a literary point of view the sixth boast, "to be in the light", forms an *inclusio* with the first boast, "we have κοινωνία with God" who is light, 1.5. Hence the section is unified by the way it begins and ends with the theme of light and treats consecutively the six boasts of the opponents. The unity of opening and closing suggests that there was a fundamental difference between our author and his opponents in their understanding of God. That difference is brought into focus in the affirmation "God is light", which is related to the boast "to be in the light" and to have κοινωνία with God who is light. Thus it would seem that the opponents claimed that they participated in the "light nature" of God. This participation was probably claimed on the basis of their experience of initiation or because they possessed the divine σπέρμα and suggests that the emphasis on being born of God in 1 Jn is due to the place of this teaching in the thought of the opponents. The same is probably true of teaching about the χρῖσμα and the σπέρμα, 2.20,27; 3.9 (cf. 5.18) which is related to the teaching about the Spirit (3.24; 4.13 but cf. 4.1-6; 2.18-27) and initiation.[43] Schulz comments as follows:

---

[42]This boast might have been developed on the basis of the tradition now in Jn 1.9 and is related to the boast to have κοινωνία with God who is light, 1 Jn 1.5f.

[43]See my "Paul and the πνευματικοί at Corinth" in *Paul and Paulinism: Essays in Honour of C. K. Barrett,* which suggests that the problem with the πνευματικοί was a consequence of the encounter between Christianity and the mystery religions. A similar situation might have occurred in the community of 1 Jn. Brown (*Epistles,* 49f.) rejects the suggestion that the opponents were "enthusiasts" such as those at Corinth because of the

As the examples show, the idea of God's seed does not occur in Pharisaic or Qumran Essene circles but is common in Hellenistic Judaism (> 543, 11ff.) and the mystery religions. But the sphere of the Hellenistic mysteries is transcended by 1 John inasmuch as the seed of God here is the Spirit who manifests Himself in His Word > 1 671, 8ff. Baptism is not primarily in view.[44]

Schulz rightly notes the source of the idea of God's seed. What he does not recognize is that this idea comes from the opponents and is modified by our author. If he is to use their expression he must modify its meaning. Thus the opponents claimed to share God's nature as his children. Against that static view of their status our author set his understanding of the dynamic relation of the believer to the Spirit.

While the opponents claimed to participate in the "light nature" of God, they did not manifest the character of the life of God that had been revealed in the historical life of Jesus. Nor did they show any concern to keep his word, the new commandment to love one another. For our author, the light of God is equated with the revelation of his love, while hatred and murder were expressions of the darkness of the world and had nothing to do with God.

The boasts to have κοινωνία with God, to know him, abide in him and to be in the light are all, in one way or another, claims to participate in the light nature of God. By virtue of this participation the opponents claimed to be sinless. However, having a different view of God and the believers' relation to him, our author asserted that sin was a dynamic problem to be dealt with by confession and forgiveness and obedience to the example and commandment of Jesus. Sinlessness was not a state which could be achieved once and for all. Though the believer could not fall into the

---

centrality of the christological controversy. But in the very chapter dealing with the πνευματικοί and tongues we note a christological problem, 1 Cor 12.3. However, while Brown denies the link with "enthusiasm" (see also, 60, n141, 452, 503) he argues that the real Pauline parallel is 1 Cor 12.3 (*Epistles,* 505). That problem is dealt with by Paul in the context of the "enthusiasts". Returning to 1 Jn it may be that χρῖσμα was appealed to by those who claimed the experience by initiation while those who spoke of participating in God by nature claimed to possess the divine σπέρμα. This distinction may have had implications also for the role of the heavenly Christ with the first while the second group claimed to participate in the "light nature" of God.

[44]*TDNT* VII, 545. See also R. Bultmann, *The Johannine Epistles,* 52 and nn36, 37. Χρῖσμα occurs 3 times in 1 Jn and nowhere else in the *NT*. On the Gnostic use of χρῖσμα see Schnackenburg *Johannesbriefe,* 252 nn2, 3, 4, 5. Schnackenburg thinks that our author could be opposing "false Gnostic" claims concerning these terms.

pattern of a life of sin, he could lapse into sin from which he would need to be restored and forgiven.

The seventh boast is introduced by the formula "If any one says ...", 4.20. The opponents boasted "I love God".[45] The seventh boast is separated from the first six by an exhortation to our author's adherents (2.12-17); a warning concerning the anti-Christ, the liar (2.18-27); a discussion of how to recognize the children of God (2.28-3.24); which leads into a discussion of how to recognize the Spirit of Truth (4.1-6); and is followed by a discussion of the nature of love, 4.7-21. It is in this discussion that our author responds to the seventh boast "I love God". His response shows that his understanding of love for God differed from the understanding of his opponents. That difference is further elaborated in 5.1-5.

Two tests of the opponents' claims emerge in this material. There is *first* the test for the claim to participate in the "nature" of God which is the equivalent of the claim to be born of God or to be children of God, though it is possible the last of these is our author's own designation as it is used by him in his critique of his opponents' claims, 5.2. Those who claim to be born of God, to participate in the "nature" of God should be godlike in behaviour. Jesus is the model of godlikeness and love is the key to this model. It is love for one another that is the test, love for the brethren.

The *second* test concerns the opponents claim to possess the Spirit (3.24; 4.1-6,13-16) which was tested in terms of the christological confession of faith. The Spirit of Truth is manifest in the true confession of Jesus Christ having come in the flesh; that Jesus is the Son of God; that Jesus is the Christ, 4.2, 6,13-16; 5.1. The Spirit of Error, of the anti-Christ, was manifest in the denial of that confession. In 5.1 we see how the true confession and hence possession of the Spirit of Truth and being born of God are two aspects of the one reality. For the moment we are concerned with the first test. We will return to the second in due course in dealing with the anti-Christ.

Because the tests were intended to reveal the error of the opponents' boasts the tests cannot have been acceptable to them and do not reveal their meaning except by negation. Hence participation in the "nature" of God did not (for them) involve loving one another, loving the brethren because

---

[45] *Ἐάν τις εἴπῃ ἀγαπῶ τὸν θεόν ...* The formula is similar to that of the first group of three boasts except that the verb is in the first person singular instead of the first person plural. This boast also speaks specifically of God.

the criticism of the opponents is not in terms of their failure to live up to an accepted ideal but of their rejection of that ideal.

Raymond Brown[46] has argued that the difference between our author and his opponents at this point was only that they belonged to different groups. He argues that the members of each group were committed to love for their own brethren but were antagonistic to those outside their own group. The basis for this view is that Brown thinks that: (1) The opponents' views would not have developed in a way that was clearly irreconcilable with the Johannine tradition upon which they intended to base their position. (2) Our author, while calling for love for one another, for the brethren, showed antagonism to his opponents calling them liars, false prophets, anti-Christs and forbade the offering of hospitality to them, 2 Jn 10-11.

This argument has some force. However, (in 2 Jn) the Presbyter's refusal of hospitality to his opponents in their mission of spreading what he considered to be destructive error need not be construed as malice or a willingness to see them starve to death. Rather it is the expression of an unwillingness to foster a mission which was (in his view) spreading falsehood. Further, if the opponents were comparatively wealthy and successful this would not have been an issue. Nor should it be concluded that the opponents could not go against the Johannine tradition. If they were "progressives" as Brown argues[47] they might well have believed that, under the guidance of the Spirit they could go beyond the Johannine tradition. Further, this test that our author devised for the opponents' claims to participate in the "nature" of God, to be born of God, would have been valueless if the opponents could respond by showing that they did love *their* brethren. While there is danger in accepting the description our author gives of his opponents it seems unlikely that his criticism would have taken the form it did had his opponents been a mirror image of his own position but in a different community. There is also a methodological problem. Had the two groups been mirror images of each other, *each deceived about the other,* how could we discover this from the picture of the opponents given in 1 Jn, since that picture is a distortion? Would we not need to know in advance that it was a distortion?

The seventh boast also suggests that this was not the case. In terms of love, what the opponents asserted was "I love God", 4.20. It might be

---

[46]See Brown (*Epistles,* 84, 85). However Brown (*Epistles,* 80) acknowledges that the opponents attributed no salvific significance to ethical behaviour. That being the case, it is unlikely that they acknowledged any obligation ($\dot{o}\phi\epsilon\acute{\iota}\lambda o\mu\epsilon\nu$) to love one another, 1 Jn 3.11; 4.11.

[47]See Brown, *Epistles,* 76, 97, 245, 264, 762.

significant that this "boast" is singular, indicating a fundamental individualism. Against this assertion our author set the test of love for the brother. "The person who boasts 'I love God' and hates *his brother* is a liar." This test represents the point at which our author's understanding of love can be distinguished from the opponents. For them love meant love for God. But what could this mean? It did not involve obedience to Jesus' word or commandments; it did not involve love for the brother. It appears that love is closely associated with the opponents' view that they participated in the "light nature" of God as asserted in the boasts to have κοινωνία with him or to be in or abide in him.

It is interesting to note that the test which proved that the claim made by the opponents, "I love God", was a lie, does not speak of loving the brethren generally (but see 3.14). The test is whether the one who makes this boast loves or hates *his brother*, 4.20-21; cf. 2.10-11; 3.10,15,17. The implications of the "his" are far-reaching. Had the opponents simply failed to love the author and his adherents but accepted the necessity of and in fact loved the members of their own group, affirming that only these were their brothers, the critique would have been pointless. The opponents could have answered, "But we do love our brothers!"

Given the antithetical style of the Johannine tradition, just as there is no half-light, only light or darkness, so there is only love or hate. The opponents affirmed no necessity of loving the brothers, whether the adherents of our author or their own group. Possibly the opponents were the larger group involved in the schism and might well have been a wealthy Gentile[48] group which found itself quite at home in the world. Members of this group would not have been dependent on "charity". This does not appear to have been true of the adherents of our author.

The charge that the opponents hated the brothers is interpreted as murder, using the example of Cain, 3.12-15. This could be an extension of thought along the lines that to fail to love is to hate, to hate is to murder, cf. Matt 5.21-22. However it is possible that the opponents not only separated from the author and his adherents but were violently antagonistic to them even to the point of causing their death. Thus the brothers included our author and his adherents. The test allows that the author and his group were the brothers of the opponents. It was the opponents who rejected this position and apparently admitted no brotherly responsibilities towards members of their own group.

---

[48]Brown (*Epistles*, 70) argues that the opponents may have been the larger group and that they made out quite well in the world.

The opponents boasted "I love God". But what would such words mean? Our author exhorted "Little children, let us not love in word or in the tongue but in deed and truth." 3.18.[49] To say "I love God" is to love in word. But what is love in (τῇ γλώσσῃ) *the tongue?* A number of aspects of the position of the opponents bear comparison with the πνευματικοί Paul encountered at Corinth.[50] It is possible that the opponents claimed that in their ecstatic outpouring in "the tongue" they were pouring out love for God. Our author called for a different kind of love, in action and reality. That love is understood in terms of showing compassion for the brother who is in need by sharing the material good things of life with him, 3.17. Such love has its source in God, who is love (4.8), and was definitively manifest in the sending of God's unique Son who gave his life, 3.16; 4.9-10. On the basis of this action and example the readers are exhorted, "we ought to love one another" (4.11), and informed that, "if we love one another God abides in us and his love is made perfect in us", 4.12.

Love for one another, the brother, is the test for a number of boasts made by the opponents and also for other positions that they held. It is the test for the claim to have κοινωνία with God who is light, for the claim to abide in God, to have the Spirit, to love God and to be born of God. Our author concluded his treatment of these themes by arguing that those who claim to love God should love his children, those who believe in Jesus Christ, 5.1-5.

2. The Anti-Christ

By arguing that "every one who believes that Jesus is the Christ is born of God" our author reveals who are the children of God, making clear that his opponents are not, 5.1. The anti-Christ denies that Jesus is the Christ, and is the liar, 2 22. It is probably for this reason that the un-Johannine (in terms of the Gospel)[51] Jesus Christ becomes characteristic in 1 Jn. The

---

[49]This could be a vaguely chiastic statement with a view to stressing the importance of action, "Be doers of the word and not hearers only". But it is puzzling that of the two pairs of words ("word and tongue" and "deed and truth") only tongue is used with the definite article (τῇ γλώσσῃ). Stylistically this spoils the balance of the sentence and draws attention to "the tongue" in a context where ecstatic utterance would be at home. See my *JWT*, 123. It is doubtful that Jn or the author of 1 Jn spoke of loving God, see *JWT* , 121ff.

[50]See notes 13, 21 and 43 above.

[51]The two uses of "Jesus Christ" in Jn 1.17 and 17.3 belong to the later strata of the Gospel which already reflect the emerging problem of the opponents.

two names together are shorthand for Jesus is the Christ in a context where there were those who denied this, see 1.3; 2.1 ; 3.23; 4.2; 5.6, 20. The affirmation that Jesus is the Christ is also prominent, 2.22; 5.1. The one who denies it is the liar, the anti-Christ. The one who believes it is born of God. Thus, like the test of love for the brother this confession of faith distinguishes the children of God from the children of the devil.

But what was it that the opponents denied when they denied Jesus is the Christ? Were they denying that Jesus was the Jewish Messiah? That does not seem likely. For them it appears to have been the equivalent of the confession that "Jesus is the Son of God", 4.15; 5.5,10. Hence our author also speaks of "his Son Jesus Christ", 1.3; 3.23; 5.20; and "Jesus his Son", 1.7. But what did the opponents intend to deny when they refused to confess "Jesus is the Son of God"? Apparently what they denied was the identity of Jesus and Christ. Jesus was the name of the human figure while Christ, Son of God, indicated the pre-existent, divine manifestation of God. That Son of God refers to that pre-existent divine element is indicated by 4.9,[52] where it is said that God sent his Son into the world.

The opponents did not deny the manifestation of the Son of God. What they denied was that Jesus Christ, the Son of God, has come in the flesh, 4.2[53] This led to the denial that Jesus Christ came by water and *blood*,

---

[52]The reference to God sending his unique Son ($\tau\grave{o}\nu$ $\upsilon\acute{\iota}\grave{o}\nu$ $\tau\grave{o}\nu$ $\mu\nu\nu\nu\gamma\epsilon\nu\hat{\eta}$) in 4.9 is relevant to the Prologue of Jn (1.14,18) and the discourse on birth from above (Jn 3.16,18) where the same terms distinguish the sonship of Jesus from the children of God (Jn 1.12). The "opponents" probably thought of the Revealer as a child of God, begotten of God, in terms similar to themselves. They claimed that they participated in the nature of God, and that his "seed" dwelt within them. The focus on being born of God in 1 Jn is a consequence of the claims of the "opponents". The theme appears in Jn 1.14,18; 3.16,18 in contexts dealing with children of God ($\tau\acute{\epsilon}\kappa\nu\alpha$ $\theta\epsilon\upsilon\hat{\upsilon}$), being born of God ($\acute{\epsilon}\kappa$ $\theta\epsilon\upsilon\hat{\upsilon}$ $\acute{\epsilon}\gamma\epsilon\nu\nu\acute{\eta}\theta\eta\sigma\alpha\nu$), and being born from above ($\gamma\epsilon\nu\nu\eta\theta\hat{\eta}$ $\check{\alpha}\nu\omega\theta\epsilon\nu$), 1.12ff.; 3.4ff. Here, as in 1 Jn, Jesus is referred to as $\upsilon\acute{\iota}\acute{o}\varsigma$ not $\tau\acute{\epsilon}\kappa\nu\nu\nu$ and his sonship is qualified by $\mu\nu\nu\nu\gamma\epsilon\nu\acute{\eta}\varsigma$. $M\nu\nu\nu\gamma\epsilon\nu\acute{\eta}\varsigma$ is used only five times in the NT, all in the conflict with the "opponents" in the later strata of Jn and in 1 Jn.

[53]The formula of the christological *confession* ($\acute{o}\mu\nu\lambda\nu\gamma\epsilon\hat{\iota}\nu$) in 4.2 is interesting and should be compared with the *confession* in 2 Jn 7. Both forms of the confession appear to have been derived from a combination of formulae used in Jn to refer to the Revealer as one $\acute{\epsilon}\rho\chi\acute{o}\mu\epsilon\nu\nu\varsigma$ $\epsilon\acute{\iota}\varsigma$ $\tau\grave{o}\nu$ $\kappa\acute{o}\sigma\mu\nu\nu$ and to the $\acute{o}$ $\lambda\acute{o}\gamma\nu\varsigma$ $\sigma\grave{\alpha}\rho\xi$ $\acute{\epsilon}\gamma\acute{\epsilon}\nu\epsilon\tau\nu$. The form in 2 Jn 7, confessing Jesus Christ $\acute{\epsilon}\rho\chi\acute{o}\mu\epsilon\nu\nu\nu$ $\acute{\epsilon}\nu$ $\sigma\alpha\rho\kappa\iota$, suggests a simple combination of the two formulae, retaining the present participle which is used in the formula in Jn (see 6.15) while I Jn has modified the tense of $\acute{\epsilon}\rho\chi\acute{o}\mu\epsilon\nu\nu\varsigma$ to give more adequate expression to the $\acute{\epsilon}\gamma\acute{\epsilon}\nu\epsilon\tau\nu$ of Jn 1.14. This suggests that either 2 Jn 7 and I Jn 4.2 were developed independently on the basis of Jn, or that

5.6; that the blood of Jesus Christ brings cleansing and forgiveness of sins, 1.7. They allowed for the baptismal manifestation of the Revealer but denied that the Revealer should simply be identified with Jesus. Hence they denied the Revealer's involvement in death and this is related to their denial of sin and the need of forgiveness and cleansing through the blood of Jesus, God's Son, and the need of the advocacy of Jesus Christ, the believer's Paraclete with the Father when they lapsed into sin.

Two important issues need to be discussed. Is it possible that any group which based its position on the Johannine tradition would deny the incarnation?[54] Second, what does the opponents' interpretation of "Christ" imply about their background?

Given that the Johannine tradition was shaped in the conflict with the Jews who denied the divine origin of Jesus it is not surprising that Jn emphasizes the incarnation. Surely Jn 1.14 makes the incarnation clear so that no Johannine Christians would baldly deny this. Such a position overlooks the gradual development of the Johannine tradition and the probability that the Prologue is one of the later strata. In fact it seems probable to me that $\sigma \acute{\alpha} \rho \xi \ \acute{\epsilon} \gamma \acute{\epsilon} \nu \epsilon \tau o$ is a later addition (by the evangelist) in response to the threat of the opponents.[55]

The use of the formulae "Jesus Christ" and "Jesus is the Christ" in a non-Messianic sense is an indication of the movement from the Jewish world to the Gentile world. Our author was responding to a Gentile Christian interpretation of the Johannine tradition, an interpretation developed by those who knew nothing of the Jewish context and conflict in which the Johannine tradition was formed. There is nothing in 1 Jn to suggest a Jewish background *for the opponents* and there are hints of a Gentile background. The position of the opponents appears to be similar to the $\pi \nu \epsilon \upsilon \mu \alpha \tau \iota \kappa o \acute{\iota}$ at Corinth who, claiming to be speaking in the Spirit

---

the confession of I Jn is a later form of that to be found in 2 Jn. However, both terms were a consequence of the situation created by the opponents.
[54]Brown (*Epistles*, 74ff.; 492ff.) does not think this possible. He argued that the opponents denied the salvific value of Jesus' life and death without denying the incarnation, or the reality of Jesus' life and death. Yet he allows for Käsemann's docetic reading of Jn 1.14 (*Epistles*, 109f.). Thus it is difficult to see why he rejects the view that the opponents were docetists.
[55]The suggestion that the author inconsistently stressed the truly human (fleshly) life of Jesus while having a low view of "the world" (see 1 Jn 2.15-17) overlooks the (at least) double sense in which "world" is used. Perhaps it would be better to talk of the paradoxical use which is a consequence of seeing the world as creation, and therefore of value and to be taken seriously (1 Jn 3.17), but because the world is not God it should not be allowed to seduce man to the desire above all else to possess it.

said "Jesus is accursed". Against them Paul asserted that no one speaking in the Spirit of God would say this and only those speaking in the Spirit would say "Jesus is Lord", 1 Cor 12.3.[56] "Jesus is Lord" meant for Paul in his context what "Jesus is the Christ", "Jesus is the Son of God", "Jesus Christ", and most explicitly, "Jesus Christ is come in the flesh" meant in the conflict with the opponents. The πνευματικοί appear to have distinguished the earthly Jesus from the heavenly Christ so that they could say "Jesus is accursed" while confessing the heavenly Christ. But Paul proclaimed *Christ* crucified (accursed), 1.23 and confessed *Jesus is* Lord, 12.3. This reversal accentuated the need to identify one Jesus Christ, because what happened to the man (crucifixion) is spoken of in terms of Christ, while the exalted status (Lord) was ascribed to Jesus. Both Paul and our author used what they considered to be the true christological confession as a test for the claim to possess the Spirit where the evidence of ecstasy and inspired utterance was used by their opponents to support their claim.

3. The Spirit of Truth and the Spirit of Error
The opponents claimed to possess the Spirit. This seems to have involved ecstatic utterance (the tongue) amongst other things, 3.18. They also stressed the significance of initiation (χρῖσμα, 2.20, 27) and the claim to be born of God, 3.9; 5.18. Their understanding of Spirit seems to have been in terms of a new nature, a divine nature, given to the initiated. This gift was the basis of immediate and complete knowledge. It meant that they participated in the nature of God, abided in him. It seems that this status, which they claimed for themselves, was similar to what they confessed in terms of Jesus. At his baptism he received the χρῖσμα ἀπὸ τοῦ ἁγίου. Thus Jesus provided the model for those who were to be initiated into enlightenment. But his earthly life had no significance for them. On the other hand those who claimed that they possessed God's σπέρμα, to be children of God by nature, had no need for Jesus at all because they knew God directly.

Against his opponents our author asserted "God has given us of his Spirit", 3.24; 4.13. The gift of the Spirit is made the evidence of abiding in God (or Christ) and of his abiding in the believer. Yet these two passages occur one each side of the passage dealing with criteria for recognizing the Spirit of Truth (God), 4.1-6. Hence, if possession of the Spirit is the test for those who claim to abide in God, or that God abides in them, the *claim* to possess the Spirit is not enough. That claim must be

---

[56]See my "Paul and the πνευματικοί at Corinth" 243 and n42, 249.

tested by the true christological confession, "Jesus Christ has come in the flesh". This is denied (or is not confessed) by the Spirit of Error, the anti-Christ, the liar, that is, the opponents.

Possession of the Spirit, being born of God, is also tested in terms of love, "Every one who loves is born of God and knows God", 4.7 cf. 8-12. This section ends with the test, "If we love one another God abides in us and his love is perfected in us" (4.12) and leads straight into evidence of the gift of the Spirit showing "that we abide in him and he in us", 4.13. Thus, both love and the gift of the Spirit are presented as criteria for the claim to abide in God and that God abides in the believer. But as has been seen, the claim to possess the Spirit itself needs to be tested. On the other hand love for one another, like the confession that Jesus Christ is come in the flesh, are criteria for which there can be no further test. This suggests that love for the brethren (one another) and the true christological confession separated our author from his opponents.

V. CONCLUSION

Our analysis has led to certain conclusions. The opponents had separated themselves from our author and his adherents. The schism had occurred because the Johannine community was now made up of two disparate groups: those who had been through the struggle with the synagogue and those who had entered the community after the breach with Judaism and consequently did not understand the Johannine tradition in the context of the struggle with Judaism. Their background was influenced by the thought and language of the mystery religions for which initiation, God's σπέρμα and birth from God all had significance.[57] From this perspective our author's community appears to us today to fit the sociological category of a sect: cut off from Judaism by excommunication and cut off from the Gentile world by a refusal to accommodate itself to a new world of cultural and religious values. On the other hand the opponents came from that Gentile world and interpreted the Johannine tradition in terms of it.

For the opponents, Jesus was a man upon whom the divine χρῖσμα had descended at his initiation, his baptism. This was understood in such a

---

[57] For such a group the OT probably held little authority and perhaps was not even directly relevant. On the other hand the Gospel (Jn) tradition was appealed to by the opponents as their authoritative source. It could be that the influence of the mystery religions made relevant our author's final warning: "Little children, guard yourselves from idols". We also need to inquire concerning the relation between the mysteries and Gnosis, especially in the light of the distinction between those who were "saved by nature" and those who were "initiated".

way that the human Jesus was distinguished from the divine Christ. Those aspects which related to his human life were regarded as insignificant, while his participation in the divine nature was confessed. As such he was an exemplar of all who were initiated after his pattern.

Some of the opponents claimed that the divine σπέρμα was abiding in them and that by virtue of this they were sinless because they participated in the divine nature. Hence they regarded themselves to be children of God because through the abiding divine σπέρμα they were begotten of God. By means of this they participated in the "light nature" of God. Hence they placed no importance on the normal human way of life with its relationships. Only love for God, κοινωνία with him, was significant. For such a group christology was not important.

In the struggle with these opponents our author returned to the Johannine tradition, affirming the necessity to confess the incarnation, Jesus Christ having come in the flesh. This was the basis of Jn's καθώς ethic which our author adopted with the consequent norm of Jesus' life in the flesh, "to walk as he walked", fulfilling his commandment to "love one another". Against those who claimed to possess God's σπέρμα, to be children of God by nature, he identified σπέρμα with χρῖσμα and related both to the initiation of Christians through the true confession of faith in Jesus Christ and the anointing with the Spirit. For him the presence of the Spirit and the status of those who possessed the Spirit as children of God were demonstrated by the true confession of faith and love for the brethren, love in action and reality.

In 1 Jn the quest for the Messiah has been transformed into the quest for an authentic christology. Here it becomes apparent that christology and community are intimately related. The faulty christology of the opponents threatened to destroy the community and 1 Jn reasserts the Johannine christology as a basis for the reestablishment of the community. To do this it was necessary to reassert the importance of Jesus life and death and the essence of his ethical teaching in the love command.

15

The Fulfilment of the Quest

Our quest for the Messiah has now run its course. The narrative of the Gospel begins with a series of inquiries that reveal the diversity of messianic expectations and express the quest for the Messiah. The ferment of expectation and hope was signalled by the embassy to John (the Baptist) to ask of him if perchance he was the Messiah. From the beginning we are made aware of the complexity of the messianic question, the multiplicity of messianic figures and the confusion surrounding the messianic identity. Certainly it may be granted that in his day John, like Jesus, raised the messianic question. But although the evangelist carefully denies any messianic significance to John he does not view him as a false Messiah. Rather he is, like Jesus, sent from God. More than any other figure in the Gospel story John stands wholly with Jesus. He is the primordial witness through whom all may come to believe. He is the first believer to whom God reveals his Messiah by a prearranged sign. He is the ideal witness who bears testimony to Jesus in terms that echo Jesus' own self-witness. No character in the Gospel story itself, apart from Jesus himself, understands the nature of Jesus' messiahship as clearly and fully as John. Indeed John's perception ranks alongside that of Jesus himself and of the narrator who has the benefit of understanding the beginning from the perspective of the end. This paradoxical treatment of John would be explicable if the evangelist himself had once been one of John's disciples and retained an admiration for him.

While John himself does not become a disciple of Jesus, two of his disciples do so on the basis of his testimony to Jesus. They come seeking Jesus and confess, "We have found the Messiah". If this might lead the reader to think that the quest for the Messiah had already reached its fulfillment at such an early stage in the story and that only repetition and anti-climax could follow, then the reader must be faced with surprises. It is true that the Prologue had already partly prepared the reader for these. But this preparation is clearer in retrospect for one who has read the Gospel than in prospect. To be sure there is repetition, but there is also development because those early confessions, which seem to penetrate the mystery of Jesus' identity, turn out to be ambiguous and in need of interpretation at a deeper level. It is the purpose of the Gospel to provide that deeper interpretation while showing how this arises from Jewish messianic expectation and is related to the earliest confessions of faith in Jesus. The original conclusion of the Gospel (20.30-31) proclaims the

Johannine christology as the authentic fulfillment of those expectations and confessions and all other quests.

By concentrating on the quest for the Messiah we have captured something of the distinctive character of the Johannine writings.[1] This distinctive character is primary evidence for the existence of a distinctive Johannine Christianity. While it can be argued that the distinctive character arises from the contribution of an author or at most a school, and this line of argument is sound I believe, it should not be forgotten that the Johannine writings have survived because they were received and read by some community or communities. It does not seem likely that Jn was read in this community (or communities) simply as an equal alongside the other Gospels. Rather Jn makes claims to provide a deep and authentic insight into the very mind of Jesus through the inspiring presence of the Spirit of Truth. Thus the distinctive christology of the Gospel is justified in the Farewell discourses through the words of Jesus which assure the readers that the Spirit will lead them into the complete truth. For the evangelist there can be no doubt that this truth is to be found in the pages of his Gospel and the figure of the BD guarantees the inspired tradition that it embodies.

The quest for the Messiah is worked out in the context of the dualistic language of the Johannine literature. Recognition of this language is a commonplace in Johannine studies. Reflection on the significance of this language is less common. Following the work of scholars like Wayne Meeks there is the recognition that this language is the expression of a distinctive social reality. If we describe that social reality in terms of a sect, understood in terms of a small community that has lost its roots (in whatever way) in society at large and experience a sense of radical alienation, then we have a basis for understanding the dualistic language. The *meaning* of the language should not, however, be reduced to its *function* of giving expression to the sense of alienation.

The dualistic language gives expression to a particular worldview. It is not sufficient to call it a dualistic world view without defining the nature of the dualism more closely. Perhaps the most useful description is a spiritual dualism, recognizing that the opposed spiritual powers have a bearing on the whole of reality. Consequently, although all things were

---

[1] The quest for the Messiah continues in 1 and 2 Jn in as much as there is a serious debate concerning Jesus. It is argued in this study that 1 and 2 Jn maintain the understanding of Jesus set out in the Gospel against a challenge to the essential unity of the divine and the human in Jesus. Thus in these letters the touchstone of the true faith has become "Jesus Christ has come in the flesh".

THE FULFILMENT OF THE QUEST

created by the λόγος, from the beginning there is evidence of the power of darkness. Indeed until the coming of the Word made flesh the power of darkness held sway. This form of dualism is characteristic of the so called "Historical Apocalypse". In it no attempt is made to explain the origin of the power of darkness though it is accepted that, until God's appointed time, the power of darkness holds sway. In such apocalyptic works the appointed time is generally viewed as imminent. But Jn, in common with the early Christian literature generally, asserts that a significant shift has already taken place with the coming of Jesus. With his coming the true light was shining in a new and critical way in a world characterized as the darkness. In particular Jn sees the signs of Jesus as manifestations of the divine glory.

It is peculiar to Jn that a second critical moment in the overthrow of the power of darkness is to be seen in the lifting up of the Son of Man. Thus the judgement is carried out in both the coming and the going of the Son of Man. This may well be a round about way of saying that the judgement is achieved through the total work of the Son of Man from coming to departure though special attention is given to the coming and going. Even so Jn asserts that Jesus' words have eschatological power in the context of his ministry (5.24-25). From this perspective Jesus also speaks of the future judging work of the Son of Man (5.27-29). That the evangelist considers that judgement is still to remain future is self-evident.[2] Consequently there is evidence in the Gospel that the Johannine Christians expected the return of Jesus. Indeed we have argued that the absence of Jesus was experienced traumatically when that return was delayed.[3]

While the evangelist reinterpreted this tradition in response to this crisis his reinterpretation did not remove the future dimension. Evidence of this is to be found not only in the scattered future eschatological sayings but also in the way the dualism remains a dominant feature. The persistent dualism requires a future eschatological resolution. Consequently it must be said that this kind of dualism implies a future eschatology and Jn is no exception. What his reinterpretation does is to shift the centre of eschatological focus to the coming and going of the Son of Man even if his work remains unfinished. Given this shift of focus the emphasis on the imminence of the return of Jesus has fallen away but it

---

[2]Some scholars think that 5.28-29 are redactional because they consider this apocalyptic dimension to be incompatible with Jn. But they have failed to take the Johannine dualism seriously.

[3]This was the crisis to which the original Farewell discourse responded.

467

has not and cannot disappear because, in the continuing history of the Johannine community, it is apparent that the power of darkness has not yet been destroyed. This was experienced in the conflict with the synagogue and later in the schism within the Johannine community.

The Gospel provides evidence that strongly suggests that it reached its present form only after a long process of gestation. Evidence of the process also sheds light on the history of the evangelist and those to whom his teaching was addressed and for whom he wrote. That process is further illuminated by the attempt to relate the Epistles to the Gospel. From the perspective of these developments it seems that the quest for the Messiah progressed through various stages. First we should allow that in Jesus' own day the quest for the Messiah was alive and that his ministry raised the messianic question. This can be admitted whether or not we think it likely that Jesus thought of himself as or taught that he was the Messiah. Second, we should recognize the diversity of messianic views in Judaism in the time of Jesus. Here as elsewhere we must allow a filtering out of diversity in the evidence that survives in the rabbinical texts. It is no real surprise that after two disastrous wars of apocalyptic and messianic dimensions the early rabbinic material shows a certain reticence about treating messianic questions. The centrality of the issue for early Christianity will also have reinforced the neglect of this theme in the rabbinic Judaism of the time.[4]

The Gospel and Epistles reveal a number of stages in the evangelist's quest for the Messiah. The collection of a number of miracle stories and the way these are presented as a basis for belief in Jesus suggests a stage when members of the synagogue were attracted to Jesus on the basis of the proclamation of the signs he performed. The use of the signs in this way arose out of Jewish tradition. The signs of Moses in the Exodus and the signs of prophets validating their mission from God provide a background here. The evidence of the sign prophets referred to by Josephus is both revealing and relevant.[5] While it is true that such prophets were concerned with deliverance (thus R.A. Horsley), because they failed to deliver they are recognized more by the signs they promised in an attempt to legitimate their role. The signs which were characteristically associated with them provide a relevant context for an understanding of the signs tradition in

---

[4]Jacob Neusner, *Messiah in Context* makes the point that the sparsity of reference to the Messiah and the casual nature of such references as do appear show that rabbinic concerns were elsewhere.

[5]See Wolfgang J. Bittner, *Jesu Zeichen im Johannesevangelium*, 24-74, 151ff.

Jn.[6] Clearly some of these sign prophets were concerned with political deliverance. This could also be said of the expectations associated with the Davidic Messiah who was characteristically associated with deliverance via armed struggle. Jn 6.14-15 portrays Jesus' rejection of this messianic role. While Georg Richter[7] is right in seeing the language concerning the mission of Jesus and the signs associated with him more closely related to the tradition of the messianic prophet than the Davidic Messiah it remains misleading to speak of the evangelist's christology as a prophetic christology. It could be that this was the view projected by the earlier use of the miracle stories in the synagogue. This view is supported by the conclusions that were drawn by those who respond positively to Jesus in the narrative of the Gospel (see 6.14-15; 9.17,30-33 and also 3.2). But the completed Gospel goes beyond a prophet christology.

For Jn the quest for the Messiah, the quest for God and the quest for life all find their fulfillment in the Jesus who is proclaimed and defended in the Gospel. Jn is quite prepared to offer evidence and to develop argument on the basis of this. He appeals to the works of Jesus as the fundamental evidence. In particular it is asserted that Jesus performed good works (10.32); he made a man whole (5.9,11,14,15); he spoke the truth (8.40). Not only does Jesus appeal to the works that he does as evidence that he is from God (10.37-38); others also draw out the implications of his signs (9.16,17,30-33; 10.21). This suggests that the miracle stories were used in the disputes with the synagogue. The form of the arguments also suggests that they were designed for response to the criticism of the synagogue.

While there is evidence of the development of the Gospel over a lengthy period of time and units of earlier tradition are sometimes visible, especially in some of the miracle stories, the case for an extensive signs source remains not only unproved but unlikely.[8] Nevertheless the signs source hypothesis has brought a focus on the *Sitz-im-Leben* of the miracle stories in Jn. It is altogether likely that this was the synagogue where the signs were proclaimed in an attempt to win its members to faith in Jesus as Messiah. This approach, it seems certain, achieved a degree of success

---

[6]See Schürer, *History* II, 403-6.
[7]See his *Studien zum Johannesevangelium* and the critique in Hans-Jürgen Kuhn, *Christologie und Wunder*, 270-351.
[8]See the summary treatment of Wolfgang Bittner, *Jesu Zeichen im Johannesevangelium*, 2-16. Perhaps the most telling criticism of the signs source hypothesis is that it leads to an unsatisfactory treatment of the signs in the completed Gospel. It also fails to do justice to the intricate relation of narrative and discourse.

provoking the decision of the Jews expressed in 9.22. This statement has rightly been the subject of concentrated study. In the midst of a series of attempts to arrest or kill Jesus, running from 5.16–12.10,[9] Jn 9 turns the focus of reaction from Jesus to those who confessed him to be the Christ. The use of the term "confess" (*ὁμολογεῖν*) has a formal ring to it, suggesting an open and public confession of faith.[10] The content of the confession that had been banned is also significant. In this context "to confess Christ" is shorthand for "to confess that Jesus is the Christ". In this particular incident no one had mentioned the title Christ, suggesting that the banned confession arose in the situation of the Johannine Christians and has been projected back into the story just as the man in his courageous confession of faith has become the ideal representative of the Johannine community. Being excluded from the synagogue he was received by Jesus and led into an adequate confession of faith in Johannine terms.

For Jn it is not the confession of Jesus as the eschatological prophet that is in view but the confession that Jesus is the Christ, 20.30-31.[11] This is not to deny that motifs associated with the eschatological prophet have contributed to his portrayal of Jesus. Manifestly they have. But the category that is used to bring together all the raw materials of his portrayal of Jesus is "Christ" understood as the Greek equivalent of "Messiah". Part of the complexity is our lack of detailed evidence concerning messianic expectation prior to the birth of Christianity. It is true that we now have access to the texts from Qumran and that these demonstrate the diversity of messianic expectations. But it would be a mistake to think that all messianic ideas from the time were gathered in and represented by these texts. Nor should we think that absence of certain views from the rabbinic texts proves that they were not to be found in the Judaism of Jesus' day. Here, in particular we have to assess the evidence concerning the signs of the Messiah. There is no evidence in the rabbinic texts that the Messiah was expected to perform miraculous signs. Should we conclude from this that the notion of a sign or wonder-working Messiah was a creation of the early Christian communities?

---

[9]The the decision to "also" kill Lazarus reiterates the previous decision to kill Jesus and adds Lazarus to the list.

[10]Compare 12.42.

[11]For this reason Bittner (*Jesu Zeichen*) is rightly critical of the hypothesis of a Johannine prophetic christology but does not allow sufficiently for the influence of prophetic motifs in the construction of the Johannine christology.

Certainly we need to recognize that there is good reason for maintaining the linguistic distinction between messiology/messianism and christology. The former term can be taken to refer to Jewish belief and the latter to Christian belief. In this case the Semitic term retains its Jewish sense while the Greek equivalent bears a Christian meaning and has become wholly identified with Jesus of Nazareth who is known as Jesus Christ or even simply Christ as if that were his name.[12] From the perspective of modern scholarship it seems that the early Christians read their beliefs in Jesus back into their messianic expectation. In other words, they read the Jewish scriptures with the hindsight belief in Jesus so that those scriptures became for them the OT. Is this the way signs became associated with their messianic expectation? Because Jesus performed signs the Messiah was expected to perform signs. But there is evidence that miraculous signs were sometimes associated with the coming Messiah. The evidence that Josephus provides concerning the sign prophets may support this view.[13] Hence it would be unwise to suggest that this element in the portrayal of Jesus was a purely Christian construction and not in any way a response to Jewish messianic expectations. That is not to say that the the notion of the signs of the Messiah and the portrayal of the signs of Jesus are not touched by Hellenistic influence or coloured in terms of some notion of the divine man. Indeed it is likely that Jewish expectations in this period were subject to these influences. While the *theios aner* hypothesis must be allowed as a possibility it is itself fraught with complex problems.[14]

In the period leading up to the Jewish war, including the time of Jesus, there was a levelling of messianic views, not in the sense of the emergence of one normative view, but in the merging of the various views so that

---

[12]Another interesting example of linguistic differentiation is the way two Greek terms that were used as equivalents in the time of Jesus became distinct so that one term ($\sigma\upsilon\nu\alpha\gamma\omega\gamma\acute{\eta}$) referred to the Jewish gathering and the other ($\acute{\epsilon}\kappa\kappa\lambda\eta\sigma\acute{\iota}\alpha$) to the Christian. In some books in the NT the equivalent use is retained though in most the exclusive use of $\acute{\epsilon}\kappa\kappa\lambda\eta\sigma\acute{\iota}\alpha$ has been adopted.

[13]It needs to be asked whether these figures were popularly thought of in messianic terms. We would not expect Josephus to acknowledge this because he regarded these figures in an extremely negative light as impostors (*AJ* xx. 97-99).

[14]There is no one unified profile of the *theios aner* and aretologies are not invariably associated with this figure in the sources. The sources to which appeal is made are widespread in terms of time and place. Some are clearly irrelevant to Jn and others so vaguely related to the *theios aner* that they are of little value for this purpose.

elements of the one became associated with the others. The early Christian proclamation of Jesus as the Messiah at first also contributed to this process. Because of this a Jewish reaction against this process became inevitable. If it is self-evidently true that Jesus and Christianity are unintelligible apart from the Judaism of Jesus' day it is also true that Judaism after 70 CE becomes increasingly unintelligible unless it is seen in its efforts to define itself over against emerging Christianity.[15] If this is true the absence of evidence of the signs of the Messiah in the Jewish sources could well be a Jewish response to the early Christian proclamation of the signs of Jesus.

But what messianic traditions are taken up by Jn in his portrayal of Jesus as Messiah? Clearly in Jn various characters in the story confess their faith in Jesus in terms of various traditional titles. But none of the titles conveys in a straightforward traditional way what Jn had in mind in terms of his christology. Thus the disciples discover that even when they have found the Messiah the quest for the Messiah goes on because they have not yet discerned who he is. What this means is that the evangelist has portrayed Jesus in such a way that he is the fulfillment of the various messianic expectations. Yet those expectations ultimately prove to be an inadequate expression of the one who is found to fulfil them. It may be that in the struggle and debate with the synagogue the evangelist was forced to elaborate and give expression to what was as yet only implicit in his portrayal of Jesus. In particular the critique of Jesus in terms of Moses and the Law seems to have been a catalyst in this development. From this perspective it was not possible simply to appeal to Moses as a witness in support of Jesus. Moses and the Law had now become the primary evidence against Jesus. In response to this Jesus is portrayed as superior to both Moses and the Law. The Law was given by Moses but grace and truth came by Jesus Christ, 1.17.[16] Likewise it is argued that it was not Moses who gave but "my Father gives the true bread from heaven", 6.32. Here the bread is first a symbol for the life-giving Law but in the subsequent discourse of Jesus it becomes clear that he, not the Law, is the life-giving bread, 6.35. Further it becomes clear that Jesus must give his flesh for the life of the world so that focus moves from Jesus' person to his action in giving his life.

---

[15]Thus Judaism would give up the Greek version of scripture known as the LXX to the Christians although it was a Jewish translation, and ἐκκλησία as distinct from συναγωγή would denote the gathering of Christians.

[16]The use of the name "Jesus Christ" here and in 17.3 signals that this is either a late stratum of the Gospel or derived from a non-Johannine tradition.

Jesus' conflict with Moses and the Law is nowhere clearer than in the disputes over sabbath observance. In these Jesus is condemned as a sabbath-breaker, 5.16,18; 9.16,24-34. It is in the context of the accusation that Jesus broke the sabbath by working on it that Jesus develops the theme of his works. The key text is 5.17 where he identifies his own works with the works of God. Thus "works" is a key theme for viewing Jesus as the Son in relation to the Father. Ultimately the confession that Jesus is the Christ has to be elaborated in terms of the Son's relation to and mission from the Father. It is true that the arguments that emerge all stress the dependence (subordination) of the Son on the Father (see 3.32,34; 5.19-30; and the many references to the Father as sender and the Son as the one sent; 10.29-30,36-38). But it should be noted that the point of the arguments concerning the dependence of the Son on the Father is to establish his authority. It is because he does the Father's will that his works are the works of God and because he speaks only what he has seen and heard from the Father that his word is the word of God. He can so speak and act because uniquely he comes from God, 3.13; 6.61-62.

By referring to 3.13; 6.61-62 we become aware that the Johannine christology has also drawn on traditions concerning the Son of Man.[17] These, like traditions concerning the eschatological prophet, Messiah, and Son of God were not only drawn from Judaism but from the tradition of interpretation within early Christianity. Thus the Johannine christology finds its point of departure in tradition comparable to what we find in the Synoptics. Indeed it may be that one or more of the Synoptics influenced the formation of Jn at later stages of its composition. But the evangelist was not closely dependent on any one of them and also had access to other tradition. As in the Synoptics the different categories are unified in their application to Jesus though this process of levelling was already taking place in the Judaism of Jesus' day. In the Gospels the process was given particular form by the figure of Jesus. Jn extends the direction of the developments to be found in the Synoptics to an extent that might have been beyond their recognition. With the Son of Man, while some of the traditional Synoptic motifs are retained by Jn, his use of this title is largely distinctive. The Son of Man is a heavenly figure. He alone has descended from heaven. It is notable that the form of the statement about

---

[17]The first reference to the Son of Man is in 1.51 where the evangelist has made use of a traditional Son of Man saying giving it distinctive meaning. See my "Christ and the Church in John 1.45-51", *L' Evangile de Jean*, 359-62.

the descent of the Son of Man is made from the perspective of his ascent although Jesus is apparently the speaker, 3.13.[18] Only the one who first descended has ascended into heaven. Thus Jn portrays the descending and ascending Son of Man. Although the language of mission always concerns the sending of the Son by the Father, which is sometimes expressed in first person language as "the Father who sent me", language about the descent of the Son of Man provides us with an equivalent to this. The subsequent ascent ($\dot{\alpha}\nu\alpha\beta\alpha\dot{\iota}\nu\epsilon\iota\nu$) of the Son of Man (3.13; 6.62) is also spoken of as his exaltation ($\dot{\nu}\psi\omega\theta\tilde{\eta}\nu\alpha\iota$, 3.14; 8.28) which Jesus also speaks of using first person language (12.32).[19] But it is in the role of the Son of Man that Jn identifies Jesus in his function of judgement as the light of the world. While the judgement was effected by the coming of the Son of Man (of the light into the world) that judgement reached its climax in the exaltation of the Son of Man. Even so the future judgement of the Son of Man on the last day remains as a significant if not central focus in the Gospel. It is a focus that becomes more prominent in 1 Jn.

Jesus speaks of the exaltation of the Son of Man and of his own exaltation. It is the narrator who informs the reader that this language tells us of the way Jesus was about to die, 12.33. Thus his death is the means of his exaltation or ascent to heaven and the means by which he draws all men to himself, 12.32. This points to the recognition of the saving function of his death. It is in his being lifted up on the cross that those who come to believe have eternal life, 3.14. This theme is also expressed in the transformation of the quest story of Jn 6 to a rejection story (6.51) and the second interpretation of the parable of Jn 10 (10.11-18).[20] Jesus is the Good Shepherd who gives his life for the sheep, that they may have life. The shepherd parable is a parable concerning the rulers in Israel and it is right to conclude that the Good Shepherd is a messianic image. The role of the Messiah is here interpreted in terms of giving his life for the sheep. Likewise when Jesus, not the Law, is proclaimed to be the bread of life it is implicit that this life-giving function can only occur when Jesus' body is broken and his blood poured out in death. Consequently we are here aware that in the conflict with the synagogue there was a shift of

---

[18]By 3.13 it is no longer Jesus who is speaking to Nicodemus (who has disappeared) but the narrator is addressing the reader directly and speaking from the perspective of Jesus' return to the Father.

[19]In a single discourse (5.19-30) we have a good example of the way the Johannine Jesus switches from first person self-reference to third person language about the Father/Son relation and concerning the Son of Man.

[20]There is thus a good case for seeing that this emphasis emerged in the second edition of the Gospel.

emphasis from the offer of salvation in response to belief in the person of Jesus to the offer of salvation as a consequence of Jesus' saving death. The footwashing symbolizes the way Jesus' service in life and death cleanses his disciples. This is signalled by placing the footwashing in the context of the final supper and in the place of the narrative concerning the broken bread and Jesus' body and the poured out wine and Jesus' blood. The narrator also signals this by saying "Having loved his own who were in the world, he loved them to the end." His death is thus an expression of his love and because his love is an expression of the love of the Father it is also an expression of God's love, 3.16; 17.23-26. Jesus' death manifests the character, extent and purpose of God's love as saving love, life-giving love. Certainly this is a redefinition of messiahship and with that a new understanding of the nature and character of God.

The significance of Jesus' death in revealing the character of God as loving (see 1 Jn 4.7–5.5) emerged in the struggle with the synagogue. It was challenged by those who did not take seriously that Jesus Christ came in the flesh. Though there were other issues that made up the full profile of the opponents of the author of 1 Jn, the refusal to confess Jesus Christ come in the flesh and consequently the failure to understand that God is self-giving love and that those who believe/love him will love one another provide us with the key to the conflict. Here the quest for the Messiah had become a quest for authentic christology and in this the quest for an authentic theology. What now becomes explicit, the concern to develop language concerning God himself, was already implicit in Jn. For the evangelist christology is in reality God-talk because Jesus as the Christ is the symbol of God in relation to his world. This is explicit in the Prologue and implicit in the language concerning the Father and the Son and the mission of the Son from the Father. The new crisis with the opponents turned the author of 1 Jn to speak of God directly. But the way he spoke of God was a consequence of his manifestation in Jesus Christ, 1 Jn 4.9-10.

The quest for the Messiah is an expression of the quest for God. For Jn there is no way to God except through Jesus as the Christ. Further it has become clear that there are, according to Jn, true and false understandings of the Christ. The true understanding is to be found in the Gospel. There Jesus speaks in a way that takes into account the work of the Spirit of Truth. Thus this Gospel provides the deepest possible understanding of Jesus as the Christ. For all the emphasis on his dependence and subordination, the purpose of the Gospel is to demonstrate the fulness of the revelation of God in him and the fulness of the gift of life that he bestows. Something of the authority which the Gospel proclaims concerning Jesus is assumed by the Gospel for itself. From a literary point of view this can be observed by the way the narrator himself speaks the language of Jesus in this Gospel. Both equally know the truth. Indeed the narrator is in a position to explain the words of Jesus better than he explains himself. What makes this possible is the continuing presence of the Messiah with his disciples through the coming of the Spirit of Truth whose task it was to keep the knowledge of Jesus alive in the believing community and to bring out the full meaning of that presence.

Bibliography of Works Cited

Achtemeier, Paul J., "Towards the isolation of the Pre-Markan Miracle Catenae", *JBL* 89 (1970), 265-91.

Achtemeier, Paul J., "The Origin and Formation of the Pre-Markan Miracle Catenae" *JBL* 91 (1972), 198-221

Alter, Robert, *The Art of Biblical Narrative*, London 1981.

Arble, M. von, "Über den Zweck des Johannesevangelium", *Theologische Quartalschrift* 42 (1861), 37-94.

Ashton, John, *Understanding the Fourth Gospel*, Oxford 1991.

Aune, D., *Prophecy in Early Christianity and the Ancient Mediterranean World*, Grand Rapids 1983.

Baldensperger, D. W., *Der Prolog des vierten Evangeliums*, Freiburg 1898.

Bammel, E., "John did no miracle", in *NTS* 18 (1971) now in C.F.D. Moule (ed.), *Miracles*, 179-202.

Banks, R.J (ed.), *Reconciliation and Hope*, Exeter 1974.

Barnett, P, "The Jewish Sign Prophets", *NTS* 27 (1981) 679-97.

Barr, James, "The Question of Religious Influence: The Case of Zoroastrianism, Judaism, and Christianity", *Journal of the American Academy of Religion* 53/2 (1985), 201-35.

Barrett, C. K., *The Gospel According to St. John*, London, 1955, 1978[2].

Barrett, C. K., *New Testament Essays*, London 1972.

Barrett, C. K., *The Gospel of John and Judaism*, London 1975.

Barrett, C. K., *Essays on John*, London 1982.

Bauckham, Richard, "Rediscovering a Lost Parable of Jesus", *NTS* 33 (1987), 84-101.

Becker, H., *Die Reden des Johanneservangeliums und der Stil der gnostischen Offenbarungsrede*, Göttingen 1956.

Becker, J., *Das Evangelium nach Johannes*, Würzburg 1979-81.

Berger, K., *The Amen-Worte Jesu*, Berlin 1970.

Bernard, J. H., *A Critical and Exegetical Commentary on the Gospel according to St. John*, Edinburgh 1928.

Betz, O., *Der Paraklet. Fürsprecher im Spätjudentum, im Johannes-Evangelium und in neu gefundenen gnostischen Schriften*, Leiden 1963.

Beutler, Johannes, *Martyria: Traditionsgeschichtliche Untersuchungen zum Zeugnisthema bei Johannes*, Frankfurt 1972.

Beutler, Johannes, "Literarische Gattungen im Johannesevangelium. Ein Forschungsbericht 1919-1980" in *ANRW* II.25.3.

Beutler, Johannes and Fortna,.R. T., (editors) *The Shepherd Discourse of John 10 and Its Context*, Cambridge 1991.

Bittner, Wolfgang J., *Jesu Zeichen im Johannesevangelium*, Tübingen 1987.

Blank, Josef, *Krisis: Untersuchungen zur johanneischen Christologie und Eschatologie*, Frieburg 1964.

Böcher, O., *Der johanneische Dualismus im Zusammenhang des nachbiblischen Judentums*, Gütersloh 1965.

Boers, H., *Neither on this Mountain nor in Jerusalem, SBLMS* 35, Atlanta 1988.

Bogart, J., *Orthodox and Heretical Perfectionism*, Chico 1977.

Boismard, M.-E., & Lamouille, A., *L'évangile de Jean*, Paris 1977.

Borgen, P., *Bread From Heaven*, Leiden 1965.

Borgen, P., "God's Agent in the Fourth Gospel" in *LOGOS was the True Light*, 121-32.

Borgen, P., *LOGOS was the true light*, Trondheim 1983.

Borgen, P., "Some Jewish Exegetical Traditions as Background for Son of Man Sayings (Jn 3.13-14 and context), in *L' Evangile de Jean*, ed. M. de Jonge, 243-58.

Borsch, F. H., *The Son of Man in Myth and History*, London 1967.

Bowman, J., "Samaritan Studies", *BJRL* (1958), 298-327.

Braun, F. M., *Jean le Theologian*, (3 vols), Paris 1959-68.

Braun, H., *Qumran und das Neue Testament*, 2 vols, Tübingen, 1966.

Brown, R. E., "The Qumran Scrolls and the Johannine Gospel and Epistles" *CBQ* 17 (1955), 403-19,559-74.

Brown, R. E., *New Testament Essays*, London 1965.

Brown, R. E., 'The Kerygma of the Gospel According to John', *Interpretation*, 21 (1967), pp. 387-400.

Brown, R. E., *The Gospel According to John*, London 1971.

Brown, R. E., *The Community of the Beloved Disciple*, New York 1979.

Brown, R. E., *The Epistles of John*, Garden City 1982.

Brunner, Emil, *Dogmatics* II, London 1952.

Buchanan, G. W., "The Samaritan origin of the Gospel of John" in *Religions in Antiquity*, edited by Jacob Neusner, 149-75.

Bühner, J.-A., *Der Gersandte und sein Weg im 4. Evangelium*, Tübingen 1977.

Bultmann, R., "Der religionsgeschichtliche Hintergrund des Prologs zum Johannes-Evangelium", in *EYXAPIΣTHPION Festschrift fur H. Gunkel*, 2 Teil, Göttingen 1923, 3-26.

Bultmann, R.,."Die Bedeutung neuerschlossenen mandäischen Quellen für das Verständnis des Johannesevangeliums", *ZNW* 24 (1925) 100-46.

Bultmann, R., *Das Evangelium des Johannes*, Göttingen 1941; 19th ed. 1968.

Bultmann, R., *Primitive Christianity in its Contemporary Setting*, London 1949.

Bultmann, R., Theology of the New Testament (2 vols) London 1955.

Bultmann, R., *History of the Synoptic Tradition*, Oxford 1968.

Bultmann, R., "John" *RGG³*, III, 840-51, Tübingen 1957-65.

Bultmann, R., *The Gospel of John*, Oxford 1971.

Bultmann, R., *The Johannine Epistles*, Philadelphia 1973.

Burkett, Delbert, *The Son of Man in the Gospel of John*, Sheffield 1991.

Burridge, Richard A., *What are the Gospels? A comparison with Graeco-Roman biography*, Cambridge 1992.

Burrows, Millar, *More Light on the Dead Sea Scrolls*, London 1958.

Carroll, K. L., "The Fourth Gospel and the Exclusion of Christians from the Synagogue" *BJRL* 40 (1957-8), 19-32.

Charlesworth, J. H. (ed.), *John and Qumran*, London, 1972.

Charlesworth, J. H. (ed.), *The Messiah: Developments in Earliest Judaism and Christianity*, Minneapolis 1992.

Collins, J. J., "The 'Son of Man' in First Century Judaism", *NTS* 38/3 (1992), 448-66.

Colwell, E. C., "A Definite Rule for the use of the Article in the Greek New Testament", *JBL* 52 (1933), 12-21.

Comfort, P. W., "The Greek Text of John according to the Early Papyri", *NTS* 36 (1990), 625-629.

Crossan, John Dominic, *The Historical Jesus: The Life of a Mediterranean Peasant*, Edinburgh 1991.

Cullmann, Oscar, *Early Christian Worship*, London 1953.

Cullmann, Oscar, *The Johannine Circle*, London 1975.

Culpepper, R. Alan, *The Johannine School*, Missoula 1975.

Culpepper, R. Alan, *Anatomy of the Fourth Gospel*, Philadelphia 1983.

Davies, W. D., *Paul and Rabbinic Judaism*, London 1965.

Davies, W.D., and Daube, D. (eds), *The Background of the New Testament and its Eschatology*, Cambridge 1964.

de Jonge, M. (ed.), *L' Evangile de Jean* , Leuven 1977.

de Jonge, M., *Jesus Stranger from Heaven and Son of God*, Missoula 1977.

de Solages, Mgr., *Jean et les synoptiques*, Leiden 1979.

Denaux, A., "The Q-Logion Mt 11.27/Lk 10.22 and the Gospel of John" (Leuven Colloquium August 1990).

Dibelius, M., *From Tradition to Gospel*, New York 1935.

Dodd, C. H., *The Gospel in the New Testament* , London 1926.

Dodd, C. H., *The Bible and the Greeks* , London 1935.

Dodd, C. H., *The Johannine Epistles*, London 1946.

Dodd, C. H., *The Interpretation of the Fourth Gospel*, Cambridge 1953.

Dodd, C. H., *Historical Tradition and the Fourth Gospel*, Cambridge 1963.

Duke, P. D, *Irony in the Fourth Gospel*, Atlanta 1985.

Dungan, David L. (ed.), *The Interrelations of the Gospels*, Leuven 1990.

Dunn, J. D. G., *Christology in the Making*, London 1990[2].

Dunn, J. D. G., "Let John be John: A Gospel for its Time" in P. Stuhlmacher (ed.) *Das Evangelium und die Evangelien*, 309-39, Michigan 1991.

Eisenmann, R., and Wise, M., *The Dead Sea Scrolls Uncovered*, Dorset 1992.

Eusebius, *Ecclesiastical History*, edited by Kirsopp Lake and J.E.L. Oulton, London 1926-32.

Fiorenza, E. S., "The Quest for the Johannine School: The Apocalypse and the Fourth Gospel" *NTS* 23 (1976-7), 402-27.

Fortna, R. T., *The Gospel of Signs*, Cambridge 1970.

Fortna, R. T., "From Christology to Soteriology", *Interpretation* 27 (1973), 31-47.

Fortna, R. T., *The Fourth Gospel and its Predecessor*, Philadelphia 1988.

Franck, Eskil, *Revelation Taught: The Paraclete in the Gospel of John*, Lund 1985.

Freed, E. D., *Old Testament Quotations in the Gospel of John*, Leiden 1965.

Freed, E. D., "The Son of Man in the Fourth Gospel", *JBL* 86 (1967), 402-09.

Freed, E. D., "Did John write his Gospel partly to win Samaritan Converts?" *Novum Testamentum*, XII (1970), 241-256.

Gärtner, B., *John 6 and the Jewish Passover*, Lund 1959.

Gardner-Smith, P., *Saint John and the Synoptic Gospels*, Cambridge 1938.

Gaster, T., *The Scriptures of the Dead Sea Sect*, London 1957.

Grayston, K., "Review of *Quest*", *Epworth Review* (May 1993), 111-2.

Haenchen, E., *John*, Philadelphia 1980.

Hanson, Anthony, "John's Citation of Psalm 82", *NTS*, 11 (1964-65), 158-62.

Hanson, Anthony, "John's Citation of Psalm 82 Reconsidered", *NTS*, 13 (1966-67), 363-7.

Hare, D. R. A., *The Son of Man Tradition*, Minneapolis 1990.

Häring, T., *Grundgedanke des ersten Johannesbriefs,*, Freiburg 1892.

Harris, J. R., *The Origin of the Prologue to St. John*, Cambridge 1917.

Harvey, A. E., *Jesus on Trial: A Study in the Fourth Gospel*, London, 1976.

Hengel, Martin, *The Johannine Question*, London 1989.

Higgins, A. J. B., *Jesus and the Son of Man*, Philadelphia 1964.

Hill, David, *New Testament Prophecy*, Richmond 1979.

Hock, R. F. and O'Neil, E. N. (eds), *The Chreia in Ancient Rhetoric*: vol 1, *The Progymnasmata* (Texts and Translations 27), Atlanta 1986.

Holladay, Carl H., *Theios Aner in Hellenistic Judaism: A Critique of the use of this Category in New Testament Christology*, Missoula 1977.

Horbury, W., "The Benediction of the *minim* and Early Jewish Christian Controversy", *JTS* 33/1 (1982), 19-61.

Horsley, R. A., "Popular Messianic Movements around the Time of Jesus", *CBQ* 46 (1984), 471-95.

Horsley, R. A, "Popular Prophetic Movements at the Time of Jesus Their Principal Features and Social Origins", *JSNT* 26 (1986), 3-27.

Houston Smith, Robert, "Exodus Typology in the Fourth Gospel", *JBL* 81 (1962).

Howard, W. F., *Christianity According to St. John* , London 1943.

Jeremias, J., "Die Berufung des Nathanael", *Angelos* 3 (1928), 2-5.

Jerenias, J., *Jerusalem, in the Time of Jesus*, London 1967.

Johnston, George, *The Spirit Paraclete in the Gospel of John*, Cambridge 1970.

Josephus, ed. H. St. J. Thackeray *et al* . (9 vols), London 1926-65.

Käsemann, E., *The Testament of Jesus*, London 1968.

Kimelman, R., "*Birkat Ha-Minim* and the Lack of Evidence for an Anti-Christian Jewish Prayer in Late Antiquity", in *Jewish and Christian Self-Definition*, Vol. 2, 226-44., ed. E. P. Sanders *et al.* Philadelphia 1981.

Kittel, G., (et al. editors) *Theological Dictionary of the New Testament* (10 vols) translated by Geoffrey W. Bromiley, Michigan 1964-76.

Klausner, Joseph, *The Messianic Idea in Israel from its Beginning to the Completion of the Mishnah*, London 1956.

Kuhn, Hans-Jürgen, *Christologie und Wunder: Untersuchungen zu Joh 1.35-51*, Pustet, 1988.

Kysar, R., *The Fourth Evangelist and His Gospel.*, Minneapolis 1975.

Kysar, R., "The Fourth Gospel: A Report on Recent Research", in *ANRW* 25.3, 2389-2480.

Kysar, Robert, *John* , Minneapolis 1986.

Law, R., *The Tests of Life*, Edinbutgh 1909.

Leivestad, Ragnar, "Exit the Apocalyptic Son of Man", *NTS* 18 (1971-72), 243-267.

Lieu, Judith, *The Second and Third Epistles of John*, Edinburgh 1986.

Lindars, B, *Behind the Fourth Gospel*, London 1971.

Lindars, B, "*ΔIKAIOΣYNH* in John 16.8 and 10" in *Festschrift für B. Rigaux*, Gembloux 1970, 275-85.

Lindars, B, *The Gospel of John*, London 1972.

Lohse, E (ed.), *Die Texte aus Qumran*, Darmstadt 1964.

MacRae, George, 'The Ego - Proclamation in Gnostic sources' in E. Bammel (ed.), *The Trial of Jesus*, London 1970, 122-134.

Macrae, G. W., "Nag Hammadi and the New Testament" in *Gnosis: Festschrift fur Hans Jonas*, Göttingen 1978.

Maddox, R., "The Function of the Son of Man in the Gospel of John" in R. Banks (ed.), *Reconciliation and Hope*, Exeter 1974, 186-204.

Manson, Wm, *The Epistle to the Hebrews*, London 1951.

Martin, R. P., *Carmen Christi*, Cambridge 1967.

Martyn J. L., "Glimpses into the History of the Johannine Community" in *Le' Evangile de Jean* ed. M. de Jonge, Leuven 1977.

Martyn, J. L., "We have found Elijah" in *The Gospel of John in Christian History*, 29-54.

Martyn, J.L, *History and Theology in the Fourth Gospel*, New York, 1968; 1979².

Martyn, J. L., *The Gospel of John in Christian History*, New York 1978.

Mathill, A. J., "Johannine Communities Behind the Fourth Gospel: Georg Richter's Analysis" in *Theological Studies* 38 (1977), 294-315.

Meeks, Wayne, "Galilee and Judaea in the Fourth Gospel", *JBL* 85 (1966), 159-69.

Meeks, Wayne, *The Prophet-King*, Leiden 1967.

Meeks, Wayne, "The Man from Heaven in Johannine Sectarianism", JBL 91/1 (1972), 44-72.

Meeks, Wayne, "Breaking Away: Three New Testament Pictures of Christianity's Separation from Jewish Communities" (93-116) in *To See Ourselves as Others See Us* ed. Jacob Neusner and E.S. Frerichs.

Mercer, Calvin, "ΑΠΟΣΤΕΛΛΕΙΝ and ΠΕΜΠΕΙΝ in John", *NTS* 36 (1990), 619-24.

Metzger, B. M., *A Textual Commentary on the Greek New Testament*, London 1971.

Minear, Paul, "The Original Functions of John 21", *JBL* 102/1 (1983), 85-98.

Minear, Paul, *The Martyrs Gospel*, New York 1984.

Moloney, F. J., *The Johannine Son of Man*, Rome 1976.

Moloney, F. J., "From Cana to Cana", *Salesianum* 40 (1978), 817-43.

Moloney, F. J., *Belief in the Word: Reading John 1-4*, Minneapolis 1993.

Morris, L. L, *The Gospel According to St.John*, Grand Rapids 1971.

Moule, C. F. D., *An Idiom Book of New Testament Greek*, Cambridge 1953.

Müller, Mogens, "Have you Faith in the Son of Man?", *NTS* 37 (1991), 291-94.

Neirynck, F, (*et al.*) *Jean et les synoptiques: Examen critique de l'exégèse de M.-E. Boismard*, Louvain 1979.

Neirynck, F., "The Anonymous Disciple in John 1", *Ephemerides Theologicae Lovanienses* LXVI/1 (April 1990), 5-37.

Neirynck, F., "The Two-Source Hypothesis" in *The Interrelations of the Gospels*, edited by David L. Dungan, 3-22.

Neusner, Jacob, *Messiah in Context*, Philadelphia 1984.

Neusner, Jacob and Frerichs, E. S., *To See Ourselves as Others See Us: Christians, Jews, "Others" in Late Antiquity*, Chico 1985.

Neusner, Jacob, Scott Green, W. and Frerichs, Ernest S. (eds), *Judaisms and Their Messiahs at the Turn of the Christian Era*, Cambridge 1988.

Neusner, Jacob, "The Formation of Rabbinic Judaism: Yavneh from AD 70-100", *ANRW* II.19.2, 3-42.

Neusner, Jacob, *Jews and Christians: The Myth of a Common Tradition*, London 1991.

Nicholson, G. C., *Death as Departure: The Johannine Descent-Ascent Schema*, Chico 1983.

Nickelsburg, G. W. E., and Stone, M. E., *Faith and Piety in Early Judaism*, Philadelphia 1983.

Nicol, W., *The Semeia in the Fourth Gospel*, Leiden 1972.

Odeberg, H., *The Fourth Gospel: Interpreted in its relation to contemporaneous religious currents in Palestine and the Hellenistic-Oriental World*, Uppsala 1929.

Okure, Teresa, *The Johannine Approach to Mission: A Contextual Study of John 4.1-32*, Tübingen 1988.

Olsson, Birger, *Structure and Meaning in the Fourth Gospel*, Lund 1974.

Overman, J. Andrew, *Matthew's Gospel and Formative Judaism*, Minneapolis 1990.

Painter, John, "Gnosticism and the Qumran Texts", *Australian Biblical Review* 17 (1969), 1-6.

Painter, John, "Eschatological Faith in the Gospel of John", in *Reconciliation and Hope* ed. R.J. Banks, Exeter 1974.

Painter, John, *John: Witness and Theologian*, London 1975 (subsequent editions 1979, 1980, 1986).

Painter, John,"Christ and the Church in John 1.45-51", in *L' Evangile de Jean* ed. by M. de Jonge, Leuven 1977, 359-62.

Painter, John, "The Church and Israel in the Gospel of John", *NTS* 25 (1978), 103-12.

Painter, John, "The Farewell Discourses and the History of Johannine Christianity", *NTS* 27 (1981), 525-43.

Painter, John, "Paul and the πνευματικοί at Corinth" in *Paul and Paulinism: Essays in honour of C. K. Barrett* , ed. M. Hooker and S. G. Wilson, London 1982, 237-50.

Painter, John, "Christology and the History of the Johannine Community in the Prologue of the Fourth Gospel", *NTS* 30 (1984), 460-74.

Painter, John, "The Johannine Epistles", *ABR* 32 (1984), 38-48.

Painter, John, "The Opponents in 1 John", *NTS* 32 (1986), 48-71.

Painter, John, "John 9 and the Interpretation of the Fourth Gospel", *JSNT* 28 (1986), 31-61.

Painter, John, *Theology as Hermeneutics: Rudolf Bultmann's Interpretation of the History of Jesus*, Sheffield 1987.

Painter, John, "Text and Context in John 5", *ABR* 35 (Oct. 1987), 28-34.

Painter, John, "The Purpose and Christology of the Fourth Gospel" in *Religions and Comparative Thought*, Delhi 1988, 387-406.

Painter, John, "Tradition and Interpretation in John 6", *NTS* 35 (1989), 421-50.

Painter, John, "Quest and Rejection Stories in John" *JSNT* 36 (1989), 17-46.

Painter, John, "Quest Stories in John 1-4" *JSNT* 41 (1991), 33-70.

Painter, John, "Tradition, History and Interpretation in John 10", in *The Shepherd Discourse of John 10 and Its Context*, ed. R.T. Fortna and J. Beutler (*SNTSMS* 69), Cambridge 1991, 53-74.

Painter, John, "Quest Stories in John and the Synoptics" in *John and the Synoptics*, ed. A. Denaux, Leuven 1992, 498-506.

Painter, John, "The Enigmatic Johannine Son of Man" in *The Four Gospels 1992* vol. 3,Louvain 1992, 1869-87.

Painter, John, "John the Evangelist as Theologian" in *In the Fulness of Time* edited by J. Pryor and D. Peterson, Sydney 1992, 95-110.

Painter, John, "Theology and Eschatology in the Prologue of John" in *SJT* 46 (1993), 27-42.

Pamment, M., "The Meaning of δόξα in the Fourth Gospel", *ZNW* 74 (1982),1/2, 12-16.

Pamment, Margaret,"Is there evidence of Samaritan influence on the Fourth Gospel", *ZNW* 73 (1982), 221-230.

Pamment, Margaret,"The Son of Man in the Fourth Gospel", *JTS* 36 (1985), 56-66.

Parker, P., "'John the Son of Zebedee and the Fourth Gospel", *JBL* 81 (1962), 35-43.

Prest, James E. (ed.), *Johannine Studies: Essays in Honour of Frank Pack*, California 1989.

Pryor, J. W., "John 4.44 and the Patris of Jesus", *CBQ* 42 (1987), 254-63.

Purvis, J. D., "The Fourth Gospel and the Samaritans", *NT* 17(1975), 161-98.

Reim, G., *Studien zum alttestamentlichen Hintergrund des Johannesevangeliums* (*SNTS MS* 22), Cambridge 1974.

Rengstorf, K. H., "σημεῖον", *TDNT* 7, Grand Rapids 1971.

Richter, G, "Die Fleischwerdung des Logos im Johannesevangelium", *NT* 14 (1972), 265ff.

Richter, Georg, *Studien zum Johannesevangelium*, ed. J. Hainz, Regensburg 1977.

Rissi, M., "Die Logoslieder im Prolog des 4 Evangeliums", *Th.Z.* (1975), 321-36.

Rissi, M., "John 1.1-18 (The Eternal Word)", *Interpretation* 31 (1977), 394-401.

Robinson, J. A. T., "The Parable of the Shepherd", *ZNW* 46 (1955), 233-40.

Robinson, J. A. T., "The Relation of the Prologue to the Gospel of St. John", *NTS* 9 (1962-63), 120-9.

Robinson, J. A. T., *Twelve New Testament Studies*, London, 1962.

Robinson, J. A. T., *The Priority of John*, London 1985.

Robinson, J. M. (ed.), *The Nag Hammadi Library*, London 1977.

Roloff, J., "Der Johanneische 'Lieblingsjünger' und der Lehrer der Gerichtigkeit", *NTS* 15 (1968-69), 129-51.

Rordorf, W., *Sunday*, London 1968.

Ruckstuhl, E., "Die johannische Menschensohnforschung 1957-1969" in J. Pfammatter and F. Fugers (eds) *Thelogische Berichte* I, Benzider 1972, 171-284.

Ruckstuhl, E, "Abstieg und Niedergang des johanneischen Menschensohn", in R. Pesch & R. Schnackenburg (eds) *Jesus und der Menschensohn*, Freiburg 1975, 314-41.

Sanders, E. P., *Judaism: Practice and Belief 63 BCE–66 CE*, Philadelphia 1992.

Sanders, J. T., *The New Testament Christological Hymns*, Cambridge 1971).

Schnackenburg, R., *Die Johannesbriefe*, Freiburg 1963.

Schnackenburg, R., *The Gospel According to St. John* (3 vols), New York 1968-82.

Schulz, S., *Untersuchungen zur Menschensohn-Christologie im Johannesevangelium*, Göttingen 1957.

Schürer, E., *The History of the Jewish People in the Age of Jesus Christ* edited by G. Vermes et al, Edinburgh 1973-87.

Scobie, C. H. H., "The Origins and Development of Samaritan Christianity", *New Testament Studies*, 19 (1972-73), 390-414.

Scott, E. F., *The Criticism of the Fourth Gospel*, Edinburgh 1905.

Schurchard, B. G., *Scripture within Scripture: The Interrelationship of Form and Function in the Explicit Old Testament Citations in the Gospel of John (SBLDS* 133), Atlanta 1992.

Segal, Alan F., *Two Powers in Heaven*, Leiden 1977.

Segovia, F. F., *The Farewell of the Word: The Johannine Call to Abide*, Minneapolis, 1991.

Sidebottom, E. M., *The Christ of the Fourth Gospel in the Light of First Century Thought*, London 1961.

Sjöberg, Erik, *Der verborgene Menchensohn in der Evangelien*, Lund 1955.

Smith, D. Moody, *The Composition and Order of the Fourth Gospel*, New Haven 1965.

Smith, D. Moody, "Johannine Christianity", *NTS* 21/2 (1976), now in his *Johannine Christianity*.

Smith, D. Moody, "The Milieu of the Johannine Miracle Source", now in his *Johannine Christianity*.

Smith, D. Moody, *Johannine Christianity*, Colombia, 1984.

Smith, D. Moody, *John Among the Gospels: The Relationship in Twentieth-Century Research*, Minneapolis 1992.

Stanton, G. N., *The Gospels and Jesus*, Oxford 1989.

Stanton, G. N., *A Gospel for a New People: Studies in Matthew*, Edinburgh 1991.

Stibbe, Mark W. G., *John as Story Teller: Narrative Criticism and the Fourth Gospel*, Cambridge 1992.

Talbert, C., "The Myth of a Descending-Ascending Redeemer in Mediterranean Antiquity", *NTS* 22 (1975-76), 418-43.

Tannehill, R. C. (ed.), *Pronouncement Stories, Semeia* 20 (1981).

Taylor, Vincent, *The Formation of the Gospel Tradition*, London 1933.

Temple, W., *Nature, Man and God*, London 1936.

Theissen, G., *The Shadow of the Galilean*, London 1987.

Thompson, Marianne Meye, *The Humanity of Jesus in the Fourth Gospel*, Philadelphia 1988.

Tiede, D. L., *The Charismatic Figure as Miracle Worker*, Missoula 1972.

Tyler, R. L., "The Source and Function of Isaiah 6.9-10 in John 12.40", in *Johannine Studies: Essays in Honour of Frank Pack*, ed. J. E. Prest.

Van Unnik, W. C., "The Purpose of St. John's Gospel", *Studia Ev.* I, 382-411.

Vermes, G., *The Dead Sea Scrolls In English*, Hammondsworth 1962.

von Wahlde, U. C., "The Terms for Religious Authorities in the Fourth Gospel: A Key to Literary Strata?" *JBL* 98 (1979), 231-53.

von Wahlde, U. C., "The Witnesses to Jesus in John 5.31-40 and Belief in the Fourth Gospel", *CBQ* 43 (1981), 385-404.

von Wahlde, U. C., "The Johannine 'Jews': A Critical Survey", *NTS* 28/1 (1982), 33-60.

von Wahlde, U. C., *The Earliest Version of John's Gospel*, Wilmington 1989.

Weder, Hans, "Die Menschwerdung Gottes: Überlegungen zur Auslegungsproblematik des Johannesevangeliums am Beispiel von Joh 6", *ZTK* 82 (1985), 325-60.

Wegner, U., *Der Hauptmann von Kafarnaum (Mt 7.28a; 8.5-10 par Lk 7.1-10): Ein Beitrag zur Q-Forschung*, (WUNT 2, Reihe 14), Tübingen 1985.

Wind, A., "Destination and Purpose of the Gospel of John", *NT* 14 (1972), 26-69.

Windisch, Hans, *Johannes und die Synoptiker*, UNT 12 (1926).

Yadin, Y., *The Scroll of the War of the Sons of Light against the Sons of Darkness*, Oxford 1962.

Zaehner, R. C., *The Dawn and Twilight of Zoroastrianism*, London 1961.

Index of Authors

This book is due for return on or before the last date shown below.